Schools of Fiction

OXFORD STUDIES IN AMERICAN LITERARY HISTORY

Gordon Hutner, Series Editor

After Critique
Mitchum Huehls

Unscripted America
Sarah Rivett

Forms of Dictatorship
Jennifer Harford Vargas

Anxieties of Experience
Jeffrey Lawrence

White Writers, Race Matters
Gregory S. Jay

The Civil War Dead and American Modernity
Ian Finseth

The Puritan Cosmopolis
Nan Goodman

Realist Poetics in American Culture, 1866-1900
Elizabeth Renker

The Center of the World
June Howard

History, Abolition, and the Ever-Present Now in Antebellum American Writing
Jeffrey Insko

Not Quite Hope and Other Political Emotions in the Gilded Age
Nathan Wolff

Transoceanic America
Michelle Burnham

Genre and White Supremacy in the Postemancipation United States
Travis M. Foster

Modern Sentimentalism
Lisa Mendelman

Speculative Fictions
Elizabeth Hewitt

Transamerican Sentimentalism and Nineteenth-Century US Literary History
Maria A. Windell

Patriotism by Proxy
Colleen Glenney Boggs

Jewish American Writing and World Literature
Saul Noam Zaritt

The Archive of Fear
Christina Zwarg

Transgression and Redemption in American Fiction
Thomas J. Ferraro

Violentologies
B.V. Olguin

The Latino Continuum and the Nineteenth-Century Americas
Carmen Lamas

Time and Antiquity in American Empire
Mark Storey

Picturesque Literature and the Transformation of the American Landscape, 1835-1874
John Evelev

Literary Neurophysiology
Randall Knoper

Writing Pain in the Nineteenth-Century United States
Thomas Constantinesco

Schools of Fiction
Morgan Day Frank

Schools of Fiction

Literature and the Making of the American Educational System

MORGAN DAY FRANK

Great Clarendon Street, Oxford, OX2 6DP,
United Kingdom

Oxford University Press is a department of the University of Oxford.
It furthers the University's objective of excellence in research, scholarship,
and education by publishing worldwide. Oxford is a registered trade mark of
Oxford University Press in the UK and in certain other countries

© Morgan Day Frank 2022

The moral rights of the author have been asserted

Impression: 1

All rights reserved. No part of this publication may be reproduced, stored in
a retrieval system, or transmitted, in any form or by any means, without the
prior permission in writing of Oxford University Press, or as expressly permitted
by law, by licence or under terms agreed with the appropriate reprographics
rights organization. Enquiries concerning reproduction outside the scope of the
above should be sent to the Rights Department, Oxford University Press, at the
address above

You must not circulate this work in any other form
and you must impose this same condition on any acquirer

Published in the United States of America by Oxford University Press
198 Madison Avenue, New York, NY 10016, United States of America

British Library Cataloguing in Publication Data

Data available

Library of Congress Control Number: 2022942795

ISBN 978–0–19–286750–6

DOI: 10.1093/oso/9780192867506.001.0001

Printed and bound by
CPI Group (UK) Ltd, Croydon, CR0 4YY

Links to third party websites are provided by Oxford in good faith and
for information only. Oxford disclaims any responsibility for the materials
contained in any third party website referenced in this work.

Contents

Preface — vi
Acknowledgements — xvi

Introduction: Irrelevance — 1

PART 1

1. The School and Society — 41
2. Against Reading — 74

PART 2

3. In Defense of Punctuality — 107
4. Interest, Disgust — 140

PART 3

5. Secret Societies — 169
6. Really, Really Secret Societies — 205

Notes — 236
Bibliography — 305
Index — 324

Preface

> [P]eople generally have more feeling for canals and roads than education.
> —Thomas Jefferson writing to Joel Barlow, December 10, 1807[1]

This book argues that the institutionalization of English literature was a signal event in the history of education in the United States. When literature appeared in classrooms, it had a transformative effect on the school. Administrators and instructors restructured the curriculum around it. They reimagined the relationship between the school and society through it. The expansion and elaboration of the educational system ultimately became possible because of it. This book insists that, to understand the school's evolving role in public life over the last two centuries, we need to acknowledge the unique influence literature has exerted on the educational system's development.

From our historical perspective, the study of literature may seem like a traditional academic endeavor. But when educators introduced English literature into the classroom, it was seen as a threatening modern incursion on the traditional curriculum, which had centered on the study of Greek and Latin. In 1827, the president and fellows at Yale College passed a resolution "inquir[ing] into the expediency of so altering the regular course of instruction in this college, as to leave out of said course the study of the dead languages." In response to this resolution, the Yale faculty produced a document now known as the "The Yale Report," proudly defending the traditional course of study: "To suppose the modern languages more practical than the ancients, to the great body of our students, because the former are now spoken in some parts of the world, is an obvious fallacy." Yet the school assumed its modern role when educators decided that this "obvious fallacy" wasn't fallacious at all. The introduction of English literature into the curriculum represented the school's acknowledgment that the ancient languages were dead and the modern languages were alive.[2]

It was the liveliness of US literary culture in particular that educational reformers claimed for the modern school system when they brought English literature into the classroom. The vitality of this culture wasn't reducible to its utility; the teaching of English literature not only indicated that the school had taken on an instrumental role within industrial society, where command of Standard English and familiarity with the vernacular canon served as credentials for the rising new middle class, while facility with Greek or Latin did not. The teaching of English literature also did much more than this. At a historical moment when the educational system was just coming into existence, the institutionalization of literature enabled the modern school to integrate itself into public life, bridging scholastic and non-scholastic experience. When I refer to the institutionalization of literature, I mean both the teaching of literature in schools and the production of literature about schools. As an object of study inside the classroom, literature invigorated the school system with unscholastic forms, practices, and affects; as an object of public attention outside the classroom, literature made the project of modern education legible to sometimes indifferent, sometimes hostile reading audiences.

Literature, in short, helped the modern school system resolve a crisis of relevance that it suffered throughout the nineteenth century. The belief that schooling lay outside the realm of true experience—that it was inauthentic or unreal—took hold at the beginning of the century, even as many in the early national period enshrined formal education as an ideal and even as schooling gradually became a more significant feature of US life. Thomas Jefferson, having tried and failed several times to pass a free-school bill through the Virginia legislature in 1806, explained in a letter to Joel Barlow that schooling was not a priority in the state, that "people generally have more feeling for canals and roads than education." Half a century later, farmers and pioneers in Yoncalla, Oregon, expressed disdain toward "all singing schools, Sabbath Schools, Spelling Schools, Grammar Schools and all debating societies," deriding spelling bees and declamations as a "sparking school or some such silly thing."[3] These sorts of accusations will appear again and again in the pages that follow. As we will see, the institutionalization of literature allowed the school system to neutralize public concerns about the relevance of formal education and establish itself as part of American life, not as an appendage to it.

This is not to suggest that literature itself hasn't benefited from its institutionalization in the school. Indeed, like formal education, literary culture has suffered its own vexed relationship to "real" experience. We can glimpse the cultural suspicion surrounding literariness as early as the eighteenth century, in Herbert Marsh's translation of Johann David Michaelis's *Introduction to the New Testament* (1793), which contrasts the ornateness of the literary with the simplicity of common language: "The writers of the New Testament in general have never pretended to the beauties of literary language; and St. Paul, who was the most able, has used in the epistles the same expressions, as he would have used in common conversation." Literariness has often provoked more severe denunciations. In 1855, an anonymous reviewer in the United States proclaimed that "affectation, literary affectation, is one of the unpardonable sins. We have no patience with it, whatever." Statements like this confirm Alexis de Tocqueville's observation that

Americans "look upon real literature with disapproval." The cultural suspicion surrounding literature and the cultural suspicion surrounding schools therefore expressed themselves in similar terms. To skeptics, both the literary and the scholastic seemed divorced from the pressing concerns of real life, as Jefferson's letter suggests, or set apart from "common" experience, as in Marsh's translation.[4]

The argument of this book is that the relationship between literary culture and formal education in the United States has proved mutually advantageous, allowing both to overcome their purported irrelevance and claim access to real social experience. This relationship, however, has not always been harmonious. Though many writers have praised the school and many educators have enthusiastically taught their students literature, the history of literary and scholastic culture in America has also been charged with antagonism. In *Moby-Dick* (1851), Herman Melville pronounced the significance of his literary endeavors by taking the school as his foil, contrasting the romance of the sea to the stultifications of formal education: Ishmael, in one of the novel's most famous lines, declares that "a whale-ship was my Yale College and my Harvard." After attending a lecture delivered by the common school reformer Horace Mann in 1839, Ralph Waldo Emerson wrote in his journal, "We are shut up in schools and college recitation rooms for ten or fifteen years, and come out at last with a bellyful of words and do not know a thing." Meanwhile John Dewey in the revised edition of *The School and Society*, published in 1915, encouraged teachers not to organize elementary education around the medium of literature. Instead of teaching Defoe's *Robinson Crusoe* or Longfellow's *Hiawatha*, "Why not," Dewey wrote, "give the child the reality with its much larger sweep, its intenser forces, its more vivid and lasting value for life"?[5]

Whether this antagonism was *more* characteristic of the relationship between literary and scholastic culture than the harmony they often enjoyed is difficult, and not strictly necessary, to determine. It's not necessary because the "antagonism" and "harmony" that have so often characterized this relationship can't truly be disentangled from one another. In order to marginalize the study of literature, modern reformers needed to include literature in the curriculum; in order to excoriate formal education, writers needed to represent it in some capacity, or simply invoke it. Better, I think, is to understand the relationship between literary and scholastic culture as fundamentally intimate. The well-documented acrimony between the two can be seen simply as a sign of their growing intimacy. This intimacy, even and especially when it took the form of bitter denunciation or mockery, has proved enormously generative. When educational reformers disparaged the study of literature, or when writers asserted the significance of their literary work against the failings of the school, these gestures only succeeded in further establishing formal education and literature in industrial society. By expressing such hostility toward each other, educators and writers were able to claim for their respective projects a greater role in US life, proclaiming their own relevance against the irrelevance of their rival. And by internalizing each other's hostility, educators and writers transcended their limitations and transformed the meaning of "education" and "literature."

I take this particular ambition—to transcend inherited institutions and forms, and to access, through this transcendence, the rich, living current of social experience—as distinctive of modern educational reform and "literature" in its modern sense. We might describe this modern sensibility as broadly anti-institutional or, following Morton White, as anti-formalist.[6] We might associate it with a Romantic worldview that took hold within nineteenth-century US culture, including educational and literary discourse. We might also identify it, as I do when discussing literature in this book, with a specific literary tradition, the American literary tradition, which has often been associated with anti-institutionalism, and with a specific literary form, the novel, which has insistently been understood as anti-formalist. Thus, my account of "literature" in this book is routed through "American literature," and my account of "American literature" is primarily routed through American novels. I focus on this specific archive in order to isolate an anti-institutional logic that gained influence within US literary culture as a whole in the period after the Civil War. The special place given to fiction in *Schools of Fiction* reflects in part the outsized role that this conception of literature came to play in cultural and educational history.

We can appreciate the supremacy of this conception of the literary in the twentieth century through Leslie Fiedler's landmark *Love and Death in the American Novel* (1960), a monograph that itself conflates literature, American literature, and American novels. For Fiedler, the novel is a "form without a theory," a genre that "defies an Aristotelian definition"; it is an "unforeseen and disruptive stranger" whose "very name was used in earlier times as a term of deprecation, as if the genre were essentially disreputable." "For traditional critics in the eighteenth century," Fiedler claimed, "it appeared to be essentially sub-literature." Of course, the qualities that make the novel so offensive to the eighteenth-century traditionalists—the qualities that make it "sub-" or "anti-literary"—are the very qualities that, to Fiedler in the mid-twentieth century, allow the novel to stand in for literature as such. To defend his conceptualization of the literary, Fiedler on the first page of his book conjures a history of literature in which the novel eventually reigns supreme over global literary culture. "The classical poetic genres revived by the Renaissance had lost their relevance to contemporary life before America entered the cultural scene; and even the lyric has provided us with occasions for few, and limited triumphs," he writes. "Not only in the United States, though pre-eminently there, literature has become for most readers quite simply prose fiction[.] ... The notions of greatness once associated with the heroic poem have been transferred to the novel; and the shift is a part of that 'Americanization of culture' which some European intellectuals continue ritually to deplore."[7]

Fiedler's compressed history of world literary culture is meant to license a chain of substitutions, where "literature" becomes "American literature," and "American literature" becomes "American novels." Whether these substitutions are credible is a question I'll bracket for just a moment: my main point here is that, through Fiedler, we can appreciate the predominance of a certain conception of literature in the mid-twentieth century, a conception that assumes "literariness" is anti-institutional and anti-formal (just like American literature and the novel, in this account, are). Though my book also focuses on American novels, it doesn't pretend, as Fiedler comes close to here, that literature, American literature, and American novels all became coextensive with one another at a certain point in history. I insist instead that the center of gravity in US literary culture shifted over the course of the postbellum period toward what I've called the modern conception of literature. And though this gravitational shift is visible in the culture's reassessment of American literature and the novel, its pull also extended beyond one national tradition and one form, without at the same time encompassing the entirety of the US literary field, which has always remained a space of contestation, made up of different conceptions of literariness vying with each other for hegemony. The poetry of Longfellow and Whittier, not to mention Browning, remained hugely influential in postbellum literary culture, even as the "Great American Novel" became an object of public fascination and, in Lawrence Buell's words, "prose fiction established itself decisively as the literary form of preference, with 'novel' as the paradigmatic form of prose fiction." Poetry also remained especially significant in the US academy for much of the twentieth century, where the poets John Crowe Ransom, Allen Tate, R. P. Blackmur, and William Empson were "welcome in English departments long before fiction writers," as Evan Kindley reminds us. Yet the entry of these poet-critics into the academy coincided with the steadily increasing scholastic prestige of the novel, marked by the publication of Robert Penn Warren and Cleanth Brooks's *Understanding Fiction* (1943), F. R. Leavis's *The Great Tradition* (1948), and Ian Watt's *The Rise of the Novel* (1957).[8]

In the end, what united the figure of the poet-critic and Fiedler, the teacher of American novels, was the conviction that literature was stubbornly resistant to the academic establishment, its protocols of study and instruction. (The poet-critics embodied this idea by occupying the margins of the academy, as teachers *and* writers of poetry. Fiedler, the *enfant terrible* of the discipline, embodied this idea too.) The reason Fiedler's own definition of the literary could plausibly describe literature in its entirety at the mid-twentieth century—and the reason indeed this definition of literature receives more attention in *Schools of Fiction* than competing ones—is that, with its blinding contempt for institutions of formal education, it grounded the study of literature in the rapidly expanding school system. A bizarre but integral feature of the modern educational experience in the United States is that teachers enthusiastically teach literary works that have nothing but terrible things to say about school. I imagine this description will sound familiar to many readers, and the paradox at its core suggests the all-important labor that literature has performed in scholastic life.

My book explains how this familiar paradox of modern pedagogy came to be. Why did certain writers before the Civil War articulate the significance of their work against the school, and why did certain educators after the Civil War insist on teaching this strain of writing as "literature"? The postbellum period is of special interest to *Schools of Fiction* as the historical moment when US literary culture, which had so often defined itself against the school, suddenly found itself enmeshed in the administrative apparatus of the school. Fiedler himself is an interesting figure in precisely these terms, a critic who insisted that literature was itself essentially anti-institutional and that his own work was also. In the preface to the first edition of *Love and Death in the American Novel*, Fiedler declares that, having eschewed footnotes or a formal bibliography, his was "not, in the customarily accepted sense of the word, an academic or scholarly book." He also explains in the same preface that his chief ambition is to "redeem our great books from the commentaries on them." Fiedler composed these proclamations from the margins of the academic establishment, at the University of Montana, and he published them not at a university press but at Criterion Books. He wrote, moreover, at a time when an unprecedented number of students received their education within the very academic apparatus that his monograph deplored, an apparatus, it should also be noted, in which his monograph eventually proved enormously influential.[9]

This book centers on a period of educational and literary history that stretches from 1861 to 1918. Over this interval of time, formal education in the United States gradually cohered into a modern system and the teaching of English literature became a standard part of the curriculum, from kindergarten all the way through graduate school. Though *Schools of Fiction* concentrates on this especially dynamic period, the book's focus also strategically widens beyond it at times to better understand its dynamism. The opening chapters explore the production of literature before the Civil War and the contradictions that attended its institutionalization after the Civil War. The subsequent chapters investigate the production of literature in the postbellum era, under the embryonic structures of the modern school, and the influence individual literary works from this period continue to exert on formal education today. This later influence is of an altogether different kind and intensity than the influence literature exerted during an earlier phase of institutional history, when its entry into the US school system provoked large-scale administrative change. As the institutional landscape has centralized over time and the school has assumed a greater role in the reproduction of the social order, literature's power to shape scholastic life has diminished accordingly. Nonetheless, its effect on the gigantic institutional complex that is the educational system remains palpable.

As Figure 1 suggests, this book maintains a rather unconventional relationship to periodization even as it recognizes the indispensability of the period concept. The book's unconventionality is a product of its desire to reconstruct the institutional conditions out of which literature has emerged at any given historical

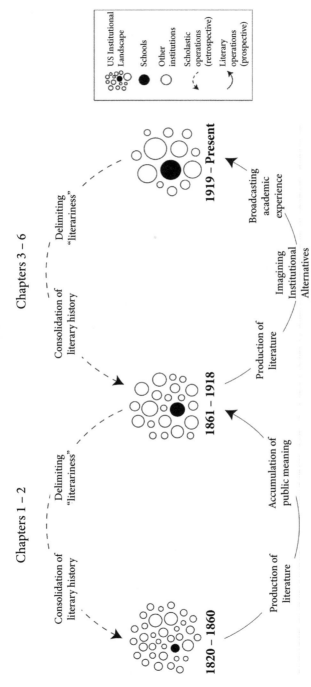

Figure 1 An overview of *Schools of Fiction*. Over the last two centuries, literature has persistently exceeded the institutional conditions that have made its existence possible. The school system has in turn metabolized certain literary works from the past for its own growth, and as it processes these works it imposes its own administrative logic onto them, retrospectively distinguishing "literary" texts from the rest of cultural production and consolidating a "literary history."

moment *and* to track literature's subsequent effect on the institutions that made its existence possible in the first place. This unconventional relationship to periodization also characterizes the book's individual chapters, which, like *Schools of Fiction* as a whole, range from their stated periods of focus sporadically so the distinctiveness of these periods can be better appreciated.

Methodologically, the book examines literature's influence on the modern school across a range of institutional sites and actors. I consider the curriculum, the textbook, and the pedagogical edition as particularly rich areas of investigation, just as many scholars have before me, but I also discuss the impact of literature on the evolution of campus culture, that boundary-zone of academic life that educational historians call the "extracurriculum," where the school system and the public try to make sense of one another. (Insofar as the origins of literary studies in higher education lie in the extracurricular activities of student societies, you might even say that the extracurriculum has been the principal site of literature's institutional influence.) This book explores the rhetoric and pedagogical theory of postbellum educational reformers as well, those architects of the modern school whose profound ambivalence toward literary culture stands as a testament to that culture's institutional significance. These were the reformers, furthermore, responsible for erecting an administrative apparatus that trained, however incompletely or unsatisfyingly, a generation of proto-modernist writers whose literary work defied that apparatus and, in defying it, facilitated its development. Enrollment numbers in English and American literature courses receive less emphasis in this book than some might expect, simply because the enduring popularity of these classes is well-established in disciplinary history and the historiography of US education.[10]

Some readers might also be surprised by the amount of time I spend attending to the content and form of actual literary works here. By no means a simple methodological reflex, this close attention to the inner workings of literature is in fact one of the book's main interventions. Unlike other disciplinary historians, who tend to see the school as the ineluctable administrator of literary culture and therefore focus on developments strictly internal to the school without attending to literature itself, I believe that literary works exert pressure upon their institutional surroundings—that they aren't simply raw and indifferent materials onto which the school imposes its administrative logic. To truly apprehend literature's institutional agency, to understand how it licenses and provokes its own institutional reception, I believe we need to attend to literary texts themselves.

Chapter 1 details the emergence of an anti-scholastic American literary tradition before the Civil War and then follows the scholastic reception of this anti-scholastic tradition in the postbellum period. Writers like Washington Irving, whose "The Legend of Sleepy Hollow" (1820) inaugurated the anti-scholastic tradition, believed that their work gave readers access to a thriving world of authentic social experience whose antithesis was the school. After the Civil War, English instructors began teaching this work in order to claim its authentic social vision for the modern educational system. Chapter 2 reveals that modern reformers in the postbellum period sought to establish the educational system at the center of industrial life by disparaging the act of reading. Reading, according to these educators, isolated and enervated individual readers, and in this sense it represented the obverse of the vibrant social life of the modern school system. This hostility toward reading was necessarily bound up with the reformers' relationship to English as a discipline, the class or department where literacy instruction occurred and where "literature" itself was increasingly understood as written material—as something you read, not something you orated or performed on a stage. As reformers expressed suspicion toward the act of reading, writers denounced reading in their work too, not to capitulate to the anti-readers but to expand the scope of literary experience. So, while English teachers taught anti-scholastic literary works to make the school un-school-like, writers such as Henry James, Edith Wharton, Theodore Dreiser, Charles Chesnutt, and Sarah Orne Jewett depicted characters not reading in order to make literature un-literary. Together, then, Chapters 1 and 2 show that literature and pedagogy after the Civil War shared an aberrant form of self-consciousness, as writers disavowed reading and educators disavowed formal education as meaningful enterprises. These disavowals reflect the complexity of the anti-institutionalism that defined the modern sensibility. Writers and educators didn't simply disavow each other but also themselves. Modern pedagogy as it evolved into a coherent program over the course of the postbellum period denounced reading *and also* schools. The modern conception of literature that eventually emerged was anti-scholastic and anti-itself.

The next chapters move forward in time, demonstrating how post–Civil War literature exceeded the institutional conditions that surrounded its production and then went on to shape formal education over the twentieth and twenty-first centuries. In Chapter 3, I argue that Henry Adams and Gertrude Stein were dissatisfied with the organization of time in schools and theorized new institutional modes—the "period" and the "continuous present"—to coordinate their reading audiences temporally. In Chapter 4, I argue that Frank Norris and Upton Sinclair cultivated a literature of disgust as a reaction to Progressive pedagogy based on student interest. In both chapters, institutional "problems"—time in Chapter 3 and feeling in Chapter 4—find literary "solutions" that are eventually incorporated into the classroom through the curriculum. By making students read about the lonely, out-of-sync college graduates in Adams's and Stein's work, instructors have paradoxically produced the standardized experience of time that Harvard president Charles Eliot sought to institutionalize through the "course unit." And by teaching the disgusting episodes that pervade postbellum literature, educators have been able to expand the emotional palate of the school, more thoroughly realizing John Dewey's vision of an all-encompassing educational system centered on the non-academic feelings of the students.

The final section of *Schools of Fiction* explores another institutional problem, beyond temporality and feeling, that post–Civil War literature has enabled the modern school to address: the problem of ideology. Before the twentieth century, the educational system lacked the social authority to function effectively as an ideological apparatus. Early campus fiction—as a product of and an active force within the liminal institutional space of student culture—broadcast the school to the public and legitimized the process that distinguished academic insiders from outsiders. It did so by taking the undergraduate secret society as its foil, an elitist student organization against which it could articulate its democratizing vision of scholastic life and on which it could base its own exclusionary meritocratic ideology. Other postbellum writers, including Thomas Dixon Jr., Charles Chesnutt, Frances Ellen Watkins Harper, and Sutton Griggs, took up the secret society in their work in order to propose competing justifications for institutional inclusion and exclusion. These alternatives have shaped the educational system upon their institutionalization as well, unsettling the meritocratic conception of the school that has served as its principle of ideological coherence for members of the new middle class and the ruling elite since the early twentieth century. Literature, in the case of Dixon, has facilitated the repressive (as opposed to ideological) operations that the school has performed on those populations whose consent is deemed unnecessary for the maintenance and reproduction of the social order. And in the case of Chesnutt and Harper, among other writers of African American literature, literature has remained indispensable to the school as it has attempted to broaden its meritocratic worldview to encompass racial difference after the protest movements of the 1960s and 1970s.

These six chapters are, needless to say, not exhaustive; I have not enumerated here all of the ways that literature has affected schools and schools have affected literature. The key insight that motivates this book is that we can't understand educational history in isolation from literary history—that the two histories are entangled with one another. This insight is fairly straightforward, but the entanglements are not. I have tried here to follow these imbricated histories and understand the significance of their complex interrelation. Though many throughout US history have doubted the value of schooling and looked askance at literary culture, the elaborate exchanges between educators and writers have endowed both nevertheless with considerable social authority. The intricacy of these exchanges is partially responsible for their success, but it also registers the precariousness of the whole performance. If *Schools of Fiction* appears to be a story of triumph—following the ascendance of literature and the educational system—it is also, we will discover, a narrative of decline, as the public significance of each has dramatically contracted in the last few decades. This decline is precisely what those advocates of literary culture and the school system feared when they excoriated each other, denounced themselves, and declared their own importance. That these gestures were ever convincing at all, that these performances worked for as long as they did, is something of a miracle, one that deserves further consideration.

Acknowledgements

I have many people to thank for their help and support on this book.

The members of my dissertation committee at Stanford—Gavin Jones, Mark McGurl, and Nancy Ruttenburg—have shaped this project from its inception. Gavin deserves special thanks for his unending patience, incisive feedback, and good cheer. I'd also like to thank other faculty members in the Stanford University Department of English for their guidance during graduate school and after—Mark Algee-Hewitt, John Bender, Judy Richardson, and Alex Woloch.

I was part of a truly special intellectual community in graduate school at Stanford. This book would not exist without Dalglish Chew, Erik Johnson, Derek Mong, J. D. Porter, Vanessa Seals, Hannah Walser, Jessie Beckman, Mary Kim, Jesse Nathan, Andrew Shepard, Justin Tackett, Josh Mann, Jonny Sensenbaugh, Amir Tevel, Allen Frost, Long Le-Khac, Claude Willan, Linda Liu, Aku Ammah-Tagoe, Luke Barnhart, Chelsea Davis, Abigail Droge, Laura Eidem, Sylvan Goldberg, Vicky Googasian, Ryan Heuser, Anita Law, Tanya Llewellyn, Frances Molyneux, Akemi Ueda, Rachel Bolten, Armen Davoudian, Erik Fredner, Juan Lamata, Hannah Smith-Drelich, Xander Manshel, Kathryn Winner, Nikil Saval, Irena Yamboliev, and Becky Richardson. I will also single out Mark Taylor, Nathan Wainstein, and Elizabeth Wilder for reading chapter-drafts in the lead up to the book's publication. Kevin Block, also in the Bay Area, is a great friend and spirited conversationalist who has provided feedback on individual chapters of the book too.

I completed this book as a visiting assistant professor in the English Department at Wesleyan University and as a lecturer in History and Literature at Harvard University. At Wesleyan, Sean McCann and Matthew Garrett have provided generous feedback on my work over the years; special thanks also go to Stephanie Weiner, Khachig Tölölyan, Joel Pfister, Susanne Fusso, Ruth Nisse, Amy Tang, Courtney Weiss-Smith, Marina Bilbija, and Sam Fallon for their advice and encouragement. I feel lucky to have supportive colleagues at Harvard like Lauren Kaminsky, Angela Allan, Duncan White, and Briana Smith.

An early version of Chapter 2 appeared in *New Literary History*, Volume 50, Issue 4, Spring 2020, pages 45–66. Copyright © 2020 Johns Hopkins University Press. An early version of Chapter 4 appeared in *NOVEL: A Forum on Fiction*, Volume 50, Issue 2, August 2017, pages 197–216. Copyright © 2017 Duke University Press. Some of the material on *Stover at Yale*'s reception history and the state of higher education in the postbellum period appeared in *Modern Language Quarterly*, Volume 80, Issue 3, September 2019, pages 311–334. Thank you to these presses for their permission to reprint.

I want to thank Gordon Hutner for his feedback on the book and for welcoming it into the Oxford Studies in American Literary History series. I am also grateful to the anonymous readers for their substantive reports on the manuscript. Thank you, finally, Katie Bishop, Jo Spillane, and Hannah Doyle at OUP for guiding the book through the publication process.

Many friendships have sustained me through the writing of this book. Casey Davis, Aditi Nagaraj, Mariana Castrellon, Laura Vollmer, Derek Tingle, Julia Roseman, Evan Tingle, Kate Levy, Eli Sevcik-Timberg, Jenn Clark, Julius Pasay, Micah Siegel, Jonathan Gienapp, Anne Twitty, Caterina Scaramelli, Ben Siegel, Ben Glaser, Priyasha Mukhopadhyay, Zack Barnett-Howell, Alanna Hickey, Andy Bruns, Naomi Levine, and Greg Ellerman are great people and I'm fortunate to have them in my life.

My family also deserves recognition for their love and forbearance: my mom, my dad, Martin, Susie, Sungmi, Eleanor, Nick, Greg, Ursula, Geoff, and Sam. I'll thank Willie individually for teaching me, you know, how to read. The Eccleses deserve my thanks as well: Chris, Cobber, Zuleika, Lydia, Isy, Betsy, and Sam. I need to thank Tony in particular for his help on the diagram.

Tasha Eccles has read every chapter of this book many times; she is my liveliest interlocutor and best friend. May this book rest easy now in print, safe from her loving and merciless scrutiny.

Introduction
Irrelevance

> The public says very little about us, and knows, I fear, even less.
> —Josiah Royce writing to Daniel Coit Gilman, September 1880[1]

In January 1887, a retired businessman named Jonas Gilman Clark announced plans to start a school in Worcester, Massachusetts. Though he originally conceived the institution as a college for poor country boys, Clark's vision had changed dramatically by the time he appointed G. Stanley Hall president in 1888. Instead of serving undergraduates, the school would become a university along the lines of Johns Hopkins, catering to the research projects of faculty and graduate students. Clark founded Clark University on a $1 million gift—at the time, the largest single gift to an educational institution in New England—and together he and Hall decided to maintain only five departments, all in the sciences: psychology, biology, chemistry, physics, and mathematics. To staff these departments, Hall raided other leading research universities, recruiting, among others, the physiologist Warren P. Lombard from Johns Hopkins, the chemists John Ulric Nef from Purdue and Arthur Michael from Tufts, and an anthropologist from Europe named Franz Boas.

In spring 1892, a little more than five years after Clark's announcement, the school all but imploded, with 70 percent of the student body and two-thirds of the faculty leaving. What happened? How could a university, founded under such favorable circumstances—the huge endowment, the illustrious faculty—prove such a spectacular failure?[2]

Clark University's near-collapse reveals some of the problems that the educational system faced during its beleaguered early years. Between the Civil War and World War I, formal education is often said to have "modernized," "bureaucratized," or undergone an "organizational revolution," and though these terms are usually understood to describe a highly rationalized, implacable process, the consolidation of a proper school system in the United States was, to the contrary, halting and dysfunctional. This dysfunction, we will discover, came about as the modern school struggled to overcome its perceived irrelevance as a social institution. Given the enthusiasm for STEM fields in our current historical moment, we might assume that Clark University's commitment to the sciences and advanced research would have sufficiently grounded its authority and guaranteed its future success. Yet the school's investment in the sciences failed to make Clark's mission comprehensible to the broader public, and this failure was principally responsible for Clark's disastrous launch.

This book will argue that literature as an object of academic study—not psychology, biology, chemistry, physics, or mathematics—ensured the reproduction and expansion of the modern educational system after the Civil War. Literature proved indispensable to the project of modern education because it helped the school system identify itself with real social experience. English literary studies assumed an unusual position within the educational system as literature's disciplinary home, the internal curricular location where the school system sought to access a world external to itself. Many other subjects entered the educational system around the same time as English and similarly upended the traditional curriculum; yet English more than these other subjects insisted, even after its institutionalization, on its essential incompatibility with academic study. It continued to associate itself with life, rather than the school. As the educational system grew and came to assume a greater role managing literature's own access to public life, the relationship between the school and the discipline only became more complex. The inability of scholars both outside and inside of English departments to recognize the significance of the discipline to the modern educational program is itself a symptom of this fraught institutional history. *Schools of Fiction* reconstructs this history, a history of mutual dependency and the frustrations, depreciations, and misrecognitions that have attended it.[3]

But let's pause for a moment and consider the challenges that the school system faced at this inchoate stage in its development, around the time of the Clark University fiasco. First, higher education was not a common feature of US life. During the 1899–1900 academic year, only 2.3 percent of the eighteen- to twenty-four-year-old population in the United States enrolled in an institution of higher education. A college-building boom during the antebellum period and the expansion of the undergraduate curriculum in the decades following the Civil War were crucial steps in the development of US higher education, yet the higher learning still remained beyond consideration for the vast majority of Americans at the beginning of the twentieth century. Colleges and universities were, furthermore, in a persistent state of financial insecurity, their existence dependent on outside benefactors and patrons. The university, with its funding problems and unintegrated programs of study, was, in the words of John Thelin, "an adolescent—gangly, energetic, and enigmatic." Though colleges fared better than universities, they were also beset by low enrollments and "formidable" attrition rates.[4]

Secondary schools suffered from problems similar to those of colleges and universities. Of the students enrolled in primary and secondary school during the 1899–1900 academic year, only 3.3 percent attended secondary school. Graduation rates remained low throughout most of the nineteenth century as well. A year or two studying the "higher branches" was often enough to distinguish prospective employees on the labor market. At Cleveland's Central High School, 51 percent of the student population were freshmen in 1862, while 27 percent were sophomores, 15 percent were juniors, and 7 percent were seniors. At Hartford's co-ed public high school, 46 percent of the students were freshmen in 1868, 29 percent were sophomores, 14 percent were juniors, and 11 percent were seniors. "To leave, or not to leave, that is the question," one Philadelphia high school student wrote in 1885, parodying Hamlet's soliloquy. "To leave, to work—/And by working, end the thousand natural/Headaches, troubles, and dissensions/That school-life is heir to—Twould be a consummation/To have no more studies." The absence of a robust high school system meant there were fewer students to attend colleges and universities. Speaking in front of the New Jersey legislature in 1871, Princeton president James McCosh described the school system as a two-story house without a staircase.[5]

Compared to the higher branches, primary schools were much more integrated into nineteenth-century US life. Between 1780 and 1840, most rural children in the North and many white children in the South attended school at some point during the year from the age of four or five until around the age of fourteen. Through the antebellum period, the one-room schoolhouse was often the only public building for miles in the rural United States, providing a central venue for community life. During the 1899–1900 academic year, the vast majority of the 15.5 million students enrolled in public primary and secondary schools—students representing 71.9 percent of the 5- to 17-year-old student-age population—were enrolled in primary schools. Yet this scholastic experience, which occurred predominantly in those one-room district schoolhouses, differed appreciably from primary schooling today. Rural schools usually operated for eight to ten weeks over the summer and a similar period over the winter. (The school superintendent of Pennsylvania lamented in 1848 that the average school term was less than five months.) Student attendance remained irregular under this abbreviated academic calendar too: during the 1899–1900 year, the average length of the primary and secondary academic term was only 144 days, about thirty-five days shorter than it is now, and each student attended an average of only ninety-nine days. Throughout the nineteenth century, many resisted the efforts of common school reformers and, later, Progressive educators to centralize the school system, lengthen the school term, regularize attendance, and standardize the curriculum.[6]

Taken as a whole, education in the nineteenth-century United States is best understood as a process that took place across a decentralized institutional landscape that included schooling—the one-room district school, the urban private-venture school, the academy, and the liberal arts college, along with their emergent modern counterparts, the state common-school system, the high school, and the university—but also extended beyond it. The church represented an especially influential formal institution for many, while an informal institution, the family, remained the most significant structuring force in the country. Along with the school, the church, and the family, a whole host of institutions contributed to the education of Americans, including various apprentice-based professions; almshouses, asylums, reformatories, and penitentiaries, which acted as surrogates for the household; lyceums that thrived during the midcentury in the Northeast and the Midwest; and books, newspapers, and other assorted reading materials that helped transmit knowledge and culture.[7]

In this decentralized institutional landscape, the school had many advocates, but it also had detractors, and there were others, too, who were simply indifferent toward it. For the indifferent, schooling was not an apprehensible feature of daily life, or, if it was apprehensible, it simply wasn't a priority. The educational historian Lawrence Cremin once described this population's relationship to education, explaining that, while the "forces of popularization in various [educational] institutions were mutually reinforcing" between 1783 and 1876, "there were groups that did not or could not partake":

> Some were isolated from the process by geographic distance: they lived far from schools, libraries, lyceums, and fairs; they were illiterate or semiliterate; and they were able to live satisfactorily according to their own values without participating in the expanding world of education. Others were isolated from the process by what one might call psychic distance. They may have been within walking distance of schools, libraries, lyceums, and fairs, but such institutions were not part of the world as they perceived it. They were either not moved to participate, or they felt they ought not to participate because the institutions were for one reason or another not for them, or they believed that the price of participation in terms of violence to their own values was not worth the conflict.[8]

Detractors of the school often vocalized the unformulated convictions of the indifferent, condemning the school as an appendage to real life. We can see this conviction in the frequent association of schools with "book-learning." While "book-learning" was not exclusively a term of derogation, it was persistently invoked throughout the nineteenth century to suggest the inadequacy of formal education.[9] In 1823, the *New England Farmer* printed excerpts from a book by the English agrarianist, pamphleteer, and politician William Cobbett, declaring that education "includes every thing with regard to the *mind* as well as the *body* of the child; but of late years, it has been so used as to have no sense applied to it but that of *book-learning*." The Reverend John H. Rice of Virginia declared in 1828 that "preachers of the gospel are mostly taught nothing but book learning. They have to do with minds and hearts; to find access to the inner man; to go to the very sources of human action; —and in preparing to do this work, they are made to study chiefly, old books, written by men in states of society, far different from ours." The school, as the institution responsible for disseminating book-learning, was thereby associated with a narrow form of education that was distinct from "education" in a more capacious and authentic sense. "A school is a building erected to deprive a child of an education," goes an old North Dakota joke. Even most of those convinced of the importance of schooling in the nineteenth century believed it should remain just one part of a larger educational process, an institution that students attended for only some of the year while they received, say, professional instruction elsewhere.[10]

Modern reformers like Hall thus faced serious obstacles as they set out to subsume the entirety of the educational process under just one institutional system. The Clark debacle indicates that the modern school at the turn of the century suffered at bottom a crisis of relevance, or rather a crisis of irrelevance. After all, Clark's implosion was not simply the result of insufficient funding or the absence of a coherent mission. Jonas Gilman Clark had plenty of money, and the university's faculty had all embraced scholarship or *Wissenschaft* as an institutional ideal. However, just a few months before the school's inauguration, on April 15, 1889, the *Worcester Telegram* published an article, "What Is Clark University," whose ambiguously punctuated headline—somewhere between a question and a statement—suggested the school system's social illegibility. The article itself consisted of a conversation between a *Telegram* reporter and Hall, who appears incapable of explaining anything whatsoever about Clark:

> "Now, President Hall, the people of Worcester know comparatively nothing about Clark University, what its policy is to be and the general character of the institution, and—"
>
> "O, really, I have nothing to say," broke in that gentleman. "It is really too early yet to say anything about our plans, for they are not yet developed. In a few weeks, however, we hope to be able to tell the public just what we propose to do." ...
>
> "Will you not state in a general way what Clark University is to be, what will be its policy, so that the public may know something about the character of the institution?"
>
> "I really cannot now, it is too early, but in a few weeks we shall be able, I hope, to tell definitely just what we propose to do; I trust we shall."[11]

The April 15 article was just the first of many attacks the *Telegram* launched against the university during the school's opening years. In 1890, the newspaper published an exposé of vivisection experiments there, accusing scientists of torturing and murdering animals.[12] In 1891, the newspaper printed a series of articles detailing Boas's research in the university labs, describing local high schoolers having "their anatomies felt" and "various portions of their bodies measured."[13] Notwithstanding the sensationalism of these later exposés, the substance of the newspaper's coverage remained the same. The purpose of the new research university was fundamentally unclear to the Worcester public, and the *Telegram*, faced with this obscure social institution, produced vivid reports of what was "actually" going on inside the school. Clark's meltdown occurred shortly after the *Telegram* published the anatomy articles. Met with growing resistance from the Worcester public and dwindling interest from other wealthy Worcester citizens, Jonas Gilman Clark began withdrawing support from the university. He gave only $18,000 to cover the school's operating expenses for its fourth year, and after 1891, Clark made no further annual gifts to the university. Relations between Hall and the faculty deteriorated. The exodus of professors and students ensued.[14]

Without a coherent picture of the modern school circulating in the popular imagination, without a common understanding of the meaning and significance of the modern educational program, even well-funded institutions with eminent faculty members could be ruined by the speculations of a local newspaper. A chasm, in short, divided the school system from the rest of public life. As Josiah Royce, a recently hired faculty member at the University of California, explained in an 1880 letter to Daniel Coit Gilman, the recently appointed president of Johns Hopkins: "The public says very little about us, and knows, I fear, even less." Both Royce and Gilman felt their own irrelevance acutely as members of research universities, yet this irrelevance was palpable for reformers of primary and secondary schools as well, those modern educators who struggled to replace the traditional institutions of formal schooling with their own all-comprehending network of institutions.

How, then, did the school system transform itself from one institution among many in a decentralized institutional landscape to the primary mechanism of US education? How did the United States become a truly schooled society? The argument of *Schools of Fiction* is that literature played a vital role in the growth and consolidation of the modern educational system. In order for the school system to move to the center of public experience—in order for the school system to evolve, in John Dewey's words, into "a genuine form of active community life, instead of a place set apart in which to learn lessons"—it needed to institutionalize literature.[15]

For all sorts of reasons, literature would seem an unlikely solution to the problems besetting the emergent educational system. If schooling has become practically unavoidable in the twenty-first century, literary culture has, according to many, largely receded from public life.[16] Moreover, the modernity of the modern curriculum is usually associated with the rise of the sciences and the marginalization of humanistic and belletristic learning. This association appears in scholarship on the history of US education, not just in public discourse. According to Laurence Veysey, by 1910, utility and research "held sway at most major institutions [of higher education] away from the eastern seaboard," whereas liberal culture "felt the illusory exhilaration of a few recent victories, but it lagged far behind in terms of actual influence, and it was soon to prove handicapped by its tie with the genteel tradition."[17] Christopher Newfield has explained that Veysey's account reflects a widely accepted "remainder theory of humanism," where "the humanities' vision of liberal culture" is treated "as a version of moral education, a kind of education central to the old college but marginal to the knowledge-creating, science-based university." The humanities, including literary studies, remain by this theory a residual form that has only managed to survive through the "undergraduate curriculum" and the "liberal arts college that ignored research."[18]

Even within literary studies, the idea that literature could transform the system of formal education has become hard to fathom. For the last forty years or so, the discipline has self-consciously sought to demystify literature as an object of study: around 1980, literary scholars began to regard literature as a product of material practices and institutions rather than as some transcendent or autonomous cultural phenomenon unto itself.[19] This demystification occurred at the tail end of a number of important developments within US intellectual life, developments in which industrial modernity was more and more often understood to involve the expansion of an oppressive disciplinary apparatus at whose center sat the school. These developments include the eruption of protests and liberation movements during the 1960s and 1970s, which identified the school system as a malign force entwined with the military-industrial complex. They also include the migration into the United States of certain strains of Western Marxist thought, such as Louis Althusser's account of ideology, which insisted that the school occupied the "*dominant* position" among Ideological State Apparatuses during capitalism's mature phase; Foucault's account of discipline and punishment in the West, with its description of the school as one of the principal sites, along with the army and the hospital, for "controlling or correcting the operations of the body"; and the Frankfurt School's account of modern society as "totally administered." The Frankfurt School proved especially influential within the student protest movements associated with the New Left, where, for instance, Mario Savio described UC Berkeley as a "knowledge factory" where "all the rough edges are taken off and smooth slick products come out."[20]

As these protest movements shaped the academy and critical theory gained legitimacy inside the research university, literary scholars divested literature of its exceptional status and eventually came to think of the school as the epicenter of cultural administration, imagining it as a factory, to adopt Savio's language, that oversaw the reproduction of literary culture just as it oversaw the reproduction of social relations more broadly. John Guillory's *Cultural Capital* (1993) represents an especially sophisticated example of this disciplinary tendency to cast the school as the institutional site where literature derives its larger social meaning. Weighing in on the canon debates of the eighties and early nineties, Guillory argued that "it is only by understanding the social function and institutional protocols of the school that we will understand how [literary] works are preserved, reproduced, and disseminated over successive generations and centuries."[21] It seems noteworthy, in retrospect, that even as Guillory challenged the assumptions that underwrote the canon debate, he nevertheless would agree with its participants that the school is the institutional site where literature takes on its larger political significance.[22]

Of course, profound differences remain between Guillory and the participants in the debate, the most meaningful of which for the purposes of this book is Guillory's conviction that the political agency of literature is entirely defined by the school; both the liberal-pluralists and the reactionaries who participated in the debate believed, by contrast, that canonical works of literature express certain ideological positions that the school serves to ratify and vitalize. As Guillory explains in *Culture Capital*, literary works instead "must be seen as the vector of ideological notions which do not inhere in the works themselves but in the context of their institutional presentation, or more simply, in the way in which they are taught."[23]

Needless to say, this particular formulation severely curtails the agency of literature: how a literary work is "taught" in school determines the political and social agency it possesses, rather than any political or social project it articulates on its own. Enshrining the school's agency and eliding literature's have become a marked trend within English scholarship over the last decade. Mark McGurl's *The Program Era* (2009)—the most influential example of this trend—argues that the educational system since the end of World War II has maintained a fundamentally programmatic relationship to literature, with certain institutional "inputs" producing a complex array of literary "outputs." McGurl's ambition is to "demonstrate that ... postwar American literature can profitably be described as the product of a system," specifically the system of higher education, with its proliferating creative writing programs. McGurl's analysis of this system yields a totalizing picture of the postwar literary field, discovering the origins of its dominant genres, "technomodernism," "lower-middle-class modernism," and "high cultural pluralism," in the creative writing injunctions, "write what you know," "show don't tell," and "find your voice." According to McGurl, the institutionalization of literary production has enriched US culture, producing not homogeneity but a more diverse and capable group of writers. *The Program Era* sets out, in this respect, to recuperate words like "institution" and "institutionalization": "The image of the institution as a prison, or of institutionalization as something that happens at a mental hospital, is obviously a satisfying and perhaps even necessary one," McGurl writes, "but it threatens to sell us on a very naive sense of how individuals actually come into being."[24] In the aftermath of *The Program Era*, scholars have taken McGurl's account of the school and applied it to school-adjacent formations, like the study abroad program, small magazines, writers' colonies, the NEA, and UNESCO. Far from entertaining the notion that literature might influence its institutional environment, the tendency in literary scholarship for several decades now has been to argue precisely the opposite.[25]

The discipline, of course, hasn't always sought to demystify its object of study as a mere institutional construct. In fact, this disciplinary tendency has developed relatively recently, and it represents an abrupt reversal of the anti-scholasticism that had energized the field since its original formation. When English first became an academic subject, it was seen as a threat to the traditional establishment. It appeared stubbornly resistant to the school's administrative regime; it conjured for students an experiential world beyond the suffocating routine of the classroom; it eluded the critical apparatus that pedagogues brought to bear in their studies. Whether conceptualized as ontologically anti-scholastic or as a by-product of scholastic administration, however, literature has not appeared to those tasked with teaching it as foundational to modern pedagogy or as a driving force behind the modern school's growth.

The scholarly failure both outside and within literary studies to grasp literature's influence on the school system is itself a consequence of the idiosyncratic institutional service that educators have called on literature to perform. As this book will go to great lengths to prove, educational reformers after the Civil War claimed for the school system a greater role in US social experience both by enthusiastically teaching literature for its anti-scholasticism and, paradoxically, by condemning literary endeavors as bookish and genteel. The contradictory pedagogical conceptions of English literature reflect the modern school's administrative imperative to overcome the traditional limitations of formal education and merge the school with life itself. Modern reformers embraced literature as intrinsically anti-scholastic and derided it as bookish because they sought to dissolve the boundary dividing the school from society.

The administrative contempt for literature's bookishness, while it enabled the architects of the modern school to claim for their institution a greater public import, has subsequently made it harder for educational historians to appreciate literature's catalytic effect on the system of formal education. For those scholars who have taught literature enthusiastically for the last 150 years, meanwhile, the failure to adequately recognize literature's institutional significance is a more complicated issue, bound up with literary studies' own vexed identity as a discipline, the educational system's increasing influence over literary culture, and the school's own shifting fortunes under the industrial and, later, postindustrial economy. When English instructors insisted that literature was anti-scholastic, the educational system was expanding rapidly under industrialization. The instructors' insistence on this point was at once a genuine expression of their suspicion toward the school system and a propulsive force in that system's expansion. The more recent conviction that the educational system is tremendously powerful, that literature is a product of its scholastic environment, has intensified precisely as the educational system—now the principal administrator of literary culture—has been strategically dismantled. This conviction has taken hold during a period of deindustrialization marked by the public divestment from education, the impending closure of many colleges and universities, and the cratering value of a bachelor's degree. English as an academic subject has felt such stresses acutely, in the form of dwindling majors and the casualization of the profession; yet these developments have not shaken scholars' belief in the school's administrative power. The crumbling of the school system has only somehow confirmed it.[26]

The persistence of this misapprehension is a barrier to the discipline's understanding of its own history and its own importance to the development of the modern school. It is also further proof of literary scholars' pathological relationship to the institution they inhabit. The recent scholarly turn, despite its rather surprising reorientation of one of the discipline's founding premises, is simply the latest exhibit in the troubled, albeit generative, history of literary and scholastic culture that this book details. By calling the discipline of literary studies pathological, I don't pretend that this book is somehow *un*pathological in its assessments, as though it weren't enmeshed in the dynamics it describes. If anything, the book is a demonstration of just how energizing pathology can be: both literature and schools have exercised a great deal of social influence as a result of their dysfunctional collaboration.

We can learn something essential about literary culture and the educational system in our bleak contemporary moment when we understand that their development over the last two centuries has emerged out of this dysfunctional collaboration. The dependence of literature on schools and schools on literature proves, fundamentally, the core fragility of both. The political imperative that follows from this insight is not necessarily the one you would expect. My book does not call for its readers to, say, work together to make the educational system newly relevant. It does not try to convince its audience to restore the educational system to its former glory, because, as these chapters will reveal, the educational system was never exactly glorious. Instead, this book enjoins its readers to acknowledge that the school is not a particularly effective instrument in political struggle, that its outsized role in the reproduction of social relations since the Second World War is contingent, as recent developments have proved. Efforts to produce a just school system are tremendously important and indeed necessary on their own. But these efforts are most transformative when they treat the school not as the engine of social change but as simply one site of struggle among many, often more significant, others. Those seeking to produce a robust and egalitarian educational system must fight to produce a just society as well.[27]

The struggle for political and economic justice, however, largely lies outside the scope of this book, which aims only to show that US schools are now, and have historically been, schools of fiction. As we'll see, prose fiction—like literature generally, only more intensely so—served as a vehicle through which the educational system reimagined its relationship to public life. The appearance of novels in school transformed the student experience inside the classroom; the appearance of the school in novels made formal education socially legible in a way it had never been before. It invested formal education with a new public meaning; it fundamentally changed formal education as an imaginative project. The conviction among literary scholars that the educational system is exceptionally powerful, all evidence to the contrary, is, then, finally, just one more indication of the school's peculiarly fictional existence. The school, as this book describes it, needed to become fictional at a particular moment in its history, and this fictiveness is a sign of the school's vulnerability, not its strength.

Outreach and Withdrawal: The Rise of the Modern School System

Though common school reform was under way in the early nineteenth century and formal education had begun to cohere into a unified system by 1860, the consolidation of the modern system—encompassing primary, secondary, and higher education—only truly took place in the years between the Civil War and the First World War. This consolidation occurred as the United States industrialized and a population of professionals, experts, managers, and salaried office workers emerged to serve the growing capitalist economy. This population has been called, at times, the "white collar masses," the "new class," the "professional-managerial class," or simply the "middle class." As the industrial economy developed, the school became the privileged site through which the new middle class reproduced itself and inflicted its Progressive vision on the rest of society. Who deserved access to wage labor and who deserved to manage wage laborers? The modern educational system provided answers to these questions.[28]

The architects of the school system reformed traditional institutions of formal education in a number of ways to support their vision of US society. They reorganized the curriculum. They divided primary and secondary school students into grades according to age rather than teaching all students as a single body in one-room classrooms. They set standard admissions requirements for college based on prescribed high school classes, and they set requirements for high schools based on prescribed elementary school classes. They made the bachelor's degree a requirement for an MD or a JD instead of having professional schools run in parallel to the undergraduate college. They organized higher education around "majors" and "departments" rather than a preset program of study that all students followed. They dropped chapel requirements, secularizing the undergraduate experience. They standardized doctoral programs through the Association of American Universities. By the end of World War I, the hegemony of the one-room school was broken, and the number of students enrolled in public elementary and secondary schools increased to 21.6 million or roughly 78 percent of the student population. Attendance rates increased sharply, too: students attended school on average 121.2 days of a 161.9-day academic year. The number of students enrolled in institutions of higher learning grew also to 597,880, or 4.7 percent of the college-age population, and the number of institutions of higher learning in operation rose from 563 in 1869–1870 to 1,041 in 1919–1920. After World War I, the school system continued its dramatic expansion until it assumed its now-familiar form in the wake of post–World War II policies, including the GI Bill of 1944, the National Defense Education Act of 1958, the Higher Education Act of 1965, and the Higher Education Amendments of 1972.[29]

None of this explains exactly how the school system obtained its considerable social authority or why its values gained legitimacy beyond its original middle-class constituents. The sharp rise in enrollments and attendance suggests that formal education took on new public relevance between the Civil War and the end of the First World War, yet the nature of the modern school's relevance and the means through which it achieved relevance are not as self-evident as certain historians have suggested.[30] In fact, some of the transformations associated with the modernization of the school are often understood to have widened the chasm dividing institutional and public life. For instance, the German ideal of *Wissenschaft* gained purchase at US institutions of higher education like Johns Hopkins, Clark University, and the University of Chicago at the turn of the twentieth century, leading to the formation of specialized disciplinary communities with their own protocols for knowledge production that were beyond the comprehension of ordinary Americans.[31] Moreover, to regulate access to credentials and expertise, the school system needed to present itself as detached from modern life, as a mechanism capable of separating the deserving from the undeserving according to professional standards unencumbered by class interests or any other kind of public investment.

Counterbalancing the institutional tendency to withdraw or stand apart from public life were a variety of what we might call outreach programs intended to establish the modern school in everyday experience and render it legible to society at large. Progressive public school reformers at the turn of the century waged a publicity campaign against rural district schools. In Colorado, state officials distributed postcards showing dilapidated one-room schools with the caption, "A National Disgrace." In Ohio, officials canvassed house to house and sent out mass mailings advocating consolidated schools. In Oklahoma, they created a new letterhead made up of two sets of drawings: "The Old Way," which showed students walking to an ugly one-room school, and the "The New Way," where students rode a bus to a modern, multistory building. The Department of Agriculture circulated a film in which children attended an attractive modern school, the girls studying cooking and sewing and the boys learning new techniques in agriculture and animal husbandry.[32]

Institutions of higher education went to even greater lengths to attract the public's attention.[33] Universities invented an executive position, the president, whose job was to attend to the public affairs of the university rather than the needs of the faculty. Thorstein Veblen sardonically explained that the president's "enterprise in publicity" "shap[ed] his ideals of scholarly endeavour and … establish[ed] his standards of expediency and efficiency in the affairs of learning."[34] Universities also created publicity departments for the first time. In his inaugural address as Harvard president, Charles Eliot insisted on the importance of attending to public opinion, and during the 1869–1870 academic year, Cornell began placing advertisements in New York newspapers. In 1896, Harry Pratt Judson, the man who would later become the second president of the University of Chicago, issued a pamphlet to attract more students to the university. In 1909, officials at Columbia planted news stories in the local press to provide advertising for the school, and the University of Texas sought a testimonial letter of praise from Woodrow Wilson to publicize the institution. In 1910, the University of Pennsylvania established a Bureau of Publicity, with a director and a suite of rooms.[35]

At the turn of the twentieth century, institutions of higher education also embraced extension school classes in order to "give to the people not in college some of the advantages enjoyed by the one-half of the 1 per cent who are able to attend campus classes," in the words of one advocate.[36] They impressed themselves on the public through the mass spectacle of college football.[37] They increased their visibility by adopting their own colors (the crimson of Harvard, the powder blue and brown of Tufts), mascots (the Michigan Wolverines, the Wisconsin Badgers), and alma maters and college hymns.[38] The resistance to academic freedom among administrators during this period may well have been less about the political investments of particular faculty members and more about controlling the public brand of their various institutions.[39] Educational historians have struggled to explain why the turn of the century—often thought of as the golden age of the research university, with its specialized disciplinary communities, siloed from the public at large and from each other—witnessed an unprecedented expansion in collegiate life, as undergraduate culture, devoted to extracurricular activities and emerging out of the liberal arts college, grew in popularity.[40] Undergraduate campus culture, however, offered a trove of representational materials for university administrations: as Harvard professor George Santayana explained in 1894, "To Harvard College belong the social and athletic traditions of the place, without which, of course, there would be no essential difference between Harvard and Clark University."[41]

We might find a similar explanation for the surprising persistence of the traditional one-room school through the early twentieth century. In the post–Civil War period, when modern reformers struggled to integrate the public school system into American life, the one-room school became a cultural icon. Poets wrote poems and writers wrote fiction about it; painters made paintings of it and hit songs memorialized it. Politically, the one-room school became a free-floating signifier. Enlisted by expansionists, it appeared in an 1899 issue of the magazine *Puck*, where a cartoon showed Uncle Sam as a teacher in a one-room school instructing students from Hawaii, Cuba, Puerto Rico, and the Philippines; enlisted by isolationists, the one-room school appeared in an 1871 Thomas Nast cartoon under attack by crocodiles shaped like Catholic bishops. Like the traditional liberal arts college, the one-room school's public legibility helps to explain its enduring success relative to its modern counterpart.[42]

Modern educational reform, then, took shape through the seemingly contradictory imperatives to withdraw and to reach out. While Ezra Cornell founded his university as "an institution in which any person can find instruction in any study," Clark's G. Stanley Hall once spoke approvingly of the "laboratory hermits" housed in universities.[43] These contradictions are perhaps most apparent in the context of the modern curriculum. After 1860, primary and secondary schools began offering subjects once considered beyond the purview of formal education; the agricultural, industrial, and fine arts began to appear on increasingly standardized curricula across the country.[44] In higher education, the liberal arts program gave way to a more capacious set of offerings as well. The traditional curriculum consisted of a four-year classical and scientific course based on the reading of Latin and Greek. Mathematics, ancient history, and religion, along with natural philosophy, chemistry, and geology, were other subjects typically offered.[45] By 1900, this course of study had been upended. Latin and Greek were dropped as requirements for a bachelor's degree, even at the most conservative institutions. New departments emerged across the natural sciences, the social sciences, and the humanities.[46] To negotiate these expanded offerings, students were no longer constrained by a prescribed sequence of courses. Rather, they enrolled in the classes they wanted to as part of an "elective system." First introduced by Francis Wayland in the 1850s at Brown University, refined by Charles Eliot at Harvard after the Civil War, and established at colleges and universities across the country by the end of the nineteenth century, the elective system influenced not just higher education but the entirety of the school system. Jettisoning formal requirements, the elective system, in Wayland's words, encouraged "every student [to] study what he chose, all that he chose, and nothing but what he chose."[47] On the one hand, these new course offerings, and this new system to navigate them, helped the school reach out to and integrate a growing population of students with a diverse set of professional interests. On the other hand, they made the school more publicly withdrawn, allowing students to take more classes within the disciplines of their choice and fostering specialized research in graduate seminars and closed-off laboratories.

The distinctive shape of the modern curriculum suggests that the emergent school system's strategic public outreach and its strategic public withdrawal might not have been altogether different strategies. After all, the internal operations of specialized, esoteric disciplines might be opaque to the public, but these operations often produce instrumental knowledge that generates much popular enthusiasm for scholarly endeavors. Indeed, the figure of the researcher, isolated in his study, poring over his books, has circulated as a legible cultural stereotype for more than a century.[48] Opacity, under certain historical conditions, can thus become a resource for publicity. And the outreach programs I've described might help the school achieve popular recognition, but when institutions over-invest in these programs they tend to undermine their own coherence as institutions, making the school indistinguishable from the mass spectacles it promotes and seeks to exploit. For instance, universities that commit too many resources to their football programs become susceptible to the criticism that higher education is merely an excuse to compete for national championships and widely televised bowl games.[49] The history of the modern school system is, to sum up, one prolonged struggle to achieve social relevance and maintain it, whether through public outreach or withdrawal or some combination of the two.

The reality of the modern US school's existence as a "media institution" that constantly seeks to win audiences is therefore very different from the picture of the school that has prevailed in critical theory, which describes the educational system as an "autonomous" or "relatively autonomous" social formation.[50] For Althusser, the school managed to become the dominant Ideological State Apparatus (ISA) under capitalism's mature phase by promoting a "universally reigning ideology of the School," which "represents the School as a neutral environment purged of ideology." Precisely because the educational system represents itself as existing outside the struggles that define social experience—that is, as a non-ideological "neutral environment"—it can in Althusser's account function as a "relatively autonomous" formation that effectively propagates ruling-class ideology.[51] Pierre Bourdieu and Jean-Claude Passeron have explained that the French school assumed its relatively autonomous role under capitalism in the eighteenth century only after a medieval phase, under the Jesuits. "Endowed by the Jesuits with particularly effective means of imposing the academic cult of hierarchy and inculcating an autarkic culture cut off from life," they write, "the French educational system was able to develop its generic tendency towards autonomization." The autarkic quality or self-sufficiency of the school, according to Bourdieu and Passeron, was appealing to the petite bourgeoisie and the intellectual factions of the bourgeoisie, who despised the nepotism of the previous social order. The educational system's Jesuitical autonomy—its sophisticated mechanisms for classifying and hierarchizing student populations according to its own internal criteria—served in the eighteenth century as the perfect instrument for disguising the reproduction of social relations under capitalism.[52]

The architects of the modern US school, however, did not develop an "autarkic culture cut off from life" but desperately sought to convince the public that scholastic credentials possessed value and that formal education offered meaningful life experience. To describe the educational system's development in terms of relevance rather than autonomy is to return the modern school to history; it is to treat the school as an institution whose social authority and very existence is perennially in question. Relevance as I understand it here is not reducible to a statistic like enrollments or state funding. (Even the tremendous expansion of the educational system over the twentieth century hasn't entirely succeeded in dispelling accusations that schooling is irrelevant.) Relevance, rather, indexes a perceived relation to meaningfulness; it encompasses stronger kinds of public recognition like authority or legitimacy while also suggesting that public recognition can take many other, much more modest, forms. For educators in higher education at the turn of the century, say, merely to have their institutions deemed "pertinent" to a larger public or for their institutions to bear a "relation to the matter at hand" was quite an achievement. Without these markers of relevance, they and their institutions languished in a kind of social oblivion.[53]

Throughout the nineteenth century, both the populations who expected to profit from industrialization and those who needed to be subdued in order to serve the rising industrial order were not entirely convinced of the modern school's value. In the 1880s, the anti-monopoly reformer Henry George warned his son, "Going to college, you will make life friendships, but you will come out filled with much that will have to be unlearned." In the 1890s, just as he was becoming one of the great philanthropists of the American school, Andrew Carnegie could still influentially compare the college student who has been "trying to master languages which are dead," to the future captain of industry, "hotly engaged in the school of experience, obtaining the very knowledge required for his triumphs." We might also remember the industrialist Silas Lapham, protagonist of William Dean Howells's *The Rise of Silas Lapham* (1885), who "went to school odd times" himself and decides his daughters, just one year shy of graduating from grammar school, "had got education enough."[54]

The development of the modern school system, in short, involved not simply overhauling the curriculum and establishing new requirements for a high school diploma or bachelor's degree. It involved turning the modern school into "a genuine form of active community life," to recall John Dewey's words. And this is where English literary culture exercised its specific influence over the development of the educational system. After all, following the logic of Carnegie's formulation, English literature was, in contrast to the classics, very much alive.

Novel Institutions

In 1895, an English professor at Yale named William Lyon Phelps offered a class on modern novels to juniors and seniors. In his *Autobiography with Letters* (1939), Phelps claimed that his was "the first course in any university in the world confined wholly to contemporary fiction." The syllabus included many novels that were published the previous year, including Hardy's *Jude the Obscure*, Twain's *Pudd'nhead Wilson*, Kipling's *The Jungle Book*, Conrad's first novel *Almayer's Folly*, as well as bestsellers *Trilby*, *The Manxman*, and *The Prisoner of Zenda*. The class made local and national headlines. On October 28, 1895, the *New York Times* declared: "A New Course in Modern Novels Introduced by Dr. William L.

Phelps. Which is Very Popular." Phelps's senior colleagues were displeased with the attention the class received. As Phelps explained, "[T]he majority of the older professors gave me distinctly to understand that unless I dropped the course at the end of its first year, I should myself be dropped from the Faculty." In a development reminiscent of the Clark University fiasco, Phelps succumbed to faculty pressure during the subsequent academic year and canceled the class. More headlines followed. "No Study of Novels at Yale," the *Times* reported on April 1, 1896. On April 12, another article proclaimed that the students enrolled in Phelps's course were "greatly astonished" when they heard that Yale had canceled the class.[55]

Histrionics attend most major institutional reforms and often quite minor ones as well. Students could now take classes on engineering, economics, and sociology—why not novels, too? The national attention Phelps's class attracted suggests that his decision to teach novels was notable even among the many upheavals that rocked turn-of-the-century formal education. Phelps insisted that he was oblivious to the controversy the class would spark. "One day in the Spring of 1895 I called on Professor Beers and told him that I should like to give a course on Modern Novels," Phelps writes in his *Autobiography*. "Rather to my surprise and greatly to my pleasure, he gave his immediate assent to this, saying there was no reason why the literature of 1895 could not be made as suitable a subject for college study as the literature of 1295." Yet surely Phelps recognized that a class on the modern novel would create controversy at Yale, a school whose curriculum was notoriously conservative. Today the ubiquity of novels on high school and college syllabi has made it difficult to appreciate the essential incompatibility between the novel and the traditional scholastic program. In part, this incompatibility was a consequence of the liberal arts college's commitment to the classics and its suspicion of vernacular languages. In part, it was the product of the novel's longtime association with popular culture.[56]

But the incompatibility of the novelistic and the scholastic goes deeper than the conservatism of certain faculty members, the traditionalists. As a literary form, the novel is notorious for its destabilizing relationship to institutional norms and conventions. This is why Mikhail Bakhtin once described it as a non-canonical genre: located on the threshold between "completed, dominant literary language" and "extraliterary language," the novel according to Bakhtin both resists fixed classification itself and denaturalizes the official genres disseminated through "academic grammar[s]," "school[s]," and "salons." To teach a novel in the traditional classroom, as Phelps did, was therefore to inject the chaos of social experience, of heteroglossia, into the rigid structures of the curriculum. It was to make the school unscholastic.[57]

Phelps's professional identity was organized around gambles like this, gambles that sought to break down the barrier dividing institutional and non-institutional experience. In the *Autobiography*, Phelps derides the traditionalists at Yale, those professors who behave "[o]fficially" one way and "on other occasions … another."

Phelps remembers one particular professor, a "most extraordinary case," from his time as an undergraduate. "[I]t was impossible for me or any other student to penetrate the barrier between this man and the class he taught," Phelps writes. Only later, after Phelps graduated, did he discover that this faculty member was an entirely different person outside of the classroom: "I discovered he was generous, kind, considerate. He was also full of fun, delighting in jokes and ridiculous puns." Phelps concludes that "this man was Jekyll and Hyde. Unofficially he was absolutely lovable; officially he was detestable." Phelps's seemingly "revolutionary and sensational" pedagogy involved his resolution that, unlike this professor, he "should be exactly the same man in the classroom as out of it; there would be no detectable difference."[58]

Phelps's course on novels in this sense reflected his broader pedagogical investment in making the official life of the classroom indistinguishable from unofficial life outside the classroom. If students read novels on their own, away from school, then Phelps would teach a class on novels. The popularity Phelps enjoyed on campus testified to the success of this project. During his first year at Yale, he taught a required English course to freshmen that was such a hit that his sophomore elective the following year attracted all but three students in the class. He brags in his *Autobiography* that his course on modern novels "was elected by two hundred and fifty men"; according to the *New York Times*, it was the largest class taught at Yale. Such enthusiasm was proof that Phelps had indeed managed to appeal to student interest beyond the narrow confines of the traditional curriculum. The newspaper coverage of the course offered more evidence that Phelps's pedagogy had begun to erode the barrier between scholastic and non-scholastic life. Where the *Telegram*'s coverage of Clark reflected the gulf dividing the public from the modern research university, with its laboratories and its devotion to *Wissenschaft*, the doting coverage of Phelps's course in the *New York Times* suggested that public experience had managed to penetrate the hallowed walls of academe by way of the contemporary novel.[59]

Phelps's justification for teaching modern novels was the same justification many other teachers marshaled when they began to assign English literature. By incorporating literary works into the curriculum, teachers claimed access to, in Lawrence Levine's words, the thriving "shared public culture" of the nineteenth-century United States. Here "literature" as a designation encompassed a more capacious set of genres and practices than it would later in the twentieth century.[60] That the curriculum shifted toward literature as the school popularized is one indication of the value educators extracted from its study. In primary schools, reading pedagogy over the first half of the nineteenth century moved away from the hornbooks and primers of the colonial era towards spellers and readers, which included an array of literary materials. Though public high schools were closely associated with the study of English from their inception in the early nineteenth century, high school literature classes specifically grew in popularity after the midcentury. Public literary culture entered institutions of higher education through extracurricular activities: students formed their own literary societies outside of class in the eighteenth and early nineteenth centuries, and these societies were eventually institutionalized. In 1855, Frank A. March taught what is believed to be the first course on English literature in US higher education at Lafayette College; the first English Department was founded at Indiana University in 1885.[61]

Although philologists like March, with their scientific methods, legitimized the study of English literature in the new research university, their rivals, the "generalists," were the ones who established English literature's significance to the modern educational system as a whole.[62] Inhabiting the boundaries of academic life themselves, the generalists were able to tap into literature's public meaning and transform the scholastic experience of all students. The educator and writer Mary E. Burt reported in 1889 that she had "seen a hundred young people in fifth and sixth grades spontaneously applaud, with no prompting from any teacher, the finest and subtlest thought in analyses of Hawthorne's Great Stone Face and the Christmas Banquet." The popularity of English classes in higher education is a further testament to literature's broader social import. During the 1893–1894 academic year, 1,383 students were enrolled at the University of California; the total enrollment of students in English courses during the first term was 873; of these, 397 were taking more than one course in English. As James Turner has explained, English literature "spread through American colleges like a contagious fever. ... By the 1880s literature was everywhere in America. Any new institution—no matter how remote, no matter how feeble—offered it instinctively."[63]

The particular power literature exercised in the school derived from its capacity to transcend the scholastic setting of traditional instruction. Woodrow Wilson, then a professor of jurisprudence at Princeton, influentially defended the study of literature in the university by insisting counterintuitively that literature couldn't actually be studied in universities. Literature, Wilson explained, "perhaps does not belong in well-conceived plans of universal instruction; for it offers many embarrassments to the pedagogic method. It escapes all scientific categories. It is not pervious to research."[64] The odd belief among educators that literature was impervious to scholastic practices influenced much of English's formation as a discipline. As I show in Chapter 1, the consolidation of an anti-scholastic canon of American literature after the Civil War follows this logic: teaching texts that claimed authentic social experience only happened outside of school helped educators make their institutions authentically "real" for students. The residue of this anti-scholasticism also clings to the pedagogical bedrock of the modern English class, close reading. The critics who developed close reading over the first half of the twentieth century saw in the practice an antidote to the pedantries of historicist scholars and philologists. By clearing away the appurtenances of the school, the student could be brought "face to face with the work itself," as Martin Wright Sampson wrote in 1894, and the literary object could "speak for itself," as John Erskine proclaimed in 1948.[65] We might even attribute the success of theory within literary studies during the 1970s and 1980s to its self-proclaimed anti-institutionalism. Or we might point to the all-too-familiar persona of the (usually male) high school English teacher, the "cool" English teacher, who happily concedes, say, that the assigned reading is dull in order to win his students' affection. The core anti-scholasticism of the discipline helps explain Stanley Fish's observation that "while in most cases antiprofessional indictments are leveled from the outside, literary antiprofessionalism is a feature of the profession itself."[66]

A class on novels, the anti-scholasticism of the American literary canon, the pedagogical practice of close reading, the charisma of theory in the English Department, the hip high school English teacher, the anti-professional professional English professor—all indicate literature's contradictory but generative role in modern institutional life. With the emergence of these classes, the experience of going to school began to resemble the experience of not being in school at all.

Educators Denounce Reading, and So Do Writers?

The study of English literature, however, met resistance not just from traditionalists, but from modern reformers as well. Although Yale president Noah Porter once declared that "[t]he critical study of English Literature cannot be overestimated," and James McCosh at Princeton wrote that "[a]s much as we appreciate other languages, we should set the *highest value* on our own," others resisted centering the curriculum on English literature.[67] This resistance expressed itself in terms that anticipated the periodic marginalization of the liberal arts over the twentieth and twenty-first centuries. For instance, in *Twenty Years at Hull-House* (1910), the Progressive reformer Jane Addams describes the dangers of a literary education. Traveling around Europe just before founding her settlement house in Chicago, Addams observes the poverty of East London and realizes that her education has been entirely deficient, that education "lumber[s] our minds with literature that only serve[s] to cloud the really vital situation spread before our eyes." The "assumption" that has caused so many problems, according to Addams, is that "the sheltered, educated girl has nothing to do with the bitter poverty and the social maladjustment which is all about her, and which, after all, cannot be concealed, for it breaks through poetry and literature in a burning tide which overwhelms her." In a dramatic moment during her European travels, Addams sees a group of impoverished women one morning from her hotel room in Saxe-Coburg and, incited to act on their behalf, loses the desire to read altogether. Though the night before (Addams explains) she was absorbed in "Gray's 'Life of Prince Albert,'" she sets it aside after the morning's events: the "book had lost its fascination." Addams's

Progressive educational philosophy emerged out of these experiences; it consisted of shifting pedagogical focus away from the study of culture and literature and toward the urgent task of urban reform.[68]

In a historical moment when literature was more and more often associated with written material—when literature was increasingly understood as something you read—the idea that reading cut readers off from authentic social experience took hold in the modern school system. Despite their suspicion of reading, reformers like Addams didn't actually oppose teaching students to read literature—indeed, Addams herself hosted communal reading groups at Hull-House. The modernization of the school system ultimately involved cultivating a contradictory relationship to literary culture. In part, the modern school embraced English literature and deemphasized the classical languages in a naked bid for relevance, grounding formal education in contemporary social practice to attract larger student populations. But, paradoxically, the modern school also embraced literature classes in order to denounce them: by representing reading as an enervating cultural activity, the architects of the school system sought to establish formal education more firmly in US experience, arrogating for their institutions the popularity and public significance of nineteenth-century literary culture.

The school's contradictory relationship to English literature had a strange effect on US literary production after the Civil War, as more and more writers received their literary training inside institutions of formal education. While reading and writing in early America was taught, if it was taught at all, through a decentralized network of institutions including church groups, the household, and the one-room school, reading and writing pedagogy in the postbellum period took place increasingly within a centralized educational system. When educators from kindergarten to graduate school identified reading as a problematic social activity, characters in post–Civil War fiction put down their novels, newspapers, or whatever reading material they had in hand.

Consider a late example of this phenomenon, Newland Archer, the protagonist of Edith Wharton's *The Age of Innocence* (1920). Archer spends an alarming amount of time in libraries, not reading. In the opening pages of the novel, Wharton explains that Archer is running late to the opera because "he had dined at seven and lingered afterward over a cigar in the Gothic library with glazed black-walnut book-cases and finial-topped chairs." At another point in the novel his sister Janey "wander[s] in on him" as he "s[its] smoking sullenly in his study." Later, having traveled to Boston to find Ellen Olenska, Archer sits "alone in the deserted library" at a club after seeing her, "turning and turning over in his thoughts every separate second of their hours together." The novel pits the act of reading against Ellen Olenska at other moments as well. Archer in one episode learns that Ellen has retreated to the country with his cousins, the van der Luydens. "He had just received a box of new books from his London book-seller, and had preferred the prospect of a quiet Sunday at home with his spoils," Wharton writes. "But he now went into the club writing-room, wrote a hurried telegram, and told the servant to send it immediately." Instead of reading in his library, Archer decides to go off in search of Ellen.[69]

It's not that Archer doesn't read. He is an avid reader: he has read Ruskin and Pater, Swinburne, Elizabeth Barrett Browning and Robert Browning, Thackeray, George Eliot, and William Morris, among many others. The Archers are known for their love of culture—"travel, horticulture and the best fiction"—in contrast to the other major clans of New York high society, the Mingotts and Mansons, who only care about "eating and clothes and money." Early in the novel, Archer even imagines that he will be able to expose his sheltered fiancée May Welland to the greater world beyond high society once they are married by teaching her to appreciate great works of literature. "[H]e contemplated her absorbed young face with a thrill of possessorship in which pride in his own masculine initiation was mingled with a tender reverence for her abysmal purity," Wharton explains. "'We'll read Faust together ... by the Italian lakes ... ' he thought, somewhat hazily confusing the scene of his projected honey-moon with the masterpieces of literature which it would be his manly privilege to reveal to his bride."[70]

As this passage indicates, Archer's fantasy of expanding his wife's horizons through the act of reading is just that, a fantasy, and his conviction that the "masterpieces of literature" will initiate May into more worldly experience only reveals the limitations of his own experience. Reading in the novel is in this sense insistently associated with the conventional leisure practices of the upper class and set in opposition to the "real world" that lies beyond mere conventionality. On one of the rare occasions that we do see Archer reading in his library, Wharton communicates this precise point. Slouched in his chair across from his wife, reading Michelet, Archer discovers that May "was simply ripening into a copy of her mother, and mysteriously, by the very process, trying to turn him into a Mr. Welland. He laid down his book and stood up impatiently." "'The room is stifling: I want a little air,'" Archer announces as he opens one of the library windows and "lean[s] out into the icy night": "The mere fact of not looking at May, seated beside his table, under his lamp, the fact of seeing other houses, roofs, chimneys, of getting the sense of other lives outside his own, other cities beyond New York, and a whole world beyond his world, cleared his brain and made it easier to breathe." After May chastises him for opening the window, Archer returns to the strictures of print and the enclosures of high society, "with a sigh ... bur[ying] his head in his book."[71]

The novel's most conspicuous characterization of reading in these terms takes place in the final chapter, when Wharton jumps forward twenty-six years and reveals Archer sitting in a library once again, not reading but contemplating the course of his life in retrospect. "It was the room in which most of the real things of his life had happened," Wharton writes.

> There his wife, twenty-six years ago, had broken to him, with a blushing circumlocution that would have caused the young women of the new generation to smile, the news that she was to have a child; and there their eldest boy, Dallas, too delicate to be taken to church in midwinter, had been christened by their old friend the Bishop of New York, the ample magnificent irreplaceable Bishop, so long the pride and ornament of his diocese. There Dallas had first staggered across the floor shouting 'Dad,' while May and the nurse laughed behind the door; there their second child, Mary ... had announced her engagement.[72]

The experiences go on and on. But of all the "real things" that have happened in the library, none involves reading. Books bear witness to the real experiences of Archer's life without being "of" these experiences.

Scenes of self-conscious not-reading appear again and again in post–Civil War literary fiction. Of course, Wharton herself didn't actually attend any institutions of formal education, and her stories and novels, like so much of the period's literary fiction, are not set within the emergent school system. These disjunctions reflect the limits of the school's influence at this historical moment, when formal education encompassed a greater portion of US experience than ever before, but still not nearly all of it. Though these scenes of not-reading appear to reproduce the educational reformers' suspicious attitude toward literary culture—suggesting that reading is a poor substitute for real social experience—in fact they represent a rejection of the reformers' anti-literary investments. The "real things of ... life" that these characters experience in fiction when they are not reading are the very experiences we readers have when we are. By disavowing reading as detached from reality, in other words, post–Civil War writers affirmed the capacity of their fiction to incorporate the reality of non-readerly life into readerly experience. Not reading in this body of literature therefore represents the literary equivalent of Phelps's class on modern novels. By teaching novels, Phelps sought to efface the scene of instruction, making classroom and not-classroom indistinguishable. When, for instance, George Hurstwood in Theodore Dreiser's *Sister Carrie* (1900) finally throws down his newspapers and goes off to work as a scab in a "real" trolley strike in Brooklyn, the novel collapses together the textual and the non-textual, insisting there is no difference between the two.

In *Schools of Fiction* I refer to these disavowals as "counter-reflexive" gestures that recurred as the modern school and modern literature came into being. Such gestures are meaningfully different from the reflexivity of post–World War II fiction that Mark McGurl documents. For him, the institutionalization of creative writing generated an abundance of metafiction—what he describes as an autopoetic "hall of mirrors" effect. This effect was the product of the school's injunction to "write what you know," which led writers with apparently disparate agendas to take as their subject the experience of writing and "the fact of fiction making."

McGurl's account, as his invocation of autopoesis indicates, builds off the insights of systems theorists, who see self-reference as "perfectly routine, not impeding but participating in the making and organizing of things," as McGurl puts it. The reflexive mode thus not only characterizes a certain phase of industrial modernity, as in Ulrich Beck's, Anthony Giddens's, and Scott Lash's account of "reflexive modernity." It also itself enacts or "participat[es] in" the creation of modern systems. The aberrant form of reflexivity that I call "counter-reflexivity"—which isn't *not* reflexive—reveals the fitfulness and instability of the process through which modern systems emerged. Straightforward self-reference wasn't always possible or desirable within literary and scholastic culture as they consolidated over time. Instead, at the turn of the century, writers wrote books where characters abruptly stop reading and teachers taught literary texts that had terrible things to say about schools.[73]

The Age of Innocence is an unusual example because it dramatizes the dialectics of counter-reflexivity in its thematic content. The novel is organized around a set of tensions—the conventional and the unconventional, the real and the ideal—whose internal relations remain unstable throughout the narrative and whose final reconciliation clarifies the novel's understanding of its own written-ness. Newland Archer, like so many fin-de-siècle Americans, finds the elaborate conventions that structure modern civilization unbearable, and Ellen Olenska's arrival in New York City presents him with an opportunity to break free of these conventions and access a more meaningful world beyond them, a world that, as we've seen, Wharton sometimes describes in the register of the "real." For Archer, the social choreography of high society is designed to cushion its constituents from all "unpleasantness," and in consequence these constituents become, in his words, "old maid[s]" "when it comes to being so much as brushed by the wing-tip of Reality." Ellen by contrast "open[s]" Archer's "eyes to things [he]'d looked at so long that [he]'d ceased to see them." According to Archer, she "look[s] at things as they are." Ellen herself in one scene encourages Archer to "look, not at visions, but at realities."[74]

Rather than truly liberating Archer from social convention, however, Ellen's entry into his life triggers a crisis where the novel's central thematic categories ("the conventional," "the unconventional," "reality," "visions") become scrambled. Under this crisis, an extramarital affair (say) can appear, on the one hand, unconventional and emancipatory and, on the other, entirely conventional and indeed stultifying.[75] Similarly, the proprieties of high society can be understood at certain moments as epitomizing the upper class's alienation from the "real world," while at others they can represent the hard obdurate stuff of real life.[76] Reading too becomes caught up in this conceptual scramble: as we've seen, it is often represented as a conventional leisure-class habit, cut-off from real life, but it also at times offers its practitioners access to unconventional experiences (albeit ones that are, too, in their own way, unreal).[77] This matrix of tensions is resolved in the novel's last chapters, as Archer's final decision to adhere to convention represents in the logic of the narrative the most unconventional act possible, and Archer's "visions," his imagination, in turn become the site for the realest experiences of his life. It's in this sense that Archer, when he sits alone outside of Ellen's Paris apartment in the novel's last pages, can experience her there as more real than really being with her. It's in this sense, too, that reading in the novel—disavowed for both its conventional and unconventional irreality—can be reclaimed as a resource for real experience, and Ellen can become, in Archer's imagination, a (real life?) character in a book that he can read. "When he thought of Ellen Olenska it was abstractly, serenely, as one might think of some imaginary beloved in a book or a picture," Wharton writes.[78] It's not that the novel has exactly reversed its polarities in these final pages, holding the unreal superior to the real, the conventional over the unconventional, and reading over not-reading; it's that the novel's key terms have converged and enriched each other through their mutual renunciation. Archer's visions can be transformed into the principal site of real experience only when their inadequacies as unreal experience have been acknowledged; the act of reading likewise can become identified with the real only after the novel has recognized its limitations, its own essential unreality.

Writers disavowing reading, teachers disavowing school. When individuals behave this way we usually describe their behavior as self-effacing or self-deprecatory. We don't have a conceptual vocabulary to describe collective formations like institutions that manifest this behavior. This isn't to say that scholars have entirely ignored the dynamics I've described, only that they've tended to describe these dynamics as ambient historical conditions, without attending to the specific institutional contexts that sustained and amplified the dynamics themselves. For instance, we might understand counter-reflexivity through Jackson Lears's account of the late Victorians, those anti-modernists who experienced "a spreading sense of moral impotence and spiritual sterility—a feeling that life had become not only overcivilized but also curiously unreal." Newland Archer's reluctance to read, examined in this light, is thus not idiosyncratic but a familiar cultural disease; Archer feels, like so many of the figures that Lears discusses, as if he has "been cut off from 'reality,'" that he has "experienced life in all its dimensions at second hand, in books rather than action." Wharton's counter-reflexivity can, in turn, be understood as a compensatory strategy designed to absorb this ambient suspicion of literature and enable the further extension and elaboration of modern literary culture.[79]

Yet the institutional specificity of these dynamics remains important, because it helps us appreciate the instability of the modernization process itself. Counter-reflexivity evolved symmetrically in scholastic and literary discourse as both desperately struggled to achieve public relevance. While the ambient suspicion surrounding one might not have originated from the other, each no doubt intensified the suspicions surrounding its rival. Max Weber, that neurasthenic whose thinking informs so much of Lears's project, wrote that bureaucracy, "[o]nce it is fully established," is "among those social structures which are the hardest to destroy."[80] These counter-reflexive gestures indicate the precarity of bureaucracy in its developmental rather than "fully established" form, the elaborate performances required to naturalize modern institutions. The enduring persuasiveness of the counter-reflexive disavowal—its stunning self-contempt, which mirrors its audience's own deepest suspicions—suggests the possibility, too, that bureaucratic structures are never entirely secure, indeed, that bureaucracy itself is not indestructible, even in its more advanced instantiations.

Moving Forward

Chapters 1 and 2 of *Schools of Fiction* provide a more extensive account of these dynamics. The opening chapters of the book begin in the early national period, with literary culture and the school system struggling to establish themselves in US life. I then examine the ascendance of modern literature and the modern school as each denounced the other and itself over the nineteenth century and into the twentieth. Moving forward, the remaining four chapters of the book execute something like a phase shift from the first two. Where the first chapters examine the production of literature outside of institutions of formal education and then the rippling consequences that followed the introduction of this literature into the classroom, the later chapters investigate the production of literature under the inchoate structures of the educational system after the Civil War and the reabsorption of this literary work back into the school over the twentieth and twenty-first centuries.

Because literary production before the Civil War occurred in a scattered institutional landscape, and literary production after the Civil War was concentrated increasingly in the educational system, the anti-scholasticism of these two periods was essentially different. For a writer like Washington Irving, it was virtually unimaginable that a work of fiction criticizing the school would one day appear in classrooms around the country. For a writer like Upton Sinclair, it felt inevitable. After the Civil War, the anti-scholasticism of literary culture came to express itself curiously and paradoxically as a scholastic endeavor. Writers at this time formalized alternative models of institutional life in their work understanding that this work could eventually find its way into a social institution that grew more capacious and sophisticated with each passing academic term. Under these conditions, Frank Norris dedicated *McTeague* (1899) to his composition instructor Lewis E. Gates; Gertrude Stein sent her undergraduate professor William James a copy of *Three Lives* (1909); and Henry Adams delivered his autobiography *The Education of Henry Adams* (1907; 1918) to Harvard president Charles Eliot in the book's first private circulation.

The bulk of *Schools of Fiction* focuses on the specific period of institutional history between 1861 and 1918, when writers first began learning to write and readers first began learning to read under the supervision of the modern educational system. As literary historians have observed, the writers of this period developed a complex relationship to the emergent class of salaried white-collar workers and professionals whose mental labor resembled their own and whose academic credentials they often shared. These writers sought to distinguish themselves from the new middle class and its institutions, particularly the school, the social apparatus that, more than any other, brought coherence to this famously incoherent class. In their anti-scholasticism, writers insisted on their superiority to the new middle class while at the same time performing labor (locating institutional inefficiencies, providing administrative solutions) that resembled the professional-managerial work they vociferously resisted.[81]

The specific form of labor these writers undertook *as* writers—that is, as school-trained producers of literature—contributed to the ambivalence of their cultural project. Earlier in the nineteenth century a prominent strain of literary culture had defined itself against the structures of formal education; now the scope and meaning of "literature" were more and more determined by a school system that had proved itself receptive to literary culture and had begun to identify "literature" with anti-scholasticism. The period of institutional history between the Civil War and World War I, from the perspective of the writers, was therefore one of confusion and possibility. After all, the educational system during this period was not the fragmented network of local institutions that obtained in the eighteenth century and early nineteenth, nor was it the post–World War system that would one day loom so large in writers' imaginations; it was instead a social institution whose structures were conspicuously malformed and plastic. Writers between the Civil War and World War I found the school system a fundamentally novel phenomenon whose inadequacies could be ignored, circumvented, or even corrected. After the First World War, writers could identify the school system's inadequacies, but they confronted this system as a given, as a fixture of twentieth-century life that they could only struggle against but never transcend or deform. The anti-scholasticism of literary culture in this subsequent period of institutional history took on a different form once again, as school-trained writers dramatized alternatively their ennui within the post–World War institutional system that circumscribed their professional lives or their botched attempts to think beyond it.[82]

Which isn't to say that literature hasn't affected the operations of the educational system after 1918, or that the "givenness" of the post–World War educational system has placed it in a realm outside of contingency. Since World War I, literature has continued to impress itself on academic experience, even as the academy no longer depends on the literary for its access to public life. The eagerness with which Norris, Stein, and Adams entrusted their writing to celebrated educators suggests one zone of contact between the literary and the scholastic. Educators, after all, read books, and this reading can affect their professional priorities and commitments. These interactions often go undocumented, however, and so recovering their history is a rather nebulous endeavor; they therefore remain largely outside the scope of this book.[83] One zone of contact between the literary and the scholastic that will receive extended attention in *Schools of Fiction* is what we might think of as the zone of representation. Once writers, educated in the modern school system, took up the academy as a subject or setting, the fictional representation of formal education began to shape public perception of the school and the lived practices of actors within it. I'll have more to say about this momentarily. Of greater significance to the later chapters of this book is the agency individual literary works have wielded as part of the school curriculum. It's this particular form of agency that literary scholarship in the wake of Guillory's *Cultural Capital* has largely discounted.

Though the institutional turn in literary studies has deprived the individual literary object of agency in the context of the curriculum, another strain of scholarship has emerged in recent years that seeks to affirm the social agency of literature. For Rita Felski, works of art "possess their own ontological dignity"; they "invite and incite us, in ways that we do not always expect and may not be able to predict; and "they orient us in certain ways and draw us down interpretative or perceptual paths." To a similar end, Caroline Levine has argued that literary forms, like all social forms, "are in motion around us, constraining materials in a range of ways and imposing their order in situated contexts where they constantly overlap other forms."[84]

Unquestionably, the agency I ascribe to literature in the curriculum more closely resembles the kinds of literary agency these scholars theorize than the depletion of agency that the institutionalists describe. The core chapters of this book argue that literary works, in their circulation through the school system, shape the operations of and the student experience within the system itself. Chapters 3 and 4, for example, are about literature's specific influence on, respectively, the temporality and feeling of scholastic life. The coordination of academic time and the emotional experience of the classroom presented problems that the architects of the modern educational system expended a great deal of energy to resolve, and the writers I discuss—Stein, Adams, Norris, and Sinclair—formalized specific solutions to these problems in their work that were later incorporated back into the school through the curriculum.

The influence individual literary objects exert on the temporality and feeling of schools is obviously just the beginning of how we might track the considerable agency they possess as part of a syllabus. Bracketing the question of political agency for a moment, consider the basic point that assigning one book rather than another in class produces disparate pedagogical results and even suggests disparate conceptions of what pedagogy is. The student experience of reading, say, *Hamlet* as opposed to *Twilight* in a high school English course determines the particular kind of social institution the school is. It also affects a whole range of experiences that students undergo while subject to the school's educational regime. It affects how students conceptualize and live the "seriousness" or "unseriousness" of the pedagogical scene; it establishes connections between the world of the classroom and the world outside of the classroom, or it severs meaningful connections between the two; it encourages certain lines of thinking, on certain kinds of topics, and not others; it might even affect the structure of students' writing.[85] One way of understanding the middle chapters of this book in particular is that they lay the foundation for a reader-response theory that operates on the scale of the institution rather than the individual reader. They develop a methodology that assumes literary objects can orient their own reception in the institutional system that enables their existence in the first place.

In the tremendous social agency Felski and Levine ascribe to literary objects, however, it's also hard not to read the same anxiety that I've suggested motivates the institutionalists.[86] In the background of these stirring claims for the social power of literature is a lingering sense that literature possesses not much social power at all. And not just in the background: often these scholars explicitly justify their research against the pervasive suspicion that literary form, far from exercising a great deal of social agency, exercises very little of it, and even this tiny amount is diminishing.[87] Anxieties about relevance surface in this scholarship's fascination with non-expert or common readers, those individuals whose reading practices haven't been contaminated by English departments and whose susceptibility to literature offers some measure of literature's enduring social meaning.[88] These anxieties also surface in this scholarship's tendency to flatten social experience in its claims for the agency of literary objects. For Felski and Levine, literature wields its agency in a world of horizontal power relations, where no one object is entirely capable of dominating all others. Felski, like Latour, "presumes the equal ontological salience of all classes of being in a mutually composed world." Levine proclaims that "no form, however seemingly powerful, causes, dominates, or organizes all others," and this ensures for her that "literary forms can lay claim to an efficacy of their own." In this flattened social world, literature comes to possess social meaning outside of the academic contexts that are traditionally understood to confine its circulation.[89]

Yet even if all forms did inhabit the same horizontal plane of social experience, it would not guarantee literary form agency. Forms don't necessarily interact with other forms. Or put differently, certain forms don't necessarily bear a meaningful relationship to the forms that structure social experience. Forms can be ignored. They can become irrelevant, and this irrelevance can deprive them of agency in ways that don't presuppose domination. This unfortunate truth is crucial for understanding the particular kind of agency literature has historically exercised in the US. The anxieties surrounding relevance in literary studies right now, manifested in the mirrored claims that literature possesses no social agency and that it pervades all of social experience, register the historical reality that literature's (and literary studies') access to social relevance, the school system, has itself lost much of its social meaning and has suffered its own crisis in recent years. It would probably reassure actors within neither literary culture nor scholastic culture to know that anxieties about relevance have been endemic to both for the last two centuries. While these anxieties have often pitted writers and educators against each other, they have also made literature and schools mutually dependent. And it is through this mutual dependency that schools and literature have imposed themselves on public life.

Nor should we forget that forms do not occupy a horizontal social plane where they confront each other as equivalents. Felski and Levine's insistence that they do has made these scholars vulnerable to attacks from the left, especially in a post-2016 political climate where it has become harder to discount the manifold ways some forms dominate others.[90] As we will see, to understand the agency of literary objects we do not need to situate them on a flat social plane. Indeed, we can probably best appreciate literature's agency in the unique role it has played, in coordination with the school, reproducing an unequal social order.

Manufacturing Consent, or Not

The final section of the book—Chapters 5 and 6—examines the role postbellum literature played in the modern school's emergence as one of the principal mechanisms of social control in the United States. Scholars whose education has taken place within the post–World War II school system have often projected their own sense of the system's legitimacy and administrative sophistication backward onto earlier periods of institutional history. But the nineteenth-century school struggled to discipline the student populations that had, in theory, surrendered themselves to its protocols. In Webster County, Nebraska, 1880, a teacher in a one-room schoolhouse was punishing a student for misbehavior, rapping him on the wrist with an eighteen-inch ruler, when "a dozen boys sprang from their seats as if by signal, seized the uplifted arm, wrested the ruler from the master's hand, and thrust the hated ruler into the stove. ... The larger boys caught up the teacher and carried him out of doors, rolled him over and over in the snow, and admonished him to 'study his lesson' for the rest of the afternoon." In a one-room schoolhouse in Kansas, a student pulled a jackknife on his instructor after undergoing successive rounds of corporal punishment. "'If you hit me again—I'll cut you to pieces,' [the student] shouted, opening the long blade and squaring himself for a finish fight." "[A]fter a moment's hesitation," the teacher "backed into the school room and closed the door."[91]

Higher education witnessed similar eruptions. Andrew White, president of Cornell, once catalogued the violence that occurred in college before the Civil War, recounting the "student brawl at the Harvard commons which cost the historian Prescott his sight" and the "fatal wounding of Tutor Dwight, the maiming of Tutor Goodrich, and the killing of two town rioters by students at Yale." According to Francis Wayland, president of Brown, a professor at the University of Virginia in the 1840s "incurred the ill will of some of the students" and was subsequently murdered. G. Stanley Hall described a series of confrontations he had with students as a faculty member at Antioch in the 1870s:

> A bullet fired in my direction lodged in the post of the store a safe rod from where I was; another was fired through the window of my room a few nights later; while at a rhetorical evening exercise where I sat on the platform, a bottle of acid was thrown through the window, evidently directed at me but fell short and broke on the edge of the platform, spoiling my clothes and the dresses of some of the girls in the front row.[92]

Needless to say, schools in the nineteenth-century United States did not exactly deploy the soft manipulations of an ideological apparatus. Instead, instructors imposed their brutal authority on a resistant population of students—and the students often triumphed over their instructors. How an ideological state apparatus becomes an ideological state apparatus, or how one ideological state apparatus can, like the modern school in Althusser's account, become "*dominant*" among many ideological state apparatuses, are questions that are treated only gesturally in critical theory. In Bourdieu and Passeron's *Reproduction*, as we've already seen, the French school developed under the Jesuits into an instrument uniquely capable of imposing the "cult of hierarchy and inculcating an autarkic culture cut off from life." Later, under the bourgeois state, the French school then "secure[d] recognition of its monopoly in the production and imposition of a unitary hierarchy."[93]

In the United States, the school did not secure recognition of its authority until the first decades of the twentieth century. This is not to say that prior to this period, unequal relations didn't structure US society, or that schools didn't benefit from these unequal relations, or even that schools weren't mobilized to naturalize these unequal relations. It's rather to say that, over the seventeenth, eighteenth, and nineteenth centuries, formal education was too decentralized and its claims to legitimacy too uncertain to impose a particular ideology on the entirety of the student-age population. For instance, Dartmouth College might have been founded as part of a colonial enterprise to educate North American indigenous populations, yet in its first two centuries of existence the institution graduated fewer than twenty Native Americans. The common school movement of the 1830s and 1840s might also have been developed in New England by Whigs to manage poor urban immigrant communities after the rise of Jacksonian democracy and universal white male suffrage, but the movement struggled to impose its ideology on students because the common school system didn't possess the administrative sophistication or social authority even within the states, Massachusetts and Connecticut, where it had the most purchase. To indoctrinate the student-age population, the educational system required a breadth and sophistication of administrative technology, as well as what I've described as a broad recognition of the school's relevance, that institutions of formal education in the United States lacked during the nineteenth century.[94]

The transformation of the school from a decentralized network of loosely affiliated institutions into a coherent system with the authority to impose values on the student-age population was eventually enacted by a cohort of institutional actors, not unlike the Jesuits, devoted to developing the range and capacities of the school itself—that is, the new middle class. This emergent class struggled for coherence and relevance in a political landscape that included industrialists—northerners and "new" southerners—who would eventually be convinced that the school could produce a submissive population of laborers; the planter aristocracy in the South that had little interest in the new middle class and the school, preferring harsher modes of social control to the softer manipulations of formal education; the remnants of the old middle class, including independent farmers, artisans, shopkeepers; predominantly immigrant industrial labor; poor southern whites; and a southern black population that fought for universal education, employment, and access to middle-class institutions. Insofar as the new middle class achieved coherence in this period, that coherence lay in an enduring commitment to expertise and to the school as the institution through which expertise could be transmitted and accredited. This commitment made the middle-class's school system potentially useful, like the Jesuits' in France, for the perpetuation of ideology.[95]

The institutionalization of literature in the educational system may, first and foremost, be understood as a development undertaken by middle-class reformers to guarantee the reproduction and growth of the school system itself. Incorporating literary culture into the classroom meant that more students would enroll in school and stay there once they enrolled.[96] By breaking down the barriers that divided scholastic and non-scholastic experience, English literature also made possible those softer academic manipulations theorists so often associate with a modern disciplinary apparatus. Rapped knuckles, unpleasant recitations, fistfights with the teacher—reformers dispensed with these relics of the traditional pedagogical program. Instead they organized the classroom around interesting and pleasant activities, like reading literature in English. Once rendered docile, students were theoretically primed for indoctrination.

Of course, the teaching of literature in schools is usually believed to carry with it more specific political power than simply establishing the proper atmospherics for indoctrination. This widespread belief is reflected in the public controversies surrounding the content of the English curriculum, whether the culture wars, the recent panic over Critical Race Theory, or really any of the other sporadic attempts by school boards to have particular works removed from high school reading lists. The idea that a work of literature will have a corrupting or salubrious influence on the world simply because it is included in the school curriculum has, however, been persistently contested within literary studies, which has called attention to the institutional settings that determine the political power of literary texts. Pierre Macherey and Etienne Balibar, building off the work of Renée Balibar and Dominique Laporte, once argued that literature performs its ideological work by displacing class struggle onto the linguistic division between literary and common language, a division that is produced and maintained by the school system. The supposedly common realm of the literary, in this account, operates as a site of freedom and mastery for members of the dominant classes who have attended college, while for members of the exploited classes, who have received only primary school education, the literary offers evidence of their own inferiority, proof that their forms of expression are "inarticulate" and "faulty."[97]

This indeed should sound similar to Guillory's argument, with its insistence that the ideological work literature performs is not effected through its representational content or its stated political investments but rather through "the conceptualization of literature itself, which is to say ... the discursive/institutional form by means of which literary works are disseminated."[98] Both arguments describe the school as the institution that invests the literary with ideological power by determining what counts as literature and who is initiated into literary practices. Insofar as the school assumes an ideological role for Guillory, Macherey, and Etienne Balibar, though, its ideological role is in turn concentrated in the act of demarcating and disseminating the literary. Reciprocity between the scholastic and the literary is assumed in these accounts, in other words, even if they each focus on the agency of the school. The school is responsible for endowing literature with political power, yet this particular responsibility then comes to determine the school's own function in the reproduction of social relations.

Recently scholars have reimagined the ideological conjunction of the literary and the scholastic. Daniel A. Clark has argued that early campus fiction, circulated in periodicals like *Collier's* and the *Saturday Evening Post*, made higher education central to American notions of social mobility and middle-class corporate professionalism.[99] Chris Findeisen also has argued that the campus novel since World War II has naturalized a mass system of higher education where "true merit is valued because the system works to recognize and reward it."[100] This scholarship endows literature with considerable agency even as the locus of this agency remains in the particular institutional environment of the school. Literature does not exercise an unmediated influence over class politics in the United States; rather, it shapes public opinion about the educational system, which then exercises influence over class politics. This recent reconceptualization of the ideological conjunction of schools and literature therefore challenges at least two of the guiding assumptions of the scholarship that preceded it. First, literature's ideological power is, as in the purportedly naive accounts of literary influence, located again in individual literary works, the dissemination of which throughout the public sphere functions in effect as propaganda for the school. Second, this ideological power surfaces in the representational content of literary texts, which Macherey and Etienne Balibar, along with Guillory, largely disregard.[101]

Chapters 5 and 6 build on this recent work by describing the institutionalization of English literature after the Civil War as a process that took place in the realm of representation as much as in the curriculum. These chapters argue that we can best appreciate the agency of early campus fiction not simply in the nebulous realm of mass culture but in the specific space of academic experience that educational historians have designated the "extracurriculum"—that is, the culture of student life and the administrative apparatus that evolved to support it. Situated on the boundary between the school and its publics, the extracurriculum has registered the educational system's shifting relationship to its social environment. In this zone of frat parties and football games, a capella groups and student demonstrations, mass culture discovers the fascination of the school just as students orient their on-campus activities toward mass culture. The extracurriculum is a liminal institutional space, a space where the inside and outside of the institution confront each other. In its circulation, early campus fiction represented the extracurriculum to a mass audience of readers while shaping the student experience within the very campus culture that produced it.[102] More so than the rest of the book, these chapters attend to dynamics specific to higher education, that network of institutions that suffered the school's crisis of relevance most acutely. The public legibility of colleges and universities had significant implications for the rest of the educational system as well, though. Once the bachelor's degree came to symbolize the summit of meritocratic excellence and achievement, the relationship between primary, secondary, and higher education was clarified and the school system could be meaningfully described as a system.[103]

Because it took the extracurriculum as its representational object—and because, as a product of the extracurriculum, it inhabited the space of confrontation between the inside and outside of academic life itself—early campus fiction inevitably came to dramatize the elaborate negotiations between institutional outreach and withdrawal that characterized the development of the educational system in the post–Civil War period. Central to these negotiations was the issue of access. Who deserved access to the school's credentials? Who would be included in the life of the campus and who would be excluded from it? And how would the exclusion of certain student-age populations find justification: explicitly or implicitly, publicly or secretly? These questions inspired much debate among a range of turn-of-the-century institutional actors, including university administrators, college students, and recent alumni who decided to translate their campus experiences into fiction.

One student organization within the extracurriculum became the principal institutional site where the debate over inclusion and exclusion was staged. That student organization was the secret society. Purportedly secret but publicly hypervisible, proudly exclusive but also potentially open to all students, secret societies reflected tensions that afflicted higher education as a whole. Colleges and universities in this period suffered a crisis of legibility even as they made increasingly sophisticated appeals to a mass audience, and they remained essentially elite institutions even as they opened themselves to more diverse student populations. Calls to abolish, reform, or enshrine the secret society at the turn of the century thus promised to clarify the school's own role in the reproduction of the social order. It is no surprise then that the institutional formation on which early campus fiction most relentlessly fixates is the secret society, and indeed campus fiction's intervention in this controversy secured higher education specifically, and the school system more broadly, in modern US social experience. It did so both by distilling the middle class's conception of the school and by convincing the ruling elite, with this vision of scholastic life, that formal education could operate as an effective ideological instrument, one capable of legitimating social inequality through its credentialing process.

In order to expand, the educational system needed to learn how to exclude. The early campus novel *Stover at Yale* (1912), written by the Progressive reformer Owen Johnson, taught the modern school this valuable lesson. Johnson's novel articulated an inclusive vision of US higher education against the secrecy of Skull and Bones, yet this denunciation of secret societies masked and advanced its own set of exclusionary practices. These practices map onto the meritocratic ideology that the modern school notoriously propagates, a secretly secretive ideology that represents the school as transparent and egalitarian while un-transparently disqualifying certain student populations, based on class, race, and gender, from receiving the highest scholastic credentials. *Stover at Yale* conjured a robust, meritocratic undergraduate culture for both the mass reading audience outside the school and the students within it, and it was this undergraduate culture that academic administrators appropriated in the years leading up to the First World War, basing the official identity of their institutions on the unofficial operations of student organizations.

Many educational reformers shared Johnson's conception of the school as a disinterested social institution that separated the deserving elite from everybody else, but other Progressives imagined different functions for formal education under industrial capitalism. Thomas Dixon Jr.'s Reconstruction Trilogy (1902–1907) suggests one alternative to *Stover at Yale*'s meritocratic understanding of institutional life. In their celebration of the Ku Klux Klan, Dixon's novels counterintuitively aspired to found modern institutions on a radical transparency. These institutions, as Dixon envisioned them, would cease to function ideologically within US society and instead enforce the social order through explicit acts of repression.

Postbellum African American fiction also presented a series of alternatives to *Stover*'s meritocratic vision of the educational system through its depiction of black secret societies. Frances Ellen Watkins Harper's *Iola Leroy* (1892) articulates its conception of post-Reconstruction institutional life with and against the clandestine prayer meetings that the novel's enslaved characters hold on plantations before the Civil War. Charles Chesnutt's *The House Behind the Cedars* (1900) thinks through Progressive-era institutional practices by intricately rendering the secret communities that form around mixed-race characters who are passing. Sutton Griggs's *Imperio in Imperio* (1899) outlines a revolutionary institutional program by portraying a secret undergraduate society that orchestrates a school uprising. Through these various fictional secret organizations, African American writers denaturalized secrecy as a principle of organizational life and attempted to reimagine the relationship between the school and the industrial order. Some of these writers believed that the twentieth-century institutional system should be less secretive, that transparency and mutual recognition between the races would ensure black equality; others believed it should be more secretive, that equality could only be achieved through the covert operations of secret institutions.

Stover at Yale has in a certain sense proved more influential than its literary alternatives: for much of the twentieth century it provided a vision of institutional life that drew a mass audience of middle-class readers to the school and convinced the ruling class that academic credentials possessed value—that, as Henry Adams explained in *The Education*, "the degree of Harvard College is worth money … in Chicago."[104] Still, the proliferation of these alternatives in postbellum fiction—and the subsequent incorporation of these fictions, including Dixon's, into the curriculum over the twentieth and twenty-first centuries—should give us pause. The school's assumption of its modern form has allegedly entailed its widespread acceptance as an independent social mechanism capable of sorting the worthy from the unworthy. This is the premise behind, in Althusser's words, the "universally reigning ideology of the School," and this is precisely the ideology that Johnson's early campus novel hoped to naturalize. But these alternatives also remind us that the reigning ideology of the school has not always reigned, that the secret of the educational system's meritocratic program has not always been well-kept. They invite us to reconsider the mechanisms through which the school has imposed order on students, not just in the period after the Civil War, when the educational system was still inchoate, but today as well. Just which student populations, we might ask, believe that the educational system disinterestedly separates the deserving from the undeserving? Just which student populations have willingly surrendered themselves to the soft disciplinary apparatus of the modern school, and which student populations have rather found in the school those harsh and coercive practices of a purportedly antiquated disciplinary regime?

Such questions mean to challenge the assumptions underwriting the modern school's role in the reproduction of social relations, specifically its status as an ideological, as opposed to repressive, apparatus. They also challenge some common assumptions about literature's capacity to manufacture consent. The proliferating alternatives to Johnson's meritocratic school system suggest that literature doesn't always interpellate readers into the dominant social order, that literature doesn't always manage to convince its audience, for instance, that the school is a just and egalitarian formal institution. The inadequacy of either literature or the school to manufacture consent on its own is reflected in the very strain of literary scholarship I've been discussing, whether Macherey and Etienne Balibar's account of literariness or Clark's and Findeisen's work on campus fiction. The scholarly tendency to conjoin the ideological operations of the literary and the scholastic suggests the insufficiency of both on their own as political instruments. The two, in effect, need each other to appear viable as ideological instruments. And just because schools and literature have appeared viable as instruments of social control to society's beneficiaries is no proof that schools and literature actually succeed in convincing everyone else that they deserve their immiseration.[105]

Coda

Not power, then, but powerlessness, and not the quiet stability of the relevant but the pettiness, jealousy, and self-laceration of the irrelevant—this is the history of US literary culture and the modern school system. The fragility of literary culture is more or less assumed at this moment in cultural history, but the fragility of the school system deserves more attention than it has received and so too does the fragility of the middle class. As the paradigmatic middle-class institution, the modern school in its vulnerability reflects the vulnerability of the class whose identity it is entangled with. The economic and political transformations that have occurred since 1973, over the historical period that Robert Brenner has described as the long downturn, have revealed the instability of a social institution and the precarity of a class, both of which appeared, during an earlier period of prosperity, invulnerable.[106] *Schools of Fiction* travels back to a time when this vulnerability was even more apparent, when the educational system was first haltingly coming into existence and when the new middle class was first gasping for air. The six chapters of the book follow the development of formal education as it migrated to the center of social experience, and they do so in order to demonstrate the unlikeliness of this migration, not its inevitability. The crucial labor that literature performed driving the school's expansion simply underscores its improbability. *Schools of Fiction* at bottom then remains interested less in recuperating the agency of literary form than in exposing the vulnerability of the educational system. My analysis sets out, ultimately, to uncover the fictions that have enabled the school to assume its modern role in US society.

PART 1

1
The School and Society

> For a long, long while, I have occasionally been visited with a singular dream. ... It is, that I am still at college,—or, sometimes, even at school,—and there is a sense that I have been there unconscionably long, and have quite failed to make such progress as my contemporaries have done; and I seem to meet some of them with a feeling of shame and depression that broods over me as I think of it, even when awake. This dream, recurring all through these twenty or thirty years, must be one of the effects of that heavy seclusion in which I shut myself up for twelve years after leaving college, when everybody moved onward, and left me behind. How strange that it should come now, when I may call myself famous and prosperous!—when I am happy, too!
>
> —Nathaniel Hawthorne, December 25, 1854[1]

Nathaniel Hawthorne had much to celebrate on Christmas Day, 1854. With the publication of *The Scarlet Letter* in 1850, he had finally begun to receive the critical and commercial recognition that had eluded him earlier in his career. The subsequent four years were some of the most productive in his life; over this interval, he published *The House of the Seven Gables* (1851), *The Blithedale Romance* (1852), *A Wonder Book* (1852), *The Life of Franklin Pierce* (1852), and *Tanglewood Tales* (1853). Thanks to the machinations of his publisher James T. Fields, Hawthorne's early writings, *Twice-Told Tales* and *Mosses from an Old Manse*, were also republished in 1851 and 1854, respectively, to capitalize on his recent success. After reading *The Scarlet Letter*, one of the leading figures in American letters, Evert Duyckinck, declared that "our literature has given to the world no truer product of the American soil ... than Nathaniel Hawthorne." The critic Edwin P. Whipple meanwhile described *The House of the Seven Gables* as "the deepest work of imagination ever produced on the American continent." Rufus Griswold called it "the purest piece of imagination in our prose literature." Living in England as a US consul, Hawthorne wrote in his journal, "I think I have been happier this Christmas than ever before,—by my own fireside, and with my wife and children about me,—more content to enjoy what I have,—less anxious for anything beyond it, in this life."[2]

What could be better? What could disturb this tranquility? Despite his many achievements, Hawthorne nevertheless felt a creeping sense of discontentment. As he explained in the same journal entry, for a "long, long while" he had "occasionally been visited with a singular dream." In this recurring dream, this nightmare, Hawthorne was somehow trapped in school, residing there "unconscionably long," having "quite failed to make such progress as [his] contemporaries." "How strange that [this dream] should come now," he concluded, "when I may call myself famous and prosperous!—when I am happy, too!"

Hawthorne is, of course, the most literary of American writers—the American writer whose work has most insistently been identified with "American literature" and indeed "literature" as categories of cultural consumption. His Christmas dream was prophetic for US literary culture in two crucial ways. First, it anticipated the particular orientation that literary culture would begin to assume toward the school system after the Civil War. While some writers in the antebellum period pronounced the significance of their work against the failings of formal education, only after the Civil War would this strain of writing start to anchor the broader cultural understanding of "literature" as such. The complex of negative emotions that Hawthorne associates with formal education—the "shame and depression" he feels when he meets his former classmates, knowing that they have progressed as he remains stuck in school—reflects the hostility toward the educational system that would eventually come to define literary endeavors. That this recurring nightmare appears to have only intensified when Hawthorne secured his place at the summit of literary culture—when he could "call" himself "famous and prosperous"—underscores the link between literariness and the aversion to schooling. Hawthorne's dream was prophetic, second, however, because it anticipated another, later phase in the history of "literature," after the school had become the primary administrator of literary culture and, toward the end of the twentieth century, literature came to be understood as a product of its scholastic environment. Hawthorne's nightmare that he is "still" at school, trapped there, unable to escape, foreshadows this later moment when the educational system's influence on literary production was experienced as all-encompassing.

Hawthorne's dream might help us, finally, appreciate the connection between these two dramatically different conceptions of literature. The antipathy toward school encoded in both Hawthorne's dream and a certain strain of literary production was a valuable resource that the educational system cultivated, injecting it into lesson plans and pedagogical editions. By claiming that literary culture provided access to a world of authentic social experience, one that not even the school could compromise, anti-scholastic writers affirmed the significance of their work; and by introducing anti-scholastic writing into the classroom, educators appropriated this uncompromised world for the school itself. Literature thereby propelled the school's expansion, enabling it to comprehend ever-larger portions of US social experience.

The first two chapters of this book describe the complex imbrication of literature and the school as each developed into what I've called its modern form over the course of the nineteenth century and into the twentieth. The modernization process, as I present it here, was fundamentally anti-formalist and anti-institutional, with writers and educators disparaging inherited forms and inherited institutions in their respective claims for their own significance. Chapter 1 examines this anti-institutionalism in relation to the school, both the literary deprecation of the school and the school system's own anti-scholasticism. Chapter 2 examines anti-institutionalism in relation to literature, both modern educational reformers' deprecation of literature and literature's own anti-literariness. In its exploration of anti-scholasticism, this first chapter focuses on a body of specifically American writings, whose reevaluation after the Civil War I take to be symptomatic of a larger transformation in literary culture as a whole. The chapter begins by excavating the origins of an anti-scholastic American literary tradition in the early nineteenth century and locating this tradition in the broader literary field. It then turns to the modern school, its enthusiastic reception of this anti-scholastic tradition after the Civil War and its eventual rejection of this tradition's rivals. As we'll see, the modern school's enthusiasm for anti-scholastic writings eventually led to the identification of this tradition with "American literature" as such. Central to this whole discussion is the idea that American literature was not simply an object of academic derision, as Elizabeth Renker has argued. American literature was in fact embraced by many teachers for its capacity to enliven the school with non-scholastic experiences.[3]

Just to be clear, I am not arguing in this first chapter that all of nineteenth-century American literature denounced formal education, nor am I claiming that educators' preference for anti-scholastic writing was detached from other ideological considerations. For much of the century, the United States enjoyed a famously heterogeneous (though not uncontentious) public culture. "Literature" under these conditions encompassed a wide variety of genres and practices, without, for instance, the stark divisions that would eventually cordon off literary from mass culture at the beginning of the twentieth century.[4] In this heterogeneous space, contributors to literary discourse—writers, readers, performers, agents, publishers—assumed no entirely consistent posture toward schooling. Some writers collaborated with educators, some ignored them, some reviled them, and some were them.[5] The process out of which a particular body of anti-scholastic writings became associated with "American literature" specifically or "literature" more broadly took place both within literary culture itself as it evolved over time and through the school as the school assumed a greater role in cultural administration. This process was also indeed the site of political contestation, with different factions in the post–Civil War period seeking to enlist "American literature" in their own respective social projects.

While anti-scholasticism remained a recurring feature of "American literature" in its development from 1861 to 1918, the American literary tradition became truly identified with the anti-scholastic only after 1918, under pressure from modernists, New Critics, and, most important, the mid-twentieth-century Americanists. This conception of American literature is usually associated with the romance tradition, and its ascendance coincides with both the rise of a truly mass system of education and the recognition within this system of American literature as a legitimate field of study. Oriented around the work of five principal American writers—Ralph Waldo Emerson, Henry David Thoreau, Nathaniel Hawthorne, Herman Melville, and Walt Whitman—the romance paradigm has been the subject of much reflection within American literary studies itself. Certain scholars understand it as a literary retreat from mass culture; others understand it as an object of mass culture itself, one instrumentalized to enforce racism, sexism, and classism domestically and US hegemony abroad.[6]

The anti-scholasticism of the romance tradition helps explain the incoherence of its historiography, where its "retreat" from mass culture into the school somehow seems to occur alongside its mass dissemination. The institutionalization of American literature (and, correspondingly, of the romance paradigm *as* American literature) should not be characterized as a literary retreat but rather as an academic takeover. This institutionalization ensured the modern school's growth, and the school's growth meant, in turn, that the increasingly exclusive body of cultural works categorized as American literature would have its own mass audience of readers—college students!—onto whom more concentrated ideological "lessons" could be impressed. As I demonstrate in Part 2 of this book, the agency literature has wielded as part of the curriculum has required this particular post–World War institutional environment, one in which millions of student readers each year are brought into contact with individual literary objects. As I explain in Part 3, too, the ideological work literature and schools have performed has taken place not just through the curriculum but also through that liminal zone of institutional space educational historians call the "extracurriculum." Right now, though, I simply want to raise the point, which will be treated in greater detail in this chapter, that the crystallization of "American literature" around the romance tradition post-1918 occurred at a crucial juncture in educational and literary history when anti-scholasticism became a defining trait of the literary and anti-scholastic writing became the most scholastic of all writing.

The key literary figure I discuss in this chapter is Washington Irving. Irving is a uniquely illuminating writer through whom to reconstruct this history, though not necessarily the most obvious. He is not, after all, one of the five foundational writers of the romance tradition. He has however remained a stubbornly canonical writer whose success in the 1820s is often credited with the founding of US literary culture after several halting attempts over the previous decades. In the 1890s, Irving's bust was installed, along with Hawthorne's and Emerson's, in the newly rebuilt Library of Congress; in 1900, Irving was elected to the Hall of Fame at New

York University, voted in with Emerson, Hawthorne, and Longfellow by university presidents, supreme court justices, and living authors. (Newspaper polls in Brooklyn and Minneapolis indicated that the general public made the same choices as the electors.)[7] Nonetheless Irving's institutionalization remains in some sense unusual but no less illuminating for that reason. He is best appreciated as either a minor major author or a major minor author. His writing has found a home in the academy, but students are just as likely to encounter it in high school or even elementary school as in college; as a regionalist, Irving has proved foundational to various attempts to construct a national literary canon, and yet in his own lifetime his glowing national reputation was driven by the recognition he received from the international literary community. Most relevant to this particular chapter, Irving is often included (though as a marginal figure) in the romance tradition, with Leslie Fiedler, for instance, describing "Rip Van Winkle" as the "first legend to seize the American imagination."[8] But Irving could just as plausibly belong to a sentimental tradition of American writing as the author of stories like "The Voyage" and "The Broken Heart," which also appeared in *The Sketch Book* (1820).

Romance and sentimentalism have confronted each other as literary antagonists for the last two centuries, and Irving's idiosyncratic position between, or rather within, the two traditions makes the shifting terms of his institutionalization especially revealing. The decisive factor in the divergent reception histories of these two opposed nineteenth-century literary traditions is, as I'll argue in my discussion of the antebellum literary field below, the orientation each assumed toward the scene of formal pedagogy. Though both romance and sentimentalism (perhaps surprisingly?) criticized traditional institutions of formal education, sentimentalism did so in the service of education reform, whereas romance did so to enshrine a literary culture that insisted it was itself unassimilable to scholastic projects. Ironically, the sentimental call for humane and modern schooling made its conception of the literary particularly ill-suited to the emergent educational system, whose ideological program it shared. Irving's specific brand of sentimentalism in the end understood itself as irreconcilable with formal education, and this, finally, and perversely, provides the key explanation for the enduring success of his writing within the educational system after the Civil War. Anti-scholasticism in effect needed to precede or attend whatever other ideological work American literature was called upon to perform. In order for the modern school to develop into one of the principal mechanisms of social reproduction in the United States, it had to learn to transform literary hostility into an engine of its own expansion.

Scholastic Horrors, Literary Adventures

What ever happened to Ichabod Crane?

In the final pages of Washington Irving's "The Legend of Sleepy Hollow," we learn that Crane—a "worthy wight" who "sojourned … in Sleepy Hollow, for the purpose of instructing the children of the vicinity"—has disappeared. The last time the townspeople saw Crane was at a party hosted by Mynheer Van Tassel, whose daughter, Katrina, Crane had failed to woo. The morning after the party, Crane, the schoolteacher, is gone: the horse he rode to the Van Tassels, Gunpowder, is "found without his saddle," and we are told that "Ichabod did not make his appearance at breakfast—dinner hour came, but no Ichabod. The boys assembled at the schoolhouse, and strolled idly about the banks of the brook; but no schoolmaster." Fearing the worst, the townspeople search the brook, "but the body of the schoolmaster was not to be discovered."[9]

Crane's whereabouts excite much speculation among the inhabitants of Sleepy Hollow. Stories proliferate about the night of the party: many believe that Crane's disappearance is the work of a local legend, the ghost of a Hessian trooper whose head was blown off by a cannonball—the headless horseman. Knickerbocker presents other, less sensational explanations for Crane's disappearance, too, however. An old farmer "who had been down to New York on a visit several years after" insists that Crane "had left the neighbourhood partly through fear of the goblin and Hans Van Ripper, and partly in mortification at having been suddenly dismissed by the heiress." The old farmer's account seems consistent with other evidence that's introduced at the end of the tale: Brom Bones, Crane's rival suitor for the hand of Katrina Van Tassel, "was observed to look exceedingly knowing whenever the story of Ichabod was related," and "always burst into a hearty laugh at the mention of the pumpkin, which led some to suspect that he knew more about the matter than he chose to tell."[10]

Was Crane carried off by a headless goblin, or did he flee Sleepy Hollow after suffering some sort of romantic humiliation? Beyond dispute is the thoroughness of his disappearance. Once the townspeople decide that Crane is really gone, Hans Van Ripper, the executor, "consign[s] to flames" the "magic books and … poetic scrawl" Crane left behind, and resolves "to send his children no more to school." "The school," Irving writes, "was removed to a different quarter of the hollow, and another pedagogue reigned in his stead." The fate of this new school and this new teacher remains outside the scope of the narrative; Crane's true replacement in "Sleepy Hollow" is instead the ever-multiplying explanations and stories that the townspeople generate in his absence. The old schoolhouse that Crane presided over, we learn, "soon fell to decay"; reports surface that the house is "haunted by the ghost of the unfortunate pedagogue," and that a plough boy "loitering homeward of a still summer evening, has often fancied his voice at a distance, chanting a melancholy psalm tune among the tranquil solitudes of Sleepy Hollow." Knickerbocker concludes at the end of "Sleepy Hollow"—the very last story published in the original US edition of *The Sketch Book*—that "old country wives maintain to this day, that Ichabod was spirited away by supernatural means; and it is a favourite story often told about the neighbourhood round the winter evening fire."[11]

The disappearance of Ichabod Crane, the country schoolteacher, and the literary outpouring that follows it came at a moment in US history when both the school system and literary culture struggled to integrate themselves into national experience. Irving, who was attempting to carve out a place for his own imaginative writings within the fragmented print networks of the early nineteenth century, found in the school a foil for his literary vision, an institution against which he could articulate the significance of literature. For Irving, that is, literature and formal education were fundamentally at odds with one another: while both served as instruments of socialization in early US life, the importance of literary culture was, as Irving conceived it, bound up with the school's deficiencies. Just as Sleepy Hollow's schoolteacher Ichabod Crane plays a far less meaningful role in the town's social organization than the legend of Ichabod Crane that emerges after his disappearance—a legend that circulates orally among the townsfolk but will one day be captured by Diedrich Knickerbocker in written form—so too, Irving insists, should schools play a far less meaningful role in the social organization of early US society than literature.

In part, Washington Irving's contempt toward the school was a matter of professional conviction, a belief he held as an aspiring writer about the role literature should play in early nineteenth-century US life. In part, Irving's contempt was personal, driven by his own terrible experiences in the classroom. The ad hoc formal education Irving received at the turn of the nineteenth century was typical for a white son of New York City merchants.[12] Instead of attending the Columbia Grammar School, one of New York's most advanced and respected (and expensive) academies, Irving was instructed by a motley assortment of the city's pedagogues. When he was about four years old he attended Ann Kilmaster's school; when he was six he entered a school led by a former soldier, Benjamin Romaine. When Romaine decided to stop teaching eight years later and go into business, Irving enrolled at Josiah A. Henderson's male seminary, which he endured for around a year until, at the age of sixteen, he ended his formal education altogether and began studying law under Henry Masterson. The institutions of formal education Irving attended were short on resources and lacking in any systematic educational plan. According to G. P. Putnam's account of Irving's life, Romaine was "a disciplinarian of the old school," and as a youth Irving "used to be greatly disgusted with his antique mode of posterior punishment of the boys after the girls were dismissed." In the words of another of Irving's biographers, Stanley T. Williams, the classroom in Henderson's male seminary was "a desert, without globes, maps, atlases, or blackboards." Conditions like these led Williams to describe Irving's formal education as possessing "a random quality": Irving was "less than half-educated."[13]

Although two of Irving's brothers did, in fact, attend Columbia College—an institution of higher education that, in 1789, could claim thirty-nine pupils, and whose graduating classes between 1784 and 1810 averaged seventeen students[14]—Washington Irving never enrolled in an institution of higher education. By all accounts there was something in Irving that rebelled against the discipline and structure of the classroom. His first teacher, Mrs. Kilmaster, notoriously scolded him as a dunce. A fellow student in Romaine's school once called Irving "a sluggish and inapt scholar of great diffidence—what teachers call stupid." Writing under one of his many pseudonyms, Geoffrey Crayon, Irving once recalled hearing a bird, the bobolink, singing outside his classroom window. "I, luckless urchin!" he remembered, "was doomed to be mewed up, during the livelong day, in that purgatory of boyhood, a school-room. It seemed as if the little varlet mocked at me as he flew by in full song."[15]

Against the crushing routine of the classroom, Irving eventually pursued a different kind of education, one that existed outside the confines of formal schooling—a literary education. An anecdote reported by one of Irving's classmates suggests the role literature played in Irving's upbringing: "[Irving's] desk," according to this classmate, "was full of the eighteenth-century romances which flooded the New York bookstalls" and Romaine, the teacher, "had a trick of stealing up behind him and snatching these dainties." Irving's love of literature was partly inculcated by his brothers William, Peter, and John, who at the turn of the nineteenth century were all active members of various New York literary societies, including the Belles Lettres Club and the Calliopean society. Washington Irving's early domestic life was saturated with literary culture, and his childhood home served as a site of oratorical performances, theatrical restagings, and readings of works like *Orlando Furioso*.[16]

This literary environment nurtured Irving's budding belletrism. In 1802, when his brother, Peter, served as editor of Aaron Burr's New York *Morning Chronicle*, Irving submitted anonymous letters to the paper under the name Jonathan Oldstyle. In 1804, when Peter helped establish an anonymous paper, the *Corrector*, Irving participated as a contributor. In 1807, after Irving had started his own literary society, the Lads of Kilkenny, he founded, along with two other members, William Irving and James Kirke Paulding, a *Spectator*-inspired anonymous paper called *Salmagundi*. Irving's first major literary success, *Salmagundi* was issued serially in twenty paperbound numbers over a year-long period, with each issue appearing in multiple editions and sub-editions. The paper thrilled and offended and delighted New York City readers; one issue even sold 800 copies in a single day. Out of *Salmagundi* grew Irving's next project, *A History of New York*, by Diedrich Knickerbocker (1809), which began as a collaborative endeavor with his brother Peter but eventually became his first single-authored work. Like *Salmagundi*, *A History of New York* was a success, earning Irving $3,000.[17]

Irving, in short, might have been inattentive as a student, but as a member of the literary community he was active and engaged. For Irving, literary pursuits were a worthy endeavor precisely because they held a social meaning that schools didn't. Thus Irving's most famous stories endow literary culture with a power of social reproduction that, from our historical perspective, is usually associated with educational institutions. His early writings compulsively describe the mechanisms of literary transmission, the ways stories pass through and hold together larger social formations: assembled from a variety of sources and handed down from one person to another, these stories exceed the life span of any single individual and accrete social meaning until they are fixed in print, where their survival will be guaranteed for future generations. The power of these stories to endure through time materially and disseminate social values counteracts the forms of mortality surveyed in the texts themselves—whether the reproductively sterile characters that crop up throughout Irving's work, like Geoffrey Crayon, Diedrich Knickerbocker, Master Simon of *Bracebridge Hall*, and Pindar Cockloft of *Salmagundi*, or the reproductively sterile societies Irving describes, like the Dutch-Americans in New York, the native Americans on the east coast, and the Alhambra. As scholars have noted, Irving's writing is fixated on the bachelor as a figure of cultural surrogacy, one capable of reproducing social values through culture when biological reproduction fails.[18] Irving's vocal support of turn-of-the-nineteenth-century literary culture, and his unique position in that culture—his work as a writer, editor, and his own literary agent—have led Andrew Piper to argue that Irving was a key participant in the international romantic bibliographic scene, which was characterized by sophisticated networks of production, textual sharing, copying, and adapting.[19]

And yet, while Piper alerts us to Irving's position in the cosmopolitan romantic-era publishing world, his account glosses over a little too quickly the difficulty Irving encountered establishing himself in this position as an American. Unlike Europe's print industry, the United States' was still inchoate. As book historians Ronald J. Zboray and Mary Saracino Zboray have argued, the publishing industry during the early national period was decentralized—a "genteel, artisan trade supported by civic patronage, religious groups, and local businesses."[20] Trish Loughran has claimed that, under these conditions, "there was no 'nationalized' print public sphere in the years just before and just after the Revolution, but rather a proliferating variety of local and regional reading publics scattered across a vast and diverse geographical space."[21] The timeline of Irving's early publications is a testament to the conditions of literary culture during the early national period: even with the success of *Salmagundi* and *A History of New York*, Irving still couldn't afford to be a full-time writer or man of letters, and it would take ten years for him to produce another work, *The Sketch Book*. In between *A History of New York* and *The Sketch Book* he moved in and out of various professional positions, some of them literary but most not. Irving during this period worked as a lawyer, a soldier, and a man of industry in his brothers' company; the most significant literary position he held was as the editor of *Analectic Magazine*, a publication that reprinted articles from various British magazines, supplemented with a little original American content. The editorship made Irving miserable, and it ended abruptly after only two years, when the *Analectic* collapsed in 1814—more evidence of literature's fragile market ecology at the time.[22]

The Sketch Book proved an enormous success on both sides of the Atlantic, catapulting Irving into a professional career as a writer, but we shouldn't forget the trouble he underwent to enjoy this first major success. Irving's struggle to establish himself as a writer during the opening decades of the nineteenth century demonstrates that the rise of a national literary culture in America was anything but natural or inevitable. It required, instead, an act of will on the part of literary ideologues. In *The Sketch Book*, Irving set out to install literary culture at the center of US life, and as part of this project, he invoked the school as a negative example, an institution that failed to provide the social benefits that literature itself could.

Pedagogues Humiliated

The students and pedagogues that appear in Irving's work usually serve as the butts of jokes, as sources of amusement, from Jeremy Cockloft, that insufferable and pedantic Columbia graduate in *Salmagundi*, to Slingsby, the likable but pathetic schoolmaster in *Bracebridge Hall* (1821).[23] Irving's most sustained and thorough critique of the school, however, occurs in "Sleepy Hollow." Although set thirty years in the past, the dilapidation of Ichabod Crane's classroom and the backwardness of his pedagogy would be familiar to any of Irving's US readers who had received a formal education in a one-room school. "His school house was a low building of one large room, rudely constructed of logs; the windows partly glazed, and partly patched with leaves of old copy books," Knickerbocker writes. "From hence the low murmur of his pupils' voices conning over their lessons … interrupted now and then by the authoritative voice of the master, in tone of menace or command, or peradventure, by the appalling sound of the birch, as he urged some tardy loiterer along the flowery path of knowledge."[24]

The comeuppance Crane receives at the end of "Sleepy Hollow," when he is attacked by the headless horseman, ultimately represents Irving's greatest act of literary self-promotion and scholastic derogation. We learn early on in "Sleepy Hollow" that Crane is susceptible to a specifically literary form of revenge. Knickerbocker tells us repeatedly that Crane loves to read: "[F]or he had read several books quite through, and was a perfect master of Cotton Mather's History of New England Witchcraft, in which, by the way, he most firmly and potently believed." Crane's credulity as a reader, the fact that he mistakes what he is reading for reality—as an upstate Quixote, of sorts—leads him to misidentify the literary for the real throughout the story. "It was often his delight, after his school was dismissed of an afternoon, to stretch himself on the rich bed of clover ... and there con over old Mather's direful tales, until the gathering dusk of evening made the printed page a mere mist before his eyes," Knickerbocker writes. "Then, as he wended his way, by swamp and stream and awful woodland, to the farm house where he happened to be quartered, every sound of nature, at the witching hour, fluttered his excited imagination." At this point in "Sleepy Hollow," Irving maintains a critical distance from his principal character, upholding the division between reality and literature even as Crane can't. The joke is that Crane makes a mistake that we readers don't, confusing the sounds of nature along the swamp and woodland for some ghostly presence that he has read about in a book.[25]

During the final confrontation with the headless horseman, though, the division between the real and the literary erodes altogether. When Crane starts riding home, "[a]ll the stories of ghosts and goblins that he had heard in the afternoon" at the Van Tassels "came crowding upon his recollection." He approaches a tree that "was connected with the tragical story of the unfortunate André"—another one of Sleepy Hollow's literary landmarks. As Crane "approached a little nearer, he thought he saw something white, hanging in the midst of the tree: he paused and ceased whistling," Knickerbocker writes. "[B]ut on looking more narrowly, perceived that it was a place where the tree had been scathed by lightning, and the white wood laid bare." Like Crane's earlier rides home, Irving continues to uphold the barrier dividing the literary and the real: although Crane "thought he saw something hanging" (i.e., Major André's dangling corpse), it turns out merely to be "white wood laid bare." But where, earlier in the story, Knickerbocker indulges in what Gerard Genette would call iterative narration to maintain a critical distance from Crane, describing his habit of "often" reading after school let out, in this scene Knickerbocker focalizes Crane's consciousness more directly, forcing the reader to suffer the flutters of imagination right along with Crane in a past tense that comes to feel disturbingly present. "Suddenly he heard a groan—his teeth chattered, and his knees smote against the saddle," Knickerbocker writes moments later; "it was but the rubbing of one huge bough upon another, as they were swayed about by the breeze."[26]

The mechanisms of language that stabilize Crane's (and the reader's) experience at the beginning of this skittish horse ride—converting the things Crane "thought he saw" or "heard" into the unthreatening stuff of everyday life, like "white wood laid bare" or "the rubbing of one huge bough upon another"—break down altogether when the headless horseman finally confronts Crane. "Just at this moment a plashy tramp by the side of the bridge caught the sensitive ear of Ichabod," Knickerbocker writes. "In the dark shadow of the grove, on the margin of the brook, he beheld something huge, misshapen, black and towering. It stirred not, but seemed gathered up in the gloom, like some gigantic monster ready to spring upon the traveller." Where before Irving calls attention to the faulty apparatus that governs Crane's perceptions, emphasizing what Crane "*thought he saw ... hanging in the* midst of the tree," here that faulty apparatus doesn't seem so faulty after all. When Crane beholds "something huge, misshapen, black and towering," that *"seemed* gathered up in gloom, *like* some gigantic monster," things as they appear turn out to be exactly what they are:

> Though the night was dark and dismal, yet the form of the unknown might now in some degree be ascertained. He appeared to be a horseman of large dimensions, and mounted on a black horse of powerful frame. ... On mounting a rising ground, which brought the figure of his fellow traveller in relief against the sky, gigantic in height, and muffled in a cloak, Ichabod was horror struck, on perceiving that he was headless! but his horror was still more increased, on observing, that the head, which should have rested on his shoulders, was carried before him on the pommel of the saddle![27]

The final encounter thus reverses the epistemological sequence of Crane's previous experiences: "appear," "seem," and "like" become, by the end of the passage, "is." What *seems* gathered up in gloom *is* gathered up in gloom; what *is like* some gigantic monster *is* a gigantic monster; what *appears* to be a headless horseman *is* a headless horseman. All of the words that, earlier, called our attention to the unreliability of Crane's impressions—ensuring we recognize that Crane is the one "perceiving," "observing," and "ascertain[ing]" the supernatural events—at this moment confirm the reliability of Crane's impressions. His perceptions and observations are licensed by the narrative and deemed "true." The stories Crane has read become real in this final scene; Crane's susceptibility to literature becomes the reader's susceptibility. Later in the story Irving provides all sorts of details that undermine the credibility of Crane's perceptions here and call into question the very status of the literary in the story—the shattered fragments of pumpkin found near Crane's hat, Brom Bones's laughter whenever he hears Crane's story, and even the "rule" the headless horseman breaks at the end of his race with Crane.[28] By the end of "Sleepy Hollow," though, these details serve to foster a thriving literary community. The controversy surrounding Crane's disappearance generates in the story healthy literary exchange; it produces a more integrated society based on the shared experience of literature and storytelling, even if that sharing originates in disagreement. So just as literary culture effloresces when Crane the schoolteacher disappears from Sleepy Hollow, so too in Crane's famous race against the headless horseman do we witness the literary overtaking and subsuming the scholastic. "All the stories of ghosts and goblins" come "crowding upon [Crane's] recollection"—until it isn't just Crane's recollection that the stories crowd upon (and crowd out), but Crane himself.

"Sleepy Hollow" is thus Irving's most powerful argument for the value of literary culture and his most thorough indictment of the school. Irving was by no means the only US writer in the nineteenth century to pit literature against formal education. Henry David Thoreau's *Walden* (1854), for instance, suggested that students should avoid the "common course" of school "where anything is professed and practised but the art of life." "Which would have advanced the most at the end of a month," Thoreau asked,

> the boy who had made his own jackknife from the ore which he had dug and smelted, reading as much as would be necessary for this,—or the boy who had attended the lectures on metallurgy at the Institute in the mean while, and had received a Rodgers' penknife from his father? Which would be most likely to cut his fingers? ... To my astonishment I was informed on leaving college that I had studied navigation!—why, if I had taken one turn down the harbor I should have known more about it.[29]

These sorts of denunciations, which offer up their authentic social wisdom against the inauthenticity of the school, aren't at all unusual for the period. In "The American Scholar" (1837), Ralph Waldo Emerson declared, "Not out of those on whom systems of education have exhausted their culture, comes the helpful giant to destroy the old or build the new, but out of unhandselled savage nature." "This is what you shall do," Walt Whitman wrote in the Preface to *Leaves of Grass* (1855). "Love the earth and sun and the animals, ... re-examine all you have been told in school or church or in any book, and dismiss whatever insults your own soul; and your very flesh shall be a great poem." And, of course, Huck leaves Aunt Sally's house, with its "sivil[izing]" structures, in the final sentences of *Adventures of Huckleberry Finn* (1884), proclaiming, "I reckon I got to light out for the Territory ahead of the rest." While Whitman and Twain in these passages position their work against all social institutions, many of the most powerful justifications for literary value in this tradition isolated the school as literature's principal antagonist and offered up the literary as an escape from the boredom and routine of the classroom. This is the meaning of Ishmael's famous line in *Moby-Dick* (1851), that "a whale-ship was my Yale College and my Harvard."[30]

The whaleship, the Mississippi River, Nature—the zone of authentic social experience in this body of writing is, by definition, anti-scholastic, asserting its claim to authenticity against the apparatuses of formal education. The expulsion of Crane and the schoolhouse from "Sleepy Hollow" is best appreciated as an origin point for this US literary tradition. Though Crane aspires to a prominent position in the communal life of Sleepy Hollow, by the end of the story all that remains of him and his institution is a blank space, an em-dash. "Ichabod endeavored to dodge the horrible missile, but too late," Knickerbocker explains during Crane's final appearance in the story. "It encountered his cranium with a tremendous crash—he was tumbled headlong into the dust, and Gunpowder, the black steed, and the goblin rider, passed by like a whirlwind.—"[31]

Pedagogues Enshrined: The Sentimental Tradition

Another strain of cultural production in the early United States maintained an entirely different relationship to education and literariness from that of Irving and his successors. Far from enforcing a strict separation between the literary and the scholastic, sentimentalism understood the two as continuous with one another. William Hill Brown proclaims in the preface to *The Power of Sympathy* (1789) that in his book "the dangerous consequences of SEDUCTION are exposed, and the Advantages of FEMALE EDUCATION set forth and recommended." Susanna Rowson in the preface to *Charlotte Temple* (1794) explains that she hopes her book may be useful to "the many daughters of Misfortune who, deprived of natural friends, or spoilt by a mistaken education, are thrown on an unfeeling world without the least power to defend themselves." Hannah Webster Foster dedicated her novel *The Boarding School* (1798) to the young ladies of America: "Convinced," she writes, "of the many advantages of a good education, and the importance of improving those advantages," and "sensible, too, that the foundation of a useful and happy life must be laid down in youth," "the author has employed a part of her leisure hours in collecting and arranging her ideas on the subject of female deportment." Such statements made even more explicit the pedagogical commitments of the books themselves, which communicated their lessons through didactic asides and parables and never shied away from the scene of instruction, either in an actual school or more typically the home, as a setting for narrative action. Professionally these sentimentalists and the ones who followed them also tended to move seamlessly between the world of formal education and the world of literature. Rowson ran an academy in and around Boston at the beginning of the nineteenth century. Harriet Beecher Stowe taught at a school while writing *Uncle Tom's Cabin* (1852). Her sister, Catherine Beecher, was a prominent domestic pedagogue and her husband, Calvin Stowe, was a school reformer. Catherine Sedgwick participated in school board activities along with the Stowes, the Beechers, and Horace and Mary Peabody Mann.[32]

For a quick comparison, we might consider one of the most famous sentimental scenes in nineteenth-century American literature, Eva St. Clare's death in *Uncle Tom's Cabin*. This scene articulates its own aesthetic mission against the failings of a traditional pedagogue, not unlike Irving's "Sleepy Hollow."[33] In the lead up to the episode, Eva's father, Augustine St. Clare, has tasked his cousin Ophelia, a Vermonter, with the education of an enslaved character, Topsy. St. Clare proposes the scheme as an experiment of sorts. "I bought her, and I'll give her to you," he explains to Ophelia. "Try, now, and give her a good orthodox New England bringing up, and see what it'll make of her." Ophelia, with her love of order and her contempt for the "shiftless," is in Stowe's novel the exemplary New Englander. Her "ideas of education," according to the narrator, were "of the kind that prevailed in New England a century ago, and which are still preserved in some very retired and unsophisticated parts, where there are no railroads." These ideas consist of teaching students to "mind when they [are] spoken to," of "the catechism, sewing, and reading," and of "whip[ping]" students "if they t[ell] lies."[34]

Needless to say, Ophelia's antiquated disciplinary methods fail to undo the educational damage Topsy has suffered under slavery, and it is instead only Eva St. Clare's pedagogy that succeeds in truly transforming Topsy into a proper Christian. So where "Sleepy Hollow" humiliates the pedagogue Ichabod Crane to reconstitute the social order under literary culture rather than formal education, *Uncle Tom's Cabin* undermines the pedagogue Ophelia to reconstitute the social order under literature *and* formal education, a renovated program where the two remain mutually reinforcing and where literature in effect serves as an instrument for modern education reform. "I don't know what to do," Ophelia confesses to her cousin at one point. "I've taught and taught; I've talked till I'm tired; I've whipped her; I've punished her in every way I can think of, and she's just what she was at first." Eva's educational program, by contrast, is enacted through tender acts of love and kindness, and this pedagogy is fully realized in the deathbed scene, as she delivers a curl of her hair to Topsy:

> "O, Miss Eva, I've been a bad girl; but won't you give me one, too?"
> "Yes, poor Topsy! to be sure, I will. There—every time you look at that, think that I love you, and wanted you to be a good girl!"
> "O, Miss Eva, I is tryin'!" said Topsy, earnestly; "but, Lor, it's so hard to be good! 'Pears like I an't used to it, no ways!"
> "Jesus knows it, Topsy; he is sorry for you; he will help you."

In the aftermath of Eva's death, Topsy is transformed into a model student; by the end of the book, she has shown "so much intelligence, activity and zeal, and desire to do good in the world" that she is "at last recommended, and approved as a missionary to one of the stations in Africa[.]" But the episode is educational as much for Ophelia the teacher as it is for Topsy the student. Having witnessed Eva's death, Ophelia says, "Topsy, you poor child ... don't give up! I can love you, though I am not like that dear little child [Eva]. I hope I've learnt something of the love of Christ from her. I can love you; I do, and I'll try to help you to grow up a good Christian girl."[35]

On the one hand, this scene can be understood as a reflection of the decentralized institutional landscape from which it emerged. It bears the traces of a range of antebellum institutions tasked with educating Americans: not just or even primarily the school, but also the church, the family, the slave plantation, and the publishing industry, with its didactic fiction and other print materials devoted to the education of readers.[36] The scene understands its own value inside this scattered institutional field and theorizes its own pedagogical force with and against the other institutions that stand alongside it. On the other hand, the scene articulates a specific disciplinary plan that proved highly influential in the increasingly centralized institutional landscape of the postbellum period. This is at least the Foucauldian reading of *Uncle Tom's Cabin* and sentimentalism that Richard Brodhead puts forward; in Eva's death scene, he claims, "the plan of discipline through love emerges from the ruins of its cultural rivals as a kind of miraculous transcendence of their apparently inevitable limits. Corporal correction in all of its still-visible forms is summoned to the task of demonstrating the glory and necessity of this softer yet surer correction." According to Brodhead, the disciplinary regime that *Uncle Tom's Cabin* ushered in found its advocates before the Civil War in middle-class educational reformers like the Stowes, Beechers, and Manns. Their program of "disciplinary intimacy," as Brodhead terms it, "generate[d] on one front an animus against corporal punishment; on another, a particular configuration of training institutions designed to support that character-building plan; and on yet another, a new place for literary reading in cultural life."[37]

Brodhead's interpretation, for all of its persuasiveness, fails to account for the specificity of *Uncle Tom's Cabin*'s institutional reception. Though sentimentalism and educational reform might have followed the same disciplinary logic, the sentimental literary tradition has not received the same amount of attention in the modern literature classroom as the anti-scholastic writings I described earlier in this chapter. If sentimentalism and the modern school shared a common middle-class political program—if, moreover, sentimentalists tended to be teachers and teachers tended to be sentimentalists—why did "Sleepy Hollow" establish itself more firmly in the school curriculum than *Uncle Tom's Cabin*? Ideological explanations for sentimental literature's exclusion aren't on their own entirely satisfying. This is largely because a novel like *Uncle Tom's Cabin*, with its rendering of Topsy's troublesome education, could be (and in fact was) recruited to promote ruling-class political projects in the decades following the Civil War and the beginning of the twentieth century—and many of these projects enlisted the school along with sentimental literature. As Brodhead suggests and as Madeleine R. Grumet once argued more comprehensively, the middle-class reformers' educational regime sought to sentimentalize formal education as a way of dulling the violent upheavals of industrialization for its student populations. Assigning sentimental literature, produced by such models of sentimental virtue as Harriet Beecher Stowe or Catherine Sedgwick, would presumably bolster this ideological program. So why not simply teach sentimental texts?[38]

The divergent institutional reception of sentimental and anti-scholastic writing raises other important questions as well. Sentimentalism's considerable social agency is usually believed to operate within mass culture or what Lauren Berlant once described as an intimate public sphere detached from the public sphere of political decision making.[39] Ann Douglas, writing in the late 1970s, can in this context insist that "[t]oday many Americans, intellectuals as well as less scholarly people, feel a particular fondness for the artifacts, the literature, the *mores* of our Victorian past." She can recount, too, her own experience as a child reading with "formative intensity" outside of school a "collection of Victorian sentimental fiction, a legacy from my grandmother's girlhood." In this extracurricular readerly environment, the scene that Douglas "remember[s] best"—the "archetypical and archetypically satisfying scene in this domestic genre"—is "the death of Little Eva in Harriet Beecher Stowe's novel, *Uncle Tom's Cabin*."[40] Douglas is of course suspicious of the immersive experience sentimentalism provides for its mass audience of readers, yet the anecdote nevertheless offers itself as proof of the considerable hold Eva's death, for instance, maintains on the popular imagination. In the educational system's quest for relevance, sentimental literature—so popular and affecting—presumably could have helped the school realize its ambition to establish itself in US social experience. Why, then, did teachers tend to leave sentimental literature off of the syllabus?

Answering these questions requires a more granular account of the process through which the literary cohered over the nineteenth and twentieth centuries. Scholars tend to describe the consolidation of American literature specifically as unfolding over three successive phases between the Civil War and World War II. In the first phase, which extended roughly over the final decades of the nineteenth century, the country's thriving shared public culture broke down as American literature became identified with a genteel tradition championed by figures like Moses Coit Tyler, Barrett Wendell, Bliss Perry, and Brander Matthews. This genteel conception took New England as the foundation for a national literary identity and subscribed to an Arnoldian understanding of culture as a mechanism of social control under the dual threats of industrialization and immigration. The second phase set in (again, roughly) at the beginning of the twentieth century and is associated with the realist tradition put in place by Vernon Louis Parrington, Fred Lewis Pattee, and Norman Foerster. This conception of American literature articulated itself against its genteel, belletristic predecessor and found in the American literary tradition a resource for a progressive but still nationalist politics. The final phase coincided with the rise of modernism and culminated with the consecration of the romance tradition in the mid-twentieth century under F. O. Matthiessen, Henry Nash Smith, R. W. B. Lewis, Richard Chase, Leslie Fiedler, Leo Marx, and Richard Poirier.[41] This third phase, too, is understood to coincide with the legitimation of American literary studies in higher education. In the 1870s, twenty-six institutions of higher education taught American authors in English literature courses, and these numbers grew over the subsequent decades. In the 1880s, at least forty-five colleges taught American literature; in the 1890s, seventy colleges and universities taught American literature courses; by the 1920s, according to Kermit Vanderbilt, "[v]ery few of America's leading universities were totally neglecting American literature ... only Duke, Notre Dame, University of the South, and some seven others." During World War II, according to Elizabeth

Renker, American literature "finally receive[d] an enthusiastic curricular embrace" because of "the practical services it could render the cause of nationalism."[42]

Though the historiography of American literature tends to break its development into these three disjointed phases, in fact its development is best appreciated as a dynamic process in which all of these positions and more are active between the mid-nineteenth century and the mid-twentieth, oftentimes jostling against each other in the work of a single critic or scholar, with one conception of the literary predominating at any given moment over its alternatives.[43] This process involved co-evolutions in literary culture, the school, and the broader industrial system where literary and scholastic value found recognition (or didn't). Within literary culture, different genres and sub-genres, canons and sub-canons, organizations, societies, magazines, and publishing houses, competed with each other for prestige and, out of this competitive jockeying, drew their own lines demarcating the literary. The school, as we'll see, expanded over this period by absorbing literature, and as it expanded it reciprocally imposed its own disciplinary regimes onto the literature it absorbed. It slotted the literary into its organization of knowledge production and instruction; it offered new justifications for literary specialization that divided expert readers from amateurs. Economic transformations after the Civil War meanwhile propelled the growth of an industrialist class that initially regarded academic credentials with suspicion and whose relationship to literary culture differed considerably from that of the earlier mercantile elites in New England and the Mid-Atlantic, as well as the remnants of an aristocratic planter class in the South and an increasingly national labor force that was developing its own cultural practices. The rising new middle class came to mediate these others not just economically but culturally too, developing programs through the school and other para-institutions (museums, foundations, lyceums) that could appeal to both its own constituents and members of the other classes that it hoped to achieve influence over. Out of these interlocking transformations, the definition of the literary underwent many shifts indeed.[44]

Sentimentalism was by no means unassimilable to every conception of American literature that emerged over this period of time, or even the dominant conceptions of American literature. *Uncle Tom's Cabin* in particular remained canonically secure—nestled comfortably within the category of American literature—through the opening decades of the twentieth century. In the immediate aftermath of the Civil War, the advocates of the genteel tradition included Stowe's novel as part of their Arnoldian social program. This program, according to Nina Baym, "display[ed] the virtues and achievements of an Anglo-Saxon United States founded by New England Puritans" and sought to instill in all citizens "those traits that they thought necessary for the future: self-reliance, self-control, and acceptance of hierarchy." Ticknor and Fields, the publishing house at the center of this literary movement, acquired the rights to Stowe's work in 1863 and reprinted *Uncle*

Tom's Cabin every year through the 1860s and 1870s. Houghton, Mifflin & Co., the successor to Ticknor and Fields, subsequently published different editions of the novel targeted at different segments of the reading population in the 1890s and the first decade of the twentieth century, marketing *Uncle Tom's Cabin* as both a bestseller and a classic. One of Houghton Mifflin's imprints, the Riverside series, published an edition of the novel addressed specifically to school readers. The Riverside series was developed by Horace Scudder, an ideologue for literary *and* scholastic culture who served as Houghton Mifflin's chief editor and a member of the Massachusetts Board of Education. Scudder, as a proto-Progressive educator, saw in the classics of American literature a far preferable alternative to the graded readers that typically organized rote classroom instruction; as a marketing visionary, he also understood that a robust educational system meant a mass audience of readers and book buyers.[45]

In the early twentieth century, Stowe remained a canonical author, with John Erskine in 1910, for instance, selecting her as one of six "leading American novelists" whom "time has already sifted out ... for special remembrance."[46] Yet after 1918, Stowe and sentimentalism were increasingly marginalized within the sphere of the literary. Even Parrington's *Main Currents in American Thought* (1927), with its (from our perspective) capacious definition of literature, suggested that Stowe's status as a literary writer was precarious. Parrington celebrated *Uncle Tom's Cabin* as a "great human document" that "stripped away the protective atmosphere from the sacred institution [of slavery], and laid bare its elementary injustice." But Parrington also conceded that the novel managed these achievements "[d]espite its obvious blemishes of structure and sentimentalism." Though scholarship on American literary history cited Stowe less frequently after 1918, her work continued to appear in the educational system during the interwar period, only in the lower levels: two editions of *Uncle Tom's Cabin* were published for school use in the twenties, one by the World Publishing Company in Cleveland and the other by Charles E. Graham and Co. in Newark, New Jersey.[47]

The hegemony of the modernist conception of American literature ultimately succeeded in severing whatever ties bound sentimentalism and Stowe's work to the realm of literature.[48] In the wake of modernism's triumph, Faye Halpern in 2018 could describe *Uncle Tom's Cabin* as an "antiliteracy manual" because it "enshrin[es] a method that counters the conventional concept of literacy that was developing in the antebellum United States" and because it resists the hermeneutics of suspicion that is foundational for twenty-first-century literary training: "[Sentimentalism] trains its readers to think of it as real, to think of its characters as actual people. However, this way of reading, becoming so immersed in the work that one can gain no critical distance from it, is exactly the way we train our undergraduates not to read."[49] Halpern's assessment no doubt fails to recognize that sentimentalism has been assimilable to certain hegemonic definitions of literacy and literariness even as it's been unassimilable to others. But it is through this very misrecognition that Halpern's argument registers the achievement of the midcentury Americanists and in fact further naturalizes their bounded conception of literariness. We have, however, still yet to arrive at an adequate explanation for the success of their paradigm after 1918 and the displacement of their rivals. This explanation, as I've suggested already and will now explain more fully, lies in the particular attitude literature was increasingly understood to assume toward the scene of formal education.

Washington Irving's Anti-Scholasticism in School

There is a strange moment at the beginning of *Tales of a Traveller with Selections from the Sketch Book* (1901)—a pedagogical edition of Washington Irving's writings—when the editor, an instructor from Teachers' College, Columbia University, named George Philip Krapp, tells teachers that Irving's work requires almost no teaching at all. "For the intelligent reading of Irving very little critical apparatus seems necessary," Krapp proclaims in the first sentence of the preface.

> In the Introduction to the present volume the endeavor has been to give a sympathetic sketch of the life of Irving, followed by a brief criticism of the group of three or four works to which the *Tales of a Traveller* and the *Sketch Book* belong. In the notes all but the most evident allusions have been explained and most of the foreign words and phrases have been translated. An occasional topic for class discussion is suggested; but generally all matters of criticism and opinion have been left untouched.[50]

It's an odd way to begin a pedagogical edition: the justifications Krapp offers for his editorial interventions are based on the premise that his interventions only minimally intervene. Assuming the passive voice, as if to efface himself from the edition altogether, Krapp presents his "critical apparatus" as if it were a source of embarrassment, something he would avoid altogether if he could. Though he concedes that his edition explains "all but the most evident allusions" and translates "most of the foreign words and phrases," he also relentlessly qualifies his editorial labor: in Krapp's words, he has provided merely a "sympathetic *sketch*," "a *brief* criticism," "*an occasional* topic for class discussion." Such qualifications betray a bizarre sort of self-consciousness at work in the preface, a pedagogy that disavows its own function as pedagogy. In another pedagogical edition of *The Sketch Book— Six Selections* (1878), edited by Homer B. Sprague, former headmaster of the Girls' High School in Boston—we see more pedagogical disavowals along the same lines, as Sprague warns the instructor not to interfere with the basic mechanisms of literary experience, and the scholastic edition renounces its own scholasticism.

"The commentary should not ... be such as to interfere with ... the story or description," the editor warns, "but simply what is necessary to a general understanding of the piece."[51]

Krapp's preface reflects American literature's idiosyncratic position within the modern school system, as well as the contradictory role literature instructors came to play within this system's development. The pedagogical force of American literature, as Krapp presents it here, lies in its capacity to transcend the scene of pedagogy. The educational labor of the literature instructor, in turn, consists of effacing his or her own educational labor. As we'll see, the incorporation of American literature into the classroom created some awkwardness even as it helped address many of the early school system's public relations problems. The self-effacing gestures so common in scholastic treatments of American literature—where the pedagogical edition disavows its own pedagogy—suggest literature's transformative powers, its capacity to break down the division between institutional and non-institutional experience. As the educational system assumed a greater role in the organization of modern society, it then exerted a corresponding influence over the production of literature, and the divergent institutional trajectories of romance and sentimentalism become explicable as a product of this feedback cycle where a certain strain of literature incited the school's growth and the school, by growing, took on a greater role adjudicating the boundaries of the literary and disseminating literature.

As one of the first American writers to appear in the school curriculum, and as a writer whose work was just as likely to be assigned in elementary and secondary school as it was in the university, Washington Irving is uniquely positioned to illuminate the impact of literature generally and American literature specifically on the educational system's development. Disciplinary historians tend to focus on the institutionalization of American literature in higher education instead of examining its reception in the school system as a whole.[52] This is, on some level, entirely understandable. The consolidation of "literature" as a cultural designation after 1918 came about with the rise of a mass system of primary and secondary education: with higher enrollments at these lower levels of the school system, the English curriculum in the research university was reimagined under the hegemony of the New Critics to invest literature with a "new kind of distinction," as John Guillory has explained. The New Critics' regime endowed literature with discursive coherence by defining it in opposition to the cultural and linguistic proficiencies students obtained in elementary and secondary classrooms.[53] But if the English Department in the research university thus came to play an outsized role in defining "literature" and "American literature" after 1918, institutions of higher education played no such role in earlier periods of literary history.

American literature textbooks appeared as early as Samuel L. Knapp's *Lectures on American Literature* (1829), and excerpts of American literature appeared regularly in the McGuffey Readers, which were first published in 1836. (These excerpts were normally in the fourth, fifth, and sixth readers.) It's difficult to calculate from the historical record the extent to which teachers incorporated these literary works into the daily rhythms of school life—textbooks tended to expose students to fragments of literature, not full texts, and in the case of the McGuffey Readers students usually didn't stay in school long enough to get beyond the third reader.[54] Nevertheless, by the end of the nineteenth century, American literature had become a mainstay in both elementary and high school education, long before it did in higher education. After conducting a study of 113 Iowa secondary schools in 1903, Mae J. Evans concluded that "American literature receives a large proportion of time in the one hundred and thirteen high schools—perhaps too large a proportion for its relative worth[.]"[55]

The shifting justifications for Irving's inclusion in the curriculum reveal the specific service literature was called upon to perform for the educational system as the system evolved. The arrival of his work in the school occurred just after the publication of *A History of the Life and Voyages of Christopher Columbus* (1828), when educators discovered in Irving a compelling figure around whom to erect a coherent national cultural identity. In an April 29, 1833, assembly of the state of New York, the committee on colleges, academies, and common schools approved a "resolution from the Senate relative to the introduction of Washington Irving's abridged Life of Columbus into the common schools." The committee's rationale for the resolution emphasized the nativeness of Irving's genius: the resolution passed not just because the committee believed Irving's book on Columbus would "have a direct tendency to raise the standard of education in the common schools of the State," but also because it would "be applauded throughout the Union as a most appropriate tribute on the part of this State to the eminent genius and meritorious labors of one of our native citizens." Just which "native citizens" Irving was "one of" appears ambiguous here, as Irving's eminence radiates through the various sites of nineteenth-century place-based affiliation, from the regional to the national to the global: *Life and Voyages* reflects well on the state of New York in the context of the larger Union, but it also reflects well on the Union in the context of the larger world. "It is unnecessary that your committee should dwell on the superior merits, as a literary production, of Washington Irving's Life and Voyages of Columbus," the resolution insists; "it has already received the stamp of public approbation, not only in this country, but in every part of the civilized world where English and American literature is known and valued."[56]

School boards and state legislatures later in the nineteenth century continued to find in Irving a figure around whom to organize a national cultural identity. In the *Seventh Annual Report of the State Commissioner of Common Schools to the Governor of the State of Ohio* (1861), the commissioner included the collected works of Washington Irving on the schedule of Ohio School Library books distributed in 1860 as part of a resolution to "furnish[] to youth ... reading matter of a high character."[57] Starting around 1844 and continuing into the twentieth century, Irving's work was excerpted regularly in the McGuffey Readers.[58] At first, the literary work that appeared with most frequency was "The Voyage," a short essay describing Geoffrey Crayon's sentimental journey by boat from the United States to England. Albeit less explicitly patriotic than his *Life and Voyages*, "The Voyage" located Irving in a legible European tradition and demonstrated the growing respectability of American literature abroad.

While Irving's sentimentalism thus served for a time to anchor the study of his work in schools, the rationale for Irving's inclusion in the classroom changed at the turn of the twentieth century, discarding his sentimentalism and enshrining his anti-scholasticism. "Rip Van Winkle" and "Sleepy Hollow" appeared more regularly in pedagogical editions and anthologies, eventually displacing *Life and Voyage* and "The Voyage." "Rip Van Winkle" appeared in the McGuffey Readers as early as 1879, and "Sleepy Hollow" as early as 1889.[59] Between 1878 and 1920, twenty-two pedagogical editions of *The Sketch Book* were published, according to Stanley T. Williams and Mary Allen Edge's *A Bibliography of the Writings of Washington Irving* (1936).[60] In 1883, Albert F. Blaisdell issued an edition of "Sleepy Hollow" for school and home; in the academic year 1899–1900, Harvard included "The Legend of Sleepy Hollow," "Rip Van Winkle," and "Tales of a Traveller" in the list of works recommended to candidates seeking entrance to the college.[61] This movement toward the anti-scholasticism of romance and away from the scholasticism of sentimentalism reflects the school's larger strategy to embed itself in public life. By teaching anti-scholastic literary works, educators began to claim for their institutions access to authentic social experience, the very social experience that writers like Irving had originally claimed for their work by situating it beyond the confines of the school.

This is why we see certain pedagogical editions of Irving's work embrace the language of student interest that came to define the modern educational program. In *Six Selections*, the instructions for reading the stories explain, "It should be the purpose of the teacher, while keeping the exercises in literature from becoming either mere tasks or pastimes, to make the lessons so interesting that they will be eagerly and vigorously studied." The minimal directions teachers provide, according to this edition, should not "interfere with the interest of the story or description"; instead they should inspire students to "search for other items that will make interesting the pieces selected for study."[62] In Chapter 4 I will provide a more in-depth account of educational reformers' commitment to structuring the emergent educational system around the interests of the student population; for now, I simply want to note that educators during this era mobilized the interest of Irving's writing to produce in schools a fundamentally un-scholastic student experience.

The disavowals of pedagogy that occur in George Philip Krapp's pedagogical edition should make more sense in this context. If explanatory notes and topics for class discussion seem to be a source of embarrassment for the editors of these editions—an incursion of stifling scholasticism into the authentic world of literary experience—the negative depiction of pedagogy in Irving's work surprisingly isn't. In fact, some pedagogical editions of *The Sketch Book* draw the students' attention to the heinousness of life in school. The suggested topics for discussion printed at the end of the "Sleepy Hollow" section in *Six Selections* encourage students to consider the representation of schools in the story. "Write a composition on 'School in Sleepy Hollow'" is one suggested activity. "When is Ichabod Crane most ludicrous?" asks another topic.[63] It's tempting to imagine the classroom activities inspired by these suggestions—students animatedly discussing the schoolteacher Ichabod Crane's various humiliations, romantic and supernatural, or arguing over the many inefficiencies of Crane's teaching methods, his use of the birch stick, "urg[ing] some tardy loiterer along the flowery path of knowledge." The reflexive work these prompts demand from students seem to undermine the project of formal education altogether. They seem to encourage students to recognize that the school is an inhumane social institution. However, these disavowals of pedagogy took place inside the classroom: through "Sleepy Hollow," educators taught students, in school, that schools offered only a limited and unpleasant imitation of social experience. By teaching literary works that renounced formal education, they set out to make the educational experience more immersive; they sought to present the school as not a school at all.

After 1918, when the literary field underwent a dramatic restructuring, Irving remained a boundary figure in the American literary tradition, his tales persisting in the primary and secondary school curriculum but also in colleges and universities. Fiedler, as we've seen, located the origins of the American literary tradition in "Rip Van Winkle," that story whose eponymous hero flees to the Catskills to escape his wife and the structures of civilization. Though Irving undoubtedly played a less significant role in the other major works of the mid-twentieth-century Americanists, his presence in this body of literary criticism seems appropriate for the minor-major or major-minor author that he has remained. While he garnered only a few passing mentions in, say, F. O. Matthiessen's *American Renaissance* (1941) and Henry Nash Smith's *Virgin Land* (1950), the opening epigraph to Leo Marx's *The Machine in the Garden* (1964) is from "The Legend of Sleepy Hollow."[64] The vehemence with which Irving's early tales renounced the school guaranteed for him inclusion in the romance tradition and underwrote the literariness of his work: these renunciations, after all, were precisely what came to define the literariness of American literature more broadly.

The Institutionalization of American Literature

The disavowal of pedagogy that we see in postbellum pedagogical editions of Irving's work recurs in scholastic editions and textbooks of American literature. In

An Introduction to the Study of American Literature (1896), Brander Matthews explains that "all dates and proper names, and all titles of books not absolutely essential, have been rigorously omitted." He goes on to insist that "[i]nterest has thus been concentrated on the literary career of each of the greater writers and on their practice of the literary art, in the hope and expectation that the student will be encouraged and stimulated to read their works for their own pleasure." Mary E. Burt's *Literary Landmarks* (1889) stresses that reading American literature taps into essentially un-scholastic forms of pleasure: "I have seen a hundred young people in fifth and sixth grades spontaneously applaud, with no prompting from any teacher, the finest and subtlest thought in analyses of Hawthorne's Great Stone Face and the Christmas Banquet." Later, she explains that this unprompted enthusiasm, inspired by literature, has the power to keep students in school: "So many pupils leave school from the fifth and sixth grades that it is of the greatest importance that the reading should be made as interesting as possible." In *American Literature* (1894), Mildred Cabell Watkins insists that the first "object" she had in mind when assembling the edition was "to make the study interesting." Along similar lines, Watkins decided to include contemporary American authors like William Dean Howells and Henry James because "it is nevertheless important that readers should learn something about the writers whose books are affording so much present enjoyment to the world." To teach American literature in school was, for these educators, a way to integrate the school more completely into American social experience by harnessing the emotional and intellectual energies that characterized life outside of school. As Mae J. Evans explains, "More valuable in human experience than the correlation of study with study is the correlation of study with life"—and "life," here, for Evans, is coextensive with literature, especially American literature.[65]

Pedagogical editions of American literature often emphasized writers' dreadful experiences in the classroom to carry this mission forward. Mildred Cabell Watkins alerts students to James Fenimore Cooper's horrible experiences in school: "The free days in the free forest made the restraints of Yale College, whither he was sent at fourteen, unbearable. He was such an indifferent student that he could not finish the course." In *A Primer of American Literature* (1909), Abby Willis Howes describes Poe's time at UVA. "On his return to America [Poe] entered the University of Virginia, where he showed a brooding disposition, an imaginative temperament, and a wayward will. He developed gambling habits, and Mr. Allan took him from college and placed him in his office." Carl Van Doren's *The American Novel* (1921) recounts Twain's early life in Hannibal, Missouri, on the banks of the Mississippi: "There Clemens passed a boyhood and youth nearly as irresponsible as Huckleberry Finn's and nearly as imaginative and mischievous as Tom Sawyer's. Neither studious by nature nor offered even tolerable opportunities for study, he left school at twelve upon the death of his father, and was apprenticed to a printer in the town."[66]

Understandably, the student experience of American literature in this institutional environment could become schizophrenic. In his memoir, *A Son of the Middle Border* (1923), Hamlin Garland recounts his first exposure to American literature while attending school in Iowa around 1878. "Our school library at that time was pitifully small and ludicrously prescriptive," he writes; despite these conditions Garland manages one day to discover "two small red volumes called *Mosses from an Old Manse*." "Of course," Garland explains, "I had read of the author, for these books were listed in my *History of American Literature*, but I had never, up to this moment, dared to open one of them. I was a discoverer." Garland's encounter with Hawthorne's work is revelatory:

> I turned a page or two, and instantly my mental horizon widened. ... Even as I walked homeward to my lunch, I read. I ate with the book beside my plate. I neglected my classes that afternoon, and as soon as I had absorbed this volume I secured the other and devoted myself to it with almost equal intensity. ... It was my first profound literary passion and I was dazzled by the glory of it.

The school plays an essential role in Garland's quasi-religious discovery of American literature even as it's abandoned almost immediately. It establishes the conditions that make Garland's initial discovery possible: the school familiarizes Garland with Hawthorne as an author through the excerpts assigned from *History of American Literature*, and it stocks Hawthorne's work in its library. And yet, though various scholastic mechanisms—the classroom assignment, the textbook, the library—all work together to produce for Garland this moment of revelation, when the actual moment of revelation comes the school proves all too easy to leave behind, as Garland proceeds to neglect his classes in favor of his book. The school's institutional force in this moment is one of self-cancelation, creating the necessary conditions for un-scholastic experience to manifest. Significantly, Garland needs to return to the school library to reclaim this anti-scholastic experience, "secur[ing]" the other volume of *Mosses* and enjoying Hawthorne once again with "equal intensity."[67]

As Stowe's reception history would suggest, however, the literary and the anti-scholastic were not perfectly co-implicated at the turn of the twentieth century. Incoherence remained in American literature as a designation, especially in its orientation to the school. Brander Matthews, for instance, could openly acknowledge that Benjamin Franklin "had no time" for a college education because he had to "work for his living from early boyhood," and that "Cooper was expelled from Yale," and that "Bryant was so dissatisfied with Williams that he left it after a single year"—all while also claiming that "the authors who came after Emerson made sure of the best education that this country could afford them." Henry A. Beers's *An Outline Sketch of American Literature* (1887), noting the preponderance of Harvard graduates among the nation's great writers, argued: "The situation of a university scholar in old Cambridge was thus an almost ideal one. Within easy reach of a great city, with its literary and social clubs, its theaters, lecture courses, public meetings, dinner parties, etc., he yet lived withdrawn in an academic retirement among elm-shaded avenues and leafy gardens." William P. Trent's *A Brief History of American Literature* (1905) recognized the truth of Beers's argument in a footnote, explaining that "the spread of literature produced by academically trained writers may counteract some of the bad effects produced upon author and book by the heterogeneous character of our national life"; yet Trent also insisted that "a more classic type of literature may be, perhaps, obtained only at the loss of raciness and originality not well to be spared." This period is often associated with the canonization of the "schoolroom poets"—Longfellow, Bryant, Lowell, Holmes, Whittier, Emerson—who mostly graduated from the same schools and were subsequently taught alongside one another in elementary and secondary school classrooms. But it was also the period when Brander Matthews told students that "Emerson was only eighteen when he was graduated, feeling that the regular course of studies had done little for him, and having therefore strayed out of the beaten path to browse for himself among the books in the library."[68]

The proponents of American realism ultimately established their hegemony over the genteel tradition by casting their colleagues and predecessors' conception of the literary as overly scholastic. In *A History of American Literature Since 1870* (1915), Fred Lewis Pattee, the first professor of American literature in the United States, at the land grant university Penn State, criticized the belletrism of his genteel predecessors. "From 1830 to 1870," Pattee writes, "the creation of literature was very little in the hands of the masses; it was in the hands of ... [a] small and provincial 'aristocracy of the intellect.'" As Pattee points out, practically all of the major mid-nineteenth-century writers either graduated from Harvard or another distinguished New England institution. "The period was dominated by college men," Pattee writes, except for "Poe, who for a time was a student at the University of Virginia and at West Point, and Whittier, who was self-educated, and two women, Margaret Fuller and Mrs. Stowe, who lived in the period when colleges were open only for men." For Pattee, the influence exerted by the traditional school on literary production led to an undemocratic national literary culture. Only after the Civil War did American literature truly come into its own, breaking the hold elite colleges had placed over intellectual life. "The war shook America awake, it destroyed sectionalism, and revealed the nation to itself," Pattee writes. "The intellectual life of the nation no longer was to be in the hands of the aristocratic, scholarly few."[69]

The displacement of the genteel tradition thus came about in the first decades of the twentieth century as actors within literary culture sought to disentangle literature from traditional institutions of formal education. Professors and instructors of American literature were often the most vehement about American literature's ontological anti-scholasticism. This belief in part grounded the "promise of American literary studies" that, according to Gerald Graff, was constitutive of the field during its original formation and has resurfaced periodically ever since, whenever the field has felt the need to rediscover its animating purpose. In the early twentieth century, faculty members like Pattee and Parrington consolidated American literature as an academic subject by suggesting its study would cut through the bureaucratic organization of the school and its English departments, "merg[ing] history and criticism in a larger cultural study that would bring literary studies into more intimate connection with American society." This project proved especially appealing as literary culture in the United States grew further estranged from its former position within public life and more deeply embedded in classroom instruction. The professionalization of American literary studies thus came to contain within itself a de-professionalizing impulse. By identifying American literature with anti-scholasticism, professors attempted to break free from the very conditions that structured their academic lives, "transcending positivistic specialization, embracing diversity as part of the whole, and even bridging the gap between high and popular American culture," in Graff's words.[70]

The expulsion of sentimentalism from the realm of the literary under the New Critics and mid-twentieth-century Americanists represents the final consummation of the literary and the anti-scholastic. Of course, in retrospect, we can see a distinct pattern emerge in the evolution of American literature as a discursive category, a pattern in which a certain conception of the literary becomes entrenched within the structures of formal education and therefore ceases to be literary altogether. The realists attacked the genteel tradition for its ties to the educational system, and the advocates of the romance tradition, subsequently, attacked the realists for failing to overcome (and in fact perpetuating) the school's bureaucratization of culture. The midcentury Americanists didn't simply base their conception of the literary on writings that explicitly renounced formal education, although, according to these scholars, the American literary tradition did indeed do that. Matthiessen, for instance, explained casually that "the bulk of Melville's reading ... did not result from any formal training, for a whale ship was his Yale College and Harvard." And Fiedler described Hannibal, Missouri, as "Mark Twain's name for the world of belongingness and security, of school and home and church, presided over by the mothers"—in short, the very world Twain's fiction, and American literature more broadly, wanted desperately to flee.[71]

For the midcentury Americanists, American literature was anti-scholastic in a more profound sense too. In its exploration of what they sometimes called the "symbolic" or the "mythic" or the "pastoral" or, simply, "romance," American literature broke free from the structures of modern scholastic life. The "[c]omplex pastoralism" of the American literary tradition, in Leo Marx's account, "acknowledges the reality of history" even as it imagines nature "as a symbolic repository of meaning and value." It thus "compels us to recognize that the aspirations once represented by the symbol of an ideal landscape have not, and probably cannot, be embodied in our traditional institutions." Lionel Trilling argued that liberalism's "organizational impulse" means that "the ideas that can survive delegation, that can be passed on to agencies and bureaus and technicians, incline to be ideas of a certain kind and of a certain simplicity: they give up something of their largeness and modulation and complexity in order to survive." "[L]iterature," according to Trilling, resists liberal institutions' organizational impulse because it is "the human activity that takes the fullest and most precise account of variousness, possibility, complexity, and difficulty."[72]

Of course, the romance tradition itself eventually became the object of a disciplinary critique that follows the very pattern I've identified. A subsequent generation of New Historicists cast the midcentury Americanists' project as a call for literature's autonomy that eventually defined the academic study of American literature. This critique necessitated in turn a "revisionary intervention" into the category of American literature itself.[73] As Jennifer Fleissner has argued, though, the New Historicists' critique mischaracterized the work of the midcentury Americanists and obscured this work's powerful Weberian diagnosis of modern life. According to Fleissner, Trilling et al. confronted the rationalization and bureaucratization of social experience in terms that weren't simply therapeutic, and as such they provide a valuable resource for overcoming a problem—modernization—that implicates the New Historicists, who once stood in judgment of them, as well as literature professors today. "[W]hat," Fleissner asks, "is our relation to rationalization? ... Americanist scholars trained in the methods of the past 25 years must come to grips not simply with our participation in this structure, but also with the possibility that the very critical methods taken on for antihegemonic purposes have in many ways served hegemony's ends."[74]

Fleissner's argument isn't inconsistent, then, with Gerald Graff's earlier characterization of the failed "promise of American literary studies." In Graff's account, the study of American literature has periodically promised to transcend the organizational divisions of academic life, yet its innovations have inevitably disappointed, as the English Department folds them back into its own unyielding structure of "patterned isolation."[75] Both Graff and Fleissner thus pit the midcentury Americanists against the modern school system's formidable administrative apparatus, and though their characterizations accurately capture the historically combative relationship between the two, these characterizations never fully acknowledge the benefits that have accrued to the school system out of this conflict. By insisting on the anti-scholasticism of American literature, the midcentury Americanists, like many Americanists before them, attempted to think beyond the institutional system that increasingly structured their daily lives, as Fleissner claims. But they also naturalized the expansion of this system and its organizational scheme of "patterned isolation." They did so by giving students access to a world as authentic and meaningful as life on board the Pequod, or in a cabin on Walden Pond, or on a raft drifting down the Mississippi. They did so by embedding within the educational system an experiential world that lay perpetually beyond the system's reach.

Conclusion

In the preface to *American Renaissance* (1941), F. O. Matthiessen provides a somewhat confusing explanation for his choice of authors—Emerson, Thoreau, Hawthorne, Melville, and Whitman. He concedes at first the obvious, that these writers weren't especially popular in their own lifetimes. "The five hundred copies of Emerson's first book, *Nature* (1836), had been disposed of so slowly that a second edition was not called for until 1849," Matthiessen explains. "Thoreau recorded in his journal that four years after the appearance of his *Week on the Concord and Merrimack* (1849) only 219 copies had been sold[.] ... Whitman set up and printed *Leaves of Grass* for himself, and probably gave away more copies than were bought[.] ... Hawthorne reported that six or seven hundred copies of *Twice-Told Tales* (1837) had been disposed of before the panic of that year descended." Matthiessen concedes, too, that the commercial failure of his subjects contrasts starkly with the "triumphant vogue of Susan Warner's *The Wide, Wide World* (1850), Maria Cummins' *The Lamplighter* (1854), the ceaseless flux of Mrs. E.D.E.N. Southworth's sixty novels." According to Matthiessen, the dismal sales record of his principal writers is not disqualifying at all, however, especially when one considers their later popularity. Matthiessen in fact proceeds to argue that his authors are worthy of study precisely because they are more popular than the popular authors of their era: "I agree with Thoreau," he writes. "'Read the best books first, or you may not have a chance to read them at all.' And during the century that has ensued, the successive generations of common readers, who make the decisions, would seem finally to have agreed that the authors of the pre-Civil War era who bulk largest in stature are the five who are my subject."[76]

This rationale, whatever confusion it might inspire, is in some sense familiar, too, as a justification for the greatness of certain literary works and the deficiency of others. Matthiessen here balances his subjects' past obscurity against their present fame, taking their early commercial struggles as an indication of their aesthetic achievement and their current success with "common readers" as its definitive proof. Whitman's brilliance finds confirmation in both his initial obscurity and his later popularity; Susan Warner's inadequacies are likewise revealed through both the "triumphant vogue" that first greeted her work and her work's subsequent disappearance from the cultural record. Matthiessen's formulation therefore indulges a fantasy where the relentless march of time guarantees the reconciliation of prestige and popularity. It is a fantasy, furthermore, where the gendered divisions that divide the masculine realm of the literary and the feminine realm of mass culture are also dissolved, once again through those common readers whose preferences appear especially legitimate because they emanate from a common-ness beyond the narrow investments of any single identity category. This is the vanishing point all culture recedes toward, Matthiessen suggests: the union of aesthetic value and commercial success in the hearts and minds of an audience of abstracted common readers.

Matthiessen articulated this fantasy under institutional conditions that he and his colleagues perceived as oppressive. Though the United States in the mid-nineteenth century might have enjoyed a bustling public culture, in the mid-twentieth century, it didn't. In the wake of the Arnoldians and the modernists, the division between prestige and popularity, aesthetic value and commercial success was stark. The breakdown of public culture along the axis of gender occurred over the post–Civil War period also, as certain actors within literary culture understood their work as under threat by a malign feminine influence. On the one hand, this threat was associated with women writers, like the sentimentalists, whose commercial success endowed them with tremendous power over the cultural landscape; on the other, it was identified with the school, whose control over the literary was often cast as emasculating. Irving's institutional reception is instructive here, because it reveals that the masculinization of literary culture coincided with the feminization of mass culture. Through Irving, that is, we can glimpse the constitutive relationship between these two processes, with sentimentalism's expulsion from the literary after roughly 1918 occurring alongside Irving's expulsion from the sentimental.[77] The school, whose role in the administration of literary culture grew over this period, only reinforced these disjunctions. It did so not simply by subjecting literature to its taxonomizing practices, which broadened the chasm between literary and non-literary writing. It did so too by propagating a conception of the literary that took the school as its antagonist. Anti-scholasticism was, after all, the great utility of literary culture within the educational system, so every writerly aspersion cast against the school became assimilable to the school's designation of literariness. American literature, therefore, underwent a process of masculinization as its production and dissemination increasingly took place under a disciplinary apparatus whose "maternal" reputation it promoted itself. Fractures within public culture thus gaped open as American literature developed as an effective instrument within the very institutional system it persistently defined itself against.

The front matter of *American Renaissance* attempts to overcome the growing fragmentation within literary culture by positing American literature as a site of reunification. Matthiessen articulates this fantasy of reunification, like so many of his predecessors and colleagues, against the system of formal education. In his acknowledgments, Matthiessen explains that, "It was hardly an accident that when I graduated from college in the early nineteen-twenties, I knew very little of our own literature except some contemporary poetry that I had read with my friends. The now encouraging, if tardy, attention that is being paid by our universities to our cultural past dates in most instances since that time." Matthiessen's description of his college experience is a misrepresentation of the historical record, per Vanderbilt, though a purposeful one. By insisting that American literature was absent from his formal education—by claiming also to write about authors whom "successive generations of common readers," that is, not scholars, have agreed "bulk largest in stature"—Matthiessen is able to invest his work with an extracurricular significance. He is able to present American literature as a cultural unity that obtains outside of the modern institutional system, through the consensus of common readers, not within it.[78]

Matthiessen's fantasy in a certain sense of course reinscribes the cultural fragmentation it seeks to overcome. By positioning his hyper-canonical writers against their sentimental contemporaries, Matthiessen asserts the boundary between literature and mass culture even as he tries to dissolve it. He insists, to be more specific, that the proper esteem common readers hold for the literary is essentially different from the improper devotion that mass audiences show toward the degraded products of sentimentalism, even though the market rewards both. The difference between the propriety of literature's commercial success and the impropriety of sentimentalism's is, for Matthiessen, largely temporal, as time distinguishes the worthy purchases of a common audience from the unworthy purchases of a mass audience. But the difference between the commercial success of the two is also really no difference at all: the market of today is by no means less pure than the market of tomorrow. Matthiessen's fantasy likewise reproduces the gender divisions it attempts to bridge by arrogating the sentimentalists' influence for his abstracted "common readers," whose disinterested literary preferences concede nothing to the feminized sentimental culture they displace.

In another sense, however, Matthiessen's fantasy has been realized, has indeed, in spite of itself, succeeded in transcending the cultural fragmentation that came about in the decades after the Civil War. It has done so through the very educational system it denounced. Through the modern school, Matthiessen's conception of the literary has effected something of a cultural reconciliation, albeit an imperfect one in which all sorts of social divisions remain intact (and are in fact reproduced). American literature, while it made the existence of the modern school and its regimes of inequality possible, has also found in modern classrooms domestically and internationally an audience of millions that has displaced its chief cultural rival. The students that make up this audience are perhaps superior to the purportedly impetuous readers of sentimental fiction, but they are also surely inferior to Matthiessen's ideal "common readers," whose unprompted reflections on culture provide the foundation for a truly robust and unfragmented literary community. Even worse, since the expansion of the school system after World War II, there are no more common readers, if by common readers we mean, as Matthiessen did, a reader disencumbered of formal education. Instead, virtually all readers are now students or erstwhile students.

For decades American literature provided proof to these students that modern experience did contain an "elsewhere" beyond the institutional system. Its presence in this capacity was probably reassuring to the students, who spent so much of their lives confined within the walls of one classroom or another. Unquestionably it offered itself as meager compensation for English instructors, who, as we'll see in the next chapter, found themselves persistently denigrated by the educational system that depended on their labor. Through literature generally and American literature specifically, these instructors could articulate their contempt toward the institution they inhabited. They could break free of the institutional system that circumscribed their professional lives. These psychodynamics might sound overly dramatic from our historical perspective, where the school system's breakdown, rather than its unrelenting expansion, tends to inspire concern. In English departments such concern has expressed itself, in a rather abrupt reversal, as awe and sometimes reverence for the modern institutional system. Scholars in recent years, that is, have depicted literature not as essentially resistant to the apparatus of formal education, but as a product of it. They have claimed to find in the study of literature evidence of the institutional system's unyielding power, confirmation that schools exercise ineluctable control over social experience and cultural production.

This misapprehension seems no less dramatic, no less untethered from historical reality than the one that preceded it. In American literature and really all of English literature, instructors for most of the twentieth century came to believe that they had discovered a site of institutional freedom. This conviction, while it ignored a whole realm of literary activity that proudly affiliated itself with institutions of formal education, was in some sense understandable. It reflected English instructors' frustrated desire to live and flourish, grow old and perish, beyond the ever-tightening grip of the school. The power scholars now attribute to the institutional system is perplexing. Even when it takes the form of critique, recent literary scholarship remains stubbornly convinced that the school system's influence is inescapable. It maintains this conviction even as the school system crumbles. The institutional turn in literary studies in this sense harbors a nostalgia for the very conditions that the midcentury Americanists so desperately wanted to escape. For scholars more recently, the idea of an all-encompassing school system might not sound so unappealing. In fact, it doesn't appear to sound unappealing at all.

2
Against Reading

[The eye] was made to look far and near, up and down, right and left, over a wide area, to see nature, follow motion, find food, game, treasures, to avoid foes and other dangers, so that to zigzag monotonously over the printed page puts a great strain upon it.
—G. Stanley Hall, *Educational Problems* (1911)

She was quite unable to read; her attention had never been so little at her command. One afternoon, in the library, about a week after the ceremony in the churchyard, she was trying to fix it a little; but her eyes often wandered from the book in her hand to the open window, which looked down the long avenue. It was in this way that she saw a modest vehicle approach the door[.]
—Henry James, *The Portrait of a Lady* (1881)[1]

In his two-volume treatise *Educational Problems* (1911), G. Stanley Hall—president of Clark University, former president of the American Psychological Association, leader of the child study movement—in short, one of the most influential educational theorists of his time—offers an extended and rousing defense of illiteracy. "Very many men have lived and died and been great, even the leaders of their age, without any acquaintance with letters," he writes. "The knowledge which illiterates acquire is probably on the whole more personal, direct, environmental and probably a much larger proportion of it practical." For Hall, an evolutionary psychologist, illiteracy is acceptable (maybe even desirable!) because humans, by not reading, manage to avoid a whole range of physical injuries and, therefore, help to ensure the well-being of the community at large. The "*near* work" literates perform, he explains, "is the chief cause of the alarming development of myopia with all the evils of excitement, choroid strain, squinting, and stooping, and the resulting congestion that follow in its train." Since these ailments are inheritable, in Hall's account, they might one day affect the species as a whole. "The men and women of coming generations ought not to be saddled with an inheritance of short-sightedness, nystagmus, with jaded retina or eye and hand centers, or with strained neuropsychic intellects," he writes. "[The eye] was made to look far and near, up and down, right and left, over a wide area, to see nature, follow motion, find food, game, treasures, to avoid foes and other dangers, so that to zigzag monotonously over the printed page puts a great strain upon it."[2]

Ultimately Hall's defense of illiteracy remains a digression—a line of argument he entertains in each of his major works but never takes to its logical conclusion. Hall, that is, never suggests that humans shouldn't learn how to read or that reading shouldn't be taught in schools. In fact, reading plays a key role in Hall's account of the modern educational system, and Hall himself, over the course of his career, taught many classes that required students to read: at Antioch, his first academic appointment, Hall served as the Bellows Professor of Mental Philosophy and English Literature, teaching a senior course in French, German, and English literature; later, after he returned to Harvard for additional graduate work, Hall obtained an instructorship in English to pay for his PhD in psychology. At different points in his professional career, Hall even wrote short stories and one science fiction novel, *The Fall of Atlantis* (1920), all extracurricularly.[3] If Hall eventually overcame his antipathy and included reading in his broader educational program, outlining with scientific precision the age he believed students ought to learn to read and the font size textbooks ought to be printed in, why in his major works does he always, at least briefly, return to the illiterate as an ideal?

Hall's theory of reading, for all its histrionics about choroid strain and congestion, was typical of post–Civil War educational reform. Unlike the teaching of writing and composition, which educational institutions assimilated more easily into their daily rhythms—starting with nineteenth-century theme exercises and culminating with twentieth-century composition and creative writing classes—the teaching of reading was vexed from the inception of the modern school.[4] As we've already seen, reading literature in class was, for many educators, a revolutionary gesture that would transform the school system by dissolving the boundaries that separated it from the rest of social experience. For other educators, however, reading instruction more generally represented a stubborn pedagogical problem. After all, traditional institutions of formal education in the United States were widely known as purveyors of "book-learning," and though this reputation wasn't always considered a liability, the modern educational system's growth depended in the eyes of its architects on transcending it.

Educational reformers' suspicion of reading instruction necessarily implicated literature. Of course, reading and literature are not self-evidently coextensive categories. You can read things other than literature, and literary culture for much of its history has been understood to include various forms of oral performance and expression. As Nancy Glazener has shown, however, the school's rise as a cultural administrator at the turn of the twentieth century led to the "intensified identification of literature with books, analysis, and written culture"; the educational system, in Glazener's account, severed literature's ties to orality.[5] The consolidation of literature in its modern sense thus involved (among other developments)

(1) the emergence of the school as a principal institution of literary administration; (2) the reduction of literature to printed material; and—here I'll add to Glazener's account—(3) the pedagogical renunciation of reading and, therefore, of literature. The pedagogical suspicion toward literature was, as we've seen, counterbalanced with a certain enthusiasm for literary works. The contradictory reception of literature—its status as both a revolutionary pedagogical instrument and a vector of a problematic textuality—in the end reflected educators' anxieties about the irrelevance of the social institution they inhabited. By representing reading as, alternately, an enlivening and enervating cultural activity, the architects of the school system sought to establish their institutions more firmly in US experience.

Skepticism toward reading was not confined to the scene of formal education. It also surfaced in the literature of the period—that is, the period's reading material. Literary fiction in the postbellum period contains many scenes where characters are explicitly and self-consciously not reading. In the opening pages of Henry Adams's *Democracy: An American Novel* (1880), we are introduced to the protagonist, Madeleine Lightfoot Lee, a widow "tortured by *ennui*." This ennui is figured in the novel's first chapter as an obsession with reading. "She had read voraciously and promiscuously one subject after another. Ruskin and Taine had danced merrily through her mind, hand in hand with Darwin and Stuart Mill, Gustave Droz and Algernon Swinburne. She had even labored over the literature of her own country." The inciting act of Adams's novel is, then, Madeleine's decision to stop this restless reading and move to Washington, DC.[6] In Henry James's *Portrait of a Lady* (1881), we first meet Isabel Archer "seated alone with a book" in her grandmother's Albany library, "her mind a good deal of a vagabond," just before she decides to stop "trudging over the sandy plains of ... German Thought" and join her aunt on a trip to Europe. In another scene, Isabel is "seated in the library" at Gardencourt "with a volume to which her attention [is] not fastened" when she learns that her uncle, Mr. Touchett, is dead. At the end of the novel, after Isabel has returned to Gardencourt and Ralph has died, she discovers that "[s]he was quite unable to read; her attention had never been so little at her command. One afternoon, in the library ... she was trying to fix it a little; but her eyes often wandered from the book in her hand to the open window, which looked down the long avenue. It was in this way that she saw a modest vehicle approach the door[.]" Lord Warburton has arrived for their final encounter, and Caspar Goodwood is set to appear just after.[7]

In this chapter, I consider the school's hostility toward reading after the Civil War alongside the many fictional episodes where characters don't read. As educational reformers identified literature with print and condemned the act of reading, characters in literary fiction dropped their books and went on to undergo a range of experiences that were more meaningful and "real" than the textual experience they left behind. Henry Adams, for instance, explains in *Democracy* that Madeleine Lightfoot Lee feels, amid her voracious and promiscuous reading, like a "passenger on an ocean steamer whose mind will not give him rest until he has been in the engine-room and talked with the engineer." By not reading, she intends to "see with her own eyes the action of the primary forces; to touch with her own hand the massive machinery of society; to measure with her own mind the capacity of the motive power."[8]

The renunciation of reading that we see in post–Civil War literary fiction would seem to reproduce the educators' suspicions, casting textual experience as subordinate to, or as an appendage of, real social experience. Yet, as we'll discover, these literary renunciations represent a complex reaction to the institutional environment of the postbellum period. Far from subscribing to the school's conception of literature, literary authors disavowed reading in their work to affirm literary experience. We might understand these scenes of not-reading as defiantly antischolastic, as a rejection of the school's mandates. But we should also see them more fundamentally as purgative: writers returned to them so often in order to purify literature of the written-ness that was coming to define its existence—in order, in some sense, to purify literature of itself. Such gestures succeeded, finally, in enshrining the printed-ness and literariness of the culture objects that these writers produced.

The proliferation of these scenes in postbellum fiction is, I'll argue, one particular manifestation of an anti-institutional impulse that I take more generally to animate modern notions of the literary. Many scholars have identified aesthetic difficulty and parody as foundational practices of modern literary culture, as elaborate position-taking strategies that allow literary works to secure their own prestige and distinguish themselves from other, non-literary cultural objects. Less often noted is the tendency of literary works to disavow, or turn away from, literariness itself. This tendency is endemic to a dominant strain of post-Romantic literary culture, but it also assumed a historically specific form under the institutional transformations that occurred between the Civil War and World War I. We can best appreciate the literalization or tropification of this self-effacing tendency—in these proliferating scenes of not-reading—by considering its relation to a school system that itself had embraced a Romantic anti-institutionalism. Just as educators expanded the scope of formal education by denouncing reading and the scholasticism of the school, writers expanded the scope of literary culture by denouncing the school and the literariness of their literary works.

Squinting and Stooping

The anxiety Hall expressed over the "zigzag" of literary consumption was in no way singular or idiosyncratic among pedagogical reformers after the Civil War. In a period when the modern school was in a state of transition, just beginning to stake a larger claim to social relevance in the United States, theorists at all levels of the educational system expressed concern about the role of reading in the classroom, and the relationship between reading and other modes of experience. According to educational theorists, reading wasn't merely *a* problem the school system needed to address, but *the* problem of modern education.

At the primary and secondary school levels, educators were resistant to reading because the classroom activities required to teach basic literacy undermined the new pedagogy being developed by reformers. Progressive educators, who believed in shaping the curriculum around the interests of students, thought the unpleasant drill-work typically used in reading lessons would lower attendance and make the school less capable of integrating a large student body. Francis Parker, an early pioneer of Progressive education, raises the problem of literacy instruction in his *Talks on Pedagogics* (1894) when he describes learning to read as a necessarily distasteful endeavor for students in primary schools. "A word in itself is a repellant object to the child's mind," he writes. "[I]f the child liked a word, if the effect of the word were pleasant to the child, if it aroused his interest, or, in other words, induced pleasing emotions, reading, as Dogberry says, would come 'by natur.'"[9]

For some theorists of primary and secondary education, though, reading posed problems that extended beyond classroom pedagogy. Perhaps more profoundly, these educators insisted that reading itself—not just learning to read—constituted a different order of experience from the experience of real life. Although John Dewey grants reading an "all-important" secondary role in the revised edition of *The School and Society* (1915), his pedagogy stresses the harms of reading. "[T]he tendency to approach nature through the medium of literature ... fails to note that there is a more straightforward road from mind to the object—direct through connection with life itself," he writes. "[T]he poem and story, the literary statement, have their place as reinforcements and idealizations, not as foundation stones. What is wanted, in other words, is not to fix up a connection of child mind and nature, but to give free and effective play to the connection already operating." Dewey's aversion to reading appears throughout his educational tracts—in long rants against reading *Robinson Crusoe* in the classroom, for instance, and in one of his favorite derogatory terms: bookish.[10]

In order to salvage reading in the school system, primary and secondary school pedagogical theorists developed a range of social reading practices. In *The Schools of To-Morrow* (1915), an account of Progressive schools John Dewey co-wrote with his daughter Evelyn, the Deweys criticize reading lessons that are oriented around mechanical drill-work and instead praise "dramatizations." "Studying alone out of a book is an isolated and unsocial performance," they write. "[T]he pupil may be learning the words before him, but he is not learning to act with other people, to control and arrange his actions and thought so that other persons have an equal opportunity to express themselves in a shared experience." These dramatizations are useful, the Deweys claim, because the production requires the students to collaborate with each other, coordinate their efforts, and learn by doing: "The fourth grade studies Greek history, and the work includes the making of a Greek house, and writing poems about some Greek myth. The children make Greek costumes and wear them every day in the classroom."[11]

In addition to dramatic work, Progressive schools also oriented reading around public speaking and storytelling. Randolph Bourne's account of William Wirt's Progressive schools in Indiana, *The Gary Schools* (1916), describes the study of expression, a mixture of elocution and dramatics. "The aim of the instruction is evidently to bring the pupils to read and speak with more intelligence and appreciation than is usually done," he writes. "It is to give the training which will bear fruit in increased expressiveness in all the studies of the school, in all writing and reciting, in 'auditorium' and 'application' work." In Evelyn Dewey's report on the Porter School in Indiana, *New Schools for Old* (1919), the school's instructor, Mrs. Harvey, teaches students to read through public performances: she "showed [the students] how to stand before the school and read aloud a new passage in such a way that the reader and the audience understood what was said." Perhaps no example from the period suggests the pervasiveness of these social modes of reading in educational theory more than Jane Addams's *Twenty Years at Hull-House* (1910). During Hull House's difficult opening days, Addams approves a communal reading group. "In the very first weeks of our residence Miss Starr started a reading party in George Eliot's 'Romola,'" Addams writes. "[T]wo members of the club came to dinner each week, not only that they might be received as guests, but that they might help us wash the dishes afterwards and so make the table ready for the stacks of Florentine photographs."[12]

Reading for primary and secondary school educators thus became palatable only when isolated encounters with printed words on a page were rerouted through communal modes of expression. At institutions of higher learning, the anxiety surrounding reading was largely extrinsic to the discipline of literary studies. The scientist Edmund Burke Huey, for instance, acknowledged in his book *The Psychology and Pedagogy of Reading* (1908) that reading and learnedness remain a modern ideal, but he also worried that "[p]rinted matter has been so diffused, and all that we do is so concerned with it, that a very considerable proportion of most people's waking time is taken up with the contemplation of reading symbols." Under these conditions, Huey concluded that "we need not be surprised that our continued and careless exercise of these unusual functions," that is, the movement of the eye while reading, "causes fatigue and, in very many cases, certain dangerous forms of degeneracy."[13]

Huey's mentor, G. Stanley Hall, devoted more attention perhaps than any of his contemporaries to the educational problem of reading, and the product of Hall's ruminations are most revealing indeed. Like other educational reformers, Hall invented activities intended to fold the solitary experience of the reader back into larger forms of social experience. In order to make reading compatible with modern life, Hall developed a theory of fast reading, where the reader "skips, skims, looks at the last section of the book, chapter-headings, glances at the preface or introduction, samples here and there." Ideally, in Hall's account, the book itself would assist the fast reader by presenting information in the most extractable format. "[E]very device of punctuation," Hall explains, "length of line, size of type, color or ink as contrasted with that of paper ... to say nothing of topical headings, inserts in the page, summaries and epitomes, chapter headings, captions, indexes, etc., all bring a relief that, slight though it may be for each, bulks large for many readers because it means so much for economic conservation of human energy." Writers would help the fast reader too, providing less text and "more and more aids in the way of synopses, resumes, epitomes, summaries of chapters and of the whole," because "[the modern reader] reads often and perhaps for the most part tentatively, and doubtful at every step whether it would pay him to go on."[14]

The fast-reading Hall theorizes is meant to give students access to collective experience without incurring the crippling effects that so often attend encounters with print. Instead of injuring their eye muscles and hurting their backs—Hall's dreaded squinting and stooping—students who read quickly obtain a higher sense of their shared human ancestry, transforming a brief interaction with a book into a form of collective enlightenment. Hall's defense of reading thus represents a blend of evolutionary biology and humanism (a humanism Hall probably learned from his lifelong friendship with Charles Eliot Norton). "In reading most poetry man reverts to the ancient days of his race, remembers its phyletic experience, falls back through millennia to the estate of his primitive for[e]bears," Hall declares. "Old echo chambers in his soul are opened and reverberate with voices that to the modern world seem strange and ghostly. This is well, for thus the man of to-day comes into and is kept in touch with his heritage[.]"[15]

With its synthetic powers, Hall's reading program seems at first to easily fit the expansionist educational vision he articulated in the second half of his career. Having withstood a series of professional disputes in the world of academic psychology and having presided over the near total collapse of Clark University, Hall developed a theory of genetic psychology and philosophy that would underwrite his educational program. Where before Hall had advocated rigorous specialization in his academic endeavors, establishing a graduate student-only research institution at Clark and championing strict scientific psychology in the *American Journal of Psychology* against philosopher-psychologists like William James and James McCosh, in the late 1890s Hall reinvented himself as an institutional prophet, a professor of the new science of education.[16] Education as a field of study, in Hall's new philosophy, would supersede all other fields, and the school would expand to oversee all other institutions. It's hard to overstate the impact of Hall's work on the subsequent development of the educational system. The pedagogy Hall proposes in articles like "The Ideal School as Based on Child Study" (1901)—a pedagogy oriented around the diverse needs of the student body, not the rigid plans of the teacher—extended the reach of formal education around the country.[17]

Just as schools would break from their traditional sphere of influence and assist in the development of modern society, so too would reading overcome its bookishness and assist in larger human endeavors—or at least that's how Hall's argument appears to work. Whenever Hall articulates the apparently limitless range of the new school system, he always has recourse to the illiterate. "We must ... reflect that a few generations ago the ancestors of all of us were illiterate," Hall writes in "The Ideal School," "[and] that Charlemagne and many other great men of the world could not read or write; that scholars have argued that Cornelia, Ophelia, Beatrice, and even the blessed mother of our Lord knew nothing of letters." In *Adolescence*, Hall proclaims: "But although some of the great men in history could not read, and while some of the illiterate were often morally and intellectually above some of the literate, the argument here is that the printed page must not be too suddenly or too early thrust between child and life."[18]

Reading in these passages is supposed to stand in for a whole host of activities that defined the narrow goals of the traditional school, while the not-reading of the illiterate allows Hall to gesture toward the broader ambitions of the emerging modern educational system. After all, the real experience that the illiterate enjoys is exactly what Hall's ideal school claims access to. When Hall finally reconciles reading and the educational system with his theory of fast reading, he therefore appears to rescue an otherwise outdated nineteenth-century practice within the sphere of his capacious social institution. And yet, despite this elegant solution to the pedagogical problems caused by reading, Hall's compulsive insistence that reading remains stubbornly problematic suggests that another issue is at stake. Each time Hall denigrates reading, he assumes that his modern school has an unproblematic relationship to social experience, which indeed it didn't. For many, the educational system was itself very much cut off from "real" life. By reintroducing a suspicion of reading, however, Hall attempts again and again to naturalize the assumption that the modern educational system is already part of social experience.

Of course, the Progressive educators' "solutions" never actually solve the problem of reading in the school system. Hall is an especially revealing figure in this respect: the theory of reading he proposes never seems able to fix the educational troubles he insists reading causes. Hall has difficulty believing anyone would be willing to accept or implement his program. Oftentimes, he imagines his ideas will provoke hostile and skeptical reactions: while discussing his own reading habits, Hall admits that "[a]ll of this work is, of course, very superficial from the standpoint of the pedagogue. I never could pass an examination on one of all these works as examinations now go." Later, he becomes even more contemptuous of literary pedagogues: "I would not exchange this habit of desultory reading in a field outside my specialty for the schoolbred habit of accurate and painstaking familiarity with a few things such as professors of literature inculcate." On the one hand, these statements offer further proof of the school's anti-scholasticism, with Hall proclaiming the importance of his modern program against the "schoolbred" habits of the "pedagogues." On the other hand, these statements suggest Hall's own understanding that his reading pedagogy is impractical and, what's more, not especially effective. Hall himself acknowledges the limitations of the program he is advocating: "Often," he admits, "I so far forget as to start reading something I have already, perhaps not so very long ago, read before."[19]

Hall's reading pedagogy ultimately demonstrates how, for educators in the modern school system, the act of reading was bound up with larger issues of institutional relevance. Hall's illiterate is meant to remind us that there is no more isolated form of human activity than reading. By insisting on the remoteness of reading as a cultural practice, post–Civil War educators set the terms through which the school system went out to conquer everyday experience.

Don't Read Henry James

The third encounter between the governess and Peter Quint's ghost in Henry James's *The Turn of the Screw* (1898) occurs when the governess is not reading a novel. "There was a roomful of old books at Bly ... [that] had reached the sequestered home and appealed to the unavowed curiosity of my youth," the governess explains. "I remember that the book I had in my hand was Fielding's 'Amelia'; and also that I was wholly awake." Evidently, however, the governess is not altogether absorbed in her reading: "I recollect in short that though I was deeply interested in my author I found myself, at the turn of a page and with his spell all scattered, looking straight up from him and hard at the door of my room." Although nothing is happening around her, the governess puts down the novel and decides to investigate: "I laid down my book, rose to my feet and, taking a candle, went straight out of the room." Outside the governess confronts the ghost of Peter Quint, and she and the ghost stare at each other in silence until the ghost leaves.[20]

The act of reading recedes somewhat strangely from this scene: the interest Fielding's novel first elicits in the governess proves less compelling than the real world that surrounds her, a world of immediate sensory experience and complicated social arrangements. Whether the governess is imagining the ghost is a question I will return to momentarily; for now, I would like to note that the ghost draws the governess's attention away from the book not because (in its ghostly way) it appears "more" literary than *Amelia*, but because, to the governess, the ghost is somehow more real: "[T]he thing was as human and hideous as a real interview," she claims; "hideous just because it *was* human." Thus the governess's access to social experience comes at the expense of a text, and when she does read in *The Turn of the Screw*, she reads the social world she inhabits, not novels. "I had restlessly read into the facts before us almost all the meaning they were to receive from subsequent and more cruel occurrences," the governess asserts at one point, and later: "[I] read into what our young friend had said to me in the fulness of its meaning," and "I suppose I now read into our situation a clearness it couldn't have had at the time[.]"[21]

What kind of self-awareness does a scene of not-reading convey? When a character in a work of prose fiction sets aside his or her book, the story draws attention to our own act of reading, at least for a moment, and interrupts the story's mimetic illusion, like much metanarrative does. Yet once this character has disposed of his or her reading material, the story in effect interrupts its own interruption of narrative realism, folding us back into the text's fictional world almost immediately. We might say, therefore, that scenes of not-reading promote a form of compromised immersiveness more closely related to another strain of metanarration, in which a story creates a second-level reality-effect by comprehensively describing the mediated-ness of the fictional text. Here, though, the interruption of the story's reality effect doesn't bring about an extended meditation on the mechanisms of fiction-making. Rather, the disavowal of reading intensifies the reading experience, more fully immersing us in the story's fictional events. From now on I'll refer to this aberrant form of self-awareness as counter-reflexivity.[22]

In some sense, not-reading appears out of place in *The Turn of the Screw*, a story that otherwise languishes in the imaginative wonders of the literary. Coming long after the social problem novels of the mid-1880s, *The Turn of the Screw* is, according to James's preface, "a fairy-tale pure and simple." The elaborate frame narrative, transcribing-a-tale-that-was-read-at-a-party-from-a-manuscript-written-by-a-governess-many-many-years-ago, seems designed specifically to cushion the story from the outside world. This effect is reinforced by the story's familiar literary setting (a gothic estate) and the familiar literary situation: "Was there a 'secret' at Bly—a mystery of Udolpho or an insane, an unmentionable relative kept in unsuspected confinement?" the governess asks shortly after her arrival. Even if she doesn't read in the narrative proper, it's clear that the governess has spent a lot of her life reading, and this sensibility permeates *The Turn of the Screw*, despite the apparent inadequacy of the reading experience that we see just before the third encounter with Peter Quint's ghost.[23]

The most important, though perhaps obvious, feature of the story's disavowal of reading, however, is that it's represented textually: we are reading a scene where reading is shown to be insufficient. When the governess sets aside her book, *The Turn of the Screw* seems to suggest that reading is a poor substitute for real social experience. Yet this move disguises the fact that the real world the governess enters after she puts down her book is itself textual, something that we can read and do read as we read James's story. The counter-reflexive episode thus grants readers access to the world of social experience by insisting that reading can't grant readers access to the world of social experience.

From its inception, the novel has manifested a suspicion of reading, whether the chivalric romances consumed by Don Quixote, the gothic novels Catherine Morland is too fond of in *Northanger Abbey*, or the popular novels that lead Emma

Bovary astray. Through the representation of reading run amok, these novels articulate a more compelling realist vision. But where these novels disavow certain kinds of reading to promote others, *The Turn of the Screw* breaks down the division between the "real" and the "textual" altogether in order to assert the fundamental continuity between the two. When the governess stops reading *Amelia*, James isn't defining his aesthetic project against Fielding's sentimental novel, a work that the governess herself suggests is of a "deprecated renown"; rather he is dissolving the hierarchies that ordinarily structure the relationship between the non-textual and the textual, between the adult world of social proprieties at Bly and the novel that "appealed to the unavowed curiosity" of the governess's "youth." The governess can read her surroundings in the same way she can read a novel of her youth because, in *The Turn of the Screw*, the boundaries dividing print and the real world of social experience are porous—in fact, non-existent. Whether the governess is the best reader in the story, correctly identifying the ghosts that possess her pupils, or whether Mrs. Grose, the story's illiterate, is actually the better reader, not seeing the ghosts at all, it's impossible to know. The literate governess and the illiterate Mrs. Grose have two mutually exclusive experiences of the events at Bly, but neither experience is proved more "real" than the other. There is no vantage point outside the story from which to judge the governess's sanity because, according to the logic of the story, and particularly of the counter-reflexive gesture, all textual experience is social, and all social experience is textual.[24]

Counter-reflexive gestures recur throughout James's work, and their recurrence suggests that James couldn't assume the compatibility of textual and social experience but needed instead to relentlessly affirm it. I've already noted some of the scenes in *The Portrait of a Lady* where Isabel Archer sets her book aside to engage in "real" social interactions. In *The Wings of the Dove* (1902), Mrs. Stringham comes upon her traveling companion Milly Theale standing on a cliff in the Swiss Alps, having "rid herself of the book" she brought with her on the hike and resolved to "tak[e] full in the face the whole assault of life[.]" The "whole assault of life" that Milly chooses in this scene is represented by her perch over the beautiful but vertiginous view, and the suggestion is that Milly's consciousness becomes legible to Mrs. Stringham because everything this view offers Milly—the danger, grandeur, and immediacy of life itself—has meaning in contrast to the book she abandons. In *The Golden Bowl* (1904), Maggie can't manage to "read her pale novel" just before her husband returns home from a trip with Charlotte Stant; upon his arrival Maggie sees something "*visibly* uncertain" "written" on his face, and though we the readers of *The Golden Bowl* already know that the reason for the Prince's embarrassment is his relationship with Charlotte Stant, from this point on the novel concerns itself with Maggie's gradual discovery of the extramarital affair and her eventual mastery over the individuals involved in it. Knowledge in this scene is thereby located outside the printed pages of books, and the moment that Maggie abandons her novel and begins reading her social environment marks her transformation into a self-conscious subject, a subject worthy of focalization, independent of the familial bonds that once sheltered her from the outside world.[25]

It might seem unlikely that James, one of the leading literary figures in US public life, would disavow the act of reading so often in his work. But James returned to scenes of not-reading precisely to realize his literary ambitions. These disavowals allowed him to absorb into his written texts the unwritten experience of social life; they allowed him to break free of the institutional categories that inhibited his work. Similar scenes surfaced in a range of literary endeavors during this period. What follows is a tour of postbellum fiction in which reading is renounced again and again. By trafficking in these renunciations, literary writers sought to transcend the printed-ness and the literariness that delimited their respective aesthetic projects. What finally united these disparate projects—modernist art novels, gritty works of social realism, regionalist fictions—was a counter-reflexive gesture that, in purging literature of its literariness, came to define the literary as such.

Scenes of Not-Reading in Postbellum America, Part 1: Dreiser and Wharton

Perhaps the most notorious scene of counter-reflexivity in post–Civil War prose fiction belongs to a novel written by Henry James's literary antithesis, Theodore Dreiser's *Sister Carrie* (1900). Soon after the titular Carrie moves to New York City with her (supposed) husband George Hurstwood, the once prosperous and self-assured Hurstwood undergoes a steady deterioration that has disturbed the novel's twentieth- and twenty-first century readers. This deterioration is represented again and again as an obsession with reading newspapers: "The disease of brooding was beginning to claim him as a victim. Only the newspapers and his own thoughts were worth while." The narrator explains just a few pages later that

> [Hurstwood] buried himself in his papers and read. Oh, the rest of it—the relief from walking and thinking! What Lethean waters were these floods of telegraphed intelligence! He forgot his troubles, in part. Here was a young, handsome woman, if you might believe the newspaper drawing, suing a rich, fat, candy-making husband in Brooklyn for divorce. Here was another item detailing the wrecking of a vessel in ice and snow off Prince's Bay on Staten Island. A long, bright column told of the doings in the theatrical world—the plays produced, the actors appearing, the managers making announcements. Fannie Davenport was just opening at the Fifth Avenue. Daly was producing "King Lear." He read of the early departure for the season of a party composed of the Vanderbilts and their friends for Florida. An interesting shooting affray was on in the mountains of Kentucky. So he read, read, read, rocking in the warm room near the radiator and waiting for dinner to be served.[26]

Reading about events in a newspaper is no substitute for really experiencing the events themselves, Dreiser suggests in this passage, which measures the newspaper's vast geographic reach—stretching from a shipwreck off of Staten Island to a "shooting affray" in the mountains of Kentucky—against the confined domestic scene of Hurstwood's reading. Reading does not expand Hurstwood's horizons; it does not expose him to a wide world otherwise unavailable to him as he "rock[s] in the warm room near the radiator." Instead, reading is a "rest" and a "relief." It is a comfort to a man increasingly incapable of living life, of participating in the kind of social experiences that the newspaper describes. "All day and all day, here he sat, reading his papers," Dreiser writes later. "The world seemed to have no attraction." Nor is the point of this passage to strategically elevate the novel over its print rival, the newspaper. The emphasis in the passage is on the inadequacy of reading as such—"he read, read, read"—and if Hurstwood is guilty of reading, so too are we the readers of Dreiser's novel. Even when Dreiser singles out Balzac's *Père Goriot* (1835) for praise later in the book—Carrie reads it on Ames's recommendation and realizes that Balzac's novel "was so strong ... that she caught nearly the full sympathetic significance of it. For the first time, it was being borne in upon her how silly and worthless had been her earlier reading, as a whole"—it is not to claim that some books offer real experience while others don't, but simply to demonstrate that some books are better than others.[27]

The culminating counter-reflexive scene in *Sister Carrie* takes place when Hurstwood, after months of reading in his rocking chair, finally drops his newspapers and resolves to participate in one of those real events that he had previously experienced secondhand. "There had been appearing in the papers about this time rumours and notices of an approaching strike on the trolley lines in Brooklyn," Dreiser explains. "Hurstwood had been reading of this thing, and wondering concerning the huge tie-up which would follow. ... Being so utterly idle, and his mind filled with the numerous predictions which had been made concerning the scarcity of labour this winter and the panicky state of the financial market, Hurstwood read this with interest." After a disagreement with Carrie, Hurstwood decides, "Damn it all! ... I can get something. I'm not down yet," and goes off to work as a scab motorman for the trolley company in Brooklyn.[28]

An extended narrative digression follows in which Hurstwood, newspapers set aside, has a firsthand encounter with "real life," thrusting himself into the war between capital and labor. Dreiser at one moment explicitly states that Hurstwood's little adventure is more real than the newspapers he has been reading. "Hurstwood, warmed and excited, gazed steadily ahead," Dreiser writes, after narrating an attack on Hurstwood's trolley. "It was an astonishing experience for him. He had read of these things, but the reality seemed something altogether new." Needless to say, Hurstwood's experience in Brooklyn proves traumatic, and after one particularly violent altercation with a crowd, where a bullet grazes his shoulder, he quits, returning to his apartment in Manhattan and to his reading.

> "Well," he said, after a time, his nature recovering itself, "that's a pretty tough game over there."
> Then he turned and saw the papers. With half a sigh he picked up the "World."
> "Strike Spreading in Brooklyn," he read. "Rioting Breaks Out in all Parts of the City."
> He adjusted his paper very comfortably and continued. It was the one thing he read with absorbing interest.[29]

The conclusion to this extended digression thus affirms its original premise. Before the episode begins, Hurstwood's reading is presented as proof of his deterioration, as evidence of his growing incapacity to take part in the real world. The moment he stops reading is then the moment that Hurstwood reenters the real world and participates in its struggles. His return to reading and to the vicarious experience of printed words at the end of the episode definitively proves what we already knew before, that Hurstwood is a husk of a man no longer capable of withstanding the pressures of the real. Printed words now buffer Hurstwood from the bruises and scratches he incurred on the job in Brooklyn; he can now comfortably read about the "Strike Spreading in Brooklyn" and the "Rioting Break[ing] Out in all Parts of the City" without exposing himself to the dangers of lived experience.

Like the disavowals of reading that we see across James's fiction, though, *Sister Carrie*'s counter-reflexivity merely allows Dreiser's book to integrate into its printed pages the reality of non-printed experience. The key insight that structures the episode is Hurstwood's realization that he "had read of these things, but the reality seemed something altogether new," and this insight, while denigrating reading, creates the illusion that Hurstwood's non-reading experiences are real, and that we readers have access to this real experience even though we are reading. We might even say that the hallmarks of social realism that characterize the episode—its thematic exploration of the violence of class struggle, its naturalist vocabulary (most apparent in its descriptions of Hurstwood's fellow scabs), its aesthetics of griminess and disgust—don't produce a reality-effect on their own but rather appear themselves to signify the real as a product of the counter-reflexive gesture.

The counter-reflexive mode in this sense unites two writers—James, Dreiser—whose literary reputations have long been opposed to one another's. Lionel Trilling once famously compared the "doctrinaire indulgence which liberal intellectuals have always displayed toward Theodore Dreiser" to the "liberal severity toward Henry James." According to Trilling, these divergent assessments were a product of each writer's relation to reality. In the liberal imagination, Trilling argues, Dreiser's novels "have the awkwardness, the chaos, and heaviness which we associate with 'reality,'" whereas James's produce "worr[y]" because they "show[] so many of the electric qualities of mind." "In the American metaphysic," Trilling writes, "reality is always material reality, hard, resistant, unformed, impenetrable, and unpleasant. And that mind is alone felt to be trustworthy which most resembles this reality by most nearly reproducing the sensations it affords. ... The 'odors of the shop' are real, and to those who breathe them they guarantee a sense of vitality from which James is debarred. The idea of intellectual honor is not real, and to that chimera James was devoted." For Trilling, the comparison of these two authors reveals in part a generic distinction between Dreiser's realism and James's romance or what Trilling elsewhere calls his "moral realism." Yet this distinction seems to contradict another point Trilling insists on, that "the difference between James and Dreiser is not of kind" but instead of a "difference ... of quality[.]" Aesthetic judgments aside, Trilling's suggestion that James and Dreiser are different in quality and not in kind is confirmed in the counter-reflexive gestures that recur in their writing. Though each author claims for his work a reality that hardly resembles that of the other's—with (to adopt Trilling's typology) James's depiction of a real world where ideas, intellect, and imagination are operative, and Dreiser's where they aren't—both assimilate these respective realities into their writing through the same trope, the counter-reflexive move, the disavowal of reading.[30]

Other realist writers in this period evinced a counter-reflexive sensibility as well. In Edith Wharton's short story "Xingu" (1911), the main character Mrs. Roby wreaks havoc at her book club when she proudly declares she hasn't read the assigned novel. This (fictional) novel is *The Wings of Death*, written by Osric Dane, a celebrated author invited to join the book club at its next meeting. Mrs. Roby "owned to having heard the name of Osric Dane; but that—incredible as it appeared—was the extent of her acquaintance with the celebrated novelist," the narrator explains. "The ladies could not conceal their surprise; but Mrs. Ballinger, whose pride in the club made her wish to put even Mrs. Roby in the best possible light, gently insinuated that, though she had not had time to acquaint herself with 'The Wings of Death,' she must at least be familiar with its equally remarkable predecessor, 'The Supreme Instant.'" "Mrs. Roby," the narrator continues,

> wrinkled her sunny brows in a conscientious effort of memory, as a result of which she recalled that, oh, yes, she *had* seen the book at her brother's, when she was staying with him in Brazil, and had even carried it off to read one day on a boating party; but they had all got to shying things at each other in the boat, and the book had gone overboard, so she had never had the chance—
>
> The picture evoked by this anecdote did not increase Mrs. Roby's credit with the club, and there was a painful pause[.][31]

Later Mrs. Roby goes on to admit that one reason she didn't read *The Wings of Death* before the meeting was that she was absorbed in a more amusing Trollope novel, but this admission simply elevates a certain kind of book (Trollope's) over another (Dane's) without detracting from the larger point of the story, which we can begin to glimpse in the passage above. Wharton, at this early moment, compares the experience of reading a book to the experience of a raucous boat party in Brazil, and the comparison is ultimately unfavorable to the book. This is the point of "Xingu": not-reading is, in the end, far superior to reading.

From the outset of the story, Wharton's vitriol is targeted at a certain kind of literary pretension. "Mrs. Ballinger," she writes in the story's opening sentences, "is one of the ladies who pursue Culture in bands, as though it were dangerous to meet alone. To this end she had founded the Lunch Club, an association composed of herself and several other indomitable huntresses of erudition." The story's satire isn't confined to these lady amateurs, however. The climax of "Xingu," after all, centers on the humiliation of the distinguished author herself, Osric Dane. Having arrived at the Lunch Club's meeting with "an air of compulsion not calculated to promote the easy exercise of hospitality," Dane evinces the same disdain for the lady amateurs as the story's protagonist Mrs. Roby. Yet Osric Dane's barely disguised contempt does not endear her to Mrs. Roby or to us, the story's readers. After Osric Dane poses a series of hostile questions to the group, which the group, flailing about, struggles to answer, Mrs. Roby reverses the power dynamics in the meeting by suggesting that the Lunch Club has been absorbed in "Xingu," a book Mrs. Roby has made up that very instant. "[Osric Dane] put down her coffee-cup, but with a look of distinct annoyance," Wharton writes. "[S]he too wore, for a brief moment, what Mrs. Roby afterward described as the look of feeling for something in the back of her head; and before she could dissemble these momentary signs of weakness, Mrs. Roby, turning to her with a deferential smile, had said: 'And we've been so hoping that to-day you would tell us just what you think of it.'"[32]

It is indeed a satisfying exchange. The great Osric Dane is made small; her literary arrogance is punished. Though the opening pages of the story suggest that the women's amateur book club is the sole object of Wharton's derision, in this climactic moment it becomes clear that Wharton's derision extends to all who believe that the act of reading makes them socially superior to anybody else. The story's moral finds expression in Wharton's description of Mrs. Plinth, one of the main power-brokers within the Lunch Club, an especially absurd figure who believes that "[b]ooks were written to read; if one read them what more could be expected?" The joke of the story "Xingu" is that no one can read the book "Xingu" because it doesn't exist. This joke exposes the act of reading for the sham that it is, a practice that, on the one hand, enforces social distinctions between insiders and outsiders and that, on the other, traps the purportedly superior insiders in an artificial world of manners and proprieties divorced from the real world of social experience enjoyed by the purportedly inferior outsiders, the non-readers.[33]

It is in some sense, however, misleading to claim, as I just did, that no one can read "Xingu," the book that Mrs. Roby has made up. In the story's climactic exchange with Osric Dane, Mrs. Roby explains that "Xingu" is "very long," "deep in places," "dangerous," a book that "[o]ne must just wade through," with some "branches" that "are very little known" and whose source is "almost impossible to get at." These metaphorics take on a greater meaning when the ladies of the book club discover, after Mrs. Roby has left to play bridge and Osric Dane has followed her out, that Xingu is actually a river in Brazil.

> Mrs. Ballinger pressed her hands to her throbbing temples. "There's nothing she said that wouldn't apply to a river—to this river!" She swung about excitedly to the other members. "Why, do you remember her telling us that she hadn't read 'The Supreme Instant' because she'd taken it on a boating party while she was staying with her brother, and some one had 'shied' it overboard—'shied' of course was her own expression."
> The ladies breathlessly signified that the expression had not escaped them.
> "Well—and then didn't she tell Osric Dane that one of her books was simply saturated with Xingu? Of course it was, if one of Mrs. Roby's rowdy friends had thrown it into the river!"[34]

In part, this discovery is simply an elaboration of the story's central joke: instead of reading Osric Dane's *The Supreme Instant*, Mrs. Roby enjoyed a "real" experience on the river Xingu, proving once again the superiority of not-reading to reading. But in part too this discovery realizes the story's joke and, in doing so, reverses its key terms. The discovery implies that Mrs. Roby has in fact "read" "Xingu"; it suggests that the river in Brazil is a text—"long," "deep," and "dangerous"—that can be read. This is of course the ultimate effect that the story's counter-reflexivity produces. Its contempt for the act of reading allows the story to integrate into itself non-readerly life, transforming Mrs. Roby's defiantly non-textual sensibility into the stuff of text. The title "Xingu" encodes this reversal as well. No character in Wharton's "Xingu" can read "Xingu," because Mrs. Roby has made the story up. But we, the readers of Wharton's "Xingu," are indeed reading "Xingu," a story whose title is indistinguishable from Mrs. Roby's unreadable and non-textual text.

Scenes of Not-Reading in Postbellum America, Part 2: Regionalism

Wharton, perhaps more often than any other writer than James, returns to scenes of not-reading throughout her work, whether in *The Age of Innocence* (1920), where we learn that Newland Archer's library is "the room in which most of the real things of his life had happened," though reading is not one of them, or in *Summer* (1917), whose protagonist Charity Royall works at a library but still "f[inds] it easier to take North Dormer as the norm of the universe than to go on reading."[35] Of course, Charity's decision to quit reading isn't held up as evidence of her greater access to "real" experience, as it is for characters in "Xingu" and *The Age of Innocence*—or at least it isn't at first. The narrator of *Summer* rather presents Charity's unwillingness to read in the novella's opening pages as proof that she is divorced from the real world outside of North Dormer. But the assumptions that ground this initial evaluation of Charity's not-reading erode over the course of the story. They erode, first, because Wharton does eventually suggest that Charity's illiteracy gives her access to a sensuous world of experience that other, more literate characters can't access. In the second chapter of the novella, Charity liberates herself from the "prison-house" of the Hatchard Memorial Library. "She was blind and insensible to many things, and dimly knew it; but to all that was light and air, perfume and colour, every drop of blood in her responded," Wharton writes. "Today," the narrator goes on to explain, "the sense of well-being was intensified by her joy at escaping from the library." The assumptions that ground the story's initial evaluation of Charity's not-reading erode, second, because the supposedly expansive world that reading first seems to grant people like Lucius Harney, Charity's erudite lover, turns out to be not expansive at all. Harney's literariness and command of language make him not, as it would first appear, more worldly but instead confine him to his own narrow, selfish sphere of experience. Charity comes to this conclusion after her encounter with Harney's "beautifully expressed" letter explaining that he will never marry her:

> [G]radually she became aware that the gist of its meaning lay in the last few words. "If ever there is a hope of realizing what we dreamed of ... "
> But then he wasn't even sure of that? She understood now that every word and every reticence was an avowal of Annabel Balch's prior claim. It was true that he was engaged to her, and that he had not yet found a way of breaking his engagement.[36]

Harney's readerly competence therefore undergoes a steady devaluation over the course of Wharton's novella, culminating in this moment when the barely literate Charity realizes the profound limits of Harney's literary sophistication. Charity's unwillingness to read becomes, correspondingly, a positive value in its own right, and the novella ends at an impasse, with Charity's ambiguous return to North Dormer as Lawyer Royall's wife signaling the story's failure to reconcile the core tensions that underlie its drama, the industrial and the pre-industrial, the literate and the illiterate. If *Summer* thus offers further evidence of Wharton's exploration of the counter-reflexive mode, it also suggests the importance of counter-reflexivity to an emergent genre of post–Civil War literature: regionalism or local color fiction.

In the frame story of Charles Chesnutt's "The Conjurer's Revenge," we come upon the narrator John and his wife Anne on a Sunday afternoon in early spring. "[M]y wife and I were seated on the front piazza," John explains, "she wearily but conscientiously ploughing through a missionary report, while I followed the impossible career of the blonde heroine of a rudimentary novel." After John "throw[s] the book aside in disgust," he sees Julius coming toward their house, and moments later John and Anne are treated to one of Julius's conjure tales. Across Chesnutt's collection *The Conjure Woman* (1899), Julius's oral performances are persistently positioned against John and Anne's otherwise disappointing interactions with print, even when John and Anne do their best to break free of textuality by, say, reading out loud to one another. In "Sis' Becky's Pickaninny," John explains that Anne's "ailment took an unexpected turn for the worse. She became the victim of a settled melancholy, attended with vague forebodings of impending misfortune." To cheer her up, John tries "read[ing] novels to her," but, he claims, "nothing seemed to rouse her from the depression into which she had fallen." Julius's arrival is welcome because John hopes Julius's stories will cure his wife of her neurasthenia. "I thought perhaps the story might interest my wife as much or more than the novel I had meant to read from"—and it does. In the opening pages of "The Gray Wolf's Ha'nt," John tries reading to his wife from a book of philosophy, with predictably disastrous results, and Anne is relieved when Julius arrives to free her from this bland textual experience: "'John,' interrupted my wife, 'I wish you would stop reading that nonsense and see who that is coming up the lane.'"[37]

Counter-reflexive is probably the best way to describe the orientation of Sarah Orne Jewett's *The Country of the Pointed Firs* (1896) also, although strictly speaking the narrator/protagonist of the book spends more of her time not writing than not reading. Having arrived in coastal Maine for the summer and rented a room from Mrs. Todd, the narrator feels guilty in the book's second vignette for helping Mrs. Todd with her herb business instead of writing. "I remembered a long piece of writing, sadly belated now, which I was bound to do," the narrator explains. "Literary employments are so vexed with uncertainties at best, and it was not until the voice of conscience sounded louder in my ears than the sea on the nearest pebble beach that I said unkind words of withdrawal to Mrs. Todd." Though the narrator goes on to rent the Dunnet Landing schoolhouse as a kind of writing retreat, she spends the remainder of the book of course not immersed in the act of writing but undergoing a variety of non-textual experiences. In one famous scene, this renunciation of the textual takes the form of not-reading, when the narrator *eats* printed words rather than reading them. At the Bowden family reunion the narrator describes the pies on offer:

> Beside a delightful variety of material, the decorations went beyond all my former experience; dates and names were wrought in lines of pastry and frosting on the tops. There was even more elaborate reading matter on an excellent early-apple pie which we began to share and eat, precept upon precept. Mrs. Todd helped me generously to the whole word *Bowden*, and consumed *Reunion* herself, save an undecipherable fragment[.][38]

Richard Brodhead reads this scene as the climax of the "healing restoration the book charts for th[e] narrator"; the narrator over the course of the book, he argues, "escap[es] from the written and its isolations into an oral culture of 'mak[ing] a visit' (58) and sociable storytelling." Brodhead refers to this process as a "disabstraction of language," and he notes, quite rightly, that the book's disavowal of the textual does not limit the reach of print but only further extends it: the narrator's non-textual travels and interactions in Maine dissolve, under the force of the counter-reflexive gesture, into the reader's experience reading the text.[39]

Now, scholars have tended to absorb the conflict between textuality and non-textuality in regionalism into what they conceive of as the broader conflict between standard language and dialect. "[D]ialect either appeared within a grammatical framework or otherwise made clear it was intended for a grammatically proper reader," Alan Trachtenberg once wrote about the genre, while explaining in the very next sentence: "This placement of speech in such a way that it is unmistakably recognized as 'low,' as culturally inferior to the *writing* of the narrator, owed as much to economics as to the social attitudes of writers[.]" The middle- and upper-class authors of regionalist fiction, then, strategically subordinated the lowly dialect speech of certain characters to their narrator's grammatically standard writing, and according to Trachtenberg they were incentivized to do so under the pressures of the literary marketplace, which was "controlled largely by major Eastern periodicals like *Atlantic*, *Century*, and *Harper's*." While Trachtenberg's argument therefore subsumes the textual/non-textual binary within the standard/dialect binary, it also recognizes no distinction between "standard" and "literary" language: the literary, that is, serves in Trachtenberg's interpretation as a vehicle of standard language. Trachtenberg's suspicious reading of regionalist fiction resonates with the account of standard language put forward by Benedict Anderson, whose history of the rise of national imagined communities centers on the erosion of the "sacred languages," like Latin, that once organized religious communities and the standardization of the vernaculars. Nationalization in Anderson's account involved the creation of standard "languages-of-power" that were propelled by the "explosive interaction between capitalism, technology and human linguistic diversity" and in which certain dialects were elevated over others and dominated the final form of national print languages.[40]

Michael North later argued that the literary and the standard were not, as Trachtenberg once assumed, interchangeable or aligned but rather essentially opposed to one another. Modernist writers, North influentially claimed, harnessed dialect's "insurrectionary opposition to the known and familiar in language," with African American dialect proving especially important: "For them [the modernists] the artist occupied the role of racial outsider because he or she spoke a language opposed to the standard. Modernism, that is to say, mimicked the strategies of dialect and aspired to become a dialect itself."[41] It's worth noting, of course, that Trachtenberg bases his account of dialect literature on the regionalist writings of the post–Civil War period, whereas North generally focuses on high modernists during the interwar period. This historical discrepancy is important because it suggests a gradual divergence of standard and literary language between the Civil War and the First World War.

Whether the standard and the literary were ever perfectly aligned at the beginning of this period, as Trachtenberg suggests, is, it should be added, not entirely clear. Gavin Jones has argued that dialect writing was an "ambivalent literary genre" that "elevated refined discourse while depicting a national language that was multifarious and strange." June Howard has also claimed that local color fiction, rather than enabling the imperial spread of the national standard over regional vernaculars, in fact coordinated the relation between the two and, in doing so, modeled for readers a critical sensibility that combines what she calls "critical regionalism" and "critical cosmopolitanism." It seems more accurate to say, therefore, that literary and standard language were never entirely coextensive after the Civil War, but instead that "literariness" emerged out of the dynamic exchanges between standard language and dialect, exchanges that eventually culminated in the high modernist repudiation of the standard during the interwar period.[42]

By disarticulating standard, dialect, and literary language in postbellum culture, we can better understand that the central drama of regionalist fiction is not simply the conflict between standard language and dialect but rather the emergence of the literary out of this conflict. Once we take literariness as the principal subject of regionalist fiction, the significance of the textual/non-textual binary reasserts itself—in fact, takes priority over the standard/dialect binary—for it was in this historical moment that the cultural jurisdiction of the literary narrowed to only written materials. This narrowing affected not just the material basis of literary culture (its printedness) but also this culture's relationship to public life. The idea that only written texts counted as literature and the idea that reading was cut off from social experience were obstacles that regionalist fiction set out to overcome by dramatizing the interaction between the writing of a narrator and the speech of other, illiterate characters.

Back to School

In what sense can we understand these counter-reflexive gestures as a reaction to the rise of the modern school and its pedagogy "against reading"? In a biographical sense, of course, these writers were among the first cohorts to receive their literary training, or rather some of their literary training, inside the modern school. The "some" here is important and reflects the school's limited sphere of influence in the post–Civil War era. The writers of this period attended class, we might say, irregularly, though this irregularity was indeed regular or typical in a historical moment when the school system remained inchoate. Wharton represents one extreme, having never gone to college herself, or any other institution of formal education for that matter. She remained, instead, school-adjacent; one of her brothers, Freddy, attended Columbia College and the other, Harry, attended Trinity Hall, Cambridge, while Wharton received her education from a governess, Anna Bahlmann, and (even less formally) from the books in her father's library.[43] Sarah Orne Jewett never went to college, but she did attend Berwick Academy, the oldest educational institution in Maine, a private school that she described as a "fitting school for the colleges" that "h[eld] a modest place below" institutions of higher education and "above the common schools."[44] Dreiser, though he served his literary apprenticeship largely at newspapers, nevertheless attended Indiana University for a year; he was admitted as a special student by the personal intervention of David Starr Jordan, one of the architects of the modern university.[45] Charles Chesnutt attended a graded school for African Americans called the Howard School, where he received a classical, rather than an industrial, education. As a teenager he worked as a teacher, first in Fayetteville and later in Charlotte, along with its neighboring rural districts; in 1880, at the age of twenty-two, he became principal of the Normal School for Colored Teachers in Fayetteville.[46] Henry James, the only one of these writers to receive his formal education almost entirely before the Civil War, had unquestionably the most manic relationship to schooling. During his childhood in New York City, his father, Henry James Sr., sent him and his brother William to ten or more schools and subjected them to at least a dozen private instructors. When the family traveled to Europe, Henry James Sr. enrolled his sons at a series of forwarding-thinking institutions in Geneva, London, Paris, and Boulogne-sur-Mer, including a Fourierite school. In 1863, Henry James finally abandoned his formal studies after spending a term at Harvard Law School and resolved to pursue a career as a writer.[47]

The irregularity of the school experience explains, in general, the rather erratic presence of formal education in postbellum US literary fiction generally and, more relevant to the current discussion, the school's modest presence in the counter-reflexive texts I've been examining.[48] As we've seen, the narrator of *The Country of the Pointed Firs* does her work in a one-room schoolhouse abandoned for summer break. In Chesnutt's "Po' Sandy," the narrator's wife Anne wants to tear down an old schoolhouse and use the lumber to build a kitchen. In *Sister Carrie*, Dreiser explains that Hurstwood's daughter Jessica attends high school, where her "decidedly ... patrician" "notions of life" are cultivated: "She met girls at the high school whose parents were truly rich and whose fathers had standing locally as partners or owners of solid businesses. ... They were the only ones of the school about whom Jessica concerned herself."[49] *The Turn of the Screw* locates the diffuse anxiety surrounding reading explicitly in the scene of formal education—the education that the governess herself is hired to superintend—linking the counter-reflexive gesture to a specific institutional setting. That this scene of formal education is antiquated, that formal education is figured in the story as the governess-pupil relation on a gothic estate rather than as the teacher-student relation in a modern classroom or even a one-room schoolhouse, indicates, again, the educational system's modest representational presence in postbellum literary fiction.

One explanation for the surprising frequency of counter-reflexive scenes in postbellum fiction, then, is the school system's (irregular) presence in the lives of literary writers. We can think about these counter-reflexive episodes not just as a "biographical" reaction to the emergence of the school system, however, but also as structurally produced. Over the postbellum period, literature as a discursive category was reconceptualized as the educational system assumed a greater role in cultural administration. Some of the consequences of this reconceptualization are apparent in the scenes of not-reading I've already discussed. For instance, the divergence of standard and literary language, which I described in the context of regionalist fiction, can be best appreciated, following John Guillory, as a product of the educational system's growth and consolidation: when more and more students began attending elementary and secondary schools, and standard English became, as a result, accessible to larger swaths of the population, literary language diverged from the standard to distinguish its adherents from the masses of high school-trained (and grammatically correct) English language users.[50] Nancy Glazener has argued that literary culture, as it entered the school, became rigidly hierarchized, with expert credentialed readers distinguishing themselves from amateur readers. "Xingu," she argues, is an example of this newly hierarchical literary culture: Wharton satirizes the non-expert lady readers of the Lunch Club as they model their organization rather pathetically on the disciplinary division of academic knowledge. Miss Van Vluyck, for instance, is in charge of "[p]hilanthropy and statistics," while Laura Glyde oversees literature. Mrs. Roby is introduced to the Lunch Club by "the distinguished biologist, Professor Foreland, as the most agreeable woman he had ever met," and this "encomium," according to the narrator, "carried the weight of a diploma[.]"[51]

Especially relevant when discussing the structural transformation of "literature" in the postbellum period is June Howard's account of regionalism and "book-learning," a term I've discussed primarily in relation to the school. For Howard, "book-learning" encompasses a whole set of values that obtained in the metropolitan center and exerted its distant force on the peripheral regions of regionalist fiction. Book-learning consists, Howard argues, of "distant sources of information," "visions of the nation," and "cosmopolitan projects," and it appears in regionalist fiction at certain times as an ideal that characters admire but also at other times as an object of characters' derision. The task of regionalism as genre, in Howard's account, is to place book-learning in proper relation to local knowledge.[52] Extending Howard's argument, we might say that regionalism's preoccupation with book-learning is also a preoccupation with, literally, "books" and "learning." These were the dual obstacles that the genre confronted as it sought to legitimize itself as a literary endeavor: the "book"-ishness that defined literature and the "learning" or school-training that readers and writers increasingly needed to receive to participate in literary culture. Regionalist literature was susceptible to the charge that it was merely book-learning, and therefore it needed to develop strategies to repel this charge.

Not just regionalism but all literary endeavors during the period could potentially be derided as "book-learning." One strategy writers of literature in the post–Civil War era deployed to defend their work from accusations of "book-learning" was, in the tradition of an earlier strain of nineteenth-century American literature, anti-scholasticism. Literary writers, that is, criticized institutions of formal education. Of course, as I argued in Chapter 1, while anti-scholasticism more and more often provided a principle of coherence for literary writing, it also made literature a particularly useful instrument within scholastic life. Another strategy that writers of literature deployed, as I've argued in this chapter, was self-renunciation or "counter-reflexivity." Because literature was becoming increasingly entangled with the very institution that it also identified as its chief antagonist—the school—"literariness" became an object of suspicion for the most literary of writers. Literary culture's suspicion of literariness often manifested in the reproach that a certain literary work or a certain literary author was genteel, as, for instance, when Fred Lewis Pattee denounced the established literary canon as an "aristocracy of the intellect."[53] When writers represented reading in their own fiction as cut off from "real life," they were, in turn, seeking to cleanse literature of the contaminating influence of institutions. They were attempting to purge their work of the very institutional category ("literature") and the very material condition (written-ness) that defined its existence.

Aside from the school's "biographical" influence over literary production, as well as its "structural" effect on literature as a cultural designation, there was also what I called in the introduction to this book an ambient suspicion surrounding reading in the postbellum period. Late Victorians felt, in Jackson Lears's words, that "they had been cut off from 'reality,' that they experienced life in all its dimensions at second hand, in books rather than action."[54] Might we understand the counter-reflexive gesture so common in fiction after the Civil War as simply a response to this ambient suspicion? My point in this chapter is not that the modern school assumed an entirely new attitude toward print and invented a new conception of literature that writers then internalized. The ambient suspicion surrounding reading in the post–Civil War era did not originate in modern educational reform, though the architects of the school system did harness this suspicion to more convincingly pronounce the social importance of their own institutions. (They also taught English literature for the same reason.) And writers did not reproduce the suspicion surrounding reading that circulated in the cultural ether, the suspicion that the modern school amplified with its pedagogy "against reading"; writers instead sought to transcend this suspicion. My point, finally, is that literary production in the postbellum period overcame a conception of reading and literariness that the school wasn't administratively powerful enough to enforce. It did so by renouncing itself. This is the convoluted process out of which literature in its modern sense and the school system in its modern form came into being: through elaborate acts of self-promotion and self-renunciation. By hating their rivals and hating themselves.

The Historical (Un)specificity of the Counter-Reflexive Gesture

None of this, however, explains the origins of the cultural suspicion surrounding reading, and none of this addresses the fact that counter-reflexive gestures have appeared in literary culture both before and after the historical period under discussion. The origins of the cultural suspicion surrounding reading are difficult to pinpoint. Notwithstanding de Tocqueville's famous observation from earlier in the nineteenth century that the "number of periodicals and occasional publications in the United States exceeds all belief," and that "scarcely a hamlet lacks its newspaper," an entrenched distrust of the authority of print and book-learning has long been endemic to the United States. Educators and writers might have derived their anti-reading rhetoric in part from this popular suspicion, but more concretely—and perhaps confusingly—they absorbed it at least in part from the same source in the Romantic period. A key forebear of both the educators' *and* the writers' mistrust of reading was the hybrid pedagogue-man-of-letters Jean-Jacques Rousseau, who described reading in *Emile* (1762) as "the scourge of infancy" and books as the "instruments of [the students'] greatest misery."[55]

As Rousseau's comments suggest, hostility toward reading was foundational to the project of Romanticism in the eighteenth century, and counter-reflexivity, specifically, surfaces in many major works of Romantic literature. It crystallizes with unusual intensity in William Wordsworth's two poems, "Expostulation and Reply" (1798) and "The Tables Turned" (1798). In "Expostulation and Reply," the speaker of the poem, William, is encouraged by his friend Matthew to cease "dream[ing]" his "time away" contemplating nature and instead to read more: "Up! up! and drink the spirit breathed/From dead men to their kind." William in response defends conversing with nature as a form of reading that is superior to reading books, and this response is elaborated in "The Tables Turned," a follow-up to "Expostulation and Reply" where the speaker, presumably still William, denounces reading as a "dull and endless strife" and exhorts his audience to "[c]lose up those barren leaves" and "[c]ome forth, and bring with you a heart/That watches and receives."[56] William's injunction—to stop reading the very poetry collection that contains "Expostulation and Reply" and "The Tables Turned"—would have been especially bewildering to readers of *Lyrical Ballads*'s second edition, which opened with these two poems.[57] Across the Atlantic, Ralph Waldo Emerson in "The American Scholar" (1837) warned of the "grave mischief" that occurs when the "sacredness which attaches to the act of creation, the act of thought, is instantly transferred to the record": "Hence, instead of Man Thinking, we have the bookworm," Emerson wrote. "Hence the book-learned class, who value books, as such; not as related to nature and the human constitution, but as making a sort of Third Estate with the world and soul. Hence the restorers of readings, the emendators, the bibliomaniacs of all degrees. This is bad; this is worse than it seems." Walt Whitman, as we saw last chapter, counseled his readers in the Preface to *Leaves of Grass* (1855) to "re-examine all you have been told in school or church or in any *book*, and dismiss whatever insults your own soul[.]"[58]

While the Romantics thus disavowed the act of reading before the institutional transformations of the post–Civil War period, the counter-reflexive gesture also post-dates the institutional dynamics of the period as well. The strain of deconstruction elaborated by Paul de Man maintains a fundamentally counter-reflexive understanding of the literary, one that announces literature's limitations and, in doing so, dissolves them altogether. In *Blindness and Insight* (1971), de Man insists that literary language registers the truth that its signs and its meaning don't coincide and thereby reveals that "sign and meaning can never coincide[.]" Literature is thus according to de Man "the only form of language free from the fallacy of unmediated expression"; it possesses what de Man, following Rousseau, describes as a "consciousness" of the "presence of nothingness" behind reality, behind the sign. The retention of literary language is a hallmark of de Manian deconstruction, and yet (as scholars have noted), though de Man retains literature as a discursive category, he does so while dramatically expanding its purview. "When modern critics think they are demystifying literature, they are in fact being demystified by it," de Man writes. "At the moment that they claim to do away with literature [by demystifying it], literature is everywhere; what they call anthropology, linguistics, psychoanalysis is nothing but literature reappearing, like the Hydra's head, in the very spot where it had supposedly been suppressed."[59]

Throughout its history, the counter-reflexive mode has therefore remained a feature of a specifically Romantic worldview—from Rousseau, Wordsworth, and Emerson to de Man, for whom Rousseau in particular was a foundational thinker—and in some sense the history I've reconstructed in the first two chapters of this book might be renarrated as a story about Romanticism, first its critique of modernity, then its migration into US cultural life, and finally its incorporation into modern US educational institutions.[60] In the last chapter, we saw that a strain of anti-scholastic writing achieved hegemony within literary culture over the course of the nineteenth century and the first half of the twentieth, and the philosophical origins of this tradition lie in Romanticism. We can, then, think of this body of literature as assisting educators as they effected the school's own Romanticization, through the teaching of, say, Washington Irving and Henry David Thoreau. Romanticism affected modern educational reform in other ways too. Johann Heinrich Pestalozzi, an avowed Rousseauian Swiss educator, and his pupil, Friedrich Fröbel, were famously influential among nineteenth-century

US reformers. John Dewey in *Democracy and Education* praised Rousseau for developing the "doctrine of accord with nature," which offered a "much less formal and abstract view of the mind and its powers." As a student, Andrew White, president of Cornell, saw Emerson deliver one of his popular lectures, and he claimed that it "made the greatest impression upon" him of any lecture that he attended. G. Stanley Hall remembered Emerson visiting Williams College in the 1860s: "[F]ew faculty attended but the students heard him gladly, and in my set a veritable Emersonian craze ran rampant." We might say, finally, that in America, both "literature" as a category of cultural consumption and the institution of the "modern school" were Romanticized as each struggled to overcome its traditional limitations, a process in which the anti-institutional gestures I've recounted over the last two chapters proliferated.[61]

The period between the Civil War and the First World War was especially chaotic and generative within this longer history, a moment when two independent paths for Romanticism (literary, scholastic) converged with one another. The meaning of these Romantic gestures changed as a consequence of the new institutional-cultural environment in which they occurred. G. Stanley Hall's renunciation of reading was crucially different from Rousseau's, even if the two inhabited the same genealogy, because Hall's was instrumentalized to propel the expansion of an institutional system that Rousseau would have found anathema. Henry James's disavowal of reading, similarly, differed in its frequency and intensity from Wordsworth's, because James's was deployed at a historical moment when the administration of culture increasingly took place within the educational system, whose expansion was itself (disorientingly) propelled by a Romantic logic.

Coda: The Denaturalization or De-Romanticization of Literature

Whether told as a story about Romanticism and the contradictions of its spread through US cultural and institutional life, or as a story about the vexed relationship between literature and schools, the dynamics that have animated these stories have, in the last forty years or so, taken on a different cast. "Literature" as cultural designation is no longer reducible to its Romantic impulses or its deep-seated anti-institutionalism. Rather, scholars have described literature as a passive product of its institutional surroundings, particularly the school's administrative apparatus. This reconceptualization of the literary took place, I would argue, when the discipline's center of gravity moved from de Manian deconstruction to the New Historicism. The critical distinction between these two schools of poststructuralism, as others have observed, is the significance (or insignificance) of the literary to each. I explained before that de Man retained the specificity of literature in a world that was, to poststructuralists, wholly textual. For Fredric Jameson, de Man is something of a liminal figure in this respect: his devotion to the literary and the aesthetic places him on the boundary of modernism and postmodernism.

De Man offers us, in Jameson's words, "the spectacle of an incompletely liquidated modernism: the positions and the arguments are 'postmodern,' ... even if the conclusions are not."[62] This distinguishes de Man in Jameson's account from the New Historicists—the two are paired in his chapter on theory in *Postmodernism* (1991)—for the New Historicists, as Jameson describes them, breathlessly move through different spheres of social experience in their analyses, discovering homologies between these spheres as they go, in a way that deprives the literary (or any other category) of a claim to transcendence. As Catherine Gallagher and Stephen Greenblatt wrote in the introduction to *Practicing New Historicism* (2000), "When the literary text ceases to be a sacred, self-enclosed, and self-justifying miracle, when in the skeptical mood we foster it begins to lose at least some of the special power ascribed to it, its boundaries begin to seem less secure and it loses exclusive rights to the experience of wonder. The house of the imagination has many mansions, of which art (a relatively late invention as a distinct category) is only one."[63]

It might be slightly more accurate to say that New Historicism didn't entirely jettison the literary or the aesthetic as much as it set out to show that these categories were themselves the product of material and institutional practices—i.e., "art (a relatively late invention ...)." (Of course, the fact that literature and art are "invention[s]"—the fact that they are the product of material and institutional practices—also makes them, despite their specificity, homologous to all other products of material and institutional practices.) This slight revision of Jameson's account reveals an often overlooked connection between the New Historicists, with their reconceptualization of the literary, and other insurgent movements within literary studies at the same historical moment. I'm referring here, first, to cultural studies and particularly the work of Raymond Williams, whose sociological methods thoroughly denaturalized "literature" as a cultural category and exercised a tremendous influence on the academic study of literature in the United States in the early 1980s. The resurgent interest in literary sociology today traces its genealogy back to this moment in disciplinary history.[64] I'm referring here, second, to the emergence of disciplinary history as a prominent sub-disciplinary formation, inaugurated by the publication of Michael Warner's "Professionalization and the Rewards of Literature" (1985) and especially Gerald Graff's *Professing Literature* (1987). The New Historicism, cultural studies, and disciplinary historiography, then, together marked a transformation in literary studies' relation to its object of study, "literature." No longer essentially anti-institutional, literariness was now understood as a product of institutions.[65]

What explains this shift? John Guillory once argued that de Man's reformulation of the literary occurred at a moment in institutional history when English departments were undergoing a large-scale capital flight. In *Cultural Capital*, he writes: "The moment of theory is determined ... by a certain defunctioning of the literary curriculum, a crisis in the market value of its cultural capital occasioned by the emergence of a professional-managerial class which no longer requires the (primarily literary) cultural capital of the old bourgeoisie."[66] We might therefore suppose that the thorough denaturalization of literature in the wake of de Manian deconstruction—undertaken by New Historicists, scholars of cultural studies, and disciplinary historians, along with John Guillory himself—indexes the final collapse of literature's market value and, in the aftermath of this collapse, literature's total demystification. James English has complicated this narrative by pointing out that the "crescendo of crisis narratives, which appeared in the wake of the cultural and curriculum wars of the late 1980s and early 1990s"—including presumably Guillory's—"coincided with a period of extraordinary growth and prosperity for English studies in the United States, when enrollments in the English major were rising faster than at any time in 30 years and faculty hiring, for a brief span, achieved near parity with the production of new PhDs."[67]

It's not entirely convincing, consequently, to describe the reformulation of "literariness" under New Historicism, cultural studies, and disciplinary historiography as a sign of the collapse of literature's market value: English classes continued to attract students throughout this period, proving that the discipline had retained the interest of the professional managerial class (PMC). A more convincing way to describe this reformulation, I'll end by suggesting, would involve scaling up analytically from the discipline to the educational system that houses it. The crisis unconsciously registered in this reformulation is not exactly specific to literary studies, in other words; it is instead a crisis of formal education writ large. The ascendance of New Historicism in the 1980s coincided, as scholars have noted, with the rise of neoliberalism and, with neoliberalism, the privatization of the educational system.[68] Christopher Newfield has described the effects of privatization in higher education, writing that "public colleges and universities have been following [a] commercialization script since 1980 or so," a script, he explains, that produces a "devolutionary cycle" in which "high student costs, stagnating educational benefits, and destabilized public college finances" result from "not public but ... private sector practices."[69] The privatization of public primary and secondary schools has had similarly damaging consequences.[70]

The idea that "literature" is an institutional construct thus took hold in literary studies at a historical moment when the US institutional system fell victim to the assault of private industry. The rise in student enrollments in the late eighties and early nineties might indicate that a bachelor's degree in English remained a desirable credential for the university's PMC graduates, but it doesn't reflect the altered meaning of the credential and of PMC membership under the long downturn. The story of the emergence of "literature" in its modern sense in the post–Civil War era—as anti-scholastic and anti-itself—therefore came to an end in the final decades of the twentieth century, when the educational system, whose growth was once enabled by literary culture and whose administrative support literary culture increasingly depended upon for its own social meaning, underwent a severe restructuring.

The final four chapters of this book set out to complicate the bedrock assumption that has oriented the discipline after 1980. They do so, first, by showing how postbellum literature transcended the scholastic conditions under which it was produced and, second, by revealing the ways this body of literature continues to shape scholastic experience today. Before turning to this next phase in the tangled history of literary and scholastic culture in the United States, I want to dwell for one last moment on the discipline of literary studies and its self-conception before the demystification of literature circa 1980, simply to underscore the strange sort of revenge that the discipline exacted on the educational system in response to the administrative rhetoric "against reading." Though scholars in recent years have been convinced of the school's administrative power, scholars earlier in the discipline's history were far more contemptuous of the school and its capacities. Faced with a scholastic apparatus that increasingly structured their daily lives, English instructors came to understand their object of study as fundamentally unassimilable to this apparatus, and in their teaching and research they gravitated toward literary works that denounced formal education, as if they could free themselves from their institutional environment by teaching the novels of James Fenimore Cooper, Herman Melville, or Mark Twain.

Where modern reformers after the Civil War claimed for the educational system access to everyday "real" American experience by denigrating the act of reading, English instructors thus insisted that literature gave students access to an uncompromised world beyond the confines of the school. When these English instructors wrote about literature or taught literary works, they didn't consider the experience writers and readers had in class or on campus, because whatever happened in class or on campus didn't seem as meaningful as whatever happened the moment literature entered other domains of social existence. For these instructors, in other words, the classroom was not a site of authentic human experience, but irrevocably cut off from it. What happened on campus didn't count as "real life" at all.

PART 2

3
In Defense of Punctuality

[A] new opposition gradually arose between them. Adele realised that Helen demanded of her a response and always before that response was ready. Their pulses were differently timed. She could not go so fast and Helen's exhausted nerves could no longer wait.
—Gertrude Stein, *Q.E.D.* (1903)

There is no educational autocrat in this country who can take out his watch at a given moment and say that at this time, from the Atlantic to the Pacific, all the children are studying arithmetic in the grammar schools.
—John Tetlow, "A Wider Range of Electives in College Admissions Requirements" (1896)[1]

In 1896, John Tetlow, principal of the Girls' High and Latin Schools in Boston, delivered a paper at the fifth annual meeting of the Harvard Teachers Association. In the paper, Tetlow expressed concern over a proposal for new college entrance requirements. He believed that this proposal, put forward by administrators in higher education, would impose academic standards on elementary and secondary schools that weren't necessarily in these schools' best interest. Tetlow worried that the new requirements would standardize American education, transforming the heterogeneous network of loosely connected, local institutions that the country then enjoyed into a single homogeneous and undifferentiated system. "We have a local option republic," Tetlow explained. "There is no educational autocrat in this country who can take out his watch at a given moment and say that at this time, from the Atlantic to the Pacific, all the children are studying arithmetic in the grammar schools."

The proposal Tetlow was responding to had originally been formulated by Harvard president Charles Eliot. For Eliot, the importance of entrance requirements extended beyond the interests of any single institution, like Harvard; to establish admissions criteria was to establish the modern educational system as a system. With the dramatic rise in the number of schools and student enrollments at the

Schools of Fiction. Morgan Day Frank, Oxford University Press. © Morgan Day Frank (2022).
DOI: 10.1093/oso/9780192867506.003.0004

turn of the twentieth century, reformers struggled to maintain academic standards across the vast "local option republic" of US formal education. If a student attended a new high school in Kansas, with its own curriculum, and then applied to Harvard, how was an admissions officer supposed to know if the applicant was prepared to attend college? How was a professor of history at Harvard supposed to know what material the student had already learned in high school and what material the student needed to learn in college? By establishing prerequisites for college, educators attempted to articulate a more coherent vision of formal education.[2] But how would educators determine these prerequisites when no existing program of study was required in all US secondary schools? In his original address, Eliot proposed a plan to translate academic standards across all educational institutions. He insisted that each individual course should have "a valuation, or coefficient, attached to it" and that this valuation should be determined by measuring the amount of time students spent in class: "I believe that the best criterion for determining the value of each subject is the time devoted to that subject in schools which have an intelligent program of studies."[3]

John Tetlow's response to Eliot is important not because it's overwhelmingly critical of the proposed admissions criteria. In fact, many of Tetlow's recommendations were already included in the new requirements, because the new requirements were meant to foster, not undermine, the heterogeneity of the school system by allowing a more diverse range of classes to count toward college entrance.[4] Tetlow's response is important, instead, because the only significant criticism it levels against Eliot's program involves the program's treatment of time. In registering his horror at a world where children across the country are studying arithmetic at the exact same moment, Tetlow actually hits on the most enduring piece of the reform, the part of the proposal that transformed US educational institutions. By 1910, after the "unit" had established itself as the primary measurement of coursework, a teacher at any moment could take out his watch and assume that every student in a particular grade across the country had spent the same amount of time that day studying arithmetic. This institutional reality was not indeed identical to the hypothetical Tetlow had conjured of perfect temporal simultaneity, but it was close. The fantasy that the modern school system ultimately realized was the fantasy of coordinated time, the temporal harmony of the student experience. At school, students would be able to live in time collectively, endure time with one another not just as members of a specific course like arithmetic, learning the multiplication tables in a room alone together for forty-five minutes, but as members of a larger scholastic community. This fantasy, instantiated in the modern curriculum, was John Tetlow's nightmare.

While educators after the Civil War struggled to organize the temporality of academic life, writers became fixated on the relationship between literature and the organization of time under industrial modernity. This relationship of course has occasioned much speculation among theorists and scholars as well.

Benedict Anderson influentially claimed that eighteenth- and nineteenth-century New World print culture helped produce new political formations, what he called the imagined community of the nation, by creating a sense of temporal simultaneity. Following Walter Benjamin, Anderson explained that, by the eighteenth century, the medieval experience of a messianic "simultaneity-along-time," where past and future are subsumed into an instantaneous present, had been replaced with the modern experience of "'homogeneous, empty time,'" where "simultaneity is, as it were, transverse, cross-time, marked not by refiguring and fulfillment, but by temporal coincidence, and measured by clock and calendar." The novel in particular, according to Anderson, functioned as "a device for the presentation of simultaneity in 'homogenous, empty time,'" and print culture in general "provided the technical means for 're-presenting' the *kind* of imagined community that is the nation."[5]

Scholars haven't always understood literature as an instrument of standard time, however. Homi Bhabha, for instance, has insisted that the temporality of the nation is intrinsically split: on the one side it is pedagogical, cultivating national consciousness through bureaucratic, economic, and cultural institutions, but on the other side it is performative, as the people struggle against the temporality the state imposes on them with their own local cultures and their own local timetables.[6] Wai Chee Dimock's *Through Other Continents* (2006) argues too that literary experience is fundamentally resistant to standardized time and thus subversive of national organizing structures. "Reading," Dimock explains, "is a common activity that can have an extraordinary effect on the mapping of time. ... It can generate bonds that deviate from the official timetable, since it is certainly not numerical chronology, not the clock and the calendar, that brings a reader into the orbit of the text." All reading according to Dimock is thus "offbeat reading": "The distance between readers and the words they read is anything but a number. In this domain, at least, time is made up not of fixed lengths but of lengths variably generated—generated by each reader in a grip of readerly passion."[7]

And yet, if we accept Dimock's account of offbeat reading—understanding literary experience, despite its formal tendency toward order and sequence, as essentially unmoored from regulated timetables, always containing segments of time "alien" to our own[8] —the relationship between literary and social experience becomes uncertain. With each reader caught in the grip of his or her own readerly passion, traversing the alien historical palimpsest that is the text, individual literary experience is out of sync not just with the temporality of the nation-state but also with everybody else's experience of time. Reading in Dimock's account is an isolating activity, an activity that's dictated by one's own temporal relationship to the words on the page and nobody else's. This is exactly how many postbellum writers represent the experience of time in an industrializing world. For characters in their books, like Adele and Helen in Gertrude Stein's *Q.E.D.* (1903), whose pulses disturbingly beat to different rhythms, being out of sync with everyone else in society doesn't feel liberating and "offbeat," as Dimock would have us believe; it feels lonely and almost unendurable. It feels, in other words, like living under what David Harvey has called the "time-space compression" of modernity.[9]

Writers in the postbellum period therefore didn't celebrate the heterogeneity, variability, or unpredictability of industrial time; like Charles Eliot in his quest to institutionalize the "course unit," they sought temporal standardization. The appeal of standard time for both writers and educators in this historical moment suggests the growing intimacy between the two as they came to inhabit the same social institutions and, perhaps of greater consequence, the same position in class relations after the Civil War. The emergence of standard time is often, as we've already seen, associated with nation-building projects and ruling-class disciplinary programs under industrial capitalism. For an educator like Eliot, though, the standardization of time promised not necessarily to drive the profits of the ruling class but to coordinate the collective endeavors of a rising class of professionals, managers, bureaucrats, and salaried white-collar employees. It promised, that is, to introduce a measure of coherence into the notoriously vague formation that is the middle class.

To the extent that the school has determined the boundaries of this class, the regularization of academic time has served to bind together its constituents and give them some modicum of a collective identity, even if this collective identity inheres only in the shared agony of hearing a school bell ring. There is no question that the middle class's elaborate systems for organizing time proved useful for industrialists in their endless hunt for surplus value. But in the course unit, as in so many other middle-class projects, the architects of the school system also formalized their own challenge to ruling class authority, forging a tool of collective action that could potentially overcome the social alienation endemic to life under industrial capitalism. To point out the ameliorating or even emancipatory qualities of standard time isn't to discount the many atrocities that have been carried out under corporate timetables. Instead it's to remember the role of what Norbert Elias once called "timing" in social life; it's to encourage us all to recognize that communal endeavors, both good and bad, require agreed-upon temporal measurements in order to come into existence; and it's to insist, finally, on the power of punctuality to help us all feel a little less alone in the world.[10] If the emancipatory potential of standard time is easily overlooked, this is undoubtedly because, while it enabled the formation of a semi-autonomous middle class, this class has regularly surrendered whatever agency it has wielded back to the ruling elite, which has found in the collective identity of the purportedly autonomous middle class a serviceable social ideal.

As the school assumed greater responsibility in the administration of social experience after the Civil War, including the administration of literature, more writers received their literary training inside the formal system of education. By no means identical to middle-class professionals and managers, the writers of this period nevertheless did resemble their peers in a number of meaningful ways: they often earned the same academic credentials, for instance, and they both performed cognitive labor within the industrial order.[11] We'll see over the next chapters that, as these writers attempted to distinguish themselves from the middle class, they ultimately undertook reform projects that were difficult to differentiate from the reformist initiatives of their professional-managerial peers.

In this particular chapter, I examine the work of two post–Civil War authors who expressed dismay about the organization of time under industrial modernity and attributed their feelings of temporal isolation to the system of formal education in the United States. For Henry Adams and Gertrude Stein, who each graduated from Harvard, albeit in different generations, Stein attending from 1893 to 1897 and Adams attending from 1854 to 1858 and teaching from 1870 to 1877, the asynchrony of modern life was a result of the school's failure to administer time properly. This critique surfaces in their work in different thematic terms. Adams's books self-consciously participate in a strain of nineteenth-century time travel literature, wallowing in the acute feelings of loneliness that sporadically afflict earlier US time travelers. Alternatively, Stein's first forays into prose fiction are filled with characters who again and again find themselves waiting for each other. Although time traveling and waiting might seem like altogether unrelated literary preoccupations, in Adams's and Stein's work, the two become representative of the temporal alienation endemic to industrial society, and in both authors' work these phenomena are shown to originate in the formal institutions of US education.

While Adams and Stein thus expose the school's failure to adequately organize the student experience of time, they also propose their own literary solutions to this institutional deficiency. Though Adams and Stein in some sense offered these solutions in defiance of the school's authority, as a means of distinguishing their literary undertakings from the undertakings of the middle-class graduates of the modern educational system, these authors also addressed their solutions to the very scholastic communities they defied. They did so literally, by sending their writings to prominent US educators. Adams delivered *The Education of Henry Adams* to Charles Eliot in the book's first private circulation. And one of the more controversial and confusing pieces of writing Adams ever produced was his "Letter to American Teachers of History" (1910), which addressed itself, as the title indicates, to American teachers of history. Gertrude Stein also sent a copy of her first book *Three Lives* (1909) to her old Harvard professor William James.[12]

Adams's and Stein's solutions have, moreover, proved impactful within the very scholastic apparatus that they once bridled against. This impact is best appreciated in the context of the curriculum: as we'll see, Adams's writing has been indispensable for scholars and teachers organizing history into discrete "periods," while the act of reading Stein's early prose fiction has enabled its scholastic audience to undergo a shared feeling of synchronicity in time, what Stein herself referred to as the "continuous present." If the institutionalization of the course unit never entirely succeeded in realizing John Tetlow's nightmare—one in which an "educational autocrat" could "take out his watch at a given moment and say that at this time, from the Atlantic to the Pacific, all the children are studying arithmetic in the grammar schools"—the teaching of Adams's and Stein's writing has nevertheless served to further harmonize the student experience, in effect compensating for the course unit's deficiencies. Postbellum literature has, in this sense, helped coordinate academic time, not to deaden individual experience, but to enable new forms of collective subjectivity.

The Course Unit

The consolidation of institutional time at the beginning of the twentieth century represents the culmination of a number of developments that took place in schools over a one-hundred-year period, including the emergence of a stable 180-day academic calendar. The course "unit" is important to this history primarily because it provided a sophisticated mechanism to coordinate the daily schedule both within individual schools and across the educational system as a whole. It is important, too, however, because it reflects educators' understanding of the sociality of the school system, the kinds of collective experience educators believed the modern school could conjure into existence. For Charles Eliot, US schools would need to provide students with a more meaningful sense of collective identity than one simply based on enrollment or "class spirit"; and academic time—what Eliot at one point referred to as the "contemporaneousness" offered by scholastic pursuits—became the medium through which this collective identity would find expression.[13]

Over the course of his professional career, Eliot served on a number of national committees where the institutional developments he initiated as a university president were translated in one form or another to the school system in its entirety. Eliot's interest in time as the key organizing element of the educational system began well before the 1890s, the decade when college admissions criteria came to the center of the reform agenda and he and John Tetlow sparred at the fifth annual meeting of the Harvard Teachers Association. One of the many seismic changes Eliot initiated at Harvard during his first years as president was the adoption of an elective system: instead of requiring students to enroll in a prescribed sequence of courses over their four years in college—all freshmen taking the same classes with each other, all sophomores taking the same classes with each other, and so on—Harvard's program of study under Eliot gave students the freedom to choose the courses they wanted to take. The elective system brought about significant administrative changes in the daily operations of US colleges and universities. Once students had this freedom within the curriculum, the bachelor's degree came dangerously close to losing its coherence as a credential. What made one sequence of college courses equivalent to another? How much education did one course provide? Did an advanced course in natural science "count" for the same amount of credit as a required freshman composition course? In his inaugural address at Harvard, delivered in 1869, Eliot emphasized the role that time would play in harmonizing the new curriculum. "Under this system the College does not demand, it is true, one invariable set of studies of every candidate for the first degree in Arts," Eliot explained, "but its requisitions for this degree are nevertheless high and inflexible, being nothing less than four years devoted to liberal culture." Though each student at Harvard could follow a unique path through coursework, enrolling in a sequence of classes all his own and different from his peers, the collective academic experience would remain united because, according to Eliot, students were traveling these various intellectual paths together in time, simultaneously, over their four years in college.[14]

The administration of time at Harvard became increasingly elaborate over the course of Eliot's presidency. Before Eliot, Harvard college catalogues listed the required "studies" that made up the curriculum; in Eliot's second year as president, the catalogues began to print individual "courses" with Arabic numerals attached to them, and the courses were grouped by department, not by class. By 1881–1882, courses were divided into "full" and "half" courses, depending on how often the course met and for how much time; by 1883–1884, the bachelor's degree could be earned by passing 18.4 courses.[15] Although Eliot wasn't the first president to institute an elective system—in the early 1850s, Francis Wayland, president of Brown, adopted an elective system when the school was faced with dwindling enrollments, but his reforms were abandoned after his retirement in 1855—the success of Harvard's program led to the adoption of the elective system at institutions of higher learning across the country. As schools adopted this curriculum, so too did they adopt Harvard's organization of time. In 1877, the requirements for a bachelor's degree at the University of Michigan were defined temporally: to graduate, students needed to complete twenty-four or twenty-six "full courses," and a full course was defined as five exercises per week during a semester. By 1893, Washington University in St. Louis adopted an elective system, requiring students to pass a certain number of full- and half-courses for graduation, and Yale, whose curriculum was much more conservative than Harvard's, implemented an elective system that began as early as sophomore year.[16]

At the beginning of the 1890s, Eliot turned his attention more deliberately to the educational system beyond Harvard, assuming the chairmanship of the influential Committee of Ten, a working group of educators assembled by the National Educational Association to recommend policy changes that would eventually standardize the US high school curriculum. The committee consisted of four college presidents, two headmasters, one principal, and William T. Harris, commissioner of education in Washington, DC. According to the *Report of the Committee on Secondary School Studies, Appointed at the Meeting of the National*

Educational Association, July, 9 1892 (1893), the first three guiding questions the Committee of Ten set out to resolve were these:

1. In the school course of study extending approximately from the age of six years to eighteen years—a course including the periods of both elementary and secondary instruction—at what age should the study which is the subject of the Conference be first introduced?
2. After it is introduced, how many hours a week for how many years should be devoted to it?
3. How many hours a week for how many years should be devoted to it during the last four years of the complete course; that is, during the ordinary high school period?

With these foundational questions, the committee had, in effect, already adopted Eliot's method of course valuation, setting national academic standards in the vocabulary of time-allotments. "The details of the time-allotment for the several studies which enter into the secondary school programme may seem to some persons mechanical, or even trivial[,] ... but such is not the opinion of the Committee of Ten," they wrote. "The Committee believe that to establish just proportions between the several subjects, or groups of allied subjects ... it is essential that each principal subject shall be taught thoroughly and extensively, and therefore an adequate number of periods a week on the school programme." The committee proposed multiple programs of study—an elective system for high schools, where students could pursue different curricular paths, depending on their interests—that were each broken down into daily periods consisting of forty-five to fifty minutes devoted to a single subject. The "period" in high school, like the "course" in college, enabled individual schools to coordinate the academic experience of their own students; it also made coursework translatable among different secondary schools and legible to institutions of higher learning, thus coordinating the academic experience nationally.[17]

The recommendations made by the Committee of Ten were implemented in slightly different forms across the educational system over the next decade. In 1897, Eliot renamed the "course" at Harvard the "point," with each point corresponding to half a year's work in a particular subject; in 1899 the Committee on College Entrance Requirements resolved to establish admissions criteria based on the "unit" rather than the "point" or "period," with each unit corresponding to a full year's work in a particular subject.[18] In 1910, after Eliot served as president of the board of trustees for the Carnegie Foundation for the Advancement of Teaching, the "unit" finally achieved widespread acceptance at educational institutions around the country.

According to the first *Annual Report* of the Carnegie Foundation, Andrew Carnegie founded the CFAT to "provid[e] in the higher institutions of learning in

America a system of retiring allowances." The goals of the CFAT extended beyond pension plans, however. In order to receive money for retiring professors, colleges and universities were required to adopt certain academic standards, and to determine these academic standards, Carnegie assembled a team of educators, led by Henry S. Pritchett, a former president of MIT. With $10 million at their disposal, the board of trustees, overseen by Eliot, produced a set of guidelines that colleges needed to follow if they wanted to receive Carnegie's money.[19]

Taking up Eliot's earlier policy recommendations, the CFAT set standards for the nation's high schools and colleges based on time-allotments. In the first *Annual Report* of the CFAT, eligible colleges were defined as institutions that had "a course of four full years in liberal arts and sciences" and required "not less than the usual four years of academic or high school preparation, or its equivalent, in addition to the preacademic or grammar school studies." The *Report* also stated that colleges could attain eligibility only by adopting the standards of the College Entrance Examination Boards, which designated admissions requirements "in terms of units, a unit being a course of five periods weekly throughout an academic year of the preparatory school."[20] Although the CFAT was established principally to influence the operation of colleges and universities, its impact extended across the educational system. After the College Entrance Examination Board endorsed the standards recommended by the CFAT in 1909, practically all high schools in the United States measured their work by the "Carnegie Unit."

Despite the industrialist Carnegie's role in the institutionalization of the course unit, Charles Eliot's crusade to standardize time in the US educational system grew out of middle-class concerns—concerns, to be more specific, about the middle class's unity as a class. The modern school's capacity to produce social unity was a topic that surfaced sometimes unexpectedly in Eliot's public statements. For instance, addressing the issue of fraternities and sororities on Harvard's campus, Eliot described the kinds of social relationships he believed the school could facilitate. While Eliot conceded in the speech that "fraternities and sororities and the social clubs in American colleges and universities, being small, exclusive, and secretive groups, seem inconsistent with democratic principles in general, and particularly with the liberal spirit of a society of scholars," he also went on to acknowledge the need for students to establish relationships with their peers. "The fact is," he explained, that "the human being wants and needs for social purposes some group or groups larger and more various than the family, but much smaller and less various than the entire community, or even than the entire membership of a society of scholars." In his qualified defense of fraternities and sororities, Eliot was thus making an argument about the school's ability to create lasting relationships under industrial modernity, relationships based on the shared endeavors of its graduates: "The limited human being, even when fairly educated, craves a limited group of congenial associates having some common interest, which, as a social bond, may as well be narrow as broad."[21]

The proper scale of social affiliation within the school remained a preoccupation for Eliot. In one speech, "Relations of American Colleges to Each Other," Eliot described the power of the elective system to produce close "congenial" associations among professional scholars, on a scale larger than the "smaller and less various" groupings he described in the fraternities speech. In Eliot's description, specialization and bureaucratization were not necessarily alienating processes; instead, they created the opportunity for new kinds of collective experience. Even as the number of colleges and universities increased, more profound forms of sociality became possible. "Under the general influence of the elective system of studies, the number of advanced students of philology, history, economics, natural science, mathematics, and philosophy began to increase in all the college faculties," Eliot explained. "[A]nd these real scholars began to associate themselves together in various learned societies for the cultivation of different fields of learning, and for mutual sympathy and support." Eliot emphasized in this particular speech the crucial role time played in integrating these professional communities. "These societies brought the professors and young teachers of the different colleges together in annual or semi-annual meetings; and these meetings developed good fellowship and the sense of a common object, namely, that of advancing American scholarship."[22]

Eliot provided his fullest account of the sociality of standard time in a 1905 speech, when he addressed a growing concern among Harvard students and alumni that "class spirit" was disappearing on campus because of the elective system. "I have heard it said many times that class spirit is declining at Harvard College, or in the Scientific School, or in the University," Eliot declared, "that class spirit is a thing of the past, going out with the elective system, of all things in the world; that mere numbers destroy it; that therefore the small college is superior to the large college." For Eliot, however, "class spirit" didn't characterize the relationship between all members of a class at once: "[I]t is perfectly clear that [class spirit] is not a universal acquaintance of each man with six hundred men. That is nonsense. There is nothing at all in that sort of acquaintance." Rather, according to Eliot, class spirit was built on the simultaneity of intellectual experience, what he called the "propinquity and contemporaneousness" of campus life. Six hundred students gain a coherent and meaningful sense of community at Harvard, Eliot argued, through the "complex influence" of contemporaneous experience:

> Here is a group of men, for instance, who enter Harvard College at the same time, and are in it together for three or four years. They are all subjected to similar influences, partly the influence of their studies, partly the influence of their society, partly the influence of the men they hear lecture or preach, or talk. It is a very complex influence[.] ... But in any case it is a contemporary influence on this group of persons that entered in one and the same year into Harvard College. Now that is a real bond of union, and that is the gist of class feeling,—the fact

that this group of men have been subjected simultaneously to these intellectual and moral influences and powers, and while they have all been growing, developing, and gathering strength and purpose. And then there is a curious effect of this contemporaneousness,—that they all get inspired by the ideals of the time, their college time, and those ideals hold right through life.[23]

This group of men, "gathering strength and purpose" at the same time together at school, did not, for Eliot, necessarily consist of an entire class, however. He went on to argue in the speech that, as the elective system has superseded the old coursework program, a more intensely contemporaneous scholastic experience has followed, one that brings together students undertaking the same intellectual and professional projects. "Your intellectual interests may be shared with seniors, juniors, sophomores, freshmen, and graduates,—with all the varieties of men that make up one of our large lecture courses, for instance," Eliot explained. "Now that indicates the width of this contemporaneousness in this Institution; and therein we differ from many other American colleges. Our classifications for purposes of study are not by class; they are much wider than that. Nevertheless, in these study groups may often be laid the foundations of mutual acquaintance, of friendship, and of prolonged association." The prolonged associations made possible by the elective system might operate on a smaller scale than the associations forged in the context of a single class, based as they are on specialized intellectual interests, but because these associations cut across classes, Eliot insists, somewhat counterintuitively, that these study groups are "wider"—having more "width of this contemporaneousness"—than the associations traditionally available in institutions of higher education. So just as Eliot explained in the "Relations" speech that learned societies can encourage faculty members to cultivate mutual sympathies that reach beyond individual institutions by meeting annually and semi-annually, in the 1905 address he maintained that the elective system could produce associations that reach beyond individual classes and courses.[24]

The propinquity and contemporaneousness of the elective system would appear perhaps only to further fragment the temporality of the school and the social experience of its constituents. No longer able to share in the "class spirit" of the traditional curriculum, students in the modern educational system instead enter into distinct disciplinary communities, each organized according to its own temporal logic, with chemistry majors undergoing one specific experience of academic time, English majors another, and so on. Yet the brilliance of Eliot's course unit is that it reconciles these proliferating temporalities under the "complex influence" of the campus experience; it makes these temporalities translatable with each other, establishing an equivalence between chemistry coursework and English coursework. The course unit thereby imposes unity on an otherwise un-unified curricular experience. It creates a common identity for the school's otherwise professionally heterogeneous graduates based on timing. The course unit, in this sense, has ensured a measure of contemporaneous and prolonged acquaintance within the vast landscape of US formal education, as college students from Colorado to Pennsylvania, from Alaska to New York, can all bond with one another over the misery of having to wake up early on a Friday morning to attend class. This kind of temporal coordination, which the modern school has evolved elaborate administrative technologies to carry out, undoubtedly falls short of the ideal Eliot articulated. Henry Adams and Gertrude Stein both were present at Harvard as Eliot's institutional reforms took hold; educated under a school system they found unsatisfyingly asynchronous, they formalized synchronicity in their writing. In doing so, we'll see, they performed a tremendous service for the educational system whose administrative apparatus they felt was inadequate.

Lonely Time Travelers

Jackson Lears's *No Place of Grace: Antimodernism and the Transformation of American Culture 1880–1920* (1981) ends with a chapter on Henry Adams. "In his restless experimentation with contrariety and process, in his refusal to rest content with unity or stasis, in his acceptance of the fragmented self in a fragmented universe, Adams prefigured the 'modern consciousness' celebrated by many avant-garde artists and intellectuals in the twentieth century," Lears writes.

> But the notion of Adams as "modernist" must be qualified. ... He clung to a wavering hope for an infinite framework of meaning, though it might seem incomprehensible to his own mind; he could never celebrate self-fulfillment, though it might seem preferable to Unitarian moralism. He preserved an enduring protest against America's emerging secular culture. He remained, to the end, an antimodern modernist.

The extended attention Lears pays to Adams in this last chapter is somewhat unusual in the larger architecture of *No Place of Grace*. While the earlier chapters in the book are each a tour de force of cultural history, demonstrating how far, say, the martial ideal spread across turn-of-the-century US life, shared by the US president Theodore Roosevelt, the philosopher William James, the poets Richard Hovey and Louise Guiney, the novelist Frank Norris, and the historian Brooks Adams, the final chapter is striking because it exchanges breadth for depth, narrowing in on a single historical figure. Adams is worthy of this attention, Lears suggests, because his work is both representative of the anti-modern impulse and its most sophisticated instantiation: "More imaginatively than any of his contemporaries, Adams explored modern dilemmas of authority," Lears writes at the beginning of the chapter. And yet, Lears is drawn to Adams not just because his work is representative of its historical moment, but also because his work "prefigure[s]" a new historical moment, the rise of a "'modern consciousness' celebrated by many avant-garde artists and intellectuals in the twentieth century."[25]

It makes sense, for Lears, then, to end his study of turn-of-the-century US culture with an extended discussion of Henry Adams, the chronologically liminal author who looks backward and forward, the "anti-modern modernist." Lears is not the only critic for whom Adams plays an indispensable periodizing role. According to John Carlos Rowe, Adams marks a rupture with the past and the emergence of a modern consciousness. In his essay, "Henry Adams's *Annis Mirabilis*: 1900 and the Making of a Modernist" (1991), Keith R. Burich writes: "Adams found hope amidst the uncertainty and doubt of the new century, particularly in its science. Adams's willingness to explore and ultimately embrace the strange and foreboding 'multiverse' ... marked his emergence as a modernist." A number of significant scholarly monographs on US literature either begin or end with Henry Adams. Jennifer Fleissner's *Women, Compulsion, Modernity* (2004) starts improbably with a reading of *The Education of Henry Adams*. Gavin Jones's *Failure and the American Writer* (2014) begins with a chapter on Adams, arguing that *The Education* contains both "a modernist ethos" of failure and a more interesting nineteenth-century investment in the "form as well as theory" of failure.[26]

Adams's status as a key periodizing figure in cultural history would, of course, seem deeply ironic, considering his famous suspicion of historiography, a suspicion Lears in the passage above gestures toward when he refers to Adams's "refusal to rest content with unity or stasis."[27] For Lears, it's precisely Adams's rejection of the cause and effect of historical narrative—his "acceptance of the fragmented self in a fragmented universe"—that makes him so easy to slip into a historical sequence, his work marking a neat transition between nineteenth-century unity and twentieth-century multiplicity. The fact that Adams, a writer known for rejecting historical narratives, is himself central to educators' historical narratives isn't exactly ironic or merely perverse; it is very much appropriate. Adams's writings might reflect a loss of historicity, but they also demonstrate the awfulness of living without a stable historical scaffolding, the terror of living without temporal bearings. Far from disavowing historiography, as many critics have suggested, Adams's work elicits the very historical narratives—the very periodization—that Adams restlessly struggled to conceive in his own lifetime and that teachers have constructed around him since.

Adams's conviction that he is unmoored in time, that he is a lonely man without a stable period, surfaces again and again in his writing. In the preface to *Mont Saint Michel and Chartres* (1904), he expends a curious amount of energy adapting two unidentified lines of Elizabethan verse. "Who reads me, when I am ashes,/Is my son in wishes" becomes under Adams's revision, at first, "Who reads me, when I am ashes, is my nephew in wishes," because, according to Adams, "[t]he relationship, between reader and writer, of son and father, may have existed in Queen Elizabeth's time, but is much too close to be true for ours." This adaptation proves problematic for Adams too, though—nephews, he explains "no longer read at all"—and so he settles on nieces, or actually just one niece. "For convenience of travel in France ... the nieces shall count as one only. As many more may come as like, but one niece is enough for the uncle to talk to, and one niece is much more likely than two to listen." Not "son" or "nephew," then, but maybe "nieces" and more likely just one "niece": it's an odd way to begin a book about medieval architecture. Adams's ambition in this exercise is to make visible the historiographic labor required to take readers on an imaginative journey through time, transporting the sixteenth-century couplet to a twentieth-century audience (with some attendant clumsiness), just as *Mont Saint Michel* will transport its twentieth-century audience to medieval France. More fundamentally, though, the awkwardness of Adams's adaptation—the forced avuncularity of the whole address—reflects the intense feelings of loneliness that always seemed to accompany him on his historical travels. Begging us to come along with Adams on his journey and end Adams's isolation, the preface further isolates.[28]

The question that perplexes Adams in *The Education* involves precisely this feeling of isolation in time. "What could become of such a child of the seventeenth and eighteenth centuries," Adams writes in the opening pages, "when he should wake up to find himself required to play the game of the twentieth?" In the book it becomes clear that this child will suffer social alienation. When Adams moves to Washington, DC, in 1892, he feels cut off from everyone else in the city: "His father and mother were dead. All his family led settled lives of their own. Except for two or three friends in Washington, who were themselves uncertain of stay, no one cared whether he came or went, and he cared least. There was nothing to care about." Adams's experience of isolation intensifies over the subsequent years: "Adams had long ceased going into society. For years he had not dined out of his own house, and in public his face was as unknown as that of an extinct statesman." "Adams found himself alone," he writes later, describing his time in DC around 1901. In the last decades of his life, Adams's social interactions appear to consist almost exclusively of sporadic trips around the world with other people's families: he travels with Senator Donald Cameron's family to South Carolina, Chicago, England, and Switzerland; he travels with the Cabot Lodges across Europe, to France, Italy, and Germany; and he travels with the Hays to Egypt.[29]

Throughout *The Education*, Adams attributes his feelings of loneliness not to any specific biographical detail, like his wife's suicide in 1885, but rather to his experience of time. He explains in the first chapter of *The Education*: "Whatever was peculiar about him was education, not character, and came to him, directly and indirectly, as the result of that eighteenth-century inheritance which he took with his name."[30] Adams indeed was not actually born in the eighteenth century— and Adams himself was not in fact a time traveler—but when he describes himself as a member of by-gone era "wak[ing] up" to play the game of the twentieth century, he locates his book within a whole nineteenth-century tradition of time traveling literature. He places himself alongside those other characters who wake up in strange historical periods, characters featured in stories such as Washington Irving's "Rip Van Winkle" (1819), Edward Bellamy's *Looking Backward: 2000–1887* (1888), and Mark Twain's *Connecticut Yankee in King Arthur's Court* (1889).

Adams often imagined historiography as a sort of time travel. In letters he wrote to John Hay describing his visits to medieval cathedrals, he cast himself as a warrior-farmer actually living in the thirteenth century. "I can almost remember the faith that gave me energy, and the sacred boldness that made my towers seem to me so daring[.] … Within I had no doubts. … There is not a stone in the whole interior which I did not treat as though it were my own child."[31] At the beginning of *Mont Saint Michel*, Adams explains that "[t]he man who wanders into the twelfth century is lost, unless he can grow prematurely young," and this confusing chronological imperative—to "grow" "prematurely" "young"—is realized in the book for readers as an experience of time travel. For instance, when Adams describes Saint Michel cathedral, he has his audience inhabit the eleventh century in the present tense: "We never fail to make our annual pilgrimage to the Mount on the Archangel's day, October 16. We expect to be called out for a new campaign which Duke William threatens against Brittany[.] … The year is 1058." Though this time-travel framing might seem playful, it is not simply meant as a joke. Adams's chronological dislocations, as he represents them in his major works, lead him to live the life of a miserable and lonely time traveler, out of sync with everybody else in society.[32]

To be sure, many of the most famous nineteenth-century time travelers suffer bouts of loneliness as they leap decades, or centuries, backward and forward in time. When Rip Van Winkle awakens after twenty years of sleep, his "heart died away at hearing of these sad changes in his home and friends, and finding himself thus alone in the world[.] … [H]e had no courage to ask after any more friends, but cried out in despair, 'Does nobody here know Rip Van Winkle?'" A similar moment of horror strikes Julian West, protagonist of Bellamy's *Looking Backward*, when, after adjusting to life in the year 2000, he appears to wake up back in the nineteenth century. "But when I had expected now surely the faces around me to light up with emotions akin to mine, they grew ever more dark, angry, and scornful," Bellamy writes. "'Put the fellow out!' exclaimed the father of my betrothed, and at the signal the men sprang from their chairs and advanced upon me." At the end of *Connecticut Yankee*, Hank Morgan travels back to the present day while leaving his wife, Sandy, and his daughter, Hello-Central, behind in the past. He mutters to himself, "Yes, I seemed to have flown back out of that age into this of ours, and then forward to it again, and was set down, a stranger and forlorn in that strange England, with an abyss of thirteen centuries yawning between me and you! between me and my home and my friends! between me and all that is dear to me, all that could make life worth living! It was awful—awfuler than you can ever imagine, Sandy." Adams, we might say, lingers on these moments of sadness in *The Education*; he dwells on these moments so that the loneliness of the time traveler comes to constitute his entire being.[33]

Against the alienating experience of time under industrial modernity, *The Education* holds up synchronized social relationships as an ideal. Adams, for instance, recounts the moment he meets his friend, Clarence King, as one of temporal synchronization. Having "wander[ed] off alone on his mule" during a trip out west in Estes Park, Adams loses track of time. "Hour after hour the sun moved westward and the fish moved eastward, or disappeared altogether, until at last when the fisherman cinched his mule, sunset was nearer than he thought." Trusting his mule to guide him back to a cabin at the entrance of the park, Adams is eventually rescued from his solitude: "As the mule came up to the cabin door, two or three men came out to see the stranger," one of whom is the geologist King. "Adams fell into [King's] arms," he writes. "As with most friendships, it was never a matter of growth or doubt. Friends are born in archaic horizons; ... they have nothing to do with the accident of space." Meeting someone at the entrance to a park in Colorado when you are wandering aimlessly on your mule does, indeed, have at least a *little* to do with the accident of space. Adams's formulation here is striking because it effaces the spatial in order to emphasize the temporal qualities of friendship. For Adams, the story of meeting Clarence King begins with disorientation in time and ends with a fortuitous moment of synchronization, and this moment of synchronization, in Adams's imagination, comes to characterize friendship as such. Friendship, according to Adams, persists through time; it is established in "archaic horizons."[34]

Periodization is appealing under these conditions because it promises to harmonize the chaotic experience of modern life, converting the isolations of a disordered temporality into a sensible order. By no means, however, does the appeal of periodization guarantee for Adams that periodization is actually possible. Consider the opening chapter of *The Education*, where Adams recounts his childhood in Massachusetts. The world of Adams's youth is divided between the strictures of Boston during the winter and the freedom of Quincy during the summer. "The chief charm of New England was harshness of contrasts and extremes of sensibility—a cold that froze the blood, and a heat that boiled it," Adams writes. "The violence of the contrast was real and made the strongest motive of education[.]" He goes on:

> Winter and summer, cold and heat, town and country, force and freedom, marked two modes of life and thought, balanced like lobes of the brain. Town was winter, confinement, school, rule, discipline; ... above all else, winter represented the desire to escape and go free. Town was restraint, law, unity. Country,

only seven miles away, was liberty, diversity, outlawry, the endless delight of mere sense impressions given by nature for nothing, and breathed by boys without knowing it.

The spatial and temporal organization of his childhood in Massachusetts reflects the central antinomy of education as Adams conceives it—the antinomy between order and disorder, unity and multiplicity. "The bearing of the two seasons on the education of Henry Adams was no fancy," Adams writes pages later. "[I]t was the most decisive force he ever knew; it ran through life, and made the division between its perplexing, warring, irreconcilable problems, irreducible opposites, with growing emphasis to the last year of study."[35]

The irony of these passages is that they present the book's central antinomy in neatly schematic terms. That is, they render the irreconcilable conflict between order and disorder as an orderly binary: as he presents it, Adams's childhood is helpfully and satisfyingly periodized between a winter term and a summer vacation. But lest we believe that Adams has succeeded in absorbing the multiplicity of experience into the unity of form, the opening chapter proceeds to undermine the binary that Adams has just established. The anecdote that structures the "Quincy" chapter involves Adams's grandfather, the former president John Quincy Adams, dragging Henry, the reluctant boy, to school one day. "[Adams] distinctly remembered standing at the house door one summer morning in a passionate outburst of rebellion against going to school," he writes. "Putting on his hat, [the former president] took the boy's hand without a word, and walked with him, paralyzed by awe, up the road to the town." Though this anecdote seems to illustrate the very schematic that Adams has elaborated—dramatically pitting authority and rule against rebellion and freedom—it also reveals the deficiency of the scheme. Adams confronts authority here during the summer, in Quincy, rather than during the winter, in Boston. The binary between winter and summer, town and country, order and disorder breaks down. Adams's periodization doesn't quite periodize.[36]

The opening chapter of *The Education* thus suggests at once the appeal of periodization and its inevitable failure. It also of course offers a critique of formal education in the United States. Far from facilitating the educational process, the school in this episode imposes its artificial order onto a disordered universe. "Summer was the multiplicity of nature," Adams writes. "[W]inter was school." Statements like this confirm Adams's earlier suggestion that an antiquated education has unfitted him for modern life, that "[w]hatever was peculiar about him was education ... and came to him, directly and indirectly, as the result of that eighteenth-century inheritance which he took with his name." The school appears in *The Education* as the formal institution most responsible for dislocating Adams in time, and its inability to adequately periodize historical experience is concretized later in the book, when Charles Eliot enlists Henry Adams to teach history at Harvard. According to Adams, the History Department had divided the study of history into "classical courses" and "modern courses." Between the two, Adams explains, "lay a gap of a thousand years" that he, the medievalist, is "expected to fill." As in the opening "Quincy" chapter, where the winter/summer periodization breaks down, the school's classical/medieval/modern periodization doesn't work either. "The task was doomed to failure for a reason which he could not control," Adams writes. "History is a tangled skein that one may take up at any point, and breaks when one has unravelled enough."[37]

Notwithstanding Adams's conviction, expressed in this same episode, that "history" is, "[i]n essence, incoherent and immoral," *The Education* frantically searches for a periodizing scheme that will bring coherence to historical experience, and it dramatizes this search for periodicity against the malfunctioning periodizations of the school. Adams's periodizing impulse expresses itself in an insistent rhetorical tick that appears throughout the opening chapters of the book. Describing his days as a schoolboy, Adams remarks that "Latin and Greek, he could, with the help of the modern languages, learn more completely by the intelligent work of six weeks than in the six years he spent on them at school." The ratio cited here—six weeks: six years—is just one of many Adams invokes in *The Education*. Sentences later, Adams makes a similar assessment: "[H]ad his father kept the boy at home, and given him half an hour's direction every day, he would have done more for him than school ever could do[.]" When Adams narrates his experience at Harvard, he offers a similar formulation: "The entire work of the four years could have been easily put into the work of any four months in after life." At another point, he sums up his entire experience within the institutions of US formal education: "Adams knew only that he would have felt himself on a more equal footing with [his contemporaries] ... had he not thrown away ten years of early life in acquiring what he might have acquired in one." Undertaking graduate study in Berlin, Adams observes that students under the German lecture system "could have learned from books or discussion in a day more than they could learn from him in a month[.]"[38]

Each of these ratios presents Adams with an opportunity to denigrate formal education for its management of time, suggesting that the student experience in school is out of sync with—indeed, slower than—the student experience outside of school, whether "at home" or "later in life." The ratio as a form presents itself as a potential solution to this academic mismanagement, however. Working not unlike Charles Eliot's course unit, Adams's ratios break up time into discrete temporal units and then make these units translatable with each other, allowing Adams to compare, say, the half hour he might have spent outside of school under the direction of his father to the entire day he actually did spend in school. And yet, if the ratios serve to coordinate time, they also register the breakdown of temporal coordination altogether. One of these ratios may make sense on its own, but when one ratio follows right after another, and then another after that, the effect tends to bewilder more than clarify. What is the relationship between these ratios? Does Adams's claim that he could have acquired in one year out of school the same education he acquired over ten years in school *include* his other claim that he could have learned Latin and Greek in six weeks with the help of modern languages, as opposed to the six years he spent on them in school? Or are the two ratios independent of each other, referring to two different school times (the time spent on languages versus the time spent on everything else), and two different out-of-school times (the time he could have dedicated to education entirely on his own or with his father)? The proliferation of these ratios throughout *The Education* confirms Adams's sense that time under the institutions of modernity is unmanageable: Adams, in attempting to orient himself in time, only succeeds in further disorienting himself.

The Education as a whole reads as a rather melancholic text that dramatizes Adams's desperate search for coherence in a fundamentally incoherent universe, a universe that Adams at one point, after the sudden death of his sister, calls a "phantasm, a nightmare, an insanity of force."[39] The pathos of Adams's quest for unity is encoded in the iterative structure of *The Education*, whose chapters, again, appear to provide a helpful and satisfying periodicity that in the end proves deficient. One indication that these chapters aren't as coherent as they appear is the erratic and unstandardized time spans they encompass: "Quincy," for instance, covers 1838 to 1848 and "Boston" 1848 to 1854; "Rome," meanwhile, covers 1859–1860 and "Diplomacy" just 1861. Most destabilizing of all is the notorious gap between Chapters XX and XXI, the twenty-year interval stretching from 1872 to 1892 that Adams doesn't narrate. These twenty years appear, on the one hand, eminently periodizable, cordoned off, as they are, into their own discrete unit. On the other hand, they are treated as an unreadable blank in the autobiographical record, unassimilated into the book and falling outside of its chapter structure. As an unintegrated supplement to Adams's educational narrative, these twenty years form a kind of anti-period that suggests the insufficiency of the organizational scheme that inexplicably excludes them.

The Education is thus propelled by a restless search for a periodizing rationale that the book never, finally, discovers. As Jennifer Fleissner has explained, the aesthetic achievement of Adams's work lies, like the church of Saint Thomas's, "not on its perfected unity but on the way that unity appears to us as inseparable from the revelation of the chaos it sought, impossibly, to overcome[.]" According to Fleissner and Lears, Adams's indefatigable but failed search for unity is at the heart of his critique of modernity—it is indeed exactly what gives his critique its force.[40] Yet Adams's critique of modernity has also proved uniquely useful for modern institutions. *The Education*'s failure to periodize is precisely what has allowed the modern school system to periodize it: for so many scholars and teachers, Adams's failure has come to mark the emergence of something distinct from what came before it, the rise of a "modern consciousness" or simply modernism.

Literary critics recently have bemoaned their discipline's dependence on the period as an organizing unit within scholarship. Eric Hayot has lamented "the near-total dominance of the concept of periodization in literary studies, a dominance that amounts to a collective failure of imagination and will on the part of the literary profession." Caroline Levine has claimed that "institutions themselves are composed of overlapping repetitions and durations, which routinely violate the frame of periodization that typically organizes historicist scholarship."[41] In both Hayot and Levine's polemics, the "period" functions as a unit of analysis that institutions impose on literature in an at best arbitrary and at worst misleading fashion. For Hayot, the period yields a certain limited set of interpretive possibilities that other concepts could also produce. The period, in consequence, according to Hayot, needs to be supplemented and challenged through the institutionalization of "a variety of competing concepts[.]" For Levine the period represents a betrayal of the very nature of institutional life. "Far from organizing social time into discrete periods," she writes, "institutions effectively compel us to live in multiple periods at once."[42]

The desire for synchronicity and periodization in Adams's writing does not indeed anticipate the "near-total dominance" the period currently enjoys in English departments across the United States. But it does suggest that periodization isn't always arbitrarily or misleadingly imposed on the objects of scholarly analysis, that sometimes a period is demanded by the objects of analysis themselves. Though institutions, in Levine's account, are "never present as such" because they "are materialized *across* time, through performative processes that cite prior events in every moment of their instantiation," the modern school system since its inception has nevertheless attempted to produce an approximately synchronous student experience, whether through the course unit or periodization. Institutions might never be present as such, pace Levine, but that is at least in part because "the present as such" does not exist, as Henry Adams discovered long ago.[43] By teaching *The Education*—by constructing historical periods around Adams's writing—educators have helped synchronize the student experience. They have imposed some measure of uniformity on the overwhelmingly non-uniform temporality of twentieth- and twenty-first-century life. The academic reception of *The Education* therefore reflects the fundamental reciprocity between a literary work and its institutional environment. Just as schools have sought to periodize literature, literature has sought to periodize schools.

Always Waiting

Fifteen years after Henry Adams left his faculty position at Harvard, Gertrude Stein enrolled at the Annex, an institute for women's education that was chartered just one year later as Radcliffe College. By all accounts Stein thrived in school, taking advantage of the many resources Harvard offered: she attended a philosophy class with George Santayana and a psychology class with Hugo Münsterberg; the composition course she took her sophomore year, English 22, was the course that, one year later, inspired Frank Norris to write *Vandover and the Brute* and *McTeague*. Stein served as secretary of the Harvard Philosophy Club and became very active in the psychology laboratory, working closely with Münsterberg and William James, eventually publishing two academic papers, "Normal Motor Automatism" (1896), co-written with Leon Solomons, another James student, and "Cultivated Motor Automatism" (1898), written alone. "I thank you above all for that model-work you have done in the laboratory and the other courses wherever I met you," Münsterberg wrote to Stein on June 10, 1895. "My contact with Radcliffe was in every way a most charming part of my Cambridge experiences. But while I met there all types and kinds of students, you were to me the ideal student, just as a female student ought to be[.]" This sort of qualified praise was not unusual for Stein. William James called her his "most brilliant woman student." After she graduated from Harvard, Stein enrolled in the medical school at Johns Hopkins, where she worked with the physiologist Franklin Paine Mall. In June 1901, she left Hopkins without earning a degree, and in 1903 she settled in Paris with her brother Leo.[44]

Although many scholars have debated whether and how Stein's experience at the Harvard laboratories and Hopkins medical school shaped her later writing— the experimentalism of her experimental work, the empiricism or anti-empiricism or the radical empiricism of her prose and poetry—few have examined the significance of the emergent school system as a whole to her work.[45] In Cambridge and Baltimore, Stein became friends with many educational reformers, including Edith Hamilton, Mabel Foote Weeks, Alfred Hodder, and Mary Mackall Gwinn.[46] Many of Stein's first attempts at fiction took up the school as a site of narrative drama, whether the themes she wrote as a student in English 22 in the 1890s or the more extensive pieces of prose fiction she wrote later, like *Q.E.D.* (1903), *Fernhurst* (1904), "Melanctha" (1909), and *The Making of Americans* (1925).[47] When Stein lived in Baltimore, she even delivered two public lectures on the higher learning, "The Value of College Education for Women" (1899) and "Degeneration in American Women" (c. 1901).[48] These polemics appear to offer two contradictory arguments about the US school system— one speaks of the benefits, and the other of the disastrous consequences of college education for women—but in fact they both articulate a continuous set of concerns about American schooling, how the educational system should operate and what kinds of preparation it should provide students. The compatibility between these two seemingly incompatible arguments about higher education lies in Stein's anxiety about institutional time, her preoccupation with the school's ability, or inability, to coordinate the social and biological clock.

The argument Stein makes in favor of college education in "The Value of College Education for Women" (1899) draws heavily on the evolutionary science she learned as an undergraduate at Harvard. According to Stein, one of the central problems facing the nineteenth-century woman was "the greater lengthening of her infancy." Stein meant by this that "a woman now takes about seven years longer to mature than her mother did. Not so very many years ago a woman was considered perfectly ready to marry at seventeen. ... [W]e now consider that former age utterly absurd and realise that a girl of 17 is hopeless[ly] immature." The more human beings develop as a species, Stein claimed in the lecture, the longer will our youth experience a prolonged period of helplessness, so even though at one time "boys of 16 and 17 were capable of ruling countries[,] of controlling armies, now they are only looked upon as infants"; and even though in the past "the demands of the world upon the woman were very much less," now "when she is beginning to have her race function as a human being" and "when the responsibilities of motherhood have become so much more complex" the modern woman begins to find "that she too needs an extended infancy in order to rightly prepare for her work in the world."[49]

How can the school help American women manage this prolonged infancy and prepare for motherhood? Instead of sending girls into society for five or six years, where they do "[n]othing in the wide world except the task of the peacock, the spreading of his tail before an admiring audience," a task that, Stein concedes, is important but "could surely be accomplished in less time and in fact used to be accomplished in less time," Stein believed girls should go to college, where they would become more capable of carrying out their evolutionary duty: the school, she says, "teaches the value and enforces obedience to these musts." "You may not have been taught how to cook [at college]," Stein declares, "but you have had the training that makes that knowledge easily acquired[.] [Y]ou may not have been taught how to run a house but you have been taught the mental habits that are most needfull [sic] for that performance."[50]

If Stein in "The Value of College Education for Women" defends the school, claiming that it assists in the evolutionary process and instrumentalizes a period of extended infancy by turning five or six years of peacocking in society into four years of serious training for motherhood, in "Degeneration in American Women," she excoriates the school for failing to use time properly, for wasting valuable biological time. The key evidence Stein cites in this lecture are statistics indicating that women who go to college bear fewer children than women who don't. "In private practice in St. Louis Engelmann finds among the Americans of American parentage 1.7 children to a marriage and Americans of foreign parentage 1.9 children to a marriage," she explains. "Among college women the results are still worse the average number of children to a marriage being 1.3 children to 1.6 while the non college women of the same class and in the same city gives a record of 2.1." Stein provides a biological and cultural explanation for this "sterility" among college graduates. Biologically, Stein claims that "the normal period of fertility for a woman is from her eighteenth to her forty fifth year and that unless labor has so to speak cleared a passage, from her twenty fifth year on there is a gradual hardening of all her genitalia making conception rarer, miscarriages more frequent and labor much more dangerous." The problem with the "modern system of education," in Stein's opinion is that "the heaviest mental strain is put upon the girl when her genitalia is making its heaviest physical demand and when her sexual desires are being constantly stimulated without adequate physiological relief, a condition that obtains to a very considerable extent in our average American college life." As a result, the school "induce[s] of necessity a weakening of the genitalia and a consequent increase of absolute and relative physiological sterility."[51]

Culturally, Stein believes that "among the educated classes in this country, that is among the educated women and among the pseudo educated women there is a strong tendency to what we may call the negation of sex and the exaltation of the female ideal of moral and methods and a condemnation and abhorrence of virility." Because college graduates exalt this female ideal, women fail to respect the matrimonial and maternal function; they fail to understand that "the only serious business of life in which they cannot be entirely outclassed by the male is that of child bearing." Stein admits that "[o]f course it is not meant that there are not a few women in every generation who are exceptions to this rule," but she also maintains that "these exceptions are too rare to make it necessary to subvert the order of things in their behalf and besides if their need for some other method of expression is a real need there is very little doubt but that the opportunity of expression will be open to them."[52]

Where Stein's biological explanation foregrounds the failure of the school system to coordinate evolutionary time with the time of civilized society—women are under the most physical and mental strain at school when their bodies should be committed to reproduction—Stein's cultural explanation also suggests, only more obliquely, that the school system's failure is a temporal one. Before, in "The Value of College Education," Stein argues that the school could correct five or six years of prolonged infancy by providing helpful training for motherhood. In "Degeneration," Stein argues instead that the time spent in school doesn't instrumentalize these wasted years, that the preparation and training women receive at school doesn't better fit them for motherhood. One of the key problems with the educational system, Stein insists, in a reversal from her last lecture, is that it makes the educated woman "mistake a knowledge of facts for training in method and makes her believe it possible for her to learn by a few lectures the things one only gets after years spent day after day in the daily round of working, listening and waiting."[53]

Stein's friends in educational reform were horrified after they read "Degeneration in American Women"—Mamie Gwinn, when she encountered the lecture, said that Stein's mother must have been a nervous invalid.[54] Stein's anxieties about academic time nevertheless persisted despite her friends' horror and became an animating force in her early writings. Although in the "Degeneration" lecture Stein maintains that the school system's unsatisfactory handling of time will have long-term consequences—a drop in fertility rate, the degeneration of the species—in her first major works the consequences of this mismanagement are much more immediate and personal. As it is in Henry Adams's work, the botched education received by the main characters in *Q.E.D.* and "Melanctha" leads to overwhelming feelings of social isolation and loneliness. For Stein, this manifests in the form of waiting.

In "Melanctha," the middle story of Stein's first published book *Three Lives* (1909), Jeff Campbell is late to a meeting with Melanctha just after the two begin their romance. "Jeff Campbell had always all his life loved to be with people, and he had loved all his life always to be thinking, but he was still only a great boy, was Jeff Campbell, and he had never before had any of this funny kind of feeling," the narrator explains. "Now, this evening, when he was free to go and see Melanctha, he talked to anybody he could find who would detain him, and so it was very late when at last he came to the house where Melanctha was waiting to receive him." We're supposed to recognize the "funny kind of feeling" Jeff Campbell experiences here as a major departure from his normal behavior: in Stein's typological understanding of human nature, Jeff Campbell is, at bottom, a thinker, someone who "loved all his life always to be thinking." But if, on one level, Jeff Campbell and Melanctha's relationship is premised on surmounting this core difference—Melanctha teaches Jeff Campbell to move beyond thinking, to feeling—on another level the "funny kind of feeling" Jeff Campbell experiences as a result of his interactions with Melanctha actually ends up exacerbating their core differences, proving that these core differences are in fact insurmountable. Though the friction between the two characters appears in any number of forms throughout the story—the repetitive movement of the plot, the circularity of their conversations—at this moment the characters' misunderstanding is figured temporally, as Jeff makes Melanctha wait for him: "Jeff came in to where Melanctha was waiting for him, and he took off his hat and heavy coat, and then drew up a chair and sat down by the fire."[55]

The temporal disjunction between Jeff and Melanctha is particularly striking at this moment in the story because, up until now, the narrator has described their relationship as synchronous. The romance between the two characters first blossoms over a series of nights when Jeff, a doctor, cares for Melanctha's dying mother. These nights are special for Jeff and Melanctha because their experience of time is harmonized, because they have the opportunity to share time together. "And so Jeff Campbell and Melanctha Herbert sat there on the steps, very quiet, a long time, and they didn't seem to think much, that they were together," Stein writes. "They sat there so, for about an hour, and then it came to Jefferson very slowly and as a strong feeling that he was sitting there on the steps, alone, with Melanctha." This synchronization eventually extends beyond the nights they spend together tending to Melanctha's mother and comes to define their relationship as a whole. "Jefferson and Melanctha now saw each other, very often," Stein writes. "They now always liked to be with each other, and they always now had a good time when they talked to one another. ... Melanctha was liking Jefferson Campbell better every day, and Jefferson was beginning to know that Melanctha certainly had a good mind[.]"[56]

Melanctha doesn't only share this feeling of simultaneity with Jeff, though; throughout the story, whenever her romantic relationships are going well, her satisfaction is registered temporally. Stein's description of Melanctha's first real romantic relationship—her relationship with Jane Harden—includes the amount of time the two spend together. "Melanctha would spend long hours with Jane in her room, sitting at her feet and listening to her stories," Stein writes. "Before the end came, the end of the two years in which Melanctha spent all her time when she was not at school or in her home, with Jane Harden, before these two years were finished, Melanctha had come to see very clear, and she had come to be very certain, what it is that gives the world its wisdom." Later, Melanctha spends all of her time with Rose: "Rose soon got to like Melanctha Herbert and Melanctha now always wanted to be with Rose, whenever she could do it."[57]

If each of the major romances in "Melanctha" starts with an intense feeling of togetherness in time, each also inevitably ends when the two characters fall out of sync with each other. Jeff's dawdling is significant in this sense because it represents how all of the relationships in the story fail, as the characters struggle to achieve synchronicity with one another. Importantly, Jeff's indecision isn't the only reason his relationship with Melanctha is asynchronous, although he is late at other times in the novel as well: "And so one evening, late, he was to go to her. He waited a little long, before he went to her. ... Melanctha sat there looking very angry, when he came in to her." Sometimes, by contrast, Melanctha makes Jeff wait for her: "Jeff waited to see if Melanctha would send any word to him. Melanctha Herbert never sent a line to him," and later, "When Jeff Campbell came to his house on Monday there was a note there from Melanctha. Could Jeff come the day after to-morrow, Wednesday? Melanctha was so sorry she had to go out that evening. She was awful sorry and she hoped Jeff would not be angry."[58]

Melanctha's isolation in time—being made to wait for others and making others wait for her—ultimately links her misery to the misery of the lonely time traveler Henry Adams. And for Stein in "Melanctha," as it is for Adams in *The Education*, the school system—that malfunctioning network of institutions tasked with each character's upbringing—bears responsibility for this asynchrony. Melanctha, we are told, "went to school" when she was young "and was very quick in all the learning[.]" Stein also explains that Melanctha's first lover, Jane Harden, attended college briefly: "Jane had had a good deal of education. She had been two years at a colored college. She had had to leave because of her bad conduct." Jeff Campbell, as a doctor, has spent the most time within the formal system of education. "The Campbell family had been very good to him and had helped him on with his ambition," the narrator explains. "Jefferson studied hard, he went to a colored college, and then he learnt to be a doctor."[59]

Q.E.D., the novel that Stein wrote in 1903 and eventually transformed into "Melanctha," in many ways makes the connection between the school and the characters' temporal misery more explicit. The novel follows the romantic drama that unfolds between three college graduates, Adele, Mabel Neath, and Helen Thomas. "All three of them were college bred American women of the wealthier class but with that all resemblance between them ended," the narrator explains. "Their appearance, their attitudes and their talk both as to manner and to matter showed the influence of different localities, different forebears and different family ideals." Many of the scenes of waiting in "Melanctha" come directly from *Q.E.D.*, as the three graduates' regional, racial, and familial differences are manifested most insistently in the narrative proper as asynchrony. As the narrator of *Q.E.D.* explains: "Their pulses were differently timed. [Adele] could not go so fast and Helen's exhausted nerves could no longer wait."[60] The fact that most of the main characters in "Melanctha" never graduated from college, and that Melanctha hasn't attended an institution of higher learning, is irrelevant, though. Read together, *Q.E.D.* and "Melanctha" demonstrate the failure of the educational system in the United States to overcome the essential differences, including temporal differences, that isolate individuals from one another. But while "Melanctha" incorporates these scenes of waiting directly from *Q.E.D.*, it also discovers a new literary mode for representing and overcoming this asynchrony through its attention to the rhythms of language.

As we've already seen in many of the passages from "Melanctha," characters yearn for a temporal harmony that finds expression in the vocabulary of "always." At one point, for instance, Stein writes that Jeff and Melanctha "always liked to be with each other," and "always now had a good time when they talked to one another"; at another point Stein writes that "Melanctha now always wanted to be with Rose, whenever she could do it." Constructions like these aren't rare in the story; the word "always" appears 743 times. Although in some cases the appearance of "always" holds more or less to the word's original meaning, referring to a phenomenon that persists for all time, and thus signaling a genuine connection between two characters, like the feeling of synchronization that Jeff and Melanctha share during their first nights together, the repetition of the word over and over again in the end undermines its more traditional definition, demonstrating the impossibility of establishing an enduring connection between characters or of maintaining true synchronization. "Jeff always loved now to be with Melanctha and yet he always hated to go to her," Stein writes at another point.

> Somehow he was always afraid when he was to go to her, and yet he had made himself very certain he would not be a coward. He never felt any of this being afraid, when he was with her. Then they always were very true, and near to one

another. But always when he was going to her, Jeff would like anything that could happen that would keep him a little longer from her.[61]

The meaning of "always" is marked as unstable from the very beginning of this passage, as Jeff oscillates between always loving *to be* with Melanctha and yet always hating *to go to her*. Though the distinction Stein draws in the passage is between Jeff's feeling when he is with Melanctha and Jeff's feeling when he is away from her, this distinction comes at the expense of "always," robbing the word of a coherent meaning. Jeff doesn't "always" seem to experience any one feeling, in other words; he seems instead to experience a shifting set of feelings, having one feeling under certain circumstances, for a brief period of time, and another under different circumstances. The impermanence of "always"—its inability to mean "always" throughout the passage—instantiates on the level of the sentence the story's larger concerns about the inability of individuals to share time with each other in a lasting way, the inability, that is, of characters to "always" be together. In this particular case, the impermanence of "always" on the level of the sentence drives the larger impermanence of "always" on the level of the story: Jeff's ambivalence as it's recapitulated in the passage causes him to search out "anything that could happen that would keep him a little longer from her," and this delay makes Melanctha wait.

The use of the word "always," then, is emblematic of Stein's larger aesthetic project and the formal innovations she inaugurated in "Melanctha." According to Stein herself, "Melanctha" transformed the representation of time in prose through its use of "insistence," a concept adjacent to, but very different from, "repetition." "[T]here can be no repetition," Stein proclaims in her essay, "Portraits and Repetition" (1935), "because the essence of that expression is insistence, and if you insist you must each time use emphasis and if you use emphasis it is not possible while anybody is alive that they should use exactly the same emphasis." Following Stein, we might say that the word "always" never repeats in "Melanctha": whatever emphasis it receives in a given instance fundamentally alters its meaning, making the word "always" refer not to some single meaning that remains stable across time but rather a meaning that shifts with every recurrence, producing an effect of immediacy and presence in the unfolding of language, what Stein in "Composition as Explanation" (1926) would call the "continuous present" or the "prolonged present." So if the insistent use of the word "always" instantiates the temporal isolation suffered by the main characters in "Melanctha"—the word affirms the fact that characters can't "always" be together, or feel the same way about each other for sustained periods of time—this insistence for Stein also has the power to produce in the act of reading an experience of simultaneity, of presence, that her characters can't realize.[62]

In her lecture "The Gradual Making of *The Making of Americans*" (1935), Stein rearticulates the aesthetic achievement of her early work:

> I began to get enormously interested in hearing how everybody said the same thing over and over again with infinite variations but over and over again until finally if you listened with great intensity you could hear it rise and fall and tell all that that there was inside them, not so much by the actual words they said or the thoughts they had but the movement of their thoughts and words endlessly the same and endlessly different.

Stein's discovery of the "rise and fall" of speech, the words not repetitive but "endlessly the same and endlessly different," is consistent with the distinction she draws between repetition and insistence in "Portraits," and the continuous present she describes in "Composition." This particular formulation is especially striking, however, because of its emphasis on the sociality of insistence. Understanding the movement of another's thoughts, endlessly the same and endlessly different, requires a shared rhythm, a temporal unity, between author and audience, speaker and listener. For Stein, this synchronization isn't easily acquired—it isn't intuitive or natural. To apprehend the continuous present and to share the rise and fall of another person's internal rhythms requires a tremendous effort on Stein's part, as she listens "with great intensity."[63]

The educational system is the institution that, over the twentieth century and into the twenty-first, has trained more readers than any other to attend to Stein's prose "with great intensity" and recognize her repetitions as insistence. Stein's prose has itself in turn shaped the modern school by harmonizing the student experience of time through the continuous present. Take these three close readings of Stein's work as evidence of the temporal harmony it has produced among readers in the academy. The first passages comes from Wendy Steiner's *Exact Resemblance to Exact Resemblance* (1978):

> Does "then" mean "at that time," "after that," or "as a result of that"? When we hear that "he was not then trying being a fat one or a very thin one" are we to think that he was trying to be a slightly thin one, or that he was not trying to be anything? And what is the relation between "trying" and "being a thin one"? Syntactically they are co-temporal—"When he was a very thin one he was ... trying being a thin one." But "trying" implies temporal-causal priority: first you try and then the result is achieved. If this is not the situation described, and the "trying" and "being" are semantically as well as syntactically co-temporal, then the "trying" is aimed at some other future "being," though it is accompanied by a related present "being." The ambiguity and complexity of this simple pair of verbs is another illustration of Stein's disruption of relationality in normal language use.

The second is from Michael North's *The Dialect of Modernism* (1994):

> Several times in the course of this story, Stein calls Jane Harden "a roughened woman" (pp. 104, 107). Thus, it would seem that her name is an appropriate one,

designating some essential hardness in her nature. Yet she is called "roughened," not "rough," and if what Stein says elsewhere is true and "people can be made by their names" then perhaps Jane was roughed up by her own name. Perhaps her "roughness" is merely an impression that others have about her. Or perhaps it designates her ability to "harden" others. But when Jeff Campbell accuses Melanctha of having "hard" ways like Jane, he exclaims, "I can't believe you mean them hardly" (p. 138) so that "hardly" means both hardly and hardly at all.

The third is from Natalia Cecire's *Experimental* (2019):

"Jeff Campbell now felt **in him** what everybody always had needed to make them really understanding, **to him**." Diegetic context illuminates the sense of the sentence: Jeff has learned that Melanctha's "understanding" (elsewhere "wisdom" and "learning") comes from her wide sexual experience and has extrapolated that such actions are *always* the condition of "understanding." Jeff apprehends this rather than knows it; he feels it "in him." The "to him" at the end of the sentence disrupts more than it clarifies; the most normative possible reading is that "to him" is redundant, and a more capacious reading would suggest that it raises semantic questions rather than putting them to rest: Does "to him" mean something different, in the context of the sentence, than "in him"? Does "to him" modify "understanding," so that the kind of understanding under consideration is specifically the kind approved by Jeff? The **preposition + him[self]** sequence in this passage thus impedes immediate grasp of the sentences' meaning, yet it does so not by "breaking" syntax but by reinforcing it, amping up its use of function words and *increasing* syntactic structure.[64]

Each of these scholars is making a different argument about Stein's work. Steiner is describing how Stein's literary portraits disrupt "relationality in normal language use" and thereby create a sense of immediacy and continuous presence. North claims that Stein's prose breaks down the power of language to attach attributes to things, and this is part of his larger argument about the masking function of dialect in Stein's work, the capacity of her writing to confront European conventions and push their contradictions (between nature and artifice, essence and accident) to radical extremes. Cecire insists that Stein's early fiction subscribes to an experimental science that aimed to invent an objective language based in abstraction rather than empirical detail. And yet, even though these critics are making different arguments, each one of their interpretations represents the act of reading as following a common temporal progression, from confusion to semantic or syntactic differentiation and finally to a conclusion. Whether the series of questions Steiner begins by posing ("Does ... ?" "are we ... ?" "and what ... ?") and then her final concluding remark ("... is another illustration of Stein's disruption of relationality"); or the set of contingent statements North makes at first ("it would seem ... " "Yet ... " "Perhaps ... " "Or perhaps ...") before he realizes that "'hardly' means both hardly and hardly at all"; or finally the questions Cecire asks ("Does ..." "Does ...") before landing on an explanation ("not by 'breaking' syntax but by reinforcing it")—all of these critics temporalize their interpretations, rendering their analysis as it emerges in the time of reading, a reading that follows the same rhythm, the same shifting emphases of Stein's language and the movement of her thoughts.

These excerpts in the end are representative of the experience Stein's work elicits from its academic readers, causing three individual, potentially idiosyncratic responses to her texts to follow a single standard pace of reading. If Stein developed the "continuous present" in response to the educational system's failures, the close readings performed by Steiner, North, and Cecire reflect how the educational system has claimed for itself the standardized time that Stein's writing elicits. Since the entry of Stein's work into the curriculum, the "continuous present" has therefore served to recalibrate academic time, providing a measure of comfort to those unfortunate students whose pulses beat at different intervals.

Coda: The Politics of Standard Time

Standard time, as the polemics I cited earlier from Benedict Anderson, Homi Bhabha, and Wai Chi Dimock indicate, is the object of much scholarly suspicion. So, too, is the course unit. In part, the suspicion surrounding the course unit stems from critics' belief that it fails to set meaningful academic standards. In part, however, this suspicion stems more predictably from the course unit's nefarious associations with ruling class interests. Early in the course unit's history, Thorstein Veblen accused it of corporatizing academic life. "Business principles take effect in academic affairs most simply, obviously and avowably in the way of businesslike administration of the scholastic routine," Veblen wrote in *The Higher Learning in America* (1918). "In all its bearings [academic] work is hereby reduced to a mechanistic, statistical consistency, with numerical standards and units; which conduces to perfunctory and mediocre work throughout, and acts to deter both students and teachers from the free pursuit of knowledge, as contrasted with the pursuit of academic credits." Clyde Barrow's *Universities and the Capitalist State* (1990) argues, too, that the Carnegie Foundation for the Advancement of Teaching was part of a larger movement that undertook to "achieve clearly identifiable and specific objectives such as the reorganization of academic labor markets and an investment of educational capital that was more favorable to business interests." In Barrow's account, the school system surrendered itself to the ruling class not simply by taking Andrew Carnegie's money but by adopting a broader corporate philosophy. The CFAT was managed by a nucleus of "corporate intellectuals": Henry S. Pritchett was not just the former president of MIT but also sat on the board of directors of the Atchison, Topeka, and Santa Fe Railroad; Nicholas Murray Butler served as president of Columbia University but also as director of the New York Life Insurance Company; Charles C. Harrison, provost at the University of Pennsylvania, had once worked in manufacturing. One of the major arguments the Carnegie Foundation marshaled in defense of the "unit" came from Morris L. Cooke, a protege of Frederick Taylor. In 1909, the CFAT published Cooke's *Academic and Industrial Efficiency*, with an introduction by Pritchett, which attempted to create a standardized statistical concept called the "student-hour." Universities were encouraged to use the student-hour to measure intellectual labor.[65]

Mark Garrett Cooper and John Marx's more recent account of the course unit in *Media U* (2018) is exceptional for its overall reluctance to take up this polemic. The argument of Cooper and Marx's book is that the research university is an institution that "bind[s] individuals into groups and certif[ies] hierarchical distinctions" through "feats of mediation." "Far more than shared syllabi, a shared measure of time spent in instruction held the postsecondary-education sector together," they write.

> Often maligned and underappreciated, the Carnegie Foundation's unit had awesome organizing power. ... [It] provided a framework to accommodate the array of institutions that composed the higher-education sector. It equally enabled the management of work within those institutions and freed them to encourage specialized courses of proliferating variety. Perhaps most significantly, it facilitated the organization of disciplines into departments and made it possible to imagine a potentially infinite series of both degrees and the departmental containers where they would be administered.

Cooper and Marx are not especially interested in the Carnegie-ism of the Carnegie unit—that is, the unit's relationship to industrial capitalism. As they explain in the book's introduction, *Media U* acknowledges that higher education has historically held an ambivalent position in the reproduction of social relations. They write, "We take it as given that the American university is propelled by a contradictory directive to flatten social hierarchy and reproduce it at the same time." To some, this formulation might seem inadequate. To "take it as given" that higher education is a political institution as well as a media institution, without explicitly explaining the connection between politics and mediation, might seem to elide the political altogether. Who or what, after all, "is propell[ing]" the university's "contradictory directive"?[66]

Yet Cooper and Marx's rather neutral framing is helpful here, I would suggest by way of conclusion, because it begins to reveal the inadequacy of a strictly corporatist account of the course unit. Such an account is inadequate, as I've tried to argue in this chapter, because it ignores the course unit's origins as an instrument of middle-class subjectivity, one conceived by educational reformers to give the graduates of the modern school a sense of collective identity and purpose.

Cooper and Marx's emphasis on the developments that the course unit made possible—"accommodat[ing] the array of institutions that composed the higher-education sector," "enabl[ing] the management of work within those institutions," and so on—usefully highlights the internal coherence that an institution must achieve before it can wield external political agency. I might mention, too, as I have already argued in this book, that the school system also needed to convince the public that academic credentials held value, that the years students spent in school were meaningful and not a waste of time. Without some administrative sophistication and broader social recognition, the modern educational system would never have come to function as an ideological instrument for a class of industrialists that sought to reduce white collar and professional labor, like all labor, to (in Veblen's words) "a mechanistic, statistical consistency." After all, the course unit evolved for decades under the supervision of educational reformers before the intervention of the CFAT, a fact suggesting that the modern school and its administrative technologies weren't simply the product of industrial capitalists.[67]

The scholarly failure to appreciate the political ambivalence of the course unit is in some sense forgivable. The organization of the school day into discrete temporal units has rarely presented itself to students as liberatory. Writing less than two decades after the institutionalization of the Carnegie unit, William Faulkner could famously narrate Quentin Compson's last day on earth as oscillating disorientingly between the stifling temporal regimentation of Harvard coursework and the temporal freedom of his own deep subjectivity.[68] For a vast majority of students, the organization of time in school is entirely apprehensible as the disciplinary project that it is—a project that, as Foucault once explained, forces its subjects to do not just "what one wishes," but also to "operate as one wishes, with the techniques, speed and the efficiency that one determines."[69] Charles Eliot, the chief architect of the course unit, believed that the coordination of scholastic time would enable new forms of collective experience and give the school's middle-class graduates a shared sense of purpose, yet overwhelming evidence indicates that the standardization of time in schools has only further alienated its students, has only indeed made them more miserable and feel more helpless under the capitalist system.

The irony of the course unit's history is in some sense the irony of the school's history and, also, the irony of the middle class's. Whatever distinct social identity the school and its middle-class graduates have achieved is, after all, one of their great assets in class warfare. The fantasy that the middle class is an independent or autonomous social formation has grounded its ideological appeal throughout the twentieth century. Eliot believed that institutional time would bring coherence to the middle class, but the middle class has tended to surrender its coherence whenever economically or politically expedient by affiliating itself with the ruling class and its political interests. This affiliation has brought with it certain advantages for professionals and administrators at the expense of the very collective identity that Eliot hoped the course unit would conjure into existence. But just because standard time has seemed to observers to operate outside of class struggle for this reason—just because, that is, standard time has appeared strictly as a weapon of ruling class domination—this doesn't mean that we should forget its emancipatory potential. For most, the standardization of time has seemed essentially oppressive, but for educators like Charles Eliot and for writers like Henry Adams and Gertrude Stein, it promised to produce a greater and more meaningful sense of collective endeavor, a richer and far less lonely existence.

4
Interest, Disgust

Now, it is very necessary that we should not flinch from seeing what is vile and debasing. There is filth on the floor, and it must be scraped up with the muck rake; and there are times and places where this service is the most needed of all services that can be performed. But the man who never does anything else, who never thinks or speaks or writes, save of the feats with the muck rake, speedily becomes, not a help but one of the most potent forces of evil.
—Theodore Roosevelt, "The Man with the Muck Rake" (1906)

Mrs. Bart had died— died of a deep disgust.
—Edith Wharton, *The House of Mirth* (1905)[1]

The turn of the twentieth century was an exceptionally disgusting time in US literary history. In 1906 Theodore Roosevelt delivered his famous "The Man with the Muck Rake" speech, reprimanding a group of journalists for thinking and speaking and writing exclusively of the filth on the floor. Although the intended targets of Roosevelt's speech were the journalists employed by William Randolph Hearst—particularly David Graham Phillips, whose series of articles, "The Treason of the Senate," exposed illicit campaign contributions—the speech's attack seems applicable not just to this specific strain of journalism but to the period's literary production more broadly.[2] In Stephen Crane's *Maggie: A Girl of the Streets* (1893), a man approaches a young unnamed prostitute, presumably the novel's protagonist: "He laughed, his brown, disordered teeth gleaming under a grey, grizzled moustache from which beer-drops dripped. His whole body gently quivered and shook like that of a dead jelly fish. Chuckling and leering, he followed the girl of the crimson legions." In the final chapter of Theodore Dreiser's *Sister Carrie* (1900), the novel's figure of downward mobility, George Hurstwood, waits with a crowd of men in front of a boarding house just before he ends his own life: "There was a face in the thick of the collection which was as white as drained veal. There was another red as brick. ... There were great ears, swollen noses, thick lips, and, above all, red, blood-shot eyes." In Edith Wharton's *The House of Mirth* (1905), the protagonist, once the darling of New York high society, dies of

Schools of Fiction. Morgan Day Frank, Oxford University Press. © Morgan Day Frank (2022).
DOI: 10.1093/oso/9780192867506.003.0005

a drug overdose, poor and alone. Like her mother before her, whose fate she is haltingly pulled toward over the course of the novel, this character, Lily Bart, dies of a deep disgust—disgusted by what surrounds her, she becomes an object of disgust herself.[3]

While writers wrote disgusting books at the turn of the century, teachers sought to organize the classroom experience around the interests of their students, and the relationship between these two seemingly unrelated developments—the emergence of a pedagogy of interest and a literature of disgust—will serve as the focus of this chapter. Student-centered pedagogy now dominates educational discourse, but this hasn't always been the case. Traditionally, formal education centered on learning goals and activities prescribed by teachers, who taught their students through strict rules, discipline, and corporal punishment, or (in the liberal arts) through disinterested inquiry.[4] One of the great ambitions of modern educational reform in the United States, however, was for schools to engage the interests and inclinations of the student population, and disgust, as writers theorized it in their work, acted as a literary rejoinder to this institutional ambition. Why did educational reformers at the turn of the century believe that student interest in particular was needed for the systemization of the modern school? And why was disgust for writers of the period the appropriate reaction to the expansion of the school system and its pedagogy of interest? If educators at the time found in interest a key mechanism for the expansion of the modern educational system, writers cultivated a literature of disgust in order to think through the limits of that system, to consider the system's boundaries. By luxuriating in disgust, turn-of-the-century authors gestured towards a range of feelings that lay beyond life in modern institutions, feelings that resisted the logic underwriting institutional growth.

It might seem implausible to suggest, as I do here, that the disgustingness of postbellum literature originated as a complex reaction to transformations in US formal education. Though scholars have yet to generate a robust account of disgust in this period, I imagine most would argue that it is simply a cultural outgrowth of industrialization and urbanization. This is at least Alfred Kazin's influential thesis in *On Native Grounds* (1942). "Our modern literature," he claims, is "rooted in that moving and perhaps inexpressible moral transformation of American life, thought, and manners under the impact of industrial capitalism." "[A]bove all," he goes on, this modern literature is "rooted in the need to learn what the reality of life was in the modern era."[5] However, Erich Auerbach's *Mimesis* (1946) provides a suggestive account of realism in the second half of the nineteenth century, albeit in a different national literary tradition, that links the emergence of disgusting literature to developments in the educational system. According to Auerbach, a sordid body of writing appeared in France alongside an urban middle-class reading public, a bourgeoisie that "had increased in numbers and, in consequence of the spread of education, had become able and willing to read." These bourgeois readers, exhausted from their daily labors, expected that literature and culture in general "should give them relaxation, recreation, and at best an easily attained intoxication[.]" In Auerbach's account, writers like Baudelaire, Flaubert, and the Goncourt's produced disgusting literature about urban poverty not as part of some political project but to advance the autonomy of the aesthetic and to distinguish their literary work from the "mass merchandise" typically consumed by the languid, educated bourgeois audience. "It is surprising but undeniable," Auerbach explains, "that the inclusion of the fourth estate in serious realism was decisively advanced by those who, in their quest for new aesthetic impressions, discovered the attraction of the ugly and pathological."[6]

More so than Auerbach, this chapter's account of the rise of disgusting literature emphasizes particular classroom practices and pedagogical theories, instead of ascribing this rise generally to the growth of an educated middle-class reading public. Auerbach nevertheless helps locate the origins of disgusting literature in a specific institutional environment where "literariness" is produced by, at once, the consolidation of a mass system of education and the rejection of formal education (as well as the rejection of formally educated readers). Because literary training in the postbellum United States occurred more and more often in the school system—that network of institutions tasked with disseminating literacy and determining the boundaries of the literary—the aesthetic practices of literary writers and the aesthetic tastes of literary readers increasingly developed in tense relation to the modern classroom. Inside this modern classroom, student interest reigned.

Conditions internal to the discipline of literary studies have made it difficult for scholars to apprehend the dynamic relationship between pedagogical interest and literary disgust. In the last decade, literary sociologists have called attention to the role institutions play in administering culture, while affect theorists have reconsidered the power of bodily sensations to condition political, ethical, and aesthetic experience. These scholarly trends suggest literature's capacity, on the one hand, to register affective intensities and, on the other, to encode thematically and formally the institutional pressures that enable literature's existence. Yet little scholarly energy has been expended in literary studies coordinating literature, institutions, and affects with one another. By examining feeling in literature and schools—especially the scholastic feelings conjured by the novels of Frank Norris and Upton Sinclair, pioneering muckrakers and naturalists—this chapter reveals a connection between domains of scholarly inquiry that are rarely thought about together.[7]

Indeed, the relationship between the disgusting literature of the turn of the century and the interest-oriented schools it emerged from reveals the work literature performs mediating the affective and institutional realms, and literature's active participation in the construction of institutional feeling. Disgust is an especially rich subject to organize this investigation around. More than any other feeling, disgust appears entangled with the operations of modern institutions. It inspires intense, aversive reactions, compelling individuals and their institutions to create boundaries, separating the clean from the unclean, the palatable from the unpalatable. And yet, if disgust provokes individuals and institutions to differentiate, the *object* of disgust nevertheless remains the vehicle through which this differentiation is effected; its expulsion ensures the proper functioning of the self or the institution that performs the expulsion. This is how turn-of-the-century writers understood the disgustingness of their work—as beyond the pale of the institutional system but also implicated with its development—and this is how theorists have understood disgust as well.[8]

Schools, however, have not expelled disgusting literature from the classroom. Teachers have not forbidden students from reading descriptions of a worker falling to his death in a vat of raw meat just before it's processed into lard, or of a patient vomiting right after her dentist proposes to her. In fact, when teachers assign Sinclair's *The Jungle* (1906) or Norris's *McTeague* (1899), students across the United States every year are required to undergo precisely these distasteful reading experiences. The ubiquity of disgust in high school and college English classes should alert us to the shaping influence literature has exercised over the school system throughout the twentieth century and into the twenty-first, injecting unscholastic emotions into the scholastic experience and expanding the feeling of formal education beyond even the ambitions of the Progressive architects of the modern school.

Interest

"The direction that I would give all teachers is: Watch the child, watch his attitude of attention. Is it spontaneous? Is the light of pleasure in his eyes? Is interest the motive which controls him? So long as that exists there is no danger." This piece of advice was offered by Francis W. Parker—the man John Dewey once called the father of Progressive education—in Parker's 1894 book, *Talks on Pedagogics*. Parker served as principal of the Cook County Normal School in Chicago and as superintendent for a number of important experimental schools between 1875 and 1900, including the Boston public schools and the schools of Quincy, Massachusetts, where he developed the Quincy Method, which eliminated harsh discipline, rote memorization, grading, and ranking systems. Parker wasn't the only educator at the time to emphasize the importance of student interest in the classroom. Joseph Mayer Rice, a journalist and educational reformer, wrote an account of the public school system in 1893 that acted as a call-to-arms for Progressive education. "When natural methods are philosophically applied by the teacher, the child becomes interested in his work, and the school is converted into a house of pleasure," he wrote. "When, on the other hand, the child is taught by mechanical methods ... he takes no interest in his work, learning becomes a source of drudgery, and the school a house of bondage." Interest was also crucial to Randolph Bourne's influential early twentieth century account of the Progressive schools in Gary,

Indiana. "The visitor," Bourne wrote, "gets the idea that children come to such a school, not because education is compulsory or because their parents send them there to get rid of them, but because what is done there is so interesting that they will not stay away."[9]

Reformers at the turn of the century situated interest at the center of a network of related terms that included pleasure, desire, curiosity, motive, attention, choice, concentration, and will. The importance of interest lay in its capacity to define the student experience inside the school along emotional and intellectual lines simultaneously. Interest, as these educators understood it, was neither a pure act of feeling nor a pure act of thinking but rather an act of thinking and feeling at once. As Dewey, the great theorizer of pedagogic interest, wrote in his 1896 essay, "Interest in Relation to Training of the Will": "Interest is in the closest relation to the emotional life, on the one side; and, through its close relation, if not identity, with attention, to the intellectual life, on the other side."[10]

The relationship between feeling and education, which modern reformers made central to their project when they seized upon interest as a governing principle, was not a new topic of fascination in US educational theory. The emotional life of pedagogy had been a major concern in religious and civic theories of education since the seventeenth century, from Jonathan Edwards's *A Treatise Concerning Religious Affections* (1746), which insisted that "[I]f it be so that true religion lies much in the affections, hence we may infer, that such means are to be desired, as have much of a tendency to move the affections," to Thomas Jefferson's "A Bill for the More General Diffusion of Knowledge" (1778), which described education as a process where citizens learn to set aside their own narrow personal desires in favor of the "publick happiness." Throughout the seventeenth and eighteenth centuries these religious and civic theories of pedagogy were implemented across a decentralized landscape of educational institutions, including one-room schools, Sunday schools, colleges, newspapers, households, and hospitals. Major shifts in the development of pedagogical interest didn't occur in US educational theory until the nineteenth century, and when they did, they coincided with the centralization of the school system.[11]

The genealogy of pedagogical interest in the United States undoubtedly runs from the continental thinkers Jean-Jacques Rousseau and Johann Heinrich Pestalozzi through Bronson Alcott, who believed, as Alcott once wrote, that educators should adapt instruction to "the genius and habits of the young mind." This pedagogical-affective tradition proved massively important to modern educational reform, and we can begin to appreciate its importance through Horace Mann's *Lectures on Education* (1845). The purpose of these lectures, which were delivered annually when Mann served as secretary of the Massachusetts Board of Education, was (in Mann's words) to "collect such information, on the great subject of Education, as now lies scattered, buried and dormant; and after digesting, and, as far as possible, systematizing and perfecting it, to send it forth to the extremist borders of the state[.]" The common school system that Mann sought to organize and perfect within the boundaries of Massachusetts would then serve as a model of public education for other state legislatures to copy. At the center of Mann's school reforms lay the problem of discipline and feeling in the classroom. "Acquirement and pleasure should go hand in hand," Mann insisted in his first lecture. "They should never part company. The pleasure of acquiring should be the incitement to acquire. ... Nature has implanted a feeling of curiosity in the breast of every child, as if to make herself certain of his activity and progress." The Massachusetts legislature, according to Mann, needed to excise fear, irritation, discomfort, and pain from the classroom; if they weren't excised, "pain [would] blend itself with the study, mak[e] part of the remembrance of it, and thus curiosity and love of learning [would be] deadened, or turned away towards vicious objects." The classroom as a site of pleasure, for Mann, meant more and better infrastructure, comfortable chairs, ventilated rooms, functioning sources of heat, and corporal punishment only as a last resort. It meant making the classroom a place of universal education, where students of different backgrounds would flock because of their desire to learn. The school would house curiosity and pleasure, and in doing so its scope would broaden; pain and fright in the classroom would lead to lower attendance, fragmentation, incoherence. "[A]dults," Mann declared in a later lecture, "have been made fools for life by sudden fright,—annulled at once, their brains turned to ashes by its consuming fires."[12]

Another key moment in the development of pedagogical interest came during Charles Eliot's presidency at Harvard. One of Eliot's key reforms was the implementation of an elective system; in 1869, Eliot insisted in his inaugural speech on the need for student choice in the curriculum. "[T]he young man of nineteen or twenty ought to know what he likes best and is most fit for," Eliot declared. "If his previous training has been sufficiently wide, he will know by that time whether he is most apt at language or philosophy or natural science or mathematics. If he feels no loves, he will at least have his hates." The freedom to choose served a dual purpose for Eliot. On the one hand it contributed to the intellectual and emotional well-being of the students: "When the revelation of his own peculiar taste and capacity comes to a young man, let him reverently give it welcome, thank God, and take courage. Thereafter, he knows his way to happy, enthusiastic work, and, God willing, to usefulness and success." On the other hand, the freedom to pursue a particular subject of study in depth reinforced Eliot's modern educational program, a program based on the independence of the disciplines, where professional producers of knowledge would be empowered to evaluate their own work and the work of their colleagues without unprofessional incursion. Eliot's program, bolstered by the elective system, in short, was one that would come to dominate the university over the twentieth century.[13]

In this sense, the rise of pedagogical interest in the nineteenth century coincided with the rise of a sophisticated, centralized school system; and the way John

Dewey and his colleagues theorized it, interest retained its meaning and coherence as an educational principle only in the context of that school system. Dewey's first article dedicated exclusively to the subject of pedagogical interest was published in 1896—"Interest in Relation to Training of the Will"—but interest would come to occupy a central role in his account of education throughout *The School and Society* (1900), *The Child and the Curriculum* (1902), *Schools of To-Morrow* (1915), *Democracy and Education* (1916), and *Experience and Education* (1938). Interest, as Dewey defined it succinctly in the 1896 article, "is the accompaniment of the identification, through action, of the self with some object or idea, because of the necessity of that object or idea for the maintenance of self-expression." He derived the word from the Latin *inter-esse*—"to be between": "The root idea of the term seems to be that of being engaged, engrossed, or entirely taken up with some activity because of its recognized worth. ... Interest marks the annihilation of the distance between the person and the materials and results of his action; it is the instrument which effects their organic union."[14]

There were different kinds of interest for Dewey, though. "Immediate interest" according to Dewey describes a blind impulsive state, where self-expression is direct, putting itself forth "with no thought of anything beyond. The present activity is the only ultimate in consciousness. It satisfies in and of itself." "Mediate interest" alternatively describes a state in which "things indifferent or even repulsive in themselves often become of interest because of their assuming relationships and connections of which we are previously unaware." Learning math on its own may be unappealing to a student; but if a student is interested in engineering, and math is a necessary tool to understand engineering, then learning math becomes much more attractive and fascinating—learning math, that is, becomes interesting. "It is all a question of relationship, whether it appeals or fails to appeal," Dewey wrote. "[A]nd while the little child takes only a near view of things, as he grows he becomes capable of extending his range, and seeing an act, or a thing, or a fact not by itself, but in its value as a part of a larger whole."[15]

The distinction between mediate and immediate interest forms the foundation of Dewey's understanding of emotion, teaching, and the relationship between the two. Blind appetite, blind passion, and blind impulse for Dewey are associated with immediate interest. Appetite, he writes, lacks any connection to its surroundings; it "is not considered from the standpoint of its bearings or relationships. ... Consequently, it is not made intelligent. It is not rationalized." However, once an emotion becomes associated with an object, once it no longer functions as an end in itself but rather as a means to an end, then the emotion is rationalized; it works "normally" as mediate interest, where effort and self-expression are required to overcome cognitive difficulty and produce a desired result. If teachers try to make a subject interesting artificially—if they reward students for doing homework, or threaten to punish students for not turning homework in on time—the results are disastrous. Artificial rewards lead to "over-stimulation and dull apathy," and the threat of punishment apart from genuine interest leads to what Dewey describes as "divided attention," in which students can mechanically carry out commands externally while "riotous, uncontrolled" imaginative play reigns internally. The correct role of the teacher is to select subjects "in relation to the child's present experience, powers, and needs" and "present the new material in such a way as to enable the child to appreciate its bearings, its relationships, its necessity for him."[16]

The importance of pedagogical interest in Dewey's educational program went beyond its power to rationalize the emotional experience of students inside the classroom. It also drove Dewey's vision of an all-encompassing school system. At one point in the revised edition of *The School and Society* (1915), Dewey describes the process of teaching students to cook. "Undoubtedly," Dewey writes, "the little child who thinks he would like to cook has little idea of what it means or costs, or what it requires. ... And it is doubtless possible to let ourselves down to that level and simply humor that interest. But here, too, if the impulse is exercised, utilized, it runs up against the actual world of hard conditions, to which it must accommodate itself." As the students' initial impulse accommodates itself to the hard conditions of the actual world, linkages, from one idea to another, form in the classroom. The children look up recipes for cooking eggs; they compare cooking vegetables and meats; they learn about the "woody fiber or cellulose" in vegetables and the "connective tissue" in meat that give each its form and structure; they study "albumen as the characteristic feature of animal food" and "starch in the vegetables"; they experiment to find out what water temperature is best for cooking the white of the eggs. Dewey stops the connections there, but why should he? The linkages that interest opens up with its "in-between-ness" can always move one step further, from eggs to animals, from animals to vegetables, from vegetables to water temperature, from water temperature to digestion, from digestion to nutrition, from nutrition to biology, and so on and so on. Each link in this way becomes connected by and in the school, and the school's scope grows to comprehend the entire globe and all of history. Dewey describes a similar cluster of interests when the students learn to sew, only on a larger scale: the students pick their own cotton, find their own wool, experiment with ways to process the material, making looms and spin wheels, and in doing so they recreate all of human civilization, "trac[ing] and follow[ing] the progress of mankind in history[.]"[17]

Dewey's educational reforms aimed to reimagine the school system as a system without boundaries—as "a genuine form of active community life, instead of a place set apart in which to learn lessons"—and interest performed a crucial role in this reimagining, not just by expanding the school's scope but also by eliminating the border between the school and the world outside the school. Without interest, Dewey explains, the school remains set apart from the whole of human experience. "When the child gets into the [traditional] classroom he has to put out of his mind a large part of the ideas, interests, and activities that predominate in his home and neighborhood," Dewey writes. "So the school, being unable to utilize this everyday experience sets painfully to work, on another tack and by a variety of means, to arouse in the child an interest in school studies." With genuine interest, however, the school can annihilate its own boundaries—the walls that separate it from the realm of lived experience—and thus the school becomes "a genuine form of active community life." Experience inside the school and experience outside the school become one and the same. The school in consequence can absorb woodwork, agriculture, the fine arts, and commerce, activities ordinarily thought to lie outside of its purview, and as it absorbs these activities, as the division between the inside and outside of the institution begins to dissolve, Dewey enacts a double-move: the school soaks up the outside world, its structures and its materials, and, at the same time, the outside world becomes a kind of school, where everything is linked to everything else as part of a greater, organic system—eggs and water temperature, wool and spinning wheel alike.[18]

And yet, it's important for Dewey that pedagogical interest can only function because of its association with other positive emotions. Negative emotions, by contrast, are associated with incoherence and disorganization, resulting from an improper understanding of mediate interest. "The teacher who tells the child he will be kept after school if he doesn't recite his geography lesson better is appealing to the psychology of mediate interest. The former English method of rapping knuckles for false Latin quantities is one way of arousing interest in the intricacies of Latin. ... They are cases of transferred interest." The problem with transferred interest, in Dewey's account, is that it isn't sufficiently connected to the things around it; it isn't bound to the organic unity in the same way that normal mediate interest is. "[I]n normal growth, the interest in one is not simply externally tied on to the other; it suffuses it, saturates, and thus transforms it," Dewey writes. "[I]n drudgery means and end remain as separate in consciousness as they are in space and time."[19]

The psychology produced by methods of "drudgery," by tedious work, by threats of pain and punishment, is an incoherent one, a divided attention in which the student's inner life and outer life aren't coordinated with each other. Negative feelings therefore hold the power to disrupt the linkages that genuine interest seeks to erect; and the organic unity, the larger whole of experience Dewey describes, which is situated in the connected world of interest, manages to establish its connections only by banishing the disorder that attends feelings like anger, pain, and irritation. Dewey's school system can swell only by pushing out an entire universe of negative feelings—and so while interest expands, it also excludes, and its exclusions create a new space outside of institutions, a space occupied by practices, behaviors, and ideas that these institutions deem unpalatable. For novelists of the time, growing up under the progressive institutions of the late nineteenth century, fiction was uniquely suited to probe the emotional terrain left uncharted by the school system.

Disgust I: What's That Funny Smell?

The climax of Frank Norris's *McTeague* takes place inside a school—"a little memorial kindergarten over on Pacific street"—when the novel's protagonist, McTeague, the dentist, murders his wife Trina and steals the money that she won in a lottery. To say the murder takes place "inside" the school is a little misleading, though. As the scene unfolds the narrative perspective bounces around, first inside the school and then outside, first bearing witness to the murder and then averting its gaze. "[A] brutal fist swung open the street door of the schoolroom and McTeague came in," Norris begins the episode. Trina locks herself in the school's cloakroom, but it's no use: "McTeague put his hand on the knob of the door outside and opened it, tearing off the lock and the bolt guard, and sending [Trina] staggering across the room." Inside the cloakroom McTeague demands the lottery money and Trina refuses. After this refusal the scene seems primed for violence, and yet Norris's description avoids much of the violence that follows:

> [Trina's] resistance was the one thing to drive [McTeague] to the top of his fury. He came back at her again, his eyes drawn to two fine twinkling points, and his enormous fists, clenched till the knuckles whitened, raised in the air.
> Then it became abominable.
> In the schoolroom outside, behind a coal scuttle, the cat listened to the sounds of stamping and struggling and the muffled noise of blows, wildly terrified, his eyes bulging like brass knobs.

The three shifts in focalization here—from Trina's perspective in the cloakroom, to the omniscient narrator abstracted and removed from the "abominable" action of the scene altogether, and finally to the cat outside the cloakroom but still inside the school—register a discursive anxiety over insides and outsides, and appropriate and inappropriate subjects of novelistic representation. These three shifts are then followed by yet another shift only moments later: after McTeague murders Trina and leaves the cloakroom, Norris turns from the cat's perspective back to the omniscient narrator's, outside the school. "The cat followed him with distended eyes as he crossed the room and disappeared through the street door," Norris writes. "The dentist paused for a moment on the sidewalk, looking carefully up and down the street."[20]

Pages later, at the end of the chapter, when Trina's body is discovered the next morning in the cloakroom, the narrative perspective undergoes a similar set of shifts. Norris starts with a description of Trina's body: "Trina lay unconscious, just as she had fallen under the last of McTeague's blows, her body twitching with an occasional hiccough that stirred the pool of blood in which she lay face downward." The perspective then moves from the cloakroom into the schoolroom, where the children are arriving. "Half way across the room one of them stopped and put her small nose in the air, crying, 'Um-o-o, what a funnee smell!'" Norris writes. "The others began to sniff the air as well, and one, the daughter of a butcher, exclaimed, 'Tsmells like my pa's shop.'" Finally, in the last sentences of the chapter, the perspective settles on the threshold of the cloakroom, as the school children are about to discover Trina's body: "[T]he tallest of the little girls swung the door of the little cloakroom wide open and they all ran in."[21]

The threshold where the narrative perspective finally settles during the murder scene operates as the site of disgust for Norris, not just in this specific chapter but in the novel as a whole. This threshold is located on the boundary dividing the inside and outside of institutional life, and from this position it marks the gradual collapse of a set of binaries that the system ordinarily depends upon for its health and proper maintenance—the rational and irrational, the civilized and uncivilized, the appropriate and inappropriate. In this in-between space, *McTeague* produces its most lurid effects, the disgust registered by so many of its readers upon its first publication. "McTeague and his companions are a sort of human garbage heap," one contemporary reviewer wrote. Another declared: "It is more repellent than one thinks fiction ought to be." "*McTeague*," another added, "is a hideous story." And these were critics who liked the novel! Other critics were less sanguine in their evaluations. One dismissed the book for being "extraordinarily repulsive"; another for being unpleasant: "It is about the most unpleasant American story that anybody has ever ventured to write"; and yet another for being gross: "grossness for the sake of grossness is unpardonable." The contemporary response to *McTeague* is perhaps best summed up by the bewildered reviewer from the *Boston Evening Transcript*: "Can it be possible that many persons can be found ... to absorb the details of the disgusting episodes which Mr. Norris presents?"[22]

Although the disgust described by these critics seems unmotivated—disgust for disgust's sake—a closer examination of the novel reveals that Norris links disgust inextricably to the work of modern institutions. He links disgust to what these institutions are, how they function, and how they fail to function. The threshold of the cloakroom in the murder scene defines the space where this disgust inheres, where the interest that connects and defines life in the school system turns into the sordidness of a brutal world without connections or rationality. Along this threshold, the logic of the institution breaks down, and the system gives way to the unsystematic. It's significant for Norris that the encounter between the children and Trina's body—where the disgust of the children's conversation could turn easily into something else entirely, something closer to terror—goes unnarrated. The scene in the schoolroom is disgusting precisely because, after jumping anxiously from inside to outside, outside to inside, the narrator lands in the in-between space of the threshold, as the routine and habit of the school day begins to fray the moment the stink of Trina's battered body drifts into the classroom. In the larger architecture of the novel, the murder scene is situated along an even greater threshold, between the industrial urban life of San Francisco where the chapter ends and the desolate landscape of Placer County, where the very next chapter begins and where nature, Norris writes, is a "vast, unconquered brute of the Pliocene epoch, savage, sullen, and magnificently indifferent to man."[23]

To understand disgust in *McTeague*, and the relationship between this disgust and the pedagogical interest theorized by Dewey, it's necessary first to articulate the multiple points of contact between Frank Norris and the institutional transformations incited by the Progressive education movement at the turn of the century. In 1894, after completing his fourth year at the University of California without earning a bachelor's degree, Norris moved across the country and enrolled at Charles Eliot's Harvard. At Harvard, Norris attended a literature class, English 22, taught by L. E. Gates, the educator Norris dedicated *McTeague* to. Harvard would have a profound effect on Norris's development as a writer, and the difference between the literature classes at Harvard and the University of California would form the basis of his polemic, "The 'English Courses' of the University of California" (1896). According to Norris, the English classes at the University of California were mechanical, rote, and—most important—insufficiently interesting. "[B]y the time he is a Junior or Senior, [the student] has lost all interest in the 'literary' courses," Norris wrote. "The 'themes' must be written, however, and the best way is the easiest. This is how he oft-times goes about it: He knows just where he can lay his hands upon some fifty to a hundred 'themes' written by the members of past classes[.] … He does not necessarily copy it. He rewrites it in his own language." In contrast to English courses at the University of California, Norris explained, classes at Harvard were much better, organized around contact with the outside world, the world of experience. "The literary student at Cambridge has but little to do with lectures, almost nothing at all with text books," he wrote. "He is sent away from the lecture room and told to look about him and think a little. Each day he writes a theme, a page if necessary, a single line of a dozen words if he likes; anything, so it is original, something he has seen or thought, not read of, not picked up at second hand." The system of education Norris encountered at Harvard was one that organized pedagogy inside lecture halls according to the world outside lecture halls; it was one that appealed to the emotional and intellectual interests of the students. "The result of this system," Norris concluded, "is a keenness of interest that draws three hundred men to the course and that fills the benches at every session of class."[24]

At Harvard, Norris would write a substantial portion of his first novel, *Vandover and the Brute*, and conceive of *McTeague*.[25] Norris's attack on the English courses at the University of California is significant not simply because it shares many of the same assumptions and much of the same language as the polemics Progressive educators were leveling against formal education at the same time. It's also significant because it extends these reform projects to the domain of the literary. The polemic demonstrates Norris's belief that a good literature course makes a good institution, and that a national literary culture requires institutional resources in order to come into being.[26]

Norris made these claims more explicit in a later essay, another polemic, "Novelists of the Future: *The Training They Need*" (1901). Norris declared at the start of the essay: "[S]o long as the fiction writers of the United States go fumbling and stumbling along in this undisciplined fashion, governed by no rule, observing no formula, setting for themselves no equation to solve, that just so long shall we be far from that desirable thing—an American school of fiction." The "American school of fiction" described in the polemic held a double meaning for Norris. On one level, the "school" of fiction referred to a movement, a literary culture, an authentic national tradition. On another level, Norris suggested somewhat jokingly, the "school" referred to an actual school. "[I]f we do not observe the rules and conform to some degree of order," Norris wrote, "we should be rapped on the knuckles or soundly clumped on the head, and by vigorous discipline taught to know that formulas (a − b) (a + b) are important things for us to observe[.]" Norris's essay advocated institutionalizing composition; it called for scholastic programs to help students cultivate habits of observation and sharpness of mind. Although by the end of the essay Norris retreated from the idea of a literal school—a classroom, four walls and a roof—he still insisted that fiction writing was something teachers could teach and students could learn. "This, then, to drop a very protracted allegory," Norris wrote, "seems to be the proper training of the novelist: The achieving less of an aggressive faculty of research, than of an attitude of mind—a receptivity, an acute sensitiveness. And this can be acquired."[27]

If Norris and Progressive reformers shared many of the same assumptions, much of the same language, and the same faith in institutions, the two also shared another, perhaps more profound point of contact, through evolutionary biology, particularly the work of Herbert Spencer. At the end of the nineteenth century, Spencer's essays made a profound impact on the whole landscape of US intellectual life, including the work of educators.[28] Norris, embedded in turn-of-the-century US educational institutions, could not escape the revolution Spencer's work effected. Norris came under the influence of evolutionary biology at the University of California, when he began an extensive reading of the works of Émile Zola, and took classes on geology and zoology taught by Joseph Le Conte, a scientist who sought to reconcile evolutionary and religious ideas.[29] But if organization, regulation, and institutions served as the bedrock of Norris's polemics on education, the influence of evolutionary biology on Norris's literary writings expressed itself in much more disturbing and contradictory ways.

In his essay on literary naturalism, "The Experimental Novel," Zola argued that the novelist's job "consists in taking facts in nature, then in studying the mechanism of these facts, acting upon them, by the modification of circumstances and surroundings, without deviating from the laws of nature. Finally, [the writer] possesses knowledge of the man, scientific knowledge of him, in both his individual and social relations." By investigating the operations of heredity and environment, literature according to Zola was capable of producing scientific knowledge, giving human beings greater control over their development. Zola thus distinguished literary naturalism's agential determinism from an agentless, nihilistic, fatalism. "'We have given the name determinism to the nearest or determining cause of phenomena,'" Zola wrote, quoting the scientist Claude Bernard. "'We never act upon the essence of phenomena in nature, but only on their determinism, and by this very fact, that we act upon it, determinism differs from fatalism, upon which we could not act at all.'"[30]

Zola's insistence that naturalism presupposes "determinism" (human beings as actors with historical and biological agency) and not "fatalism" (human beings as passive subjects, without agency, historical or otherwise) seems particularly ironic in retrospect, considering the most famous twentieth-century charges leveled against naturalism claimed just the opposite: that naturalism as a genre, unlike realism, weakly submits to the forces of history rather than acting upon them. This, of course, is the line Lukács pursued in his essay, "Narrate or Describe?," arguing in favor of the realism of Scott, Balzac, and Tolstoy against the naturalism of Zola and Flaubert. Where, for Lukács, the realist novel narrates characters' lives emerging and unfolding in direct involvement with historical events, the naturalist novel instead gets stuck in description: characters don't learn or grow but are rather non-acting spectators who remain subject to external forces. Lukács excoriates the fatalism of the naturalists: "The writers' fatalism, their capitulation (even with gnashing teeth) before capitalist inhumanity, is responsible for the absence of development in these 'novels' of development."[31]

The contradictions that naturalism manifests—power slipping into powerlessness, action into inaction—weren't particular to the literary production of the period but were symptomatic of the larger contradictions that attended the institutionalization of evolutionary biology at the turn of the century. As professors across the social sciences began to incorporate Spencer's ideas into their work, the results were a mixed bag of policy suggestions: advocates for a laissez-faire society emerged, but so too did advocates for greater social intervention. This was especially true of the institutionalization of evolutionary science in education. Some educators argued in the wake of evolutionary biology that social growth was produced not through the activities of individuals or institutions, but through the inexorable (and, from a human perspective, passive) work of the evolutionary process. Others argued that human cognition and state institutions were in fact part of the evolutionary process and insisted that collective social action and education functioned as a means through which human beings shape their surrounding environment. Lawrence Cremin, following what Richard Hofstadter once termed the "dual potentiality" of Social Darwinism in American thought, described this contradictory reception of Spencer's work in educational life: "[W]e know full well that

William Graham Sumner's doubts about the power of popular schooling derived from his study of Spencer; but then, so did Lester Frank Ward's enthusiasm for the extension of educational opportunity."[32]

This, then, is the threshold that naturalism in general and Frank Norris's work in particular inhabits: on the one side, rationality, action, determinism, and institutions, and on the other side, irrationality, inaction, fatalism, and the corrosion of institutional life. And disgust, as Norris depicts it in *McTeague*, becomes the presiding affective response to life on this threshold. By writing disgusting books, Norris set out to explore the practices that lie on the borders of an increasingly borderless educational system. For Norris, the literary imagination inhabits the disgusting region where institutions falter and the school can grow no more.[33]

Norris conceptualizes disgust in one of the novel's early scenes, when McTeague and Trina first meet in McTeague's dental parlors, after Trina has fallen off of a swing and injured herself. McTeague examines Trina's mouth and discovers that hers is a "curious case" of "necrosis," in which the roots of a broken tooth are still stuck in the gum, "loose, discolored, and evidently dead," but with "no vascular connection between the root and the gum." While examining Trina's mouth, McTeague finds himself strangely attracted to her—interested in her—and because of this interest he sets his mind to fixing the problem: "McTeague began to like her better and better[.] ... He became interested; perhaps he could do something, something in the way of a crown or bridge. ... He began to study the situation very carefully, really desiring to remedy the blemish." Following Dewey's logic precisely, McTeague's interest in Trina becomes an interest in Trina's dead tooth. And as a result of this interest, McTeague resolves to overcome the cognitive difficulty presented by the necrosis, literally bridging gaps and making connections:

> It was the first bicuspid that was missing, and though part of the root of the second (the loose one) would remain after its extraction, [McTeague] was sure it would not be strong enough to sustain a crown. All at once he grew obstinate, resolving, with all the strength of a crude and primitive man, to conquer the difficulty in spite of everything. He turned over in his mind the technicalities of the case. No, evidently the root was not strong enough to sustain a crown; besides that, it was placed a little irregularly in the arch. But, fortunately, there were cavities in the two teeth to either side of the gap—one in the first molar and one in the palatine surface of the cuspid; might he not drill a socket in the remaining root and sockets in the molar and cuspid, and partly by bridging, partly by crowning fill in the gap? He made up his mind to do it.[34]

If McTeague's determination to "bridge" Trina's broken tooth represents a textbook execution of Deweyan interest—interest overcoming an obstacle, creating connections, and expanding the mind's capacities—it also demonstrates the unraveling of Deweyan interest. The operations on Trina's mouth take weeks to perform, during which time McTeague's interest extends itself and McTeague begins to recognize the charm and delight of women: "It was not only [Trina] that he saw and felt, it was woman, the whole sex, an entire new humanity, strange and alluring, that he seemed to have discovered." The moment interest exposes McTeague to the greater whole of life, and womankind, interest itself starts to decompose, revealing not a world organized by reason and connections and institutions, but an irrational world, ruled only by blind passion. "[McTeague's] narrow point of view was at once enlarged and confused, and all at once he saw that there was something else in life besides concertinas and steam beer," Norris writes. "Everything had to be made over again. His whole rude idea of life had to be changed. The male virile desire in him tardily awakened, aroused itself, strong and brutal. It was resistless, untrained, a thing not to be held in leash an instant."[35]

It's precisely when interest begins to unravel, and McTeague struggles between reason and passion in the "foul atmosphere" of the dental parlor, that the novel becomes disgusting. At one point during the operation Norris describes McTeague "kiss[ing] Trina, grossly, full on the mouth," and later, after Trina wakes from the ether, McTeague proposes to her:

> McTeague came nearer to her, repeating the same question. "No, no," she cried, terrified. Then, as she exclaimed, "Oh, I am sick," was suddenly taken with a fit of vomiting. It was the not unusual after effect of the ether, aided now by her excitement and nervousness. McTeague was checked. He poured some bromide of potassium into a graduated glass and held it to her lips.
>
> "Here, swallow this," he said.[36]

Disgust—linked etymologically to mouths and orality—appears here on the threshold between the inside and outside of Trina's body, as substances once contained within her stomach pour out ("fit of vomiting"), and as substances once outside of her stomach are incorporated in ("'swallow this'"). The eruption of bodily fluids in the scene reflects a corresponding upheaval in the educational process, a movement from the inside to the outside of institutional logic. In Norris's account, as in Dewey's, the emotional thrill of interest pushes McTeague to overcome an intellectual challenge, the one posed by Trina's necrosis. And yet, unlike in Dewey's writing, Norris here insists that while this thrill incites reason at first, it also undoes reason. It's significant that the threshold of disgust Norris settles on in the murder scene is between the schoolroom (the site of rationality and the institution) and the cloakroom (the site of irrationality and behaviors that can't be institutionalized). Norris, that is, situates the outside of the institution inside the institution. Interest thus breaks down into disgust not by reaching some external barrier but through its own inner logic and momentum.

Although some critics have convincingly described Norris as a technocrat, an adherent of the technologies of management and systemization that were emerging at the end of the nineteenth century, it seems important to note that insofar as Norris remained an adherent of the system, his literary production was inevitably pulled toward the margins of that system, the disgusting boundary where that system broke down.[37] *McTeague*, after all, is only sparsely populated by characters who are embedded in the rising institutional structures of the turn of the century—characters like the "Other Dentist" on Polk Street who "just graduated from the college, a poser, a rider of bicycles." By contrast, the characters and events that occupy the most space in *McTeague* are the ones that inhabit the threshold of these institutional structures, where the influence of these institutions begins to deteriorate.[38]

No one character embodies this liminal space of institutions more than McTeague himself—the dentist who never went to dental school, put out of work by a dentist who did go to dental school—but the waning of institutional influence is visible practically everywhere the narrative turns and everywhere disgust manifests: for instance in the infamous scene where Trina removes her lottery money from the bank, brings it back to her room above the kindergarten, and pleasures herself with it. "Not a day passed that Trina did not have it out where she could see and touch it," Norris writes. "One evening she had even spread all the gold pieces between the sheets, and had then gone to bed, stripping herself, and had slept all night upon the money, taking a strange and ecstatic pleasure in the touch of the smooth flat pieces the length of her entire body."[39] The scene feels illicit not just because Trina's pleasure is onanistic, but also because Trina has deprived the money of value by removing it from Uncle Oelbermann's store, where it was accruing interest and producing and reproducing value. The scene feels illicit, that is, because the money, like Trina herself, has absented itself from the realm of reproduction—and this reproductive failure extends equally to the schoolhouse beneath Trina as well. Schools in the novel fail in their function as schools—like the money on the bed malfunctions as money, and, Norris suggests, like Trina malfunctions as a woman and a mother—insofar as the schools don't fulfill their role in the reproduction of the social order. The novel's disgusting fascination with unreproductive behavior, and especially with the mouth as the primary site of sexual excitation—when McTeague bites Trina's hands "crunching and grinding them with his immense teeth," when Marcus Schouler crams a billiard ball into his mouth, when Zerkow makes Maria Macapa describe the gold of her childhood, so soft "you could bite into it and leave the dent of your teeth"—points to this crisis in individual and institutional functioning.[40] The apparatuses that are supposed to guarantee the reproduction of human life and culture in the San Francisco of *McTeague* lie just beyond the scope of the expanding institutions of the turn of the century; and as a result, these apparatuses falter and fail.

Frank Norris professed a faith in science and organization in his essays and, from this vantage point inside the system, mobilized disgust in his literary work as a way of articulating the boundaries of US institutions, where life inside the system begins to deteriorate on its way out of the system. Another writer at this time mobilized disgust in his writing, too, but from a different institutional perspective. This writer, Upton Sinclair, also conceived of disgust as residing on the threshold of institutional life, yet for Sinclair, who hoped to enact revolutionary change from outside of the system, disgust came instead to mark the process of incorporation, where life outside institutions irrevocably gets swallowed up in the system's expansion.

Disgust II: How the Sausage Is Made

Late in the summer of 1905, Upton Sinclair founded a nationwide organization called the Intercollegiate Socialist Society (ISS) to encourage socialism on college campuses. Sinclair had originally conceived of the society a year earlier, but it wasn't until September 1905 that the organization actually began to take shape, as more than fifty supporters gathered at Peck's Restaurant in downtown New York City for the society's first meeting. By the end of the night, the founding members had managed to establish the ISS's bylaws and elect Jack London the organization's first acting president. Sinclair, the driving force behind the society, having convened the first meeting and solicited the endorsement of nine public intellectuals, including London, Clarence Darrow, and Charlotte Perkins Gilman, was elected vice president. In the weeks that followed the inaugural meeting of the ISS, Sinclair decided to capitalize on Jack London's growing popularity by arranging a series of on-campus visits across the country. London, whose lecture was eventually published as the essay "Revolution," spoke to packed auditoriums in Cambridge, New York City, and New Haven about the rise of a revolutionary army that would one day rule the world. "[The revolutionaries] intend nothing less than to destroy existing capitalist society and to take possession of the whole world," London proudly declared. "If the law of the land permits, they fight for this end peaceably, at the ballot-box. If the law of the land does not permit, and if they have force meted out to them, they resort to force themselves. They meet violence with violence."[41]

Responses to London's speech varied widely at the different institutions he visited. At Harvard, where London delivered his first lecture in the series, he received a standing ovation and afterward stayed up all night discussing socialism with a group of students. In New York City he was also received warmly: as Upton Sinclair would later recount in his *Autobiography*, a "roar of cheers" broke out when "our hero and his wife were walking down the aisle." At Yale, though, the lecture caused a scandal. Local New Haven libraries stopped circulating London's books after the speech, and the *New York Times*, which hadn't commented on London's appearance in New York, decried the lecture at Yale for encouraging violence and class warfare—"the war of one class in society against other classes." Four days after the Yale controversy, the *Times* published a letter from Sinclair that dampened London's fiery rhetoric and downplayed London's call for revolutionary violence. For instance, according to Sinclair, London's declaration that a "blood-red banner will soon be waving wildly in all winds" was misrepresented in the *Times* coverage: London in the speech went on to explain to his audience that the blood-red banner "as used by the Socialists ... is a symbol of the Brotherhood of Man, and not of war and destruction."[42]

In the end, the founding of the ISS and the controversy at Yale reflected the uneasiness of the marriage between revolutionary politics and formal education that Sinclair was trying to arrange in the opening years of the twentieth century. Sinclair's decision to locate his radical political agenda inside the school system was itself somewhat counterintuitive. Sinclair's own political education didn't take place inside the school system at all—not during his time at the City College of New York, where he spent five years, or at Columbia University, where he spent another desultory four. "I had had nine years of college and university," he wrote, "and I hadn't learned that the modern socialist movement existed." Sinclair's political education, instead, occurred during a single crashing moment in 1902, when one of his friends by chance happened to give him a socialist pamphlet. "It was like the falling down of prison walls about my mind," Sinclair later remembered.[43]

Following the language of Sinclair's revelation, the school system seems like one of the last places Sinclair would want to situate his radical politics. If, as Jack London insisted in his college lectures, the aim of the Socialist Party was to "destroy existing capitalist society and to take possession of the whole world," then college campuses in particular would seem an unlikely place for the socialists to start. On tour, London wasn't doing anything to "destroy" existing social infrastructure, and he wasn't addressing the army of revolutionaries he described in his speech. Instead, the campuses he visited—Harvard, Yale—were bastions of economic and social privilege. For Sinclair in September 1905, though, these contradictions weren't contradictions at all. "Since the professors refused to teach the students about modern life, it was up to the students to teach themselves": this was the logic underwriting the formation of the ISS. If the revolutionary energy gathering outside educational institutions managed to infiltrate these institutions and appropriate institutional resources, then, according to Sinclair, political change could be effected on a mass scale.[44]

Only during London's lecture tour would the tensions in Sinclair's vision of radical education begin to manifest. In New York, London's crowd consisted mostly of residents of the lower east side, not college students; and after the Yale controversy, Sinclair's letter to the *Times*—already in its very form a gesture of curtailed radical energy—made the society's revolutionary platform seem much more moderate.

What began, in other words, as Jack London's incendiary call for a revolutionary army, once passed through the school system, became instead Upton Sinclair's frustrated letter to the editor of the *New York Times*. The Yale controversy, in short, was one of the first confrontations between Sinclair's revolutionary politics and the formal system of education. The results of this confrontation were the deradicalization of Sinclair's radical tendencies, and—as the ISS spread to college campuses across the country—the absorption of a more palatable version of London's revolutionary fervor into the school system. Finally, then, Sinclair's efforts demonstrated not the revolutionary transformation of the formal system of education but the formalization and attenuation of revolutionary politics.[45]

While Sinclair struggled to organize the political education of millions of Americans through the ISS, he was also busy struggling to depict the political education of just a single fictional character, Jurgis Rudkus, the protagonist of his novel *The Jungle*. The first chapter of *The Jungle* had appeared on February 25, 1905, in the socialist newspaper *Appeal to Reason*. Sinclair's fee for the serialization of his novel was $500, and although the opening chapters of *The Jungle* increased the circulation of the *Appeal*, by the spring Sinclair needed more money, and his editors at the newspaper and at Macmillan (the publishing house where he was hoping to sell the completed novel) were growing increasingly skeptical. In April, an editor at Macmillan, George Brett, somehow managed to be both anxious about and bored with *The Jungle*—anxious because the novel was sure to draw lawsuits from the meatpacking industry, and bored because the novel's plot kept getting derailed by long didactic passages advocating socialism. By September 23, less than two weeks after the inaugural meeting of the ISS at Peck's Restaurant, Macmillan pulled Sinclair's book deal. A few days later, in early October, Sinclair's editor at the *Appeal*, Fred Warren, fell asleep listening to Sinclair read the final chapters of the novel. By the first week of November, faced with a lagging interest among readers, Warren stopped publishing the novel in the *Appeal* altogether.[46]

The obstacles Sinclair confronted during the founding of the ISS were thus mirrored in the obstacles he confronted during the composition of *The Jungle*. Both, in effect, were manifestations of the same set of tensions that plagued Sinclair's attempts to theorize radical education. Sinclair's certainty that socialism was a necessary political movement was accompanied by a great deal of uncertainty—uncertainty over who should be taught, what should be taught, where the teaching should happen, and how to present the teaching in a way that wouldn't produce hostility or indifference.

Although Sinclair's dissatisfaction with *The Jungle*'s commercial and political success after the novel's publication is well known—"I aimed at the public's heart, and by accident I hit it in the stomach," he would write a few months after the Pure Food and Drug Act was passed[47]—far less attention has been paid to the ways in which this failure was inscribed in the novel during its composition. When Sinclair finally did manage to publish *The Jungle* at Doubleday, Page and Company, almost three months following MacMillan's decision to drop the novel, it was only after he agreed to a series of compromises with his editors.[48] The novel's publication date—February 26, 1906, three weeks after the letter to the *New York Times* editor—testifies to Sinclair's abridged revolutionary ambitions for the book. If Sinclair's defense of Jack London's "Revolution" speech articulated a more moderate platform for revolutionary education and, in consequence, enabled the ISS's incorporation into the school system, then *The Jungle* registers Sinclair's concerns surrounding incorporation in its very subject matter, which restages the drama that accompanied the founding of the ISS.

Incorporation is central to the thematics of *The Jungle*—not just business or legal incorporation, although these are certainly two of the novel's larger preoccupations, but more basically, incorporation in the sense of bringing the outside in. The most disgusting moments in *The Jungle* involve the process of incorporation, when materials that are supposed to remain on the outside threaten, through the production and consumption of food, to enter our insides. Chicago satirist Peter Finlay Dunne's famous caricature of President Roosevelt reading the novel over breakfast and refusing to eat his morning sausage located *The Jungle*'s political efficacy in the disgust it produced in its readership, and yet this caricature also links disgust to issues of incorporation more broadly. The caricature ends with Teddy insisting that the outside remain outside, that the outside not come in, by "throwin' sausages out iv th' window."[49] Dunne's caricature of presidential disgust is one of the enduring legacies of the novel, and it's no accident that the particular food-item foregrounded in the caricature is sausage. Even in *The Jungle*—one of the most famous and disgusting novels in American literary history, a novel that's famous for being disgusting—the scenes involving sausage stand out as more disgusting than others.[50] It's precisely in the sausage scenes, where the novel's disgust reaches a pitch, that the relationship between disgust and incorporation, and between disgust and the institutions of US life more generally, becomes most clearly articulated.

The sausage room doesn't appear until the thirteenth chapter of *The Jungle*, and when it does it's only after the characters have been exposed to every other horror in the meatpacking plant. In part, Sinclair's decision to save sausage until the end is meant to follow the logic of Chicago meat production. If Sinclair begins by exposing the Rudkus family to the killing room, where the cows and pigs are first brought to be slaughtered and butchered, and next takes the family to the pickling room, where older, oftentimes partially spoiled meat is preserved for future use, then it makes sense that Sinclair would expose the family last of all to the sausage room, where the discarded pieces of meat—the pieces of meat with no further use—are processed into something that can be used. "It was only when the whole ham was spoiled," Sinclair explains, "that it came into the [sausage] department[.]" In part, also, Sinclair's decision to save the sausage until the end is meant to reflect the family's desperation. Only after Jurgis injures his ankle, loses his job on the killing floor, and finds a worse job in the company's fertilizer plant, and only after the other family members take on jobs—Jurgis's wife Ona sews covers for hams, the children start selling newspapers—does Jurgis's step-mother-in-law Teta Elzbieta begin to work in the sausage room, a last-ditch effort to make enough money for the family to stay in their home. The sausage room thus represents both a culmination of the Rudkus family's entanglement with Chicago's meatpacking industry and the last lesson the characters receive on the industrial conditions of meat production. Once Teta Elizbieta starts working in the sausage room, the industry in its entirety becomes legible to the characters in the novel and, by extension, Sinclair's readers: "[The family] could now study the whole of the spoiled-meat industry on the inside, and read a new and grim meaning into that old Packingtown jest,—that they use everything of the pig except the squeal."[51]

In its very form, the sausage itself also comes to represent Sinclair's deepest anxieties surrounding incorporation. One of the defining features of sausage is that it doesn't correspond to a discrete part of an animal, as most items in a butcher shop do. That is, a sausage isn't a leg, a wing, a thigh, a breast, or a rack of ribs; it consists instead of undifferentiated minced meat and a blend of spices, which are then mixed together and enclosed by a thin intestinal casing that forms the meat into sausage-shaped cylinders or "links." What goes into the sausage remains a mystery to consumers: while the outside wrapper makes the spiced meat inside recognizable as sausage, it also insistently reminds us that we will never really know what is inside the sausage we are consuming. The thin casing thus structures the experience of eating sausage by upholding the precarious boundary between inside and outside; in forming this boundary it tethers the reassuring signifier "sausage" to the potentially horrifying signified "sausage meat." With each bite of a sausage, our very legitimate suspicion that we don't know what we are eating must be surmounted by the belief that sausage meat, and sausage meat alone, is enclosed in the sausage skin. The thrill and delight and terror of eating sausage is produced by this formal separation of inside and outside.

The industrial system of production is disgusting in *The Jungle* because of the instability of these boundaries, the ease with which the outside becomes incorporated into the inside. "There was never the least attention paid to what was cut up for sausage," Sinclair writes. "Cut up by the two-thousand-revolutions-a-minute flyers, and mixed with half a ton of other meat, no odor that ever was in a ham could make any difference." Sinclair's description of the production process begins with an account of spoiled ham being churned into sausage, but it then quickly degenerates into a catalogue of invasions, a list of non-food items that have managed to penetrate the sausage's intestinal membrane, becoming integrated into the sausage itself. The items in this catalogue include dirt and sawdust and spit: "There would be meat that had tumbled out on the floor, in the dirt and sawdust, where the workers had tramped and spit uncounted billions of consumption germs"; also dirty rainwater: "There would be meat stored in great piles in rooms; and the water from leaky roofs would drip over it"; and dead rats, rat feces, and rat poison: "[A] man could run his hand over these piles of meat and sweep off handfuls of the dried dung of rats. These rats were nuisances, and the packers would put poisoned bread out for them; they would die, and then rats, bread, and meat would go into the hoppers together"; also dirty water, used for hand washing, because workers "made a practice of washing [their hands] in the water that was to be ladled into the sausage"; and debris from the factory waste barrels: "in the barrels would be dirt and rust and old nails and stale water—and cart load after cart load of it would be taken up and dumped into the hoppers with fresh meat, and sent out to the public's breakfast." At one point in Sinclair's account, the sausage's inner contents literally become foreign: "[T]here would come all the way back from Europe old sausage that had been rejected, and that was mouldy and white," and this spoiled foreign meat would then be made edible through a chemical treatment, "dosed with borax and glycerine, and dumped into the hoppers, and made over again for home consumption."[52]

So much of the disgust in *The Jungle* as a whole involves just these sorts of invasions—in one of the novel's more notorious scenes, for instance, workers at the factory are described falling into steaming industrial vats, where they are cooked and processed until "all but the bones of them had gone out to the world as Durham's Pure Leaf Lard!"[53] These invasions suggest that disgust is a fundamentally liminal phenomenon in the book, marking the moments when the outside transgresses in. When Sinclair describes workers dumping dead rats into the hoppers with the rest of the sausage meat, the novel suggests that not just the sausage skin is violated, but also the reader's body. The rats are integrated from the outside to the inside of the sausage, and, when we readers eat and digest the sausage, the rats go from the outside to the inside of us as well. The anxiety that disgust registers in *The Jungle* is the same anxiety that Sinclair experienced in relation to the institutions of US life at the time. As the educational system swallowed up the revolutionary fervor of Jack London's speech at Yale, so too does the meatpacking industry in *The Jungle* swallow up dust and dirt, rats and rat poison, chemicals, nails, and anything else in its path. The disgust of *The Jungle* reflects the repulsiveness of a system that incorporates everything that surrounds it, and its capacity to metabolize the things it incorporates in the service of its own expansion.

If disgust encodes the tensions that attended *The Jungle*'s composition—the founding of the ISS, the battles with the editors at the *Appeal* and Macmillan— it also anticipates the novel's reception, not just its immediate political effects, and the quickness with which food legislation passed in its wake, but also its incorporation into the formal system of education in the United States.[54] *The Jungle* has become firmly embedded in the US school system over the twentieth and twenty-first centuries—and not as literature but as history. Daniel J. Cohen's

"By the Book: Assessing the Place of Textbooks in U.S. Survey Courses" (2005) found *The Jungle* to be among the top five supplementary texts assigned in undergraduate history survey courses in the United States, ahead of Thomas Paine's *Common Sense*, Harriet Beecher Stowe's *Uncle Tom's Cabin*, and *The Autobiography of Malcolm X*. In 2006, Christopher Phelps's "How Should We Teach 'The Jungle'?" (2006), published in the *Chronicle of Higher Education*, pointed out the danger of history teachers situating the novel in the "comforting narrative of liberal progress," and instead encouraged history teachers to think of the novel less as history and more as a novel: "as both a transcription of social life and a work of literary imagination, as both reportage and social criticism." Even articles that have more forcefully contested the use of the novel in history courses—like Louise Carroll Wade's "The Problem with Classroom Use of Upton Sinclair's *The Jungle*" (1991)—testify to the novel's status as an enduring presence in the American history curriculum.[55]

The Jungle's prominence in secondary school American history courses can be traced as far back as 1925, when it appeared in Henry Eldridge Bourne and Elbert Jay Benton's textbook, *American History*, but it wasn't until the late thirties that the novel's place in the pedagogy of US history was secured. This rise to pedagogical prominence was largely propelled by the historians Charles and Mary Beard, whose textbook, *The Making of American Civilization* (1937), placed the novel within a Progressive narrative of state intervention against the unfettered interests of capitalism. "With startling realism Upton Sinclair described the meat-packing industry in Chicago as a sample of operations by 'big business,'" the Beards write. "Indeed President Theodore Roosevelt was so affected by the book that he called Sinclair to the White House and talked with him about laws which might remove the abuses pictured in that story." In the decades following the Beards' account, *The Jungle* proved a mainstay in American history textbooks, demanding at least a sentence or two in chapters about Progressivism, Theodore Roosevelt, or both.[56]

While the Beards leave out the socialism that takes up most of the novel's final third and fail to mention the often tense relationship Sinclair and Roosevelt maintained in real life,[57] they also include, in their reference to the novel's "startling realism," at least a sense of the disgusting reactions *The Jungle* elicited. The whitewashing of socialism and the inclusion of disgust prove, in fact, to be the two features that characterize most of, if not all, the descriptions of *The Jungle* in history textbooks. Riegal and Haugh (1947) recount "the public's horror at the disclosures of Upton Sinclair's *The Jungle*"; Hofstadter et al. (1957) call the novel "nauseatingly realistic"; Bernard et al. (1968) mention the "unhealthful, shocking conditions" in Sinclair's portrayal of the Chicago yards; Bailey et al. call Sinclair's novel a "revolting tract" that "described in noxious detail the filth, disease and putrefaction in Chicago's damp, ill-ventilated slaughterhouses"; and Ahlquist et al. even include language from the original sausage room scene: "Sinclair described the Chicago stockyards and meatpacking plants. To kill rats, Sinclair wrote, 'the packers would put poisoned bread out for them; they would die, and then rats, bread, and meat would go into the hoppers together.' Out of that, sausage was made for 'the public's breakfast.'" Far from making the novel unpalatable to US institutions, the disgust *The Jungle* provoked is exactly what the educational system has held onto in its absorption of the novel. Disgust has come to define the very terms by which *The Jungle* has been incorporated.[58]

It therefore seems fitting that movements from the inside out are represented much less frequently in *The Jungle* than movements from the outside in. Even *The Jungle*'s larger project—to expose the inner workings of Chicago's meatpacking industry to the public, which would seem to move in the other direction, from the inside out—manifests itself in the narrative proper as a fundamentally incorporative move, enfolding "you" the reader into the world of the meatpacking factory, as the narrator sporadically resorts to the second person over the course of the book. Also, in more thematic terms, despite the "sickening" stench that permeates the novel's descriptions of the city of Chicago, characters almost never vomit in *The Jungle*. The one time characters do vomit—when Jurgis comes home from his first day at the fertilizer plant—Sinclair refuses to linger on the details and, instead, quickly moves on to a more detailed account of Jurgis's daily life at the plant.[59] *McTeague* offers a useful contrast to *The Jungle* in this respect. Where *The Jungle*'s representation of disgust comes from Sinclair's position outside of the institutions he wants to upend and centers on issues of incorporation, with little attention paid to vomit, *McTeague*'s representation of disgust originates from Norris's position inside educational institutions, and in consequence his disgust travels in the opposite direction, with vomit receiving much more narrative attention. So even though only one scene in *McTeague* actually features vomit (when McTeague kisses Trina during her oral surgery, and Trina wakes up and vomits), this scene plays a much larger role in the novel's overall design than the single mention—the one sentence—of vomit in *The Jungle*. If disgust occupies a place on the threshold of educational institutions in both of these books, marking the boundary where insides come outside and outsides come inside, Norris and Sinclair can be understood to inhabit the two sides of the threshold: Norris, standing inside, imagines the degeneration of life as it crosses the threshold outside, and Sinclair, standing outside, watches with horror as revolutionary energy crosses the threshold in.

In the afterword to *Ugly Feelings* (2005), Sianne Ngai asks why "[t]heories, poetics, and ethics of 'desire' abound" while for some reason in the academy "disgust seems to have resisted engendering these forms of attention." It is "not that the idiom of disgust is inherently more 'radical' ... or that agonistic emotion has better rather than simply different possibilities to offer [than desire]," according to Ngai. Rather, it is that "the academically routinized concept of 'desire' is simply more concordant, ideologically as well as aesthetically, with the aesthetic, cultural, and political pluralisms that have come to define the post-modern than an emotional idiom defined by its vehement exclusion of the intolerable."[60] But if, for Ngai, the fully administered postwar system of higher education finds the centripetal pull of desire more conducive to its cultural and political program than the centrifugal force of disgust, the disgusting literature of the turn of the century alerts us to the indispensable labor disgust has nonetheless carried out on behalf of the educational system. Students are more likely to encounter *The Jungle* in the classroom than anywhere else in their lives, and the same is true of *McTeague* and the other disgusting novels of the period. Insofar as the turn of the century has become legible as a coherent literary-historical period in schools—a period that saw the rise of social realism, naturalism, and muckraking—its coherence lies in the very disgust writers at the time evoked to demarcate and constrain the scholastic.

McTeague and *The Jungle*, for all of their disgustingness, have by no means inhibited or restricted the kinds of emotions students experience in school. The ultimate reintegration of these novels into the classroom—and the reintegration of literary disgust more broadly—in fact signals a further broadening of the school's emotional palate. Battered corpses and rat feces may continue to remain outside the scope of the high school curriculum, but the novelistic representation of battered corpses and rat feces has proved an uncontroversial, if not welcome, addition to lesson plans across the country. Emerging out of a disorganized institutional landscape in the process of organizing itself, literary disgust has irrevocably shaped twentieth- and twenty-first-century institutional feeling, the way we feel in schools and the way schools train us to feel.

Conclusion

Upton Sinclair spent much of his private and professional life after the publication of *The Jungle* restaging the confrontation between his revolutionary educational program and the formal school system in the United States. In 1906, he squandered $16,000—half the proceeds from *The Jungle*—establishing his own Brook Farm–type community, Helicon Hall, in an abandoned boys' school in Englewood, New Jersey.[61] (He nearly convinced John Dewey to invest in Helicon Hall, and even though Dewey never invested money in the institution, he remained on the community's board of directors, visiting Helicon Hall often, along with William James.)[62] After the failure of Helicon Hall, Sinclair promised publicly in 1909 to create a boys' school with a curriculum focused on physical activities and diet, the students subsiding each day on "an ounce or two of nuts, a dish of soaked wheat with a little olive oil, and some dates, and an apple or two to finish off."[63] In the twenties he published two muckraking books on US education, one on the university system, *The Goose-Step* (1922), the other on the secondary school system,

The Goslings (1924). His novel *Oil!* (1927) ends with the protagonist, an oil scion named Bunny, deciding to use his money to found a labor college.

In 1957, after these confrontations had played out and Sinclair entered the final decade of his life, he would have the unique privilege of witnessing his own incorporation into the system of education in the United States. That year, Sinclair agreed to donate his papers and manuscripts to the libraries at Indiana University, and significantly, his reaction to his own institutionalization, as he recorded it in the *Autobiography*, is not one of disgust. By the late fifties, so much of US life would be administered, so much of it would take place inside the system first erected by the Progressives, then expanded under the New Deal, and finally consolidated in the post-war military-industrial complex, that the institutional borders disgust relied on for its lurid effects at the turn of the twentieth century would seem, from Sinclair's perspective, to have disappeared altogether. The packers from Indiana arrive at Sinclair's house, and it's as if he realizes in this moment that once he surrenders his work to the school system, there will be nothing of him left outside the system. In claiming his papers, the formal institutions of US education have finally managed to claim him, and Sinclair's response suggests not abhorrence or fear or anger but bewilderment, resignation, and maybe, even, a little relief:

> One of the great sights of my life was the arrival of a huge van from a storage company, and the packing of those treasures. ... Into those boxes went all the priceless foreign editions, the original manuscripts, the manila folders with the two hundred and fifty thousand letters. The whole job was done in three or four hours, and off went our lifetime's treasure. Off went the bust by the Swedish sculptor, Carl Eldh, and the large photograph of Albert Einstein with the poem to me, written in German; off went all the books, pamphlets and manuscripts[.] ... The collection rolled away, and the place seemed kind of empty—all those storerooms and nothing in them!

For Sinclair, the era of disgust had long passed away.[64]

PART 3

5
Secret Societies

We may observe, even in school classes, how small, closely attached groups of comrades, through the mere formal fact that they form a special group, come to consider themselves an elite, compared with the rest who are unorganized; while the latter, by their enmity and jealousy, involuntarily recognize that higher value. In these cases secrecy and pretense of secrecy (*Geheimnistnerei*) are means of building higher the wall of separation, and therein a reinforcement of the aristocratic nature of the group.
—Georg Simmel, "The Sociology of Secrecy and of Secret Societies" (1906)

Yale's annual secret society elections were held to-day on the campus, each member of three societies from the class of 1907 slapping a member of the class of 1908 between the shoulders by way of an official notification.
—"Yale's Society Elections," *New York Times* (1907)[1]

In 1831, Alexis de Tocqueville traveled to the United States and noted, approvingly, the prevalence of voluntary associations: "Americans of all ages, conditions, and all dispositions constantly unite together," he wrote in the second volume of *Democracy in America* (1840). In 1904, Max Weber visited the United States and was less sanguine in his evaluation of the social landscape. Voluntary associations for Weber were "the typical vehicles of social ascent into the circle of the entrepreneurial middle class," serving to "diffuse and to maintain the bourgeois capitalist business ethos among the broad strata of the middle classes[.]" "The entire life of a typical Yankee of the last generation led through a series of such exclusive associations," he went on, "beginning with the Boys' Club in school, proceeding to the Athletic Club or the Greek Letter Society or to another student club of the same nature, then onward to one of the numerous notable clubs of businessmen and the bourgeoisie, or finally to the clubs of the metropolitan plutocracy." Weber was by no means unfamiliar with voluntary associations before coming to the United States. When he attended school in Heidelberg, he joined a dueling fraternity where he learned, in the words of one biography, to "hold his own in drinking bouts as well as duels," and his face, after he graduated, "carried the conventional dueling scar." Yet even Weber was shocked by the proliferation of these organizations in America during his trip.[2]

Foremost among the voluntary associations that structured civil society in the postbellum United States was the secret fraternal order. More than a quarter of adult men in the country belonged to at least one fraternal lodge by 1896. These fraternal lodges were sharply graded by class: Freemasons attracted the greatest percentage of businessmen, merchants, professionals, and better-paid clerks, while the Knights of Pythias was made up largely by members of the working class, and the Odd Fellows occupied a space in between the other two.[3] Weber's colleague Georg Simmel eventually produced a robust theoretical account of these particular voluntary associations. In his essay, "The Sociology of Secrecy and of Secret Societies," which was translated and published in the January 1906 issue of the *American Journal of Sociology*, Simmel argued that the distribution of secrecy in society was undergoing a dramatic shift under industrial modernity: he wrote that "politics, administration, justice, have lost their secrecy and inaccessibility in precisely the degree in which the individual has gained possibility of more complete privacy, since modern life has elaborated a technique for isolation of the affairs of individuals, within the crowded conditions of great cities[.]" Secret societies fascinated Simmel in part because they reversed this larger trend in the relationship between secrecy and the social. Rather than further individualizing secrecy, the secret society socialized it.[4]

If Simmel's article suggests the prominence of secret societies in fin-de-siècle culture, it also indicates the extent to which these organizations had infiltrated school life, and not merely as an object of academic study. The editor of the *American Journal of Sociology*, Albion Woodbury Small, was himself a member of one of those "small, closely attached groups of comrades" in "school classes" whose secret practices, Simmel explained, "are means of building higher the wall of separation, and therein a reinforcement of the aristocratic nature of the group"—Small belonged to a fraternity, Delta Kappa Epsilon or "Deke." Perhaps his experience in this fraternity as an undergraduate at Colby College motivated Small to translate Simmel's article (to this day, a relatively minor one) and include it in the pages of the *American Journal of Sociology*; undoubtedly Small's membership in the fraternity played a role in his decision to serve in administration as a graduate dean at the University of Chicago. A profile published in the *University of Chicago Magazine* emphasized Small's fraternal background. As a former member of a fraternity, the profile declared, "Dr. Small has never lost his interest in undergraduate students and their perennial stunts."[5]

As we'll see over the next two chapters, a variety of institutional actors—loyal alumni and Progressive university administrators, Baptist ministers and former abolitionists—sought to understand formal education as an instrument of class struggle through the secret societies that proliferated on campus and off, as well as (more capaciously) through "secrecy" as a feature of organizational life. Simmel is unique among these actors for his unneurotic insistence that secrecy is simply an intrinsic feature of social experience. More like Simmel's colleague Weber, the writers I discuss in these chapters—Owen Johnson and Thomas Dixon Jr. in Chapter 5, and Frances Ellen Watkins Harper, Charles Chesnutt, and Sutton Griggs in Chapter 6—believed that secret societies wielded tremendous power in class relations. The significance these writers ascribed to secret organizations derived from their intuition that the reproduction of the conditions of production was dictated by invisible institutional collectives or (to use the language of Progressivism) "combinations." According to Fredric Jameson, the paranoid conspiracy films of the 1970s and 1980s reflect a range of attempts to conceive the social totality under late capitalism; the secret societies that appeared in the not unparanoid fiction of the turn-of-the-century United States suggest that this thematic characterizes the effort to fathom class relations as such.[6]

An influential strain of critical theory has long understood the modern institutional system in general and the school in particular as fundamentally secretive. In his essay "Ideology and Ideological State Apparatuses" (1970), Louis Althusser famously argued that the school occupied the "*dominant* position" among Ideological State Apparatuses; under capitalism's mature phase, he claimed, the relationship between the exploited and the exploiter is "naturally covered up and concealed by a universally reigning ideology of the School," an ideology that "represents the School as a neutral environment purged of ideology[.]" Pierre Bourdieu and Jean-Claude Passeron's *Reproduction in Education, Society and Culture* (1970) deployed a similar argument, using similar metaphorics, insisting that the school's relative autonomy as a social institution allows it to disguise the reproduction of social hierarchies. The "hidden services" the school "renders to certain classes," they wrote, "conceal[] social selection under the guise of technical selection and legitimat[e] the reproduction of the social hierarchies by transmuting them into academic hierarchies." The language of concealment and invisibility seems to enter all of Bourdieu's analysis of the French educational system. In *The State Nobility* (1996), he argued that the "invisible action" of the school is "effected through the statutory assignation ... that results from attaching students to a place and a status that are socially distinguished from the commonplace, which we might think of as a type of *marking* that creates a magical boundary between insiders and outsiders[.]"[7]

More recently, Sara Ahmed's examination of diversity workers in institutions of higher education, *On Being Included* (2012), investigates "what diversity does by focusing on what diversity obscures, that is, by focusing on the relationship between diversity and racism as a way of making explicit a tendency that is reproduced by staying implicit." For Ahmed, the modern school's racism is reinforced and disguised by the invocation of diversity. Universities, she claims, regularly have recourse to "non-performative" speech acts—a neologism Ahmed adapts from

J. L. Austin and Judith Butler—in which "the failure of the speech act to do what it says is not a failure of intent or even circumstance, *but is actually what the speech act is doing*." Uncovering the ideological work the school performs under these conditions doesn't simply involve unmasking "what the surface hides," as it would under traditional ideology critique. It involves, rather, a critique of "*how things surface*, which is to say, a critique of what recedes," and it's in this context that Ahmed understands her analysis as phenomenological, invested in discovering "how something becomes given by not being the object of perception."[8]

The modern school for each of these thinkers is ideological insofar as it obscures not only the perpetuation of the social order but also its own role in the reproduction process. The school visibly distinguishes the "deserving" from the "undeserving" and in doing so *in*visibly reproduces an unequal society, separating the dominators from the dominated, those inside social power from those outside. The school in this strain of critical theory is, in short, a secret society, and this is why Bourdieu in *The State Nobility* refers to scholastic culture—the vocabulary, jokes, and dispositions shared by students in elite French higher education—as the "'freemasonry' of the grandes écoles."[9] In this chapter, I argue that the metaphorics of secrecy that surround the school are not accidental: in the opening decades of the twentieth century, the US educational system deliberately set out to *transform itself into a secret society*. Administrators in higher education enacted this transformation, in one sense, by embracing and publicizing secret societies on campus after years of trying to suppress them. They enacted it, in another sense, by denouncing the secrecy of secret societies—by representing this secrecy as undemocratic—while they secretly adopted the societies' undemocratic admissions practices.

Literature facilitated the school system's transformation into a secret society and, in turn, enabled the school system to secure recognition as an ideological instrument. It did so in part by broadcasting undergraduate campus culture, and the secret societies contained in it, to a mass audience of readers. Though the traditional district one-room school had become a free-floating cultural signifier in the decades after the Civil War, appearing in fiction, poetry, and hit songs, the modern educational system nevertheless faced a representational deficit during this period. The emergence of campus fiction as a genre at the end of the century made the modern school unprecedentedly legible. It resolved the educational system's representational crisis by showing readers why a bachelor's degree—the system's crown jewel, the reward that justified the whole unpleasant endeavor of primary school, high school, and college—was valuable.[10]

Campus fiction shaped the public perception of formal education, but it also shaped formal education itself. It could influence the inside and outside of the academic experience—and bridge the two together—because it occupied the liminal institutional space that educational historians call the "extracurriculum." Thorstein Veblen at the time recognized the influence of the extracurriculum or undergraduate culture on the operations of higher education. He argued that educational institutions felt the need to attend to students' "other interests" for fear of "losing their custom and their good will, to the detriment of the university's standing in genteel circles and to the serious decline in enrolment which their withdrawal would occasion." "Hence," he wrote, "college sports come in for an ever increasing attention and take an increasingly prominent and voluminous place in the university's life; as do also other politely blameless ways and means of dissipation, such as fraternities, clubs, exhibitions, and the extensive range of extra-scholastic traffic known as 'student activities.'"[11]

As simultaneously a product of this emergent undergraduate culture, a representation of it, and an active force within it, early campus fiction occupied the threshold of scholastic life, and from this position it proposed solutions to one of the great institutional challenges of the period: where and how schools would establish the "magical boundary" between academic "insiders and outsiders." As I will demonstrate below, early campus fiction sought to legitimize higher education as *the* social mechanism capable of distinguishing true leadership and rewarding true merit.

This isn't to say that campus fiction's meritocratic solution to the problem of college and university admissions, or that the modern school's adoption of this solution, has entirely naturalized the educational system's role in the reproduction of social relations. In fact, the alternatives to early campus fiction's meritocratic ideology indicate that the school's capacity to invisibly reproduce unequal social relations, and that literature's capacity to naturalize the school's role in social reproduction, are not as great as scholars and theorists have claimed.[12] Campus fiction's meritocratic conception of the educational system might have proved compelling for the school's middle-class clientele and "genteel" benefactors, yet the controversies surrounding the educational system's allegedly secret operations indicate that this meritocratic ideology didn't altogether succeed in subduing those populations it was meant to. Though literature and schools since at least the 1970s have been understood, separately and together, as uniquely effective instruments for naturalizing unequal class relations and interpellating subjects into the social order, the literary works that I examine in this chapter and the next suggest that schools and literature aren't especially effective political tools, that neither performs especially well that task—indoctrination—that supposedly distinguishes both as modern ideological instruments. The "secret" that schools reproduce social inequality has not, in other words, been especially well kept.

The Skull and the Snake

The final episode of Owen Johnson's early campus novel *Stover at Yale* (1912) takes place during Tap Day, as the novel's protagonist, Dink Stover, eagerly waits to see if

Yale's most elite senior society, Skull and Bones, will induct him. "Tap Day arrived at last, cloudy and misty," Johnson writes. "The morning was interminable, a horror. They did not even joke about the approaching ordeal." Although over the course of the novel Stover has grown increasingly suspicious of the society system at Yale, the novel's climax derives its suspense from the question of whether Stover—star football player, big man on campus—is going to be elected. When Stover is indeed finally "tapped" for the society, the moment proves disorienting at first but in the end cathartic:

> It was a shout of electrifying drama, the voice of his society speaking to the college.
> Someone caught Stover. He straightened up, trying to collect his wits, utterly unprepared for the shock. About him pandemonium broke loose. Still dazed, he felt Hungerford leap at him, crying in his ears:
> "God bless you, old man. It's great, great—they rose to it. It's the finest ever!"
> He began to move mechanically towards his room, seeing nothing, hearing nothing. He started towards the library, and someone swung him around. He heard them cheering, then he saw hundreds of faces, wild-eyed, rushing past him; he stumbled and suddenly his eyes were blurred with tears, and he knew how much he cared, after the long months of rebellion, to be no longer outside, but back among his own with the stamp of approval on his record.[13]

It's difficult to appreciate the novelty of such a scene from our contemporary moment, when the cultural fascination with student organizations has come to seem natural, indulged in popular movies from *Animal House* (1978) to *The Skulls* (2000) to *Old School* (2003) to *Pitch Perfect* (2012) to *Neighbors* (2014). This fascination isn't new, however: campus fiction has always gravitated toward the student "society" in its various forms, even at the inception of American campus fiction as a genre at the turn of the twentieth century. James Gardner Sanderson's popular collection *Cornell Stories* (1898) centers on the shenanigans of the members of Rho Tau, Beta Chi, and Chi Delta Sigma houses. One of the first episodes in Burt Standish's *Frank Merriwell at Yale* (1903) involves an elaborate hazing ritual performed by members of the sophomore society Delta Kappa: the protagonist Frank Merriwell is kidnapped by a group of masked men, and under the supervision of a Mephisto he is dunked in a tub of ice water, made to crawl through a piano box filled with sawdust, and mock-executed under a guillotine. *Stover at Yale*, often cited as the first American campus novel—the novel that served as "somewhat of a text-book" for Amory Blaine, protagonist of F. Scott Fitzgerald's *This Side of Paradise* (1920)[14]—can be seen as yet another origin point for this tradition, despite (and as we'll see, precisely because of) its core ambivalence toward the society system. But why? Why did the student society, particularly the secret society, become so central to campus fiction at the turn of the century? Why did the secret society become the institutional fixture around which campus fiction developed such a rich and enduring representational vocabulary?

Answering these questions requires a better understanding of the not-so-secret history of secret societies. The fact that educational historians haven't had much trouble unearthing the history of secret societies is precisely the point; from their inception, secret societies have been legible to the public. They are part of higher education's official history—not, as we might expect, its unofficial history. The visibility of secret societies is a product of the unique position these organizations have held on the boundary of academic experience and the influence these organizations have exercised on the institutional system from this boundary location. By the late nineteenth century, the secret society had installed itself in the culture of college campuses, one of the organizations that Thorstein Veblen lamented was taking "an increasingly prominent and voluminous place in the university's life." Educational historian Frederick Rudolph understood the importance of the "extracurriculum" for the history of higher education and recuperated it in his landmark *The American College and University* (1962), explaining the contribution of student organizations to what he called the "collegiate way," the notion that "a curriculum, a library, a faculty, and students are not enough to make a college. ... [The collegiate way] is what every American college has had or consciously rejected or lost or sought to recapture."[15]

The origins of the college secret society lie in the post-Revolutionary era. In the mid-eighteenth century, the colonial college developed its own distinctive culture through its robust system of extracurricular literary societies, which consisted of faculty members and students gathering together outside of class to educate themselves for the demands of public life. At the turn of the nineteenth century, however, campus culture evolved as relations between the faculty that enforced the curriculum and the students who were expected to submit to it began to deteriorate. At Princeton, hostilities boiled over: in 1807 two-thirds of the student body barricaded itself in Nassau Hall after two students were suspended for drinking. Much structural damage ensued, and in the end, 125 students were suspended, seventy never to return. It was in the aftermath of these sorts of confrontations, which occurred on campuses across the country, that students banded together to form secret fraternities.[16]

The first fraternity, Kappa Alpha, was founded at Union College in 1825. In a perhaps incongruous symbolic pairing, the organization yoked the trappings of Greek antiquity with those of freemasonry, adopting some of the fraternal order's rituals and terminology, and claiming the key watch as its emblem. Soon after the founding of Kappa Alpha, two other fraternities formed at Union, and in 1831 these organizations spread across the state to Hamilton College. By 1850, campuses throughout New England and the Midwest hosted fraternities. Compulsory chapel attendance and grueling Latin and Greek recitations made these fraternities especially appealing. In a fraternity, students of a certain social standing could secretly indulge all of those behaviors normally forbidden by the faculty. By the end of the nineteenth century, student societies were ubiquitous. In most places, they took the form of secret fraternities, but there were notable local variations, especially at the most elite institutions, from the finals clubs at Harvard (Porcellian, A.D., Fly), to the secret societies at Yale (Skull and Bones, Keys, Book and Snake, Wolf's Head), to the eating clubs at Princeton (Ivy, Cottage, Cap and Gown). According to Lincoln Steffens, who arrived at the University of California in 1885, deciding "which fraternity to join" was one of the first "socially important" questions students asked themselves upon entering college.[17]

The turn of the twentieth century, however, witnessed an upheaval in the "collegiate way," as Progressives began to question the role of the society in campus life. We've already seen in Chapter 3 the ambivalence Charles Eliot, president of Harvard, expressed toward fraternities and secret societies. For Eliot, social clubs in institutions of higher education, "being small, exclusive, and secretive groups" seemed "inconsistent with democratic principles in general, and particularly with the liberal spirit of a society of scholars." And yet, Eliot ultimately offered a begrudging defense of these organizations. "The limited human being, even when fairly educated," Eliot explained, "craves a limited group of congenial associates having some common interest, which, as a social bond, may as well be narrow as broad."[18] Woodrow Wilson was less ambivalent toward these societies; he spent a good deal of his energy as president of Princeton fighting a losing battle against the school's entrenched eating clubs.

The increasing democratization of higher education at the beginning of the twentieth century incited these controversies. Earlier in the nineteenth century, secret societies thrived in an undergraduate culture that was understood to reward the best from each class, but the entrance of a broader, more diverse body of students onto college campuses sowed doubts about the societies' selection process. "[T]he celebrated 'collegiate ideal' began to fall short after 1900," educational historian John Thelin has explained. "The recurrent concern was that collegiate rewards were not, as promised, based primarily on talent and merit but had become a matter of favoritism and nepotism." To remove the social divisions in campus culture under the society system, Progressive reformers encouraged students to live in on-campus housing and invented the "student union" as an architectural feature of colleges around the country, a communal structure that allowed all members of the student body to gather together, not in their own individual societies.[19]

Owen Johnson, writing in 1912, made the institutional debate surrounding secret societies central to the narrative of *Stover at Yale*. For Johnson, the crisis in the society system was brought about by the changing student demographics on college campuses. "The fraternities and secret societies, which were formerly intellectual in their purpose and leanings, were the convenient instruments at hand when the great social struggle outside swept into the colleges and overwhelmed them," he explained in a *New York Times* interview conducted after the publication of the novel. "They were supported in opposition to the spontaneous democracy that finds its natural leaders and natural groupings."[20] From the opening scene of the novel, Johnson goes to great lengths to demonstrate that the "great social struggle" outside the school has indeed entered campus life. When Stover disembarks from the train in New Haven, he is immediately "[b]uffeted by the crowd," swinging "down the crowded street to the heart of the city[.] ... The jumble of the city was in his ears, the hazy crowded panorama in his eyes, at his side the passing contact of strangers. Everything was multiplied, complex, submerging his individuality." Later in the book, freshmen walk to class: "The windows were open, crowded with eager heads; the street corners clustered with swiftly assembling groups[.]" Before the big football game against Princeton, Stover travels "silently through the surging, arriving multitude, all intoxicated with the joy and zest of the great game."[21]

The principal drama of *Stover at Yale* is whether Stover can assert his own individual superiority in the middle of all these crowds—whether he can successfully "fre[e] himself from the thralling oblivion of the mass"—and how the secret society can assist in this sorting process. The argument in favor of the society system is presented early in the novel by the character Le Baron, a student one year older than Stover who is already a member of a sophomore society. "[I]t's the best system there is, and it makes Yale what it is today," Le Baron explains to Stover. "It makes fellows get out and work; it gives them ambitions, stops loafing and going to seed, and keeps a pretty good, clean, temperate atmosphere about the place." For Le Baron, secret societies are a reward for students who distinguish themselves as the natural leaders of their class, those destined to take a prominent role in public life after graduation. "I'm frankly aristocratic in my point of view," Le Baron concedes to Stover. "You may think the world begins outside of college. It doesn't; it begins right here. You want to make the friends that will help you along, here and outside. Don't lose sight of your opportunities, and be careful how you choose."[22]

Against Le Baron, Johnson introduces other characters—Progressives—whom Stover is increasingly drawn toward over the course of the novel. Foremost among these characters is Brockhurst, based on one of Johnson's Yale classmates, a man named Henry Hunt, who went on to become mayor of Cincinnati.[23] According to Brockhurst, the society system undermined the mission of higher education by embracing secrecy. "The harm is that this mumbo jumbo, fee-fi-fo-fum, high cockalorum business is taken seriously," Brockburst explains to Stover toward the end of the novel. "By George it *is* a return of the old idol-worship idea[.] ... It's wrong, fundamentally wrong—it's a crime against the whole moving spirit of university history—the history of a struggle for the liberation of the human mind." Brockhurst's rhetoric reappears throughout the novel. Instead of embracing "piffle," "bosh," and "mumbo-jumbo," societies according to the Progressive characters should be transparent, with the understanding, typical of the era, that such transparency will produce better outcomes, with the true leaders of the class rising to the top.[24]

Johnson voiced these criticisms of the society system explicitly in a five-part essay published in *Collier's*, "The Social Usurpation of Our Colleges" (1912). According to Johnson, the impulse that "exalt[s] the idea of social success to the stifling of the broader and more vital ambitions" is one and the same as the impulse "to convert our universities ... into social clearing houses"; it is an impulse, Johnson claimed, that "express[es] itself in open or silent clubs, secret societies, or general fraternities." Rather than encouraging the search for knowledge, or preparing students for future leadership roles, the society system in Johnson's estimation existed to preserve class distinctions, using secrecy to mask undemocratic principles of social selection. Under the society system, students with wealth and privilege were cordoned off from the rest of the student population, an arrangement that was damaging to students both with and without social privilege.[25]

Put in somewhat different terms, the secret society is anathema to many of the characters in *Stover at Yale* because it is fundamentally *un*secretive. As Johnson depicts it in the novel, the society system exercises such a decisive role in the life of the campus because it broadcasts its secrecy out in the open and in doing so mystifies class relations among the student body. After all, the *New York Times* had been covering Tap Day ceremonies at least as early as 1893, reporting to eager readers which students were most likely to be tapped, and which students eventually were.[26] In this context, the school doesn't "liberat[e]" minds; it becomes a place where the mind luxuriates in mystery and magic. This is apparent in the very first Tap Day scene represented in the novel, during Stover's freshman year. "On the fateful Thursday in May, shortly after half past four, [Stover] and Tough went over to the campus," Johnson writes. "By the fence the junior class, already swallowed up by the curious body of the college, were waiting the arrival of the senior elections which would begin on the stroke of five." As the crowds gather, Stover begins to notice that secrecy isn't especially secretive, that secrecy can elicit the most intense expressions of public interest and curiosity. "He looked over at the herd huddled under the trees by the fence. It was all a spectacle still—dramatic, but removed from his own personality," Johnson writes. "[H]e noticed, above the ghost-like heads of the crowd, the windows packed with spectators drawn to the spectacle."[27]

The view Stover adopts at the end of the novel offers itself up as an alternative to this particular form of secrecy, the kind that draws "spectators ... to the spectacle." Before the novel's final Tap Day, Stover approaches an alum of Skull and Bones to make his opinions on the matter clear: "That Skull and Bones, which does a great good here—I believe it—also does a great deal of harm; all of which is unnecessary and a weakness in its system. In a word, I've come to the point where I believe secrecy is un-American, undemocratic, and stultifying; and, as I say, totally unnecessary. I should always be against it." And yet, despite Stover's insistence that he should "always be against" the society's secrecy, he remains, even in his denunciations, not against the society itself, acknowledging the "great good" Skull and Bones does for Yale. In fact, whenever Stover voices his criticisms of the society system, he never suggests that it should be abolished altogether. "With the aims and purposes of Skull and Bones he was in thorough sympathy," Johnson writes, "but the more he freely acknowledged their influence for democracy and simplicity at Yale, the more he revolted at the unnecessary fetish of it all." Even the novel's most radical condemnations of the societies affirm their right to exist. As Brockhurst tells Stover:

> "This is what I'd do: drop the secrecy—this extraordinary muffled breathless guarding of an empty can—retain the privilege any club has of excluding outsiders, stop the childishness of getting up and leaving the room if some old lady happens to ask are you a Bones man or a Keys man. Instead, when a Bones man goes to see a freshman whom he wants to befriend, have him say openly as he passes the chapter house:
> "That's my society—Skull and Bones. It stands as a reward of merit here. Hope you'll do something to deserve it."[28]

The solution to the problems besetting the society system that Johnson offered in his *Collier's* articles adopts this pattern—abolishing secrecy, not the society[29]—and it's in this context that we can begin to understand the larger project of *Stover at Yale*, and the stakes of the novel's climax, when Stover is finally tapped for Skull and Bones. Against the mystery and secrecy of the society system, Johnson proposes a vision of campus life that is oriented fundamentally around a cleaner form of publicity. Instead of a publicity that mystifies, in other words, Johnson calls for a publicity that democratizes. The final pivotal scene of the novel enacts these values in a couple of different senses. In the diegetic world of the novel, this Tap Day episode represents a transformation in the society system—it demonstrates the willingness of the secret society to become more open and democratic in its practices. The final scene is still a spectacle for everyone in attendance, like the first Tap Day was, only this time the public that has assembled bears witness to the tapping of Stover, a critic of the society's secrecy. The eruption that occurs after the "tapping"—when Stover hears the crowds "cheering" for him after the selection and sees "hundreds of faces, wild-eyed, rushing past him"—takes place because everyone present has witnessed an affirmation of transparency, the willingness of the societies to reform. "[T]hey rose to it," Stover's friend Hungerford explains. "It's the finest ever!" The final scene enacts these values in a material sense as well: as the book circulates through the public sphere, it gives a mass reading audience—positioned as spectators alongside the crowds in the novel—a glimpse into a Tap Day ceremony at one of the country's most elite college campuses, disseminating a vision of campus life that is changing for the better, at its core meritocratic.

It makes sense that the American campus novel would come into existence under these conditions, with *Stover at Yale*, one of the first examples of the genre, imposing itself on a mass audience of readers by embracing transparency and publicity in its content and form. Perhaps more surprising than the influence of Johnson's novel on literary history, however, is its influence on educational history. From the start of *Stover at Yale*, Johnson is reflexive about the power of print culture to shape the internal operations of the school and the public perception of it. We learn on the first page of the novel that at his prep school, Lawrenceville, Stover had been "the big man in a big school," a position with "sovereign responsibilities," responsibilities that meant "his slightest action had a certain public importance." Stover's mannerisms and habits are taken up by his peers, shaping the entirety of student culture. "His walk had been studiously imitated by twenty shuffling striplings," Johnson explains. "His hair, parted on the side, had caused a revolution among the brushes and stirred up innumerable indignant cowlicks. His tricks of speech, his favorite exclamations, had become at once lip-currency."[30]

At Yale, Stover experiences this publicity on an even greater scale; his name first circulates among the students at the college as his reputation builds, and later it appears in newspapers, spreading across a broader public, shaping local and national opinion. After Stover sees his name for the first time in the *Evening Register*—"STOVER, A FRESHMAN, PLAYS SENSATIONAL GAME"—he is shocked. "The thing was too incredible. He stood stupidly looking at it," Johnson writes. "There was no answer Stover could give to that first throbbing sensation at seeing his name—his own name—in print. It left him confused, a little frightened." Later in the novel, after the big game against Princeton, Stover sees his name in print again and the experience is less shocking, more a source of pride, and increasingly something Stover accepts as natural. "To have seen the burning letters S-T-O-V-E-R actually vibrating on the front pages of metropolitan papers," Johnson writes, "to have gazed on his distinguished (though slightly smudged) features, ruined by an unfeeling photographer ... —to have felt these heavenly sensations at the age of eighteen could not be lightly disguised."[31]

Stover at Yale is thus deeply preoccupied with the publicity surrounding the campus and the effect of this publicity on the campus itself. Upon its publication, Johnson's novel exercised an immediate, local influence on secret societies at Yale. We can see its impact in a series of *New York Times* articles that appeared in the aftermath of the book's publication.[32] In the buildup to the Tap Day ceremony in 1912, the newspaper reported that the novel caused much debate among Yale students and alumni. In a May 10, 1912 article, Yale seniors criticized *Stover at Yale*: one student claimed that the novel was "Too much fiction," another that it "harms the college by giving outsiders a wrong impression of Yale." The very next day, the

New York Times published a follow-up article that viewed the novel more favorably. A former captain of the Yale football team praised *Stover at Yale*, explaining that it took "ten or fifteen years" for him "to outgrow the view of life he had taken with him from college." The novel ensured that the 1912 Tap Day ceremony was especially charged for participants. "More excitement and a higher feverish interest than has been known in years centres around the 'Tap Day' exercises held Thursday on the Yale campus," the *Times* reported. There were two reasons for all the excitement, the article explained. First, "[t]here are more prominent men, more representatives of leading American families in the incoming senior class than in years," and second, "the recent agitation over the senior societies, stirred by Owen Johnson's novel, 'Stover at Yale,' has created widespread interest as well as caustic comment."[33]

Stover at Yale's influence on the 1912 Tap Day remained ambiguous, however. The two most notable "tappings," according to the *New York Times*, were not merit-based choices that Johnson would approve but students from prominent families: Skull and Bones elected George B. Cortelyou Jr., whose father was Theodore Roosevelt's private secretary, and Keys elected Vanderbilt Webb, grandson of W. K. Vanderbilt. Not until the next academic year did the force of *Stover at Yale*'s message really shape Yale's culture. In March 1913, students in Yale's sophomore class publicly protested the society system, claiming that it should "lose its features of mystery, and should not be entangled with general college affairs." In April, these sophomores launched an anti-secrecy campaign, which Johnson publicly supported. Tap Day in 1913 then represented the society system's willingness to embrace Johnson's proposals for campus life. "Mr. Johnson, in his recent letter to The Times, suggested that the senior societies recruit their lists from an agreed-upon roll of accomplishment, composing a society of one hundred and submitted by the junior class," a May 17 article reported. "If such a roll had been formulated, we dare say that most of the men tapped on Thursday would have been included. The revolt of the sophomores against the assumption of secrecy and social exclusiveness in the senior societies has borne fruit."[34] Johnson's novel remained a touchstone in undergraduate culture at Yale through the 1930s, when Kingman Brewster invoked the novel in support of a reform movement he led with Richard Bissell, Whitney Griswold, Sherman Kent, Max Millikan, and Eugene Rostow.[35]

Stover at Yale attracted attention at other institutions as well. "[T]hey who agree with Johnson in his attacks on college abuses are awaiting eagerly the results of 'Stover' during the coming college year," the *Berkeley Gazette* announced in 1912. "One of the most widely read novels of last year has been Owen Johnson's 'Stover at Yale,' " a writer declared in the supplement to the *University Missourian* in 1913. "Without discussing the merits of Mr. Johnson's fiction or philosophy, one can safely say that this arraignment has raised in every big university the question of the fitness and success of its own social organization." "You may have notist [*sic*] lately a book by a Yale graduate, 'Stover at Yale,' " Stanford president David Starr Jordan said to students at Reed College. "[I]f you ever go to Yale University ... the one answer to any question as to why this or that or the other thing is done is, 'Why, that's the way we have always done at Yale.' It comes to be a hevy [sic] burden of tradition. Reed College starts free from the weight of the burden which the old has imposed on the new. There is no machine or tradition so good that it is not our part to make it better."[36]

For generations, the novel anchored the popular perception of Yale in particular and the college experience more generally. In 1957, Calvin Trillin enrolled at Yale under the encouragement of his father, an immigrant grocery store owner and *Stover at Yale* enthusiast. After his (Calvin's) arrival on campus, a committee on general education chaired by Whitney Griswold lamented the "false myth of Yale" that continued to hamper the school—"the Yale glorified and made famous by Owen Johnson and the rest." Institutional historian Helen Lefkowitz Horowitz in 1987 declared *Stover at Yale* "the best-known depiction of college life," a work secondary school students once supposedly consulted "in preparation for the manly trials to come" in college. According to Horowitz, these high school students treated the novel, in other words, like the "twenty shuffling striplings" at Lawrenceville treated Stover, imitating his walk, haircut, and tricks of speech. Fitzgerald's Amory Blaine—a *Princeton* undergraduate—wasn't, in short, the only student to treat *Stover at Yale* as a "text-book."[37]

The considerable influence of the novel is explicable in the context of the emergent educational system's representational deficit, or what I described in the introduction to this book as the modern school's crisis of relevance. To overcome the chasm that divided the modern school from the popular imagination, administrators developed "outreach" programs to make institutional life legible to the public. Schools, for instance, developed publicity departments that brought photojournalists to campus, and these photojournalists published their work in articles with titles like, "The American Undergraduate," "Life at a Girls College," "College Life at Princeton—Old and New," and "On Knowing College Men."[38] Campus fiction—which appeared with increasing regularity in popular periodicals like *Saturday Evening Post*, *Munsey's*, *Cosmopolitan*, and *Collier's Weekly*, and in individual editions through publishing houses like Putnam's, Charles Scribner's, and Street and Smith—contributed to the heightened visibility of higher education. It gave mass audiences a clearer understanding of what went on inside institutions of higher education and explained why college offered valuable life experience.[39] It wielded this power not exactly in an official capacity as part of a college administration but not exactly in an unofficial capacity either. It did so as an outgrowth of that liminal institutional space nestled between campus and the world beyond it, the extracurriculum. By advertising undergraduate culture to the public, it in turn shaped the rituals within the culture that produced it.

The Secret of Meritocracy

Stover at Yale's influence was only possible in this specific site of conjuncture, where the inside and the outside of the school system converged with one another. In this liminal space, Johnson's novel treated the secret society as its foil, a negative example against which it could articulate a democratic vision of campus life. However, the novel's vision of undergraduate life ultimately isn't as democratic as it first appears. *Stover at Yale*'s celebration of openness and publicity in fact obscures its own fundamental investment in hierarchy and exclusion. Johnson's Progressive critique of the secret society had secrets of its own.

The novel's Progressive commitments are embodied in the character Tom Regan, Stover's best friend on campus. Stover initially meets Regan on his first train ride to New Haven: "He saw a man of twenty-two or -three, with the head and shoulders of a bison, sandy hair, with a clear, blue, steady glance, heavy hands, and a face already set in the mold of stern purpose." Regan has spent his adolescence wandering from city to city in the West—"Des Moines, Iowa, at the last," he explains to Stover. Regan is attracted to Yale because of its meritocratic system of student life—"It's a college where you can stand on your own feet, all square to the wind"—and during school vacations, Regan lives his Progressivist worldview. He works in coal mines and drives cabs, and he does so to have the "opportunity to meet the fellow who gets the grind of life—to understand what he thinks of himself, and especially what he thinks of those above him. I won't have many more chances to see him on the ground floor, and some day I've got to know him well enough to convince him."[40]

Over the course of the book, Stover finds himself preferring characters like Regan over the more traditional society men—characters who are Anglo-Saxon Progressives from the American West, not just Brockhurst and Regan, but Nathaniel Pike and Swazey, "a man of twenty-five or six ... rough, uncouth, with thick head and neck ... one ear maimed by a scar, badly dressed, badly combed, and badly shod." These are the men who won't be chosen for the senior societies but ought to be, the men who, if the system were truly meritocratic, would be tapped. However, *Stover at Yale* doesn't only argue that these less-privileged Progressives should be included in elite secret societies; it also projects, through the novel's investment in publicity, a more open representation of campus life that includes these men's stories. "'Wonder what Regan's story is—the whole story?'" Stover thinks at one point. "'And Pike and all the rest of—' He hesitated, and then added, '—of the fellows who don't count.'" To Yale's snobbish society system, these stories don't "count," but for Johnson's highly influential novel they do.[41]

In stark contrast to the openness the novel displays toward these Progressives, there remains a population of racially marked characters whose stories continue not to count, characters who remain on the margins of the narrative. Among these characters is the Italian barber who appears in one scene as the butt of a joke, when Stover's friends McNab and Waters, never ones to take their studies too seriously, skip work to play pranks in New Haven, tricking the barber into cutting the hair of a dog they find on the street. When McNab and Waters fail to pay, the barber tries to chase them down. "Dagos have no sense of humor," Waters explains. "Here he comes with a razor—scud for it!" In a similar comic interlude later in the novel, McNab and Waters trick their friends into overpaying for Cuban cigars. The pranksters welcome "a couple of *Cuba libre* dagos" into Stover's room, and Stover and his friend McCarthy pay the "chocolate patriots" $14 a box for cigars that their friends pay only $5 for.[42]

Just before the final Tap Day episode, the whole narrative ecosystem of *Stover at Yale* threatens to shut down when one of these marginalized characters enters the representational space of the novel in a more permanent and meaningful way. This character is a love interest, Fanny Le Roy, "rather pretty, dark with Irish black eyes," who emerges in the final third of the novel to seduce Stover away from the campus, its politics and struggles, and from Jean Story, the daughter of a Yale alum and Skull and Bones member, whom Stover had previously pursued romantically. "He did not realize how often he met [Fanny], leaving his troubled roommates with a curt excuse, nor how rapidly he consumed the distance to their meeting place," Johnson writes. "He had talked to her at first seriously of serious things, then gradually, laughing in a boyish way, half tempted, he began to pay her compliments." The temptation Fanny represents to Stover is almost irresistible—"He wondered what he might do with her. ... He put out his arms and took her in them, and stood a long moment, looking at her lips"—but before this relationship can derail the book entirely, Fanny excuses herself, sending Stover a note explaining that they can't be together. "I'm going away, it's best for you and me I know it. I would care too much and I'm not good enough for you," Fanny writes. In the aftermath of the breakup, Stover begins to realize what was at stake in his attraction to Fanny, and in talking over the whole ordeal with his friends, Regan divulges a secret about his own mysterious past.

> "What's terrible about it," [Stover] said, talking out his soul, "is that there's so much good in them. And yet what can you do? They're human, they respond, you can't help pitying them—wanted to be decent, to help—and you can't. It's terrible to think that there are certain doors in life you open and close, that you must turn your back on human lives sometimes, that things can't be changed, Lord, but it's a terrible thing to realize."
>
> He stopped, and he heard Regan's voice, moved as he had never heard it, say: "That's my story—only *I* married."
>
> Suddenly, as though realizing for the first time what he had said, he burst out: "Good God, I never meant to tell. See here, you men, that's sacred—you understand."

And Dink and Joe, looking on his face, realized all at once why a certain gentler side of life was shut out to him[.][43]

In this conversation, we see how Johnson contains the threat that Fanny introduces into the narrative. From Stover's first encounter with Fanny, we are meant to understand her presence as a distraction from the novel's investment in publicity and the representational possibilities of the system of higher education. Stover comes across Fanny after he agrees to go for a carriage ride outside the city with two of his more worldly classmates. In the carriage, the Yale students come across Fanny with a friend, and Johnson describes them as "a rather noticeable type" and later, "an obvious type[.]" At the outset, then, Johnson emphasizes the power of these ethnically marked women to demand attention, and this impression is confirmed as the plot unfolds. After the girls join the Yale students in the carriage, Fanny is suddenly stricken with pain, and Stover alone, without the support of his other classmates, resolves to drive her through New Haven to the hospital, despite the controversy that will ensue. Johnson writes: "Stover turned the horses' heads into the thoroughfare, looking straight ahead, aware soon of the men who saw him in the full light of day, driving through the streets of New Haven in such inexplicable company."[44]

The danger Fanny represents in the novel is therefore the danger of bad publicity, of misplaced and unwanted attention. If the novel rejects Fanny and the other racialized characters as unfit for the representational possibilities of campus life, Stover's conversation with his roommates and Regan's final confession demonstrate why this rejection is necessary and justifiable. In *Stover at Yale*, the secret society is flawed because it excludes lower-class Anglo-Saxons so the wealthy can hold onto the privileges they've inherited. The society system would be more democratic, in Johnson's estimation, if it were more transparent, allowing the Tom Regans of the world to compete in open competition with the sons of established New York families. As we see here, however, the novel assumes that racial outsiders—the Italian barber, the Hispanic cigar salesmen, Fanny LeRoy—can't compete in this meritocratic system. The kind of racism Stover articulates in the conversation with his roommates is willing to concede that "there's so much good" in these characters, that "[t]hey're human," and that "you can't help pitying them," all while understanding that paying attention to these characters won't do anyone any good. This is because, according to Stover, these characters are doomed for another life altogether—one of servitude, not of leadership. "[W]hat can you do?" Stover asks his friends. The answer *Stover at Yale* gives is that you ignore these people; you keep these people outside the representational space of the novel. You must, as Stover explains, "turn your back on human lives sometimes," with the knowledge that "things can't be changed."

This point is reinforced in Regan's surprise confession. Unlike Stover, who managed (however inadvertently) to free himself from his romantic entanglements,

Regan, we learn, married his Fanny LeRoy. If Regan divulges this secret accidentally—"Good God," he exclaims, "I never meant to tell"—the mishap serves as an educational moment for everybody, not just the characters in the conversation but the readers of the novel as well. Here we are taught what a real secret looks like and how we're supposed to keep it. Until this moment, Regan's wife has never been mentioned in the novel, and we are never led to believe he is married. There are no clues—there is no foreshadowing—to suggest that this woman might exist. Even after the revelation occurs, when Regan suddenly "realiz[es] for the first time what he had said," there is no further mention of his wife: his friends register the sanctity of this information, and no one refers to Regan's marriage again in *Stover at Yale*. In a book that is oriented around the secret society—where characters spend their time debating the merits and faults of the society system, attending Tap Day ceremonies, and striving to be worthy of election—Regan's wife is the only real secret in the narrative. She and Fanny LeRoy stand in for all excluded social populations, those potential students who, in the world of the novel, are ill-equipped and incapable of participating in campus life, and know it.

The Progressive reform of higher education in the opening decades of the twentieth century would in the end embrace the exclusionary practices that *Stover at Yale* formalized and that campus culture adopted. It did so by reimagining the relationship between the school and (the secret) society. In the decades following the novel's publication, as the public elementary and secondary school system grew and institutions of higher education attracted record numbers of high school graduates, admissions policies became selective for the first time. Earlier in the nineteenth century, admission to institutions of higher education hadn't been especially selective, because colleges relied heavily on enrollments for their survival, and there weren't very many candidates to choose from. Exclusivity nevertheless operated relentlessly in campus culture, with societies taking it upon themselves to distinguish the elect. With the rise of selective admissions, exclusionary practices were shifted from the social organizations on campus to the school administration. Institutions of higher education, led by presidents like Lawrence Lowell at Harvard and deans like Frederick P. Keppel at Columbia, began implementing admissions quotas. By the 1930s, ethnic quotas imposed originally at Ivy League schools and other elite east coast institutions had spread to the Midwest, the West, and the South.[45]

Undergraduate campus culture, under *Stover at Yale*'s influence, had provided the model of selective admissions that these administrators were following. Though the administrators had maintained an agonistic relationship to secret societies for much of the nineteenth century, by the beginning of the twentieth, they welcomed the secret society as they came to see campus culture as a guarantee of institutional health and stability. Helen Lefkowitz Horowitz has shown that colleges and universities "harnessed and co-opted college life" during this period, with "the particular institutions and traditions of a segment of the student body ... established as the official institutions and traditions of the college." For instance, yearbooks—now indispensable to the scholastic experience, produced and disseminated through the official organs of administration—were originally made by individual student organizations within universities and colleges. Secret societies were appropriated as well: some were transformed into honor societies, while "tap day" at many schools served, according to Horowitz, as a campus-wide celebration.[46] Elizabeth A. Armstrong and Linda T. Hamilton have demonstrated that, to this day, institutions of higher education remain dependent on secret societies as a way of attracting affluent students who don't require need- or merit-based financial aid. The "party pathway" through college, as they call it, is fundamental to the identity of US higher education, and it plays a key role in the process through which "[c]lass disparities become invisible, embedded—at every stage of achievement—in [academic] credentials themselves."[47]

It's in this sense that, at the beginning of the twentieth century, the modern educational system transformed itself into a secret society: it denounced the secrecy of secret societies while publicizing these societies and (secretly) awarding its credentials according to their undemocratic criteria. John Thelin explains that to deal with the social friction caused by the growing student population, administrators and admissions officers began accepting the exclusionary logic of the society men, those future loyal alumni and donors whose support the institution needed. "When serious problems surfaced and factions within the campus clashed," Thelin writes, "the customary response of college officials was, ironically, to side with the 'college system' and reinforce the exclusionary tendencies of the dominant student organizations."[48]

The Progressives' call for the democratization of higher education was therefore coextensive with the school system's embrace of secret societies and their exclusionary practices, and this contradiction marks the assumption of the school as an ideological apparatus. Much more than the begrudging language of "separate but equal" that justified Jim Crow institutions in the South, the relentless Progressive rhetoric of meritocracy in elite northern institutions constitutes the school's modern ideological program. This was the moment in US history when the educational system presented itself as non-discriminatory in order to more effectively discriminate. When President Lowell of Harvard first attempted to implement a quota system publicly in 1922, he was met with fierce resistance from Jewish and African American alumni and the Boston public; however, when Lowell worked covertly—proposing merely a fixed number of undergraduates (1,000 students per class) instead of strict quotas—he succeeded in defining the demographic makeup of Harvard's undergraduate population. Yale followed Harvard's example, adopting an informal quota—"sawing wood and saying not a word," as Robert Nelson Corwin, an admissions chair for the Sheffield Scientific School at Yale, described it—which ensured that members of the excluded populations wouldn't publicly criticize the school and demand that Yale be taxed.[49]

Whether these quota systems were entirely covert or secretive is, of course, a matter of perspective. When Harvard asked applicants for their race and religion, or when Yale demanded (more subtly?) the full name and birthplace of the applicant's father and the maiden name of the applicant's mother, prospective students were indeed explicitly told that these institutions were considering race as a criterion for admission. For these students, the ideological work of the school was never truly a secret. If, in fact, the modern educational system has ever in its ideological operations truly succeeded in masking its role in the reproduction of social relations, or if its effectiveness as a political instrument has always depended on visible and explicit acts of domination and control, are questions that Thomas Dixon Jr.'s work and its institutionalization raise. Even the invisibility of Tom Regan's marriage in *Stover at Yale*—the kind of secrecy, I've argued, that the Progressive educational system at least in part aspired toward when it assumed its modern role in the reproduction of the social order—never remains a perfect secret: it rises to visibility for a brief moment to be suppressed once again. Visibility was, counterintuitively, central to Thomas Dixon Jr.'s understanding of the institutional system and his celebration of the "Invisible Empire" of the Ku Klux Klan. For Dixon, the revelation of secrets and the exposure of secret societies would serve as the foundation for a truly Progressive society.

The Hood and the Cross

Tuskegee Institute celebrated its silver jubilee anniversary on January 22, 1906, with a night of speeches at Carnegie Hall. For Tuskegee's president, Booker T. Washington, the event was just the first stop in a long fundraising tour through the North; in the boxes that night were prominent philanthropists Mrs. John D. Rockefeller, Isaac N. Seligman, and Mrs. Henry H. Rogers, among others. As Washington entered Carnegie Hall, a messenger approached him with a note from Thomas Dixon Jr., author of two recently published novels, *The Leopard's Spots* (1902) and *The Clansman* (1905), that each celebrated the Ku Klux Klan's role in undermining Reconstruction-era policies. (Both would also be adapted in 1915, by Dixon and D. W. Griffith, into the film *Birth of a Nation*). In the past Dixon had defended Washington's work at Tuskegee, citing Washington in a sermon as proof that "[t]he negro *can* cultivate the friendship of the Southern white man" if he surrenders political freedoms. Since publishing this sermon, however, Dixon had become increasingly suspicious of Washington. The note Washington received on his way into the silver jubilee read:

Sir: In response to your appeal for funds I hereby offer to contribute $10,000 from the profits of "The Clansman" to Tuskegee Institute provided you give complete and satisfactory proof that you do not desire Social Equality for the Negro and that your School is opposed to the Amalgamation of the races. Sincerely,

Thomas Dixon Jr.[50]

This was not the first time Dixon had attempted to confront Washington publicly over the issue of "Social Equality for the Negro." In August 1905, Dixon wrote an article for the *Saturday Evening Post*, "Booker T. Washington and the Negro" (1905), that addressed what Dixon saw as the inadequacies of Washington's educational program. In the same year, Dixon also published an unsigned article in the Charlestown *News and Courier* claiming that Washington maintained an intimate relationship with the white philanthropist Robert C. Ogden. (Dixon insisted that the two men had hugged publicly.)[51] As a former state legislator, occasional Baptist minister, aspiring actor and playwright, and successful novelist, Dixon's obsession with Booker T. Washington, the president of a black industrial college in Alabama, would appear somewhat curious. Education, however, was essential to Dixon's vision of Progressive social reform at the turn of the century, persisting across his various occupational guises. Dixon himself received an exceptional formal education for the time, earning his undergraduate degree from Wake Forest in 1883 and securing a fellowship afterward to pursue graduate work in history and politics at Johns Hopkins, where he attended seminars led by Herbert Baxter Adams. Also at Hopkins, Dixon befriended Woodrow Wilson, and in 1886, after leaving graduate school and being elected to the North Carolina legislature, Dixon set out to appropriate funds to found a department of history and political science at the University of North Carolina, where he hoped Wilson would work as a professor.[52]

Dixon's time in the emergent educational system made him acutely aware of the school's capacity, or incapacity, to enact large social transformations. According to Dixon, the most urgent problem confronting the United States at the turn of the century was no longer the sectional rivalries that induced the Civil War but rather the "Negro problem"; and, in Dixon's estimation, the solution to the Negro problem specifically *did not* lie in the school. In an era that witnessed the dramatic growth of the educational system, Dixon conceived of the modern school as an institution with limits—an institution that couldn't, and shouldn't, serve the nation's black population. A character in *The Leopard's Spots* sums up Dixon's educational philosophy: "The more you educate [the African American], the more impossible you make his position in a democracy. Education! Can you change the colour of his skin, the kink of his hair, the bulge of his lips, the spread of his nose, or the beat of his heart, with a spelling book? The Negro is the human donkey. You can train him, but you can't make of him a horse."[53]

Dixon elaborated this scholastic philosophy in the *Saturday Evening Post* article, insisting that Washington's industrial program of education suffered from two key flaws. The first flaw, entirely in keeping with the passage from *The Leopard's Spots*, is that there are fundamental biological realities that make African American education a futile endeavor: "[N]o amount of education of any kind, industrial, classical or religious, can make a Negro a white man or bridge the chasm of the centuries which separate him from the white man in the evolution of human civilization." The second flaw—which isn't exactly consistent with the first—is that education for African Americans would inevitably lead to social equality, and with social equality, according to Dixon, there would follow either race mixing or violent conflict. "The trouble with Mr. Booker T. Washington's work is that he is silently preparing us for the future heaven of Amalgamation," Dixon writes. "[O]r *he is doing something equally dangerous*, namely, he is attempting to build a nation inside a nation of two hostile races. In this event he is storing dynamite beneath the pathway of our children—the end at last can only be in bloodshed."[54]

These polemics begin to explain why Booker T. Washington loomed so large in Dixon's imagination, inspiring a series of erratic confrontations between the two. As a novelist and political reformer who saw America's future as necessarily white and understood efforts to promote black educational opportunity as alternately futile and dangerous, Dixon's strange fixation on Washington is more comprehensible. And yet, Dixon's obsession with Washington extended beyond Washington's public prominence as an educator. Dixon found Washington so disturbing because he believed that Washington's professed and actual beliefs weren't aligned. In Dixon's imagination, that is, a chasm existed between the explicit social program Washington advocated publicly and the implicit social program he secretly planned to enact.

Coming over a decade after Washington's speech at the Cotton States and International Exposition in Atlanta, Georgia, Dixon's demand in his silver jubilee note for "complete and satisfactory proof" that Washington opposed "Social Equality for the Negro" and the "Amalgamation of the races" seems excessive. In the "Atlanta Compromise" speech, Washington had famously gone out of his way to explain to his audience that he wasn't calling for social equality, declaring: "In all things that are purely social we can be as separate as the fingers, yet one as the hand in all things essential to mutual progress." What further proof did Dixon need—or what further proof could Washington provide—to make it absolutely clear that Washington wasn't calling for social equality?[55]

For all its paranoia, however, Dixon's note is unusually insightful about the particular mechanisms of Washington's political ascent at the turn of the century. After all, Washington's long-standing reputation as one of the most influential African American figures of the period, if not the most, assumes that his considerable influence came about as a result of deft and surreptitious political maneuvering.

Both his detractors and defenders agree that Washington managed to obtain political power precisely because what he said and what he meant didn't always align. According to detractors, the Hampton-Tuskegee model of industrial education didn't open up a path for political and social equality among the races, as Washington claimed it someday would, but rather further consolidated the system of racial capitalism in the South, producing a class of docile black laborers. According to defenders, Washington's political program only *appeared* accommodationist; in fact, Washington worked tirelessly behind the scenes to advance civil liberties for African Americans under Jim Crow.[56]

By sensing that there was a hidden motivation behind Washington's stated claims—by demanding "complete and satisfactory proof" that Washington did not support social equality among the races—Dixon thus articulated the assumption underlying the most influential "readings" of Booker T. Washington over the twentieth and twenty-first centuries. As we'll see, Dixon's investment in a politics of public transparency—and his anxiety about secrecy—made him especially sensitive to the gap between the stated and unstated, the overt and covert, that Washington is thought to have manipulated at the turn of the century. Though Dixon is remembered almost exclusively for his Reconstruction Trilogy of novels commemorating the heroic deeds of the Ku Klux Klan—perhaps the most notorious secret society in US history—his fiction remains profoundly suspicious of secrecy and, in fact, formalizes an aesthetic, political, and institutional program committed to public transparency. The irony here is that Dixon's devotion to transparency in the trilogy, which celebrates the KKK, was much more radical than Owen Johnson's devotion to transparency in *Stover at Yale*, which critiques secret societies at Yale.

The greatest danger to southern life under Reconstruction as Dixon represents it in *The Leopard's Spots* is a network of secret societies that sets out to empower African Americans after the Civil War. "The summer of 1867! Will ever a Southern man or woman who saw it forget its scenes?" Dixon writes. "A group of oath-bound secret societies, The Union League, The Heroes of America, and The Red Strings dominating society, and marauding bands of negroes armed to the teeth terrorising the country, stealing, burning and murdering." The Union League in particular is the organization responsible in the novel for rigging elections and arming the freedmen who terrorize the white characters. *The Clansman* provides a more in-depth examination of the formation of the Union League, exposing this specific oath-bound society as part of a larger conspiracy undertaken after Abraham Lincoln's assassination to subject white southerners to black rule. In the novel, the Union League is founded by Austin Stoneman, a character based on Thaddeus Stevens who plans to "secure the future of [the Republican] party and the safety of this nation" through "the confiscation of the millions of acres of land owned by the white people of the South and its division among the negroes and those who fought and suffered in this war[.]"[57]

In the Reconstruction Trilogy, the rise and fall of the Union League is told twice, first in *The Leopard's Spots* and then again in *The Clansman*. (*The Leopard's Spots*, the first installment, follows the life of Charles Gatson from his childhood during Reconstruction to his election as governor of North Carolina afterward, and the next two novels in the trilogy dilate, respectively, on the two historical moments described in the first novel.) In fact, the Klan is heroic in the first two novels of the trilogy insofar as it works to undermine the political program of the Union League. "The success of the Ku Klux Klan was so complete, its organisers were dazed," Dixon writes in *The Leopard's Spots*. "Its appeal to the ignorance and superstition of the Negro at once reduced the race to obedience and order. Its threat against the scalawag and carpet-bagger struck terror to their craven souls, and the 'Union League,' 'Red Strings,' and 'Heroes of America' went to pieces with incredible rapidity." In *The Clansman*, which devotes all of its narrative attention to southern life under Reconstruction, the success of the Ku Klux Klan again means the demise of the Union League and its secretive practices: "[T]he arms furnished the negroes by the State and National governments were in the hands of the Klan. The League began to collapse in a panic of terror."[58]

If the Reconstruction Trilogy therefore examines secrecy as an emergent and dangerous force in the political realm, the more mundane romance plots that the novels pursue also improbably thematize secrecy. In *The Leopard's Spots*, the principal love interest, the southerner Sallie Worth, is playfully chastised by her friend, the northerner Helen Lowell, for her peculiar courtship rituals. "You Southern girls are so queer," Helen says. "The moment you like a man you're as sly as a cat, and deny that you even know him. When I find the man I love I don't care who knows it, if he loves me." Helen's comment isn't simply an incidental observation about regional difference; Charles Gatson spends most of *The Leopard's Spots* in a state of anxiety brought about by the romantic experience, worrying over the hidden secret of Sallie Worth's true affection. "He longed to pour out to her his passion, but feared her answer," Dixon writes. "He was sure she loved him. And yet he was not sure. She was so skilled in the science of self defence, so subtle a mistress of all the arts of polite society in which the soul's deepest secrets are hid from the world, he was paralysed now as the moment drew near." The third and final novel in the trilogy, *The Traitor* (1907), coordinates the mystery of the romance and political plots. The protagonist John Graham spends much of the novel trying to discover whether another character, Stella Butler, actually loves him; Stella Butler spends much of the novel trying to discover whether John Graham is the Grand Dragon of the Klan in North Carolina. "There should be no shadows between those who thus love, should there?" Stella asks John during one of their courtship scenes. "Not one," John replies moments later. "Every secret of my life shall be laid bare before I'd dare claim you as my wife."[59]

Whether in romance or politics, secrecy thus remains throughout the Reconstruction Trilogy a disturbing fact of social life that characters need to confront and overcome. In each of these novels, clandestine oath-bound societies are exposed;

the hidden affairs of the heart are brought to light. The melodramatic style of these novels reflects not simply Dixon's budding ambitions in the theater but also the more profound impulse in his work to make the manifest latent, to bring secrets to light. According to Peter Brooks, in melodrama "[n]othing is spared because nothing is left unsaid," and this makes melodrama a preeminently modern mode, aspiring to "uncover[]" in a post-revolutionary and post-sacred world the Manichean forces disguised behind everyday occurrences and to reveal "a moral universe which, though put into question, masked by villainy and perversions of judgment, does exist."[60]

Dixon's commitment to exposing the unseen and invisible to public attention might place his trilogy within a legible generic tradition, but it also creates formal problems that threaten to break down the apparatus of narrative altogether. In the Reconstruction Trilogy, secrets are often revealed as—and sometimes even before—they're introduced as secrets. For instance, Dixon sporadically hints in *The Clansman* that the main characters are engaged in some sort of conspiracy. At one point, Marion Lenoir asks Ben Cameron, one of the novel's protagonists and the Grand Dragon of the Klan in North Carolina, why he disappears so often at night:

> "[W]hat I want to know is what you are doing out so late every night since you've come home, and where you were gone for the past week?"
> "Important business," he answered soberly.
> "Business—I expect!" she cried. "Look here, Ben Cameron, have you another girl somewhere you're flirting with?"
> "Yes," he answered slowly, coming closer and his voice dropping to a whisper, "and her name is Death."[61]

The function of this exchange seems relatively straightforward: Dixon reveals that one of the novel's protagonists is devoting his time to "important business," but withholds what that important business is—a classic example, it would seem, of Roland Barthes's hermeneutic code, those units of narrative "whose function it is to … constitute an enigma and lead to its solution." This exchange undermines the operations of the hermeneutic code, however, because the "enigma" that's introduced isn't really an enigma at all. We know that Ben Cameron, the protagonist of *The Clansman*, is a clansman before this scene even occurs. There is nothing covert about his suggestion that he is "flirting" with a "girl" whose name "is Death"—certainly not to readers and even probably to Marion, who places "her trembling hand unconsciously on his arm" after she hears his not especially subtle declaration.[62]

At another moment in *The Clansman*, Austin Stoneman, the Thaddeus Stevens character, explains to his co-conspirators that his "full plans are not for discussion at this juncture," and then immediately reveals his intention to "secure the future of [the Republican] party and the safety of this nation" through "the confiscation of the millions of acres of land owned by the white people of the South[.]"⁶³ Here Dixon again disforms the hermeneutic code, collapsing the distance between the enigma and its revelation as Stoneman discusses his full plans the moment after he explains they "are not for discussion." In both of these examples—the "secret" of Ben Cameron's late nights, and the "secret" of Austin Stoneman's plans for Reconstruction—the internal structure of the Reconstruction Trilogy militates against any kind of sustained narrative mystery: Dixon has already demonstrated in *The Leopard's Spots* the historical fact that the Ku Klux Klan heroically defeated the Union League, so it isn't especially mysterious when, in a sequel called *The Clansman*, the main character disappears for extended periods of time without telling people where he's going (because obviously he's working with the Klan), or when the novel's villain, a character responsible for the political organization of the South after the Civil War, has a secret plan for Reconstruction (because obviously he's forming the Union League).

But if Dixon's Reconstruction Trilogy is invested in an aesthetic, political, and institutional program of transparency, whatever formal awkwardness ensues, why then do the novels take as their subject the heroic role of a secret society, the Klan, and its "invisible empire"? Dixon himself is not unaware of this tension within the novels. The Klan's secretive practices, for all of their political efficacy during Reconstruction, create anxiety for the more responsible characters in the trilogy. As Dr. Cameron explains to his son Ben in *The Clansman*, "[A] secret society such as you have planned means a conspiracy that may bring exile or death. I hate lawlessness and disorder. We have had enough of it. Your clan means ultimately martial law." Elsie Stoneman, Ben Cameron's future wife, is also queasy about the Klan's work. "[T]his is wrong—this wild vengeance is a crime you are doing, however great the provocation," she says. "You are a conspirator[.] ... You are committing murder!" Dixon himself criticized the Klan for similar reasons as Elsie and Dr. Cameron during the organization's revival in the twenties.⁶⁴

The structure of Dixon's trilogy in effect formalizes this anxiety, licensing the Klan's secrecy but only under specific historical conditions. In *The Leopard's Spots*, the Klan's success is followed by its abrupt dissolution. "The Klan has done its work. The carpet-baggers have fled. The state is redeemed from the infamies of a negro government, and we have a clean economical administration, and we can keep it so as long as the white people are a unit without any secret societies," Major Dameron, the head of the Klan, declares. It's in this sense that *The Traitor*, Dixon's post-Reconstruction novel, which is sometimes thought to be exceptional within the trilogy for its explicit renunciation of the Klan, in fact merely fulfills Dixon's promise in *The Leopard's Spots* to disband the organization. In the opening pages of *The Traitor*, John Graham dissolves the Klan, declaring, "Our work is done. We have rescued our state from Negro rule. We dissolve this powerful secret order in time to save you from persecution, exile, imprisonment and death."⁶⁵

In the end, however, the novels' depiction of the Klan is justified for reasons that go beyond these anxious containment strategies. Dixon in the novels celebrates the heroic deeds of the Klan not to uphold or justify the organization's secret practices but rather to expose these practices to public view. Dixon establishes his relationship to the Klan in the dedication to the original 1905 Doubleday, Page & Co. edition of *The Clansman* (Figure 2):

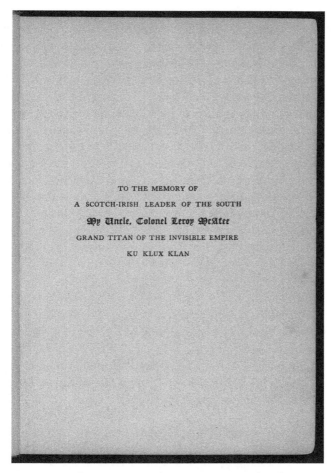

Figure 2 Dedication Page. Thomas Dixon Jr., *The Clansman* (Doubleday, Page, 1905).
Credit: Houghton Library, Harvard University, PZ3 .D646.

Dixon's dedication deploys the primary rhetorical tactic the novel reverts to again and again in the pages that follow. The disjunction on full display here between the invisibility of the "invisible empire" and the exaggerated visibility of the dedication itself—a visibility that is performed in both the capitalizations and the flamboyant medieval-ish script of "My Uncle, Colonel Leroy McAfee"—is a source not of embarrassment in the novel but rather of pride. In fact, the whole force of the dedication lies in exploiting precisely this discrepancy, making the visible *more visible* by positioning it against the invisible. The dramatic unmasking of Dixon's uncle Colonel Leroy McAfee in the dedication is only possible because McAfee has been masked in the first place. Dixon's investment in the Klan can be understood along these lines as part of a publicity campaign whose publicity is made all the more spectacular for its foundation in secrecy.

Throughout *The Clansman*—the most extensive and avowedly pro-Klan novel in the trilogy—Dixon's rhetoric follows the unmasking procedure performed in the dedication, making the Klan's once invisible practices now visible to a national audience of readers.[66] "The organization was governed by the Grand Wizard Commander-in-Chief, who lived at Memphis, Tennessee," Dixon explains in the preface to the novel, divulging many of the Klan's most important secrets in the very first sentences of the book. "The Grand Dragon commanded a State, the Grand Titan a Congressional District, the Grand Giant a County, and the Grand Cyclops a Township Den." When the Klan rises to visibility in the novel, after Marion Lenoir is raped by a troop of freedmen and commits suicide, Dixon continues to reveal the organization's inner workings to the public. One of the most dramatic episodes in the novel involves a secret meeting where Marion's rapist Gus is tried according to Klan law. "[L]et the Grand Scribe read the objects of the Order on which your authority rests,' the Grand Cyclops announces at the beginning of the trial.

> The Scribe opened his Book of Record, "*The Prescript of the Order of the Invisible Empire*," and solemnly read:
> "To the lovers of law and order, peace and justice, and to the shades of the venerated dead, greeting:
> "This is an institution of Chivalry, Humanity, Mercy, and Patriotism: embodying in its genius and principles all that is chivalric in conduct, noble in sentiment, generous in manhood, and patriotic in purpose[.]"[67]

In short, Dixon's paean to the Klan deploys a rhetoric of transparency that appears so radically transparent because it is set against the Klan's secrecy. If one of the defining narrative modes of the trilogy is explanatory—giving readers access to the inner workings of a secret society—what is ultimately explained in the novels' many explanatory passages, as we can see in the trial scene above, is a complex but internally coherent institutional system. Following the Scribe's reading from the Book of Record, Dixon provides an in-depth account of Gus's trial, revealing the Klan's rules as they are established in *The Prescript of the Order of the Invisible Empire*. The Klan's systematicity distinguishes it from the organizational incoherence of the Union League and the official mechanisms of administration governing the South under Reconstruction. The Klan's prescribed dress, its elaborate rituals and terminology, and its rigid hierarchies (from Grand Dragon to Titan to Giant to Cyclops) stand in stark contrast to the marauding bands of freedmen in the novel and the political corruption undermining the integrity of the electoral process and the South Carolina state legislature. The secret that Dixon unmasks in *The Leopard's Spots*, *The Clansman*, and *The Traitor* is thus the power of white organization and white institutions.

Of course, the Klan's success in the trilogy effects a return to institutional stability in the South, restoring the region's social institutions to the white characters and reducing the once disobedient black population to "obedience and order." With the South's institutions once again in the hands of the whites, organizations like the Klan are no longer necessary: secret institutions have, in effect, become public, with the Klan's impressive organizational regime coming to define the "clean economical administration" of the post-Reconstruction government writ large, to use Major Dameron's expression from *The Leopard's Spots*. In the logic of the trilogy, the distinction between Gus's trial during Reconstruction in *The Clansman* (conducted in secret according to the rules of the Klan) and an official trial in a state courtroom after Reconstruction is negligible. John Graham in *The Traitor* can serve heroically as the Grand Dragon of the unlawful Klan during Reconstruction while fiercely defending the law after Reconstruction because, in Dixon's account, the Klan during Reconstruction is more law-abiding than the law itself, and the law after Reconstruction is essentially Klan law, the law of the white Progressive state.[68]

Under these post-Reconstruction social conditions, the invisibility of the invisible empire is, for Dixon, not only unnecessary but unacceptable, and the task of the artist or educator consists of upholding the integrity of white civilization by insisting, publicly and explicitly, on the exclusion of African Americans from modern institutional life. Dixon's abiding concern with the social and political danger posed by secrecy is, in this sense, perfectly consistent with his celebration of the Klan's work during Reconstruction. It's only by apprehending Dixon's radical commitment to public transparency as the foundation for American institutional life that we can truly understand his fiction and its specific relationship to the non-ideological work the modern school system has performed over the twentieth century and into the twenty-first.

On State Apparatuses, Repressive and Ideological

Surely no one in the 1980s and 1990s had Thomas Dixon Jr. in mind when the culture wars raged and English departments were divided over the question of which texts did or didn't belong in the curriculum; and yet Dixon was, undoubtedly, one of the beneficiaries of the fight to expand the canon during this period. In part, the inclusion of the previously excluded Dixon followed the broader logic driving the extension of the canon: by returning to Dixon's work, scholars were able to devote attention to issues of race and identity that had been obscured or erased under the traditional English curriculum. In part, however, the renewed interest in Dixon's work represented a serious challenge to the expansion of the canon—not because of the white supremacism Dixon championed, but because his fiction was mobilized as part of an influential argument meant to dispute the multiculturalism that subtended the liberal-pluralist critique of the traditional curriculum.

I'm referring here to Walter Benn Michaels's account of Thomas Dixon Jr.'s work in "Race into Culture," an article published in the summer 1992 issue of *Critical Inquiry* that was later adapted and elaborated in the monograph *Our America* (1995).[69] In "Race into Culture," Michaels sets out to construct a "Cultural Genealogy of Cultural Identity" (as he announces in the essay's subtitle), tracking different conceptions of race through the twentieth century, from Dixon's white supremacy to the anti-essentialist identity politics that were hegemonic in the academy, according to Michaels, when he was writing. Michaels's essay argues that Dixon's "Progressive racism," which centered on racial hierarchy and white superiority, gave way in the 1920s to "pluralist racism," which "represent[ed] a theoretical intensification of racism" by emphasizing racial essence and difference rather than hierarchy: under the regime of racial pluralism, Michaels writes, "one prefers one's own race not because it is superior but because it is one's own."[70]

The rhetorical force of Michaels's claims in the essay is unmistakable: though pluralists in the twenties founded their conception of race against the rising tide of nativist organizations like the Ku Klux Klan—Horace Kallen dramatically declared in *Culture and Democracy in the United States* (1924) that "[t]he alternative before Americans is Kultur Klux Klan or Cultural Pluralism"—Michaels insisted that the racial politics of the cultural pluralists and the racial politics of the Klan were more alike than it might at first seem. The essentialism secreted in the pluralist conception of race, Michaels explains, persists even into contemporary anti-essentialist accounts of identity. Michaels acknowledges at one point that just because "the origins of cultural pluralism in America are so deeply intertwined with conceptual advances in racism" it "does not mean that contemporary cultural pluralism must also rest on an essentially racial base"—however, he goes on to write, "I have also tried to show ... that it does rest on such a base."[71]

"Race into Culture" thus represents Michaels's first foray into what is now a decades-long battle against identity politics. Increasingly Michaels's polemics have targeted the educational system as the institutional apparatus through which anti-racism finds its larger, pernicious significance. Where the power of Michaels's "Race into Culture" came from exposing the racist, essentialist assumptions underlying anti-essentialist constructions of identity—i.e., "The modern concept of culture is not, in other words, a critique of racism; it is a form of racism"[72]—the power of Michaels's more recent work has come from exposing anti-racism as a set of practices and positions that, taken in up in US scholastic life, further legitimize capitalism by naturalizing the inequalities it creates. As Michaels observes in "The Political Economy of Anti-Racism" (2018), "During the years in which American universities have been fighting (with mixed success) for race-based affirmative action, their students have been becoming richer, so rich that, today, at elite institutions, the number of students of color, even if there aren't all that many, nonetheless greatly exceeds the number of poor students."[73]

Michaels's point isn't simply that ending discrimination succeeds in redistributing economic benefits more proportionally across racial and gender demographics without addressing the underlying conditions of inequality. His point is that the primary effect of anti-discriminatory policies in the US school is to make the elite population of students it consecrates appear deserving of their wealth. "The problem with affirmative action," Michaels writes in *The Trouble with Diversity* (2006), "is not (as is often said) that it violates the principles of meritocracy; the problem is that it produces the illusion that we actually *have* a meritocracy." Calling for economic diversity instead of racial diversity is "doomed to fail" as well, in Michaels's argument. He writes in "The Political Economy of Anti-Racism":

> Even if we could overcome the practical obstacles; even if we could turn the elite colleges into schools for the 99%; even if we could go one step farther and make it possible for everyone to go to college, and one step farther than that and make it possible for every college to be as good as Harvard's supposed to be, it would still make no contribution to economic equality. In this utopia, we'd all have the equivalent of a Harvard degree. But we'd be entering a job market in which there wasn't very much demand for that degree. … [I]nstead of selling inequality (as we do now), colleges would be selling the justification for it. As in, we gave you the chance to get a first-rate education; if you couldn't make it pay, that's on you. Which is precisely—in a period of inequality—what makes the appeal to education so prevalent. The more vividly a society depends on exploited labor, the more eager it is to tell the exploited they had a fair chance to become exploiters.[74]

All of this is primarily to say that the reproduction of social relations under capitalism since the early twentieth century has occurred under an institutional regime that, according to Walter Benn Michaels, originated with the rejection of Thomas Dixon Jr.'s particular brand of Progressivism. Against Dixon's harsh and explicit political messaging, now relegated to the historical past, the modern school system (as Michaels represents it) deploys more sophisticated and covert forms of indoctrination. In "Race into Culture," Michaels exposes the ideological operations of the modern school by demonstrating the hypocrisy of the pluralists and anti-essentialist identitarians, whose cultural accounts of identity disguise a more profound essentializing impulse; in the passage I just quoted from "The Political Economy of Anti-Racism," Michaels takes the ideology of the modern school to an extreme with an extended hypothetical. In this hypothetical, where everyone goes to college and every college is as good as Harvard is supposed to be, the school perfectly realizes its ideological function, invisibly reproducing the structure of social relations by eagerly "tell[ing]"—or we might say "convincing"—"the exploited they had a fair chance to become exploiters."

As Werner Sollors pointed out in his original review of *Our America*, however, one of the major weaknesses of Michaels's argument is precisely its genealogical ambitions, its failure to adequately explain how an ideological paradigm that came into existence in the twenties became institutionalized and remained intact through the late twentieth century.[75] Against Michaels's insistence on the (near simultaneous) emergence and hegemony of racial pluralism, Sollors in his review gestures to David Hollinger's history of race and institutions in *Postethnic America* (1995), which (as Sollors recapitulates it) sees pluralism as "only one contender among many" conceptions of race in the twenties, including Dixon-style hierarchical racism, then as marginalized by "a social vision in the Roosevelt years and a universalist and assimilationist position in the antifascist war and early Cold War years," and finally as "resuscitated" and institutionalized after the social movements of the sixties.[76] The significance of Sollors's observation for the purposes of this particular chapter is that it simply indicates the possibility that the racist institutionalism that Dixon articulates in his fiction persisted deeper into the twentieth century than an account like Michaels's would suggest. Placing Dixon's institutional vision alongside Owen Johnson's, as I have in this chapter, might seem to reinforce the narrative that Michaels constructs in "Race into Culture," with Dixon's overt, hierarchical white supremacism overtaken by Johnson's covert racial practices early in the twentieth century. However, my real intention in reading these two literary works alongside one another is to show that the modern school's role in the reproduction of social relations has not merely involved disseminating the ideology of meritocracy—that the educational system has in fact persistently resorted to repressive practices that, as a "modern" institution, it allegedly dispensed with long ago.

That Dixon's particular style of racism didn't instantly disappear from institutional life is evident from the various overt and explicit racial policies of the modern school that—like Jim Crow segregation—never seriously pretended that all student populations were equal and organized access to educational institutions accordingly. That Dixon's vision of explicit white superiority wasn't rendered obsolete is also evidenced by the enduring presence of his work in the school system itself throughout much of the twentieth century, a presence that is belied by my earlier reference to the English department's "recuperation" of his fiction in the nineties. Dixon's work, in fact, has played a much larger role in the school system than literary scholars would probably suspect. While Dixon internalized an account of Reconstruction put forward by Dunning School historians, his fiction helped publicize this account to generations of post-Reconstruction schoolchildren through history textbooks. Donald Yacovone has recently undertaken a study of 3,000 US history textbooks from roughly 1800 to the 1960s, discovering in their pages explicit white supremacist accounts of the nation's history that "instill in generations of young American students a version of history no different than that found in Thomas Dixon Jr.'s pro-Klan *The Leopard's Spots* (1902) and *The Clansman* (1905), and usually not as well written."[77]

Yacovone's allusion to Dixon isn't accidental. In *The Growth of the American People* (1934), the University of Chicago historian Marcus Jernegan, according to Yacovone, relied "on the toxic scholarship of Claude Bowers, George Fort Milton, and even Thomas Dixon Jr." to describe "the Freedmen's Bureau as an organ for 'race hatred,'" while the Ku Klux Klan appears in the textbook as "the bulwark against carpetbag corruption." In *The Story of Our America*, a 1951 history textbook written by Gertrude Van Duyn Southworth and John Van Duyn Southworth, and adopted by the state of Indiana for the seventh and eighth grades, Yacovone found "an image of white-robed, galloping Klansmen (with similarly robed horses) borrowed from the 1915 film *The Birth of a Nation* to illustrate how the Klan and similar groups defeated corrupt carpetbag and scalawag governments and their Negro tools to restore respectable whites to their justly dominant position."[78]

Dixon's fiction, in short, appeared in the curriculum well into the twentieth century, and its presence there was not meant to reassure students that they were all equal members of an inclusive and meritocratic academic community, contrary to Michaels's description of the modern school. It served instead to notify students that certain populations were eligible for scholastic credentials and others weren't. This notification took place in an institutional context quite different from the one where literary objects are typically believed to exercise their political agency. Dixon's fiction was not taught in literature classes, and its inclusion in the curriculum was not intended to win students over to, say, a particular conception of the aesthetic. Rather, it appeared in primary and secondary school history classes, mediated through primary and secondary school history textbooks, where its aesthetic value and political investments were not subject to debate or interpretation. In an educational system that increasingly embraced a rhetoric of meritocracy, history textbooks greeted students with celebratory images and descriptions of white-robed, galloping Klansmen. These descriptions and images served to undergird a social order that did not demand the consent but only the abjection of its lowliest subjects.[79] Althusser, of course, qualified the ideological work that Ideological State Apparatuses perform, explaining that "every State Apparatus, whether Repressive or Ideological, 'functions' both by violence and by ideology"—only the Repressive State Apparatus functions "massively and predominantly *by repression*," whereas the Ideological State Apparatus functions "massively and predominantly *by ideology*." The enduring presence of Dixon's work in the curriculum suggests something more fundamental about the ideological operations of the school as a social institution than Althusser's qualification would imply.[80]

Consider, for instance, Michaels's hypothetical about universal higher education, which he invokes as evidence that promoting economic equality through the school is "doomed to fail." In what sense, however, is this particular hypothetical destined for failure? Michaels's argument is that giving every college-age student a bachelor's degree would do little to change inequality; it would merely expand the number of graduates competing for elite, high-paying jobs but not the number of jobs themselves. The graduates who were hired for these jobs would then seem, in the end, worthy of their rewards. Mass education, as Michaels renders it in the hypothetical, legitimizes rather than undercuts the capitalist system: hence "failure."

The critique of mass education that Michaels extracts from this hypothetical is a fairly familiar, Marxist one; however, it seems important to note that in its specifics Michaels's critique of mass education remains somewhat idiosyncratic, differing in crucial ways from the Marxist critique put forward by a thinker like Pierre Bourdieu. In Bourdieu's sociological investigations of the French school, we again see the ideological work performed by a mass system of education, only for Bourdieu, the system is "mass" not in the sense that every student is guaranteed a degree from an elite institution of higher education, but because almost all of the student-age population is *enrolled* in the school from an early age. Over the course of primary, secondary, and higher education, the school then allows some students, richly endowed with cultural or economic capital (or both), to earn prestigious degrees and others, without these forms of capital, to drop out or settle for degrees with less prestige attached to them.[81]

The distinction between Michaels's and Bourdieu's systems of mass education—the distinction, that is, between universal enrollment and universal credentialing—is meaningful because it draws attention to the somewhat awkward position the school inhabits as a social institution tasked with reproducing class relations. In one of his first essays translated into English, "Cultural Reproduction and Social Reproduction" (1973), Bourdieu explains that academic credentials are fundamentally "weak currency." "[T]he possession of a diploma, as prestigious as it may be, is in any case less and less capable of guaranteeing access to the highest positions and is never sufficient to guarantee in itself access to economic power," Bourdieu writes. Membership in the "dominant sections of the dominant classes," conversely, "is relatively independent of the chances of gaining access to higher education for those individuals from sections closest to economic and politico-administrative power[.]" In other words, for really wealthy and powerful people, the school's credential isn't especially meaningful. Academic success, rewards, and merit are only truly meaningful, in fact, Bourdieu explains, to those who forget that other forms of capital, like economic capital, exist. For those in possession of these forms of capital, meanwhile, it isn't especially difficult to achieve academic success, and academic success isn't necessary to retain wealth or power, either.[82]

It's precisely because academic credentials are "weak" in Bourdieu's account that the school must anxiously manage the students it does and doesn't deem worthy of its highest degrees, going to great lengths to ensure that the students it consecrates will eventually possess economic and symbolic capital. To make a degree valuable—or rather, to make a degree appear valuable—the educational system thus awards its highest diplomas primarily to students who are already in possession of economic and symbolic capital, while winnowing out the rest. The kind of universal higher education that Michaels describes in his hypothetical is "doomed to fail," therefore, not necessarily because the school fails to effect structural change under capitalism, but rather—and more profoundly—because the school itself is no longer capable of performing its ideological function. Once every college-age student is in possession of the same bachelor's degree, the degree ceases to have value altogether and, in consequence, the pretense of meritocracy falls apart. With no distinctions in academic capital, high-paying jobs would obviously—instead of covertly—reproduce existing relations under capitalism. Michaels's hypothetical of an educational system that is perfectly and entirely ideological—functioning through the illusion of meritocracy produced by universal degree-conferral—actually represents the collapse of the ideology of the modern school and, in all likelihood, the collapse of the modern school itself.

Even those educational systems whose authority appears entirely secure, like France's, thus occupy a precarious position as they carry out the reproduction of social relations. From one side, formal education is tasked with convincing the working class that the school distributes its credentials fairly while it programmatically denies this class access to its highest credentials; from the other side, formal education is tasked with convincing the ruling elite that they should covet credentials that they have no real need for. The presence of Dixon's work on the syllabus is not merely a reminder, pace Althusser, that the school is never purely ideological, that the educational system will inevitably resort to at least some overt and repressive techniques as it disqualifies student populations from the credentialing process. More fundamentally, the presence of Dixon's work on the syllabus is proof of the limits of the school's ideological project, proof that the school, as it's sought to establish its value as an instrument of social control, has failed in the United States to win over the constituencies it's supposed to have won over. It has failed to perform the service—manufacturing consent—that purportedly differentiates it from other institutions. If instructors in recent years have tried to use Dixon's fiction to help students think critically about early twentieth-century US history and culture, this pedagogical reorientation has not succeeded in dismantling the repressive institutional regime that Dixon's writing helped call into existence earlier in the twentieth century. Even as teachers introduce it in new pedagogical situations, Dixon's fiction serves as a reminder of the violent mechanisms that the school can't quite seem to do without.[83]

Conclusion

In the 1920s, the Ku Klux Klan's ascent was felt on college campuses around the country. Members of elite institutions of higher education often set out to distinguish their exclusionary practices from the Klan's; at Princeton, student editorials denounced the Klan as "un-American" and in 1924 more than eight hundred students rioted against the appearance of hooded kleagles. At Harvard, however, the response was more complicated. In 1923, the *Crimson* published an article suggesting that Klan had already infiltrated the campus: its headline read, "Ku Klux Klan at Harvard Awaits Moment to Strike." In response, James Weldon Johnson, then the secretary of the NAACP, sent a telegram to Lawrence Lowell and the Harvard Board of Overseers asking university officials to expel those responsible for bringing the Klan to Harvard. "It would be better to close the university," Johnson explained, "than to permit it to become a vehicle for disseminating the poison of race and religious hatred upon which the infamous Klan depends in recruiting its members." Though the *Crimson* article turned out to be a Halloween prank, historian Marcia Graham Synnott cites the whole incident, including Johnson's telegram, as "an ominous sign of the times," evidence that nativism had begun to penetrate campus life.[84]

It seems worth emphasizing—in addition to Synnott's main point that scholastic and Klan practices began to interpenetrate during this historical moment[85]—that James Weldon Johnson's reaction to the prank reflects his own sensitivity to the potential dangers of secret organizations operating within the education system, his belief that the school could be fundamentally reconfigured by a secret society. As an African American living under Jim Crow, Johnson had every right to be suspicious of the forces governing academic administration in the United States. In Chapter 6, though, we'll see that secret societies entered the African American institutional imagination in much more complex and diverse ways than Johnson's letter to Lowell would suggest. Far from seeing the secret society only as a pernicious agency in academic life, certain African American writers, including Johnson himself, understood the secret society as a potentially emancipatory organization, an organization that played a vital role in black community life under slavery and might reshape Jim Crow institutions at the turn of the twentieth century. Whether the unique power of the secret society should be instrumentalized after slavery, however, or whether African Americans should seek public recognition through the existing structures of the institutional system, remained a contested issue within the black middle class, a subject of much concern and speculation.

6
Really, Really Secret Societies

> To the grand architect of the universe,
> And in memory of the
> Long line of illustrious brethren
> In the grand lodge above,
> And to the cause of truth and right
> This volume is
> Fraternally and affectionately dedicated by
> The author.
> —William Grimshaw's *Official History of Freemasonry among Colored People in North America* (1903)

> It is a difficult thing for a white man to learn what a colored man really thinks; because, generally, with the latter an additional and different light must be brought to bear on what he thinks; and his thoughts are often influenced by considerations so delicate and subtle that it would be impossible for him to confess or explain them to one of the opposite race. This gives to every colored man, in proportion to his intellectuality, a sort of dual personality; there is one phase of him which is disclosed only in the freemasonry of his own race.
> —James Weldon Johnson's *The Autobiography of an Ex-Colored Man* (1912)[1]

There is a famous passage early in James Weldon Johnson's *Autobiography of an Ex-Colored Man* (1912) where the unnamed narrator offers a reformulation of W. E. B. Du Bois's "double consciousness." Because his thoughts "are often influenced by considerations so delicate and subtle that it would be impossible for him to confess or explain them to one of the opposite race," the "colored man," according to Johnson's narrator, possesses a "dual personality." Alongside his public identity, he maintains a private identity, "disclosed only in the freemasonry of his own race." Johnson's expression "dual personality" invites us to see a connection between his account of black subjectivity and Du Bois's, but if we focus too hard on this connection we risk overlooking the much more bizarre part of Johnson's formulation.

We risk overlooking, that is, Johnson's invocation of freemasonry to describe racial experience. For Johnson, race isn't *like* a secret society; race *is* a secret society.

Johnson's reference to freemasonry in *The Autobiography of an Ex-Colored Man* played off of a larger public curiosity about African American secret societies at the turn of the twentieth century. While black "Prince Hall Freemasonry" came into existence in the late eighteenth century, interest in the African American freemason reached new heights when Johnson was writing, a period that witnessed the publication of works like William H. Upton's *Negro Masonry, Being a Critical Examination of Objections to the Legitimacy of the Masonry Existing among the Negroes in America* (1902) and William Grimshaw's *Official History of Freemasonry among Colored People in North America* (1903).[2] A few years before the release of Johnson's *Autobiography of an Ex-Colored Man*, a character in one of Sutton Griggs's novels complained that too many African Americans were attracted to the status benefits bestowed on members of secret societies. "The thought that he will enter a realm where much wisdom abides operates to draw the Negro to the secret society," Griggs wrote. "Then, too, if he is a member of such a body, he has, in the fact of membership, a passport bearing testimony as to his social standing." According to Griggs's character, membership in a secret society was a status symbol, a marker of class difference. For Johnson, as we've seen, however, the secret society provided a rich metaphor for racial identity, a metaphor Johnson could elaborate over the course of an entire book on passing: after all, *The Autobiography of an Ex-Colored Man* begins by describing the narrator's experience in the language of the secret: "I know that in writing the following pages I am divulging the great secret of my life, the secret which for some years I have guarded far more carefully than any of my earthly possessions[.]"[3]

The secret society became the subject of much speculation in black discourse at the turn of the twentieth century for the same reason that it did in the culture at large—because it promised to explain the existence of inequality and perhaps transform the institutions responsible for reproducing it. In the aftermath of the Civil War, the social order underwent a dramatic upheaval as the industrial economy assimilated a population of the formerly enslaved. Who stood to benefit under this new regime and how this new regime would find justification were questions of tremendous significance not only for industrialists but also for southern planters, immigrant industrial laborers, the independent farmers, artisans, and shopkeepers of the old middle class, and poor southern whites, as well as, of course, the freed population that had fought for its own emancipation and now sought restitution from the system that had profited off of its labor in the past. In the middle of this struggle, too, was a newly empowered class of managers, professionals, white-collar workers, and salaried employees whose Progressive vision promised to rationalize the process through which the social order was reproduced. With this middle class at its helm, the school system after the Civil War assumed the task of reproducing and legitimizing the inequalities of industrial society through its credentialing operations. The secret society held fascination in these decades because it seemed to provide a rationale for the institutional system's (and the school's) distribution of rewards. For some, it helpfully formalized and reinforced existing hierarchies; for others, it was responsible for the injustice of the system; for yet others, it was a potentially transformative organization, one capable of overcoming the system's glaring faults.

The system's faults were indeed glaring for black writers. As James Anderson has argued, the formerly enslaved population led the charge for universal education in the South in the wake of the Civil War, but after Reconstruction this demand for adequate schooling was obstructed by a ruling class that "called for the special instruction of former slaves" and developed a "new curriculum," which "offered the possibility of adapting black education to [its] particular needs and interests[.]"[4] This new curriculum was the Hampton Model of industrial education developed first by Samuel Chapman Armstrong and later spearheaded by Booker T. Washington at Tuskegee. The point of bringing up Tuskegee here is not to relitigate the argument between Du Bois and Washington but to suggest that there were specific historical conditions that, on the one hand, made the school an especially significant institution for African Americans in political struggle, and on the other hand, prevented African Americans from accessing formal education and changing it on their own terms.[5] As the Tuskegee Machine increasingly dictated the scope and content of black formal education, literature came to function as an outlet for African American writers' frustrations with the modern school system.

The secret society appeared meaningfully different in this body of literature than in, say, Owen Johnson's *Stover at Yale* or white Progressive discourse more broadly because of those specific historical conditions black writers faced. For instance, the black secret society was—with at least one important exception, which I discuss later in this chapter—an off-campus phenomenon. Few institutions of higher education offered college-level instruction for black students; the two best endowed institutions, Hampton and Tuskegee, focused their curricula on agricultural and industrial education, not the liberal arts, where campus culture thrived. At the two prominent institutions that did provide college-level instruction, Howard University and Fisk University—neither of which received the kind of northern industrial philanthropy that Hampton and Tuskegee did—students and faculty tended to focus on their studies, not the hijinks of the extracurriculum. Only in the 1920s, after Fisk and Howard capitulated to northern industrialists, did campus culture begin to seep into African American colleges and universities.[6]

Other differences between black and white literary representations of the secret society will become apparent as this chapter unfolds. For our present purposes, I simply want to underscore the fact that, notwithstanding these differences, the secret society remained ubiquitous in black middle-class discourse just as it did in white middle-class discourse at the turn of the twentieth century, as Johnson's reference to the "freemasonry" of race in *The Autobiography of an Ex-Colored Man* suggests. As a graduate of Atlanta University, the first black executive secretary of the NAACP, and the Spence Chair of Creative Literature at Fisk University, James Weldon Johnson was enmeshed in the formal institutions of the black middle class throughout his life. That a writer as institutionally attuned as Johnson invoked the secret society in his first major work indicates its position at the center, rather than the periphery, of black institutional consciousness at the time.

And yet, though secrecy remains an abiding preoccupation throughout *The Autobiography of an Ex-Colored Man*, the book's attitude toward it remains fundamentally ambivalent. Whether the novel renounces the narrator's decision to hide his racial identity, depicting it as harmful to his sense of self, or whether the novel remains attracted to the idea of a hidden racial identity, depicting it as an opportunity for self-fashioning and social mobility—it's hard to say. The narrator in the last lines of the novel admits, "My love for my children makes me glad that I am what I am," while at the same time lamenting that "I have sold my birthright for a mess of pottage." The narrator's regret in the final sentence of the novel that he has been forced to keep his true inner life a secret belies the fact that he is continuing to keep secrets (for instance, he still hasn't revealed his real name).[7]

Johnson's ambivalence toward the secret in *The Autobiography of an Ex-Colored Man* makes him a somewhat anomalous figure. Secrecy and secret societies tended to polarize black discourse rather than inspire ambivalence. Many endorsed the secret society because it offered its own (non-academic) credential for the African American middle class, a "passport," in Griggs's words, "bearing testimony as to ... social standing." We can see this attitude toward the secret society in the pages of the *Colored American Magazine*, which devoted more attention to fraternal orders and African American business leaders once Booker T. Washington wrested control of the periodical from Pauline Hopkins.[8] We can also see this attitude fictionalized in Paul Laurence Dunbar's *The Sport of the Gods* (1902), where, in the opening chapters of the book, Berry Hamilton belongs to a secret society, the "Tribe of Benjamin," that distinguishes the Hamiltons from other African Americans in their southern community.[9] Others, however, denounced secrecy as a foundation for postbellum institutional life. In doing so, these African Americans demystified the racism embedded in the middle class's meritocratic worldview and sought to embed themselves in this class's institutions. Still others embraced secret societies to radically alter the system itself. These individuals saw in secrecy institutional possibilities that extended beyond the assimilationist ambitions of the freemasons and the Elks. For them, secret organizations more closely resembled the ad hoc institutional formations that emerged under slavery and Reconstruction than black freemasonry, which often mimicked white fraternal orders.[10] This chapter is organized around two opposing attitudes toward the secret society—the first section examines writers who denounced the secret society, the second a single writer who embraced it for its radical political potential, not its conservatism—and Johnson's ambivalence puts him on the boundary between these conflicting positions.

For decades the dissemination and preservation of these literary works took place primarily outside the system of formal education, but in the aftermath of the student protest movements of the 1960s and 1970s they truly entered the school, and with their entry they have transformed the educational system and its role in the reproduction of social relations. The institutionalization of these works—which has involved the creation of administrative departments and programs to teach them, such as Ethnic Studies and African American Studies—has inspired much ambivalence among contemporary observers. While this institutionalization is often believed to have facilitated the expansion of educational opportunity in the United States and the development of counter-hegemonic epistemologies, it is also persistently understood to have inaugurated a shift in the school's ideological program—it is read, that is, as a sign that the educational system has neoliberalized. These accusations are just as likely to come from scholars working within Ethnic Studies programs as they are from scholars external to them.[11] As I will explain in greater depth later in the chapter, the belief that the ruling class has instrumentalized the teaching of African American and other ethnic literatures to further consolidate its power strikes me as somewhat misguided. The educational system might have incorporated African American literature into the syllabus in the late twentieth century to more convincingly present itself as a multicultural institution capable of credentialing a diverse and deserving population of middle-class students, but this renovated ideological project has taken hold as the school's function in US society has changed dramatically under the long economic downturn. Though deindustrialization and globalization might have inspired administrators in the United States to expand the school's meritocratic program, these processes have also made ideology increasingly dispensable as a mechanism of social control, rendering the United States' principal ideological apparatus—the school—dispensable too. I will devote more attention to the political consequences of teaching these literary works, however, only after I've examined their relationship to the institutional system they emerged from earlier, at the turn of the twentieth century.

Shadows Uplifted

We can begin to understand the significance of the secret society in the postbellum black literary imagination through two key passages. The first is from Frances Ellen Watkins Harper's *Iola Leroy* (1892); the second is from Charles Chesnutt's *The House Behind the Cedars* (1900):

"Good mornin', Bob how's butter dis mornin'?"
"Fresh; just as fresh, as fresh can be."

"Oh, glory!" said the questioner, whom we shall call Thomas Anderson, although he was known among his acquaintances as Marster Anderson's Tom.

His informant regarding the condition of the market was Robert Johnson. ... There seemed to be an unusual interest manifested by these men in the state of the produce market, and a unanimous report of its good condition. Surely there was nothing in the primeness of the butter or the freshness of the eggs to change careless looking faces into such expressions of gratification, or to light dull eyes with such gladness. What did it mean?

Between the colored glass bottles in the window he could see a young woman, a tall and slender girl, like a lily on its stem. ... Her face was partly turned away from the window, but as Tryon's eye fell upon her, he gave a great start. Surely, no two women could be so much alike. The height, the graceful droop of the shoulders, the swan-like poise of the head, the well-turned little ear,—surely, no two women could have them all identical! But, pshaw! The notion was absurd, it was merely the reflex influence of his morning's dream.

She moved slightly; it was Rena's movement. Surely he knew the gown, and the style of the hair-dressing! She rested her hand lightly on the back of a chair. The ring that glittered on her finger could be none other than his own. ... When Rena's eyes fell upon the young man in the buggy, she saw a face as pale as death, with starting eyes, in which love, which once had reigned there, had now given place to astonishment and horror. She stood a moment as if turned to stone. One appealing glance she gave,—a look that might have softened adamant. When she saw that it brought no answering sign of love or sorrow or regret, the color faded from her cheek, the light from her eye, and she fell fainting to the ground.[12]

However different these passages might seem after an initial comparison, both suggest the prominence of the secret society in post-Reconstruction African American discourse and both reflect, more specifically, the suspicion certain members of the African American middle class held toward secrecy as a feature of modern institutions. The passage in *Iola Leroy* is from the opening paragraphs of the novel—two enslaved characters are having a conversation at a market in North Carolina during the last days of the Civil War—and it is meant, on first reading, to be confusing. The exchange is confusing for reasons that aren't simply structural, the fact that, since these are the first lines of the novel, we are just beginning to figure out who is speaking and where they are. The exchange is confusing, in addition to these factors, because of the incongruity between the subject of the characters' conversation (butter) and the joy this subject elicits from the speakers ("Oh, glory!"). "What did it mean?" the narrator asks. In the very next sentence we learn that these enslaved characters are not, in fact, discussing butter; instead they are exchanging, in code, news of the North's latest victory. "During the dark days of the Rebellion," the narrator explains, "some of the shrewder slaves, coming in contact with their masters and overhearing their conversations, invented a phraseology to convey in the most unsuspected manner news to each other from the battle-field."[13] During the Civil War, Harper suggests, secret languages allowed these characters to forge meaningful social bonds. Talking to each other about the freshness of the butter or the quality of the eggs at the market is a way for them to disseminate information and assert a degree of collective agency.

But if the opening lines of the novel are disorienting, thrusting the reader into a conversation between two characters spoken entirely in a secret language, this disorientation doesn't last very long. The characters' secret language doesn't remain secret, as Harper reveals their "phraseology." "[U]nder [an] apparently careless exterior there was an undercurrent of thought which escaped the cognizance of th[e] masters," she writes. "In conveying tidings of the war, if they wished to announce a victory of the Union army, they said the butter was fresh, or that the fish and eggs were in good condition. If defeat befell them, then the butter and other produce were rancid or stale." The trajectory followed in this opening scene—from secrecy to transparency, from the latent to the manifest—is central to the project of *Iola Leroy* as a whole; it's representative of how the book understands the function of literature and the struggle for African American social and political equality at the turn of the century.[14]

The second passage, from *The House Behind the Cedars*, concerns itself not with the preservation of secrecy, like the first lines of *Iola Leroy*, but with its exposure. In this pivotal moment, George Tryon realizes for the first time that the woman he is engaged to, Rowena Warwick, is not the white woman he thought she was. She is, rather, Rena Walden, the novel's protagonist, a mixed-race woman who is passing for white. Tryon discovers here, in the words of the narrator, "Rena's secret," the very thing she's been trying to hide from him, "the worm in the bud, the skeleton in the closet."[15]

Tryon's discovery is the result of a series of highly improbable coincidences, the same conspiracy of unlikelihoods that precede and bring about the other set pieces in the novel. In this particular set piece, the conditions of Tryon's revelation are exceedingly improbable. Rena has traveled to Patesville, North Carolina (where she was born), from Clarence, South Carolina (where she is passing), because she dreamed, three times, that her mother was dying. Tryon has traveled to Patesville because he arrived back in Clarence from a business trip earlier than expected, and decided, with Rowena's abrupt departure, to travel to Patesville in order to collect a claim owed to his family. Tryon doesn't know where Rowena is when he decides to go to Patesville—she sends him a letter explaining simply that she has "been called away to visit a sick-bed"—and yet even this single coincidence isn't enough to guarantee the revelation of Rena's secret identity. The network of agents tasked by Rena and her brother John either directly or indirectly to keep their ancestry secret—their mother Molly Walden, Judge Straight, Frank Fowler—ensures that a revelation will occur only under the most contrived circumstances. As Molly renarrates the events to her son John in a letter afterward, "Frank saw [Tryon] up street and run all the way down here to tell me, so that [Rena] could keep out of his way," but Rena "was still up town waiting for the doctor and getting me some camphor gum for my camphor bottle." And "Judge Straight must have knowed something about it, for he sent me a note to keep Rena in the house," but the little boy the judge sends to Molly "did n't bring [the note] till Rena was already gone up town, and, as I couldn't read, of course I didn't know what it said."[16]

The narrator, in his more grandiloquent moments, describes these concatenations as the inner workings of "Fate," and yet this set piece—the first of the novel, and its most elaborate—represents less a commentary on the metaphysics of free will and more a meditation on the sociology of the secret itself. The peculiar agency the secret wields in the episode is one of self-cancelation, bending human and nonhuman actors toward its own exposure—from Rena's dreams in Clarence, to the claim that sends Tryon to Patesville in the first place, to the "gingerbread" that tempts the "little boy" entrusted to deliver the note from Judge Straight, delaying his trip to Molly Walden's house.[17] Rena's secret in effect possesses its own volition: it wants to come out. Even the suspenseful "near-misses" that take place before Tryon's discovery testify to the will the secret exercises in effecting its own revelation. For instance, as Tryon waits in Judge Straight's office shortly after he arrives in town, he apprehends, half-asleep, a conversation going on out in the hall—a conversation between Rena and the judge's attendant, Dave—and he wakes up just in time to hear, or to think he has heard, "a light footfall descending the stairs," but not in time to see who the footfall actually belongs to.[18]

In its final moment of exposure, Chesnutt therefore denaturalizes the organizational apparatus that forms around secrets. Secret societies are a source of interest elsewhere in Chesnutt's work—*The Marrow of Tradition* (1901) follows Major Carteret and his associates' covert attempts to undermine Reconstruction-era policies, a satire of Thomas Dixon Jr.'s secret societies—and in *The House Behind the Cedars*, characters find themselves in what we might think of as an informal secret society whose boundaries are constantly being negotiated. Secrets, in *The House Behind the Cedars*, in other words, can't remain secret, and in their unveiling, they produce ever-widening networks of association, forging unexpected, yet profound, connections between characters. When Tryon sees Rena at the drugstore, and she sees him, the two characters share a look that only they—and not onlookers, like Dr. Green—can understand, a look of recognition in which (as the focalization shifts, inhabiting a space shared by both characters but belonging fully to neither) Tryon's face appears to Rena "pale as death," and Rena appears to Tryon "fainting to the ground."

Ultimately, both *Iola Leroy* and *The House Behind the Cedars* remain suspicious of the secret society. In the two novels, secrecy remains untenable, or inappropriate, as a foundation for African American institutional life in post-Reconstruction society. This conviction emerged out of the two writers' middle-class backgrounds and their unsatisfying encounters with the US institutional system, particularly the school. Although Chesnutt himself did not earn a high school degree or attend college, he started teaching at the age of sixteen, and by his early twenties he was named principal of the Colored Normal School in Fayetteville, North Carolina.[19] Even after he abandoned his career as an educator and established himself as a writer, Chesnutt remained an active member in middle-class African American institutions. He served on the local branch of the NAACP. He kept a regular correspondence with Booker T. Washington and published an essay in 1901 expressing admiration for Tuskegee. He replaced W. E. B. Du Bois on the Committee of Twelve for the Advancement of the Interests of the Negro Race in 1905. When Chesnutt's writing career began to falter, however, his institutional commitments waned too as he sought to maintain his middle-class life as an attorney and stenographer.[20]

Harper received an exceptional formal education before the Civil War as a free African American at her uncle's school in Baltimore, the William Watkins Academy for Negro Youth, which emphasized biblical studies, the classics, and elocution. With this education, she became the first female teacher at the Union Seminary, a school near Columbus, Ohio, founded by the AME Church, although she left after a short time, presumably because the seminary lacked sufficient support. In 1852, she took another teaching position in Little York, Pennsylvania, but again left after she began suffering bouts of illness and despondency. Harper's political energies were soon channeled through institutions outside the school. She started publishing her poetry and essays in abolitionist newspapers. She also began a career as a lecturer and joined a number of anti-slavery societies and voluntary organizations, including the Maine Anti-Slavery Society, the Ohio State Anti-Slavery Society, American Women's Suffrage Association, the National Council of Women, and the Women's Christian Temperance Union. She participated in the First Congress of Colored Women in the United States, and in 1896 she joined the historic meeting of the National Federation of Afro-American Women and the Colored Women's League, a meeting that led to the formation of the National Council of Negro Women.[21] Out of these experiences, Harper and Chesnutt, like so many others at the time, took up the secret society in their fiction as a subversive and potentially transformative organization in the post-Reconstruction United States. As we will see, however, Harper and Chesnutt concluded that the secret society was inadequate as a foundation for institutional politics.

Secret societies don't appear especially harmful or nefarious in the first half of *Iola Leroy*, which is set during the Civil War years. In fact, secret societies emerge in these pages as the primary mechanism of association for the main characters as they suffer under the oppressive and dehumanizing conditions of slavery. Shortly after the opening exchange between Robert and Tom, we learn that both belong to a secret society that gathers at night for covert prayer meetings. "Las' Sunday we had a good time," Aunt Linda explains to Robert. "I war jis' chock full an' runnin' ober. ... An' I want you to come Sunday night an' tell all 'bout the good eggs, fish, and butter." Robert in particular plays an important role in these secret prayer meetings. As he explains later in the novel, "I used to get the morning papers to sell to the boarders and others and when I got them I would contrive to hide a paper, and let some of the fellow-servants know how things were going on. And our owners thought we cared nothing about what was going on." Robert, as one of the only literate enslaved characters, tells others what's "going on" during these secret prayer meetings, and consequently the meetings serve an indispensable social function on the plantation. "[W]e contrived to hold secret meetings in spite of their caution," Robert claims later. "We knew whom we could trust."[22]

If, in the first half of the novel, the secret society enables the enslaved characters to coordinate with each other and wield agency collectively, in the second half of the novel, which is set after the Civil War, secrecy no longer serves as a necessary or even useful institutional strategy. In these later chapters, Harper presents readers with a whole range of institutions capable of fostering racial equality during Reconstruction. These institutions include, most noticeably, and perhaps unexpectedly, the family. Though earlier in the novel Harper represents the family under slavery as a profoundly broken social institution, she represents it after emancipation as the center of social experience, an institution that structures the characters' lives and their relations to each other. The second half of *Iola Leroy* unfolds according to the logic of reunion, with the characters finding lost family members and discovering that they are all in fact related to each other. The title of the novel—*Iola Leroy*—is somewhat misleading, read in this light. The novel is less about the character Iola Leroy than it is about the network of characters that forms around her. The fact that Iola Leroy doesn't even appear until the fifth chapter of *Iola Leroy* reflects the novel's interest in this larger social network. Where all of the characters are formally separated from one another in the first half of the novel, with the siblings Iola and Harry temporally and geographically dislocated from each other and from their uncle Robert, in the second half the novel straightens out, with all of the characters reunited and occupying the same narrative space on the same narrative timeline.

Other institutions, beyond the family, also help reintegrate the characters into postbellum US society. Robert discovers his lost mother at a church gathering, where "there were remnants of broken families—mothers who had been separated from their children before the war, husbands who had not met their wives for years." Iola finds her brother Harry at a "Methodist Conference" in Georgia. At the end of the novel, many of the characters resolve to become teachers in North Carolina: Iola, we learn, is "going to teach in the Sunday-school," and Harry and his wife Lucille "are at the head of a large and flourishing school." In the last sustained episode of the novel, Harper depicts a *"conversazione,"* a literary society meeting in which "some of the thinkers and leaders of the race" gather together "to consult on subjects of vital interest to our welfare." At the meeting, characters read papers with titles such as, "Negro Emigration," "Patriotism," "Education of Mothers," and "Moral Progress of the Race." A poem is read too, called "A Rallying Cry."[23]

At times, Harper seems to insist on the continuity between these emergent institutional formations and the secret society meetings held under slavery. As Robert rides to the church gathering where he will find his mother, he "indulge[s] pleasant reminiscences ... when, with Uncle Daniel and Tom Anderson, he attended secret prayer-meetings." These reminiscences return when Robert approaches the church itself, passing "the place where [the enslaved characters] held [their] last prayer-meeting." But if, in these moments, Robert's nostalgia appears to link the project of the prayer meeting during slavery with the project of the church gathering after slavery, later in the novel Harper suggests that postbellum institutions break altogether from their predecessors. At the very end of the book, Robert distinguishes the conversazione from the secret prayer meetings:

> "I," said Robert, "was thinking of the wonderful changes that have come to us since the war. When I sat in those well-lighted, beautifully-furnished rooms, I was thinking of the meetings we used to have in by-gone days. How we used to go by stealth into the lonely woods and gloomy swamps, to tell of our hopes and fears, sorrows and trials. I hope that we will have many more of these gatherings. Let us have the next one here."[24]

The reason that the conversazione is exhilarating for Robert is its transparency, instantiated in those "well-lighted" rooms where the characters discuss subjects vital to their welfare. Robert believes this transparency is a "wonderful chang[e]" from the prayer meetings on the plantation, where characters were forced to travel "by stealth into the lonely woods and gloomy swamps." The conversazione as it's represented in the novel enacts these postbellum institutional values. It offers characters a chance to share their ideas out in the open, in public, as they debate whether to emigrate to Africa, with Bishop Tunset affirming that "Africa is to be redeemed to civilization," and Miss Delany insisting that "America ... is the best field for human development." The characters also argue over patriotism, with Reverend Cantnor delivering a paper in which "the white man was extolled as the master race," and speaking "as if it were a privilege for the colored man to be linked to his destiny[.]" Professor Gradnor responds by arguing that "our country needs ... truth more than flattery." The conversazione guarantees public recognition for the characters, as they justify themselves to each other and to the larger audience of *Iola Leroy*'s readers. Significantly, there is no room for interiority during the conversazione; characters express their thoughts in dialogue or not at all. The conversazione scene reads like a transcript, like the minutes taken by an extremely diligent scribe.[25]

The renunciation of secrecy in favor of transparency occurs again and again in the second half of the book. The mixed-race characters in the novel, for instance, are vehemently opposed to passing as white. Harry insists on serving in a black regiment during the Civil War, even though he could easily be taken for a white man, a decision that perplexes a white recruitment officer: "[Y]ou are the d–d'st fool I ever saw—a man as white as you are turning his back upon his chances of promotion! But you can take your choice." When Iola decides not to marry Dr. Gresham—a white man who might not know her family background—she thinks to herself, "To the man I marry my heart must be as open as the flowers to the sun. I could not accept his hand and hide from him the secret of my birth[.]" Iola reiterates this point later, after it becomes clear that Dr. Gresham does know her background, explaining to him that she won't hide her race from his family, that she has "too much self-respect to enter your home under a veil of concealment," and that she is "not willing to live under a shadow of concealment[.]"[26] The man Iola does marry, Dr. Latimer, is another mixed-race character who refuses to pass. This renunciation of secrecy and concealment even manifests in the physical description of characters: critics in the past have noticed Harper's tendency to describe Iola as "flush," flushing being a "cardiovascular event" that, unlike blushing, is "an essentially internal event" that surfaces on the skin as "an expression of untutored feelings."[27] Harper's commitment to light and transparency against concealment and shadows is foregrounded in the novel's subtitle, *Shadows Uplifted*.

Post–Civil War institutional life for African Americans, as Harper depicts it in the novel, thus depends on a commitment to public visibility, with the formerly enslaved characters gaining access to and recognition within those institutions that they were previously barred from under slavery—the family, the school, the church, the literary society. The novel itself is self-conscious about the power of literature to summon into existence this new institutional life. Harper affirms the institutional force of literary objects during the conversazione, when characters read and discuss the poem, "A Rallying Cry." But she also—and more significantly—affirms the institutional power of literature in the hymn Iola sings while working as a nurse during the Civil War. It is this hymn that brings her and Robert together for the first time: "'That,' said he, looking earnestly into Iola's face, 'was my mother's hymn. I have not heard it for years. Where did you learn it?'" The hymn reappears later, reconnecting Robert with his mother at the church gathering: "Robert raised the hymn which Iola had sung for him when he was recovering from his wounds, and Iola, with her clear, sweet tones, caught up the words and joined him in the strain. When the hymn was finished a dear old mother rose from her seat."[28]

If *Iola Leroy* is more invested in understanding the network of affiliations that ties characters together than the psychology of any individual character, literary objects like the hymn are significant in the novel because they produce these networks. Once again, the public circulation of these literary objects gives them their power. The capacity of the hymn to make visible previously invisible connections between characters depends on its public performance; in the novel, the public space of the church gathering or the conversazione is where latent connections between characters reside, waiting to be activated. With its queasiness about keeping anything secret, *Iola Leroy* presents itself as ready for public recognition, a text capable of eliciting the institutional forms it thematizes in its pages. The novel aspires to a state of pure surface and transparency, with no depth or hidden meaning; the secret, while indispensable for enslaved life on the plantation, has no place whatsoever in the formal makeup of the novel.

In *The House Behind the Cedars*, secrecy is not so much renounced as it is shown to be an untenable feature of African American institutional life. This distinction, while seemingly of little significance, appears more consequential when understood in relation to the two novels' depiction of passing, the practice that signifies, in Everett Stonequist's words, that "group conflict is so severe that the individual is compelled to resort to subterfuge." While in *Iola Leroy* passing is unquestionably bad, in *The House Behind the Cedars*, passing represents an opportunity for characters too tempting to forgo. The scholarly response to passing in Chesnutt's work can be characterized as ambivalent—some see passing as fundamentally pernicious, part of the psychic turmoil Chesnutt's mixed-race characters suffer, while others see it as genuinely subversive—but whether the secret of passing is, in the final diagnosis, good or bad seems less important to Chesnutt than the fact that in the novel it's impossible for the characters to keep anything secret in the first place.[29]

The initiating action of the book—John's decision to include Rena in his plans and encourage her to pass with him—comes about, according to the narrator, because of the unbearable feelings of isolation John experiences as the holder of a secret. "He had no fear that the family secret would ever be discovered," the narrator explains, "and yet he could not but feel, at times, that if peradventure ... it should become known, his fine social position would collapse like a house of cards. Because of this knowledge, which the world around him did not possess, he had felt now and then a certain sense of loneliness[.]" Somewhat counterintuitively, the vulnerability John feels as a keeper of a secret doesn't cause him to protect his secret, limiting the number of individuals who know about it, but rather to spread it, bringing another person, Rena, in on the secret. "[T]here was a measure of relief in having about him one who knew his past, and yet whose knowledge, because of their common interest, would not interfere with his present or jeopardize his future," the narrator explains.[30]

Rena undergoes a similar experience of isolation when she begins to pass, after John sends her to school. Rena, with "no schoolmate from her own town, no relative or friend of the family near by," is, according to the narrator, "too fresh from her prison-house to doubt that sympathy would fail before the revelation of the secret[.]" In the lead up to the pivotal revelation scene, the novel tracks the gradual expansion of the secret society, the network of characters who are "in" on the secret of Rena's ancestry. Judge Straight improbably comes across a letter from "Rowena Warwick" lodged among the papers Tryon brings to Patesville. "While he held the sheet in his hand, it dawned upon him slowly that he held also one of the links in a chain of possible tragedy which he himself ... had had a hand in forging," Chesnutt writes. "It is the Walden woman's daughter, as sure as fate! Her name is Rena. Her brother goes by the name Warwick. She has come to visit her sick mother. My young client, Green's relation, is her lover—is engaged to marry her—is in town and is likely to meet her!" Frank Fowler travels to Clarence to see Rena in her new surroundings and discovers that she is passing: "[H]e had seen her: she was happy; he was content in the knowledge of her happiness. She was doubtless secure in the belief that her secret was unknown. Why should he, by revealing his presence, sow the seeds of doubt or distrust in the garden of her happiness?"[31]

However improbable the discovery of the secret is in practice—for Judge Straight, rapidly translating "Rowena" into "Rena," through Warwick and Molly Walden, which is no easy feat, and for Frank, seeing Rena at a medieval festival in Clarence—once a character is "initiated" into the secret, he becomes yet another member of the novel's secret society, the group charged with protecting the facts of Rena's ancestry from outsiders. In Frank's case, there is a proliferation of secrecy that accompanies the initial exposure, as Frank resolves, once he gains knowledge of Rena's secret, to keep his own secret from Rena—that he knows about her secret. The secret in *The House Behind the Cedars* is an essentially social phenomenon, constantly exceeding whatever boundaries individuals erect around it, finding new communities to circulate through, communities that are, at the same time, bounded and contained but also soon to be exceeded in their own right. Tryon's dramatic discovery is representative in this respect. Once he figures out who "Rowena" actually is, he doesn't make the secret broadly public; he decides to keep it a secret. "I need scarcely assure you that I shall say nothing about this affair," Tryon writes to John after the revelation, "and that I shall keep your secret as though it were my own." In the world of *The House Behind the Cedars*, we might say that there is no such thing as a "secret" one person keeps to him- or herself: there is only the "secret society."[32]

One of the principal narrative activities of *The House Behind the Cedars* consists of mapping this ever-expanding secret network, and it seems significant that this network remains a greater object of attention and interest for Chesnutt than the other formal institutions the novels treats only glancingly. The amount of narrative attention Chesnutt devotes to the school system in particular represents a stark contrast to the amount of narrative attention he devotes to the informal secret society. Although Rena, after she is "outed," decides to take a self-sacrificing career as a teacher, finding in the school "a worthy field of usefulness," in the end the task of promoting social equality through the educational system proves too burdensome for her. "Rena was unusually fatigued at the close of her school Wednesday afternoon," Chesnutt writes. "She had been troubled all day with a headache. ... The pupils seemed unusually stupid. A discouraging sense of the insignificance of any part she could perform towards the education of three million people with a school term of two months a year hung over her spirit like a pall."[33]

But if the secret society remains the central object of narrative attention in *The House Behind the Cedars*, more so than the school, ultimately whatever institutional possibilities the society affords prove insufficient to the characters' needs. The informal secret society is appealing because it offers the novel's mixed-race main characters an opportunity for social mobility and collective agency after Reconstruction. Yet the secret society, as the novel depicts it, fails the central characters just as the school does. In part, this is because of dynamics internal to the secret society itself, what I've described as the self-cancelation mechanisms built into its structure: the secret's compulsion to spread to new publics, thereby undermining the stability of whatever communal structures are organized around it. In part, this is because the slow painful dissolution of the secret society prevents the characters, no matter how devoted they are to it, from leading their own self-determining lives.[34]

Harper's and Chesnutt's essential pessimism about secrecy as the foundation for postbellum institutional life characterizes one particular strain of middle-class African American thought. Their literary work, which encodes this pessimism, proved tremendously influential in the school system later in the twentieth century, when the black middle class and their cultural products finally achieved a modicum of recognition within the US educational system—when the shadows surrounding African American literature were uplifted. But before examining the institutional reception of Harper's and Chesnutt's work, we should turn to another strain of African American literature, one that saw in the secret society a revolutionary answer to the problems afflicting post-Reconstruction institutions.

Equality or Death

There is a pivotal scene in Sutton Griggs's *Imperium in Imperio* (1899) where one of the novel's protagonists, Belton Piedmont, starts a secret society at his college. Belton's decision occurs after a trip to the college's sister institution, where he passes the school's dining room and sees the school's "colored teacher enjoying a meal with the white teachers." Because the one black teacher at Belton's university is not allowed to eat at the same table as his white colleagues, Belton finds that he "could not enjoy the sight as much as he would have liked, from thinking about the treatment his teacher was receiving." Returning to his own college, Stowe University, Belton, we learn, "called together all the male students. He informed them that they ought to perfect a secret organization and have a password. They all agreed to secrecy and Belton gave this as the password: 'Equality or Death.'" The group, after it's formed, conspires to change the school's dining hall policy; one morning, during a chapel exercise, the students leave a letter of protest on the president's desk. The president tries to dismiss the students, but they refuse to leave. "He rang the gong a second time and yet no one moved," Griggs writes.

"All remained still. At a signal from Belton, all the students lifted their right hands, each bearing a small white board on which was printed in clear type: 'Equality or Death.'" The teachers eventually agree to the society's demands.[35]

For the narrator, the secret society's success represents a transformation in black identity at the turn of the twentieth century: "The cringing, fawning, sniffling, cowardly Negro which slavery left, had disappeared, and a new Negro, self-respecting, fearless, and determined in the assertion of his rights was at hand." The chapter ends with an extended meditation on this "new Negro" and the longer history in which he is embedded:

> Ye who chronicle history and mark epochs in the careers of races and nations must put here a towering, gigantic, century stone, as marking the passing of one and the ushering in of another great era in the history of the colored people of the United States. Rebellions, for one cause or another, broke out in almost every one of these schools presided over by white faculties, and as a rule, the Negro students triumphed.
>
> These men who engineered and participated in these rebellions were the future leaders of their race. In these rebellions, they learned the power of combinations, and that white men could be made to capitulate to colored men under certain circumstances. In these schools, probably one hundred thousand students had these thoughts instilled in them. These one hundred thousand went to their respective homes and told of their prowess to their playmates who could not follow them to the college walls. In the light of these facts the great events yet to be recorded are fully accounted for.
>
> Remember this was Belton's first taste of rebellion against the whites for the securing of rights denied simply because of color. In after life he is the moving, controlling, guiding spirit in one on a far larger scale; it need not come as a surprise. His teachers and school-mates predicted this of him.[36]

The campus uprising in *Imperium in Imperio* is notable for its spectacular efficacy. In this fictional scene, characters, living under the deprivations of Jim Crow, identify an institutional failure and fix it, heralding the emergence of the "new Negro" more than two decades before the publication of Alain Locke's anthology of the same name. Griggs's depiction of the secret society is unusual within turn-of-the-century African American culture, and not just because of Griggs's enthusiasm for it, in contrast to, say, Harper's and Chesnutt's suspicion. In *Iola Leroy* and *The House Behind the Cedars*, the secret society emerges as a response to the inadequacies of the US institutional system, including the school, but importantly it doesn't operate in the educational system itself. In *Imperium in Imperio*, by contrast, Belton's secret society forms within an institution of higher education, and in this sense the Stowe University uprising scene resembles an early piece of campus fiction, in the vein of *Frank Merriwell at Yale* or *Stover at Yale*. (Griggs, having attended public schools in Dallas and having graduated from a Baptist institution of higher education, Bishop College, in 1890, seems to have been uniquely sensitive to campus culture.)[37] The African American secret society, while publicly denounced by many black authors, and virtually unimaginable as a scholastic phenomenon, becomes for Griggs in this scene a vital force within a radical black politics.

The campus uprising scene occurs at an especially important point in the novel too. On the one hand, it affirms the institutional possibilities of secrecy that earlier episodes only hint at. Before Belton and Bernard Belgrave's graduation from their one-room schoolhouse, there is an oratory competition, which the two "[s]ecretly and silently" prepare for, Bernard with the help of his white teacher, Mr. Leonard, and Belton with the help of a sympathetic congressman. Though Bernard and Belton each covertly train for the competition, Belton's secret training more closely resembles the campus uprising later in the novel. He not only prepares for the competition but also devises a prank to undermine the institution that hosts the event. Belton sneaks into the schoolhouse at night and digs "a large hole running from the floor of the wood-shed to a point under the platform of the school room"; when he loses the competition, he flings open the trapdoor and his abusive teacher Mr. Leonard falls through, humiliated. Insofar as Belton at Stowe socializes the covert methods he developed in the one-room schoolhouse, the uprising scene represents a continuation, and a culmination, of the scholastic practices the novel gestures toward earlier. On the other hand, the campus uprising scene forecasts the appearance in later chapters of the Imperium, the secret government operating within the United States that is made up of more than 7 million African Americans. The Imperium's government, Belton explains to Bernard, is "complete in every detail, exercising the sovereign right of life and death over its subjects[.]" Where the students at Stowe University object to the school's dining hall policy and hold up signs that say "Equality or Death," the members of the Imperium "are determined to secure the protections for their lives and the full enjoyment of all rights and privileges due American citizens. They take a solemn oath, offering their very blood for the cause." This is the rebellion "on a far larger scale" the narrator alludes to above, the rebellion that Belton serves as "the moving, controlling, guiding spirit" of.[38]

And yet, there is some awkwardness that attends the scene's endorsement of secrecy as a subversive force in institutional life. It's revealing and a little confusing that the narrator at the end of the episode calls on "[y]e who chronicle history" to erect "a towering, gigantic, century stone," to mark the transition from the old to the "new Negro." Although secrecy functions as the enabling condition of Belton's "combination," the narrator here advocates not more secrecy but less, calling for a monument of public recognition. There is a certain formal awkwardness that attends the novel's endorsement of secrecy as well. If we accept that this scene is central to Griggs's understanding of institutional politics—if we believe that Griggs is really affirming the secret society as an effective agent to combat the injustices of the Jim Crow school system—then wouldn't any depiction of the secret society (like the one Griggs provides) represent in some sense a betrayal of its mission? Wouldn't Griggs, in communicating to us the existence of the secret society, even while endorsing it, become a traitor, the same kind of "traitor" that Berl Trout is, the character who, in the novel's elaborate frame narrative, delivers the manuscript exposing the Imperium to Sutton Griggs?[39]

The incongruity between the secret society and the "towering, gigantic, century stone" the narrator calls for thus draws attention to the larger formal awkwardness between the endorsement of secrecy as a political or institutional strategy and the novelization of this endorsement. What would a really truly secretive novel look like, one whose meaning is so obscured, buried so deep, as to be undiscoverable to its readers? This is the kind of novel *Imperium in Imperio* aspires to be. To read the rest of Griggs's work through the campus uprising scene—rather than, say, allowing subsequent events in *Imperium in Imperio*, or his other novels, or his nonfiction writing, to inflect our reading of the scene—is not only licensed by a logic internal to the scene itself. (Once we accept the political efficacy of the secret, all other public statements become worthy of suspicion.) It's also key to understanding Griggs's distinctive qualities as a writer, those features of his work that have confused and frustrated readers in the past.

It's not at all obvious, of course, that we should read Griggs's work in light of the secret society episode and not the other way around. As in *Iola Leroy*, perhaps, the novel could endorse secrecy under certain oppressive conditions but dispense with it once those conditions are ameliorated. *Imperium in Imperio* provides plenty of evidence in fact to support such a reading. If the campus uprising scene represents secrecy as an effective strategy for institutional change, over the course of the novel the characters' confidence in the efficacy of the secret appears to erode. Nowhere is this more apparent than in the final chapters of the novel, when Bernard and Belton, both now prominent members in the Imperium's political structure, advocate two different paths for the future of the organization. According to Belton, who has become more conservative since his graduation from Stowe, the Imperium should renounce secrecy and deal with white society out in the open. "Before we make a forward move," Belton declares in front of the Imperium, "let us pull the veil from before the eyes of the Anglo-Saxon that he may see the New Negro standing before him humbly, but firmly demanding every right granted him by his maker and wrested from him by man." The first resolution in Belton's plan for the Imperium, along these lines, is that "we no longer conceal from the Anglo-Saxon the fact that the Imperium exists[.]" According to Bernard, who has been radicalized after his time in college, the Imperium should remain secret and pursue a more aggressive course of military action. Bernard's final proposal resolves that the organization should "[r]econsider our determination to make known the existence of our Imperium," and also "[q]uietly purchase all Texas land. ... Build small commonplace huts on these lands and place rapid fire disappearing guns in fortifications dug beneath them. All this is to be done secretly, the money to be raised by the issuance of bonds by the Imperium."[40]

The final chapters of the novel, in which Belton and Bernard lay out their competing plans for the future of the Imperium, proceed more or less dialogically, with the values of secrecy and transparency openly debated. This dialogism—along with Belton's martyrdom and Berl Trout's defection—has led certain critics to conclude that Griggs's novel fails to chart a coherent plan for a black political future, secret or otherwise, and others to claim that the novel does indeed offer a coherent political program, only one that favors the conservative course of action, with its transparency, over the radical course of action, with its secrecy.[41] There is much evidence that one could cite, from both *Imperium in Imperio* and Griggs's other writings, to argue for Griggs's essential conservatism and his opposition to the secret program Bernard outlines in the novel's final chapter. In the logic of *Imperium in Imperio*'s frame narrative, Sutton Griggs, the publisher of the manuscript, is aligned with the defectors Belton and Berl Trout; he is another agent willing to expose the Imperium to the US public. We have already seen Griggs articulate his critique of secret societies in another document—*Dorlan's Plan*, a dissertation on the race problem appended to Griggs's third novel, *Unfettered* (1902). In this dissertation, which was supposedly penned by a character in *Unfettered*, the secret society serves as a "passport bearing testimony as to ... social standing." This critique is by no means identical to the one Belton puts forward in *Imperium in Imperio*, yet both would appear to indicate that Griggs is uneasy with secret organizations, whether (real) fraternal orders or (fictional) secret black governments like the Imperium.

All of this finally is just to say that secrecy, though it emerges as a force for institutional change in the campus uprising scene, appears more or less renounced by the end of *Imperium in Imperio* and in the rest of Griggs's writings. As I suggested before, however, to take seriously the political logic of the campus uprising scene is to look at this other evidence with suspicion and distrust; it's to read the renunciation of the secret society that takes place at the end of the novel not as a true disavowal but as a more effective means of enforcing and maintaining secrecy. The narrator suggests an interpretation like this is possible in the extended aside after the campus revolt at Stowe. "Remember," the narrator insists, "this was Belton's first taste of rebellion against the whites. ... In after life he is the moving, controlling, guiding spirit in one on a far larger scale[.]" While the prolepsis here is meant to point out the continuity between Belton's secret society at Stowe and the unnamed, shadowy Imperium that promises to appear later, the narrator's formulation is striking in retrospect for its *in*accuracy. We learn in the final chapters of the novel that Belton is not, actually, the "moving, controlling, guiding spirit" of the Imperium—he is, conversely, out of sync with it, a dissenter. Rather than a straightforward prolepsis, the narrator's remarks produce a discrepancy between the story the campus uprising scene forecasts and the story the novel eventually tells.

The narrator's reference to Belton as the "moving, controlling, guiding spirit" of the Imperium after the campus uprising finds an interesting counterpoint later in the novel, when Belton first recruits Bernard to the organization. During this conversation, Belton explains to Bernard that he has worked for the Imperium since college. "While I was at Stowe University, though a young man, I was chairman of the bureau of education and had charge of the work of educating the race upon the doctrine of human liberty," Belton tells Bernard.[42] This is the first time the reader has heard about Belton's actual work in the Imperium, however. In the chapters set at Stowe University, Griggs never mentions Belton's position as chairman of the bureau of education. So, where the narrator's proleptic invocation of the Imperium after the campus uprising scene highlights the discrepancy between the story the scene foreshadows and the story the novel tells, Belton's analeptic confession to Bernard highlights the discrepancy between the story the novel has already told and the story Belton is projecting backward. In both cases, these discrepancies reveal a disjunction between the novel's "official" story and what is happening or has happened or will happen; they suggest there are undisclosed events taking place beneath the surface of the reported narrative.

Griggs supplies other evidence to suggest that the novel's ultimate disavowal of secrecy is itself merely a facade, a mask meant to hide an inaccessible set of secret operations beneath the manifest content of the narrative. Even in the final chapters of the novel, where the secret appears to lose its institutional force, with Belton calling for the Imperium to "pull the veil from before the eyes of the Anglo-Saxon," *Imperium in Imperio* persistently undermines the assumptions supporting such appeals to transparency. Read in isolation, the back and forth between Belton and Bernard seems entirely straightforward, one of many examples from the period of prominent black intellectuals charting opposing paths for the future of African Americans under Jim Crow. Read in the context of the rest of the novel, however, the positions Belton and Bernard advocate appear disturbingly unmotivated, emanating from a place beyond the reader's understanding. It should come as a surprise, after all, that the character who champions the conservative course of action—the character who calls for transparency and peace—is Belton, who, for most of the novel, carries out a radical political program. It should also come as a surprise that the character who champions the radical course of action—the character who calls for secrecy and militancy—is Bernard, who, for most of the novel, remains conservative. It is Belton, in other words, who humiliates their white teacher at school, forms a secret society at Stowe, and leads a campus uprising. Alternatively, it is Bernard who is the son of a prominent white politician and raised in relative luxury, and it is Bernard who is nurtured by their white teacher, attends Harvard, and establishes himself as a leading political figure within the more traditional structures of governance.

Griggs does indeed provide some narrative explanation to account for the abrupt transformation in each character's worldview. On the one hand, Belton, before he attends college, is encouraged by his benefactor, the newspaperman V. M. King, to recognize "that there are two widely separated classes of [white people], and that there is a good side to the character of the worst class. Always seek for and appeal to that side of their nature." Also, before Belton graduates from college, the president of Stowe comes to his apartment and explains to him "what an unholy passion revenge" is; and after Belton graduates from college and returns home, the narrator proclaims that "[r]evenge was dead in [Belton's] bosom." On the other hand, Bernard is radicalized after the woman he is about to marry, Viola, commits suicide, because (as she outlines in her suicide note) she has read a book about the dangers of intermarrying and resolved to "never marry a mulatto man" like Bernard. The suicide note ends by exhorting Bernard to "dedicate [his] life to the work of separating the white and colored races."[43]

Although in most realist novels these kinds of experiences are understood to impress themselves on the characters' psychology—rounding out their subjectivities, motivating their actions, and paving the way for future growth—in *Imperium in Imperio* these kinds of experiences provide only possible and ultimately inadequate explanations for why characters behave the way that they do. To cite just one example of this phenomenon: Belton, working as a teacher in Louisiana, is hanged from a tree for seven minutes by members of a KKK-style organization, shot in the head, and dragged to a doctor's house, where he manages to regain consciousness, murder the doctor, and escape. The failed lynching undermines the conservative stance Belton assumes at the end of the novel, because (surely!) it seems as though it should be sufficient to (re-)radicalize him, the character who has only recently come to understand "what an unholy passion revenge" is. The failed lynching calls into question the radical stance Bernard assumes at the end of the novel as well, because (again, surely!) if the failed lynching didn't radicalize Belton, Viola's suicide wouldn't radicalize Bernard. To put all of this more simply, experience, while helpful in the traditional realist novel, providing a window into a character's inner life, confuses more than it clarifies in *Imperium in Imperio*, making subjectivity and motivation seem inaccessible, not accessible. If at the end of the novel Griggs appears to endorse Belton's transparency over Bernard's secrecy, the reasons each character adopts his respective political position are clouded in mystery; both characters' inner motivations remain during and after the scene profoundly untransparent, a secret each one is keeping just to himself.

Plot twists like Viola's suicide and Belton's failed lynching are characteristic of Griggs's writing; and while they make it very difficult to truly understand any individual character's psychology, they also serve in Griggs's novels more broadly to draw attention to the inaccessibility of all intention, especially authorial intention. Below I've summarized a few examples of the typical Griggsian plot twist. I've added in brackets before the plot twist whatever exposition I felt was necessary for understanding it in the context of its larger narrative, and I've added in parentheses after the plot twist the amount of space, by word count, Griggs devotes to it in the novel.

[In *Imperium in Imperio*, Belton escapes after he murders the doctor who planned to dissect him.] Belton flees to Baton Rouge, asks the governor to intervene in his case; the governor refuses and turns Belton over to the police; Belton is tried and convicted of the murder of Dr. Zackland; Belton speaks to a reporter for a liberal newspaper, who broadcasts his (Belton's) story around the country; Bernard reads about Belton's trial and argues Belton's case in front of the Supreme Court; the decision of the lower court is reversed; Belton is granted a change of venue, a new trial, and in the end he is acquitted. (400 words)

[Dolly Smith, a character in *Overshadowed* (1901), is charged by James Benson Lawson, an ex-governor's son, to enlist Erma Wysong, the novel's protagonist, as his mistress.] To exact revenge on the family, Dolly brings Lawson to court and exposes his and the ex-governor's illicit affairs with black women; after the trial, the ex-governor goes insane, Lawson goes to jail, and Dolly is tarred and feathered. (762 words)

[Ramon Mansford, a minor character in *The Hindered Hand* (1905), is engaged to Alene Daleman, a prominent white southern citizen, who is murdered in her room one night; Bud Harper, a central character, is suspected of the murder and is lynched; Ramon is suspicious about the crime; he dyes his skin and infiltrates the black community to find the real murderer.] Ramon interrogates various members of the black community and discovers, from Bud Harper's father, that it was not, in fact, Bud who was lynched, but his brother, Dave; Ramon also learns that Dave (who has just been introduced into the narrative) was sentenced to prison for twenty years after an altercation with a police officer, only he managed to serve a sentence of just two years by switching places with another inmate, a consumptive; returning home, but keeping away from his family, Dave overheard that Arthur Daleman Jr. (Alene's brother) planned to rape Foresta Crump (his brother Bud's fiance), and believing that Foresta was welcoming Arthur's affections, Dave one night attacked Arthur and the woman he believed was Foresta, but was actually Alene, killing Alene. (1343 words)[44]

These plot twists are dramatic and life-altering—Belton is convicted of murder, Dolly Smith is tarred and feathered, Ramon discovers the real killer of Alene Daleman—yet they don't really impress themselves on the narrative in any meaningful way. Griggs's plot twists are marked by their abruptness and their inexplicability: the fact that they are abrupt is what makes them inexplicable. When the relationship between story time and discourse time becomes increasingly out of proportion—the first expanding, the second shrinking—we lose the frameworks through which we typically understand literary intention and motivation. As we've already seen, the compressed nature of Griggs's plot twists, unfolding in a mere 400 or 1,000 words, elides any possibility of character interiority: when Viola abruptly commits suicide, for instance, there is no character space in which the character of Viola might emerge, too few words to sufficiently explain why she has decided to do what she has done. At the same time, and more extremely, the abruptness of these plot twists also makes it difficult to discern the operation of authorial intention. In certain respects the dramatic plot twist draws attention to the power the author wields in the narrative, making it seem as though the reversals in a character's fortunes are a product of the decisions made by a hidden and omnipotent author-figure rather than the decisions made by the character him- or herself. But in other respects the arbitrariness of the plot twist also makes it impossible to determine what logic, if any, governs these authorial interventions.

Griggs's novels are reflexive about the omnipotence and inaccessibility of authors. In the first chapter of *Overshadowed*, when two principal characters are separated because one of them is leaving for college, the narrator opines about the hidden mechanics behind such plot developments: "[T]he unseen power that ordains that two souls shall journey through earth together, also chooses, it would seem, the hallowed spot; chooses the precious and never to be forgotten *moment* when soul is unveiled to soul; chooses the exact degree of the development that shall exist in each at the hour of the mating." In one of the last episodes of *Unfettered*, Dorlan (author of *Dorlan's Plan*) goes up in a hot air balloon as he waits to hear Morlene's reaction to his dissertation, and thinks to himself: "There must be a great force somewhere directing the affairs of the universe. His plannings puzzle me." In *Imperium in Imperio*, when Viola first rejects Bernard's proposal, she insists that "[a] power higher than either you or I has decreed it otherwise."[45] In each of these moments Griggs's texts self-consciously express a conviction that the improbable events described in the narrative are authored by a single omnipotent figure capable of making motivated decisions—the unseen power in *Overshadowed* "choos[es]" where and when two characters will be together, and the great force in *Unfettered* "direct[s] the affairs of the universe," and the higher power in *Imperium in Imperio* "decree[s]" that Viola and Bernard won't be together. And yet, alongside this conviction is another suggestion, that the unseen power, the great force, the higher power, can't be apprehended, that whatever omnipotent figure is guiding the course of the characters' lives possesses motives that are incomprehensible. This point is made most explicitly by Dorlan—who acknowledges that the plannings of the great force "puzzle" him—but it remains implicit in the other examples as well: the invocation of the unseen, higher power, is, as a rhetorical gesture, an expression of helplessness, an admission that the events of the novel are dictated by forces beyond any readily apparent logic or plan.

Griggs's plot twists in particular and Griggs's novels in general posit a radical theory of authorship that represents authorial intention as constantly impinging on the world of fiction, only in ways and for reasons that are entirely undisclosed to readers—a theory of authorship that represents authorial intention, in other words, as a secret society that no reader has access to. In the past, critics have explained away these features of Griggs's writing as aesthetic deficiencies. "[S]cholars," Caroline Levander writes, "have historically viewed the literary value of Griggs's writing as compromised by its awkward style, heavy didacticism, excessive polemics, and improbable plot twists."[46] Griggs's literary offenses (which Levander enumerates here but does little to dispute) reflect what we might think of as Griggs's "overstyle." Overstyle—a term I'm adapting from D. A. Miller, who has identified an "understyle" in Alfred Hitchcock's movies—describes the set of intrusive and apparently unmotivated aesthetic choices that I take to be characteristic of Griggs's fiction. According to Miller, Hitchcock "cultivate[s] alongside his manifest style with its hyper-legible images, a secret style that sows these images with radical duplicity." The mistakes that make up Hitchcock's understyle are noticeable only to someone Miller describes as the "Too-Close Viewer," and rather than being easily assimilated into a totalizing account of Hitchcock's work, they militate against such totalizing schemes: "In inviting us to *account* for continuity errors, Hitchcock's style would not be pointing to a secret coherence that, once unveiled, makes the oeuvre whole, but rather to a teasing insistence on [the] disjuncture that asks to be factored in even when it doesn't add up."[47] The dissonance the Too-Close Viewer experiences when he recognizes Hitchcock's understyle—deciding whether the mistakes in Hitchcock's work are merely accidents of film production or whether they are mistakes that Hitchcock has deliberately planted—is, in Miller's analysis, constitutive of understyle itself, the very experience understyle is supposed to elicit in its viewers.

Griggs's overstyle produces a similar feeling of viewerly (or readerly) dissonance, only it creates this feeling not through visual quirks perceptible only to the superhuman Too-Close Viewer, but through intrusive and inexplicable acts of authorial intervention recognizable to even the most boorish readers. Overstyle invites dismissal along the lines that Levander describes. Like understyle, the reader can always disregard Griggs's interventions as aesthetically deficient, mere mistakes. But it also encourages readers to recuperate these interventions as aesthetically motivated and compellingly integrated into the larger project of *Imperium in Imperio*: these interventions function as markers of the novel's commitment to secrecy. If, according to Miller, "[b]ehind the impersonal detachment of a sovereign stylist, there often stands a damaged or disparaged person," we might understand the difference between understyle's all-but-imperceptible quirks and overstyle's all-too-perceptible interventions as a product of the different forms of social disparagement Hitchcock and Griggs suffered. The covert mistakes that make up Hitchcock's understyle produce their dissonant effects by both challenging and confirming Hitchcock's prowess as a filmmaker. They are, as Miller explains, simultaneously "[l]ittle rebellions of filmmaking contingencies against Hitchcock's mastery" and further proof of Hitchcock's mastery, possessing what Miller describes as a "strange aptness to [Hitchcock's] work as *dis*harmonies."⁴⁸ In contrast, the overt mistakes that make up Griggs's overstyle produce their dissonant effects not from the assumption of Griggs's mastery but from its opposite. Overstyle plays off of the racialist conviction, circulating since the eighteenth century, that African Americans' failure to produce great works of literature was evidence of their inferiority and justification for their enslavement. Where understyle hides itself in the almost imperceptible continuity errors of Hitchcock's apparently perfect films, overstyle hides itself in the unmistakable authorial intrusions of Griggs's supposedly deficient novels. To sum up all of these points, grasping Griggs's unique qualities as a writer requires an appreciation of just how thoroughly his fiction adopts the strategies of the secret society. Griggs's novels, in effect, set out to recede from visibility, exercising their influence covertly, under cloak and dagger.

The Institutionalization of African American Literature

African American literature remained for much of the twentieth century a discursive category whose meaning took on coherence largely outside the system of formal education. When African American literary works began appearing regularly on the school syllabus, those advocating their inclusion often adopted the anti-secrecy rhetoric of *The House Behind the Cedars* and *Iola Leroy*. Consider, for instance, Toni Morrison's influential *Playing in the Dark* (1992): here is a polemic that understands itself as overcoming "a certain set of assumptions conventionally accepted among literary historians and critics and circulated as 'knowledge.'" These assumptions, according to Morrison, "hold[] that traditional, canonical American literature is free of, uninformed, and unshaped by the four-hundred-year-old presence of, first, Africans and then African-Americans in the United States." Against this set of assumptions Morrison argues that the Africanist presence is "one of the most furtively radical impinging forces on the country's literature" and that its existence remains furtive or secret not just in individual literary texts but also in the educational system responsible for preserving and disseminating American literature. *Playing in the Dark* diagnoses this institutional problem but also sets out to correct it by demonstrating "how inextricable Africanism is or ought to be from the deliberations of literary criticism and the wanton, elaborate strategies undertaken to erase its presence from view."⁴⁹

Morrison's justification for studying African American literature thus mirrored the institutional project of Chesnutt's and Harper's work. Morrison's aim is to bring recognition to a previously unrecognized Africanist presence, to expose the secret of Africanism to public view through a critical act of noticing. "To notice is to recognize an already discredited difference," she writes. "To enforce its invisibility through silence is to allow the black body a shadowless participation in the dominant cultural body. According to this logic, every well-bred instinct argues *against noticing*[.]" It is precisely *by noticing* that Morrison insists we can produce institutional and social change. Through the act of noticing, we can better apprehend "what makes intellectual domination possible; how knowledge is transformed from invasion and conquest to revelation and choice; what ignites and informs the literary imagination, and what forces help establish the parameters of criticism."[50] The circulation of *Iola Leroy* and *The House Behind the Cedars* through the school system—a circulation that was facilitated by Collier Books's decision to reissue *The House Behind the Cedars* in 1969 and Beacon Press's decision to reprint *Iola Leroy* in their Black Women Writers series in 1987[51]—signaled that the educational system had indeed begun to recognize the once scholastically invisible cultural products of a minority population as "literature."

Now, the incorporation of African American literature into the school has produced much skepticism even as many have celebrated it as a marker of progress. Jodi Melamed has described literary studies as the privileged instrument for propagating liberal multiculturalism after 1964: "Literary studies at U.S. universities socialized future members of the professional-managerial class, whether white, of color, or international, into progressive constituencies for regressive public policies and a grossly unequal system of global capital accumulation." According to Melamed, literary studies' socializing function has taken on added meaning during the most recent phase of liberal anti-racism—a phase Melamed calls "neoliberal multiculturalism"—helping members of the middle class "learn[] to see themselves as part of a multinational group of enlightened multicultural global citizens" and "preparing them for their role in global civilizing/disqualifying regimes."[52] Roderick Ferguson has argued that the emergence of ethnic studies programs in the aftermath of the student protest movements of the sixties and seventies represented a reordering of social power. According to Ferguson, systems of power routed through the state, the school, and capital responded to these protest movements by transforming the students' revolutionary demands into an affirmative program of recognition. One of the signature achievements of this new reordering as Ferguson presents it was to "make the pursuit of recognition and legitimacy into formidable horizons of pleasure."[53]

Adopting Ferguson's terms, we might say that the institutionalization of *Iola Leroy* and *The House Behind the Cedars* enabled the school system's evolution from a mode of power that "disciplined difference in the universalizing names of canonicity, nationality, or economy" into a mode of power that now "discipline[s] through a seemingly alternative regard for difference and through a revision of the canon, national identity, and the market."[54] Without these literary works, the US school system could not plausibly present itself to the world as a multicultural social institution or claim to disinterestedly bestow its credentials on a diverse student population. The recognition Harper and Chesnutt once sought from the US institutional system they have therefore received, only this recognition has served to interpellate subjects into an unequal global order, one that celebrates, rather than represses, diversity and difference. To summarize this line of thinking—and to situate it more explicitly within the history that I've unfolded over the last five chapters—we might say that the institutionalization of African American literature has shaped the modern school by allowing it to extend its meritocratic ideology to a population of students who, after the rapid economic growth of the post–World War II period and the success of the Civil Rights movement, became eligible for school's highest credentials.[55] The school had assumed its role as an instrument of ideology earlier in the twentieth century by institutionalizing one anti-scholastic body of literature; teaching post-Reconstruction African American literature that criticized formal education has now served to extend the school's ideological reach.

For all of its persuasiveness, this description of the institutionalization of African American literature fails to grapple with the shifting role of ideology in class struggle and the shifting role of the school as an ideological apparatus under deindustrialization. We can begin to understand these shifting roles through Melinda Cooper's recent work, which offers up a variation on some of the arguments I've just discussed. Cooper claims that the student protest movements of the sixties and seventies challenged the sexual normativity of the Fordist family wage and, in doing so, inspired an alliance between neoliberals and new social conservatives. This alliance went on to dramatically reimagine the political economy of the United States. Beginning in the 1980s, the welfare state's redistributive services were steadily rolled back; radical cuts to state and federal health, education, and welfare budgets ensued. In the realm of higher education, Democrats and Republicans came to share the assumption that students should pay for college by taking on debt instead of receiving direct, government-funded grants. Tuition fees at public universities have subsequently skyrocketed, and the generalization of student loans has served, in Cooper's words, as a form of *"regressive taxation"* that marks a transformation in the school's disciplinary regime. "Credit comes at a higher price for the poor," Cooper writes. "Assuming the same initial burden of debt, a student with no assets or savings is more likely to have to defer, refinance, or default on a loan, accumulating a much longer temporal burden of interest payments than the student who can pay on schedule."[56]

Cooper would claim that the school remains, under this regime, an essentially ideological instrument. "With each reauthorization of the Higher Education Act of 1965, successive governments since Reagan have utterly transformed the structures of college funding while never formally renouncing the democratic promise of the 1960s," Cooper writes. "In principle, we all have access to a college education, no matter how much we or our parents earn. Yet, private credit does not merely obscure the effects of class; it also actively exacerbates inequality by forcing those without income or collateral to pay higher rates for the same service." The school's rhetoric of diversity is implicated in this renovated disciplinary project as well, according to Cooper. "[T]he economic conditions that had enabled minorities to challenge the institution in the first place were profoundly revised [after the liberation movements of sixties and seventies and, later, the culture wars], leading not to the crude exclusion of times past but to highly conditional forms of private debt-based inclusion," Cooper explains. "Students may specialize in African American or ethnic studies even while the public investment strategies that allowed low-income minorities to attend college in the first place have been radically stripped back. Others may take a major in queer studies even while the institutional accreditation of this knowledge is utterly dependent on parental wealth and familial forms of economic obligation."[57]

Even as it insists on the ideological work that the school continues to perform, Cooper's account can help us understand that the school has also become increasingly obsolete as an instrument of social control. The dramatic rise in student debt might have allowed legislators and administrators for decades to publicly affirm the democratic promise of higher education while using the school covertly as an engine of inequality, as Cooper claims, but it has also, importantly, eviscerated these institutions and left them in a state of extreme vulnerability. Rising tuition rates have made students and families increasingly reluctant to pay for a bachelor's degree, threatening one of the most important revenue streams for colleges and universities: tuition. As these institutions have reached a "tuition limit," higher education has, since 2011, shed 2 million students. Since 2016, sixty-one small private liberal arts colleges have closed or merged, and a similar number of public institutions have been consolidated into larger public systems. For the years 2018 and 2019, the credit rating agency Moody's downgraded the higher education sector from "stable" to "negative." In 2019, the governor of Alaska proposed a $135 million cut to the University of Alaska system. (He eventually compromised to a $70 million cut over three fiscal years.) The pandemic has only intensified this crisis: in April 2020 the American Council on Education predicted a 15 percent decline in enrollment and $45 billion in lost revenue across the sector. "However individual schools navigate the rapids ahead, it appears inevitable that many will head toward bankruptcy," Simon Torracinta wrote in the spring of 2020.[58]

The pandemic has, in this sense, merely accelerated a process that began in the eighties, a process that has involved the disassembly of the modern educational system, whose emergence coincided with the growth of US industry. Under the political economy of the post-1980 United States, apparatuses beyond educational institutions will continue to discipline an ever-growing percentage of the population, apparatuses engineered not to manufacture consent but to enforce the social order through coercive and often violent means. The downwardly mobile middle class will struggle to preserve its economic privileges and status benefits in a deprofessionalized "gig economy" that, despite its celebration of entrepreneurialism and flexibility, most effectively disciplines indebted workers by offering them only low-paid, contingent positions.[59] The downwardly mobile working class, meanwhile, will increasingly find itself altogether surplus to the needs of the capitalist economy, unable to access wage labor and without the welfare state's social safety net. As others have noted, deindustrialization has entailed not simply the dismantling of this safety net but the creation of institutions—most notably, the system of mass incarceration—charged with disciplining racialized surplus populations.[60] The celebration of diversity in schools—which has occurred along with the deterioration of the modern educational system, the rise of the gig economy, and the expansion of punitive state apparatuses—appears to be less the triumphant culmination of the school's meritocratic program and more a desperate, and not especially convincing, attempt on the part of administrators to sure-up the legitimacy of their institutions. After all, outside the ever-shrinking middle class, the legitimacy or relevance of higher education is increasingly in doubt: for those aspiring to enter the middle class, college tuition is becoming too expensive, and for ruling elites, middle-class institutions are less and less necessary to train the workforce or justify social inequality. At its lower levels, the school has even begun to resemble those punitive apparatuses it otherwise has sought to distinguish itself from.[61]

All of this should temper the suspicion that has surrounded the institutionalization of African American literature. We do not now, nor does it appear we ever will, live in the dystopia that some scholars imagine we do, where a global multicultural ruling class maintains its power through an affirmative program of minority difference. As the economy tightens and as class disparities become even more spectacular, whatever soft power schools and literature (and literature in schools) have historically wielded in the United States will give way to other, harder modes of domination. The decision to discontinue ethnic studies programs at the outset of the COVID-19 pandemic is simply one indication that the celebration of diversity and inclusion will not characterize the looming social order.[62] Should African American literature remain in the curriculum, reading it will not brainwash students into believing that we live in a fair society where economic inequality is justified. At worst, administrators will publicize the diversity of the curriculum in a cynical attempt to show prospective students and patrons that their institutions still have value. At best, the teaching of African American literature will provide an opportunity to consider the history of social relations, the erosion of the middle class, and the production of surplus life. Of course, all of this assumes that the US system of higher education will continue to resemble its current form in the future, and that this system will employ instructors and faculty members who teach literature, and that some of this literature will have been produced by African Americans. None of these assumptions is exactly certain, and this fact provides further proof of the limited agency that both literature and schools exercise as ideological instruments.

But what about a book like *Imperium in Imperio*, one that understands literature's power in the vocabulary of secrecy and invisibility rather than recognition?

In what sense has it impressed itself on scholastic experience? Before venturing too far into the realm of speculation, I should note that the logic of Griggs's revolutionary program was present in the culture-war debates, just as the renunciation of secrecy appeared in these debates as well. To apprehend the presence of Griggs's program in these debates requires inverting Toni Morrison's claims. It requires attending to arguments in which the invisibility of the Africanist presence is not symptomatic of a deep-seated white cultural pathology but a positive quality in its own right. This is the substance of Henry Louis Gates Jr.'s famous distinction between "signification" and "Signification." "In the extraordinarily complex relationship between the two homonyms," Gates writes, "we both enact and recapitulate the received, classic confrontation between Afro-American culture and American culture. ... The relationship that black 'Signification' bears to the English 'signification' is, paradoxically, a relation of difference inscribed within a relation of identity." Hidden within the dominant white signifier "signification" is the subversive black "Signification," which Gates describes at various points as offering a "*shadowy* revision of the white term," as operating through "the *obscuring* of apparent meaning," as "a mode of *encoding* for self-preservation," and as "the figurative difference between the literal and the metaphorical, between surface and latent meaning." According to Gates, the power of the black vernacular lies specifically in the secrets it keeps, in its capacity to imitate or repeat discourse with a difference, to "say one thing but to mean quite another."[63]

In the moments when Gates attempts to offer an account of the emergence of Signifyin(g), he ends up hypothesizing, in the absence of concrete historical evidence, that the origins of the practice lie in a sort of secret society. Gates argues that the "(re)naming ritual ... apparently took place anonymously and unrecorded in antebellum America." It came about when "[s]ome black genius or community of witty and sensitive speakers emptied the signifier 'signification' of its received concepts and filled this empty signifier with their own concepts." Although Gates is careful to avoid any positivist claims about the historical conditions that led the "witty and sensitive speakers" to replace signifying with Signifyin(g), he remains nevertheless committed to the idea that the distinction between signification and Signification is not a matter of historical coincidence but the deliberate production of a subversive and anonymous community. The lack of documentary evidence surrounding this community simply testifies to its unique power. As Gates explains, the "historically nameless community of remarkably self-conscious speakers of English defined their ontological status as one of profound difference vis-a-vis the rest of society," and this profound difference would only have been legible to the initiated. To the uninitiated, it wouldn't have been legible at all.[64]

So, where Morrison saw the Africanist presence in American literary history as suffering a "furtiv[e]" and "invisible" existence and set out to remedy this state of affairs through a critical act of noticing, Gates celebrated the black vernacular tradition for its capacity to assert difference within identity, to produce latent meaning beneath manifest content. Though Morrison's critical act of noticing appears to be an entirely sensible response to the invisibility of the Africanist presence in literary scholarship, Gates's study of Signifyin(g) seems incongruous with the practice itself. Signifyin(g) "obscur[es] ... apparent meaning" and "encod[es] for self-preservation," yet Gates as a scholar does the opposite, revealing the latent meaning previously obscured, decoding what Signifyin(g) encodes. To say that Gates's scholarly work truly mirrors or enacts something like Griggs's radical institutional program doesn't, in this sense, seem quite accurate.

Nor would the recuperation of Griggs's work at the beginning of the twenty-first century appear to realize the institutional strategies Griggs's work proposes. *Imperium in Imperio*, like *Iola Leroy*, registers an awareness of literature's power to affect the development of institutional structures—Belton's college, after all, is called Stowe University "in honor of Mrs. Harriet Beecher Stowe, author of 'Uncle Tom's Cabin'"[65]—but where *Iola Leroy* has belatedly received the institutional recognition that the novel itself demanded, *Imperium in Imperio* has received the institutional recognition that the novel itself eschewed. After a century of neglect, Griggs's book became institutionally visible when the Modern Library published a paperback edition of *Imperium in Imperio* in 2003, with an introduction by Cornel West, and when Tess Chakkalakal and Kenneth Warren edited a collection of scholarly essays on Griggs in 2013. The reversal in Griggs's institutional fortunes—from obscurity to visibility—replays the awkward transition *Imperium in Imperio* makes from the secret society's successful uprising at Stowe to the narrator's call for a "towering, gigantic, century stone" to mark the occasion.

It would appear, then, that Griggs's radical vision has never been realized in the system of formal education, even as that system has taken up Griggs's novels. *Imperium in Imperio* is therefore something of a limit case for this book, a work of literature that circulates through the educational system but not on its own terms, a work of literature that has been enlisted into an institutional program without exerting symmetrical or reciprocal pressure against the program itself. But it's a limit case only if we assume that the secret institutional collectives that Griggs's work hopes to conjure into existence have never in fact existed. It's a limit case only if we believe that the absence of documentary evidence is proof that these secret institutional collectives don't exist and never have. On the contrary, this absence could just as plausibly provide proof that secret collectives are thriving. Insofar as this chapter has contributed to the institutional conversation surrounding *Imperium in Imperio* and concentrated more academic attention on the book, it has in effect betrayed the institutional strategies that Griggs's novel so compellingly puts forward. To carry this project forward by tracking down historical evidence of really, really secret societies would only further that betrayal. I'm afraid I've said too much already.

Notes

Preface

1. Thomas Jefferson to Joel Barlow, December 10, 1807, Library of Congress, Manuscript/Mixed Material, https://www.loc.gov/item/mtjbib017974/.
2. *Reports on the Course of Instruction in Yale College; By a Committee of the Corporation and the Academical Faculty* (New Haven: Hezekiah Howe, 1828), 3, 39.
3. Quoted in David B. Tyack, *The One Best System: A History of American Urban Education* (Cambridge: Harvard University Press, 1974), 20.
4. Johann David Michaelis, *Introduction to the New Testament*, vol. 1, part 1, trans. Herbert Marsh (Cambridge: J. Archdeacon Printer, 1793), 14. See *Oxford English Dictionary*, s.v. "Literary v. 5," accessed January 13, 2022, https://www-oed-com.ezp-prod1.hul.harvard.edu/view/Entry/109067?redirectedFrom=literary. "Carlyle and His Imitators," in *The Keepsake*, ed. J. T. Headley (New York: Leavitt and Allen, 1855), 141. Alexis De Tocqueville, *Democracy in America*, trans. Gerald Bevan (New York: Penguin, 2003), 352.
5. Herman Melville, *Moby-Dick* (New York: W.W. Norton, 2002), 101. *Journals of Ralph Waldo Emerson, with Annotations*, vol. 5, ed. Edward Waldo Emerson and Waldo Emerson Forbes (Boston: Houghton Mifflin, 1911), 250. John Dewey, *The School and Society*, revised ed. (Chicago: University of Chicago Press, 1915), 154–155.
6. See Morton White, *Social Thought in America* (New York: Viking Press, 1952).
7. Leslie Fiedler, *Love and Death in the American Novel* (Champaign: Dalkey Archive, 2008), 40–41, 23.
8. Lawrence Buell, *The Dream of the Great American Novel* (Cambridge: Harvard University Press, 2014), 27. Evan Kindley, *Poet-Critics and the Administration of Culture* (Cambridge: Harvard University Press, 2017), 8.
9. Fiedler, *Love and Death*, 9, 11.
10. I discuss English department enrollments in the introduction, fn 63.

Introduction

1. Quoted in Laurence R. Veysey, *The Emergence of the American University* (Chicago: University of Chicago Press, 1970), 16.
2. See William A. Koelsch, *Clark University, 1887–1987: A Narrative History* (Worcester: Clark University Press, 1987), and Dorothy Ross, *G. Stanley Hall: The Psychologist as Prophet* (Chicago: University of Chicago Press, 1972).
3. For rhetorical purposes, I tend to conflate "English literary studies" and "literary studies" in this book, even though there are, of course, profound differences between the

history of English and the history of, say, comparative literature. Moreover, my discussion of the development of literary studies is confined to the United States, even though I recognize that, as Gauri Viswanathan has argued, the "intertwined genealogies of the discipline invariably begin and end at a point extending far beyond England's [or the United States's] national borders." But if, in these senses, *Schools of Fiction* offers an account of literary studies that is far narrower than the designation "literary studies" would seem to imply, it also offers, in another sense, a broader conceptualization of the discipline, one that stretches from reading and writing classes in primary schools to the English department in the research university. I'll also mention here that, while I take English literary studies as the "disciplinary home" of literature, *Schools of Fiction* also at times examines literature's impact on the school system through history classes and interdisciplinary programs, like African American and Ethnic Studies. Gauri Viswanathan, Preface to *Masks of Conquest* (New York: Columbia University Press, 2015), xiv.

4. John R. Thelin, *A History of American Higher Education* (Baltimore: Johns Hopkins University Press, 2004), 153, 175. For enrollment rates during the 1899–1900 academic year, see *120 Years of American Education: A Statistical Portrait*, ed. Thomas D. Snyder (US Dept. of Education, Office of Educational Research and Improvement, National Center for Education Statistics, 1993), 76. According to Christopher Newfield, institutions of higher education before World War II experienced "endless insecurity," financially speaking. Christopher Newfield, *Ivy and Industry: Business and the Making of the American University, 1880–1980* (Durham: Duke University Press, 2003), 24–25. Thelin explains that in the colonial era, the "combination of forgone income and the cost of two or three years of college tuition and expenses made a college education unaffordable, or at least unappealing, to the vast majority of colonists. Class distinctions within the colony were sharp, and the colleges became increasingly distant from the world and experience of most American families" (25). During the "new national period" (1785–1860), higher education remained a "scarce commodity" and a "rare experience," for similar reasons: tuition fees and forgone income. "[I]n those areas where the American economy showed signs of enterprise and growth," Thelin writes, "a college degree—even if affordable and accessible—was perceived as representing lost time for making one's fortune" (70).

5. Enrollment rates are from *120 Years of American Education*, 34. See William J. Reese, *The Origins of the American High School* (New Haven: Yale University Press, 1995), 208–213, for a nuanced account of secondary school enrollment statistics in the nineteenth century, when non-standardized curricula made it difficult to determine which institutions offered students access to the higher branches of learning. See also Reese, 237–238, for more on the high school's struggle to retain students, along with the Hamlet parody. McCosh compared the school system to "a house built at great expense by a friend of mine; it was two stories high, and commodious and elegant in every respect, but he forgot to put a stair to lead from the lower to the upper floor." Quoted in Burton Bledstein, *The Culture of Professionalism* (New York: W. W. Norton, 1978), 279.

6. Statistics on primary schools between 1780 to 1840 are from Carl F. Kaestle, *Pillars of the Republic* (New York: Hill and Wang, 1983), 15. Statistics for the 1899–1900 academic year are from *120 Years of American Education*, 34. The reference to

the Pennsylvania school superintendent is from Kaestle, *Pillars*, 111. For more on nineteenth-century primary education, including the agon between one-room district schools and common-school reformers, see Kaestle and Jonathan Zimmerman, *Small Wonder* (New Haven: Yale University Press, 2015). Kaestle and Zimmerman both cite the one-room school as proof of the organic relationship between school and society in early America and the nation's native enthusiasm for formal education. "[U]nlike England," Kaestle writes, "America witnessed virtually no opposition to popular education per se" (x), arguing that the "proliferation of private-venture schools in the cities and neighborhood district schools in rural areas was a response to popular demand" (4). Zimmerman writes at one point, *"Americans believe deeply in education,"* explaining that *"since the mid-nineteenth century ... most of them have attended school for at least part of their lives"* (12). For Zimmerman, the one-room school is evidence of this deep-seated belief: "[O]ne-room schools provided a central venue for community life in rural America. ... Often the only public building for miles, one-room schools hosted political rallies, election-day voting stations, and a wide variety of social events: marriages, funerals, picnics, dances, and more" (37). I attempt to complicate Kaestle's and Zimmerman's characterizations in this paragraph and the ones that follow it.

7. The historiography of American education has, counterintuitively, maintained a vexed relationship to the institution of the school. Bernard Bailyn once famously called for educational historians to move beyond their narrow focus on formal schooling and understand education as a more holistic process. "[B]y limiting education to formal instruction," he explained, "[educational historians] lost the capacity to see it in its full context and hence to assess the variety and magnitude of the burdens it had borne and to judge its historical importance." Bernard Bailyn, *Education in the Forming of American Society* (Chapel Hill: University of North Carolina Press, 1960), 9. Lawrence Cremin worked throughout his career to expand the scope of educational historiography beyond the school, arguing in his three-volume *American Education* that education in the United States involved the evolution of a "common paideia" across a range of institutions. See Lawrence A. Cremin, *American Education: The National Experience, 1783–1876* (New York: Harper and Row, 1980), 498, for an extended description of this paideia. Rather than focusing exclusively on just one institution, i.e., the school, Cremin's history of education in the United States thus examines what he calls the institutional "configurations" that educated Americans. My description in the preceding paragraph of the various institutions that contributed to the education of Americans in the nineteenth century is drawn from *The National Experience*, 371–414. I'll note in passing that the relationship between "schooling" construed narrowly and "education" construed broadly is itself historically specific—that the consolidation of the educational system, in fact, involved collapsing these two terms together, as the modern school claimed for itself educational functions once distributed across a range of other institutions.

8. Cremin, *American Education: The National Experience*, 485. Kaestle himself—whom I cite above and who insists on the popularity of formal education in the United States—provides plenty of evidence to suggest that for much of the nineteenth century, formal education was simply not a priority for many Americans. We might consider, for instance, his description of immigrant communities in urban areas, who "did not

see extended schooling as an advantage or who could not afford to forgo the income of their children." Kaestle, *Pillars*, 60. (Enrollment rates in cities, even northern cities, fell far behind enrollment rates in rural districts.) We could also consider Kaestle's description of urban workers' "moderate support or indifference" (146) toward formal education: though in the 1830s workingmen's organizations "supported a more egalitarian public school system," the "hard times of the 1840s turned workers toward issues of wages and hours." "By 1850," Kaestle writes, "the trade unions were almost silent on educational issues" (140–141). The most glaring evidence of the nation's indifference toward schooling is of course the South, where, under the slave system, formal education proved a less important part of the overall educational process. See Kaestle's account of low enrollments in the South (192–217). Attendance in the Mid-Atlantic states wasn't spectacular either: "Communities in Pennsylvania and New Jersey appear to have been slower to provide widespread local schooling before state intervention. Rates in these states rose from around 20 percent in 1840 to 40 percent in 1860" (106).

9. The *OED* defines book-learning as "Learning or knowledge acquired from books, esp. (frequently somewhat *depreciative*) as opposed to practical knowledge or common sense; the study of books." *Oxford English Dictionary*, s.v. "Book learning," accessed January 14, 2022, https://www-oed-com.ezp-prod1.hul.harvard.edu/view/Entry/357163?redirectedFrom=book+learning. The expression's origins lie in the sixteenth century, and its use as a term of depreciation, associated with the school, was apparent as early as the eighteenth century, when Samuel Johnson wrote in the *Rambler* that "several hints had been dropped of the uselessness of universities, the folly of book learning, and the aukwardness of scholars." Samuel Johnson, *The Works of Samuel Johnson*, vol. 4 (London: G. Offor, 1818), 13. Needless to say, the cultural suspicion surrounding book-learning also implicated literature, which at the turn of the twentieth century was increasingly identified with written materials. I discuss this point at greater length in Chapter 2.

10. William Cobbett, "Excerpts from 'Cottage Economy,'" in *The New England Farmer*, vol. 2, ed. Thomas G. Fessenden (Boston: William Nichols, 1824), 38, emphasis in the original. John H. Rice, "The Ministerial Character and Preparation Suited to Our Country, the World, and the Age," in *Home, the School, and the Church*, vol. 1, ed. C. Van Rensselaer (Philadelphia: William S. Martien, 1850), 171. The old North Dakota joke is quoted in Zimmerman, *Small Wonder*, 48.

11. "What Is Clark University," *Worcester Telegram*, April 15, 1889, 1.

12. The *Telegram* published the vivisection articles on March 9, 12, 16, 23, and 30, 1890, and April 13, 1890.

13. "Wave of Public Censure," *Worcester Telegram*, March 5, 1891, 1. The *Telegram* published the anatomy articles on March 5, 8, and 22, 1891.

14. "The *Telegram*'s sensationalized and abusive treatment hurt and bewildered the founder ... and from these and other incidents, added to the lack of local financial response, he drew the not unreasonable conclusion that his new university was not wanted in Worcester." Koelsch, *Clark University*, 34.

15. John Dewey, *The School and Society*, revised ed (Chicago: University of Chicago Press, 1915), 14.

16. John Guillory famously described literature's "retreat" from mass culture into the university in the mid-twentieth century. John Guillory, *Cultural Capital: The Problem of Literary Canon Formation* (Chicago: University of Chicago Press, 1993), 166, 167. Gerald Graff also once argued that the "rise of literature as a college subject with its own departments and programs coincided with the collapse of the communal literary culture" of the nineteenth century. Gerald Graff, *Professing Literature: An Institutional History* (Chicago: University of Chicago Press, 2007), 20. Literary scholars more recently have elaborated this narrative. Nancy Glazener argues that "the reorganization of knowledge around disciplinary expertise ... distanced [literature] from forms of literary study and literary authority operating in public culture." Nancy Glazener, *Literature in the Making* (New York: Oxford University Press, 2016), 120. Joseph North has bemoaned the demise of publicly engaged literary criticism and the "scholarly turn" toward historicism and contextualism that culminated in the 1970s and 1980s. Joseph North, *Literary Criticism: A Concise Political History* (Cambridge: Harvard University Press, 2017), 4–6. However, Rachel Sagner Buurma and Laura Heffernan have resisted this tendency by insisting that the classroom is a more porous institutional site than disciplinary historians have allowed; examining the classroom, they claim, "evade[s] the deadening impasse of disciplinary autocritique without reinstating a formalist vision of our practice that must ignore the ways that we connect students, publics, texts, and histories in our everyday professional lives." Rachel Sagner Buurma and Laura Heffernan, "The Common Reader and the Archival Classroom: Disciplinary History for the Twenty-First Century," *New Literary History* 43, no. 1 (Winter 2012): 116. Deidre Lynch has resisted this narrative too, arguing that "[w]e produce a partial picture only when we narrate the prehistory of English departments as though it were simply the story of the separation of a specialist caste of interpreters from a general reading public. ... [T]hat narrative leaves us unable to assess the entanglements of the institutional and the intimate within the informal, everyday practice of English studies, within that psycho-pedagogy of everyday life that defines the discipline's real effectivity just as much as our publications in literary criticism do." Deidre Lynch, *Loving Literature: A Cultural History* (Chicago: University of Chicago Press, 2015), 12.

17. Veysey, *The Emergence of the American University*, 257.

18. Newfield, *Ivy and Industry*, 43–44. Newfield revises the remainder theory of humanism, arguing that the humanities and managerial culture "have been false opposites"; the humanities, he claims, "have provided an aesthetic—and deeply personal—basis for a craft labor view of professional life" (4). In the body of Newfield's argument, however, the humanities remain the institutional inferior. "[L]iberal humanism persisted, and still persists," Newfield writes, "to unsettle professional and managerial life, often acting as a critical or antagonistic position, jostling its institutional superior, the technosciences, while drawing on radical and noncapitalistic traditions" (47). It's worth pointing out, as I have already done, however, that English was considered a threatening modern incursion on the traditional liberal arts curriculum when it first appeared in institutions of formal education, though it is now included under the umbrella of the liberal arts. See Graff, *Professing Literature*, especially chapters 2 and 3.

19. In Chapter 2, I provide a more in-depth account of the demystification of literature within literary studies circa 1980. For now I'll simply say that this demystification coincided with the rise of New Historicism, cultural studies, and the writing of disciplinary history.
20. Louis Althusser, "Ideology and Ideological State Apparatuses (Notes towards an Investigation)," in *Lenin and Philosophy, and Other Essays*, trans. Ben Brewster (New York: Monthly Review Press, 2001), 103. Michel Foucault, *Discipline and Punish*, trans. Alan Sheridan (New York: Vintage, 1995), 136. Savio, quoted in Parker Donham, "Savio Blasts Kerr's 'Knowledge Factory,'" *Harvard Crimson*, December 12, 1964, https://www.thecrimson.com/article/1964/12/12/savio-blasts-kerrs-knowledge-factory-pmario/.
21. Guillory, *Cultural Capital*, vii.
22. This is, for instance, how Guillory frames the canon debate: "In recent years the debate about the literary canon has entered a new phase, with the emergence in the university and in the popular media of a strong conservative backlash against revisions of the curriculum." Guillory, *Cultural Capital*, 3.
23. Guillory, *Cultural Capital*, ix.
24. Mark McGurl, *The Program Era: Postwar Fiction and the Rise of Creative Writing* (Cambridge: Harvard University Press, 2009), x, xi–xii.
25. See, for instance, Margaret Doherty, "State-Funded Fiction: Minimalism, National Memory, and the Return to Realism in the Post-Postmodern Age," *American Literary History* 27, no. 1 (Spring 2015); Kathryn Roberts, "Writing 'Other Spaces': Katherine Anne Porter's Yaddo," *Modernism/modernity* 22, no. 4 (November 2015); Evan Kindley, *Poet-Critics and the Administration of Culture* (Cambridge: Harvard University Press 2017); Amy Hungerford, *Making Literature Now* (Stanford: Stanford University Press, 2016); Merve Emre, *Paraliterary: The Making of Bad Readers in Postwar America* (Chicago: University of Chicago Press, 2017); Dan N. Sinykin, "The Conglomerate Era: Publishing, Authorship, and Literary Form, 1965–2007," *Contemporary Literature* 58, no. 4 (Winter 2017); and Sarah Brouillette, *UNESCO and the Fate of the Literary* (Stanford: Stanford University Press, 2019).

    This is not to suggest that literary scholars since 1980 have been entirely incapable of attributing agency to literary works, or of arguing, more specifically, that literary works have exerted their agency on the school itself. Merve Emre once asked, "In what social contexts can literary representations of human behavior give rise to lived practices of self-cultivation?" before going on to demonstrate that Henry James's work incited the development of the paraliterary institution of the study abroad program. Merve Emre, "Jamesian Institutions." *American Literary History* 27, no. 2 (Summer 2015): 226. Emre's article therefore has a different emphasis than Emre's book *Paraliterary*, which is more interested in the McGurlian examination of "bad readers and the institutions that spawned them in postwar America" (3). Mark Vásquez has argued that literary culture in the nineteenth-century United States did not passively absorb but actively "appropriat[ed] ... a hybrid of sermonic and instructional discourses" in order to "promote self-change and social reform." Mark Vásquez, *Authority and Reform* (Knoxville: University of Tennessee Press, 2003), xxii. Angela Sorby has argued that popular poetry at the turn of the twentieth century "helped to construct" "simultaneously nurturing and disciplinary communities," including the school. Angela Sorby, *Schoolroom Poets* (Durham: University of New Hampshire Press, 2005), xlv. Jaime Osterman Alves has explored how "adolescent girls, real and imagined, ... 'talked back' to teacher, parent, and culture." Jaime Osterman Alves, *Fictions of Female Education in the Nineteenth Century* (New York: Routledge, 2009), 8. The most significant recent attempt to recuperate the agency of literary form can be found within the movement known as "post-critique," which is especially interested in discovering literature's agency outside of school, among non-expert readers. (I discuss post-critique's central figure, Rita Felski, later in this introduction.)

But while there are, therefore, many examples over the last few decades of literary scholars who have neither hollowed out literature's social agency nor enshrined the school as an omnipotent formal institution, I would argue that these accounts have yet to dislodge the assumption that currently orients the discipline, the assumption that literature is, generally speaking, a product of history, with "history" here understood through Foucault as a discursive system that governs human behavior and thought at any given moment in time. One piece of evidence I'll mention here to support my sense of the state of the discipline is that no literary scholar has argued, as I do in this book, that English literature is foundational to the modern educational system, despite evidence that is readily accessible in the historiography of US education and the English department. The bedrock assumption of the discipline has simply made this argument difficult to truly fathom. Outside the discipline, the scholarly work that most directly anticipates my argument here is Maxine Greene's *The Public School and the Private Vision* (1965), which insists that the canonical works of the American Renaissance offered a critique of the early educational system and, in doing so, anticipated or "intimated" the project of Progressive educational reform at the turn of the twentieth century. For instance, Greene writes at one point: "There were intimations in Thoreau's own writing, hints at alternative modes of educating—teaching children not to comply but to think and be themselves. The uncertainties, however, would persist for generations. ... Whatever resolutions could be found would be, in time, incorporated into the schools, since it was largely in the schools that Americans were to learn how and what to be." Maxine Greene, *The Public School and the Private Vision* (New York: New Press, 2007), 82.

26. For more on the state of higher education at the time this book was written, see Christopher Newfield, *The Great Mistake* (Baltimore: Johns Hopkins University Press, 2016); Tressie McMillan Cottom, *Lower Ed* (New York: New Press, 2017); Dan Nemser and Brian Whitener, "The Tuition Limit and the Coming Crisis in Higher Education," *New Inquiry*, March 26, 2018, https://thenewinquiry.com/the-tuition-limit-and-the-coming-crisis-of-higher-education/; Adrianna Kezar, Tom DePaola, and Daniel T. Scott, *The Gig Academy* (Baltimore: Johns Hopkins University Press, 2019); and Simon Torracinta, "Extinction Event," *n+1*, May 28, 2020, https://www.nplusonemag.com/online-only/online-only/extinction-event/. For more on the state of primary and secondary school education under neoliberal reforms, see Noliwe Rooks, *Cutting School* (New York: The New Press, 2020); Sonya Douglass Horsford, Janelle T. Scott, and Gary L. Anderson, *The Politics of Education Policy in an Era of Inequality* (New York: Routledge, 2019), particularly chapter 1; and Eric Blanc, *Red State*

Revolt (New York: Verso, 2019), also chapter 1. For more on the state of literary studies, see Benjamin Schmidt, "The Humanities Are in Crisis," *The Atlantic*, August 23, 2018, https://www.theatlantic.com/ideas/archive/2018/08/the-humanities-face-a-crisisof-confidence/567565/; and Mark Garrett Cooper and John Marx, *Media U* (New York: Columbia University Press, 2017), chapter 8.

27. I am hardly the first scholar to advance this polemic. Cottom argues that the growth of for-profit colleges in the twenty-first century reflects a broader economic transformation where "the private sector has shifted the cost of job training onto the workers, and the public sector has not provided a social policy response"; the solution to this crisis, according to Cottom, is not for schools to close the skills gap, as one so often hears, but for everybody to undertake a large-scale project of social transformation. "This requires politics," Cottom writes. Cottom, *Lower Ed*, 181, 182. Joshua Clover has insisted that in order to renovate the system of higher education as it faces the economic realities of the long downturn, we need to resort to political strategies beyond the school itself: "[I]f there is to be something ahead, an emancipation of learning, it will not be discovered in the hearts and minds of administrators and legislators persuaded to see the error of their ways, but in a transformation of the society beyond the edges of campus." Joshua Clover, "Who Can Save the University?" *Public Books*, June 12, 2017, https://www.publicbooks.org/who-can-save-the-university/. Piya Chatterjee and Sunaina Maira have explained that the "university is an institution within an imperial nation-state … and so any struggle waged within or against it must not romanticize its progressive possibilities and must be squarely situated within a struggle that extends beyond its hallowed walls." Piya Chatterjee and Sunaina Maira, *The Imperial University* (Minneapolis: University of Minnesota Press, 2014), 43. Related to these polemics, too, is Abigail Boggs and Nick Mitchell's critique of recent crisis narratives and their nostalgia for the post–World War II system of higher education: "The valorization of the public university … repeats the forgetting of the dispossession at the university's origins while simultaneously drumming up a sense of crisis regarding the potential consequences of its downfall." Abigail Boggs and Nick Mitchell, "Critical University Studies and the Crisis Consensus," *Feminist Studies* 44, no. 2 (2018): 441.

28. My narrative of the rise of the modern educational system in the United States draws principally from Frederick Rudolph, *The American College and University: A History* (Athens: University of Georgia Press, 1990); Patricia A. Graham, *Progressive Education from Arcady to Academe: A History of the Progressive Education Association, 1919–1955* (New York: Teachers College Press, 1967); David Nasaw, *Schooled to Order* (New York: Oxford University Press, 1979); Marcia Graham Synnott, *The Half-Opened Door* (Westport: Greenwood Press, 1979); Roger L. Geiger, *To Advance Knowledge: The Growth of American Research Universities, 1900–1940* (New York: Oxford University Press, 1986); David O. Levine, *The American College and the Culture of Aspiration, 1915–1940* (Ithaca: Cornell University Press, 1986); Helen Lefkowitz Horowitz, *Campus Life* (Chicago: University of Chicago Press, 1987); James Anderson, *The Education of Blacks in the South, 1860–1935* (Chapel Hill: University of North Carolina Press, 1988); and Craig Steven Wilder, *Ebony & Ivy* (New York: Bloomsbury, 2013), along

with the works I've already cited by Bledstein, Tyack, Kaestle, Reese, Thelin, Newfield, and Zimmerman, not to mention Lawrence Cremin's monumental three-volume series, *American Education* (New York: Harper and Row, 1972, 1980, 1988).

29. Statistics come from *120 Years*, 34, 75.
30. David O. Levine, for instance, describes the rise of a "culture of aspiration" that fueled the expansion of higher education after the First World War. "For the first time young people looked primarily to education as the avenue to economic and social mobility, businessmen and professionals looked to the college for its talent and its stamp of legitimacy, and society looked to the university for the benefits of its research." World War I changed people's minds about the value of a college degree, according to Levine, bringing about "a social consensus about the value of higher education." Levine, *The American College and the Culture of Aspiration, 1915–1940*, 14, 23.
31. Thomas Bender has argued that this period marked a decisive phase when "[k]nowledge and competence increasingly developed out of the internal dynamics of esoteric disciplines rather than within the context of shared perceptions of public needs." Thomas Bender, *Intellect and Public Life* (Baltimore: Johns Hopkins University Press, 1993), 10.
32. These endeavors are described in Zimmerman, *Small Wonder*, 81–82. See chapter 2 for more on the Progressive publicity campaign that sought to "protect rural citizens from themselves" (81).
33. The failure of *Wissenschaft* on its own to legitimize the university is one fact that meaningfully differentiates the history of higher education in the United States and continental Europe. Chad Wellmon has argued the modern university first emerged in late eighteenth-century Germany when "fundamental shifts in the media environment, combined with the atrophy of the theological basis of the medieval university … forced the university to reimagine its justification." To justify its existence, Wellmon explains, the university would have to present itself as embodying "a new order of knowledge which was self-organizing, internally coherent, and distinct. It would have to distinguish itself from the market and more public forms of information distribution. In this modern research university, the bibliographic order of knowledge would give way to a disciplinary order of knowledge with its distinctions between general reader and specialized scientist [*Wissenschaftler*]. This disciplinary order organized knowledge by forming those who produced it." Chad Wellmon, *Organizing Enlightenment* (Baltimore: Johns Hopkins University Press, 2015), 16–17.
34. Thorstein Veblen, *The Higher Learning in America* (New York: B. W. Huebsch, 1918), 254.
35. For these early publicity campaigns and the emergence of publicity departments in higher education, see Veysey, *The Emergence of the American University*, 325–326.
36. Quoted in Lawrence A. Cremin, *American Education: The Metropolitan Experience, 1876–1980* (New York: Harper and Row, 1988), 245. See 243–246 for more on the university extension school movement.
37. In the postbellum period, "much academic knowledge was socially useful, but it was not nearly as accessible or as visible as commercial spectacle," according to Brian

Ingrassia. "Athletics, especially the prototypical big-time sport of football, filled this cultural gap by making universities appear meaningful to the public." Brian M. Ingrassia, *The Rise of Gridiron University: Higher Education's Uneasy Alliance with Big-Time Football* (Lawrence: University Press of Kansas, 2012), 3.

38. See Thelin, *A History of American Higher Education*, 159–161, for a fuller account of these "institutional symbols."
39. "[R]esistance to academic freedom was not so much a matter of principle as it was an aspect of public relations." Veysey, *The Emergence of the American University*, 410.
40. Thelin has described this as the "interesting riddle of American higher education between 1890 and 1910." Thelin, *A History of American Higher Education*, 154. Geiger calls this phenomenon the "collegiate syndrome" that afflicted research universities during the interwar period, when the emphasis on campus *life*, with its fraternities and sporting events and college newspapers, replaced campus *studies*—when "[g]oing to college was evaluated in terms of what one did, rather than what one learned; with whom one associated, rather than by whom one was taught." Geiger, *To Advance Knowledge*, 115.
41. George Santayana, "The Spirit and Ideals of Harvard University," in *Educational Review*, vol. 7 (New York: Henry Holt, 1894), 320.
42. See Zimmerman, *Small Wonder*, chapter 2, which exhaustively documents the one-room schoolhouse's circulation through popular culture between the Civil War and World War I. As Zimmerman explains, the "chaos and dislocations of the war, and the swift urbanization that followed it, fueled nostalgia for a simpler time" (63). John Greenleaf Whittier's wildly popular poem "In School Days" (1870) rendered the one-room school as an emblem of this "simpler time." "Bad boy" fiction, which so often took as its setting the rural one-room school before the Civil War, tapped into a similar set of associations, as did Winslow Homer's widely circulated painting *Snap the Whip* (1872) and the hit song "School Days" (1909), which sold more than 3 million copies in sheet music. The statistics on one-room school attendance are from Zimmerman, *Small Wonder*, 17.
43. Cornell quoted in Bledstein, *The Culture of Professionalism*, 285–286. G. Stanley Hall, "The University Idea," *The Pedagogical Seminary* 15, no. 1 (1908): 104.
44. Here is Cremin's description of the primary school curriculum by the mid-nineteenth century: "spelling, reading, writing, grammar, arithmetic, geography, and history were the staples that ... had become readily available in most settled regions." Cremin, *American Education: The National Experience*, 394. Here is Cremin's description of the curriculum after 1876: "The most obvious shifts in curricula ... involved the admission of new subjects at all levels, the transformation and reorganization of the substance of traditional subjects, the movement of some subjects from one level to another, and the addition of so-called extracurricular activities at all levels." The expansion of subjects at the elementary level included more instructional attention to "art, music, drama, dance, and physical training," and at the secondary level to "arts, physical training, vocational education, and so-called personal development subjects, including drivers education." Cremin, *American Education: The Metropolitan Experience*, 549.
45. This was the "prescribed course" that, according to "The Yale Report" (1828), contained "those subjects only which ought to be understood, as we think, by every one

who aims at a thorough education." *Reports on the Course of Instruction in Yale College; By a Committee of the Corporation and the Academical Faculty* (New Haven: Hezekiah Howe, 1828), 18.

46. See Thelin, *A History of American Higher Education*, chapters 3, 4, and 5. "Between 1860 and 1890," he writes, "American institutions of higher education responded pragmatically, albeit imperfectly, to the challenge of competing with the attractions of a commercial and industrial economy. They did so by adding new curricula that were intended to attract new kinds of students—all as a supplement to their historical missions and traditional audiences" (108). By 1910, he goes on to explain, "[n]ew students could choose the bachelor of arts course, usually characterized by the classical languages," but they could also "opt for any number of other programs: medicine, law, engineering, business, theology, or agriculture" (153).
47. Quoted in William Greene Roelker, *Francis Wayland* (Worcester: American Antiquarian Society, 1944), 44.
48. Michael Warner once described the stereotype of the professional scholar along the lines of George Eliot's Casaubon: "As a teacher and mentor, he is a failure. His setting is a solitary office. He is conspicuously absent from the circles in which the teacher is thought of so warmly. Those with whom he associates communicate with him by writing—especially through published articles." Michael Warner, "Professionalization and the Rewards of Literature: 1875–1900," *Criticism* 27, no. 1 (1985): 22–23.
49. George L. Cross, president of the University of Oklahoma, famously came before the state legislature in the early 1950s and defended the school's budget by explaining, "We want to build a university our football team can be proud of." Quoted in Ira Berkow, "Sport of the Times; The Grapes of Wrath at Oklahoma," *New York Times*, February 18, 1989, 49. Inverting the cliché, Cross showed the ease with which college football can subsume the mission of the college (or university) itself. The public outcry that followed Louisiana State University's decision to invest $28 million in its football team's locker room is further evidence of the dangers a university risks when it overextends itself in the realm of commercial spectacle. See Will Jarvis, "LSU Just Unveiled a $28-Million Football Facility. The Flood-Damaged Library Is Still 'Decrepit,'" *Chronicle of Higher Education*, July 22, 2019, https://www.chronicle.com/article/LSU-Just-Unveiled-a/246750.
50. See Cooper and Marx, *Media U*.
51. Althusser, "Ideology and Ideological State Apparatuses," 105, 100.
52. Pierre Bourdieu and Jean-Claude Passeron, *Reproduction in Education, Society and Culture*, 2nd ed., trans. Richard Nice (New York: Sage, 2000), 149–150.
53. See *Oxford English Dictionary*, s.v. "Relevance, v.2," accessed January 15, 2022, https://www-oed-com.ezp-prod1.hul.harvard.edu/view/Entry/161891?redirectedFrom=relevance. One exception to critical theory's disinterest in the problem of relevance is Adorno, although he theorizes irrelevance in the domain of aesthetics, not social reproduction. Adorno writes: "If art cedes its autonomy, it delivers itself over to the machinations of the status quo; if art remains strictly for itself, it nonetheless submits to integration as one harmless domain among others." The harmlessness of the work of art that exists entirely for itself is the condition that I'm calling irrelevant. For Adorno, this irrelevance is just as great a threat to the emancipatory value of art

as surrendering to the logic of industry. Theodor Adorno, *Aesthetic Theory*, trans. Robert Hullot-Kentor (Minneapolis: University of Minnesota Press, 1997), 237.
54. Henry George, *The Life of Henry George, by His Son* (London: William Reeves, 1900), 356. Andrew Carnegie, *The Empire of Business* (Doubleday, Page, 1902), 110. William Dean Howells, *The Rise of Silas Lapham* (New York: Penguin, 1986), 9, 26.
55. William Lyon Phelps, *Autobiography with Letters* (New York: Oxford University Press, 1939), 297, 301. "New Professors at Yale," *New York Times*, October 28, 1895, 10. "No Study of Novels at Yale," *New York Times*, April 1, 1896, 2. "Modern Novels at Yale," *New York Times*, April 12, 1896, 16.

See Graff, *Professing Literature*, 124, for a brief account of Phelps's course on modern novels. Despite Phelps's insistence that his class was the first of its kind, Brander Matthews claimed that he taught a course at Columbia in 1891 on the modern novel. And when Yale announced the cancellation of Phelps's course in April 1896, the *Times* ran another article reporting on the novel course offered at Princeton. See "Princeton Surprised at Yale," *New York Times*, April 12, 1896, 16. Non-elite institutions of higher education were usually on the forefront of curricular experiments like these, a fact that casts even more doubt on Phelps's claims. The readings for Phelps's 1895 class may have been different from the novels he lists in his *Autobiography*. The *Yale Daily News* reported on September 30, 1895, that "Dr. Phelps' course in English novels has been slightly changed." The new syllabus included "1, Lorna Doone; 2, Marcella; 3, A Modern Instance; 4, Esther Waters; 5, A Gentleman of France; 6, Treasure Island; 7, The Luck of Roaring Camp; 8, The Phantom Rickshaw; 9, A Suburban Pastoral; 10, Trilby." "English Novels," *Yale Daily News*, September 30, 1895, 1.
56. Phelps, *Autobiography with Letters*, 297. We've already encountered the suspicions of the traditionalists in "The Yale Report." Authors and publishers had been trying to establish a high cultural tradition for the novel and dispel its lowly associations since the end of the eighteenth century. See Michael Gamer, "A Select Collection: Barbauld, Scott, and the Rise of the (Reprinted) Novel," in *Recognizing the Romantic Novel*, ed. Jillian Heydt-Stevenson and Charlotte Sussman (Liverpool: Liverpool University Press, 2008) and Homer Obed Brown, *Institutions of the English Novel* (Philadelphia: University of Pennsylvania Press, 1998). McGurl's *The Novel Art* suggests that this project was still in process at the turn of the twentieth century, when Henry James started writing modernist art novels. Mark McGurl, *The Novel Art: Elevations of American Fiction after Henry James* (Princeton: Princeton University Press, 2001).
57. Mikhail Bakhtin, *The Dialogic Imagination*, ed. Michael Holquist, trans. Caryl Emerson and Michael Holquist (Austin: University of Texas Press, 1981), 67, 382.
58. Phelps, *Autobiography with Letters*, 202, 282–283.
59. Phelps, *Autobiography with Letters*, 298. "Yale and Dr. W. L. Phelps," *New York Times*, November 7, 1895, 15. Phelps himself insisted that he did not foresee and actively shunned the publicity the class drew. "When I gave the first lecture in the Autumn, I hoped the course would attract no attention from outside of academic halls; for in those days, newspaper notoriety was often fatal to a university career," Phelps wrote in his *Autobiography with Letters*. "It is hard to say just how this publicity began, for I gave no interviews, nor did I mention the subject anywhere" (298). Phelps was being disingenuous. The *Times* quotes Phelps at length in their coverage of the class, as he

expounds his anti-formalist teaching philosophy. "The study of the novel should be a study of the spirit of the times, for the man who reads the novel of to-day keeps track of not only the taste of the times, but of the spirit and the tendencies of the times," he told the newspaper. "New Professors at Yale," 10. Phelps's openness to publicity undoubtedly contributed to the *Times*'s flattering coverage: "Phelps is delightfully in touch with the men, so much so that he is in many ways the most valuable teacher there is in the English department," the newspaper gushed. "Yale and Dr. W. L. Phelps," 15. The media coverage "outside of academic halls" very much enacted Phelps's pedagogical mission to render indistinguishable the official and the unofficial.

60. Lawrence Levine, *Highbrow/Lowbrow* (Cambridge: Harvard University Press, 1988), 30. Nancy Glazener's account of "literature in the making" in part builds off Levine. See Glazener, *Literature in the Making*, chapters 1–4 especially.

61. Primary school "readers," according to Cremin, "brought together stories, verse, expositions, historical accounts, essays, speeches and excerpts from belles-lettres." After 1783, the material included in the readers underwent a "shift" from "an overwhelming emphasis on religious prose and poetry to a more diverse fare of stories about animals, birds, and children. ... Increasingly, too, orations from Revolutionary days, biographies of Revolutionary heroes, and other patriotic material found its way into the readers." Cremin also explains that "particularly" in the McGuffey series (which appeared in 1836) "there were substantial sections from such English authors as Shakespeare, Milton, Addison, Scott, and Dickens, and such American authors as Longfellow, Hawthorne, and Bryant." Cremin, *American Education: The National Experience*, 391, 392. The first high school in the United States was founded in Boston as the "English Classical School" in 1821, only to be renamed the "English High School" in 1824. "English" here was meant to signify the school's commitment to modern subjects and non-classical languages, in contrast to the classical course of instruction offered at the academies. See Reese, *The Origins of the American High School*, 1–2. In high schools, according to Reese, "[l]iterature classes grew in popularity after the 1850s. Access to Shakespeare and Pope helped acquaint future opinion makers with the literary allusions that peppered both prose and oral discourse. ... More American literature appeared on reading lists after the midcentury, joining the familiar British and Western standards. ... Still, the journey from Beowulf to Browning remained the preferred path to erudition" (116). Literature's prominent role in the high school curriculum was further cemented when institutions of higher education began listing "English masterpieces" on entrance exams and preparatory reading lists in the postbellum period. See Glazener, *Literature in the Making*, 302–303, fn 6. See Graff, *Professing Literature*, chapters 2–7 for the standard account of literary culture's migration into institutions of higher education.

62. Disciplinary historians have diminished the contributions of the generalists to the development of English as an academic subject. The generalists appear as a residual formation in the first wave of disciplinary history published in the 1980s, even as their conflict with the philologists is widely acknowledged in this scholarship to have produced the discipline itself. See Warner, "Professionalization and the Rewards of Literature: 1875–1900," 20, and Graff, *Professing Literature*, 3–4, 84. More recently, the generalists have dropped out of disciplinary history almost altogether, though their

chief predecessor, Matthew Arnold, has been retained. If for Veysey and Graff the generalists' liberal culture was fundamentally Arnoldian, for Mary Poovey, Arnold's criticism didn't ground the generalists' dilettantish anti-professionalism but rather served to justify the expertise of professional literary scholars. Mark Taylor, too, has argued that literary criticism is "organized discursively around the recession or decline of agency" that Arnold's "lower criticism" modeled. Insofar as these recent accounts emphasize the enduring influence of Arnold's thought on the evolution of the discipline, they complicate the conflict described in the first wave of disciplinary history between the doomed Arnoldian generalists and the philologists. Insofar as these accounts represent the development of the discipline as an evolution toward specialization and expertise, however, they seem to me to miss something essential about the role literary studies has played in the evolution of the school system as a whole. The institutional success of literary studies is not entirely explicable in the terms of professionalism, specialization, and expertise; its success was due in fact to its methodological *il*legitimacy, its renunciation of those very values and practices associated with the formation of disciplinary communities. Mary Poovey, "The Model System of Contemporary Literary Criticism," *Critical Inquiry* 27, no. 3 (Spring 2001). Mark Taylor, "The Lower Criticism," *Representations* 150 (Spring 2020): 34.

63. Mary E. Burt, *Literary Landmarks: A Guide to Good Reading for Young People* (Boston: Houghton, Mifflin, 1890), 29–30. English enrollment statistics from the University of California are from *English in American Universities*, ed. William Morton Payne (Boston: D. C. Heath, 1895), 99–100. James Turner, *Philology* (Princeton: Princeton University Press, 2014), 255. Other enrollment statistics confirm Turner's assessment and indicate that the University of California was no aberration. English courses were "everywhere very popular": "The thousand odd students at Yale (and Sheffield), at Harvard, at the Universities of Michigan, and even of Nebraska, give eloquent testimony to the popularity of English teaching, to say nothing of the eight hundred and seventy-three reported by California, the six hundred and twenty-nine by Chicago, and the four hundred and fifty by Stanford." *English in American Universities*, 24.

Despite the rhetoric of crisis that has persisted within literary studies since the discipline's formation, English was a consistently popular major throughout the twentieth century and into the twenty-first. James English has recently undertaken a statistical analysis of undergraduate majors, focusing on a period after literary studies had established itself in the twentieth century as (in Bill Readings's words) the "discipline entrusted by the nation-state with the task of reflecting on cultural identity," and after the explosive growth of English majors in the late 1960s and early 1970s. The period that attracts English's attention is instead the one that stretches from the 1982–1983 academic year to the 2007–2008 academic year, when the discipline allegedly underwent a massive decline. English concludes, "Considered strictly in terms of US higher educational enrollments over the past quarter century, English is the dominant field in the fastest rising sector [humanities], as well as a field whose share of undergraduate majors is larger than that of the combined computer and information sciences and larger than those of math, physics, chemistry, and geology put together." James English, *The Global Future of English Studies* (West Sussex: Wiley-Blackwell, 2012), 16–17. Bill Readings, *The University in Ruins* (Cambridge: Harvard University Press,

1999), 70. Even the dramatic drop in English literature's "share" of majors after the financial crisis of 2008 has obscured the fact that English is one of only six majors—along with mathematics, psychology, political science and government, history, and biology—that is essentially ubiquitous in US higher education, achieving what Mark Garrett Cooper and John Marx call a "reach" of over 90 percent. (Reach, a metric Cooper and Marx adapt from television broadcasting, is a measurement of "the percentage of students who could have chosen to finish a program because it was available at their institutions.") "In other words, after 2011, whether you went to a small and specialized PhD-granting institution or to a gigantic university, you could expect to find someone majoring in English, Biology, Mathematics, Psychology, Political Science, or History," they write. "Out of nearly one thousand baccalaureate programs tracked at PhD-granting institutions, these six degrees, and only these degrees, can be regarded as ubiquitous." Mark Garrett Cooper and John Marx, *Media U* (New York: Columbia University Press, 2017), 189, 192.

64. Woodrow Wilson, "Mere Literature." *The Atlantic*, 72 (Boston: Houghton, Mifflin, 1893), 821.
65. Martin Wright Sampson quoted in *English in American Universities*, 95. John Erskine, *My Life as a Teacher* (Philadelphia: Lippincott, 1948), 24. Graff explains that "the dream of the generalists" persisted in the pedagogy of the New Critics: "If only literature itself could be allowed to work its potential magic, all would be well." Graff, *Professing Literature*, 171.
66. Stanley Fish, "Profession Despise Thyself: Fear and Self-Loathing in Literary Studies," *Critical Inquiry* 10, no. 2 (December 1983): 353. Guillory argues that the rise of theory in English departments is explicable in the context of the bureaucratization of professorial labor, with the master theorists (foremost among them Paul de Man) retaining an "'anti-institutional' charisma." Guillory, *Cultural Capital*, 259. The figure of the "cool" English teacher has been relentlessly parodied on the internet. See, for instance, CollegeHumor, "Hardly Working: Cool English Teacher," YouTube video, 2:51, May 20, 2008, https://www.youtube.com/watch?v=lILCc6AZ10c.
67. Noah Porter, "The American Colleges and the American Public," in *The New Englander*, ed. George P. Fisher, Timothy Dwight, and William L. Kingsley (New Haven: Stafford, 1869), 95. McCosh, quoted in Th. W. Hunt, "The Place of English in the College Curriculum," in *Transactions of the Modern Language Association, 1884–5*, vol. 1 (Baltimore: Modern Language Association, 1885), 131.
68. Jane Addams, *Twenty Years at Hull-House* (New York: Penguin, 1998), 51, 53.
69. Edith Wharton, *The Age of Innocence* (New York: Scribner, 1996), 24, 103, 263, 146.
70. Wharton, *The Age of Innocence*, 53, 27.
71. Wharton, *The Age of Innocence*, 311–313.
72. Wharton, *The Age of Innocence*, 360.
73. McGurl, *The Program Era*, 53, 49. See also Ulrich Beck, Anthony Giddens, and Scott Lash, *Reflexive Modernization* (Stanford: Stanford University Press, 1994).
74. Wharton, *The Age of Innocence*, 135, 105, 94, 304, 306.
75. Many characters challenge the conventions governing New York high society in *The Age of Innocence*, from Julius Beaufort, with his extramarital affairs, to Mrs. Manson

Mingott, with her various social "audacities." Archer and Ellen's rather depressing realization in the famous scene at the Met is that even if they were to carry out their most transgressive plans (running off to Japan, or carrying on an affair in New York), they would still simply be adhering to conventional scripts: "Don't let us be like all the others!" Ellen tells Archer. Wharton, *The Age of Innocence*, 32, 327.

76. Though Archer often insists that high society is essentially divorced from the real world, at other times he insists that it is the realest of all worlds. For instance, when he arrives in St. Augustine to visit the Wellands, he thinks to himself: "Here was the truth, here was reality, here was the life that belonged to him." Wharton, *The Age of Innocence*, 158.

77. For instance, when Archer finally opens his box of new books from his London bookseller, Wharton presents us with another scene of failed reading. "[T]hough he turned the pages with the sensuous joy of the book-lover," Wharton writes, "he did not know what he was reading, and one book after another dropped from his hand." The only book he can be said to properly read in the scene is a collection of Rossetti poems, and this reading experience, described in the register of the Romantic as exhilaratingly unconventional, ultimately proves unsatisfying because it remains untethered from reality. "All through the night he pursued through those enchanted pages the vision of a woman who had the face of Ellen Olenska," Wharton writes. "[B]ut when he woke the next morning, and looked out at the brownstone houses across the street, and thought of his desk in Mr. Letterblair's office, and the family pew in Grace Church, his hour in the park of Skuytercliff became as far outside the pale of probability as the visions of the night." Wharton, *The Age of Innocence*, 156–157.

78. Wharton, *The Age of Innocence*, 362.

79. Jackson Lears, *No Place of Grace* (Chicago: University of Chicago Press, 1994), 5, 48. Wharton is often read through the framework Lears established. See Nancy Bentley, "'Hunting for the Real': Wharton and the Science of Manners," in *The Cambridge Companion to Edith Wharton*, ed. Millicent Bell (Cambridge: Cambridge University Press, 1995); and Jennifer Fleissner, "Wharton, Marriage, and the New Woman," in *The Cambridge History of the American Novel*, ed. Leonard Cassuto, Clare Virginia Eby, and Benjamin Reiss (Cambridge: Cambridge University Press, 2011).

80. Max Weber, *From Max Weber: Essays in Sociology*, trans. and ed. H.H. Gerth and C. Wright Mills (New York: Oxford University Press, 1946), 228.

81. For the relationship between the modernists and the emergent class of experts and professionals, see, for instance, Louis Menand, *Discovering Modernism: T. S. Eliot and His Context* (New York: Oxford University Press, 1987); Thomas Strychacz, *Modernism, Mass Culture, and Professionalism* (Cambridge: Cambridge University Press, 1993); and McGurl, *The Novel Art*. Lisi Schoenbach has more recently examined a group of "pragmatic modernists" in order to argue against the common perception of modernism as a movement "synonymous with an oppositional stance" and the belief within literary studies that "institutions, traditions, and habits are anathema to the very project of modernism." I'm claiming here, through Menand, Strychacz, and McGurl, that the modernists' pragmatic critique of institutions like the school was not a break from but a particular phase in the history of literary anti-institutionalism. Lisi Schoenbach, *Pragmatic Modernism* (New York: Oxford University Press, 2011), 13.

82. Andrew Hoberek has argued that post-1945 fiction encodes the crisis of the new middle class as it moved further and further away from property ownership and entrepreneurism, the traits that defined the old middle class: "Threatened with proletarianization through the loss of its property to big capital, the middle class translates this loss into narratives of individual dispossession that enforce its cultural dominance rather than seeking a potentially more useful affiliation with those already outside the magic circle of capital." Andrew Hoberek, *The Twilight of the Middle Class* (Princeton: Princeton University Press, 2005), 32. Stephen Schryer has argued that the post-1945 crisis of the middle class led to a transdisciplinary project, undertaken by writers, literary critics, and sociologists, to create a "public-minded but antimanagerial cultural elite dedicated to national education but indifferent or hostile to pragmatic reform." This "fantasy of the new class," according to Schryer, was "at once a response to the knowledge elite's newfound prominence in U.S. society and a reflection of that elite's ongoing powerlessness." Stephen Schryer, *Fantasies of the New Class* (New York: Columbia University Press, 2011), 11, 14.

83. In later chapters, I will occasionally remark on, for instance, Gertrude Stein's friendship with the educator and classicist Edith Hamilton, and Upton Sinclair's attempt to convince John Dewey to invest in a Brooks-Farm-type utopian experiment in Englewood, New Jersey. These anecdotes are, as we'll see, suggestive but not dispositive.

84. Rita Felski, "Latour and Literary Studies," *PMLA* 130, no. 3 (2015): 739. Caroline Levine, *Forms* (Princeton: Princeton University Press, 2015), 11.

85. In a 300-level seminar I took my junior year of college titled, "Faulkner and the Thirties," the professor remarked at the end of the semester that having read seven Faulkner novels over the last few months, we students in our papers had begun to write windy Faulknerian sentences.

86. How "tremendous" is the social agency that these scholars ascribe to literature? Felski, for instance, would claim that her understanding of literary agency is far more modest than the agency that, say, Marxists invest literature with. In *Uses of Literature* (2008), Felski follows Amanda Anderson and positions her research against the "frequent attempts to endow literary works with … aggrandized agency." However, her various writings over the last decade have traded the Marxists' belief in literature's profound political power for a belief in its extensive presence across social experience. See below. Rita Felski, *Uses of Literature* (Malden: Wiley-Blackwell, 2008), 8.

87. Felski, for instance, writes: "Our students … are migrating in droves toward vocationally oriented degrees in the hope of guaranteeing future incomes to offset sky-rocketing college bills. The institutional fiefdoms of the natural and social sciences pull in ever heftier sums of grant money and increasingly call the shots in the micro-dramas of university politics. In the media and public life, what counts as knowledge is equated with a piling up of data and graphs, questionnaires and pie charts, input-output ratios and feedback loops. Old-school beliefs that exposure to literature and art was a sure path to moral improvement and cultural refinement have fallen by the way-side, to no one's great regret. In such an austere and inauspicious climate, how do scholars of literature make a case for the value of what we do? How do we come up with rationalizations for reading and talking about books without reverting to the canon-worship of the past?" Felski, *Uses of Literature*, 2.

88. See Buurma and Heffernan, "The Common Reader and the Archival Classroom: Disciplinary History for the Twenty-First Century," for a critique of literary studies' fascination with common readers as evidence that the discipline has overly internalized Bourdieu. I tend to see post-critique's interest in non-expert readers as a recent variation on the discipline's abiding anti-scholasticism. Unschooled readers are, for these scholars, superior to their schooled counterparts.
89. Felski, "Latour and Literary Studies," 737. Levine, *Forms*, 17.
90. For critiques of Felski and/or Levine from the left, see Lee Konstantinou, "Critique Has Its Uses," *American Book Review* 38, no. 5 (July/August 2017); and Bruce Robbins, "Fashion Conscious Phenomenon," *American Book Review*, 38, no. 5 (July/August 2017). Anna Kornbluh has attempted to reconcile Levine and Marx by arguing that the "forms in art may themselves theorize the forms in life, and questions of social configuration may be abstractly posed in art in ways that the concretude of experience blocks." For Kornbluh, Felski's Latourian methodology promotes a "horizontal flat ontology" while Levine "countenances no hierarchy in which some forms reveal, theorize, or mediate others." Anna Kornbluh, *The Order of Forms* (Chicago: University of Chicago Press, 2019), 6, 1, 168 fn 13.
91. Loulie Ayer Beall, "Early School Experiences in Nebraska," *Nebraska History* 33 (July–September 1942): 200–201. John Ise, *Sod and Stubble: The Story of a Kansas Homestead* (New York: Wilson-Erickson, 1936), 234. These examples are cited in the first chapter of Annette Fuentes, *Lockdown High* (New York: Verso, 2011).
92. Andrew D. White, *Autobiography of Andrew D. White*, vol. I (New York: Century, 1905), 353. Francis Wayland and H. L. Wayland, *A Memoir of the Life and Labors of Francis Wayland, D.D. LL.D.*, vol. 2 (New York: Sheldon, 1867), 93. G. Stanley Hall, *Life and Confessions of a Psychologist* (New York: D. Appleton, 1923), 202. See Bledstein, *The Culture of Professionalism*, 232–236, for a more extensive account of the old-time college's failures as an instrument of discipline. "The traditional social institutions Americans inherited from the eighteenth century were too informal and loose—too external in forms of discipline—to structure a young life in rapid motion," Bledstein writes at another moment (213).
93. Althusser, "Ideology and Ideological State Apparatuses," 103. Bourdieu and Passeron, *Reproduction*, 149–150.
94. See Nasaw, *Schooled to Order*, Part I, for an account of the ideological foundations of the common school movement and the movement's failure to truly school kids "to order." "If the reformers' ultimate objectives had been to establish within their lifetimes common schools that would be universally attended by rich and poor alike, they failed," Nasaw writes. "If it was to coax or coerce the Irish Catholics into their common schools, they failed. If it was to diminish to insignificance community control of local schools, they failed. If it was to eliminate poverty, pauperism, criminality, intemperance, workplace indiscipline, political unrest, and social disorder, they failed again" (83).

See Wilder, *Ebony and Ivy*, chapter 4, and especially 114, for an account of Dartmouth College's failing Indian education program. Wilder is of course not making the point that I am here. He insists instead that the school effectively propagated settler-colonial ideology, a claim that, to me, seems overstated. Wilder undoubtedly proves that institutions of higher education in North America soaked up capital from the merchant class and the planter class—often in the form of actually enslaved people—and then set out to do the bidding of these classes. But so many of the examples that the book cites suggest the school's failure to carry out the ideological services it had been enlisted to perform. We might point to Dartmouth's failed Indian education program, or Harvard's, for that matter. See 41–42. Other examples abound. If academics "formed an important and boisterous lobby against abolitionism," naming themselves "the racial guardians of the United States" and championing colonization through the American Colonization Society, the influence of these academics remained profoundly limited: as Wilder points out, not even their students internalized the principles of colonization (266). See also 269–270. If academics were early developers of race science before the Civil War, they had a hard time legitimizing their scientific practices to the wider public. "Between the Revolution and the Civil War," Wilder writes, "seventeen separate mobs attempted to stop dissections and resurrections" (207). By emphasizing the failure of early US schools to function effectively as ideological instruments, I by no means intend to sanitize their history. Early American education simply reflects the unique mixture of incompetence and cruelty that has so often characterized the reign of the ruling classes in the United States.

95. My account of the emergence of the school's "modern" role in the reproduction of social relations synthesizes a number of important works, specifically Anderson, *The Education of Blacks in the South*; Bledstein, *The Culture of Professionalism*; Nasaw, *Schooled to Order*; Newfield, *Ivy and Industry*; Tyack, *The One Best System*; and Barbara Ehrenreich and John Ehrenreich, "The Professional-Managerial Class," in *Between Labor and Capital*, ed. Pat Walker (Boston: South End Press, 1979).

96. As Bourdieu and Passeron explain, formal education needs to reproduce itself before it can play a larger role in the process of social reproduction. It must, that is, "*produce and reproduce the institutional conditions whose existence and persistence (self-reproduction of the system) are necessary both to the exercise of its essential function of inculcation and to the fulfillment of its function of reproducing a cultural arbitrary which it does not produce (cultural reproduction), the reproduction of which contributes to the reproduction of the relations between the groups or classes (social reproduction).*" Bourdieu and Passeron, *Reproduction*, 54.

97. Pierre Macherey and Etienne Balibar, "Literature as an Ideological Form: Some Marxist Propositions," trans. Ian McLeod, John Whitehead, and Ann Wordsworth, *Oxford Literary View* 3, no. 1 (1978): 12.

98. Guillory, *Cultural Capital*, 135. See 71–82 for Guillory's discussion of Macherey and Balibar in his extended account of the "historical forms of the literary canon."

99. "Mass magazines formed the principal cultural forum where the perception of college was recrafted and worked into the cultural horizon of the plain middle-class businessman. The magazines did not reflect a changing reality in the image of college portrayed on their pages; they actively created this ideal out of a response to the sense of crisis perceived among their male readers." Daniel A. Clark, *Creating the College Man* (Madison: University of Wisconsin Press, 2010), 18.

100. Christopher Findeisen, "'The One Place Where Money Makes No Difference': The Campus Novel from *Stover at Yale* through *The Art of Fielding*," *American Literature* 88, no. 1 (2016): 82.

101. Macherey and Balibar explain, for instance, that "the objectivity of literature, i.e. its relation to objective reality by which it is historically determined, is not a relation to an 'object' which it represents, is not representative." Macherey and Balibar, "Literature as an Ideological Form," 7. Travis M. Foster offers another account of campus fiction that invests its representational content with political power: the "genre's representations of camaraderie ... manifested an extraordinary ability to accommodate multiple social tensions," of which post–Civil War "sectional reconciliation and white cohesion" was "the most urgent." Travis M. Foster, "Campus Novels and the Nation of Peers," *American Literary History* 26, no. 3 (2014): 464.
102. Harold Lloyd's *The Freshman* (1925) reflexively dramatizes the exchanges between scholastic and mass culture as it is mediated through the extracurriculum. The film's main character, Harold "Speedy" Lamb, models his behavior when he first sets off to college on the campus movies and campus novels he has read; for example, each time he meets a new classmate he performs a little jig he has seen in the (fictional) campus movie *The College Hero*. At first this jig makes Lloyd a laughingstock among his peers, and it is only when Lloyd stops imitating campus life as he's learned about it through mass culture and starts being himself that he can, during the film's climactic football game, claim the title of "big man on campus." The moment Speedy stops imitating mass campus culture is thus also complicatedly the moment he becomes an example of it, and those characters who once mocked Speedy's jig begin imitating it themselves. For a more recent example, we might consider that exemplary and loathsome fixture of undergraduate culture, the "toga party." While students at fraternities held toga parties long before *Animal House* (1978), it was surely only after the success of the film that toga parties became omnipresent in the extracurriculum.
103. Cremin suggests that the social illegibility of higher education in the mid-nineteenth century prevented the school system from truly cohering: "While a unitary system of schooling—embracing primary school, then intermediate school, then high school, grammar school, or academy, and then college (or theological seminary, medical school, or law school)—had begun to emerge by the 1850s and 1860s, the precise place of the college in that system and indeed the precise character of the system itself were neither well defined nor universally understood." Cremin, *American Education: The National Experience*, 403.
104. Henry Adams, *The Education of Henry Adams: An Autobiography* (Boston: Houghton Mifflin, 2000), 305–306.
105. Chapters 5 and 6 contribute to recent conversations in Marxist scholarship surrounding the production of subjects and subjectivity under capitalism. These conversations over the last decade or so have centered on the particular kinds of subjectivity produced under neoliberalism. While Wendy Brown has argued, by way of Foucault, that neoliberalism produces entrepreneurial subjects through "soft, rather than hard, power," others, including Ruth Wilson Gilmore, see neoliberalism as involving an expansion in the state's punitive capacities. Wendy Brown, *Undoing the Demos: Neoliberalism's Stealth Revolution* (Princeton: Zone Books, 2015), 47. Ruth Wilson Gilmore, *Golden Gulag* (Berkeley: University of California Press, 2007). Annie McClanahan has argued against "nondeterministic" or "antieconomistic" theories of subjectivity altogether, not just in the neoliberal period. She suggests that we might think of

Gramscian models of hegemony as taking hold in academic discourse, alternately, as part of an effort to "reconcile Karl Marx and Michel Foucault (by way of Louis Althusser as well as Gramsci)," or as a product of "the influence of cultural Maoism ... on intellectual thought after 1968," or as "a phenomenon specific to the New Left and to the shift, in the 1970s and 1980s, toward theories of culture and discourse as the primary or only remaining sites of political contestation," or, finally, she writes, "We might even yoke it to the particular, and particularly vexing, position of the professoriat, at once potentially radical organic intellectuals and purest representatives of the 'managerial elite' that ... rebound in power under neoliberalism." Chapters 5 and 6 attempt to explore further the questions of when (if ever) and how an institution like the school has operated as an ideological instrument. Annie McClanahan, "Serious Crises: Rethinking the Neoliberal Subject," *Boundary 2* 46, no. 1 (2019): 109.
106. See Robert Brenner, "The Economics of Global Turbulence," *New Left Review* 229 (May/June 1998).

Chapter 1

1. Nathaniel Hawthorne, *Passages from the English Note-Books of Nathaniel Hawthorne*, vol. 1 (Leipzig: Tauchnitz, 1871), 147–148.
2. Evert Duyckinck, "Nathaniel Hawthorne: *The Scarlet Letter*," *Literary World*, no. 165 (March 30, 1850): 324–325. Edwin P. Whipple, "Review of New Books: *The House of the Seven Gables*," *Graham's Magazine* 38, no. 6 (June 1851): 467. Rufus W. Griswold, "Nathaniel Hawthorne," *International Magazine*, May 1, 1851, 159. Hawthorne, *Passages from the English Note-Books*, 147. For the standard account of Hawthorne's canonization in the wake of *The Scarlet Letter*, see Richard Brodhead, *The School of Hawthorne* (New York: Oxford University Press, 1986), chapter 3, particularly pages 51–63.
3. Renker argues that colleges and universities resisted the study of American literature through "total curricular exclusion" and "various forms of strategic marginalization" until the mid-twentieth century, when it could serve the cause of nationalism. Elizabeth Renker, *The Origins of American Literature Studies* (Cambridge: Cambridge University Press, 2007), 1. Even as Renker describes the marginalization of American literary studies in higher education, she often notes the "upward pressure" of student demand against the top-down injunctions of administrators and university scholars. Mount Holyoke, for instance, "showed consistent interest post-1920 not only in maintaining but also in building the number of American literature classes ... particularly in response to the bottom-up force of student demand" (62). At Ohio State in the early 1920s, Renker explains, the "Introduction to American Literature" survey was popular, in part because it had no prerequisites and in part too presumably because students wanted to take the class. Unlike composition, for instance, American literature was not a required course, but it still drew huge numbers (114). The account I put forward here largely differs from Renker's in its emphasis: we both agree that American literature classes were popular in institutions of higher education and that administrators and scholars denounced the study of American literature. But where Renker sees these trends as a sign of American literature's degraded status within the educational

system, I see them as a testament to American literature's institutional significance. As I explain in the next chapter, the institutionalization of literature was a contradictory process that involved both the eager absorption *and* strategic marginalization of literary culture in the curriculum. When "modern" scholars and administrators derided the study of literature generally or American literature specifically, they did so in order to arrogate for their institutions the popularity literature then enjoyed.

4. For an account of the heterogeneity of nineteenth-century US culture, see Lawrence Levine, *Highbrow/Lowbrow* (Cambridge: Harvard University Press, 1988). For an account of literature's evolving meanings from the eighteenth century to the twenty-first, see Nancy Glazener, *Literature in the Making* (New York: Oxford University Press, 2016).

5. Allison Speicher suggests this writerly ambivalence in her account of "common school fiction" between the 1830s and 1880, describing this body of work as "multivocal and untidy, reflecting the messiness of the school experience [it] present[s]." Speicher here is characterizing the various positions writers assumed vis-à-vis common school reform; there were also, of course, many writers who were uninvolved with or unmoved by the debate over formal education. Mark Vásquez's *Authority and Reform* (2003) suggests this writerly ambivalence too with its argument that literary culture "appropriat[ed] ... a hybrid of sermonic and instructional discourses" in order to "promote self-change and social reform." Vásquez's emphasis on "appropriation" helpfully captures the competitiveness and affinity that characterized the relationship between these spheres in the nineteenth century. Just as writers assumed no entirely consistent posture toward the school, educators assumed no entirely consistent posture toward literature. Often, but by no means always, teachers and writers worked collaboratively, and literary scholars have written compellingly about these collaborations. Derek Pacheco, for instance, has examined a coterie of literary-pedagogical reformers—Nathaniel Hawthorne, Elizabeth Peabody, Margaret Fuller, and Horace Mann—and explored "the ways in which [these reformers] articulate[d] interlocking moral and economic imperatives in their search for educational commodities that could help them navigate a still-amorphous literary market." Angela Sorby has explored postbellum educators' fondness for Longfellow and the rest of the schoolroom poets. Allison Speicher, *Schooling Readers* (Tuscaloosa: University of Alabama Press, 2016), 17. Mark Vásquez, *Authority and Reform* (Knoxville: University of Tennessee Press, 2003), xxii. Derek Pacheco, *Moral Enterprise* (Columbus: Ohio State University Press, 2013), 2. Angela Sorby, *Schoolroom Poets* (Durham: University of New Hampshire Press, 2005), especially chapter 1.

I am obviously interested in the friction, rather than the harmony, between writers and educators, in large part because I believe this friction helps explain how "literature" developed as a discursive category over the twentieth century. It's worth pointing out that the literary-pedagogical coterie Pacheco discusses saw their projects falter in the 1840s, with each "mov[ing] on to endeavors beyond the scope of this study" in later decades. (Hawthorne, for instance, failed as a writer of children's books in the 1840s and only returned to the genre after establishing himself as a writer of literary fiction.) Pacheco, 15. It's worth noting also that Sorby's main examples belong to a literary tradition that, in the early twentieth century, would find its status as "literature" diminished. This is not to say that the schoolroom poets didn't meaningfully affect the operations of the modern school; I am simply interested here in examining "literature" as it transformed over time and in understanding how this transformation affected and was affected by the school system.

6. Here is Lawrence Buell's account of the historiography of the romance tradition. (This account is filtered through Buell's interest in the history of the Great American Novel, so it emphasizes romance fiction exclusively rather than the entirety of the romance tradition.) He writes: "On the one hand, reenvisionment of the field of U.S. fiction as a cohort of masterfully intricate symbolic performances that could not be interpreted without initiation and hard work looked suspiciously like a defensive firewall designed to protect high culture against an emergent mass culture. On the other hand, it created an 'ideal order of eternal objects' that celebrated American art and civilization, consolidating the authority of American literature studies in the process, and in a way conveniently marketable as an export commodity to showcase U.S. exceptionalism at the very moment when enthusiasm for American culture was starting to take off in a big way around the world." Lawrence Buell, *The Dream of the Great American Novel* (Cambridge: Harvard University Press, 2014), 51.

Buell's description is meant to suggest the incoherence of this historiography. On the one hand, there is John Guillory's account of the New Critics (and, Buell suggests, their Americanist counterparts as well), which insists that they cultivated "a kind of recusant literary culture, at once faithful to the quasi-sacred authority of literature but paying tribute at the same time to the secular authority of a derogated mass culture." On the other hand, there is David Shumway's account, which argues that "[t]he disciplinary form of American literature studies ... came to serve American nationalism quite effectively" and that "[t]he importance of the 'American Adam' or the 'pastoral myth' was not mainly what they told us about America, but that they guaranteed the cultural significance of its literature." Shumway here appears to stand in for the New Historicist critique of the romance paradigm; for examples of the origins of this critique, see Nina Baym, "Melodramas of Beset Manhood: How Theories of American Fiction Exclude Women Authors," *American Quarterly* 33, no. 2 (Summer 1981) and Paul Lauter, "Race and Gender in the Shaping of the American Literary Canon: A Case Study from the Twenties," *Feminist Studies* 9, no. 3 (Autumn 1983). John Guillory, *Cultural Capital: The Problem of Literary Canon Formation* (Chicago: University of Chicago Press, 1993), 175. David R. Shumway, *Creating American Civilization: A Genealogy of American Literature as an Academic Discipline* (Minneapolis: University of Minnesota Press, 1994), 21.

7. See Brodhead, *School of Hawthorne*, 52, for an account of the American literary canon at the turn of the twentieth century.

8. Leslie Fiedler, *Love and Death in the American Novel* (Champaign: Dalkey Archive, 2008), 339.

9. Washington Irving, *History, Tales, and Sketches* (New York: Library of America, 1983), 1060, 1085–1086.

10. Irving, *History, Tales, and Sketches*, 1086.

11. Irving, *History, Tales, and Sketches*, 1086–1087.
12. Carl F. Kaestle explains that from 1780 to 1830, parents in cities like New York "sought schooling from an array of independent pay schools and academies. The most affluent families hired private tutors or patronized select boarding schools, while private-venture day schools served those in the middle ranks[.]" Carl F. Kaestle, *Pillars of the Republic* (New York: Hill and Wang, 1983), 51.
13. George P. Putnam, "Memories of Distinguished Authors: Washington Irving," *Harper's Weekly* 15, no. 752 (May 1871): 493. Stanley T. Williams, *The Life of Washington Irving* (New York: Oxford University Press, 1935), 12, 14.
14. These numbers are provided by Williams, *The Life of Washington Irving*, 14.
15. The fellow student is quoted in Williams, 11. Washington Irving, *Chronicles of Wolfert's Roost and Other Papers* (Leipzig: Tauchnitz, 1855), 27.
16. The classmate is quoted in Williams, *The Life of Washington Irving*, 12. For more on Irving's literary domestic life, see Williams, 17.
17. For a more detailed account of the publication history of *Salmagundi* and *A History of New York*, see Williams, *The Life of Washington Irving*, 173–175 and Henry Pochmann, "Washington Irving: Amateur or Professional," in *Critical Essays on Washington Irving*, ed. Ralph M. Aderman (Boston: G. K. Hall, 1990), 156–158.
18. For bachelorhood in Irving's work, see Michael Warner, "Irving's Posterity," *ELH* 67, no. 3 (Fall 2000), which argues that "[l]iterary reproduction is, for Irving, the ultimate form of surrogacy: a mode of cultural reproduction in which bachelors are, at last, full at home" (792).
19. See Andrew Piper, *Dreaming in Books: The Making of the Bibliographic Imagination in the Romantic Age* (Chicago: University of Chicago Press, 2009), especially 147-148.
20. Ronald J Zboray and Mary S. Zboray, *Literary Dollars and Social Sense: A People's History of the Mass Market Book* (New York: Routledge, 2005), xi. Zboray and Zboray argue that the North American print scene lagged well behind the British industry, which itself lagged well behind publishing centers on the continent (xvii).
21. Trish Loughran, *The Republic in Print: Print Culture in the Age of U.S. Nation Building, 1770–1870* (New York: Columbia University Press, 2007), xix.
22. Pochmann, "Washington Irving: Amateur or Professional?" describes Irving's difficult journey from amateur dabbler to professional writer.
23. Diedrich Knickerbocker's landlords mistake him for a schoolmaster in the frame story of *A History of New York*, and Knickerbocker is indignant at the comparison. "What is more, [my wife] even offered, merely by way of making things easy, to let him live scot-free, if he would teach the children their letters," the landlord explains; "but the old gentleman took it in such dudgeon, and seemed so affronted at being taken for a schoolmaster, that she never dared to speak on the subject again." The figure of the pedagogue is literally pushed to the margins of *A History*, when the landlords hire a schoolmaster to add supplementary footnotes: "Upon this we got a very learned school-master, who teaches our children, to prepare it for the press, which he accordingly has done[.]" Irving, *History, Tales, and Sketches*, 375, 376.
24. Irving, *History, Tales, and Sketches*, 1061.
25. Irving, *History, Tales, and Sketches*, 1063, 1063–64.

260   NOTES

26. Irving, *History, Tales, and Sketches*, 1081, 1082. Gérard Genette, *Narrative Discourse: An Essay in Method*, trans. Jane E. Lewin (Ithaca: Cornell University Press, 1983), 116.
27. Irving, *History, Tales, and Sketches*, 1082–1083, 1083.
28. At the end of the famous chase scene, Crane is surprised when the headless horseman doesn't disappear once they reach the bridge, a detail that seems to undermine either the legends that circulate about the headless horseman or Crane's experience during the episode, suggesting that it's not, in fact, the ghost of a trooper who is chasing him but rather Brom Bones in disguise. "He recollected the place where Brom Bones' ghostly competitor had disappeared. 'If I can but reach that bridge,' thought Ichabod, 'I am safe.' Just then he heard the black steed panting and blowing close behind him; he even fancied that he felt his hot breath. Another convulsive kick in the ribs, and old Gunpowder sprung upon the bridge; he thundered over the resounding planks; he gained the opposite side, and now Ichabod cast a look behind to see if his pursuer should vanish, according to rule, in a flash of fire and brimstone. Just then he saw the goblin rising in his stirrups, and in the very act of hurling his head at him." Irving, *History, Tales, and Sketches*, 1084–1085.
29. Henry David Thoreau, *Walden, Civil Disobedience, and Other Writings*, ed. William Rossi (New York: W. W. Norton, 2008), 38–39.
30. Ralph Waldo Emerson, "The American Scholar," in *Nature and Selected Essays*, ed. Lazer Ziff (New York: Penguin, 2003), 94–95. Walt Whitman, "Preface 1855—*Leaves of Grass*, First Edition," in *Leaves of Grass and Other Writings*, ed. Michael Moon (New York: W.W. Norton, 2002), 622, 242–243, 250–252. Mark Twain, *The Adventures of Huckleberry Finn* (New York: Penguin, 2003), 307. Herman Melville, *Moby-Dick* (New York: W. W. Norton, 2002), 101.
31. Irving, *History, Tales, and Sketches*, 1085.
32. William Hill Brown, *The Power of Sympathy*, ed. William S. Kable (Columbus: Ohio State University Press, 1969), 5. Susanna Rowson, *Charlotte Temple*, ed. Marion L. Rust (New York: W. W. Norton, 2011), 5. Hannah Webster Foster, *The Coquette and the Boarding School*, ed. Jennifer Harris and Bryan Waterman (New York: W. W. Norton, 2013), 136. See Marion L. Rust, Introduction to *Charlotte Temple*, ed. Marion L. Rust (New York: W. W. Norton, 2011) for Rowson's experiences as a teacher. See Richard Brodhead, *Cultures of Letters* (Chicago: University of Chicago Press, 1993), particularly chapter 1, for a more extensive account of the relationship between sentimentalism and nineteenth-century educational reform. I address Brodhead's argument below.
33. Sentimentalists often critiqued traditional schooling in their work. See, for instance, Whitman's "Death in the School-Room" (1841), in which the narrator reassures readers that "[w]e are waxing toward that consummation when one of the old-fashioned schoolmasters, with his cowhide, his heavy birch-rod, and his many ingenious methods of child-torture will be gazed upon as a scorned memento of an ignorant, cruel, and exploded doctrine." Walt Whitman, "Death in the School-Room," *United States Magazine and Democratic Review*, August 1841, 177. Another later example is Louisa May Alcott's *Little Women* (1868–1869), where Mrs. March pulls Amy from school in chapter 7 after she is the victim of corporal punishment in the classroom. Louisa May Alcott, *Little Women* (New York: Penguin, 1989).

34. Harriet Beecher Stowe, *Uncle Tom's Cabin or, Life Among the Lowly* (New York: Penguin, 1986), 354, 357.
35. Stowe, *Uncle Tom's Cabin*, 407, 420, 612, 432.
36. Jane Tompkins, for instance, argues that sentimental fiction models itself on the educational tracts published by the Tract Society. See Jane Tompkins, *Sensational Designs* (New York: Oxford University Press, 1985), 152–154.
37. Brodhead, *Cultures of Letters*, 40, 17–18. Brodhead is careful to explain that "disciplinary intimacy," while omnipresent in antebellum culture, wasn't an institutional reality until a later historical moment: "It needs to be insisted that the middle-class social model, like the disciplinary plan that gave it its sense of mission, was far from being socially established in the antebellum decades. Even where it was accepted as an ideal, we always find intriguing disparities between this scheme and the organizations of actual lives in this period. ... But if this model was not established then, the antebellum decades were the time when the newly defined middle class began its push to establish its model as a social norm; and it is as an agent in this assertion that the theory of discipline through love (together with its anticorporal insistences) had its force. This theory supplied an emerging group with a plan of individual nurture and social structure that it could believe in and use to justify its ways; more, it helped shape and empower the actual institutions through which that group could impress its ways on others" (26–27).
38. The trajectory of Brodhead's argument is consistent with Grumet's in *Bitter Milk* (1988). Grumet writes: "The feminization of teaching became a form of denial as the female teachers in the common schools demanded order in the name of sweetness, compelled moral rectitude in the name of recitation, citizenship in the name of silence, and asexuality in the name of manners." Madeleine R. Grumet, *Bitter Milk* (Amherst: University of Massachusetts Press, 1988), 44.
39. See Lauren Berlant, *The Female Complaint* (Durham: Duke University Press, 2008), especially chapter 1.
40. Ann Douglas, *The Feminization of American Culture* (New York: Knopf, 1977), 3.
41. These three phases map more or less onto the schematic provided in chapter 13 of Gerald Graff, *Professing Literature: An Institutional History* (Chicago: University of Chicago Press, 2007).
42. Kermit Vanderbilt, *American Literature and the Academy: The Roots, Growth, and Maturity of a Profession* (Philadelphia: University of Pennsylvania Press, 1986), 84, 110, 126, 257. Renker, *The Origins of American Literature Studies*, 9.
43. For instance, the modernist conception of the literary is, as I've suggested, normally thought to have become active only after the First World War. But Henry James published his modernist art novels after the failure of his social-realist experiments in the 1880s, as Mark McGurl has argued—and indeed the origins of the modernist conception of the literary can be found even earlier in the nineteenth century, in the work of, say, Hawthorne and Poe. Similarly, the genteel tradition of American literature is often associated with Matthew Arnold; yet, as Mary Poovey has demonstrated, Arnold's understanding of organic form could be instrumentalized by formalists and modernists as well as the genteel. Mark McGurl, *The Novel Art: Elevations of American Fiction after Henry James* (Princeton: Princeton University Press, 2001), chapters 1

and 2. Mary Poovey, "The Model System of Contemporary Literary Criticism," *Critical Inquiry* 27, no. 3 (Spring 2001).

44. Accounts of this process include Nancy Glazener, *Reading for Realism* (Durham: Duke University Press, 1997), Alan Trachtenberg, *The Incorporation of America* (New York: Farrar, Straus and Giroux, 2007), and Michael Denning, *Mechanic Accents* (New York: Verso, 1987), along with Glazener, *Literature in the Making*; Shumway, *Creating American Civilization*; McGurl, *The Novel Art*, and Brodhead, *The School of Hawthorne*.

45. Nina Baym, "Early Histories of American Literature: A Chapter in the Institution of New England," *American Literary History* 1, no. 3 (Autumn 1989): 459–460. For a comprehensive account of *Uncle Tom's Cabin*'s publishing history, see Claire Parfait, *The Publishing History of Uncle Tom's Cabin, 1852–2002* (Aldershot: Ashgate, 2007). For more on genteel literary culture and its publishing apparatus, see Baym, "Early Histories of American Literature" and Brodhead, *The School of Hawthorne*, particularly chapter 3. For more on Scudder, see Brodhead, *The School of Hawthorne*, 58–60. In Brodhead's account, Stowe remains a decidedly peripheral figure in the genteel literary movement, a figure who "crashed Fields's system." Brodhead explains that "Ticknor and Fields became [Stowe's] publisher too, but only after she changed her European travel plans so as to ride home on the same ship with Fields in 1860, having, as she told Mrs. Fields, 'some other particular *business* to arrange with your husband'" (225 fn 22). I would argue that Brodhead is struggling in this footnote to fathom the literariness of Stowe's work during a historical moment (the late twentieth century) when the conjunction of the literary and the sentimental had become practically unthinkable.

46. John Erskine, *Leading American Novelists* (New York: Henry Holt, 1910), vii. Erskine named Stowe along with Charles Brockden Brown, James Fenimore Cooper, William Gilmore Simms, Nathaniel Hawthorne, and Bret Harte.

47. Vernon Louis Parrington, *Main Currents in American Thought*, vol. 2 (New York: Harcourt, Brace, 1930), 376. For the scholastic editions of *Uncle Tom's Cabin*, see Harriet Beecher Stowe, *Uncle Tom's Cabin or, Life Among the Lowly, Abridged for School Use with Sixty Illustrations* (Cleveland: World Publishing, c. 1920) and Harriet Beecher Stowe, *Uncle Tom's Cabin Abridged for Use in Schools with Sixty Illustrations* (Newark: Charles E. Graham, c. 1920). For more information on the World Publishing Company edition, see "This low-priced edition ... ," *Uncle Tom's Cabin & American Culture*, University of Virginia, accessed January 17, 2022, http://utc.iath.virginia.edu/childrn/wpchp.html.

48. Tompkins notes that the literary field underwent a radical restructuring under the New Critics: between the publication of Fred Lewis Pattee's *Century Readings for a Course in American Literature* (1919) and the publication of Perry Miller's *Major Writers of America* (1962), Tompkins writes, "the notion of who counted as a major writer and even the concept of the 'major writer' had altered dramatically," with Pattee's single volume study "contain[ing] hundreds of writers" and Miller's much larger study "contain[ing] only twenty-eight." Tompkins, *Sensational Designs*, 187.

49. Faye Halpern, "Beyond Contempt: Ways to Read *Uncle Tom's Cabin*," PMLA 133, no. 3 (2018): 637.

50. George Philip Krapp, Preface to *Tales of the Traveller with Selections from the Sketch Book*, ed. (Chicago: Scott, Foresman, 1901), 5.
51. Homer B. Sprague, "Suggestion for Teachers," in *Six Selections from Irving's Sketch-Book: With Notes, Questions, Etc., for Home and School Use*, ed. Homer B. Sprague (Boston: Ginn, 1878), xii.
52. Vanderbilt concedes, for instance, that "there is not space in this book to pursue the study of American literature at the precollege level," but suggests nevertheless that "the high schools were still, as in previous decades, more realistically attuned to our national literature than were the hidebound arbiters of college curricula." Vanderbilt, *American Literature and the Academy*, 191.
53. Guillory, *Cultural Capital*, xi. Guillory argues that literature became associated with conceptual and linguistic difficulty when "Standard English ... became the possession of nearly everyone with a grade-school education" (171). The reorganization of the "literary" under the New Critics after the rise of mass primary and secondary education helps explain not just the divergence of "literary" and "mass" culture, as Guillory argues. It also helps explain the hierarchization *within* literary culture between works that appear on the primary and high school syllabus and works that appear on the college and graduate school syllabus. Take, for instance, the schoolroom poets. Angela Sorby writes that the schoolroom poetic tradition was most firmly in place "between 1865 and 1917," and that it continued to be read "until at least the mid-twentieth century." The schoolroom poets were, of course, foundational to the genteel tradition that I've already described, and so their prominence in postbellum culture and postbellum institutions is not at all surprising. Sorby's more surprising revelation is that schoolroom poetry persisted after 1918 in the elementary and secondary school curriculum, as well as in adjacent institutions (museums, theaters, newspapers, magazines). Across these institutional spaces, Sorby writes, readers read the schoolroom poets to "perform (and perhaps negotiate) their roles as middle-class strivers." Placing Sorby and Guillory's arguments alongside one another, we can better understand the schoolroom tradition after 1918 as "lesser" literature, a literature that served as a vehicle of an aspirational middle-class subjectivity and national consciousness—a literature against which "more" and "better" literary works (the ones that are taught in college) asserted their greater literariness. Sorby, *Schoolroom Poets*, xiii, xxix.
54. See Samuel L. Knapp, *Lectures on American Literature: With Remarks on Some Passages of American History* (New York: Elam Bliss, 1829). "Most students probably did not get beyond the third [*McGuffey Reader*]. Not only were school terms short and attendance sporadic, but by the time children turned thirteen or fourteen, they were needed to work on farms and in factories, which made anything beyond basic literacy a luxury." Elliot J. Gorn, Introduction to *The McGuffey Readers: Selections from the 1879 Edition*, ed. Elliott J. Gorn (Boston: Bedford Books, 1998), 27. In the mid-nineteenth century, moreover, assigned reading in primary school was necessarily irregular and unstandardized, because students didn't have access to the same textbooks. A historian of Wisconsin education once wrote that "each child would bring to school whatever the family happened to have, often books that had been brought along by his parents when they came to Wisconsin. There were sometimes as many different textbooks in use in a school as there were children in attendance." Quoted in Kaestle, *Pillars*, 17.

55. Mae J. Evans, "How Much Work Is Done in American Literature in the High School, and by What Methods?" *School Review* 11, no. 8 (October 1903): 649. "The average time devoted to English literature, estimating five recitations weekly, six months of American to eight months of British," Evans writes (649). As William J. Reese explains, American literature began appearing on high school reading lists after the mid-nineteenth century. William J. Reese, *The Origins of the American High School* (New Haven: Yale University Press, 1995), 116.

56. "In Assembly, April 29, 1833," *Documents of the Assembly of the State of New York* 4, no. 333 (April 1833): 1.

57. *Seventh Annual Report of the State Commissioner of Common Schools to the Governor of the State of Ohio: For the Year Ending August 31 1860* (Columbus: Richard Nevins, 1861), 74.

58. For Irving's appearance in the McGuffey Readers see, for instance, William H. McGuffey, *McGuffey's Rhetorical Guide, or, Fifth Reader of the Eclectic Series: Containing Elegant Extracts in Prose and Poetry, with Copious Rules and Rhetorical Exercises* (Cincinnati: Winthrop B. Smith, 1844); *McGuffey's Newly Revised Rhetorical Guide, or, Fifth Reader of the Eclectic Series: Containing Elegant Extracts in Prose and Poetry, with Copious Rules and Rhetorical Exercises* (Cincinnati: Winthrop B. Smith, 1853); *McGuffey's New Sixth Eclectic Reader: Exercises in Rhetorical Reading, with Introductory Rules and Examples* (Cincinnati: Winthrop B. Smith, 1857); *McGuffey's New Fifth Eclectic Reader: Selected and Original Exercises for Schools* (Cincinnati: Wilson, Hinkie, 1866); *McGuffey's Sixth Eclectic Reader*, revised ed. (Cincinnati: Van Antwerp, Bragg, 1879); *McGuffey's Alternate Sixth Reader* (Cincinnati: Van Antwerp, Bragg, 1889); *McGuffey's Fifth Eclectic Reader*, revised ed. (New York: American Book Company, 1907); *McGuffey's Sixth Eclectic Reader*, revised ed. (New York: American Book Company, 1921).

59. For "Rip Van Winkle," see McGuffey, *McGuffey's Sixth Eclectic Reader*, revised ed. (Cincinnati: Van Antwerp, Bragg, 1879). For "Sleepy Hollow," see *McGuffey's Alternate Sixth Reader* (Cincinnati: Van Antwerp, Bragg, 1889).

60. Stanley T. Williams and Mary A. Edge, *A Bibliography of the Writings of Washington Irving* (New York: B. Franklin, 1970). Twenty-two pedagogical editions is only a rough estimate—not a perfect count. The texts I tagged as "pedagogical" in the bibliography were the ones explicitly marked "for school use." Other editions, not just pedagogical ones, may have appeared in schools.

61. See Washington Irving, *The Legend of Sleepy Hollow by Washington Irving*, ed. Albert F. Blaisdell (New York: Maynard, Merrill, 1883). See *Annual Reports of the President and the Treasurer of Harvard College, 1899–1900* (Cambridge: Harvard University Press, 1901), 95.

62. Washington Irving, *Six Selections from Irving's Sketch-Book: With Notes, Questions, Etc., for Home and School Use*, ed. Homer B. Sprague (Boston: Ginn, 1878), xi, xii, iii.

63. Irving, *Six Selections*, 69.

64. Leo Marx, *The Machine in the Garden* (New York: Oxford University Press, 2000), 3.

65. Brander Matthews, *An Introduction to the Study of American Literature* (New York: American Book Company, 1896), 5. Mary E. Burt, *Literary Landmarks: A Guide to Good Reading for Young People* (Boston: Houghton, Mifflin, 1890), 29–30, 67. Mildred

Cabell Watkins, *American Literature* (New York: American Book Company, 1894), 3, 3–4. Evans, "How Much Work Is Done," 652.
66. Watkins, *American Literature*, 44. Abby Willis Howes, *A Primer of American Literature* (Boston: D. C. Heath, 1909), 51. Carl Van Doren, *The American Novel* (New York: Macmillan, 1921), 159.
67. Hamlin Garland and Alice B. Stephens, *A Son of the Middle Border* (New York: Macmillan, 1922), 219.
68. Matthews, *An Introduction*, 95. Henry A. Beers, *An Outline Sketch of American Literature* (New York: Chautauqua Press, 1887), 161. William P. Trent, *A Brief History of American Literature* (New York: D. Appleton, 1905), 237 fn 1.
69. Fred Lewis Pattee, *A History of American Literature Since 1870* (New York: Century, 1917), 11, 10–11, 15. The aristocracy of the intellect, according to Pattee, includes William H. Prescott, John Lothrop Motley, Francis Parkman, James Russell Lowell, Charles Eliot Norton, Thomas Wentworth Higginson, Richard Henry Dana Sr., William Ellery Channing, Daniel Webster, George Ticknor, Edward Everett, George Bancroft, Henry Wadsworth Longfellow, and Oliver Wendell Holmes, along with Emerson, Thoreau, and Hawthorne.
70. Graff, *Professing Literature*, 214.
71. F. O. Matthiessen, *American Renaissance: Art and Expression in the Age of Emerson and Whitman* (New York: Oxford University Press, 1941), 121–122. Fiedler, *Love and Death*, 462–463.
72. Marx, *The Machine in the Garden*, 363, 364. Lionel Trilling, *The Liberal Imagination* (Garden City: Doubleday, 1953), xii–xiii. Lisi Schoenbach identifies Trilling as a representative figure of the discipline who remains invested in "a romanticized ideal" of modern literature as "an adversarial art that can flourish only outside institutions and free of habits." For Schoenbach, this investment has deformed literary studies' conception of modernism: "[S]tudies of modernism have been dominated too long by a central ideology of modernism: the ideology of rupture, opposition, and anti-institutionality." Lisi Schoenbach, *Pragmatic Modernism* (New York: Oxford University Press, 2011), 12.

I'll note here too that, if the New Critics and mid-century Americanists succeeded in establishing the hegemony of the anti-scholastic conception of literature, they were also at times very much aware of the paradoxical nature of their success. Trilling describes the experience of exposing his students to the revolutionary works of modernism inside an academic setting. "I venture to say that the idea of losing oneself to the point of self-destruction, of surrendering oneself to experience without regard to self-interest or conventional morality, of escaping wholly from societal bonds, is an 'element' somewhere in the mind of every modern person who dares to think of what Arnold in his unaffected Victorian way called 'the fulness of spiritual perfection.' But the teacher who undertakes to present modern literature to his students may not allow that idea to remain in the *somewhere* of his mind; he must take it from the place where it exists habitual and unrealized and put it in the conscious forefront of his thought. … I press the logic of the situation not in order to question the legitimacy of the commitment, or even the propriety of expressing the commitment in the college classroom (although it does seem odd!), but to confront those of us who do teach modern literature with the striking actuality of our enterprise." Lionel Trilling, "On the Teaching of Modern Literature," in *Beyond Culture* (New York: Viking Press, 1965), 30. Fiedler too was outraged by the American fascination with the "Good Bad Boy"—that archetypal character who, like Tom Sawyer, defies institutional norms and injunctions but in ways that endear him to institutional authorities: "In our national imagination, two freckle-faced boys, arm in arm, fishing poles over their shoulders, walk toward the river; or one alone floats peacefully on its waters, a runaway Negro by his side," Fiedler writes. "They are on the lam, we know ... from all the reduplicated female symbols of 'sivilization.' ... Such figures become constantly more false in their naivete, in their hostility to culture in general and schoolteachers in particular; and it scarcely matters whether they are kept in the traditional costume of overalls or are permitted jeans and sweaters decorated with high-school letters." Fiedler, *Love and Death*, 271.

73. Donald Pease writes that the mid-century Americanists "disclos[e]" themselves "as ideological when [they] produc[e] an *imaginary separation* between the cultural and the public sphere." It was this imaginary separation between the cultural (especially the literary) and the public sphere that the New Americanists sought to bridge. Donald Pease, "New Americanists: Revisionist Interventions into the Canon," in *Revisionary Interventions into the Americanist Canon*, ed. Donald Pease (Durham: Duke University Press, 1994), 8.

74. Jennifer Fleissner, "After the New Americanists: The Progress of Romance and the Romance of Progress in American Literary Studies," in *A Companion to American Literary Studies*, ed. Caroline F. Levander and Robert S. Levine (New York: Wiley-Blackwell, 2011), 180.

75. As Graff explains, the failure of American literary studies "has to do, again, with that dynamics of 'patterned isolation' with which we have been concerned before in this book. This is a pattern that has welcomed innovations, but so isolated them that their effect on the institution as a totality is largely nullified. American literature and cultural studies were merely *added* to the existing departments and fields, which did not have to adapt to them, quarrel with them, or recognize their existence to any sustained degree. Their influence has finally been assimilated, but quietly and in uncontroversial fashion." Graff, *Professing Literature*, 224–225.

76. Matthiessen, *American Renaissance*, x, x–xi.

77. Julie Ellison offers an account of sentimentalism that differs appreciably from the one narrated by feminists in the 1980s; the sentimental tradition, for Ellison, consists not strictly of antebellum American writers like Stowe, Susan Warner, and Maria Susanna Cummings, but of authors like Philip Freneau, Charles Brockden Brown, Royal Tyler, Phillis Wheatley, Sarah Wentworth Morton, and Ann Eliza Bleecker. According to Ellison, the "strategies of [sentimental] female authors only make sense in the context of the early cultural prestige of masculine tenderheartedness. The literature of sensibility respond[ed] to the reorganization of masculine experience in an expansionist parliamentary culture." Julie Ellison, *Cato's Tears and the Making of Anglo-American Emotion* (Chicago: University of Chicago Press, 1999), 9.

78. Matthiessen, *American Renaissance*, xvii.

Chapter 2

1. G. Stanley Hall, *Educational Problems*, vol. 2 (New York: D. Appleton, 1911), 445–446. Henry James, *The Portrait of a Lady* (New York: Penguin, 2011), 614.
2. Hall, *Educational Problems*, 443, 411, 445–446.
3. For a more in-depth account of Hall's literary output, see Dorothy Ross, *G. Stanley Hall: The Psychologist as Prophet* (Chicago: University of Chicago Press, 1972), 95, 257, 430. Also see Ross, 51, 63 for Hall's time at Antioch and Harvard.
4. The legions of instructors who have complained about teaching first-year composition testify to the fact that the school system assimilated composition "more easily" than reading (but still not easily). These complaints can be found as early as the late nineteenth century, when the "daily theme" exercise was invented. Looking back on his career as professor of English at Penn State University from 1895 to 1928, Fred Lewis Pattee asked, "Has not the daily theme in the colleges … been a damage to our literature?" Although Pattee bemoaned his school's composition instruction, describing the daily theme as a "goose-step drill" that "regiment[s] our writing youth with rules and patterns and … frown[s] on all who are out of step and original," his complaints signal just how widespread daily composition had become in English departments around the country at the time. Fred Lewis Pattee, *Penn State Yankee* (State College: Pennsylvania State College, 1953), 175.
5. Nancy Glazener, *Literature in the Making* (New York: Oxford University Press, 2016), 201. As Glazener goes on to explain, the "separation of speech from English" was "accomplished gradually over a number of decades." This separation occurred under the disciplinary divisions of the school and its mandate to distinguish expert credentialed readers from the amateurs in public literary culture; it "distanc[ed] academic literary studies further from public literary culture. Indeed, speech instructors' sense of their lower status within English departments may have been a byproduct of the deepening expert-amateur divide that privileged print. It wasn't just that academic literary studies and public literary culture had parted ways: academics also secured their expert status by disallowing features of public literary culture that might count as entertainment" (201).
6. Henry Adams, *Democracy: An American Novel* (New York: Meridian, 1983), 13, 17.
7. James, *The Portrait of a Lady*, 22, 25, 215, 614.
8. Adams, *Democracy*, 17.
9. Francis W. Parker, *Talks on Pedagogics* (New York: E. L. Kellogg, 1894), 195–196.
10. John Dewey, *The School and Society*, revised ed (Chicago: University of Chicago Press, 1915), 85, 142. See 154–155 for the extended rant against *Crusoe*. "Bookish" in Dewey's vocabulary stands for everything that's wrong with traditional schooling: learning that is rote, mechanized, unsocial, unembodied. He writes in *Democracy and Education*: "Formal instruction, on the contrary, easily becomes remote and dead—abstract and bookish, to use the ordinary words of depreciation." And later: "For when the schools depart from the educational conditions effective in the out-of-school environment, they necessarily substitute a bookish, a pseudo-intellectual spirit for a social spirit." John Dewey, *Democracy and Education* (New York: Macmillan, 1916), 9, 46. "Bookish" is also a word Hall adopts: "[T]he ideal child … will not be bookish, but will already

know a few dozen well-chosen books[.]" G. Stanley Hall, "The Ideal School as Based on Child Study," in *Journal of Proceedings and Addresses of the Fortieth Annual Meeting of the National Education Association* (Chicago: University of Chicago Press, 1901), 482. For a subsequent generation of intellectuals, Dewey's educational philosophy represented an anti-intellectualism endemic to American culture. Richard Hofstadter once wrote: "What many of Dewey's followers have done, with or without complete license from the master himself, is to attack the ideas of leadership and guidance, and the values of culture and reflective life, in favor of certain notions of spontaneity, democracy, and practicality." Richard Hofstadter, *Anti-Intellectualism in American Life* (New York: Knopf, 1963), 362. For Hofstadter on Hall, see 369–372.

11. John Dewey and Evelyn Dewey, *Schools of To-Morrow* (New York: E. P. Dutton, 1915), 124–126. Dramatization was one of the most popular forms of reading instruction implemented by Progressive educators. See Evelyn Dewey, *New Schools for Old* (New York: E. P. Dutton, 1919), 300, and Randolph S. Bourne, *The Gary Schools* (Cambridge: MIT Press, 1970), 52, for contemporary accounts of dramatization.

12. Bourne, *The Gary Schools*, 114. Dewey, *New Schools for Old*, 149. Jane Addams, *Twenty Years at Hull-House* (New York: Penguin, 1998), 70.

13. Edmund Burke Huey, *The Psychology and Pedagogy of Reading* (New York: Macmillan, 1908), 8.

14. Hall, *Educational Problems*, 477, 446, 478. Hall brags in *Educational Problems* about how much he read in college as part of an extracurricular "Junto": "It was thus that I rushed through Emerson, Carlyle, Macaulay, John Stuart Mill (everything but his Logic and Political Economy)," Hall writes, "Ruskin, DeQuincey, The Spectator-Tatler Series, Webster's Orations and some of Burke, Coleridge, Lamb, Tennyson, Wadsworth, Pope, Dryden, Byron, Bulwer-Lytton, much of Goethe and Schiller (in English), Shelley, Milton, Whittier, Longfellow, and many, I think I may say very many more, but not Browning despite my efforts" (480–481). Not Browning, despite his efforts: Hall's various qualifications are meant to testify to his otherwise comprehensive knowledge of human culture. He has only read "some" of Burke et al. and "much" of Goethe et al.; the "only" literary figure Hall appears not to have read is Browning.

15. Hall, *Educational Problems*, 485. Hall grew up in Ashfield, Massachusetts, where Charles Eliot Norton spent his summers. The two first met when Hall was on vacation from Williams College as an undergraduate, and their relationship continued through Hall's time at Harvard and beyond. See Ross, *G. Stanley Hall*, 20, 60, 82, 87, 110–112.

16. For more on the founding of Clark University and the exodus of two-thirds of the faculty in 1892, see Ross, *G. Stanley Hall*, 186–230. For more on the founding of the *American Journal of Psychology*, Hall's waning influence there, and his eventual falling out with William James, see Ross, 170–185, 230–50. For more about the shift in Hall's thinking after these two cataclysms, see Ross, 251–275.

17. Educational historian Lawrence Cremin describes the significance of Hall's work on the school system: "The shift was truly Copernican, its effects, legion. On the one hand, it hastened the acceptance of academic studies long barred from the school by reason of tradition, custom, or simple apathy. On the other hand, it opened the pedagogical floodgates to every manner of activity, trivial as well as useful, that seemed in some

way to minister to 'the needs of children.'" Lawrence A. Cremin, *The Transformation of the School* (New York: Knopf, 1961), 104.
18. Hall, "The Ideal School as Based on Child Study," 475. G. Stanley Hall, *Adolescence*, vol. 2 (New York: D. Appleton, 1905), 461. This last example is revealing syntactically, allowing Hall to present two ideas that aren't in tension as if they are. Of course, if some great men couldn't read and were better off for it, then the argument Hall presents makes sense—yes! children shouldn't be forced to read too suddenly or too early—and there's no need for Hall to add "but" and "although" at the beginning of the sentence.
19. Hall, *Educational Problems*, 481–482.
20. Henry James, *The Turn of the Screw and Other Short Fiction* (New York: Bantam, 1981), 47–49.
21. James, *The Turn of the Screw and Other Short Fiction*, 48, 33, 67, 98.
22. For a more comprehensive account of metanarrative and metanarration, see Monika Fludernik, *An Introduction to Narratology* (New York: Routledge, 2006), 60–63.
23. Henry James, *The Art of the Novel* (Chicago: University of Chicago Press, 2011), 171. James, *The Turn of the Screw*, 21.
24. Shoshana Felman has offered a very convincing poststructuralist reading of *The Turn of the Screw* along these lines. Shoshana Felman, "Turning the Screw of Interpretation," *Yale French Studies* no. 55/56 (1977): 94–207. I address the relationship between counter-reflexivity and poststructuralism below.
25. Henry James, *The Wings of the Dove* (New York: Oxford University Press, 1984), 89. Henry James, *The Golden Bowl* (Oxford: Oxford University Press, 1999), 306, 308.
26. Theodore Dreiser, *Sister Carrie* (New York: Modern Library, 1999), 438, 453–454.
27. Dreiser, *Sister Carrie*, 467, 649.
28. Dreiser, *Sister Carrie*, 531, 534.
29. Dreiser, *Sister Carrie*, 554–555, 561.
30. Lionel Trilling, *The Liberal Imagination* (Garden City: Doubleday, 1953), 8, 10–11, 9. For Trilling's description of James's moral realism, see the chapter "The Princess Casamassima," especially 84.
31. Edith Wharton, "Xingu," in *Roman Fever and Other Stories* (New York: Berkley, 1981), 18–19.
32. Wharton, "Xingu," 16, 25, 28.
33. Wharton, "Xingu," 21.
34. Wharton, "Xingu," 30–31, 41.
35. Edith Wharton, *The Age of Innocence* (New York: Scribner, 1996), 360. Edith Wharton, *Ethan Frome & Summer* (New York: Modern Library, 2001), 100. Sheila Liming offers an extensive account of Wharton's relationship to libraries (both real and fictional), and while Liming doesn't address "not reading" as a recurring feature of Wharton's writing, she does explain that libraries for Wharton were not divorced from real social experience but a site of it. Liming writes: "[T]hough it was Wharton's intention that the library should be used for reading, she did not foresee that reading as being chiefly of the solitary sort. When Wharton gathered friends at The Mount—as she did often, inviting them in small groups—the library was often the center of activity, a background for conversations taking place with and about books, within a space that enabled discourse in the form of reading aloud. ... This is another way of saying that

these kinds of social spaces enable an inspection of the social means of production because social space is, after all, 'a materialization of social being.'" Sheila Liming, *What a Library Means to a Woman* (Minneapolis: University of Minnesota Press, 2020), 43–44.
36. Wharton, *Ethan Frome & Summer*, 106–107, 213.
37. Charles W. Chesnutt, *Stories, Novels, and Essays* (New York: Library of America, 2002), 46, 58, 59, 70.
38. Sarah Orne Jewett, *The Country of the Pointed Firs and Other Stories* (New York: Modern Library, 2000), 7, 114–115.
39. Richard Brodhead, *Cultures of Letters* (Chicago: University of Chicago Press, 1993), 148. For Brodhead, *The Country of the Pointed Firs* dramatizes the narrator's escape from the city to the vacation town—from what he (following Jewett) calls the "cold page" of modern urban life to the oral folk culture of Dunnet Landing. The narrator's thematic escape is, according to Brodhead, in turn, formal as well: the book translates into its printed pages the (unprinted) experience of going on vacation. Brodhead writes: "Dunnet Landing is here offered as a place interchangeable with other places and possessable through print: reading it, consuming its representation in writing, will either remind us of the parallel vacation spot we already 'own' or supply us with such a spot if we don't yet 'possess' one" (148–149).
40. Alan Trachtenberg, *The Incorporation of America* (New York: Farrar, Straus and Giroux, 2007), 189 (emphasis in the original), 190. Benedict Anderson, *Imagined Communities* (New York: Verso, 2006), 45.
41. Michael North, *The Dialect of Modernism* (New York: Oxford University Press, 1998), np.
42. Gavin Jones, *Strange Talk* (Berkeley: University of California Press, 1999), 15. June Howard, *The Center of the World* (New York: Oxford University Press, 2018), 15.
43. For Freddy and Harry's educational history, see Hermione Lee, *Edith Wharton* (New York: Vintage, 2008), 26. For more on Wharton's relationship to her governess, see *My Dear Governess: The Letters of Edith Wharton to Anna Bahlmann*, ed. Irene Goldman-Price (New Haven: Yale University Press, 2012). See also Liming, *What a Library Means to a Woman*, chapter 1, which examines the library in Wharton's work as a space of self-making (especially of autodidacticism outside the realm of formal education).
44. Sarah Orne Jewett, Preface to *A Memorial of the One Hundredth Anniversary of the Founding of Berwick Academy* (Cambridge: Riverside Press, 1891), v-vi. Berwick Academy had a formative influence on Jewett. She helped assemble a memorial for the school's centennial; she also contributed articles to the school magazine, *The Berwick Scholar*. See Terry Heller, *Sarah Orne Jewett Text Project*, accessed April 5, 2021, http://www.sarahornejewett.org/soj/sj-index.htm.
45. See Joseph Katz, "Theodore Dreiser at Indiana University," *Notes and Queries* 13, no. 3 (1966). Here is Dreiser's account of his college acceptance: "[H]ow I ever came to get into the University without preliminary examinations. ... I cannot say. Apparently the correspondence between Miss Field [Dreiser's high school teacher] and Dr. Jordan resulted in my being admitted without examination, and so the coast was clear." Theodore Dreiser, *Dawn: An Autobiography of Early Youth*, ed. T. D. Nostwich (Santa Rosa: Black Sparrow Press, 1998), 375.

46. I discuss Chesnutt in greater depth in Chapter 6. For a quick overview of Chesnutt's relationship to formal education, see Brodhead, *Cultures of Letters*, 179–180. Brodhead argues that Chesnutt was able to pursue a literary career because he was a member of Du Bois's "talented-tenth": "What we see behind Chesnutt is an early stage in the emergence of a black professional class in the post–Civil War decades. This new class ... was largely formed in the new black normal schools and colleges of the postbellum period, and formed there in a double sense. Such schools are where black members of educated professions (teachers especially) got their education proper. And these schools were the scenes of their resocialization, their reacculturation into a Northern, bourgeois-based culture of self-discipline and high-achieverism that molded their ambitions and profoundly differentiated them from other groups. Chesnutt's ambition for a literary career is by no means a standard issue of such schools. But he won the preconditions for his ambition ... through the schooling in which he was so centrally enmeshed." Brodhead, *Cultures of Letters*, 183–184.
47. For more on the James's unusual upbringing, see Leon Edel, *The Life of Henry James*, vol. I. (New York: Penguin, 1977), 93–197, and R. W. B. Lewis, *The Jameses: A Family Narrative* (New York: Doubleday, 1991), 71–103.
48. By the turn of the twentieth century, the one-room district school had established itself in the popular imagination, but the high school and college experience were just beginning to circulate through mass and literary culture. I will devote more attention to representations of the school during this period in Chapter 5.
49. Dreiser, *Sister Carrie*, 114.
50. Guillory claims that assigning difficult literature whose meaning could only be extracted through close reading distinguished elite college and university graduates from the mass of elementary and high school graduates, who had access to standard language but not the symbolic capital embedded in "literature." John Guillory, *Cultural Capital: The Problem of Literary Canon Formation* (Chicago: University of Chicago Press, 1993), chapter 3.
51. Glazener, *Literature in the Making*, 141–142. Wharton, "Xingu," 24, 17–18.
52. Howard, *The Center of the World*, 48.
53. Fred Lewis Pattee, *A History of American Literature Since 1870* (New York: Century, 1917), 11.
54. Jackson Lears, *No Place of Grace* (Chicago: University of Chicago Press, 1994), 48.
55. Alexis De Tocqueville, *Democracy in America*, trans. Gerald Bevan (New York: Penguin, 2003), 215. *Rousseau's Émile or Treatise on Education*, abridged, and annotated by William H. Payne (New York: D. Appleton, 1911), 81.
56. William Wordsworth, "Expostulation and Reply," in *Wordsworth's Poetry and Prose*, ed. Nicholas Halmi (New York: W.W. Norton, 2014), 58: 4, 7–8. William Wordsworth, "The Tables Turned; An Evening Scene, on the Same Subject," in *Wordsworth's Poetry and Prose*, ed. Nicholas Halmi (New York: W.W. Norton, 2014), 60: 9, 30–32. The speaker in "Expostulation and Reply" defends his decision not to read by claiming that not-reading is a form of reading in which nature and the mind reciprocally "impress" themselves upon each other: "'Nor less I deem that there are Powers/Which of themselves our minds impress,/That we can feed this mind of ours/In a wise passiveness'" (59: 21–24).

57. Wordsworth's famous preface was first published in the 1800 edition as well.
58. Ralph Waldo Emerson, "The American Scholar," in *Nature and Selected Essays*, ed. Lazer Ziff (New York: Penguin, 2003), 88. Walt Whitman, "Preface 1855—*Leaves of Grass*, First Edition," in *Leaves of Grass and Other Writings*, ed. Michael Moon (New York: W. W. Norton, 2002), 622: 250–252, my emphasis.
59. Paul de Man, *Blindness and Insight* (New York: Oxford University Press, 1971), 17, 18. According to Guillory, the scope of the literary expanded under de Manian deconstruction and literary theory more broadly: "The equation of literature with rhetoric is not exclusive to de Manian deconstruction; it rather describes an identification which is more or less accepted within most versions of literary theory. It is by means of a shift onto the terrain of rhetoric that theory opens the literary syllabus to nonliterary works: theory discovers the 'rhetorical' in these works and in finding rhetoric it *refinds literature*. By referring all language to rhetoric the literary critic can read anything, but in practice this has meant reading non literary texts *as literary*." Guillory, *Cultural Capital*, 180. Glazener also notes the expansion of the literary in the wake of "literary and cultural theory; the influence of cultural studies, popular cultural studies, middlebrow studies, studies of fan cultures, and performance studies; and the canon wars." However, she argues too that the effects of this expansion were "muffled" because "familiar forms of analysis and figures from older canons continued to appear in curricula and scholarship." Glazener, *Literature in the Making*, 217.
60. I acknowledge that the Romantic lineage I've constructed, which extends into de Manian deconstruction, is not uncontroversial. Despite de Man's reverence for Rousseau, his relationship to Romanticism is notoriously fraught. Somewhat quizzically, de Man insists in the preface to *The Rhetoric of Romance* (1984) that *Allegories of Reading* (1979)—a book that would appear to be entirely about Romanticism—is "in no way a book about romanticism or its heritage." (Later in the same volume de Man would claim that an "affinity ... with Rousseau" can "well be considered to be a valid definition of romanticism as a whole"—and of course *Allegories of Reading* is enamored of Rousseau.) Paul de Man, *The Rhetoric of Romanticism* (New York: Columbia University Press, 1984), vii, 10.

According to Denise Gigante, Romanticism became ideologically suspect in the wake of de Manian deconstruction: "For those literary critics, historians, and theorists seeking to unmask the ideology of organic form—or Romantic ideology properly so-called, ideology in its deep heart's core—the discontinuities laid bare through the mechanics of artificial form (allegory) perform a useful critical function: because they cannot be glossed over through philosophical ideas about unity in multëity, they denaturalize, de-romanticize if you will, material reality, its conditions and forms. Seen as coterminous with organicism, Romanticism has thus become something of an embarrassment to literary historians." Of course, de Man's preference for allegory over symbolism by no means places his thinking outside the Romantic tradition. The shifting fortunes of various Romantic concepts (allegory, symbol, organic form) within literary studies, and the disparate scholarly projects these concepts have been enlisted to justify, are examples to me of the contradictions that have attended what I call below the "Romanticization" of US literary culture and the US educational system. These contradictions have only intensified as a Romanticized US literary culture has had to

make sense of itself within a Romanticized US educational system. Denise Gigante, *Life: Organic Form and Romanticism* (New Haven: Yale University Press, 2009), 34.
61. Andrew D. White, *Autobiography of Andrew D. White*, vol. I (New York: Century, 1905), 29. For more about Emerson's influence on modern educational reformers, see Burton Bledstein, *The Culture of Professionalism* (New York: W. W. Norton, 1978), 259–268. G. Stanley Hall, *Life and Confessions of a Psychologist* (New York: D. Appleton, 1923), 163. Dewey, *Democracy and Education*, 163. Dewey also went on to criticize Rousseau's "doctrine of accord with nature," claiming that it "meant a rebellion against existing institutions, customs, and ideals" (137). Dewey probably more than any other modern educator self-consciously sought to reconcile Romanticism and institutionality. For a quick sense of Pestalozzi's influence on American educational reform, see Lawrence A. Cremin, *American Education: The National Experience, 1783–1876* (New York: Harper and Row, 1980), 79, 85; for Fröbel's, see Lawrence A. Cremin, *American Education: The Metropolitan Experience, 1876–1980* (New York: Harper & Row, 1988), 547.
62. Fredric Jameson, *Postmodernism, or, the Cultural Logic of Late Capitalism* (Durham: Duke University Press, 1991), 255. Jameson goes to great lengths to show that de Man, in whose work "something suspiciously resembling aesthetic evaluation and literary study itself becomes triumphantly reestablished" (252), is not simply a traditionalist. Jameson does so by arguing that de Man's aesthetics are essentially ascetic and puritanical: "Aesthetic experience is thus again valorized [in de Man's writing], but *without* those tempting aesthetic pleasures that always used to seem its very essence, as though art were a pill one had to swallow in spite of its sugarcoating" (255). It's in this sense that, for Jameson, modernism is "incompletely liquidated" in de Man's work.
63. Catherine Gallagher and Stephen Greenblatt. *Practicing New Historicism* (Chicago: University of Chicago Press, 2000), 12.
64. For an example of this "literary" denaturalization, see the entry on "literature" in Raymond Williams, *Keywords* (New York: Oxford University Press, 1983). James English has explained that the "'sociology of literature' was something an American graduate student could not help but be aware of in the early 1980s": "The Birmingham scene was attracting considerable transatlantic attention. [Raymond] Williams's major early works were well known[.] ... [I]n the early 1980s his *Keywords* and *Writing in Society* both appeared in U.S. editions." James F. English, "Everywhere and Nowhere: The Sociology of Literature After 'the Sociology of Literature,'" *New Literary History* 58, no. 2 (Spring 2010): vii. Williams was also clearly an influence on Guillory's *Cultural Capital*: for instance, Guillory refers at one point to Williams's "very useful discussions of the ... term 'literature[.]'" It's strange, in this respect, that cultural studies remains largely peripheral to Guillory's analysis in *Cultural Capital*. At the end of his chapter on theory, Guillory remarks, "It is not yet clear whether a 'cultural studies' curriculum has been conceived which does not replicate the theoretical and hermeneutic paradigms of literary interpretation [specifically the rhetorical analysis of literary theory]. There is also evidence to suggest that cultural studies' new opening of the syllabus to popular or mass cultural works has been accompanied by a closure of the syllabus to the

same High Cultural philosophical texts which were so important to the dissemination of theory. Such a cultural studies syllabus would certainly not be inclusive of cultural products generally. If literary criticism is ever to conceptualize a new disciplinary domain, it will have to undertake first a much more theoretical reflection on the historical category literature; otherwise I suggest that new critical movements will continue to register their agendas symptomatically, by ritually overthrowing a continually resurgent literariness and literary canon." Guillory, of course, argues that the canon controversies and these methodological battles were a symptom of literature's loss of cultural capital. He does not, however, include his own project within the domain of cultural studies—one of his clearest methodological predecessors—nor does he reflect on the symptomatology of his own project, what his own "theoretical reflection on the historical category literature" suggests about this whole state of affairs. Guillory, *Cultural Capital*, 68, 265.

65. We might point to Graff's famous injunction—"teach the conflicts"—as evidence of this new conception of the literary as institutionally produced. Graff's injunction assumes that literary works can't bring coherence to their own institutional reception. "Texts," he explains, "don't tell us what to say about them." Gerald Graff, Preface to *Professing Literature: An Institutional History* (Chicago: University of Chicago Press, 2007), xviii.
66. Guillory, *Cultural Capital*, xii.
67. James English, *The Global Future of English Studies* (West Sussex: Wiley-Blackwell, 2012), 7.
68. Joseph North has argued that literary studies in the late seventies and early eighties embraced a "historicist/contextualist paradigm" that "was symptomatic of the wider retreat of the left in the neoliberal period and was thus a small part of the more general victory of the right." Joseph North, *Literary Criticism: A Concise Political History* (Cambridge: Harvard University Press, 2017), 3.
69. Christopher Newfield, *The Great Mistake* (Baltimore: Johns Hopkins University Press, 2016), 3–4.
70. See, for instance, Lesley Bartlett, Marla Frederick, Thaddeus Gulbrandsen, and Enrique Murillo, "The Marketization of Education: Public Schools for Private Ends," *Anthropology & Education Quarterly* 33, no. 1 (March 2002) and chapter 1 of Sonya Douglass Horsford, Janelle T. Scott, and Gary L. Anderson, *The Politics of Education Policy in an Era of Inequality* (New York: Routledge, 2019). Noliwe Rooks describes the transformation of public primary and secondary schools under neoliberalism as yet another example in US history of "segrenomics," where "separate, segregated, and unequal forms of education have provided the opportunity for businesses to make a profit selling school." Noliwe Rooks, *Cutting School* (New York: New Press, 2020), 2. Across these sources, the neoliberalization of public primary and secondary schools is understood to involve the celebration of "choice" in schooling—through, say, voucher programs or charter schools—as well as the casualization of teaching and the outsourcing of school administration to for-profit organizations, i.e., Rooks, *Cutting School*, 3–4, and Bartlett et al., "The Marketization of Education," 6.

Chapter 3

1. Gertrude Stein, *Writings 1903–1932* (New York: Library of America, 1998), 40; John Tetlow, "A Wider Range of Electives in College Admissions Requirements," *Educational Review* 11 (January–May 1896): 429.
2. In an 1879 speech, Joseph F. Tuttle, the president of Wabash College, described the incoherent training a typical incoming college student received: "[A] little Latin, a little English, a little mathematics, and a little natural science, with a male or female youth thrown in as a unifier! and we call the attenuated compound a 'Freshman.'" Quoted in William J. Reese, *The Origins of the American High School* (New Haven: Yale University Press, 1995), 74.
3. Charles Eliot, "A Wider Range of Electives in College Admissions Requirements," *Educational Review* 11 (January–May 1896): 421.
4. John Tetlow explains in the opening sentences of his response that he is in sympathy with the proposals, and that he "shall endeavor to maintain the same general thesis; but ... shall, of course, approach the subject from a somewhat different point of view." Tetlow, "A Wider Range of Electives," 428. He isn't being coy when he writes this. In fact, he and Eliot were professionally like-minded, and the two served on the influential Committee of Ten together. I explain this committee's work in more detail below.
5. Benedict Anderson, *Imagined Communities* (New York: Verso, 2006), 24–25.
6. Homi K. Bhabha, "DissemiNation: Time, Narrative, and the Margins of the Modern Nation," in *Nation and Narration*, ed. Homi K. Bhabha (New York: Routledge, 1990).
7. Wai Chee Dimock, *Through Other Continents: American Literature Across Deep Time* (Princeton: Princeton University Press, 2006), 133. Other scholars have followed Dimock's insistence that literary culture inherently resists standard time. Lloyd Pratt has argued that "[d]espite its often well-articulated wish that the nation share a consistent experience of time around which its members might unite, the available evidence contradicts the idea that this experience of national simultaneity actually came to pass [in the nineteenth-century United States]. This literature combined the temporalities of everyday life with the untimely chronotypes that its conventions of genre demanded and then redistributed both of them to Anglophone readers. This literature pluralized time. It did not purify it." Lloyd Pratt, *Archives of American Time: Literature and Modernity in the Nineteenth Century* (Philadelphia: University of Pennsylvania Press, 2010), 5. For an alternative account of the heterogeneous temporality of the nation, see Thomas M. Allen, *A Republic in Time: Temporality and Social Imagination in Nineteenth-Century America* (Chapel Hill: University of North Carolina Press, 2008).
8. Dimock, *Through Other Continents*, 132. As Gérard Genette writes, "[E]ven if the sequentiality of its components can be undermined by a capricious, repetitive, or selective reading, that undermining nonetheless stops short of perfect analexia: one can run a film backwards, image by image, but one cannot read a text backwards, letter by letter, or even word by word, or even sentence by sentence, without its ceasing to be a text." Gérard Genette, *Narrative Discourse: An Essay in Method*, trans. Jane E. Lewin (Ithaca: Cornell University Press, 1983), 34.

9. See David Harvey, *The Condition of Postmodernity* (Cambridge: Blackwell, 1990).
10. For a sociologist like Elias, it's impossible to think about time as a phenomenon that functions independently of collective human activity. "The study of time submitted here conveys a different picture," he writes. "The isolated individual no longer stands at the centre. Nature is no longer a world of objects existing outside the individual; society no longer only a circle of others among whom the individual finds himself as if by chance. Calendar time illustrates in a simple way how the individual is embedded in a world in which there are many other people, a social world, and many other natural processes, a natural universe." According to Elias, "the verbal form 'to time' makes it more immediately understandable that the reifying character of the substantival form, 'time,' disguises the instrumental character of the activity of timing." Unsurprisingly, Elias entertains a somewhat morbid fascination with tardiness in his essay: "[I]n a society with a high standard of individual self-control as regards time, one can observe over and again individuals who are compulsively unpunctual." Norbert Elias, *Time: An Essay*, trans. Edmund Jephcott (Cambridge: Blackwell, 1992), 28, 43, 19.
11. This has led Mark McGurl to describe modernism as an anti-bourgeois bourgeois aesthetic. See Mark McGurl, *The Novel Art* (Princeton: Princeton University Press, 1993), particularly the Introduction.
12. Charles Eliot returned his copy of *The Education of Henry Adams* without a word, positive or negative. Later he was reported to comment, "An overrated man and a much overrated book." Although the two were in disagreement on certain issues, they also shared a common hatred of traditional eighteenth-century American schooling. See Brook Thomas, "The Education of an American Classic: The Survival of Failure," in *New Essays on The Education of Henry Adams*, ed. John Carlos Rowe (Cambridge: Cambridge University Press, 1996). For a more in-depth account of Adams's bizarre "Letter to American Teachers of History," see Jennifer Fleissner, "The Ordering Power of Disorder: Henry Adams and the Return of the Darwinian Era," *American Literature* 84, no. 1 (2012): 31–60. And see *The Flowers of Friendship: Letters Written to Gertrude Stein*, ed. Donald Gallup (New York: Knopf, 1953), 22, for evidence that William James acknowledged the copy of *Three Lives* Stein sent to him in 1910.
13. My account of the course unit draws on Thorstein Veblen, *The Higher Learning in America* (New York: B. W. Huebsch, 1918); Ellsworth Tompkins and Walter H. Gaumnitz. *The Carnegie Unit: Its Origin, Status, and Trends* (Washington, DC: US Government Printing Office, 1954); Dietrich Gerhard, "The Emergence of the Credit System in American Education Considered as a Problem of Social and Intellectual History," *Bulletin of the American Association of University Professors* 41, no. 4 (1955): 647–668; Clyde W. Barrow, *Universities and the Capitalist State: Corporate Liberalism and the Reconstruction of American Higher Education, 1894–1928* (Madison: University of Wisconsin Press, 1990): and Mark Garrett Cooper and John Marx, *Media U* (New York: Columbia University Press, 2017). I address this body of scholarship in the coda below.
14. Charles Eliot, "Inaugural Address as President of Harvard College," in *Educational Reform: Essays and Addresses* (New York: Century, 1898), 13–14.

15. See Samuel Eliot Morison, *Three Centuries of Harvard 1636–1936* (Cambridge: Harvard University Press, 1936), 344–346 and Samuel Eliot Morison, *The Development of Harvard University: Since the Inauguration of President Eliot 1869–1929* (Cambridge: Harvard University Press, 1930), xliii.
16. See Gerhard, "The Emergence of the Credit System," 653–654.
17. *Report of the Committee on Secondary School Studies Appointed at the Meeting of the National Educational Association July 9 1892* (Washington, DC: US Government Printing Office, 1893), 6, 42.
18. In his annual report for the 1897–1898 academic year, Eliot writes: "A 'point' is estimated to represent approximately a half-year's work in one study, of four or five lessons a week, in school, or a 'half course' in College." *Annual Reports of the President and the Treasurer of Harvard College 1897–98* (Cambridge: Harvard University Press, 1899), 101. The "Special Report of the Committee on College-Entrance Requirements," published in 1899, states: "*Resolved*, That the committee recommends that the number of constants be recognized in the following proportion, namely: four units in foreign languages (no language accepted in less than two units), two units in mathematics, two in English, one in history, and one in science." "Special Report of the Committee on College-Entrance Requirements," in *Journal of Proceedings and Addresses of the Thirty-Eighth Annual Meeting* (Chicago: University of Chicago Press, 1899), 661.
19. *Annual Report—Carnegie Foundation for the Advancement of Teaching* (New York: The Foundation, 1906), 7.
20. *Annual Report—Carnegie Foundation*, 38.
21. Charles Eliot, "Sororities and Fraternities," Harvard University, President's Office, Records of the President of Harvard University, Charles W. Eliot, 1869–1930, Box 241, 1. Courtesy of the Harvard University Archives.
22. Charles Eliot, "Relations of American Colleges to Each Other," Harvard University, President's Office, Records of the President of Harvard University, Charles W. Eliot, 1869–1930, Box 241, 2–3. Courtesy of the Harvard University Archives.
23. Charles Eliot, "Address of President Charles William Eliot. Harvard Union. January 9 1905," *Harvard Monthly* 41, no. 5 (February 1906): 239, 241, 242.
24. Eliot, "Address," 243.
25. Jackson Lears, *No Place of Grace* (Chicago: University of Chicago Press, 1994), 296–297, 262.
26. See John Carlos Rowe, *Henry Adams and Henry James: The Emergence of a Modern Consciousness* (Ithaca: Cornell University Press, 1976); Keith R. Burich, "Henry Adams's *Annis Mirabilis*: 1900 and the Making of a Modernist," *American Studies* 32, no. 2 (Fall 1991): 104; Jennifer Fleissner, *Women, Compulsion, Modernity: The Moment of American Naturalism* (Chicago: University of Chicago Press, 2004); Gavin Jones, *Failure and the American Writer* (Cambridge: Cambridge University Press, 2014), 7.
27. Adams writes in *The Education*: "Historians undertake to arrange sequences,—called stories, or histories—assuming in silence a relation of cause and effect. These assumptions, hidden in the depths of dusty libraries, have been astounding, but commonly unconscious and childlike; so much so, that if any captious critic were to drag them to light, historians would probably reply, with one voice, that they had never supposed

themselves required to know what they were talking about." Henry Adams, *The Education of Henry Adams: An Autobiography* (Boston: Houghton Mifflin, 2000), 382.
28. Henry Adams, *Mont Saint Michel and Chartres* (New York: Penguin, 1986), 5.
29. Adams, *The Education*, 4, 318, 331, 355. For the trips with the Cameron's, see 332; with the Lodges, see 353, 367; with the Hays, see 360.
30. Adams, *The Education*, 7.
31. Quoted in Lears, *No Place of Grace*, 276. Lears explains that in this letter, "[a]s in other letters" to Hay, Adams "fancied himself a medieval warrior-farmer" (276).
32. Adams, *Mont Saint Michel*, 7, 10–11.
33. Washington Irving, *History, Tales, and Sketches* (New York: Library of America, 1983), 780–781. Edward Bellamy, *Looking Backward* (Mineola: Dover, 1996), 160. Mark Twain, *A Connecticut Yankee in King Arthur's Court* (Berkeley: University of California Press, 1984), 447. Gavin Jones offers an extended comparison of "Rip Van Winkle" and *The Education* along these lines: "If 'Rip Van Winkle' is finally a tale of recovery when the outcast Rip is welcomed back into the community, then the *Education* dwells in the gap of time that Irving opens." Jones, *Failure*, 8.
34. Adams, *The Education*, 311. Shared temporality is foundational to Adams's understanding of friendship in *The Education*. He writes at one point: "As usual, Adams found himself fifty years behind his time, but a number of belated wanderers kept him company, and they produced on each other the effect or illusion of a public opinion. They straggled apart, at longer and longer intervals, through the procession, but they were still within hearing distance of each other" (259). If Adams's friendships are based on a shared experience of time, a common feeling of belatedness, it seems important that even in affirming these friendships Adams suggests their fragility, as he and his friends continue to "straggl[e] apart," from one another, "at longer and longer intervals." The sad fact that even the best of friends must someday become unsynchronized with each other is suggested in *The Education* through the virtual absence of Clarence King after the "Failure" chapter described above. It is also suggested in the final sentences of *The Education*, when Adams imagines returning to society along with his two best friends, King and Hay, more than thirty years in the future, on their hundredth birthdays. These last sentences indulge a fantasy of *un*lonely time travel ("Perhaps some day—say 1938, their centenary—they might be allowed to return together for a holiday, to see the mistakes of their own lives made clear in the light of the mistakes of their successors" [505]), yet the fantasy is compromised from the very beginning, marked as merely a fantasy. After all, it's not really Adams, Hay, and King's centenary. While it's true that Hay and Adams were born in the same year, 1838, Clarence King wasn't born until 1842. Even in Adams's fantasies, time isn't perfectly coordinated.
35. Adams, *The Education*, 7–8, 9. The capacity to read order and structure into the disorder of historical experience constitutes for Adams education as such: "From cradle to grave this problem of running order through chaos, direction through space, discipline through freedom, unity through multiplicity, has always been, and must always be, the task of education" (12).
36. Adams, *The Education*, 12–13.
37. Adams, *The Education*, 9, 300, 302.

38. Adams, *The Education*, 301, 38, 60, 64–65, 75.
39. Adams, *The Education*, 288.
40. Fleissner, "The Ordering Power of Disorder," 55.
41. Eric Hayot, "Against Periodization; or, On Institutional Time," *New Literary History* 42, no. 4 (2011): 740. Caroline Levine, *Forms* (Princeton: Princeton University Press, 2015), 52.
42. Hayot, "Against Periodization," 742. Levine, *Forms*, 60.
43. Levine, *Forms*, 62. Levine's description of the "overlapping repetitions and durations" that constitute institutional life is indebted to Wai Chee Dimock's description of the reading process, where "time is made up not of fixed lengths but of lengths variably generated." See Levine, 54. Dimock traces her account of "offbeat reading" back to Einstein's critique of Newtonian physics, which is the same critique that Henry Adams explores (via Karl Pearson's *The Grammar of Science*) in *The Education*. As I suggested before, if for Dimock and Levine there is something liberating about the nonuniformity of time, for Adams the nonuniformity of time produces misery.
44. Münsterberg quoted in *The Flowers of Friendship*, 4. William James quoted in Alice P. Albright, "Gertrude Stein at Radcliffe: Most Brilliant Women Student," *Harvard Crimson*, February 18, 1959, http://www.thecrimson.com/article/1959/2/18/gertrude-stein-at-radcliffe-most-brilliant. See Brenda Wineapple, *Sister Brother: Gertrude and Leo Stein* (New York: G. P. Putnam's Sons), 1996, 48–154, for more on Gertrude's experiences in institutions of higher education and the relationships she formed there.
45. For the influence of the laboratory on Stein's work, see B. F. Skinner, "Has Gertrude Stein a Secret?," in *Critical Essays on Gertrude Stein*, ed. Michael J. Hoffman (Boston: G. K. Hall, 1986); Lisa Ruddick, *Reading Gertrude Stein: Body, Text, Gnosis* (Ithaca: Cornell University Press, 1990); Steven Meyer, *Irresistible Dictation: Gertrude Stein and the Correlations of Writing and Science* (Stanford: Stanford University Press, 2001); Liesl M. Olson, "Gertrude Stein, William James and Habit in the Shadow of War," *Twentieth Century Literature* 49, no. 3 (Autumn 2003): 328–359; Lisi Schoenbach, *Pragmatic Modernism* (New York: Oxford University Press, 2011); and Natalia Cecire, *Experimental: American Literature and the Aesthetics of Knowledge* (Baltimore: Johns Hopkins University Press, 2019).

    Sean McCann has drawn attention to Stein's eventual departure from her Progressive contemporaries and her critique of the faulty institutions of US life, but in the end McCann's focus is more on Stein's relationship to Progressive politics than her relationship to Progressive educational institutions. "As a student in Cambridge and Baltimore, [Stein] experienced first hand the rapid rise of the research university and the enthusiasm for expert knowledge it produced," McCann writes. "And as a member of several, overlapping groups of friends excited by the new opportunities and advantages that higher education provided, she knew well a number of young people who were involved in both the growing political movements to reshape American institutions and the closely related social-scientific theories that would often be called on to justify those changes. Her close friends at the turn of the century were aspiring scientists, educators, advocates for women's suffrage, and antiparty activists in the movement for urban reform." Sean McCann, *A Pinnacle of Feeling: American*

Literature and Presidential Government (Princeton: Princeton University Press, 2008), 37.

46. Hamilton served as the first head of the Bryn Mawr preparatory school. Weeks taught on the staff at Dr. Sachs's preparatory school in New York City; later she was associated with Barnard College, first as a teacher and eventually as an assistant dean. Hodder was a professor and Gwinn an instructor at Bryn Mawr College.
47. See Stein's republished themes in Rosalind S. Miller, *Gertrude Stein: Form and Intelligibility* (New York: Exposition Press, 1949), especially "An Annex Girl," "Ocean Symphony," "In a Psychological Laboratory," "April 13 1895," "April 25 1895," "April 26 1895," and "Kindergarten Just Got Out."
48. Brenda Wineapple discovered the "Degeneration" lecture in the mid-1990s. References are to the version of the lecture reprinted in *Sister Brother*. See Wineapple, *Sister Brother*, 151–154, 411–414.
49. Gertrude Stein, "The Value of College Education for Women." Archives and Manuscripts Collection, Baltimore Museum of Art, 2013, http://cdm15264.contentdm.oclc.org/cdm/ref/collection/p15264dc/id/454, 7–8.
50. Stein, "The Value of College Education," 8–10.
51. Gertrude Stein, "Degeneration in American Women," in *Sister Brother: Gertrude and Leo Stein* (New York: G. P. Putnam's Sons, 1996), 411, 412.
52. Stein, "Degeneration in American Women," 413.
53. Stein, "Degeneration in American Women," 413.
54. See Wineapple, *Sister Brother*, 151–154, for more on the context of and the reaction to the "Degeneration" lecture.
55. Stein, *Writings*, 163.
56. Stein, *Writings*, 150, 155.
57. Stein, *Writings*, 139, 211.
58. Stein, *Writings*, 185–186, 204, 213.
59. Stein, *Writings*, 128, 138, 144.
60. Stein, *Writings*, 3–4, 40. Adele's unpunctuality in *Q.E.D.* follows the exact same course as Jeff Campbell's in "Melanctha." "When the time came for keeping her engagement Adele for some time delayed," Stein writes. "In Helen's room she found a note explaining that being worried as it was so much past the hour of appointment, she had gone to the Museum as Adele had perhaps misunderstood the arrangement" (21). An early Stein critic once remarked on the importance of timing to Stein's work, but this intuition hasn't been adequately pursued in subsequent scholarship. In *Intellectual America* (1941), Oscar Cargill writes: "The author, with extraordinary penetration, has seen that it is not always the jarring of wills, the conflict of violent natures, which makes the course of love uncertain; she has discovered with the help of her medical science, that the element of 'timing' is an important one in passion." Quoted in Miller, *Gertrude Stein*, 34.
61. Stein, *Writings*, 155, 211, 163.
62. Gertrude Stein, "Portraits and Repetition," in *Lectures in America* (Boston: Beacon Press, 1985), 167. Gertrude Stein, "Composition as Explanation," in *Gertrude Stein: Selections*, ed. Joan Retallack (Berkeley: University of California Press, 2008), 220.

63. Gertrude Stein, "The Gradual Making of *The Making of Americans*," in *Lectures in America* (Boston: Beacon Press, 1985), 137.
64. Wendy Steiner, *Exact Resemblance to Exact Resemblance: The Literary Portraiture of Gertrude Stein* (New Haven: Yale University Press, 1978), 70. Michael North, *The Dialect of Modernism* (New York: Oxford University Press, 1998), 74. Cecire, *Experimental*, 110.
65. Veblen, *The Higher Learning in America*, 222. Barrow, *Universities and the Capitalist State*, 74, along with chapter 3. See also Morris Llewellyn Cooke, *Academic and Industrial Efficiency: A Report to the Carnegie Foundation for the Advancement of Teaching* (New York, 1910).
66. Cooper and Marx, *Media U*, 1, 20–21, 2.
67. Carnegie himself, as I suggested in the introduction, needed to be convinced of the value of formal education before he became a great educational philanthropist. In his *Gospel of Wealth* (1889), Carnegie advised his readers that "[i]f any millionaire is at a loss to know how to accomplish great and indisputable good with his surplus, here is a field which can never be fully occupied, for the wants of our universities increase with the development of the country." Yet he regularly made public statements denigrating the overeducated, and he often suggested that not going to school was more educational than going to school. In one of the essays collected in *The Empire of Business* (1902), "How to Win a Fortune," first published in 1890, he noted the absence of college graduates among the nation's leading businessmen and wrote: "The millionaires who are in active control started as poor boys, and were trained in that sternest but most efficient of all schools—poverty." The "prize-takers," he explained later in the same essay, have "too many years the start of the graduate. ... [W]hile the college student has been learning a little about the barbarous and petty squabbles of a far-distant past, or trying to master languages which are dead ... the future captain of industry is hotly engaged in the school of experience[.]" One reviewer at the time noted the contradiction in Carnegie's attitudes toward formal education: "These convictions [about the superiority of the prize-taker's education over the college student's] have not prevented the man who expresses them from creating a fund of ten million dollars, the income of which is to be used for assisting young Scotchmen to attend the universities of their native land." Andrew Carnegie, *The Gospel of Wealth* (New York: Carnegie Corporation, 2017), 24. Andrew Carnegie, *The Empire of Business* (New York: Doubleday, Page, 1902), 109, 110. M. W. Hazeltine, "Mr. Andrew Carnegie's New Book," *North American Review* 175, no. 548 (July 1902): 65. See also Ethan W. Ris for an account of Carnegie's progression from "fierce skepticism about college education to strong support for it." Ethan W. Ris, "The Education of Andrew Carnegie: Strategic Philanthropy in American Higher Education, 1880–1919," *Journal of Higher Education* 88, no. 3 (2017): 402. I take Carnegie to be representative of the industrial class's relationship to formal education: the emergence of the modern university and the modern curriculum coincided with the industrialists' conversion to the school's mission. And middle-class reformers were responsible for effecting this conversion.
68. "You taking a cut this morning?" Shreve asks Quentin in the opening pages of "June Second, 1910":
"Is it that late?"

[Shreve] looked at his watch. "Bell in two minutes." William Faulkner, *The Sound and the Fury*, ed. David Minter (New York: W. W. Norton, 1994), 49.
69. Michel Foucault, *Discipline and Punish*, trans. Alan Sheridan (New York: Vintage, 1995), 138.

Chapter 4

1. Theodore Roosevelt, "The Man with the Muck Rake," in *American Political Speeches*, ed. Terry Golway (New York: Penguin, 2012), 43. Edith Wharton, *The House of Mirth* (New York: Penguin, 1993), 35.
2. See Doris Kearns Goodwin, *The Bully Pulpit* (New York: New York: Simon & Schuster, 2013), 480–487, for more on "The Man with the Muck Rake" speech.
3. Stephen Crane, *Maggie: A Girl of the Streets and Other Tales of New York*, ed. Larzer Ziff (New York: Penguin, 2000), 78. Theodore Dreiser, *Sister Carrie* (New York: Modern Library, 1999), 653.
4. In the 1830s and 1840s, common school reformers like Horace Mann criticized the one-room district school's use of corporal punishment to discipline its student populations. I discuss Mann in greater detail below. For more on disinterestedness in the American liberal arts tradition, see Louis Menand, *The Marketplace of Ideas* (New York: W. W. Norton, 2010), 55.
5. Alfred Kazin, *On Native Grounds* (New York: Harcourt Brace, 1995), xxii–xxiii.
6. Erich Auerbach, *Mimesis: The Representation of Reality in Western Literature*, trans. Willard R. Trask (Princeton: Princeton University Press, 2003), 501, 502, 504, 505.
7. The fact that affect studies and literary sociology have so rarely been thought about together is perhaps surprising, considering that the two share a common lineage in disciplinary history through the figure of Raymond Williams. In his *Marxism and Literature* (1977), Williams, a literary sociologist, influentially called for an examination of "structures of feeling"—that is, of "meanings and values as they are actively lived and felt[.]" Williams's interest in structures of feeling was motivated by his methodological preference for Gramsci's "hegemony" as a site of analysis over Althusser's "ideology," a structure of feeling being in effect the lived experience of the hegemonic. Williams's preference for hegemony over ideology therefore also demanded a shift in critical focus away from the formal institutions of Althusser's "ideological state apparatus." For Williams, a structure of feeling precedes both institutions and formations as "social experience that is still *in process*"; by the time a structure of feeling has been "formalized, classified, and ... built into institutions and formations," a new structure of feeling "will usually have begun to form, in the true social present." Institutions are in this sense twice or even three-times removed from a structure of feeling, and, as such, they are not especially productive as an object of critical investigation. "Structures of feeling" would thus appear to conjoin the study of affect and the study of institutions, but instead it divides the two. Raymond Williams, *Marxism and Literature* (New York: Oxford University Press, 1977), 132. Merve Emre's *Paraliterary* (2017) helpfully begins to think through the connection between affect studies and literary sociology by exploring in one chapter the "dense apparatus of institutions, literary and

paraliterary texts, and human agents" that "connected practices of reading American literature to norms governing how and what one learned to feel towards others" in the mid-twentieth century. Emre's account focuses on discourses of institutional/literary feeling that were defined "through and against the ... more dominant reading practice" of the "dispassionate and avowedly non-concupiscent teachings of the New Critics[.]" Rather than consigning aberrant feelings to the institutional periphery, as Emre does, my account seeks to recuperate the disgustingness of dominant scholastic practices. Merve Emre, *Paraliterary: The Making of Bad Readers in Postwar America* (Chicago: University of Chicago Press, 2017), 56, 57.

8. The extensive body of scholarly and theoretical work on disgust includes Julia Kristeva, *Powers of Horror*, trans. Leon S. Roudiez (New York: Columbia University Press, 1982), William Miller, *The Anatomy of Disgust* (Cambridge: Harvard University Press, 1997), Winfried Menninghaus, *Disgust: The Theory and History of a Strong Sensation*, trans. Howard Eiland and Joel Golb (Albany: State University of New York Press, 2003), Martha C. Nussbaum, *Hiding from Humanity: Disgust, Shame, and the Law* (Princeton: Princeton University Press, 2005), and Sianne Ngai, *Ugly Feelings* (Cambridge: Harvard University Press, 2005). Drawing on this work, Benedict Robinson has explained that the invention of disgust "should be understood in relation to the emergence of a social world in which the work of producing and maintaining social boundaries was increasingly performed by forms of cultural competence, a socioaesthetics in which the visceral judgment of the senses is linked to other forms of boundary-drawing." Benedict Robinson, "Disgust c. 1600," *ELH* 81, no. 2 (Summer 2014): 555.

9. Francis W. Parker, *Talks on Pedagogics* (New York: E. L. Kellogg, 1894), 135. J. M. Rice, *The Public-School System of the United States* (New York: Century, 1893), 23. Randolph S. Bourne, *The Gary Schools* (Cambridge: MIT Press, 1970), 135.

10. John Dewey, "Interest in Relation to Training of the Will," in *The Early Works of John Dewey: 1882–1898*, ed. Jo Ann Boydston (Carbondale: Southern Illinois University Press, 1972), 113.

11. Jonathan Edwards, *A Treatise Concerning Religious Affections* (Bedford: Applewood Books, 2009), 148–149. Thomas Jefferson, *Writings* (New York: Library of America, 1984), 365.

12. Alcott, quoted in Lawrence A. Cremin, *American Education, The National Experience, 1783–1876* (New York: Harper and Row, 1980), 85. Horace Mann, *Lectures on Education* (Boston: W. M. B. Fowle and N. Capen, 1845), 11, 20–21, 22, 313. During his tenure as a secretary of the Massachusetts board of education, Mann found himself embroiled in a controversy surrounding corporal punishment. "That corporal punishment, considered by itself, and without reference to its ultimate object, is an evil, probably none will deny," Mann wrote. "Yet, with almost three thousand public schools in this State, composed of all kinds of children, with more than five thousand teachers, of all grades of qualification, to govern them, probably the evils of corporal punishment must be endured" (45). Richard Brodhead cites Mann's critique of corporal punishment (belied by the ambivalence of this last statement) as a reflection of the antebellum

middle class's theory of socialization, a theory that Brodhead calls "disciplinary intimacy." See Richard Brodhead, *Cultures of Letters* (Chicago: University of Chicago Press, 1993), chapter 1, especially pages 23–27.

13. Charles Eliot, "Inaugural Address as President of Harvard College," in *Educational Reform: Essays and Addresses* (New York: Century, 1898): 12. Louis Menand has described Eliot as "the greatest professionalizer in the history of American higher education." Louis Menand, *The Metaphysical Club* (New York: FSG, 2001), 230.
14. Dewey, "*Interest in Relation to Training of the Will*," 121, 122.
15. Dewey, "*Interest in Relation to Training of the Will*," 125, 126, 126.
16. Dewey, "*Interest in Relation to Training of the Will*," 129, 136–137, 127.
17. John Dewey, *The School and Society*, revised ed (Chicago: University of Chicago Press, 1915), 38, 38–39, 20.
18. Dewey, "*Interest in Relation to Training of the Will*," 14, 75. According to Sianne Ngai, "the interesting" first emerged as an aesthetic category under the German Romantics as a "specifically modern response to novelty and change … and, more precisely, to novelty as it necessarily arises against a background of boredom, to change against a background of sameness." The interesting is defined by its "low or minimal affect, its functional and structural generality, its seriality, its eclecticism, its recursiveness, and its future-oriented temporality." According to Ngai, the interesting has "a deeply pedagogical dimension" and the "capacity to produce knowledge" through both the way it "suspends a once-and-for-all appraisal, for a 'continuing attention directed at the object' that might help us figure out why it made us go 'Huh?' in the first place," and the way it "redefines the process of aesthetic evaluation as including the other's subsequent demand for us to justify it." But for Dewey, pedagogically speaking, interest functions not through the utterance of aesthetic appraisal but as a high affect mode unto itself, taking the deferrals and seriality that "the interesting" vocalizes and transforming them into a totalizing system. Sianne Ngai, "Merely Interesting," *Critical Inquiry* 34, no. 4 (Summer 2008): 789–790, 815.
19. Dewey, "*Interest in Relation to Training of the Will*," 128.
20. Frank Norris, *Novels and Essays*, ed. Donald Pizer (New York: Library of America, 1986), 509, 523–525.
21. Norris, *Novels and Essays*, 526, 527.
22. "A Western Realist," *Washington Times*, April 23, 1899, 20. Reprinted in *Frank Norris: The Critical Reception*, ed. Joseph R. McElrath Jr. and Katherine Knight (New York: Burt Franklin, 1981), 46. "A New and Promising American Novelist," *New York Tribune*, March 5, 1899, ill. Supp. Reprinted in *Frank Norris: The Critical Reception*, ed. Joseph R. McElrath Jr. and Katherine Knight (New York: Burt Franklin, 1981), 29. Charles F. Lummis, "Another California Novel," *Land of Sunshine* 11 (1889): 117. Reprinted in *Frank Norris: The Critical Reception*, ed. Joseph R. McElrath Jr. and Katherine Knight (New York: Burt Franklin, 1981), 52. "Novels of the Week," *Spectator* 83 (November 4, 1899): 662. Reprinted in *Frank Norris: The Critical Reception*, ed. Joseph R. McElrath Jr. and Katherine Knight (New York: Burt Franklin, 1981), 52. "Summer Reading," *Review of Reviews*, June 1899: 749. Reprinted in *Frank Norris: The Critical Reception*, ed. Joseph R. McElrath Jr. and Katherine Knight (New York: Burt Franklin, 1981), 51. Edward Abbot and Madeline Vaughn Abbot,

"McTeague," *Literary World* 30 (April 1, 1899): 99. Reprinted in *Frank Norris: The Critical Reception*, ed. Joseph R. McElrath Jr. and Katherine Knight (New York: Burt Franklin, 1981), 45. "A Rough Novel," *Boston Evening Transcript*, March 22, 1899, 10. Reprinted in *Frank Norris: The Critical Reception*, ed. Joseph R. McElrath Jr. and Katherine Knight (New York: Burt Franklin, 1981), 38.

23. Norris, *Novels and Essays*, 528.
24. Norris, *Novels and Essays*, 1110, 1111.
25. Although the McElrath and Crisler biography of Frank Norris downplays the role Harvard played in the composition of *Vandover* and *McTeague*, even its qualifications testify to the tremendous amount of conceptual and practical labor that happened within the university system: "Though he may not have begun in 1889 the *Vandover* we now know, he had already conceptualized to some degree such a work by the time he came to Harvard. And when he returned to San Francisco ... he had at least made considerable progress with the manuscript, perhaps considering it finished. But it was not until the end of the decade that he brought this novel to anything like completion[.] ... And *McTeague*, as Norris testified in his inscription to Gates, was in only 'embryonic' form by the close of the spring 1895 semester." Joseph R. McElrath Jr. and Jesse S. Crisler, *Frank Norris: A Life* (Champaign: University of Illinois Press, 2006), 160.
26. Norris can be read in this respect as a proto-Program Era writer, and Harvard as *the* proto-Program Era institution of creative writing. Mark McGurl finds one of the origins of the Program Era in Harvard's 47 Workshop, a playwriting class Thomas Wolfe attended in 1919. See Mark McGurl, *The Program Era* (Cambridge: Harvard University Press, 2009), chapter 1. As McElrath and Crisler suggest in their biography, though, the English 22 class Norris attended shared striking similarities with later creative writing programs. "In other words," they write, "Norris found himself on 27 September 1894, when classes commenced, in a workshop situation like those now conducted in creative writing programs of colleges and universities across the United States." McElrath and Crisler, *Frank Norris*, 154.
27. Norris, *Novels and Essays*, 1152, 1152, 1154.
28. The first of Herbert Spencer's essays to appear in the United States were his essays on education, published in 1860. Cremin speaks of Spencer's vast influence over the educational landscape of the late nineteenth century when he writes: "In contemplating the needs for knowledge that were emerging in metropolitan America, Herbert Spencer's question, 'What knowledge is most worth?' could not be avoided. And the various ways in which various groups of Americans answered that question and pressed their answers in the affairs of schools, colleges, cultural agencies, workplaces, philanthropic foundations, and government institutions remained at the heart of the politics of education throughout the twentieth century." Lawrence A. Cremin, *American Education: The Metropolitan Experience 1876–1980* (New York: Harper & Row, 1988), 377.
29. Donald Pizer has traced the influence of evolutionary thought in Norris's work from Darwin to Spencer to Le Conte. "The central themes of Norris's novels," Pizer writes, "are closely related to the foremost intellectual dilemma of his time: the conflict

between traditional concepts of God, man, and nature and a growing body of scientific knowledge impinging on those concepts." Donald Pizer, *The Novels of Frank Norris* (Bloomington: Indiana University Press, 1966), 3.

30. Émile Zola, "The Experimental Novel," in *The Experimental Novel and Other Essays*, trans. Belle M. Sherman (New York: Haskell House, 1964), 9, 29.
31. Georg Lukács, "Narrate or Describe?," in *Writer and Critic and Other Essays*, ed. and trans. Arthur Kahn (London: Merlin Press, 1970), 146.
32. Richard Hofstadter, *Social Darwinism in American Thought*, revised ed. (Boston: Beacon Press, 1955) 201. Lawrence A. Cremin, Foreword to *Herbert Spencer on Education*, ed. Andreas M. Kazamias (New York: Teachers College Press, 1966), vii.
33. My claim, that naturalism and the disgust naturalism luxuriates in are located on the threshold of institutional life, owes a debt to Jennifer Fleissner's *Women, Compulsion, Modernity* (2004), which situates the compulsiveness of American naturalism in-between (i.e., on the threshold of?) the genre's omnipotent "plots of triumph" and helpless "plots of decline": "[N]aturalism's most characteristic plot ... is neither the steep arc of decline nor that of triumph, but rather by an ongoing, nonlinear, repetitive motion—back and forth, around and around, on and on." Jennifer L. Fleissner, *Women, Compulsion, Modernity* (Chicago: University of Chicago Press, 2004), 9.
34. Norris, *Novels and Essays*, 279–280, 280.
35. Norris, *Novels and Essays*, 281.
36. Norris, *Novels and Essays*, 282, 284, 286.
37. Mark Seltzer has described naturalist writers as male technocrats obsessively setting out to manage female nature: "[W]hat unites these stories," Seltzer writes, "is the desire to project an alternative to biological reproduction, to displace the threat posed by the 'women people' (the reduction of men to 'mere animalcules' in the process of procreation) and to devise a counter-mode of reproduction (the naturalist machine)." Mark Seltzer, *Bodies and Machines* (New York: Routledge, 1992), 32. "Technocrat" might be too narrow a designation for Norris's own class position or the site of his class preoccupations: scholars have also read *McTeague* (and naturalism more broadly) as encoding the middle class's anxieties about its own liminality. June Howard argues that the "brute" in naturalism is a "representation of the relation of a relatively privileged class to conditions of existence that produce [a] range of inconsistent fears." June Howard, *Form and History in American Literary Naturalism* (Chapel Hill: University of North Carolina Press, 1985), 95. Gavin Jones reads *McTeague* as an expression of a specifically lower-middle-class worldview, "an intermediate class, situated in between the exploitative capitalist class and the proletariat, aspiring to a higher lifestyle yet prone to impoverishment and its anxieties." Gavin Jones, "The Embarrassment of Naturalism," *Amerikastudien/American Studies* 55, no. 1 (2010): 48.
38. Norris, *Novels and Essays*, 281. Norris's obsession with the threshold of institutional life can also be seen in his theory of romance and naturalism. Where realism, he argues, confines itself to "the smaller details of everyday life, things that are likely to happen between lunch and supper," naturalism sets itself on the extremes of life, where everything "is extraordinary, imaginative, grotesque even" (1107). Naturalism is thus a subset of romance, which "is the kind of fiction that takes cognizance of variations from the type of normal life" (1166).

39. Norris, *Novels and Essays*, 514–515.
40. Norris, *Novels and Essays*, 479, 304, 296.
41. Jack London, *The Radical Jack London: Writings on War and Revolution*, ed. Jonah Raskin (Berkeley: University of California Press, 2008), 143. For more about the founding of the ISS, see Anthony Arthur, *Radical Innocent: Upton Sinclair* (New York: Random House, 2006), 63–64, and Max Horn, *The Intercollegiate Socialist Society, 1905–1921: Origins of the Modern American Student Movement* (Boulder: Westview Press, 1979), 1–16.
42. Upton Sinclair, *The Autobiography of Upton Sinclair* (New York: Harcourt, Brace & World, 1962), 114. "Class War," *New York Times*, February 1, 1906, 8. Upton Sinclair, "The Call of the Wild: Jack London Put an 'If' on the Condemned Constitution," *New York Times*, February 5, 1906, 8. It's a little unclear whether London's speech at Yale was the same as the speeches he delivered in New York and at Harvard. Sinclair, who wasn't at Yale, insisted in his letter to the *Times* that the manuscripts for all the speeches were the same—and yet, the *Times*'s reaction to London's Yale speech suggests London may have deviated from the written script. See Horn, *The Intercollegiate Socialist Society*, 12–15, for more on London's campus visits.
43. Sinclair, *The Autobiography*, 329, 101.
44. Sinclair, *The Autobiography*, 113.
45. Sinclair's radical politics smashed against the school system throughout his professional career, particularly in the twenties, with his muckraking accounts of education, *The Goose-Step* (1922) and *The Goslings* (1924). In these books, Sinclair advocated an educational program centered on the study of labor conditions. In general, though, these books were focused less on solutions and more on problems, as Sinclair insisted over and over again that the early twentieth-century educational system "is not a public service, but an instrument of special privilege; its purpose is not to further the welfare of mankind, but merely to keep America capitalist." I will give a more detailed account of Sinclair's troubled relationship with the school system, including his relationship to Progressive educators, later in the chapter. Upton Sinclair, *The Goose-Step: A Study of American Education* (self-pub, 1923), 18.
46. See Arthur, *Radical Innocent*, 59–69, for a more detailed account of the publication of *The Jungle*.
47. Upton Sinclair, "What Life Means to Me," in *The Jungle*, ed. Clare Virginia Eby (New York: W. W. Norton, 2003), 351. For Sinclair, the food legislation that Roosevelt signed into law on June 30, 1906 was an indication of *The Jungle*'s failure, not its success. In the years following the novel's publication, Sinclair would go on record explaining how, despite the novel's many political achievements, he failed in his goal of writing the *Uncle Tom's Cabin* of wage slavery: "I wished to frighten the country by a picture of what its industrial masters were doing to their victims; entirely by chance I had stumbled on another discovery—what they were doing to the meat-supply of the civilized world" (351).
48. The Doubleday, Page and Co. edition of *The Jungle* is two-thirds the length of the serialized *Appeal* edition and represents the last of Sinclair's stumbling efforts to get the novel published after it was passed over by five publishing houses and Sinclair tried to self-publish it. Sinclair "never fully admitted the degree to which he was forced

to compromise his original intentions," Anthony Arthur explains in his biography of Sinclair. When Sinclair first met with the Doubleday editors, he "agreed to sit down with [them] and take out anything in *The Jungle* that seemed libelous or likely to offend readers needlessly." One point of contestation, Arthur explains, was the novel's title, which according to the editors was too provocative, linking the forces of capitalism to the violence of the wilderness. Although in the end Sinclair did refuse to change the novel's title, he still "dropped almost all reference other than the title itself to the world as a jungle." Arthur, *Radical Innocent*, 68–69.

49. F. P. Dunne, "Mr. Dooley on the Food We Eat," *Collier's*, June 23, 1906, 15–16.
50. Often when academics inventory the novel's disgusting passages they go immediately to the sausage scenes, following in Dunne's footsteps. See Irving F. Ahlquist, George O. Roberts, and David C. King, *Addison Wesley United States History* (Menlo Park: Addison-Wesley, 1984), 440–441; Thomas A. Bailey, David M. Kennedy, and Lizabeth Cohen, *The American Pageant*, 11th ed. (Boston: Houghton Mifflin, 1998), 691; and Christopher Phelps, "How Should We Teach 'The Jungle'?" *Chronicle of Higher Education* 52, no. 26 (March 2006): https://www.chronicle.com/article/how-should-we-teach-the-jungle/. "Worst of all," Arthur writes, "was the making of sausages." Arthur, *Radical Innocent*, 55.
51. Upton Sinclair, *The Jungle*, ed. Clare Virginia Eby (New York: W. W. Norton, 2003), 132, 131.
52. Sinclair, *The Jungle*, 132.
53. Sinclair, *The Jungle*, 97.
54. After the Pure Food and Drug Act passed, Albert J. Beveridge proclaimed: "In the history of reforms which have been enacted into law ... there has never been a battle which has been won so quickly and never a proposed reform so successful in the first contest." Quoted in Goodwin, *The Bully Pulpit*, 464.
55. Daniel J. Cohen, "By the Book: Assessing the Place of Textbooks in U.S. Survey Courses," *Journal of American History* 91, no. 4 (March 2005): 1405–1415. Phelps, "How Should We Teach 'The Jungle'?" Louise Carroll Wade, "The Problem with Classroom Use of Upton Sinclair's *The Jungle*," *American Studies* 32, no. 2 (Fall 1991): 79–101.
56. Henry Eldridge Bourne and Elbert Jay Benton, *American History* (Boston: D. C. Heath, 1925). Charles A. Beard and Mary R. Beard, *The Making of American Civilization* (New York: Macmillan, 1937), 593–594. For examples of *The Jungle*'s presence in US history textbooks, see, for instance, Mabel B. Casner and Ralph Henry Gabriel, *The Rise of American Democracy* (New York: Harcourt, 1938), 627; Robert E. Riegel and Helen Haugh, *United States of America: A History* (New York: Scribner's, 1947), 612; David Saville Muzzey, *Our Country's History* (Boston: Ginn, 1957), 424; Richard Hofstadter, William Miller, and Daniel Aaron, *The United States: The History of the Republic* (Englewood Cliffs: Prentice-Hall, 1957), 649; Henry F. Graff and John A. Krout, *The Adventure of the American People* (New York: Rand McNally, 1959), 475; Ruth Wood Gavian and William A. Hamm, *United States History* (Boston: D. C. Heath, 1960), 536–537; Richard N. Current, Alexander DeConde, and Harris L. Dante, *United States History* (Glenview: Scott, Foresman, 1967), 238; Laureat Bernard, Ralph Brande, and Don Sharkey, *America and Its People* (New York: Sadlier, 1968), 593–594; Ahlquist

et al., *Addison Wesley United States History*, 440–441; and Bailey et al., *The American Pageant*, 691.
57. See Arthur, *Radical Innocent*, 77–84, for the interpersonal difficulties that accompanied Roosevelt and Sinclair's attempts to bring about social change.
58. Riegel and Haugh, *United States of America*, 612. Hofstadter et al., *The United States*, 649. Bernard et al., *America and Its People*, 400. Bailey et al., *The American Pageant*, 691. Ahlquist et al., *Addison Wesley United States History*, 440–441.
59. See Sinclair, *The Jungle*, 27, 38, 97, 129, for other instances of Chicago's "sickening" atmospherics. Here is the whole sentence that describes the vomiting, followed by Jurgis's return to the plant: "[Jurgis] smelt so that he made all the food at the table taste, and set the whole family to vomiting; for himself it was three days before he could keep anything upon his stomach—he might wash his hands, and use a knife and fork, but were not his mouth and throat filled with the poison? And still Jurgis stuck it out! In spite of the splitting headaches he would stagger down to the plant and take up his stand once more" (127).
60. Ngai, *Ugly Feelings*, 332, 344.
61. In his *Autobiography*, Sinclair describes gathering an investment group and buying two or three acres of land that was once a boys' school for $36,000. Sinclair, *The Autobiography*, 129. Arthur claims Sinclair put up $16,000 of his own money for 160 shares of the property. Arthur, *Radical Innocent*, 91. Kevin Mattson describes the building as a former "juvenile detention institution." Kevin Mattson, *Upton Sinclair: And the Other American Century* (Hoboken: John Wiley, 2006), 70.
62. See Sinclair, *The Autobiography*, 132-133 for Sinclair's account of his relationship with John Dewey and William James. See Arthur, *Radical Innocent*, 91–92, for an account of Dewey's interest in Helicon Hall but ultimately his decision not to invest. In 1913 Sinclair enrolled his son David in a Progressive school outside of New York City. See Sinclair, *The Autobiography*, 195.
63. Mattson, *Upton Sinclair*, 80.
64. Sinclair, *The Autobiography*, 305.

Chapter 5

1. Georg Simmel, "The Sociology of Secrecy and of Secret Societies," *American Journal of Sociology* 11, no. 4 (January 1906): 486–487. "Yale's Society Elections," *New York Times*, May 24, 1907, 2.
2. Alexis De Tocqueville, *Democracy in America*, trans. Gerald Bevan (New York: Penguin, 2003), 596. Max Weber, *From Max Weber: Essays in Sociology*, trans. and ed. H. H. Gerth and C. Wright Mills (New York: Oxford University Press, 1946), 308, 309. H.H. Gerth and C. Wright Mills, "A Biographical View," in *From Max Weber: Essays in Sociology*, trans. and ed. H. H. Gerth and C. Wright Mills (New York: Oxford University Press, 1946), 7.
3. Richard White has explained that by 1896, "roughly 5.5 million of the country's 19 million adult men belonged to one or more fraternal lodges." According to White, these lodges "did not embrace fraternité"; "most," he explains, "were racially segregated, and the various lodges reflected clear class distinctions." In White's account, the

lodges "provided a counterpoint to the gendered evangelical home, mimicking it while purging it of women, and proclaiming their respect for and support of it." Richard White, *The Republic for Which It Stands: The United States During Reconstruction and the Gilded Age, 1865–1896* (New York: Oxford, 2017), 169, 170–171.
4. Simmel, "The Sociology of Secrecy and of Secret Societies," 469.
5. "Chicago Deans," *University of Chicago Alumni Magazine* 15, no. 1 (November 1922): 17.
6. See Fredric Jameson, *The Geopolitical Aesthetic* (Bloomington: Indiana University Press, 1992).
7. Louis Althusser, "Ideology and Ideological State Apparatuses (Notes towards an Investigation)," in *Lenin and Philosophy, and Other Essays*, trans. Ben Brewster (New York: Monthly Review Press, 2001), 103, 105. Pierre Bourdieu and Jean-Claude Passeron, *Reproduction in Education, Society and Culture*, 2nd ed., trans. Richard Nice (New York: Sage, 2000), 152–153. Pierre Bourdieu, *The State Nobility* (Stanford: Stanford University Press, 1996), 102.
8. Sara Ahmed, *On Being Included* (Durham: Duke University Press, 2012), 14, 117, 185, 21.
9. Bourdieu, *The State Nobility*, 83.
10. For the emergence of the one-room school as a free-floating cultural signifier, see Jonathan Zimmerman, *Small Wonder* (New Haven: Yale University Press, 2015), especially chapter 2. See also Allison Speicher, *Schooling Readers* (Tuscaloosa: University of Alabama Press, 2016), which examines a genre of "common school fiction" in the nineteenth-century United States.
11. Thorstein Veblen, *The Higher Learning in America* (New York: B. W. Huebsch, 1918), 102.
12. As I explained in the introduction to this book, Daniel A. Clark has argued that the emergence of campus fiction helped make higher education central to American notions of social mobility. Christopher Findeisen similarly has claimed that *Stover at Yale* (1912)—one of the centerpieces of this chapter—founded a genre, the campus novel, that proved highly influential in the post–World War II period. According to Findeisen, *Stover at Yale* dramatizes the "competition for symbolic prestige" at the turn of the century, and though at the time of its publication this was mostly an innocuous gesture because "the university ha[d] no economic function because its students [were] already wealthy," in the postwar period the campus novel performed pernicious social work by naturalizing a system where "true merit is valued because the system works to recognize and reward it." Daniel A. Clark, *Creating the College Man* (Madison: University of Wisconsin Press, 2010), 9–10. Christopher Findeisen, "'The One Place Where Money Makes No Difference': The Campus Novel from *Stover at Yale* Through *The Art of Fielding*," *American Literature* 88, no. 1 (2016): 81.
13. Owen Johnson, *Stover at Yale* (New York: Macmillan, 1968), 303, 307.
14. Fitzgerald writes: "[Amory] read voluminously all spring, the beginning of his eighteenth year: 'The Gentleman from Indiana,' 'The New Arabian Nights,' 'The Morals of Marcus Ordeyne,' 'The Man Who Was Thursday,' which he liked without understanding; 'Stover at Yale,' that became somewhat of a text-book[.]" F. Scott Fitzgerald, *This Side of Paradise* (New York: Charles Scribner's Sons, 1970), 33.

15. Frederick Rudolph, *The American College and University: A History* (Athens: University of Georgia Press, 1990), 87. Rudolph's attention to the "extracurriculum," though once controversial, has proved massively influential in educational historiography. John Thelin has explained that "in making the bold decision to emphasize student life within the history of higher education, [Rudolph] contributed an analytic model of the extracurriculum that transcends the particular episodes and cases he described. Although he gave specific attention to the literary societies, evangelical groups, debating teams, eating clubs, and athletic teams of the nineteenth and the early twentieth centuries, the truly significant finding is the residual pattern: such activities tended to go through a life cycle of being founded by and for students outside the formal course of study; successful activities then faced official sanctions or abolition, but, persistence as a 'renegade' activity ultimately led to faculty and administrative acquiescence and, ultimately, official adoption." John R. Thelin, "Rudolph Rediscovered," in *The American College and University: A History* (Athens: University of Georgia Press, 1990), xii–xiii.
16. See Helen Lefkowitz Horowitz, *Campus Life* (Chicago: University of Chicago Press, 1987), chapter 2, and Rudolph, *The American College and University*, chapter 7 for histories of fraternities and secret societies.
17. Lincoln Steffens, *The Autobiography of Lincoln Steffens* (New York: Harcourt, Brace, 1931), 120.
18. Charles Eliot, "Sororities and Fraternities." Harvard University. President's Office. Records of the President of Harvard University, Charles W. Eliot, 1869–1930, Box 241, 1. Courtesy of the Harvard University Archives.
19. John R. Thelin, *A History of American Higher Education* (Baltimore: Johns Hopkins University Press, 2004), 188. See chapter 5, especially pages 192–193, for more on the history of the student union.
20. "College as a Means of Stifling Thought," *New York Times*, March 25, 1912, 20.
21. Johnson, *Stover at Yale*, 8–9, 29, 96.
22. Johnson, *Stover at Yale*, 53, 19, 21. Le Baron at this moment is giving voice to the ideology of Rudolph's "collegiate way," an ideology with its origins at Yale. According to Thelin, Yale installed itself as the model of campus life in the second half of the nineteenth century precisely because its culture produced such strong public leaders. "This American collegiate ethos radiated from the influential core at Yale," Thelin writes. "The key to the 'college system' was 'Yale's democracy'—the proposition that campus activities provided a free forum in which students might demonstrate their talents and be judged on their merits by student peers. ... This was what made Yale famous as a training ground for future leaders: it provided the critical formula whereby American individualism could be reconciled with cooperation. Yale was America's college." Thelin, *A History of American Higher Education*, 166–167.
23. Johnson was very open about the inspiration for Brockhurst's character. See "College as a Means of Stifling Thought" and "Danger in the Snobbery of American Colleges," *New York Times*, March 31, 1912.
24. Johnson, *Stover at Yale*, 274, 27, 27, 30. For more on the Progressives' investment in publicity as a weapon of reform, see Jonathan Auerbach, *Weapons of Democracy* (Baltimore: Johns Hopkins University Press, 2015).

25. Owen Johnson, "The Social Usurpation of Our Colleges. I-Introductory Article," *Collier's*, May 15, 1912, 10.
26. See "Yale University," *New York Times*, May. 29, 1893, 11.
27. Johnson, *Stover at Yale*, 166, 166, 168.
28. Johnson, *Stover at Yale*, 300, 299, 274–275.
29. In the *Collier's* articles, Johnson advocates not another *secret* society but what we might think of as a *super* society, one that would be truly meritocratic and transparent, and would supersede all other societies. He writes: "There is one practical way to offset or to remedy the errors of undergraduate judgment, to reward the men of late development, and to bring into useful contact with the university those who could influence it for the best, and that is to establish what would be equivalent to a graduate Order of Merit, an organization possessing all the social attractions of a clubhouse, membership to which should be offered only to graduates of six years' standing, and that only for the most distinguished achievement. In other words, if our colleges are to continue on the basis of arbitrary social selection, what is imperatively needed is a corrective organization that would transcend all undergraduate organizations, that would be the greatest ambition to a college man and present to the outer world a true test of a college career." Johnson, "The Social Usurpation of Our Colleges," 39.
30. Johnson, *Stover at Yale*, 1–2.
31. Johnson, *Stover at Yale*, 65–66, 115.
32. Articles on *Stover at Yale* appeared in the *New York Times* on these dates: March 25 and 31, 1912; April 28, 1912; May 10, 11, 12, 17, 19, and 28, 1912; June 16, 1912; March 25, 1913; April 14, 1913; May 1, 12, and 17, 1913.
33. "Attack 'Stover at Yale,'" *New York Times*, May 10, 1912, 1. "College Men Agree with Owen Johnson," *New York Times*, May 11, 1912, 8. "Yale Juniors Now in Fix of 'Stover,'" *New York Times*, May 10, 1912, 12.
34. "Juniors Must Reform, Too," *New York Times*, March 17, 1913, 1. "'Tap Day' at Yale," *New York Times*, May 17, 1913, 10. For the sophomore's anti-secrecy campaign, see "Yale's Society's Revolt," *New York Times*, May 1, 1913, 10.
35. See Geoffrey Kabaservice, *The Guardians* (New York: Henry Holt, 2004), 62.
36. "Owen Johnson Recovered," *Berkeley Daily Gazette*, September 27, 1912, 4. W. W. Hawkins, "The Average Student at the University of Missouri: His Intellectual and Social Life," *University Missourian*, February 16, 1913, 3. David Starr Jordan, "At the Laying of the Corner-Stone of the Dwelling Hall," *Reed College Record*, no. 4 (December 1912): 29.
37. Calvin Trillin, *Remembering Denny* (New York: FSG, 1993), 92. Horowitz, *Campus Life*, 98.
38. See Thelin, *A History of American Higher Education*, 156–160.
39. This, as I've explained already, is the argument of Clark, *Creating the College Man*, which examines stories set in college that appeared in *Collier's* and the *Saturday Evening Post* from 1899 to 1915, and *Munsey's* and *Cosmopolitan* from 1893 to 1912.
40. Johnson, *Stover at Yale*, 6, 121.
41. Johnson, *Stover at Yale*, 56, 186.
42. Johnson, *Stover at Yale*, 88, 128, 130.
43. Johnson, *Stover at Yale*, 283, 294, 295, 296, 297.

44. Johnson, *Stover at Yale*, 282, 283, 286.
45. See David O. Levine, *The American College and the Culture of Aspiration, 1915–1940* (Ithaca: Cornell University Press, 1986), and Marcia Graham Synnott, *The Half-Opened Door* (West Port: Greenwood Press, 1979) for a more extensive account of the quota system.
46. Horowitz, *Campus Life*, 111.
47. Elizabeth A. Armstrong and Laura T. Hamilton, *Paying for the Party* (Cambridge: Harvard University Press, 2013), 219. "When the university structures the interests of a constituency into its organizational edifice, we say that it has created a 'pathway,'" Armstrong and Hamilton write. "The party pathway is built around an implicit agreement between the university and students to demand little of each other. Extremely affluent students with middling academic credentials are the ideal candidates. They cost the university the least, as they are not eligible for need-based aid, are less competitive for merit scholarships, do not demand much time with faculty, and do not require remedial assistance. Legacy policies … and comparatively low academic standards make it easier for universities to admit more of these students." Sororities and fraternities are key mechanisms within the party pathway; they provide solutions to the institutional problem of "how to systematically, and in large-scale fashion, generate 'fun'" for affluent students (15).
48. Thelin, *A History of American Higher Education*, 197.
49. Corwin quoted in Synnott, *The Half-Opened Door*, 155. See Synott, chapters 3, 4, and 5 for an account of Lowell's quota system and its adoption at Yale. Synnott explains that it "cannot be known for sure" whether Yale accepted Corwin's proposal for a formal quota on Jewish students, and therefore she insists that "considerable evidence point[s] to the existence of an *informal* quota" (155). We can say, though, that the impossibility of determining the distinction between a formal and an informal quota—the distinction between explicit and implicit discrimination in admissions practices—is very much a product of Corwin's "sawing wood and not saying a word" strategy.
50. Thomas Dixon Jr., "A Friendly Warning," in *Dixon's Sermons* (New York: F. L. Bussey, n.d.), 117–118. *Booker T. Washington Papers*, vol. 8, ed. Louis R. Harlan and Raymond W. Smock (Champaign: University of Illinois Press, 1979), 508. Dixon's suspicion may have first been aroused by Washington's refusal to review *The Leopard's Spots* after Dixon sent him a copy. (Dixon had assumed that Washington would approve of the novel's message.) See Dixon to Washington, March 4, 1902, in *Booker T. Washington Papers*, vol. 6, ed. Louis R. Harlan and Barbara Kraft (Champaign: University of Illinois Press, 1977), 413.
51. See Hugh C. Bailey, *Liberalism in the New South* (Coral Gables: University of Miami Press, 1969), 90, and John David Smith, "'My Books Are Hard Reading for a Negro': Tom Dixon and His African American Critics, 1905–1939," in *Thomas Dixon Jr. and the Birth of Modern America*, ed. Michele K. Gillespie and Randall L. Hall (Baton Rouge: Louisiana State University Press, 2006), 51.
52. See Thomas D. Clark, Introduction to *The Clansman* (Lexington: University Press of Kentucky, 1970), xii.
53. Thomas Dixon Jr., *The Leopard's Spots* (Ridgewood: Gregg Press, 1967), 464.

54. Thomas Dixon Jr., "Booker T. Washington and the Negro," *Saturday Evening Post*, August 19, 1905, 1, 2.
55. Booker T. Washington, *Up from Slavery* (New York: Oxford World's Classics, 2008), 128.
56. A Washington detractor, James Anderson, argues that Washington "urged the development of a black laboring class" and was "silent on the questions of black voting and officeholding"; therefore "his espousal of the Hampton Idea gave it more legitimacy than Armstrong ever did or could have. Somehow, the retrogressive and repressive tenets of the Hampton Idea rang differently when spoken by an ex-slave." A Washington defender, Robert J. Norrell, describes Washington as a "behind-the-scenes civil-rights activis[t]" and an "underground resistance operative" who deployed the indirect tactics of the "fox" rather than the direct tactics of the "lion" in his quest to improve black life at the turn of the century. James Anderson, *The Education of Blacks in the South, 1860–1935* (Chapel Hill: University of North Carolina Press, 1988), 73. Robert J. Norrell, *Up from History* (Cambridge: Harvard University Press, 2009), 189, 185.
57. Dixon, *The Leopard's Spots*, 101. Thomas Dixon Jr., *The Clansman* (Lexington: University Press of Kentucky, 1970), 98.
58. Dixon, *The Leopard's Spots*, 155. Dixon, *The Clansman*, 341.
59. Dixon, *The Leopard's Spots*, 248, 270. Thomas Dixon Jr., *The Traitor* (New York: Doubleday, Page, 1907), 203, 205.
60. Peter Brooks, *The Melodramatic Imagination* (New Haven: Yale University Press, 1976), 4, 15, 20.
61. Dixon, *The Clansman*, 300–301.
62. Roland Barthes, *S/Z*, trans. Richard Miller (New York: FSG, 1974), 17. Dixon, *The Clansman*, 301.
63. Dixon, *The Clansman*, 98.
64. Dixon, *The Clansman*, 262, 334, 335. During the reemergence of the modern Ku Klux Klan in the 1920s, Dixon "condemned the secret organization for ignoring civilized government and encouraging riot, bloodshed, and anarchy." Michele K. Gillespie and Randall L. Hall, Introduction to *Thomas Dixon Jr. and the Birth of Modern America* (Baton Rouge: Louisiana State University Press, 2006), 13.
65. Dixon, *The Leopard's Spots*, 171. Dixon, *The Traitor*, 53–54.
66. One could argue that Dixon's novelistic practices aren't a betrayal of the Klan's secretive practices but rather their purest fulfillment. As Elaine Frantz Parsons has argued, the dialectic between secrecy and publicity was central to the Klan's rise during Reconstruction. "The Ku-Klux's liminal status enabled northerners to maintain an ambiguous relationship to southern white-on-black violence," Parsons writes. "Ku-Klux claimed the ability to move undetected through the silent and darkened rural southern landscape, but they intended for accounts of their deeds to be published and circulated through a national newspaper exchange and wire system. That is, they claimed to be invisible to their local southerners, but visible to a national audience." Elaine Frantz Parsons, *Ku-Klux: The Birth of the Klan During Reconstruction* (Chapel Hill: University of North Carolina Press, 2015), 9–10.
67. Dixon, *The Clansman*, 1, 320.

68. My interpretation of Dixon's novels is consistent with Walter Benn Michaels's reading of the Reconstruction Trilogy. "[I]n Dixon," Michaels writes, "the state is saved by the Klan[.] ... Or rather, since Dixon actually imagines no pre-existing state to be saved from the empire by the Klan, the state is constituted or prefigured by the Klan, which offers racial identity as a kind of rehearsal for the collective identity required by the new modes of national citizenship. ... His point, then, is not the defence of the white state but the creation of the state through whiteness." Walter Benn Michaels, "Race into Culture," *Critical Inquiry* 18, no. 4 (Summer 1992): 663. I engage with Michaels's account in more detail below.
69. Michaels also published an earlier essay on Dixon—"The Souls of White Folk"—that was reworked in "Race into Culture" and *Our America* (1995). Walter Benn Michaels, "The Souls of White Folk," in *Literature and the Body: Essays on Populations and Persons*, ed. Elaine Scarry (Baltimore: Johns Hopkins University Press, 1988). Walter Benn Michaels, *Our America* (Durham: Duke University Press, 1995).
70. Michaels, "Race into Culture," 669.
71. Horace Kallen, *Culture and Democracy in the United States* (New York: Boni and Liveright, 1924), 43. Michaels, "Race into Culture," 684.
72. Michaels, "Race into Culture," 683.
73. Walter Benn Michaels, "The Political Economy of Anti-Racism," *nonsite.org*, issue 23, February 11, 2018, nonsite.org/article/the-political-economy-of-anti-racism.
74. Walter Benn Michaels, *The Trouble with Diversity* (New York: Henry Holt, 2006), 85. Walter Benn Michaels, "The Political Economy of Anti-Racism."
75. "Michaels's broadly sketched period piece offers no historical account of why the paradigm shifted when it did, nor of why (or if) it has remained in place since then." Werner Sollors, "Review of *Our America* by Walter Benn Michaels," *Modern Philology* 96, no. 4 (May 1999): 551.
76. Sollors, "Review of *Our America*," 551–552. See David Hollinger, *Postethnic America* (New York: Basic Books, 1995).
77. Donald Yacovone, "Textbook Racism," *Chronicle of Higher Education*, April 8, 2018, www.chronicle.com/article/How-Scholars-Sustained-White/243053. Yacovone has elaborated these findings in *Teaching White Supremacy* (New York: Pantheon, 2022).
78. Yacovone, "Textbook Racism."
79. The presence of Dixon's work in history textbooks complicates John Guillory's incisive point in *Cultural Capital* (1993) that literary works "must be seen as the vector of ideological notions which do not inhere in the works themselves but in the context of their institutional presentation, or more simply, in the way in which they are taught." A textbook, after all, aims to collapse together the "ideological notions" that "inhere" in the literary work itself with their "institutional presentation[.]" Put differently, the textbook obviates the instructor; it teaches itself. I address another complication that Dixon's reception history introduces to Guillory's argument below. John Guillory, *Cultural Capital: The Problem of Literary Canon Formation* (Chicago: University of Chicago Press, 1993), ix.

80. Althusser, "Ideology and Ideological State Apparatuses," 97, 98.
81. Bourdieu describes these as "processes of elimination" that take place "throughout the whole of the period spent in education[.]" Pierre Bourdieu, "The School as a Conservative Force: Scholastic and Cultural Inequalities," in *Contemporary Research in the Sociology of Education*, ed. John Eggleston, trans. J. C. Whitehouse (London: Methuen, 1974), 32.
82. Pierre Bourdieu, "Cultural Reproduction and Social Reproduction," in *Power and Ideology in Education*, ed. Jerome Karabel and A. H. Halsey (New York: Oxford University Press, 1977), 507.
83. The recuperation of Dixon's work in English departments in the wake of the culture wars therefore represents another complication to Guillory's argument in *Cultural Capital*—that literary works "must be seen as the vector of ideological notions which do not inhere in the works themselves but in the context of their institutional presentation, or more simply, in the way in which they are taught." Perhaps no longer used to champion white supremacy in the classroom, Dixon's fiction is now taught alongside W. E. B. Du Bois's *Souls of Black Folk* and David W. Blight's *Race and Reunion*, presumably to expose students to the nation's troubled racial history. In Chapter 6, I'll have more to say about multiculturalism and the rise of what many, including Michaels, have denounced as the neoliberalization of the school system. For now I'll simply say that the celebration of diversity in schools has occurred alongside the ruling class's divestment from ideology as a mechanism of social control and its embrace of punitive institutions or "repressive apparatuses." The increasing intimacy of, say, elementary schooling and policing is one indication that the educational system's ideological operations are becoming more and more unsettled under the emerging social order. In this historical moment, we can thus confidently invert Guillory's formulation and say that a literary work's "ideological notions" (I might suggest, instead, its political investments) will inhere not in its institutional presentation or the way it's taught but in the work itself: Dixon's fiction communicates to its readers the historical reality, belied by the scene of progressive pedagogy, that the school is fundamentally repressive. Guillory, *Cultural Capital*, ix. To understand the institutional presentation of Dixon's work in the contemporary educational system, see the entries for *The Leopard's Spots* and *The Clansman* on the *Open Syllabus Project*, which offers a "Most Frequently Assigned With" metric. *Open Syllabus Project*, accessed January 21, 2022, http://opensyllabusproject.org/.
84. Synnott, *The Half-Opened Door*, 25.
85. Evidence of the Klan's presence at Harvard in the 1920s continues to surface. An article in the *Harvard Crimson* recently unearthed a pair of photo negatives in the Boston Public Library's digital archives showing "10 men in bright white sheets, pointy hats, and cut-out eye holes, posed around the John Harvard Statue" during Class Day 1924. The photo description reads: "Harvard Klass Kow & Klans—students having fun." Simon J. Levien, "The Crimson Klan," *Harvard Crimson*, Mach 25, 2021, https://www.thecrimson.com/article/2021/3/25/harvard-klan-scrut/.

Chapter 6

1. William Grimshaw, *Official History of Freemasonry among Colored People in North America* (New York: Broadway Publishing, 1903), np. James Weldon Johnson, *Writings* (New York: Library of America, 2004), 15-16.
2. For a helpful overview of the historiography of the black secret society, see Paul Lawrence Dunbar, "Hidden in Plain Sight: African American Secret Societies and Black Freemasonry," *Journal of African American Studies* 16, no. 4 (2012): 622-637.
3. Sutton Griggs, *Unfettered* (New York: AMS Press, 1971), 242. Johnson, *Writings*, 1.
4. James Anderson, *The Education of Blacks in the South, 1860-1935* (Chapel Hill: University of North Carolina Press, 1988), 31.
5. Du Bois in *Dusk of Dawn* (1940) looked back on his confrontations with the "Tuskegee Machine" and reframed his criticism of Washington's work. He claimed that the Tuskegee Machine was pernicious not because it undermined his own proposal of higher education for the talented tenth, but because it "concentrate[d] influence" under one institutional framework. "After a time almost no Negro institution could collect funds without the recommendation or acquiescence of Mr. Washington," Du Bois writes. "Few political appointments were made anywhere in the United States without his consent. Even the careers of rising young colored men were very often determined by his advice and surely his opposition was fatal." The tendency to reduce African American pedagogical theory during this period to a single debate between Du Bois and Washington is symptomatic of the dynamic that Du Bois identifies here. W. E. B. Du Bois, *Writings* (New York: Library of America, 1986), 607.
6. It's in this context that Du Bois could proclaim in a 1930 Howard University commencement address: "Our college man today is, on average, a man untouched by real culture. He deliberately surrenders to selfish and even silly ideals, swarming into semiprofessional athletics and Greek letter societies, and affecting to despise scholarship and the hard grind of study and research." Quoted in John R. Thelin, *A History of American Higher Education* (Baltimore: Johns Hopkins University Press, 2004), 187. In *Dusk of Dawn*, Du Bois described his experience at Harvard in the late 1880s as intellectually stimulating precisely because he was socially ostracized and denied entrance to undergraduate campus culture. "In general, I asked nothing of Harvard but the tutelage of teachers and the freedom of the library," he wrote. "I was quite voluntarily and willingly outside its social life. I knew nothing of and cared nothing for fraternities and clubs." To the members of the Porcellian or the Fly, Du Bois was merely—to adopt that famous early twentieth-century campus derogatory epithet, as Du Bois himself does—a "grind[.]" Du Bois, *Writings*, 579, 580. See Thelin, *A History of American Higher Education*, 186-187, for an account of campus life in African American institutions of higher education.
7. Johnson, *Writings*, 127. *The Autobiography of an Ex-Colored Man*, as I describe it here, occupies a liminal place in Werner Sollors's typology of passing: on the one hand, passing is a source of psychic conflict, with "some characters ... withhold[ing] public acknowledgement of their closest of kin and dearest friends when they are in the presence of their new white allies or spouses"; on the other hand, "[p]assing may ... lead an individual who succeeds in it to a feeling of elation and exultation, an experience

of living as a spy who crosses a significant boundary and sees the world anew from a changed vantage point, heightened by the double consciousness of his subterfuge." Werner Sollors, *Neither Black Nor White Yet Both: Thematic Explorations of Interracial Literature* (New York: Oxford University Press, 1997), 253.

8. See Eurie Dahn and Brian Sweeney, "A Brief History of *The Colored American Magazine*," Digital Colored American Magazine, accessed August 15, 2018, http://coloredamerican.org/?page_id=70.

9. The Hamiltons' elevated class position, which Dunbar signals through Berry's membership in a fraternal order, inspires envy within the southern black community: but then again, the narrator asks sardonically, "[W]hen has not the aristocrat been the target for the plebeian's sneers?" Paul Laurence Dunbar, *The Sport of the Gods and Other Essential Writings*, ed. Shelley Fisher Fishkin and David Bradley (New York: Modern Library, 2005), 323. Membership in a black secret society continued to be coveted as a marker of class and prestige within the African American community throughout the twentieth century. Adolph Reed, writing in the late 1970s, described the black middle class's leadership in the civil rights movement as motivated in part by the limited social mobility this class was afforded at the midcentury: "Where ideology demanded nuclear physics and corporate management, black upward mobility rested with mortuary service and the Elks Lodge!" Adolph Reed, "Black Particularity Reconsidered," *Telos*, no. 39 (Spring 1979): 80.

10. Du Bois's *Black Reconstruction* (1935), for instance, describes secret schools that operated in the South during the decades leading up to the Civil War. "The most noted of the clandestine schools for free colored children was opened in Savannah in 1818 or 1819 by a colored Frenchman named Julien Froumontaine, from Santo Domingo," Du Bois writes. "Up to 1829, this school was taught openly. After December 22 1829, it was made a penal offense to teach a Negro or free person of color to read or write. Froumontaine's school, however, flourished clandestinely for many years[.]" W. E. B. Du Bois, *Black Reconstruction* (New York: Oxford University Press, 2016), 528. Richard White has described the formation of the African American "Council" or "Committee" in Shreveport, Louisiana, in 1873 as "a secret intelligence-gathering body that functioned in the area. Its members used only their first names; their meetings were secret; and neither politicians nor preachers could belong. The committee kept a record of Southern violence in Louisiana and other states." Richard White, *The Republic for Which It Stands: The United States During Reconstruction and the Gilded Age, 1865–1896* (New York: Oxford, 2017), 278.

11. Notable critics of ethnic studies external to the discipline include Kenneth Warren, who argues that African American cultural projects—including the Black Aesthetic movement, black literary feminisms, Afrocentrisms, and cultural studies—form part of a hegemonic bourgeois scheme that insists that "the truth about black political hopes and desires lies hidden within apparently nonpolitical activities." Kenneth W. Warren, *So Black and Blue: Ralph Ellison and the Occasion of Criticism* (Chicago: University of Chicago Press, 2003), 33. As I discussed last chapter, Walter Benn Michaels has also highlighted the "trouble with diversity" in higher education over the last few decades. See, for instance, Walter Benn Michaels, *The Trouble with Diversity* (New York: Henry Holt, 2006). Scholars working within Ethnic Studies have persistently

leveled even more devastating critiques of these programs than Warren and Michaels. In 1991, for instance, Ruth Wilson Gilmore argued that the "object status of African American women in the Academy is that of Decorative Beasts. ... Decorative Beasts are alibis for the Academy, living symbols whose occasional display is contingent on the Academy's need to illustrate certain ideological triumphs: capitalism, for example, or Christianity, equality, democracy, multiculturalism." Ruth Wilson Gilmore, "Decorative Beasts: Dogging the Academy in the Late 20th Century," *California Sociologist* 14, no. 1–2 (1991): 113. In 1995, David Palumbo-Liu understood that higher education's celebration of diversity could serve as a "mode of managing a crisis of race, ethnicity, gender, and labor in the First World and its relations with the Third as late capitalism has fostered the uneven flow of capital, products, materials, and labor across more porous borders." David Palumbo-Liu, Introduction to *The Ethnic Canon*, ed. David Palumbo-Liu (Minneapolis: University of Minnesota Press, 1995), 6. Later in this chapter, I address more recent critiques along these lines put forward by Roderick Ferguson and Jodi Melamed.

12. Frances Ellen Watkins Harper, *Iola Leroy* (New York: Penguin, 2010), 7–8. Charles W. Chesnutt, *Stories, Novels, and Essays* (New York: Library of America, 2002), 360.
13. Harper, *Iola Leroy*, 8.
14. Harper, *Iola Leroy*, 8.
15. Chesnutt, *Stories, Novels, and Essays*, 318.
16. Chesnutt, *Stories, Novels, and Essays*, 331, 367.
17. Chesnutt, *Stories, Novels, and Essays*, 348. "'So one of old Duncan McSwayne's notes went so far as that?,'" the judge asks Tryon. "'Well, well, I don't know where you won't find them'" (340).
18. Chesnutt, *Stories, Novels, and Essays*, 339.
19. In an 1882 speech, "Methods of Teaching" (1882), delivered to the North Carolina State Teachers Educational Association in Raleigh, Chesnutt reveals his familiarity with recent developments in pedagogy, referencing the work of earlier continental educational theorists like Johann Heinrich Pestalozzi and contemporary American educators like Francis Parker. Anticipating later debates between Du Bois and Washington, Chesnutt in the speech charted a middle path between industrial modes of education just then emerging and a liberal arts model of education for African Americans. For more on "Methods of Teaching," see SallyAnn H. Ferguson, "Signifying the Other: Chesnutt's 'Methods of Teaching'" in *Passing in the Works of Charles W. Chesnutt*, ed. Prothro Wright and Ernestine Pickens Glass (Jackson: University Press of Mississippi, 2010).
20. For more on Chesnutt's retreat from activism, see Joseph R. McElrath Jr., Robert C. Leitz III, and Jesse S. Crisler, Introduction to *Charles W. Chesnutt: Essays and Speeches*, ed. Joseph R. McElrath Jr., Robert C. Leitz III, and Jesse S. Crisler (Stanford: Stanford University Press, 1999), and Jesse S. Crisler, Robert C. Leitz, III, and Joseph R. McElrath Jr., Introduction to *An Exemplary Citizen: Letters of Charles W. Chesnutt, 1906–1932*, ed. Jesse S. Crisler, Robert C. Leitz, III, Joseph R. McElrath Jr. (Stanford: Stanford University Press, 2002). Though Chesnutt was elected to replace Du Bois on the Committee of Twelve for the Advancement of the Interests of the Negro Race in 1905, he was not exactly an active committee member; he did not answer letters in a

timely fashion from the committee's secretary, and he deferred many of his decisions to more prominent committee members, like Booker T. Washington. And though Chesnutt eventually became a member of a local branch of the NAACP, he did not draw a salary from the national office, like Du Bois, James Weldon Johnson, and William Pickens did. In an article, "Possibilities of the Negro" (1903), Du Bois chided Chesnutt for attending more to his professional life than his duties as a black activist and author. Instead of writing novels and stories, Chesnutt, according to Du Bois, indulged the "peculiar temptation," of "money making"—"[W]hy leave some thousands of dollars a year for scribbling about black folk?" Du Bois asked. Quoted in McElrath et al., "Introduction," xxix fn 7. He was being sarcastic.

21. See Frances Smith Foster, Introduction to *A Brighter Day Coming*, ed. Frances Smith Foster (New York: Feminist Press, 1990) for Harper's biography, especially her institutional affiliations.
22. Harper, *Iola Leroy*, 11, 36, 36.
23. Harper, *Iola Leroy*, 137, 146, 213, 184. Elizabeth McHenry has helpfully explained the importance of the literary society in both *Iola Leroy* and post-Reconstruction African American life. *Iola Leroy*, according to McHenry, "dramatizes the process of transformation to race consciousness and pious activism experienced by the members of the fictional literary society" and in doing so "offers itself as a means of making that process available to its readers." Elizabeth McHenry, *Forgotten Readers: Recovering the Lost History of African American Literary Societies* (Durham: Duke University Press, 2002), 188.
24. Harper, *Iola Leroy*, 134, 134, 198.
25. Harper, *Iola Leroy*, 187, 189, 190.
26. Harper, *Iola Leroy*, 97, 85, 89, 177.
27. Geoffrey Sanborn, "Mother's Milk: Frances Harper and the Circulation of Blood," *ELH* 72, no. 3 (2005): 695.
28. Harper, *Iola Leroy*, 107, 137.
29. Stonequist, quoted in Sollors, *Neither Black Nor White Yet Both*, 248. For scholarship on passing in Chesnutt's fiction, see, for instance, Cynthia A. Callahan, "The Confounding Problem of Race: Passing and Adoption in Charles Chesnutt's The Quarry," *MFS Modern Fiction Studies* 48, no. 2 (Summer 2002): 314–340, and John Sheehy, "The Mirror and the Veil: The Passing Novel and the Quest for American Racial Identity," *African American Review* 33, no. 3 (Fall 1999): 401–415. Ambivalence toward passing in *The House Behind the Cedars* is inscribed in the description of the house behind the cedars itself: "On dark or wintry days, the aspect of this garden must have been extremely sombre and depressing, and it might well have seemed a fit place to hide some guilty or disgraceful secret," the narrator explains. "But on the bright morning when Warwick stood looking through the cedars, it seemed, with its green frame and canopy and its bright carpet of flowers, an ideal retreat from the fierce sunshine and the sultry heat of the approaching summer." Chesnutt, *Stories, Novels, and Essays*, 275.
30. Chesnutt, *Stories, Novels, and Essays*, 312.
31. Chesnutt, *Stories, Novels, and Essays*, 328, 345, 351–352.
32. Chesnutt, *Stories, Novels, and Essays*, 369.

33. Chesnutt, *Stories, Novels, and Essays*, 401, 445.
34. My argument that Chesnutt is pessimistic about the institutional possibilities of secrecy might seem counterintuitive, especially since the critical recuperation of Chesnutt's work was premised on the idea that there lurked a secret, subversive voice under the veneer of his seemingly inoffensive stories about southern plantation life. According to Eric Sundquist, Chesnutt's work exploited a "counterpossibility" embedded in turn-of-the-century ethnology, which characterized black language as having "failed to meet civilized standards." This counterpossibility, as Sundquist describes it, was that black language represented "the sign of a secret world kept out of range of the middle-class mind, much as the coded languages of slavery had been deliberately kept out of the range of the masters." Sundquist's reading inevitably puts more weight on the conjure stories, and particularly the figure of Uncle Julius, with his unique ability to "signify upon and destroy, even while wearing the disguise of, plantation literature and the racial conceptions that supported it." Sundquist himself acknowledges, however, that Chesnutt's writing underwent a shift after the conjure tales, a shift that meant that by the time he wrote *The Marrow of Tradition*, he had disavowed conjure. My reading of *The House Behind the Cedars* describes this shift from the conjure of the early tales to what we might think of as the explicitness of the *The Marrow of Tradition* as one in which the secret has, thematically and formally, been renounced. We can better understand Chesnutt's changing fortunes in the white publishing world through the lens of this renunciation: if William Dean Howells originally supported Chesnutt as a "sweet" African American writer, he would eventually cool to Chesnutt's later work for its confrontational subject matter. In a letter Howells wrote to Henry Blake Fuller in 1901 after reading *The Marrow of Tradition*, he exclaimed, "Good Lord! How such a negro must hate us." Quoted in McElrath et al., *Charles W. Chesnutt*, xxiv. Eric Sundquist, *To Wake the Nations: Race in the Making of American Literature* (Cambridge: Harvard University Press, 1993), 311, 450.
35. Sutton Griggs, *Imperium in Imperio* (New York: Modern Library, 2003), 44–45.
36. Griggs, *Imperium in Imperio*, 46–47.
37. Lavelle Porter describes *Imperium in Imperio* as one of the first black academic novels. See Lavelle Porter, *The Blackademic Life* (Evanston: Northwestern University Press, 2019), chapter 2. For Griggs's educational background, see Tess Chakkalakal and Kenneth W. Warren, Introduction to *Jim Crow, Literature, and the Legacy of Sutton E. Griggs*, ed. Tess Chakkalakal and Kenneth W. Warren (Athens: University of Georgia Press, 2013). Griggs was interested in campus culture beyond the secret society; in his fifth and final novel, *Pointing the Way* (1908), he offers a vivid description of a college football game. See Sutton Griggs, *Pointing the Way* (New York: AMS Press, 1974), chapter 10, "Conroe Driscoll."
38. Griggs, *Imperium in Imperio*, 26, 129, 125.
39. Griggs, *Imperium in Imperio*, 5.
40. Griggs, *Imperium in Imperio*, 163, 163, 167.
41. Dickson Bruce, for instance, believes that "Griggs seems to have been especially unaware and unable to come to grips with the ambiguities that were so strong in black ideas and concerns during the late nineteenth and early twentieth centuries."

Dickson Bruce, *Black American Writing from the Nadir: The Evolution of a Literary Tradition, 1877–1915* (Baton Rouge: Louisiana State University Press, 1992), 156. Maria Karafilis argues that *Imperium in Imperio* "lays out several strategies for political action without wholeheartedly endorsing any." Maria Karafilis, "Oratory, Embodiment, and US Citizenship in Sutton E. Griggs's 'Imperium in Imperio,'" *African American Review* 40, no. 1 (Spring 2006): 140. Kenneth Warren provides the most convincing account of Griggs's conservatism, insisting that "despite Griggs's penchant for staging debates among his characters—and despite the variegated surface of his fictions—he does lay out a rather consistent program for political action in the South that centers on responding to disenfranchisement." Kenneth Warren, "Perfecting the Political Romance: The Last Novel of Sutton Griggs," in *Jim Crow, Literature, and the Legacy of Sutton E. Griggs*, ed. Tess Chakkalakal and Kenneth W. Warren (Athens: University of Georgia Press, 2013), 260.

42. Griggs, *Imperium in Imperio*, 133.
43. Griggs, *Imperium in Imperio*, 36–37, 56, 79, 119.
44. Griggs, *Imperium in Imperio*, 108–109. Sutton Griggs, *Overshadowed* (Freeport: Books for Libraries Press, 1971), 120–123. Sutton Griggs, *The Hindered Hand* (Miami: Mnemosyne, 1969), 117–121.
45. Griggs, *Overshadowed*, 12. Griggs, *Unfettered*, 210. Griggs, *Imperium in Imperio*, 113.
46. Caroline Levander, "Sutton Griggs and the Borderlands of Empire," in *Jim Crow, Literature, and the Legacy of Sutton E. Griggs*, ed. Tess Chakkalakal and Kenneth W. Warren (Athens: University of Georgia Press, 2013), 30.
47. D. A. Miller, *Hidden Hitchcock* (Chicago: University of Chicago Press, 2016), 4, 18.
48. Miller, *Hidden Hitchcock*, 1, 16.
49. Toni Morrison, *Playing in the Dark* (Cambridge: Harvard University Press, 1992), 5, 8–9.
50. Morrison, *Playing in the Dark*, 10, 8.
51. In 1969, the University of Michigan Press also reprinted many of Charles Chesnutt's most important works in paperback. For more on the recuperation of *Iola Leroy*, see Eric Gardner, "Rediscovering Frances Ellen Watkins Harper," *OUPBlog*, October 17, 2015, https://blog.oup.com/2015/10/frances-harper-forest-leaves/.
52. Jodi Melamed, *Represent and Destroy* (Minneapolis: University of Minnesota Press, 2011), 36, 46.
53. Roderick A. Ferguson, *The Reorder of Things* (Minneapolis: University of Minnesota Press, 2012), 12–13.
54. Ferguson, *The Reorder of Things*, 6.
55. See Gavin Wright, *Sharing the Prize* (Cambridge: Harvard University Press, 2013) for an account of the economic transformations that preceded the civil rights movement and the economic consequences that followed in the movement's wake.
56. Melinda Cooper, *Family Values* (New York: Zone Books, 2017), 247.
57. Cooper, *Family Values*, 250–251, 252–253
58. The evidence I cite in the paragraph above is from Simon Torracinta, "Extinction Event," *n+1*, May 28, 2020, https://www.nplusonemag.com/online-only/online-only/extinction-event/. On the "tuition limit," see Dan Nemser and Brian Whitener, "The

Tuition Limit and the Coming Crisis in Higher Education," *New Inquiry*, March 26, 2018, https://thenewinquiry.com/the-tuition-limit-and-the-coming-crisis-of-higher-education/: "[T]he higher-education sector, which is facing, at all levels, a tuition limit, appears to be entering a period of sustained crisis," they write.

In 2017, Annie McClanahan explained, "Between 2001 and 2013, the average wage for workers with a bachelor's degree declined 10 percent. The current unemployment rate among recent college graduates is nearly identical to the national average rate of unemployment. Of those fortunate enough to have a job, half of university graduates have jobs that do not require a college degree. Because this is happening at the same time that college costs have increased many times faster than the rate of inflation, and given the costs of paying off student debt, 25% of US universities, by one estimate, now offer students a negative return on their 'investment.' For many students today, then, the cost of an education is greater than the lifetime income gains." In McClanahan's account, this is all an indication that the university is "becoming much less successful at guaranteeing positive economic outcomes for its graduates." McClanahan writes: "Precisely because the university is increasingly disconnected from the economy as a whole—because it is increasingly irrelevant to or superfluous within an economy that now needs fewer educated workers than ever before—the language of human capital and economic outcomes has emerged as a kind of defense mechanism against the potentially revolutionary political consequences of this reality." Annie J. McClanahan, "Becoming Non-Economic: Human Capital Theory and Wendy Brown's *Undoing the Demos*," *Theory & Event* 20, no. 2 (2017): 516–517.

59. Wendy Brown has argued that neoliberalism "configures human beings exhaustively as market actors, always, only, and everywhere as *homo oeconomicus*." Under this regime, "[a] student might undertake charitable service to enrich her college application profile" and "a parent might choose a primary school for a child based on its placement rates in secondary schools who have high placement rates in elite colleges[.]" The scholastic examples are not incidental here: for Brown, neoliberalism has "shr[unk]" the "value of higher education"—and really, in her account, all education—to "individual economic risk and gain, removing quaint concerns with developing the person and citizen or perhaps reducing such development to the capacity for economic advantage." Wendy Brown, *Undoing the Demos* (New York: Zone Books, 2015), 31, 23. Annie McClanahan has claimed quite convincingly that Brown's description of neoliberalism as the "becoming-economic of the non-economic" is actually a description of a particular class's experience of the economic realities of the long downturn; it is the "introduction of economic exigencies into the lives of a group—white, educated, upper middle-class citizens of the developed world—formerly protected from them." McClanahan goes on to insist that the people most directly subjected to neoliberal disciplinary regimes aren't deluded by the rhetoric of entrepreneurialism but instead experience "a kind of irrational exuberance from below": McClanahan's students "do not believe that they will own homes like their parents do, they do not believe that they will move up the ladder of social mobility, they do not believe they will have stable, meaningful work. They do not think their degree is an investment in their future[.] ... They do not think they will ever be out of debt." McClanahan, "Becoming Non-Economic," 512, 519, 518. For the "gig"-ification of higher education itself,

see Adrianna Kezar, Tom DePaola, and Daniel T. Scott, *The Gig Academy* (Baltimore: Johns Hopkins University Press, 2019).

60. For more on the policing of surplus populations under deindustrialization, see Ruth Wilson Gilmore, *Golden Gulag* (Berkeley: University of California Press, 2007), and Chris Chen, "The Limit Point of Capitalist Equality," *Endnotes*, no. 3 (September 2013), https://endnotes.org.uk/issues/3/en/chris-chen-the-limit-point-of-capitalist-equality. Chen is self-consciously seeking to reconcile two strains of thought—Marxism and Afropessimism—that have been understood as hostile to each other. Chen's essay centers the history of capitalism on unwaged rather than wage labor and takes Frank Wilderson's description of the black subject—terrorized outside of those industrial settings, like the factory, where workers are traditionally the victims of exploitation—as the figure of the proletariat as such. See Frank Wilderson III, "Gramsci's Black Marx: Whither the Slave in Civil Society?" *Social Identities* 9, no. 2 (2003): 225–240.

61. Elementary and secondary schools have increasingly outsourced their disciplinary procedures to juvenile courts and the police, who maintain an active presence on campuses around the country. Far from embracing a disciplinary program in which difference is insidiously affirmed, these schools have enforced an allegedly antiquated regime in which race remains quite obviously a site of domination. Though black children made up 16 percent of the student population during the 2011-2012 academic year, they accounted for 31 percent of in-school arrests. Black students were also three times more likely to be expelled than white students, and black girls were suspended at higher rates than girls of any other race or ethnicity and at higher rates than most boys too. See "Civil Rights Data Collection: Data Snapshot (School Discipline)," United States Department of Education Office for Civil Rights, March 21, 2014, https://www2.ed.gov/about/offices/list/ocr/docs/crdc-discipline-snapshot.pdf.

62. See Colleen Flaherty, "Canaries in a 'Toxic Mine,'" *Inside Higher Ed*, May 5, 2020, https://www.insidehighered.com/news/2020/05/05/professors-ohio-u-say-faculty-cuts-cant-just-be-blamed-covid-19 for an account of the "May Day Massacre" at Ohio University, where both non-tenure-track and tenure-track faculty were told that their contracts wouldn't be renewed. These cuts included the one tenure-track faculty member in the school's African American studies program and the one full-time instructional faculty member in the women's and gender studies program. Even before the pandemic, there were many high-profile cases across the country where assistant professors in ethnic studies programs were denied tenure. Kate Taylor, "Denying a Professor Tenure, Harvard Sparks a Debate over Ethnic Studies," *New York Times*, October 14, 2021, https://www.nytimes.com/2020/01/02/us/harvard-latinos-diversity-debate.html.

63. Henry Louis Gates Jr., *The Signifying Monkey: A Theory of Afro-American Literary Criticism* (New York: Oxford University Press, 1988), 45, 49, 53, 67, 82, 82. Emphases mine.

64. Gates, *The Signifying Monkey*, 46, 47.

65. Griggs, *Imperium in Imperio*, 38

Bibliography

120 Years of American Education: A Statistical Portrait. Edited by Thomas D. Snyder. US Department of Education, Office of Educational Research and Improvement, National Center for Education Statistics, 1993.
Abbot, Edward, and Madeline Vaughn Abbot. "McTeague." *Literary World*, April 1, 1899, 99. Reprinted in *Frank Norris: The Critical Reception.* Edited by Joseph R. McElrath Jr. and Katherine Knight, 45–46. New York: Burt Franklin, 1981.
Adams, Henry. *Democracy: An American Novel.* New York: Meridian, 1983.
Adams, Henry. *The Education of Henry Adams: An Autobiography.* Boston: Houghton Mifflin, 2000.
Adams, Henry. *Mont Saint Michel and Chartres.* New York: Penguin, 1986.
Addams, Jane. *Twenty Years at Hull-House.* New York: Penguin, 1998.
Adorno, Theodor. *Aesthetic Theory.* Translated by Robert Hullot-Kentor. Minneapolis: University of Minnesota Press, 1997.
Ahlquist, Irving F., George O. Roberts, and David C. King. *Addison Wesley United States History.* Menlo Park: Addison-Wesley, 1984.
Ahmed, Sara. *On Being Included.* Durham: Duke University Press, 2012.
Albright, Alice P. "Gertrude Stein at Radcliffe: Most Brilliant Women Student." *Harvard Crimson*, February 18, 1959. http://www.thecrimson.com/article/1959/2/18/gertrude-stein-at-radcliffe-most-brilliant.
Alcott, Louisa May. *Little Women.* New York: Penguin, 1989.
Allen, Thomas M. *A Republic in Time: Temporality and Social Imagination in Nineteenth-Century America.* Chapel Hill: University of North Carolina Press, 2008.
Althusser, Louis. "Ideology and Ideological State Apparatuses (Notes towards an Investigation)." In *Lenin and Philosophy, and Other Essays*, 85–126. Translated by Ben Brewster. New York: Monthly Review Press, 2001.
Alves, Jaime Osterman. *Fictions of Female Education in the Nineteenth Century.* New York: Routledge, 2009.
Anderson, Benedict. *Imagined Communities.* New York: Verso, 2006.
Anderson, James. *The Education of Blacks in the South, 1860–1935.* Chapel Hill: University of North Carolina Press, 1988.
Annual Report—Carnegie Foundation for the Advancement of Teaching. New York: The Foundation, 1906.
Annual Reports of the President and the Treasurer of Harvard College 1897–98. Cambridge: Harvard University Press, 1899.
Annual Reports of the President and the Treasurer of Harvard College, 1899–1900. Cambridge: Harvard University Press, 1901.
Armstrong, Elizabeth A., and Laura T. Hamilton. *Paying for the Party.* Cambridge: Harvard University Press, 2013.
Arthur, Anthony. *Radical Innocent: Upton Sinclair.* New York: Random House, 2006.
"Attack 'Stover at Yale.'" *New York Times*, May 10, 1912.
Auerbach, Erich. *Mimesis: The Representation of Reality in Western Literature.* Translated by Willard R. Trask. Princeton: Princeton University Press, 2003.

Auerbach, Jonathan. *Weapons of Democracy*. Baltimore: Johns Hopkins University Press, 2015.
Bailey, Hugh C. *Liberalism in the New South*. Coral Gables: University of Miami Press, 1969.
Bailey, Thomas A., David M. Kennedy, and Lizabeth Cohen. *The American Pageant*. 11th ed. Boston: Houghton Mifflin, 1998.
Bailyn, Bernard. *Education in the Forming of American Society*. Chapel Hill: University of North Carolina Press, 1960.
Bakhtin, Mikhail. *The Dialogic Imagination*. Edited by Michael Holquist, translated by Caryl Emerson and Michael Holquist. Austin: University of Texas Press, 1981.
Barrow, Clyde W. *Universities and the Capitalist State: Corporate Liberalism and the Reconstruction of American Higher Education, 1894–1928*. Madison: University of Wisconsin Press, 1990.
Barthes, Roland. *S/Z*. Translated by Richard Miller. New York: FSG, 1974.
Bartlett, Lesley, Marla Frederick, Thaddeus Gulbrandsen, and Enrique Murillo. "The Marketization of Education: Public Schools for Private Ends." *Anthropology & Education Quarterly* 33, no. 1 (March 2002): 5–29.
Baym, Nina. "Early Histories of American Literature: A Chapter in the Institution of New England." *American Literary History* 1, no. 3 (Autumn 1989): 459–488.
Baym, Nina. "Melodramas of Beset Manhood: How Theories of American Fiction Exclude Women Authors." *American Quarterly* 33, no. 2 (Summer 1981): 123–139.
Beall, Loulie Ayer. "Early School Experiences in Nebraska." *Nebraska History* 33 (July–September 1942): 195–204.
Beard, Charles A., and Mary R. Beard. *The Making of American Civilization*. New York: Macmillan, 1937.
Beck, Ulrich, Anthony Giddens, and Scott Lash. *Reflexive Modernization*. Stanford: Stanford University Press, 1994.
Beers, Henry A. *An Outline Sketch of American Literature*. New York: Chautauqua Press, 1887.
Bellamy, Edward. *Looking Backward*. Mineola: Dover, 1996.
Bender, Thomas. *Intellect and Public Life*. Baltimore: Johns Hopkins University Press, 1993.
Bentley, Nancy. "'Hunting for the Real': Wharton and the Science of Manners." In *The Cambridge Companion to Edith Wharton*. Edited by Millicent Bell, 47–67. Cambridge: Cambridge University Press, 1995.
Berkow, Ira. "Sport of the Times; The Grapes of Wrath at Oklahoma," *New York Times*, February 18, 1989.
Berlant, Lauren. *The Female Complaint*. Durham: Duke University Press, 2008.
Bernard, Laureat, Ralph Brande, and Don Sharkey. *America and Its People*. New York: Sadlier, 1968.
Bhabha, Homi K. "DissemiNation: Time, Narrative, and the Margins of the Modern Nation." In *Nation and Narration*. Edited by Homi K. Bhabha, 291–322. New York: Routledge, 1990.
Blanc, Eric. *Red State Revolt*. New York: Verso, 2019.
Bledstein, Burton. *The Culture of Professionalism*. New York: W. W. Norton, 1978.
Boggs, Abigail, and Nick Mitchell. "Critical University Studies and the Crisis Consensus." Feminist Studies 44, no. 2 (2018): 432–463.
Booker T. Washington Papers. Vol. 6. Edited by Louis R. Harlan and Barbara Kraft. Champaign: University of Illinois Press, 1977.

Booker T. Washington Papers. Vol. 8. Edited by Louis R. Harlan and Raymond W. Smock. Champaign: University of Illinois Press, 1979.

Bourdieu, Pierre. "The School as a Conservative Force: Scholastic and Cultural Inequalities." In *Contemporary Research in the Sociology of Education.* Edited by John Eggleston, translated by J.C. Whitehouse, 32–46. London: Methuen, 1974.

Bourdieu, Pierre. "Cultural Reproduction and Social Reproduction." In *Power and Ideology in Education.* Edited by Jerome Karabel and A. H. Halsey, 487–510. New York: Oxford University Press, 1977.

Bourdieu, Pierre. *The State Nobility.* Stanford: Stanford University Press, 1996.

Bourdieu, Pierre and Jean-Claude Passeron. *Reproduction in Education, Society and Culture.* 2nd ed. Translated by Richard Nice. New York: Sage, 2000.

Bourne, Henry Eldridge and Elbert Jay Benton. *American History.* Boston: D.C. Heath and Co., 1925.

Bourne, Randolph S. *The Gary Schools.* Cambridge: MIT Press, 1970.

Brenner, Robert. "The Economics of Global Turbulence." *New Left Review* 229 (May/June 1998): i–265.

Brodhead, Richard. *Cultures of Letters.* Chicago: University of Chicago Press, 1993.

Brodhead, Richard. *The School of Hawthorne.* New York: Oxford University Press, 1986.

Brooks, Peter. *The Melodramatic Imagination.* New Haven: Yale University Press, 1976.

Brouillette, Sarah. *UNESCO and the Fate of the Literary.* Stanford: Stanford University Press, 2019.

Brown, Homer Obed. *Institutions of the English Novel.* Philadelphia: University of Pennsylvania Press, 1998.

Brown, Wendy. *Undoing the Demos: Neoliberalism's Stealth Revolution.* New York: Zone Books, 2015.

Brown, William Hill. *The Power of Sympathy.* Edited by William S. Kable. Columbus: Ohio State University Press, 1969.

Bruce, Dickson. *Black American Writing from the Nadir: The Evolution of a Literary Tradition, 1877–1915.* Baton Rouge: Louisiana State University Press, 1992.

Buell, Lawrence. *The Dream of the Great American Novel.* Cambridge: Harvard University Press, 2014.

Burich, Keith R. "Henry Adams's *Annis Mirabilis*: 1900 and the Making of a Modernist." *American Studies* 32, no. 2 (Fall 1991): 103–116.

Burt, Mary E. *Literary Landmarks: A Guide to Good Reading for Young People.* Boston: Houghton, Mifflin, 1890.

Buurma, Rachel Sagner, and Laura Heffernan. "The Common Reader and the Archival Classroom: Disciplinary History for the Twenty-First Century." *New Literary History* 43, no. 1 (Winter 2012): 113–135.

Callahan, Cynthia A. "The Confounding Problem of Race: Passing and Adoption in Charles Chesnutt's The Quarry." *MFS Modern Fiction Studies* 48, no. 2 (Summer 2002): 314–340.

"Carlyle and His Imitators." In *The Keepsake*, edited by J. T. Headley, 140–146. New York: Leavitt and Allen, 1855.

Carnegie, Andrew. *The Empire of Business.* New York: Doubleday, Page, 1902.

Carnegie, Andrew. *The Gospel of Wealth.* New York: Carnegie Corporation, 2017.

Casner, Mabel B., and Ralph Henry Gabriel. *The Rise of American Democracy.* New York: Harcourt, 1938.

Cecire, Natalia. *Experimental: American Literature and the Aesthetics of Knowledge.* Baltimore: Johns Hopkins University Press, 2019.

Chakkalakal, Tess and Kenneth W. Warren. Introduction to *Jim Crow, Literature, and the Legacy of Sutton E. Griggs*. Edited by Tess Chakkalakal and Kenneth W. Warren, 1–20. Athens: University of Georgia Press, 2013.

Chatterjee, Piya, and Sunaina Maira. *The Imperial University*. Minneapolis: University of Minnesota Press, 2014.

Chen, Chris. "The Limit Point of Capitalist Equality." *Endnotes*, no. 3 (September 2013). https://endnotes.org.uk/issues/3/en/chris-chen-the-limit-point-of-capitalist-equality.

Chesnutt, Charles W. *Stories, Novels, and Essays*. New York: Library of America, 2002.

"Chicago Deans." *University of Chicago Alumni Magazine* 15, no. 1 (November 1922): 17.

"Civil Rights Data Collection: Data Snapshot (School Discipline)." United States Department of Education, Office for Civil Rights. March 21, 2014, https://www2.ed.gov/about/offices/list/ocr/docs/crdc-discipline-snapshot.pdf.

Clark, Daniel A. *Creating the College Man*. Madison: University of Wisconsin Press, 2010.

Clark, Thomas D. Introduction to *The Clansman*, v–xviii. Lexington: University Press of Kentucky, 1970.

"Class War." *New York Times*, February 1, 1906.

Clover, Joshua. "Who Can Save the University?" *Public Books*, June 12, 2017. https://www.publicbooks.org/who-can-save-the-university/.

Cobbett, William. "Excerpts from 'Cottage Economy.' " In *The New England Farmer*, vol. 2. Edited by Thomas G. Fessenden, 38–39. Boston: William Nichols, 1824.

Cohen, Daniel J. "By the Book: Assessing the Place of Textbooks in U.S. Survey Courses." *Journal of American History* 91, no. 4 (March 2005): 1405–1415.

"College as a Means of Stifling Thought." *New York Times*, March 25, 1912.

"College Men Agree with Owen Johnson." *New York Times*, May 11, 1912.

CollegeHumor, "Hardly Working: Cool English Teacher," YouTube video, 2:51, May 20, 2008, https://www.youtube.com/watch?v=lILCc6AZ10c.

Cooke, Morris Llewellyn. *Academic and Industrial Efficiency: A Report to the Carnegie Foundation for the Advancement of Teaching*. New York, 1910.

Cooper, Mark Garrett and John Marx. *Media U.* New York: Columbia University Press, 2017.

Cooper, Melinda. *Family Values*. New York: Zone Books, 2019.

Cottom, Tressie McMillan. *Lower Ed*. New York: New Press, 2017.

Crane, Stephen. *Maggie: A Girl of the Streets and Other Tales of New York*. Edited by Larzer Ziff. New York: Penguin, 2000.

Cremin, Lawrence A. *American Education: The Colonial Experience, 1607–1783*. New York: Harper & Row, 1970.

Cremin, Lawrence A. *American Education: The National Experience, 1783–1876*. New York: Harper and Row, 1980.

Cremin, Lawrence A. *American Education: The Metropolitan Experience, 1876–1980*. New York: Harper & Row, 1988.

Cremin, Lawrence A. *The Transformation of the School*. New York: Knopf, 1961.

Cremin, Lawrence A. Foreword to *Herbert Spencer on Education*. Edited by Andreas M. Kazamias vii–viii. New York: Teachers College Press, 1966.

Crisler, Jesse S., Robert C. Leitz III, and Joseph R. McElrath Jr. Introduction to *An Exemplary Citizen: Letters of Charles W. Chesnutt, 1906–1932*. Edited by Jesse S. Crisler, Robert C. Leitz III, and Joseph R. McElrath Jr., xvii–xxxiv. Stanford: Stanford University Press, 2002.

Current, Richard N., Alexander DeConde, and Harris L. Dante. *United States History*. Glenview: Scott, Foresman, 1967.

Dahn, Eurie, and Brian Sweeney. "A Brief History of *The Colored American Magazine*." *The Digital Colored American Magazine*. Accessed August 15, 2018. http://coloredamerican.org/?page_id=70.
"Danger in the Snobbery of American Colleges." *New York Times*, March 31, 1912.
De Man, Paul. *Blindness and Insight*. New York: Oxford University Press, 1971.
De Man, Paul. *The Rhetoric of Romanticism*. New York: Columbia University Press, 1984.
Denning, Michael. *Mechanic Accents*. New York: Verso, 1987.
Dewey, Evelyn. *New Schools for Old*. New York: E. P. Dutton, 1919.
Dewey, John. *Democracy and Education*. New York: Macmillan, 1916.
Dewey, John. "Interest in Relation to Training of the Will." In *The Early Works of John Dewey: 1882–1898*. Edited by Jo Ann Boydston, 111–150. Carbondale: Southern Illinois University Press, 1972.
Dewey, John. *The School and Society*. Revised ed. Chicago: University of Chicago Press, 1915.
Dewey, John, and Evelyn Dewey. *Schools of To-Morrow*. New York: E. P. Dutton, 1915.
Dimock, Wai Chee. *Through Other Continents: American Literature Across Deep Time*. Princeton: Princeton University Press, 2006.
Dixon, Thomas, Jr. "Booker T. Washington and the Negro." *Saturday Evening Post* 178, no. 8 (August 19, 1905): 1–2.
Dixon, Thomas, Jr. *The Clansman*. Doubleday, Page, 1905.
Dixon, Thomas, Jr. *The Clansman*. Lexington: University Press of Kentucky, 1970.
Dixon, Thomas, Jr. "A Friendly Warning." In *Dixon's Sermons*, 112–120. New York: F. L. Bussey, no date.
Dixon, Thomas, Jr. *The Leopard's Spots*. Ridgewood: Gregg Press, 1967.
Dixon, Thomas, Jr. *The Traitor*. New York: Doubleday, Page, 1907.
Doherty, Margaret. "State-Funded Fiction: Minimalism, National Memory, and the Return to Realism in the Post-Postmodern Age," *American Literary History* 27, no. 1 (Spring 2015): 79–101.
Donham, Parker. "Savio Blasts Kerr's 'Knowledge Factory.'" *Harvard Crimson*, December 12, 1964, https://www.thecrimson.com/article/1964/12/12/savio-blasts-kerrs-knowledge-factory-pmario/.
Douglas, Ann. *The Feminization of American Culture*. New York: Knopf, 1977.
Dreiser, Theodore. *Dawn: An Autobiography of Early Youth*. Edited by T. D. Nostwich. Santa Rosa: Black Sparrow Press, 1998.
Dreiser, Theodore. *Sister Carrie*. New York: Modern Library, 1999.
Du Bois, W. E. B. *Black Reconstruction*. New York: Oxford University Press, 2016.
Du Bois, W. E. B. *Writings*. New York: Library of America, 1986.
Dunbar, Paul Laurence. *The Sport of the Gods and Other Essential Writings*. Edited by Shelley Fisher Fishkin and David Bradley. New York: Modern Library, 2005.
Dunbar, Paul Lawrence. "Hidden in Plain Sight: African American Secret Societies and Black Freemasonry." *Journal of African American Studies* 16, no. 4 (2012): 622–637.
Dunne, F. P. "Mr. Dooley on the Food We Eat." *Collier's*, June 23, 1906.
Duyckinck, Evert. "Nathaniel Hawthorne: *The Scarlet Letter*." *Literary World*, no. 165 (March 30, 1850): 323–325.
Edel, Leon. *The Life of Henry James*. Vol. 1. New York: Penguin, 1977.
Edwards, Jonathan. *A Treatise Concerning Religious Affections*. Bedford: Applewood Books, 2009.
Ehrenreich, Barbara, and John Ehrenreich. "The Professional-Managerial Class." In *Between Labor and Capital*. Edited by Pat Walker, 5–45. Boston: South End Press, 1979.

Elias, Norbert. *Time: An Essay*. Translated by Edmund Jephcott. Cambridge: Blackwell, 1992.

Eliot, Charles. "Address of President Charles William Eliot. Harvard Union. January 9 1905." *Harvard Monthly* 41, no. 5 (February 1906): 237–254.

Eliot, Charles. "Inaugural Address as President of Harvard College." In *Educational Reform: Essays and Addresses*, 1–38. New York: Century, 1898.

Eliot, Charles. "Relations of American Colleges to Each Other." Harvard University. President's Office. Records of the President of Harvard University, Charles W. Eliot, 1869–1930, Box 241. Courtesy of the Harvard University Archives.

Eliot, Charles. "Sororities and Fraternities." Harvard University. President's Office. Records of the President of Harvard University, Charles W. Eliot, 1869–1930, Box 241. Courtesy of the Harvard University Archives.

Eliot, Charles. "A Wider Range of Electives in College Admissions Requirements." *Educational Review* 11 (January–May 1896): 417–432.

Ellison, Julie. *Cato's Tears and the Making of Anglo-American Emotion*. Chicago: University of Chicago Press, 1999.

Emerson, Ralph Waldo. "The American Scholar." In *Nature and Selected Essays*. Edited by Lazer Ziff, 83–105. New York: Penguin, 2003.

Emre, Merve. "Jamesian Institutions." *American Literary History* 27, no. 2 (Summer 2015): 226–255.

Emre, Merve. *Paraliterary: The Making of Bad Readers in Postwar America*. Chicago: University of Chicago Press, 2017.

English in American Universities. Edited by William Morton Payne. Boston: D. C. Heath, 1895.

English, James F. "Everywhere and Nowhere: The Sociology of Literature after 'the Sociology of Literature.'" *New Literary History* 58, no. 2 (Spring 2010): v–xxiii.

English, James. *The Global Future of English Studies*. West Sussex: Wiley-Blackwell, 2012.

"English Novels." *Yale Daily News*, September 30, 1895.

Erskine, John. *Leading American Novelists*. New York: Henry Holt, 1910.

Erskine, John. *My Life as a Teacher*. Philadelphia: Lippincott, 1948.

Evans, Mae J. "How Much Work Is Done in American Literature in the High School, and by What Methods?" *School Review* 11, no. 8 (October 1903): 647–654.

Faulkner, William. *The Sound and the Fury*. Edited by David Minter. New York: W. W. Norton, 1994.

Felman, Shoshana. "Turning the Screw of Interpretation." *Yale French Studies*, no. 55/56 (1977): 94–207.

Felski, Rita. "Latour and Literary Studies." *PMLA* 130, no. 3 (2015): 737–742.

Felski, Rita. *Uses of Literature*. Malden: Wiley-Blackwell, 2008.

Ferguson, Roderick A. *The Reorder of Things*. Minneapolis: University of Minnesota Press, 2012.

Ferguson, SallyAnn H. "Signifying the Other: Chesnutt's 'Methods of Teaching.'" In *Passing in the Works of Charles W. Chesnutt*. Edited by Prothro Wright and Ernestine Pickens Glass, 9–22. Jackson: University Press of Mississippi, 2010.

Fiedler, Leslie. *Love and Death in the American Novel*. Illinois: Dalkey Archive, 2008.

Findeisen, Christopher. "'The One Place Where Money Makes No Difference'": The Campus Novel from *Stover at Yale* Through *The Art of Fielding*." *American Literature* 88, no. 1 (2016): 67–91.

Fish, Stanley. "Profession Despise Thyself: Fear and Self-Loathing in Literary Studies." *Critical Inquiry* 10, no. 2 (December 1983): 349–364.

Fitzgerald, F. Scott. *This Side of Paradise*. New York: Charles Scribner's Sons, 1970.
Flaherty, Colleen. "Canaries in a 'Toxic Mine.'" *Inside Higher Ed*. May 5, 2020. https://www.insidehighered.com/news/2020/05/05/professors-ohio-u-say-faculty-cuts-cant-just-be-blamed-covid-19.
Fleissner, Jennifer. "After the New Americanists: The Progress of Romance and the Romance of Progress in American Literary Studies." In *A Companion to American Literary Studies*. Edited by Caroline F. Levander and Robert S. Levine, 173–190. New York: Wiley-Blackwell, 2011.
Fleissner, Jennifer. "The Ordering Power of Disorder: Henry Adams and the Return of the Darwinian Era." *American Literature* 84, no. 1 (2012): 31–60.
Fleissner, Jennifer. "Wharton, Marriage, and the New Woman." In *The Cambridge History of the American Novel*. Edited by Leonard Cassuto, Clare Virginia Eby, and Benjamin Reiss, 452–469. Cambridge: Cambridge University Press, 2011.
Fleissner, Jennifer. *Women, Compulsion, Modernity: The Moment of American Naturalism*. Chicago: University of Chicago Press, 2004.
The Flowers of Friendship: Letters Written to Gertrude Stein. Edited by Donald Gallup. New York: Knopf, 1953.
Fludernik, Monika. *An Introduction to Narratology*. New York: Routledge, 2006.
Foster, Frances Smith. Introduction to *A Brighter Day Coming*. Edited by Frances Smith Foster, 3–40. New York: Feminist Press, 1990.
Foster, Hannah Webster. *The Coquette and the Boarding School*. Edited by Jennifer Harris and Bryan Waterman. New York: W. W. Norton, 2013.
Foster, Travis M. "Campus Novels and the Nation of Peers." *American Literary History* 26, no. 3 (2014): 462–483.
Foucault, Michel. *Discipline and Punish*. Translated by Alan Sheridan. New York: Vintage, 1995.
Fuentes, Annette. *Lockdown High*. New York: Verso, 2011.
Gallagher, Catherine, and Stephen Greenblatt. *Practicing New Historicism*. Chicago: University of Chicago Press, 2000.
Gamer, Michael. "A Select Collection: Barbauld, Scott, and the Rise of the (Reprinted) Novel." In *Recognizing the Romantic Novel*. Edited by Jillian Heydt-Stevenson and Charlotte Sussman, 119–155. Liverpool: Liverpool University Press, 2008.
Gardner, Eric. "Rediscovering Frances Ellen Watkins Harper." *OUPBlog*. October 17, 2015. https://blog.oup.com/2015/10/frances-harper-forest-leaves/.
Garland, Hamlin, and Alice B. Stephens. *A Son of the Middle Border*. New York: Macmillan, 1922.
Gates, Henry Louis Jr. *The Signifying Monkey: A Theory of Afro-American Literary Criticism*. New York: Oxford University Press, 1988.
Gavian, Ruth Wood, and William A. Hamm. *United States History*. Boston: D. C. Heath, 1960.
Geiger, Roger L. *To Advance Knowledge: The Growth of American Research Universities, 1900–1940*. New York: Oxford University Press, 1986.
Genette, Gérard. *Narrative Discourse: An Essay in Method*. Translated by Jane E. Lewin. Ithaca: Cornell University Press, 1983.
George, Henry. *The Life of Henry George, by His Son*. London: William Reeves, 1900.
Gerhard, Dietrich. "The Emergence of the Credit System in American Education Considered as a Problem of Social and Intellectual History." *Bulletin of the American Association of University Professors* 41, no. 4 (1955): 647–668.

Gerth, H. H., and C. Wright Mills. "A Biographical View." In *From Max Weber: Essays in Sociology*. Translated and edited by H. H. Gerth and C. Wright Mills, 3–31. New York: Oxford University Press, 1946.
Gigante, Denise. *Life: Organic Form and Romanticism*. New Haven: Yale University Press, 2009.
Gillespie, Michele K., and Randall L. Hall. Introduction to *Thomas Dixon Jr. and the Birth of Modern America*, 1–22. Baton Rouge: Louisiana State University Press, 2006.
Gilmore, Ruth Wilson. "Decorative Beasts: Dogging the Academy in the Late 20th Century." *California Sociologist* 14, no. 1–2 (1991): 113–135.
Gilmore, Ruth Wilson. *Golden Gulag*. Berkeley: University of California Press, 2007.
Glazener, Nancy. *Literature in the Making*. New York: Oxford University Press, 2016.
Glazener, Nancy. *Reading for Realism*. Durham: Duke University Press, 1997.
Goodwin, Doris Kearns. *The Bully Pulpit*. New York: Simon & Schuster, 2013.
Gorn, Elliot J. Introduction to *The McGuffey Readers: Selections from the 1879 Edition*. Edited by Elliott J. Gorn, 1–36. Boston: Bedford Books, 1998.
Graff, Gerald. Preface to *Professing Literature: An Institutional History*, vii–xxii. Chicago: University of Chicago Press, 2007.
Graff, Gerald. *Professing Literature: An Institutional History*. Chicago: University of Chicago Press, 2007.
Graff, Henry F., and John A. Krout. *The Adventure of the American People*. New York: Rand McNally, 1959.
Graham, Patricia A. *Progressive Education from Arcady to Academe: A History of the Progressive Education Association, 1919–1955*. New York: Teachers College Press, 1967.
Greene, Maxine. *The Public School and the Private Vision*. New York: New Press, 2007.
Griggs, Sutton. *The Hindered Hand*. Miami: Mnemosyne, 1969.
Griggs, Sutton. *Imperium in Imperio*. New York: Modern Library, 2003.
Griggs, Sutton. *Overshadowed*. Freeport: Books for Libraries Press, 1971.
Griggs, Sutton. *Pointing the Way*. New York: AMS Press, 1974.
Griggs, Sutton. *Unfettered*. New York: AMS Press, 1971.
Grimshaw, William. *Official History of Freemasonry among Colored People in North America*. New York: Broadway, 1903.
Griswold, Rufus W. "Nathaniel Hawthorne." *International Magazine*, May 1, 1851.
Grumet, Madeleine R. *Bitter Milk*. Amherst: University of Massachusetts Press, 1988.
Guillory, John. *Cultural Capital: The Problem of Literary Canon Formation*. Chicago: University of Chicago Press, 1993.
Hall, G. Stanley. *Adolescence*. Vol. 2. New York: D. Appleton, 1905.
Hall, G. Stanley. *Educational Problems*. Vol. 2. New York: D. Appleton, 1911.
Hall, G. Stanley. "The Ideal School as Based on Child Study." In *Journal of Proceedings and Addresses of the Fortieth Annual Meeting of the National Education Association*, 474–488. Chicago: University of Chicago Press, 1901.
Hall, G. Stanley. *Life and Confessions of a Psychologist*. New York: D. Appleton, 1923.
Hall, G. Stanley. "The University Idea." *Pedagogical Seminary* 15, no. 1 (1908): 92–104.
Halpern, Faye. "Beyond Contempt: Ways to Read *Uncle Tom's Cabin*." *PMLA* 133, no. 3 (2018): 633–639.
Harper, Frances Ellen Watkins. *Iola Leroy*. New York: Penguin, 2010.
Harvey, David. *The Condition of Postmodernity*. Cambridge: Blackwell, 1990.
Hawkins, W.W. "The Average Student at the University of Missouri: His Intellectual and Social Life." *University Missourian*, February 16, 1913.

Hawthorne, Nathaniel. *Passages from the English Note-Books of Nathaniel Hawthorne*. Vol. 1. Leipzig: Tauchnitz, 1871.
Hayot, Eric. "Against Periodization; or, On Institutional Time." *New Literary History* 42, no. 4 (2011): 739–756.
Hazeltine, M. W. "Mr. Andrew Carnegie's New Book." *North American Review* 175, no. 548 (July 1902): 61–70.
Heller, Terry. *Sarah Orne Jewett Text Project*. Accessed April 5, 2021. http://www.sarahornejewett.org/soj/sj-index.htm.
Hoberek, Andrew. *The Twilight of the Middle Class*. Princeton: Princeton University Press, 2005.
Hofstadter, Richard. *Anti-Intellectualism in American Life*. New York: Knopf, 1963.
Hofstadter, Richard. *Social Darwinism in American Thought*. Revised ed. Boston: Beacon Press, 1955.
Hofstadter, Richard, William Miller, and Daniel Aaron. *The United States: The History of the Republic*. Englewood Cliffs: Prentice-Hall, 1957.
Hollinger, David. *Postethnic America*. New York: Basic Books, 1995.
Horn, Max. *The Intercollegiate Socialist Society, 1905–1921: Origins of the Modern American Student Movement*. Boulder: Westview Press, 1979.
Horowitz, Helen Lefkowitz. *Campus Life*. Chicago: University of Chicago Press, 1987.
Horsford, Sonya Douglass, Janelle T. Scott, and Gary L. Anderson. *The Politics of Education Policy in an Era of Inequality*. New York: Routledge, 2019.
Howard, June. *The Center of the World*. New York: Oxford University Press, 2018.
Howard, June. *Form and History in American Literary Naturalism*. Chapel Hill: University of North Carolina Press, 1985.
Howells, William Dean. *The Rise of Silas Lapham*. New York: Penguin, 1986.
Howes, Abby Willis. *A Primer of American Literature*. Boston: D. C. Heath, 1909.
Huey, Edmund Burke. *The Psychology and Pedagogy of Reading*. New York: Macmillan, 1908.
Hungerford, Amy. *Making Literature Now*. Stanford: Stanford University Press, 2016.
Hunt, Th. W. "The Place of English in the College Curriculum." *Transactions of the Modern Language Association, 1884-5*. Vol. 1, 118–132. Baltimore: Modern Language Association, 1885.
"In Assembly, April 29, 1833." *Documents of the Assembly of the State of New York* 4, no. 333 (April 1833): 1–3.
Ingrassia, Brian M. *The Rise of Gridiron University: Higher Education's Uneasy Alliance with Big-Time Football*. Lawrence: University Press of Kansas, 2012.
Irving, Washington. *Chronicles of Wolfert's Roost and Other Papers*. Leipzig: Tauchnitz, 1855.
Irving, Washington. *History, Tales, and Sketches*. New York: Library of America, 1983.
Irving, Washington. *The Legend of Sleepy Hollow by Washington Irving*. Edited by Albert F. Blaisdell. New York: Maynard, Merrill, 1883.
Irving, Washington. *Six Selections from Irving's Sketch-Book: With Notes, Questions, Etc., for Home and School Use*. Edited by Homer B. Sprague. Boston: Ginn, 1878.
Ise, John. *Sod and Stubble: The Story of a Kansas Homestead*. New York: Wilson-Erickson, 1936.
James, Henry. *The Art of the Novel*. Chicago: University of Chicago Press, 2011.
James, Henry. *The Golden Bowl*. Oxford: Oxford University Press, 1999.
James, Henry. *The Portrait of a Lady*. New York: Penguin, 2011.

James, Henry. *The Turn of the Screw and Other Short Fiction*. New York: Bantam, 1981.
James, Henry. *The Wings of the Dove*. New York: Oxford University Press, 1984.
Jameson, Fredric. *The Geopolitical Aesthetic*. Bloomington: Indiana University Press, 1992.
Jameson, Fredric. *Postmodernism, or, the Cultural Logic of Late Capitalism*. Durham: Duke University Press, 1991.
Jarvis, Will. "LSU Just Unveiled a $28-Million Football Facility. The Flood-Damaged Library Is Still 'Decrepit.'" *Chronicle of Higher Education*, July 22, 2019, https://www.chronicle.com/article/LSU-Just-Unveiled-a/246750.
Jefferson, Thomas. *Thomas Jefferson to Joel Barlow*. December 10, 1807. Manuscript/Mixed Material. Library of Congress, www.loc.gov/item/mtjbib017974/.
Jefferson, Thomas. *Writings*. New York: Library of America, 1984.
Jewett, Sarah Orne. *The Country of the Pointed Firs and Other Stories*. New York: Modern Library, 2000.
Jewett, Sarah Orne. Preface to *A Memorial of the One Hundredth Anniversary of the Founding of Berwick Academy*, iii–viii. Cambridge: Riverside Press, 1891.
Johnson, James Weldon. *Writings*. New York: Library of America, 2004.
Johnson, Owen. "The Social Usurpation of Our Colleges. I-Introductory Article." *Collier's*, May 15, 1912.
Johnson, Owen. *Stover at Yale*. New York: Macmillan, 1968.
Johnson, Samuel. *The Works of Samuel Johnson*. Vol. 4. London: G. Offor, 1818.
Jones, Gavin. "The Embarrassment of Naturalism." *Amerikastudien/American Studies* 55, no. 1 (2010): 45–61.
Jones, Gavin. *Failure and the American Writer*. Cambridge: Cambridge University Press, 2014.
Jones, Gavin. *Strange Talk*. Berkeley: University of California Press, 1999.
Jordan, David Starr. "At the Laying of the Corner-Stone of the Dwelling Hall." *Reed College Record*, no. 4 (December 1912): 24–30.
Journals of Ralph Waldo Emerson, with Annotations. Vol. 5. Edited by Edward Waldo Emerson and Waldo Emerson Forbes. Boston: Houghton Mifflin, 1911.
"Juniors Must Reform, Too." *New York Times*, March 17, 1913.
Kabaservice, Geoffrey. *The Guardians*. New York: Henry Holt, 2004.
Kaestle, Carl F. *Pillars of the Republic*. New York: Hill and Wang, 1983.
Kallen, Horace. *Culture and Democracy in the United States*. New York: Boni and Liveright, 1924.
Karafilis, Maria. "Oratory, Embodiment, and US Citizenship in Sutton E. Griggs's 'Imperium in Imperio.'" *African American Review* 40, no. 1 (Spring 2006): 125–143.
Katz, Joseph. "Theodore Dreiser at Indiana University." *Notes and Queries* 13, no. 3 (1966): 100–101.
Kazin, Alfred. *On Native Grounds*. New York: Harcourt Brace, 1995.
Kezar, Adrianna, Tom DePaola, and Daniel T. Scott. *The Gig Academy*. Baltimore: Johns Hopkins University Press, 2019.
Kindley, Evan. *Poet-Critics and the Administration of Culture*. Cambridge: Harvard University Press, 2017.
Knapp, Samuel L. *Lectures on American Literature: With Remarks on Some Passages of American History*. New York: Elam Bliss, 1829.
Koelsch, William A. *Clark University, 1887–1987: A Narrative History*. Worcester: Clark University Press, 1987.
Konstantinou, Lee. "Critique Has Its Uses." *American Book Review* 38, no. 5 (July/August 2017): 15–18.

Kornbluh, Anna. *The Order of Forms*. Chicago: University of Chicago Press, 2019.
Krapp, George Philip. Preface to *Tales of the Traveller with Selections from the Sketch Book*, 5–6. Edited by George Philip Krapp. Chicago: Scott, Foresman, 1901.
Kristeva, Julia. *Powers of Horror*. Translated by Leon S. Roudiez. New York: Columbia University Press, 1982.
Lauter, Paul. "Race and Gender in the Shaping of the American Literary Canon: A Case Study from the Twenties." *Feminist Studies* 9, no. 3 (Autumn 1983): 435–463.
Lears, Jackson. *No Place of Grace*. Chicago: University of Chicago Press, 1994.
Lee, Hermione. *Edith Wharton*. New York: Vintage, 2008.
Levander, Caroline. "Sutton Griggs and the Borderlands of Empire." In *Jim Crow, Literature, and the Legacy of Sutton E. Griggs*. Edited by Tess Chakkalakal and Kenneth W. Warren, 21–48. Athens: University of Georgia Press, 2013.
Levien, Simon J. "The Crimson Klan." *Harvard Crimson*, March 25, 2021. https://www.thecrimson.com/article/2021/3/25/harvard-klan-scrut/.
Levine, Caroline. *Forms*. Princeton: Princeton University Press, 2015.
Levine, David O. *The American College and the Culture of Aspiration, 1915–1940*. Ithaca: Cornell University Press, 1986.
Levine, Lawrence. *Highbrow/Lowbrow*. Cambridge: Harvard University Press, 1988.
Lewis, R. W. B. *The Jameses: A Family Narrative*. New York: Doubleday, 1991.
Liming, Sheila. *What a Library Means to a Woman*. Minneapolis: University of Minnesota Press, 2020.
London, Jack. *The Radical Jack London: Writings on War and Revolution*. Edited by Jonah Raskin. Berkeley: University of California Press, 2008.
Loughran, Trish. *The Republic in Print: Print Culture in the Age of U.S. Nation Building, 1770–1870*. New York: Columbia University Press, 2007.
Lukács, Georg. "Narrate or Describe?" In *Writer and Critic and Other Essays*. Edited and translated by Arthur Kahn, 110–148. London: Merlin Press, 1970.
Lummis, Charles F. "Another California Novel." *Land of Sunshine* 11 (1889): 117. Reprinted in *Frank Norris: The Critical Reception*. Edited by Joseph R. McElrath Jr. and Katherine Knight, 52. New York: Burt Franklin, 1981.
Lynch, Deidre. *Loving Literature: A Cultural History*. Chicago: University of Chicago Press, 2015.
Macherey, Pierre, and Etienne Balibar. "Literature as an Ideological Form: Some Marxist Propositions." Translated by Ian McLeod, John Whitehead, and Ann Wordsworth. *Oxford Literary View* 3, no. 1 (1978): 4–12.
Mann, Horace. *Lectures on Education*. Boston: Wm. B. Fowle and N. Capen, 1845.
Marx, Leo. *The Machine in the Garden*. New York: Oxford University Press, 2000.
Matthews, Brander. *An Introduction to the Study of American Literature*. New York: American Book Company, 1896.
Matthiessen, F.O. *American Renaissance: Art and Expression in the Age of Emerson and Whitman*. New York: Oxford University Press, 1941.
Mattson, Kevin. *Upton Sinclair: And the Other American Century*. Hoboken: John Wiley, 2006.
McCann, Sean. *A Pinnacle of Feeling: American Literature and Presidential Government*. Princeton: Princeton University Press, 2008.
McClanahan, Annie J. "Becoming Non-Economic: Human Capital Theory and Wendy Brown's *Undoing the Demos*." *Theory & Event* 20, no. 2 (2017): 510–519.
McClanahan, Annie. "Serious Crises: Rethinking the Neoliberal Subject." *Boundary 2* 46, no. 1 (2019): 103–132.

McElrath, Joseph R., Jr., and Jesse S. Crisler. *Frank Norris: A Life.* Champaign: University of Illinois Press, 2006.
McElrath, Joseph R., Jr., Robert C. Leitz III, and Jesse S. Crisler. Introduction to *Charles W. Chesnutt: Essays and Speeches.* Edited by Joseph R. McElrath Jr., Robert C. Leitz III, and Jesse S. Crisler, xxiii–xxxvii. Stanford: Stanford University Press, 1999.
McGuffey, William H. *McGuffey's Alternate Sixth Reader.* Cincinnati: Van Antwerp, Bragg, 1889.
McGuffey, William H. *McGuffey's Fifth Eclectic Reader.* Revised ed. New York: American Book Company, 1907.
McGuffey, William H. *McGuffey's New Fifth Eclectic Reader: Selected and Original Exercises for Schools.* Cincinnati: Wilson, Hinkie, 1866.
McGuffey, William H. *McGuffey's New Sixth Eclectic Reader: Exercises in Rhetorical Reading, with Introductory Rules and Examples.* Cincinnati: Winthrop B. Smith, 1857.
McGuffey, William H. *McGuffey's Newly Revised Rhetorical Guide, Or, Fifth Reader of the Eclectic Series: Containing Elegant Extracts in Prose and Poetry, with Copious Rules and Rhetorical Exercises.* Cincinnati: Winthrop B. Smith, 1853.
McGuffey, William H. *McGuffey's Rhetorical Guide, Or, Fifth Reader of the Eclectic Series: Containing Elegant Extracts in Prose and Poetry, with Copious Rules and Rhetorical Exercises.* Cincinnati: Winthrop B. Smith, 1844.
McGuffey, William H. *McGuffey's Sixth Eclectic Reader.* Revised ed. Cincinnati: Van Antwerp, Bragg, 1879.
McGuffey, William H. *McGuffey's Sixth Eclectic Reader.* Revised ed. New York: American Book Company, 1921.
McGurl, Mark. *The Novel Art: Elevations of American Fiction after Henry James.* Princeton: Princeton University Press, 2001.
McGurl, Mark. *The Program Era: Postwar Fiction and the Rise of Creative Writing.* Cambridge: Harvard University Press, 2009.
McHenry, Elizabeth. *Forgotten Readers: Recovering the Lost History of African American Literary Societies.* Durham: Duke University Press, 2002.
Melamed, Jodi. *Represent and Destroy.* Minneapolis: University of Minnesota Press, 2011.
Melville, Herman. *Moby-Dick.* New York: W. W. Norton, 2002.
Menand, Louis. *Discovering Modernism: T. S. Eliot and His Context.* New York: Oxford University Press, 1987.
Menand, Louis. *The Marketplace of Ideas.* New York: W. W. Norton, 2010.
Menand, Louis. *The Metaphysical Club.* New York: FSG, 2001.
Menninghaus, Winfried. *Disgust: The Theory and History of a Strong Sensation.* Translated by Howard Eiland and Joel Golb. Albany: State University of New York Press, 2003.
Meyer, Steven. *Irresistible Dictation: Gertrude Stein and the Correlations of Writing and Science.* Stanford: Stanford University Press, 2001.
Michaelis, Johann David. *Introduction to the New Testament.* Vol. 1, part 1. Translated by Herbert Marsh. Cambridge: J. Archdeacon Printer, 1793.
Michaels, Walter Benn. *Our America.* Durham: Duke University Press, 1995.
Michaels, Walter Benn. "The Political Economy of Anti-Racism." *nonsite.org,* no. 23 (February 11, 2018): nonsite.org/article/the-political-economy-of-anti-racism.
Michaels, Walter Benn. "Race into Culture." *Critical Inquiry* 18, no. 4 (Summer 1992): 655–685.
Michaels, Walter Benn. "The Souls of White Folk." In *Literature and the Body: Essays on Populations and Persons.* Edited by Elaine Scarry, 185–210. Baltimore: Johns Hopkins University Press, 1988.
Michaels, Walter Benn. *The Trouble with Diversity.* New York: Henry Holt, 2006.

Miller, D. A. *Hidden Hitchcock*. Chicago: University of Chicago Press, 2016.
Miller, Rosalind S. *Gertrude Stein: Form and Intelligibility*. New York: Exposition Press, 1949.
Miller, William. *The Anatomy of Disgust*. Cambridge: Harvard University Press, 1997.
"Modern Novels at Yale." *New York Times*, April 12, 1896.
Morison, Samuel Eliot. *The Development of Harvard University: Since the Inauguration of President Eliot 1869–1929*. Cambridge: Harvard University Press, 1930.
Morison, Samuel Eliot. *Three Centuries of Harvard 1636–1936*. Cambridge: Harvard University Press, 1936.
Morrison, Toni. *Playing in the Dark*. Cambridge: Harvard University Press, 1992.
Muzzey, David Saville. *Our Country's History*. Boston: Ginn, 1957.
My Dear Governess: The Letters of Edith Wharton to Anna Bahlmann. Edited by Irene Goldman-Price. New Haven: Yale University Press, 2012.
Nasaw, David. *Schooled to Order*. New York: Oxford University Press, 1979.
Nemser, Dan. and Brian Whitener. "The Tuition Limit and the Coming Crisis in Higher Education." *New Inquiry,* March 26, 2018. https://thenewinquiry.com/the-tuition-limit-and-the-coming-crisis-of-higher-education/.
"A New and Promising American Novelist." *New York Tribune*, March 5, 1899, ill. supp. Reprinted in *Frank Norris: The Critical Reception*. Edited by Joseph R. McElrath Jr. and Katherine Knight, 29–30. New York: Burt Franklin, 1981.
"New Professors at Yale." *New York Times*, October 28, 1895.
Newfield, Christopher. *The Great Mistake*. Baltimore: Johns Hopkins University Press, 2016.
Newfield, Christopher. *Ivy and Industry: Business and the Making of the American University, 1880–1980*. Durham: Duke University Press, 2003.
Ngai, Sianne. "Merely Interesting." *Critical Inquiry* 34, no. 4 (Summer 2008): 777–817.
Ngai, Sianne. *Ugly Feelings*. Cambridge: Harvard University Press, 2005.
"No Study of Novels at Yale." *New York Times*, April 1, 1896.
Norrell, Robert J. *Up from History*. Cambridge: Harvard University Press, 2009.
Norris, Frank. *Novels and Essays*. Edited by Donald Pizer. New York: Library of America, 1986.
North, Joseph. *Literary Criticism: A Concise Political History*. Cambridge: Harvard University Press, 2017.
North, Michael. *The Dialect of Modernism*. New York: Oxford University Press, 1998.
"Novels of the Week." *Spectator* 83 (November 4, 1899): 662. Reprinted in *Frank Norris: The Critical Reception*. Edited by Joseph R. McElrath Jr. and Katherine Knight, 52–53. New York: Burt Franklin, 1981.
Nussbaum, Martha C. *Hiding from Humanity: Disgust, Shame, and the Law*. Princeton: Princeton University Press, 2005.
Olson, Liesl M. "Gertrude Stein, William James and Habit in the Shadow of War." *Twentieth Century Literature* 49, no. 3 (Autumn 2003): 328–359.
Open Syllabus Project. Accessed January 21, 2022. http://opensyllabusproject.org/
"Owen Johnson Recovered." *Berkeley Daily Gazette*, September 27, 1912.
Pacheco, Derek. *Moral Enterprise*. Columbus: Ohio State University Press, 2013.
Palumbo-Liu, David. Introduction to *The Ethnic Canon*. Edited by David Palumbo-Liu, 1–27. Minneapolis: University of Minnesota Press, 1995.
Parfait, Claire. *The Publishing History of Uncle Tom's Cabin, 1852–2002*. Aldershot: Ashgate, 2007.
Parker, Francis W. *Talks on Pedagogics*. New York: E. L. Kellogg, 1894.

Parrington, Vernon Louis. *Main Currents in American Thought*. Vol. 2. New York: Harcourt, Brace, 1930.
Parsons, Elaine Frantz. *Ku-Klux: The Birth of the Klan During Reconstruction*. Chapel Hill: University of North Carolina Press, 2015.
Pattee, Fred Lewis. *A History of American Literature Since 1870*. New York: Century, 1917.
Pattee, Fred Lewis. *Penn State Yankee*. State College: Pennsylvania State College, 1953.
Pease, Donald. "New Americanists: Revisionist Interventions into the Canon." In *Revisionary Interventions into the Americanist Canon*. Edited by Donald Pease, 1–37. Durham: Duke University Press, 1994.
Phelps, Christopher. "How Should We Teach 'The Jungle'?" *Chronicle of Higher Education* 52, no. 26 (March 2006): https://www.chronicle.com/article/how-should-we-teach-the-jungle/.
Phelps, William Lyon. *Autobiography with Letters*. New York: Oxford University Press, 1939.
Piper, Andrew. *Dreaming in Books: The Making of the Bibliographic Imagination in the Romantic Age*. Chicago: University of Chicago Press, 2009.
Pizer, Donald. *The Novels of Frank Norris*. Bloomington: Indiana University Press, 1966.
Pochmann, Henry. "Washington Irving: Amateur or Professional." In *Critical Essays on Washington Irving*. Edited by Ralph M. Aderman, 155–166. Boston: G. K. Hall, 1990.
Poovey, Mary. "The Model System of Contemporary Literary Criticism." *Critical Inquiry* 27, no. 3 (Spring 2001): 408–438.
Porter, Lavelle. *The Blackademic Life*. Evanston: Northwestern University Press, 2019.
Porter, Noah. "The American Colleges and the American Public." In *The New Englander*. Edited by George P. Fisher, Timothy Dwight, and William L. Kingsley, 69–113. New Haven: Stafford, 1869.
Pratt, Lloyd. *Archives of American Time: Literature and Modernity in the Nineteenth Century*. Philadelphia: University of Pennsylvania Press, 2010.
"Princeton Surprised at Yale." *New York Times*, April 12, 1896.
Putnam, George P. "Memories of Distinguished Authors: Washington Irving." *Harper's Weekly* 15, no. 752 (May 1871): 492–496.
Readings, Bill. *The University in Ruins*. Cambridge: Harvard University Press, 1999.
Reed, Adolph. "Black Particularity Reconsidered." *Telos*, no. 39 (Spring 1979): 71–93.
Reese, William J. *The Origins of the American High School*. New Haven: Yale University Press, 1995.
Renker, Elizabeth. *The Origins of American Literature Studies*. Cambridge: Cambridge University Press, 2007.
Report of the Committee on Secondary School Studies Appointed at the Meeting of the National Educational Association July 9, 1892. Washington, DC: Government Printing Office, 1893.
Reports on the Course of Instruction in Yale College; By a Committee of the Corporation and the Academical Faculty. New Haven: Hezekiah Howe, 1828.
Rice, J. M. *The Public-School System of the United States*. New York: Century, 1893.
Rice, John H. "The Ministerial Character and Preparation Suited to Our Country, the World, and the Age." In *Home, the School, and the Church*. Vol. 1. Edited by C. Van Rensselaer, 164–172. Philadelphia: William S. Martien, 1850.
Riegel, Robert E., and Helen Haugh. *United States of America: A History*. New York: Scribner's, 1947.
Ris, Ethan W. "The Education of Andrew Carnegie: Strategic Philanthropy in American Higher Education, 1880–1919." *Journal of Higher Education* 88, no. 3 (2017): 401–429.

Robbins, Bruce. "Fashion Conscious Phenomenon." *American Book Review*, 38, no. 5 (July/August 2017): 5–6.
Roberts, Kathryn. "Writing 'Other Spaces': Katherine Anne Porter's Yaddo." *Modernism/modernity* 22, no. 4 (November 2015): 735–757.
Robinson, Benedict. "Disgust c. 1600." *ELH* 81, no. 2 (Summer 2014): 553–583.
Roelker, William Greene. *Francis Wayland*. Worcester: American Antiquarian Society, 1944.
Rooks, Noliwe. *Cutting School*. New York: New Press, 2020.
Roosevelt, Theodore. "The Man with the Muck Rake." In *American Political Speeches*. Edited by Terry Golway, 37–41. New York: Penguin, 2012.
Ross, Dorothy. *G. Stanley Hall: The Psychologist as Prophet*. Chicago: University of Chicago Press, 1972.
"A Rough Novel." *Boston Evening Transcript*, March 22, 1899, 10. Reprinted in *Frank Norris: The Critical Reception*. Edited by Joseph R. McElrath Jr. and Katherine Knight, 38-39. New York: Burt Franklin, 1981.
Rousseau's Èmile or Treatise on Education. Abridged, translated, and annotated by William H. Payne. New York: D. Appleton, 1911.
Rowe, John Carlos. *Henry Adams and Henry James: The Emergence of a Modern Consciousness*. Ithaca: Cornell University Press, 1976.
Rowson, Susanna. *Charlotte Temple*. Edited by Marion L. Rust. New York: W. W. Norton, 2011.
Ruddick, Lisa. *Reading Gertrude Stein: Body, Text, Gnosis*. Ithaca: Cornell University Press, 1990.
Rudolph, Frederick. *The American College and University: A History*. Athens: University of Georgia Press, 1990.
Rust, Marion L. Introduction to *Charlotte Temple*, xi–xxix. Edited by Marion L. Rust. New York: W. W. Norton, 2011.
Sanborn, Geoffrey. "Mother's Milk: Frances Harper and the Circulation of Blood." *ELH* 72, no. 3 (2005): 691–715.
Santayana, George. "The Spirit and Ideals of Harvard University." In *Educational Review*, Vol. 7, 313–325. New York: Henry Holt, 1894.
Schmidt, Benjamin. "The Humanities Are in Crisis." *The Atlantic*, August 23, 2018, https://www.theatlantic.com/ideas/archive/2018/08/the-humanities-face-a-crisisof-confidence/567565/.
Schoenbach, Lisi. *Pragmatic Modernism*. New York: Oxford University Press, 2011.
Schryer, Stephen. *Fantasies of the New Class*. New York: Columbia University Press, 2011.
Seltzer, Mark. *Bodies and Machines*. New York: Routledge, 1992.
Seventh Annual Report of the State Commissioner of Common Schools to the Governor of the State of Ohio: For the Year Ending August 31, 1860. Columbus: Richard Nevins, 1861.
Sheehy, John. "The Mirror and the Veil: The Passing Novel and the Quest for American Racial Identity." *African American Review* 33, no. 3 (Fall 1999): 401–415.
Shumway, David R. *Creating American Civilization: A Genealogy of American Literature as an Academic Discipline*. Minneapolis: University of Minnesota Press, 1994.
Simmel, Georg. "The Sociology of Secrecy and of Secret Societies." *American Journal of Sociology* 11, no. 4 (January 1906): 441–498.
Sinclair, Upton. *The Autobiography of Upton Sinclair*. New York: Harcourt, Brace & World, 1962.
Sinclair, Upton. "The Call of the Wild: Jack London Put an 'If' on the Condemned Constitution." *New York Times*, February 5, 1906.
Sinclair, Upton. *The Goose-Step: A Study of American Education*. Self-published, 1923.

Sinclair, Upton. *The Jungle*. Edited by Clare Virginia Eby. New York: W. W. Norton, 2003.
Sinclair, Upton. "What Life Means to Me." In *The Jungle*. Edited by Clare Virginia Eby, 348–353. New York: W. W. Norton, 2003.
Sinykin, Dan N. "The Conglomerate Era: Publishing, Authorship, and Literary Form, 1965–2007." *Contemporary Literature* 58, no. 4 (Winter 2017): 462–491.
Skinner, B. F. "Has Gertrude Stein a Secret?" In *Critical Essays on Gertrude Stein*. Edited by Michael J. Hoffman, 64–71. Boston: G. K. Hall, 1986.
Smith, John David. "'My Books Are Hard Reading for a Negro': Tom Dixon and His African American Critics, 1905–1939." In *Thomas Dixon Jr. and the Birth of Modern America*. Edited by Michele K. Gillespie and Randall L. Hall, 46–79. Baton Rouge: Louisiana State University Press, 2006.
Sollors, Werner. *Neither Black Nor White Yet Both: Thematic Explorations of Interracial Literature*. New York: Oxford University Press, 1997.
Sollors, Werner. "Review of *Our America* by Walter Benn Michaels." *Modern Philology* 96, no. 4 (May 1999): 550–552.
Sorby, Angela. *Schoolroom Poets*. Durham: University of New Hampshire Press, 2005.
"Special Report of the Committee on College-Entrance Requirements." In *Journal of Proceedings and Addresses of the Thirty-Eighth Annual Meeting*, 632–677. Chicago: University of Chicago Press, 1899.
Speicher, Allison. *Schooling Readers*. Tuscaloosa: University of Alabama Press, 2016.
Sprague, Homer B. "Suggestion for Teachers." In *Six Selections from Irving's Sketch-Book: With Notes, Questions, Etc., for Home and School Use*. Edited by Homer B. Sprague, xi–xiv. Boston: Ginn, 1878.
Steffens, Lincoln. *The Autobiography of Lincoln Steffens*. New York: Harcourt, Brace, 1931.
Stein, Gertrude. "Composition as Explanation." In *Gertrude Stein: Selections*. Edited by Joan Retallack, 215–225. Berkeley: University of California Press, 2008.
Stein, Gertrude. "Degeneration in American Women." In *Sister Brother: Gertrude and Leo Stein*, 411–414. New York: G. P. Putnam's Sons, 1996.
Stein, Gertrude. "The Gradual Making of *The Making of Americans*." In *Lectures in America*, 135–164. Boston: Beacon Press, 1985.
Stein, Gertrude. "Portraits and Repetition." In *Lectures in America*, 165–206. Boston: Beacon Press, 1985.
Stein, Gertrude. "The Value of College Education for Women." Archives and Manuscripts Collection, Baltimore Museum of Art, 2013. https://cdm16075.contentdm.oclc.org/digital/collection/p15264dc/id/454.
Stein, Gertrude. *Writings 1903-1932*. New York: Library of America, 1998.
Steiner, Wendy. *Exact Resemblance to Exact Resemblance: The Literary Portraiture of Gertrude Stein*. New Haven: Yale University Press, 1978.
Stowe, Harriet Beecher. *Uncle Tom's Cabin Abridged for Use in Schools with Sixty Illustrations*. Charles E. Graham, c. 1920.
Stowe, Harriet Beecher. *Uncle Tom's Cabin or, Life Among the Lowly*. New York: Penguin, 1986.
Stowe, Harriet Beecher. *Uncle Tom's Cabin or, Life Among the Lowly, Abridged for School Use with Sixty Illustrations*. Cleveland: World, c. 1920.
Strychacz, Thomas. *Modernism, Mass Culture, and Professionalism*. Cambridge: Cambridge University Press, 1993.
"Summer Reading." *Review of Reviews* June 1899: 749. Reprinted in *Frank Norris: The Critical Reception*. Edited by Joseph R. McElrath Jr. and Katherine Knight, 51. New York: Burt Franklin, 1981.

Sundquist, Eric. *To Wake the Nations: Race in the Making of American Literature*. Cambridge: Harvard University Press, 1993.
Synnott, Marcia Graham. *The Half-Opened Door*. Westport: Greenwood Press, 1979.
"'Tap Day' at Yale." *New York Times*, May 17, 1913.
Taylor, Kate. "Denying a Professor Tenure, Harvard Sparks a Debate over Ethnic Studies." *New York Times*, October 14, 2021. https://www.nytimes.com/2020/01/02/us/harvard-latinos-diversity-debate.html.
Taylor, Mark. "The Lower Criticism." *Representations* 150 (Spring 2020): 32–60.
Tetlow, John. "A Wider Range of Electives in College Admissions Requirements." *Educational Review* 11 (January–May 1896): 417–432.
Thelin, John R. *A History of American Higher Education*. Baltimore: Johns Hopkins University Press, 2004.
Thelin, John R. "Rudolph Rediscovered." In *The American College and University: A History*, ix–xxiii. Athens: University of Georgia Press, 1990.
"This low-priced edition ... ." *Uncle Tom's Cabin & American Culture*. University of Virginia, accessed January 17, 2022. http://utc.iath.virginia.edu/childrn/wpchp.html.
Thomas, Brook. "The Education of an American Classic: The Survival of Failure." In *New Essays on The Education of Henry Adams*. Edited by John Carlos Rowe, 23–46. Cambridge: Cambridge University Press, 1996.
Thoreau, Henry David. *Walden, Civil Disobedience, and Other Writings*. Edited by William Rossi. New York: W. W. Norton, 2008.
De Tocqueville, Alexis. *Democracy in America*. Translated by Gerald Bevan. New York: Penguin, 2003.
Tompkins, Ellsworth, and Walter H Gaumnitz. *The Carnegie Unit: Its Origin, Status, and Trends*. Washington, DC: US Government Printing Office, 1954.
Tompkins, Jane. *Sensational Designs*. New York: Oxford University Press, 1985.
Torracinta, Simon. "Extinction Event." *n+1*, May 28, 2020. https://www.nplusonemag.com/online-only/online-only/extinction-event/.
Trachtenberg, Alan. *The Incorporation of America*. New York: Farrar, Straus and Giroux, 2007.
Trent, William P. *A Brief History of American Literature*. New York: D. Appleton, 1905.
Trillin, Calvin. *Remembering Denny*. New York: FSG, 1993.
Trilling, Lionel. "On the Teaching of Modern Literature." In *Beyond Culture*, 3–30. New York: Viking Press, 1965.
Trilling, Lionel. *The Liberal Imagination*. Garden City: Doubleday, 1953.
Turner, James. *Philology*. Princeton: Princeton University Press, 2014.
Twain, Mark. *The Adventures of Huckleberry Finn*. New York: Penguin, 2003.
Twain, Mark. *A Connecticut Yankee in King Arthur's Court*. Berkeley: University of California Press, 1984.
Tyack, David B. *The One Best System: A History of American Urban Education*. Cambridge: Harvard University Press, 1974.
Van Doren, Carl. *The American Novel*. New York: Macmillan, 1921.
Vanderbilt, Kermit. *American Literature and the Academy: The Roots, Growth, and Maturity of a Profession*. Philadelphia: University of Pennsylvania Press, 1986.
Vásquez, Mark. *Authority and Reform*. Knoxville: University of Tennessee Press, 2003.
Veblen, Thorstein. *The Higher Learning in America*. New York: B. W. Huebsch, 1918.
Veysey, Laurence R. *The Emergence of the American University*. Chicago: University of Chicago Press, 1970.
Viswanathan, Gauri. Preface to *Masks of Conquest*, xi–xxiii. New York: Columbia University Press, 2015.

Wade, Louise Carroll. "The Problem with Classroom Use of Upton Sinclair's *The Jungle*." *American Studies* 32, no. 2 (Fall 1991): 79–101.
Warner, Michael. "Irving's Posterity." *ELH* 67, no. 3 (Fall 2000): 773–799.
Warner, Michael. "Professionalization and the Rewards of Literature: 1875–1900." *Criticism* 27, no. 1 (1985): 1–28.
Warren, Kenneth. "Perfecting the Political Romance: The Last Novel of Sutton Griggs." In *Jim Crow, Literature, and the Legacy of Sutton E. Griggs*. Edited by Tess Chakkalakal and Kenneth W. Warren, 254–282. Athens: University of Georgia Press, 2013.
Warren, Kenneth W. *So Black and Blue: Ralph Ellison and the Occasion of Criticism*. Chicago: University of Chicago Press, 2003.
Washington, Booker T. *Up from Slavery*. New York: Oxford World's Classics, 2008.
Watkins, Mildred Cabell. *American Literature*. New York: American Book Company, 1894.
"Wave of Public Censure." *Worcester Telegram*, March 5, 1891.
Wayland, Francis, and H. L. Wayland. *A Memoir of the Life and Labors of Francis Wayland, D.D. LL.D.* Vol. 2. New York: Sheldon, 1867.
Weber, Max. *From Max Weber: Essays in Sociology*. Translated and edited by H. H. Gerth and C. Wright Mills. New York: Oxford University Press, 1946.
Wellmon, Chad. *Organizing Enlightenment*. Baltimore: Johns Hopkins University Press, 2015.
"A Western Realist." *Washington Times*, April 23, 1899, 20. Reprinted in *Frank Norris: The Critical Reception*. Edited by Joseph R. McElrath Jr. and Katherine Knight, 46–48. New York: Burt Franklin, 1981.
Wharton, Edith. *The Age of Innocence*. New York: Scribner, 1996.
Wharton, Edith. *Ethan Frome & Summer*. New York: Modern Library, 2001.
Wharton, Edith. *The House of Mirth*. New York: Penguin, 1993.
Wharton, Edith. "Xingu." In *Roman Fever and Other Stories*, 16–43. New York: Berkley, 1981.
"What Is Clark University." *Worcester Telegram*, April 15, 1889.
Whipple, Edwin P. "Review of New Books: *The House of the Seven Gables*." *Graham's Magazine* 38, no. 6 (June 1851): 467–468.
White, Andrew D. *Autobiography of Andrew D. White*. Vol. 1. New York: Century, 1905.
White, Morton. *Social Thought in America*. New York: Viking Press, 1952.
White, Richard. *The Republic for Which It Stands: The United States During Reconstruction and the Gilded Age, 1865–1896*. New York: Oxford, 2017.
Whitman, Walt. "Death in the School-Room." *United States Magazine and Democratic Review*, August 1841, 177–181.
Whitman, Walt. "Preface 1855—*Leaves of Grass*, First Edition." In *Leaves of Grass and Other Writings*. Edited by Michael Moon, 616–636. New York: W. W. Norton, 2002.
Wilder, Craig Steven. *Ebony & Ivy*. New York: Bloomsbury, 2013.
Wilderson III, Frank. "Gramsci's Black Marx: Whither the Slave in Civil Society?" *Social Identities* 9, no. 2 (2003): 225–240.
Williams, Raymond. *Keywords*. New York: Oxford University Press, 1983.
Williams, Raymond. *Marxism and Literature*. New York: Oxford University Press, 1977.
Williams, Stanley T. *The Life of Washington Irving*. New York: Oxford University Press, 1935.
Williams, Stanley T., and Mary A. Edge. *A Bibliography of the Writings of Washington Irving*. New York: B. Franklin, 1970.
Wilson, Woodrow. "Mere Literature." *The Atlantic*, vol. 72, 820–828. Boston: Houghton, Mifflin, 1893.

Wineapple, Brenda. *Sister Brother: Gertrude and Leo Stein*. New York: G. P. Putnam's Sons, 1996.
Wordsworth, William. "Expostulation and Reply." In *Wordsworth's Poetry and Prose*. Edited by Nicholas Halmi, 58–59. New York: W. W. Norton, 2014.
Wordsworth, William. "The Tables Turned; an Evening Scene, on the Same Subject." In *Wordsworth's Poetry and Prose*. Edited by Nicholas Halmi, 59–60. New York: W. W. Norton, 2014.
Wright, Gavin. *Sharing the Prize*. Cambridge: Harvard University Press, 2013.
Yacovone, Donald. *Teaching White Supremacy*. New York: Pantheon, 2022.
Yacovone, Donald. "Textbook Racism." *Chronicle of Higher Education*, April 8, 2018. www.chronicle.com/article/How-Scholars-Sustained-White/243053.
"Yale and Dr. W.L. Phelps." *New York Times*, November 7, 1895.
"Yale Juniors Now in Fix of 'Stover.'" *New York Times*, May 10, 1912.
"Yale University." *New York Times*, May 29, 1893.
"Yale's Society Elections." *New York Times*, May 24, 1907.
"Yale's Society's Revolt." *New York Times*, May 1, 1913.
Zboray, Ronald J., and Mary S. Zboray. *Literary Dollars and Social Sense: A People's History of the Mass Market Book*. New York: Routledge, 2005.
Zimmerman, Jonathan. *Small Wonder*. New Haven: Yale University Press, 2015.
Zola, Émile. "The Experimental Novel." In *The Experimental Novel and Other Essays*. Translated by Belle M. Sherman, 1–54. New York: Haskell House, 1964.

Index

Note: The abbreviation 'n' after a page number refers to an endnote.

A

Academic and Industrial Efficiency (Cooke) 137
academic standards 107, 108, 111, 113–14, 115, 275 n2
academies *x*, 164, 198, 213, 270 n44, 298 n11
   relevance of formal education 3, 7, 27, 248 n61, 255 n103
   school and society 45, 47, 54, 62, 95, 259 n12
Adams, Henry *xiv*, 26, 27–8, 36, 76–7
   temporality and 111, 112, 118, 119, 120–6, 130, 131, 139, 276 n12, 277 n27, 278 nn34–35
Adams, Herbert Baxter 189
Adams, John Quincy (Henry Adam's grandfather) 123
Addams, Jane 20–1, 79
administration and administrators *see* cultural administration and administrators
admissions criteria: higher education 107, 108, 112, 186–7
Adolescence (Hall) 81, 269 n18
Adorno, Theodor 246 n53
Adventures of Huckleberry Finn (Twain) 53
Aesthetic Theory (Adorno) 246 n53
affect 28, 29, 142, 235, 282 n7, 284 n18
African American "Council"/ "Committee" 298 n10
African American Studies *see* ethnic studies
African American writers and literature *xv*, 36, 204, 205–9
   black identity and secret societies 219–29
   hidden identity 205–9, 210–11, 298 n10
   institutionalization of 209, 229–35
   significance of secret societies in 209–19
   see also American Literature; black education; writers
Afropessimism 304 n60
Age of Innocence, The (Wharton) 21–5, 90, 251 nn75–77
agency 29, 30, 33, 37, 44, 252 nn86–7
Agriculture, Department of 12
Ahlquist, Irving F. et al. 163–4
Ahmed, Sara 171–2
Alaska, University of 232
Alcott, Bronson 144

Alcott, Louisa May 260 n33
Allegories of Reading (de Man) 99, 272 n60
Almayer's Folly (Conrad) 16
Althusser, Louis 7, 15, 31, 36, 171, 201, 202, 203, 282 n7
Alves, Jaime Osterman 241 n25
"always": meaning and usage 132–4
'Amelia' (Fielding) 82, 84
American College and the Culture of Aspiration, The (Levine) 244 n30
American College and University, The (Rudolph) 175, 291 n15
American Council on Education 232
American Education: The National Experience 1783–1876 (Cremin) 4, 238 nn7–8, 245 n44, 248 n61, 255 n103, 285 n28
American History (Bourne and Benton) 163
Americanists 44, 60, 64, 68, 69, 258 n6, 265 n72, 266 n73
American Journal of Psychology 80
American Journal of Sociology 170
American Literature and the Academy (Vanderbilt) 57, 263 n52
American literature *ix*, 8, 252 n82
   anti-scholasticism 41–2, 43, 44–5, 47–53, 56, 60–4, 67–9, 71, 72, 73, 256 n3, 257 n4
   institutionalization of 64–9, 265 n72
   pedagogical editions *xiii*, 42, 60–1, 63, 64, 65, 66, 264 n60
   sentimentalism 54, 55, 56–60, 260 n33, 260 n36
   see also African American writers and literature
American Literature (Watkins) 65
American Novel, The (Van Doren) 65
American Renaissance (Matthiessen) 64, 70, 71–2
American Scholar, The (Emerson) 53, 98–9
"American school of fiction" 152
Analectic Magazine 49–50
Anderson, Amanda 252 n86
Anderson, Benedict 93, 109, 136
Anderson, James 207, 294 n56
Animal House (film) 174, 255 n102

INDEX 325

antebellum period 3, 42, 45, 55, 59, 261 n37, 266 n79
see also postbellum period
anti-institutionalism *vii, viii, ix, x, xi, xiii, xiv*
  reading and not-reading 77, 100, 101
  relevance of formal education 20, 43, 250 n66, 251 n81
anti-intellectualism 78, 267 n10
Anti-Intellectualism in American Life (Hofstadter) 267 n10
Antioch College/University 75
anti-scholasticism *vii, viii, ix, x, xiii, xiv, xv,* 4–5, 8–9, 16, 19, 20
  American literature 41–2, 44–5, 47–53, 56, 60–4, 67–9, 71–3, 256 n3, 257 n4
  educational reform 41, 42, 43, 44
  elementary education 61, 62, 64, 67, 263 n53, 263 n54
  literary culture 26, 27, 67–8
  reading and not-reading 77, 81, 97, 99, 102
  Washington Irving and 60–4
  see also formal education
Appeal to Reason (newspaper) 159, 162, 287 n48
apprentice-based professions 4
Archives of American Time (Pratt) 275 n7
Ariosto, Ludovico 48
aristocracy of the intellect 265 n69, 271 n53
Armstrong, Elizabeth A. 187, 293 n47
Armstrong, Samuel Chapman 207
Arnold, Matthew 57, 71, 250 n62, 261 n43, 265 n72
Arthur, Anthony 287 n48, 289 nn61–2
Association of American Universities 11
"Atlanta Compromise" speech (Washington) 190
Atlanta University 208
attendance rates 3, 11–12, 78, 145, 239, 263 n54
Auerbach, Erich 141, 142
Austen, Jane 83
Austin, J. L. 172
authorial intention 225, 227–8
Authority and Reform (Vásquez) 241 n25, 257 n5
Autobiography of an Ex-Colored Man, The (Johnson) 205, 206, 208, 209
Autobiography with Letters (Phelps) 16, 17, 18, 247 nn55–6, 247 n59
Autobiography of Malcolm X, The 163
Autobiography (Sinclair) 157, 166, 289 nn61–2
autonomy: educational systems 15, 171, 246 n53

B
bachelorhood 49, 259 n18
bachelor's degree 9, 11, 14, 16, 34, 112, 113, 151, 246 n46

secret societies 172, 202, 203, 232, 302 n58
"Bad boy" fiction 245 n42
Bailey, Thomas A. et al. 163
Bailyn, Bernard 238 n7
Bakhtin, Mikhail 17
Balibar, Etienne 33, 34, 37, 254 n97, 255 n101
Balibar, Renée 33
Balzac, Honoré de 86
Barlow, Joel *vi, vii*
Barrow, Clyde 136
Barthes, Roland 193, 194
Baym, Nina 58, 262 n45
Beacon Press 230
Beard, Charles and Mary 163
Beck, Ulrich 24
"Becoming Non-Economic: Human Capital Theory and Wendy Brown's Undoing the Demos" (McClanahan) 302 n58, 303 n59
Beecher, Catherine (sister of Harriet Beecher Stowe) 54, 56
Beers, Henry A. 66–7
Bellamy, Edward 121
Belles Lettres Club (New York) 48
Bender, Thomas 244 n31
Benton, Elbert Jay 163
Berkeley Gazette 181
Berlant, Lauren 56
Bernard, Claude 153
Bernard, Laureat et al. 163
Berwick Academy (Maine) 95, 270 n44
Beveridge, Albert J. 288 n54
"Beyond Contempt: Ways to Read Uncle Tom's Cabin" (Halpern) 60, 262 n49
Bhabha, Homi 109, 136
Bibliography of the Writings of Washington Irving, A (Williams and Edge) 63
"Bill for the More General Diffusion of Knowledge, A" (Jefferson) 144
Birth of a Nation, The (film) 188, 201
Bissell, Richard 181
Bitter Milk (Grumet) 261 n38
Black American Writing from the Nadir (Bruce) 301 n41
black education 95, 131, 132, 189–90, 191, 197, 271 n46, 294 n56
  see also African American literature
Blackmur, R. P. *x*
"Black Particularity Reconsidered" (Reed) 298 n9
Black Reconstruction (Du Bois) 298 n10
black secret societies 36
  black identity and 219–29
  hidden identity 205–9, 210–11, 298 n10

black secret societies (*Continued*)
    institutionalization of African American literature 209, 229–35
    significance of in African American literature 209–19
Blaisdell, Albert F. 63
Bleecker, Ann Eliza 266 n77
Blight, David W. 296 n83
blind appetite/passion/impulse 146
Blindness and Insight (de Man) 99, 272 nn59–60
Boarding School, The (Foster) 54
Boas, Franz 1, 5, 239 n13
Bodies and Machines (Seltzer) 286 n37
Boggs, Abigail 243 n27
"Booker T. Washington and the Negro" (Dixon) 189, 190
bookishness 9, 78, 81, 96, 267 n10
"book-learning" 4, 5, 75, 96–7, 98, 99, 239 n9
Boston Evening Transcript 150
boundaries/borders *xiii*, 9, 19, 34, 75, 110
    disgust (literary) and 141, 142–3, 147, 148, 150, 156–7, 164, 165, 166, 286 n38
    secret societies 171, 173, 175
Bourdieu, Pierre 15, 31, 32, 171, 172, 202–3, 254 n96, 296 n81
Bourne, Henry Eldridge 163
Bourne, Randolph 79, 143–4
Bowers, Claude 201
Bracebridge Hall (Irving) 49, 50
Brenner, Robert 37
Brett, George 159
Brewster, Kingman 181
Brief History of American Literature, A (Trent) 67
Brodhead, Richard 56, 92, 93, 261 n37, 262 n45, 270 n39, 271 n46, 283 n12
Brooks, Cleanth *x*
Brooks, Peter 193
Brown, Charles Brockden 262 n46, 266 n77
Browning, Robert *x*
Brown University 14, 31, 113
Brown, Wendy 255 n105, 303 n59
Brown, William Hill 54
Bruce, Dickson 301 n41
Bryant, William Cullen 66, 67 n69
Buell, Lawrence *x*, 258 n6
Bureau of Publicity (University of Pennsylvania) 13
Burich, Keith R. 119
Burt, Mary E. 19, 65, 249 n63
Butler, Judith 172
Butler, Nicholas Murray 136–7
Buurma, Rachel Sagner 240 n16

"By the Book: Assessing the Place of Textbooks in U.S. Survey Courses" (Cohen) 162–3

C
Caine, Sir Hall 16
California, University of 6, 19, 151, 176, 249 n63
Calliopean society (New York) 48
campus culture *xiii*, 34, 35, 44, 245 n40, 301 n37
    institutional time 115, 116–17, 220–1
    secret societies 172–3, 174, 175, 186, 291 n15, 291 n22
    see also higher education
campus fiction *xv*, 33, 34, 35, 37, 254 n99, 255 n34
    ideological state apparatuses (ISAs) 197–204
    meritocracy and 173, 183–8
    secret societies 172–3, 174–82, 183, 290 n12
    white supremacy 188–94, *195*, 196–7
"Campus Novels and the Nation of Peers" (Foster) 255 n101
campus uprisings 31, 204, 220–1, 222, 223, 224
canons and sub-canons (national literary) *vii*, 7, 8, 17, 19, 20, 44, 45, 58, 241 nn21–22
capitalism 7, 11, 15, 137, 138, 141, 158, 233, 255 n105, 304 n60
    secret societies 171, 191, 199, 202, 203
Cargill, Oscar 280 n60
Carnegie, Andrew 16, 114–15, 281 n67
Carnegie Foundation for the Advancement of Teaching (CFAT) 114–15, 136–7, 138
Cato's Tears and the Making of Anglo-American Emotion (Ellison) 266 n77
Cecire, Natalia 135, 136
Central High School (Cleveland) 3
Century Readings for a Course in American Literature (Pattee) 262 n48
Cervantes 83
CFAT *see* Carnegie Foundation for the Advancement of Teaching
Chakkalakal, Tess 235
"Charity Royall" (fictional librarian) 90–1
Charles E. Graham and Co. (publishers) 59
Charles Scribner's (publishers) 182
Charlotte Temple (Rowson) 54
Chase, Richard 57
Chatterjee, Piya 243 n27
Chen, Chris 304 n60
Chesnutt, Charles *xiv*, *xv*, 36, 91–2, 95, 171, 271 n46, 299 nn19–20, 300 n29, 301 n34
    secret societies 209, 211–13, 217–19, 220, 229, 230
Chicago, University of 12, 13, 170
Child and the Curriculum, The (Dewey) 146
child study movement 74

INDEX 327

"Christmas Banquet" (Hawthorne) 19, 65
Church, The 3, 4, 21, 55, 214–15, 216
City College of New York 158
"Civil Rights Data Collection: Data Snapshot (School Discipline)" 304 n61
Civil Rights movement 231, 302 n55
Civil War *xi*, *xiii* 11, 67
  secret societies 191, 206, 210–11, 212, 213–17
Clansman, The (Dixon) 188, 189, 191, 192, 193–4, 195*f*, 196, 197, 201
Clark, Daniel A. 33, 37, 254 n99, 290 n12
Clark, Jonas Gilman 1–2, 6, 239 n12–14
Clark University 1–2, 5, 6, 12, 13, 14, 18, 74, 80, 239 nn12–14
classism and class politics 33, 35, 44
  secret societies 171, 173, 178, 185, 203
"class spirit" 112, 116, 117
close reading 19–20
Clover, Joshua 243 n27
Cobbett, William 4
Cohen, Daniel J 162–3
College Entrance Examination Boards 115
college football 13, 15, 244 n37, 246 n49, 301 n37
  secret societies 35, 36, 173–4, 177, 290 n12
colleges *see* higher education
"collegiate way" 175, 176, 245 n40, 291 n22
Collier Books 230
Collier's Weekly (periodical) 33, 178, 179, 182, 292 n29
Colorado 12
Colored American Magazine 208
colored colleges 131, 132
Colored Normal School (Fayetteville) 213
Columbia 13
Columbia College 47–8, 50, 95
Columbia Grammar School (New York) 47
Columbia University 60, 158, 186, 247 n55
Committee on College Entrance Requirements 114
Committee of Ten (National Educational Association) 113–14
Committee of Twelve for the Advancement of the Interests of the Negro Race 213, 299 n20
"Common Reader and the Archival Classroom: Disciplinary History for the Twenty-First Century, The" (Buurma and Heffernan) 240 n16
common readers 72
"common school fiction" 257 n5
common school movement 31, 32, 62, 145, 253 n94, 282 n4
Common Sense (Paine) 163
"Composition as Explanation" (Stein) 133, 134

"Conjurer's Revenge, The" (Chesnutt) 91–2
Conjure Woman, The (Chesnutt) 92
Connecticut 32
Connecticut Yankee in King Arthur's Court (Twain) 121–2
Conrad, Joseph 16
continuous present *xiv*, 111, 133, 134–6
Cooke, Morris L. 137
Cooper, James Fenimore 65, 66, 103, 262 n46
Cooper, Mark Garrett 137, 138, 249 n63
Cooper, Melinda 231–2
Cornell Stories (Sanderson) 174
Cornell University 13, 14, 31, 100
corporal punishment 30
corporatization: education systems 136–8, 281 n67
Corrector 48
Cortelyou Jr., George B. 181
Corwin, Robert Nelson 188
Cosmopolitan 182
Cottom, Tressie McMillan 243 n27
counter-reflexivity 23–6, 83, 84, 85, 86, 87, 88, 90, 91, 92, 94–100
Country of the Pointed Firs, The (Jewett) 92, 93, 95, 270 n39
course units *xiv*, 108, 110, 111, 112–18, 124, 126, 136, 137–8, 277 n18
Covid-19 pandemic 232, 233, 304 n62
Crane, Stephen 140
Crayon, Geoffrey *see* Irving, Washington
Creating American Civilization: A Genealogy of American Literature as an Academic Discipline (Shumway) 258 n6
Creating the College Man (Clark) 33, 254 n99, 290 n12
creative writing programs 8, 21, 27, 75, 110
Cremin, Lawrence 4, 153–4, 238 nn7–8, 245 n44, 248 n61, 255 n103, 268 n17, 285 n28
Crisler, Jesse S. 285 nn25–6
Criterion Books *xi*
Critical Inquiry 195 nn68–9, 198
Critical Race Theory 33
critical regionalism/cosmopolitanism 94
critical theory 15, 171, 172, 246 n53
"Critical University Studies and the Crisis Consensus" (Boggs and Mitchell) 243 n27
Cross, George L. 246 n49
"Cultivated Motor Automatism" 127
cultural administration and administrators *vi*, *xi*, *xiii*, 71, 142, 245 n39, 256 n3
  reading and not-reading 75, 76, 96, 100, 103
  relevance of formal education 7, 9–10, 32, 34, 35
  secret societies 172, 182, 186–7
  temporality 110, 111, 113

328   INDEX

Cultural Capital: The Problem of Literary Canon Formation (Guillory) 7, 8, 61, 240 n16, 241 n21-2, 250 n66, 254 n98, 258 n6, 295 n79, 296 n83
   agency of literature 28, 33, 34, 255 n101
   cultural studies 101, 273 n64
   New Critics 258 n6, 263 n53
   reading and not-reading 96, 102, 271 n50, 272 n59
cultural pluralism 198, 199, 200
"Cultural Reproduction and Social Reproduction" (Bourdieu) 202-3
cultural studies 101 n64, 102
Culture and Democracy in the United States (Kallen) 198
Cultures of Letters (Brodhead) 56, 93, 261 n37, 270 n39, 271 n46, 283 n12
Cummins, Maria Susanna 70, 266 n77
curriculum *vi, viii, xi, xiii*, 3, 6, 61, 62, 78, 145, 233
   development of modern school system 14, 16-19, 28, 32, 56, 245 nn44-6, 248 n61
   "elective system" in higher education 14, 112, 113, 116, 117, 145
   institutional time 107, 108, 126-36
   secret societies 198, 201-2, 203, 207
   undergraduate 2, 7, 112-13, 117
Cutting School (Rooks) 274 n70

D

Darrow, Clarence 157
Dartmouth College 31, 253 n94
Dawn: An Autobiography of Early Youth (Dreiser) 95, 270 n45
"Death in the School-Room" (Whitman) 260 n33
"Decorative Beasts" (Gilmore) 298 n11
dedications 26, 54
Defoe, Daniel *viii*, 78 n10
"Degeneration in American Women" (Stein) 127, 128-30
de Man, Paul 59, 99, 100, 101, 102, 272 nn59-60
Democracy: An American Novel (Adams) 76-7
Democracy in America (De Tocqueville) 98, 169, 271 n55
Democracy and Education (Dewey) 99, 100, 146, 267 n10, 273 n61
determinism 153, 154
De Tocqueville, Alexis 98, 169, 271 n55
Dewey, Evelyn 78, 79, 268 n11
Dewey, John *viii, xiv*, 6, 16, 78, 79, 252 n83, 268 n11
   democracy and formal education 99, 100, 146, 267 n10, 273 n61

student interest 143, 144, 145-6, 147-8, 151, 154, 155, 165, 289 n62
Dialect of Modernism, The (North) 134-5, 135-6
dialects 93-4
"Diedrich Knickerbocker" (fictional character) 46, 47, 48, 49, 50, 51, 259 n23
Dimock, Wai Chee 109, 110, 136, 275 n7, 279 n43
disciplinary communities 12, 13
disciplinary history *xiii*, 61, 101, 102, 240 n16, 248 n62, 282 n7
discipline and punishment 47, 54, 55, 233, 260 n33, 261 n37, 282 n4, 304 n61
   social control and 30-1, 32, 36
   student interest 141, 145, 146, 147, 148, 152, 284 n18
"Disgust c. 1600" (Robinson) 283 n8
disgust (literary) *xiv*, 140, 261 n43, 283 n8, 286 nn37-38
   Norris and violence 26-8, 127, 142, 143, 149-57, 164, 165, 285 nn25-6, 285 n29, 286 nn37-8
   Sinclair and revolutionary politics *xiv*, 26, 142, 143, 157-66, 252 n83, 287 n42, 287 n45, 287 nn47-8, 288 n50, 289 nn59-62
   student interest 141, 142, 143-8, 151, 152, 154, 155, 165, 289 n62
   see also realism and reality
diversity 68, 93, 123, 171-2, 199, 231, 233, 296 n83, 298 n11
Dixon Jr., Thomas *xv*, 35, 36, 171, 195*f*, 196, 198, 199, 200, 203-4, 212, 294 n64, 295 n79, 296 n83
   Reconstruction Trilogy 188-94, 197, 201, 294 n66, 295 n68
doctoral programs 11
Don Quixote (Cervantes) 83
Dorlan's Plan (Griggs) 223, 227
"double consciousness" 205
Doubleday, Page and Company (publishers) 159-60, *185*, 287 n48
Douglas, Ann 56-7, 261 n40
dramatizations 78-9, 268 n11
Dream of the Great American Novel, The (Buell) 258 n6
Dreiser, Theodore *xiv*, 23, 140
   reading and not-reading 85-90, 95, 270 n45
"dual personality" 206
Du Bois, W.E.B. 205, 207, 213, 296 n83, 297 nn5-6, 298 n10, 299 n20
Du Maurier, George 16
Dunbar, Paul Laurence 208, 298 n9

Dunne, Peter Finlay 160
Dusk of Dawn (Du Bois) 297 nn5–6
Duyckinck, Evert 41

E

"Early Histories of American Literature" (Baym) 58, 262 n45
Ebony and Ivy (Wilder) 253 n94
Edge, Mary Allen 63
education *see* formal education
educational history and historians 175, 238 n7
   relevance of informal education, *xii, xiii, xv*, 3, 4, 6, 9, 10, 13, 27
Educational Problems (Hall) 74, 77, 79, 80, 81, 82, 268 nn14–15
educational reform
   anti-scholasticism 41, 42, 43, 44
   institutional time 108, 127, 137, 138
   post-Civil War modernization process 43, 56, 63, 75, 78, 97
   reading and not-reading 99, 103
   relevance of formal education *xiv*, 3, 9, 11, 12, 14, 20, 32, 35
   student interest 141, 144–5, 147
educational tracts 261 n36
Education of Blacks in the South, 1860–1935, The (Anderson) 207, 294 n56
Education in the Forming of American Society (Bailyn) 238 n7
Education of Henry Adams, The (Adams) 26, 36, 111, 119, 120–6, 131, 276 n12, 277 n27, 278 nn34–35
educators *vi*, 110, 144, 152, 163, 218, 219
   feminization of teaching 261 n38
   fictional 44–7, 48, 49, 50, 57, 61, 63, 265 n72
   humiliation of 30, 31, 32, 50–3, 64, 221, 224
   reading and not-reading 75, 78, 79, 98, 103, 267 n4, 271 n46
   relevance of formal education 18, 20, 28, 30, 250 n66, 252 n83
   school and society 43, 61, 67, 72–3, 257 n5
   sentimentalism and 54, 55, 56–60, 61, 63, 260 n33, 261 n36
Edwards, Jonathan 144
"elective system": higher education 14, 112, 113, 116, 117, 145
elementary education 172, 201, 202, 238 n6, 245 n44, 248 n61, 304 n61
   anti-scholasticism 61, 62, 64, 67, 263 n53, 263 n54
   imposition of academic standards 107, 108
   reading and not-reading 78, 79, 96, 102, 271 n50, 274 n70
   relevance of formal education 2, 3, 11, 14, 18, 33, 34

see also higher education; high schools; secondary education
Elias, Norbert 110, 276 n10
Eliot, Charles *xiv*, 13, 14, 26, 176
   course units 108, 110, 111, 112–18, 124, 126, 136, 137–9, 277 n18
   institutional time 107, 123, 276 n12
   student interest 145, 151
Eliot, George 79
Ellison, Julie 266 n77
"Embarrassment of Naturalism, The" (Jones) 286 n37
Emerson, Ralph Waldo *viii*, 44, 45, 53, 67, 70, 98–9, 100, 265 n69
Emile (Rousseau) 98
emotions *xiv*, 28, 144, 147, 148
Empire of Business, The (Carnegie) 281 n67
Empson, William *x*
Emre, Merve 241 n25, 282 n7
"English Classical School" (Boston) 248 n61
"'English Courses' of the University of California" (Norris) 151
English, James 102, 249 n63, 273 n64
enrollment and enrollment rates 12, 19, 32, 61, 102, 107–8, 113, 186, 232, 237 n5, 249 n63
Erskine, John 20, 59, 262 n46
essentialism 198, 199
Ethnic Canon, The (ed. Palumbo-Liu) 298 n11
Ethnic Studies 209, 230, 232, 233, 298 n11, 304 n62
Evans, Mae J. 62, 65, 264 n55
"Eva St. Clare" (fictional character) 54–7
"Everywhere and Nowhere: The Sociology of Literature After 'the Sociology of Literature'" (English) 273 n64
evolutionary biology 80, 152, 153, 285 n29
evolutionary time 128–30
Exact Resemblance to Exact Resemblance (Steiner) 134, 136
Experience and Education (Dewey) 146
Experimental (Cecire) 135, 136
"Experimental Novel," (Zola) 152–3
"Expostulation and Reply" (Wordsworth) 98, 271 n56
expression: study of 79
extension school classes 13
"extracurriculum" *see* campus culture
eye health: reading 74–5, 79, 80

F

Failure and the American Writer (Jones) 119, 121, 278 n33
Fall of Atlantis, the (Hall) 75
families 3, 4, 21, 55, 115, 144, 214, 216, 231, 263 n54

Fantasies of the New Class (Schryer) 252 n82
fast reading 79, 80, 81, 268 n14
Faulkner, William 138, 252 n85, 281 n68
feeling xiv, 28, 144, 146, 147, 148
Felski, Rita 29, 30, 252 nn86–87, 253 n89–90
Feminization of American Culture, The (Douglas) 56–7, 261 n40
Ferguson, Roderick 230
Fernhurst (Stein) 127
Fictions of Female Education in the Nineteenth Century (Alves) 241 n25
Fiedler, Leslie ix–x, xi, 45, 57, 68, 265 n72
Fielding, Henry 82–3, 84
Fields, James T. (publisher) 41, 58–9, 262 n45
Findeisen, Christopher 33, 37, 290 n12
First Congress of Colored Women in the United States 213
First World War 11, 12, 27–8, 35, 94, 100, 244 n30, 261 n43
Fish, Stanley 20, 250 n66
Fisk University 207, 208
Fitzgerald, F. Scott 174, 182, 290 n14
Flaubert, Gustave 83–4
Fleissner, Jennifer 69, 119, 125, 286 n33
Foerster, Norman 57
food production/consumption 159, 160–2, 287 n47
Forgotten Readers: Recovering the Lost History of African American Literary Societies (McHenry) 300 n23
formal education 1, 3, 4, 8, 80, 216, 218, 230, 235, 243 n27
 decentralization 28, 30, 31, 32, 55, 144
 hostility towards reading 74–82
 institutionalization of English literature vi–vii, xi, xii, xiii, xv, 6, 32, 43, 256 n3
 literature and expansion of 2, 6–10, 19, 26, 37, 42, 43, 241 n19, 241 n25, 248 n62, 249 n63
 relevance to public life vi–vii, viii, x, xv, 2, 5, 6, 12, 14, 15, 17, 20–1, 26, 34, 240 n16, 246 n53
 rise of modern school system 11–16
 social control in United States 30–7, 56, 57, 58, 232, 254 n99, 263 n53
 see also anti-scholasticism; Progressive education
Form and History in American Literary Naturalism (Howard) 286 n37
Forms (Levine) 279 n43
for-profit colleges 243 n27
Foster, Hannah Webster 54
Foster, Travis M. 255 n101
Foucault, Michel 7, 138, 241 n25, 255 n105, 282 n69

France 15, 31, 32, 141, 202, 203
Frankfurt School 7
Franklin, Benjamin 66
Frank Merriwell at Yale (Standish) 174, 220
Frank Norris: A Life (McElrath and Crisler) 285 nn25–26
fraternity 170, 173, 175–6, 176–7, 178, 208, 223, 289 n3, 298 n9
Freedmen's Bureau 201
Freemasonry 170, 172, 175, 205–6, 208
Freneau, Phillip 266 n77
Freshman, The (film) 255 n102
Fröbel, Friedrich 99
Fuller, Margaret 67, 257 n5

G
Gallagher, Catherine 101
Garland, Hamlin 66
Gary Schools, The (Bourne) 79, 143–4
Gates Jr., Henry Louis 234–5
Gates, Lewis E. 26, 151
Geiger, Roger L. 245 n40
gender 35, 44, 54, 67, 70, 71, 72, 95
 higher education and 127, 128–9, 131, 132
Genette, Gerard 51, 275 n8
genres and sub-genres 8, 17, 43, 57, 58, 153, 275 n7, 286 n33
 campus fiction 172, 174, 180, 255 n101, 257 n5, 290 n12
 regionalism 91, 93, 94, 96
George, Henry 16
Germany 124
GI Bill (1944) 12
Giddens, Anthony 24
Gigante, Denise 272 n60
gig economy 232, 233
Gilman, Charlotte Perkins 157
Gilman, Daniel Coit 6
Gilmore, Ruth Wilson 298 n11
Glazener, Nancy 75, 96, 240 n16, 267 n5, 272 n59
Global Future of English Studies, The (English) 249 n63
Golden Bowl, The (James) 84
"Good Bad Boy" 265 n72
Goose-Step, The (Sinclair) 165, 287 n45
Gorn, Elliot J. 263 n54
Goslings, The (Sinclair) 166, 287 n45
Gospel of Wealth (Carnegie) 281 n67
governesses 82–3, 84, 95–6
"Gradual Making of The Making of Americans, The" (Stein) 133–4
graduation rates 2

INDEX 331

Graff, Gerald 67, 69, 101, 240 n16, 266 n75, 274 n65
Gramsci, Antonio 282 n7
"Gramsci's Black Marx: Whither the Slave in Civil Society?" 304 n60
"Great American Novel" x, 44, 258 n6
"Great Stone Face" (Hawthorne) 19, 65
Great Tradition, The (Leavis) x
Greek vi, vii, 14, 124, 125
Greenblatt, Stephen 101
Greene, Maxine 241 n25
Griffith, D. W. 188
Griggs, Sutton xv, 36, 171, 206, 208, 219–29, 233–4, 235, 301 n37, 301 n41
Grimshaw, William 205, 206
Griswold, Rufus 41
Griswold, Whitney 181, 182
Growth of the American People, The (Jernegan) 201
Grumet, Madeleine R. 261 n38
Guillory, John 7, 8, 61, 240 n16, 241 n21–2, 250 n66, 254 n98, 258 n6, 295 n79, 296 n83
  agency of literature 28, 33, 34, 255 n101
  cultural studies 101, 273 n64
  New Critics 258 n6, 263 n53
  reading and not-reading 96, 102, 271 n50, 272 n59
Gwinn, Mary (Mamie) Mackall 127, 129, 280 n46

H

Half-Opened Door, The (Synnott) 204, 293 n49
Hall, G. Stanley 1, 5, 14, 31
  reading and not-reading 74, 75, 77, 79–80, 81, 82, 100, 267 n10, 268 nn14–15, 268 n17, 269 nn18–19
Halpern, Faye 59–60, 262 n49
Hamilton College 175
Hamilton, Edith 127, 252 n83, 280 n46
Hamilton, Linda T. 187, 293 n47
Hampton-Tuskegee model of industrial education 191, 207, 294 n56, 297 n5
Hardy, Thomas 16
Harper, Frances Ellen Watkins xv, 36, 171, 209–11, 212–13, 220, 222, 229, 230, 235, 300 n23
Harrison, Charles C. 137
Harris, William T. 113
Harte, Bret 262 n46
Hartford (public high school) 3
Harvard Board of Overseers 204
Harvard Crimson 204, 296 n85
Harvard Teachers Association 107, 112
Harvard University 13, 14, 26, 36, 53, 66–7, 68, 75, 224
  Adams and 123–4, 126
  institutional time 107, 108, 111, 112, 113, 114, 115, 116–17, 118, 277 n18
  revolutionary politics 157, 158
  secret societies 176, 186, 187, 200, 204, 296 n85, 297 n6
  Stein and 126–7, 128
  student interest 145, 151, 285 n25
  see also Yale University
Harvey, David 110
Haugh, Helen 163
Hawthorne, Nathaniel 19, 41–2, 44, 45, 65, 66, 70, 257 n5, 262 n46, 265 n69
Hayot, Eric 125–6
Heffernan, Laura 240 n16
Helicon Hall (farm community) 165, 289 n62
Henderson, Josiah A. 47
"Henry Adams's Annis Mirabilis: 1900 and the Making of a Modernist" (Burich) 119
Herbert Spencer on Education (Cremin) 153–4
hermeneutic code 193–4
Heroes of America, The 191, 192
Hiawatha (Longfellow) viii
higher education 64, 157, 237 nn4–5, 239 n12, 239 n14, 243 n27, 244 n30, 245 n46, 249 n63, 255 n103
  admissions criteria 107, 108, 112–13, 115
  gender and 127, 128–9, 131, 132
  ideological state apparatuses (ISAs) 197–204
  institutionalization of literature 61, 209, 229–35, 302 n58, 303 n59
  institutional time 137, 138
  legitimation of literary studies 57, 58
  meritocracy and 173, 183–8
  reading and not-reading 79, 102, 271 n48, 271 n50
  relevance of formal education 1, 2, 5, 7, 9, 10, 12–14, 15–17, 33, 34, 35
  revolutionary politics 157–9, 165
  school and society studies 43, 47–8, 256 n3
  secret societies 169, 171–2, 173, 175–6, 199, 202, 203, 204, 207, 231–2, 290 n12, 291 n15
  student interest 144, 151, 285 n25
  white supremacy 188–94, 195, 196–7
  see also campus culture; elementary education; high schools; secondary education
Higher Education Act (1965) 12, 231
Higher Education Amendments (1972) 12
Higher Learning in America, The (Veblen) 136, 138, 172–3, 175

332   INDEX

high schools 172, 248 n61, 263 n52, 264 n55, 271 n48, 271 n50
   institutional time 113, 115
   reading and not-reading 95, 96
   relevance of formal education 3, 11, 16, 18, 19
   see also elementary education; higher education; secondary education
Hindered Hand, The (Griggs) 226
History of American Higher Education, A (Thelin) 176, 187, 245 n40, 291 n22
History of American Literature Since 1870, A (Pattee) 66, 67, 97, 265 n69, 271 n53
history and historians 111, 119, 121, 124, 126, 163, 201, 277 n27, 295 n79
History of the Life and Voyages of Christopher Columbus, A (Irving) 62, 63
History of New York, A (Irving) 48, 49, 50, 259 n23
History, Tales, and Sketches (Irving) 50, 51, 259 n23, 260 n28
Hitchcock, Alfred 228–9
Hoberek, Andrew 252 n82
Hodder, Alfred 127, 280 n46
Hofstadter, Richard 153, 163, 267 n10
Hollinger, David 200
Holmes, Oliver Wendell 67, 265 n69
Homer, Winslow 245 n42
honor societies 187
Hope, Sir Anthony 16
Hopkins, Pauline 208
hornbooks 18
Horowitz, Helen Lefkowitz 182, 187
Houghton, Mifflin & Co (publishers) 59
House Behind the Cedars, The (Chesnutt) 36, 209, 211–13, 217–19, 220, 229, 230, 300 n29, 301 n34
House of Mirth, The (Wharton) 140–1
House of the Seven Gables, The (Hawthorne) 41
Howard, June 94, 96, 286 n37
Howard University 207
Howells, William Dean 16, 65, 301 n34
Howes, Abby Willis 65
"How Much Work Is Done in American Literature in the High School and by What Methods?" (Evans) 62, 65, 264 n55
"How Should We Teach 'The Jungle'?" (Phelps) 163
"How to Win a Fortune" (Carnegie) 281 n67
Huey, Edmund Burke 79
Hull-House 20–1, 79
humanism 6, 7, 80, 240 n18
Hunt, Henry 177, 291 n23
hymns 216–17

I

"Ichabod Crane" (fictional schoolteacher) 44–7, 50–1, 52, 55, 64, 260 n28
"Ideal School as Based on Child Study" (Hall) 80, 81, 267 n10, 268 n17, 269 n18
Ideological State Apparatuses (ISA) 7, 15, 31, 187, 197–204, 231, 282 n7, 296 n83
"Ideology and Ideological State Apparatuses" (Althusser) 171
ideology xv, 7, 8, 15, 33–4, 35, 36, 37, 45
illiteracy 74–5, 81, 82, 84, 91, 94
immediate interest 146
Imperial University, The (Chatterjee and Maira) 243 n27
Imperium in Imperio (Griggs) 36, 219–20, 221–7, 228, 233–4, 235
Indiana University 19, 95, 166, 270 n45
industrialization vi–vii, viii, xiv, 57, 58, 141, 151, 209
   corporatization of education systems 136–8, 281 n67
   deindustrialization 231, 232–3, 304 n60
   food production/consumption 159, 160–2, 287 n47
   institutional time 107, 108, 110, 111, 114–15
   relevance of formal education 7, 9, 11, 16, 27, 32, 36
   secret societies 170, 206–7
Ingrassia, Brian 244 n37
"In School Days" (poem) 245 n42
institutional time 3, 107, 108, 111–18, 123, 126–36, 276 n12, 277 n18
institutions and para-institutions 101, 123, 214–15, 238 n8
   disgust (literary) 142–3, 150
   school and society *xiii, xiv*, 3, 4, 8, 25, 27, 33, 35, 58
instructors *see* educators
Intellect and Public Life (Bender) 244 n31
Intellectual America (Cargill) 280 n60
Intercollegiate Socialist Society (ISS) 157, 158, 159, 160, 162
"Interest in Relation to Training of the Will" (Dewey) 144, 146
'Introduction to The McGuffey Readers' (Gorn) 263 n54
Introduction to the New Testament (Michaelis) vii, viii
Introduction to the Study of American Literature, An (Matthews) 65, 66
Iola Leroy: Shadows Uplifted (Harper) 36, 209–11, 212, 213–17, 220, 222, 229, 230, 235, 300 n23
Irving, Peter (Washington's brother) 47, 48

Irving, Washington *xiii*, 26, 71, 99, 121, 259 n18, 259 n23, 260 n28, 278 n33
  anti-scholasticism 44–9, 55, 56, 60–4
  humiliation of educators 50–3
Irving, William (brother of Washington) 47, 48
"Ishmael" (fictional character) *viii*, 53
isolation and loneliness 120–1
ISS *see* Intercollegiate Socialist Society
Ivy and Industry (Newfield) 6–7, 240 n18

J
James, Henry *xiv*, 65, 74, 241 n25, 261 n43
  reading and not-reading 76, 82–5, 87, 88, 90, 95–6, 100
"Jamesian Institutions" (Emre) 241 n25
Jameson, Fredric 100, 101, 171, 273 n62
James, William 26, 80, 111, 127, 165, 289 n62
'Jeremy Cockloft' (fictional student) 50
Jefferson, Thomas *vi–vii*, *viii*, 144
Jernegan, Marcus 201
Jesuits 15, 31, 32
Jewett, Sarah Orne *xiv*, 92, 93, 95, 270 n39, 270 n44
Jim Crow laws 187, 191, 200, 204, 220, 222, 224
Johns Hopkins University 6, 12, 127, 189
Johnson, James Weldon 204, 205–6, 208, 209, 299 n20
Johnson, Owen 191, 200, 207, 220, 290 n12, 291 n22, 292 n29
  campus fiction 35, 36, 171, 173–4, 176–82, 183
Johnson, Samuel 239 n9
Jones, Gavin 94, 119, 121, 278 n33, 286 n37
Jordan, David Starr 95, 182
Jude the Obscure (Hardy) 16
Judson, Harry Pratt 13
Jungle Book, The (Kipling) 16
Jungle, The (Sinclair) 143, 159–65, 287 nn47–8, 288 n50, 289 n59

K
Kaestle, Carl F. 237 n6, 238 n4, 238 n8, 259 n12
Kallen, Horace 198
Kappa Alpha (fraternity) (Union College) 175
Karafilis, Maria 301 n41
Katz, Joseph 270 n45
Kazin, Alfred 141
Kent, Sherman 181
Keppel, Frederick P. 186
Kilmaster, Ann (educator) 47, 48
Kindley, Evan *x*
Kipling, Rudyard 16
Knapp, Samuel L. 61, 263 n54
Knights of Pythias 170
"knowledge factories" 7

Kornbluh, Anna 253 n90
Krapp, George Philip (editor) 60, 61, 63–4
Ku-Klux: The Birth of the Klan During Reconstruction (Parsons) 294 n66
Ku Klux Klan 35, 188–94, *195*, 196–7, 204, 225, 294 n64, 294 n66, 296 n85

L
Lads of Kilkenny (literary society) 48
Lafayette College 19
Lamplighter, The (Cummins) 70
language: standard/dialect/literary *vi*, *vii*, 14, 21
  reading and not-reading 93–4, 96, 99, 271 n50
  Stein and 133–4, 135, 136
Laporte, Dominique 33
Lash, Scott 24
Latin *vi*, *vii*, 14, 93, 124, 125
"Latour and Literary Studies" (Felski) 29, 30, 253 nn89–90
Leading American Novelists (Erskine) 59, 262 n46
learnedness 79
Lears, Jackson 25, 26, 97, 118, 119, 125
Leaves of Grass (Whitman) 53, 70, 99
Leavis, F. R. *x*
Le Conte, Joseph 152, 285 n29
Lectures on American Literature (Knapp) 61, 263 n54
Lectures on Education (Mann) 144–5
"Legend of Sleepy Hollow, The" (Irving) *xiii*, 44–51, 52, 53, 55, 56, 63, 64, 260 n28
Leopard's Spots, The (Dixon) 188, 189, 190, 191, 192, 194, 197, 201
lesson plans 42, 66
"Letter to American Teachers of History" (Adams) 111
Levander, Caroline 228
Levine, Caroline 29, 30, 126, 252 n86, 253 n90, 279 n43
Levine, David O. 244 n30
Levine, Lawrence 18
Lewis, R. W. B. 57
liberal arts colleges 3, 7, 13, 14, 17, 232, 245 n40
liberal culture 6–7, 68–9, 87
Liberal Imagination, The (Trilling) 69, 265 n72
libraries 22–3, 44, 66, 67, 76, 90, 91, 95, 269 n35
Library of Congress 44
Life: Organic Form and Romanticism (Gigante) 272 n60
Liming, Sheila 269 n35
"Limit Point of Capitalist Equality, The" 304 n60

literariness *vii–viii*, *x*, *xiif*, 37, 42, 60, 64, 142, 262 n45, 263 n53
    reading and not-reading 71, 77, 85, 94, 97, 101, 102
literary agency 29, 30, 33, 37, 44, 252 nn86–7
Literary Criticism: A Concise Political History (North) 240 n16, 274 n68
literary culture 240 n16, 241 n25
    anti-scholasticism 26, 27, 67–8
    feminization/masculinization of 56, 70, 71, 72, n77, 261 n38, 266 n77
    postbellum period *xi*, *xiii*, *xiv*, *xv*, 30–7, 257 n5
    reading and not-reading 75, 77, 94, 96, 98, 99, 101 n64, 102–3, 267 n5, 272 nn59–60
    relevance of formal education *vii*, *viii*, *ix*, *x*, *xi*, *xiii*, *xv*, 4, 6, 7, 9, 10, 16, 19, 23, 32, 37
    school and society 42, 43, 44, 47, 49, 52, 58, 61, 257 n5, 258 n6, 263 n53
Literary Landmarks: A Guide to Good Reading for Young People (Burt) 19, 65, 249 n63
literary-pedagogical reformers 257 n5
literary production 21, 26–7, 29, 97, 252 n85
    disgust (literary) 140, 153, 156
    school and society 42, 49, 61, 67
literary societies 19, 48, 58, 175, 214, 215, 216, 300 n23
literary sociology 101, 142, 273 n64, 282 n7
literary studies *xiii*, 103, 126, 142, 230, 236 n3, 282 n7
    higher education and legitimation of 57, 58, 68, 69, 73, 266 n75
    relevance of formal education 2, 7, 10, 19, 28, 33, 248 n62, 249 n63, 256 n3
literary transmission 49
"Literature as an Ideological Form: Some Marxist Propositions" (Macherey and Balibar) 33, 34, 254 n97, 255 n101
Literature in the Making (Glazener) 75, 96, 240 n16, 267 n5, 272 n59
literature *viii*, 8, 18, 27
    agency and 29, 30, 33, 37, 44, 252 nn86–7
    "counter-reflexive" gestures 23–6
    denaturalization/de-romanticization of 100–3
    educational hostility towards 74–82
    expansion of modern education 2, 6, 7, 9, 10, 19, 26, 37, 42, 44, 61, 241 n19, 241 n25, 248 nn62–3
    institutionalization of *vi–vii*, *xi*, *xii*, *xiii*, *xv*, 6, 32, 43, 44, 256 n3
    relevance of formal education 2, 6, 7, 9, 10, 26, 37, 248 nn62–3
Little Women (Alcott) 260 n33
Lloyd, Harold 255 n102

local color fiction *see* regionalism
Locke, Alain 220
Lombard, Warren P. 1
London, Jack 157, 158–9, 160, 162, 287 n42
Longfellow, Henry Wadsworth *viii*, *x*, 45, 257 n5, 265 n69
Looking Backward: 2000–1887 (Bellamy) 121
Loughran, Trish 49
Louisiana State University 246 n49
Love and Death in the American Novel (Fiedler) *ix–x*, *xi*, 265 n72
Loving Literature: A Cultural History (Lynch) 240 n16
Lowell, James Russell 265 n69
Lowell, Lawrence 186, 187, 204, 293 n49
Lower Ed (Cottom) 243 n27
Lukács, Georg 153
lyceums 4, 58
Lynch, Deidre 240 n16
Lyrical Ballads (Wordsworth) 98, 272 n57

M

McCann, Sean 279 n45
McClanahan, Annie 255 n105, 302 n58, 303 n59
McCosh, James 3, 20, 80
McElrath Jr., Joseph R. 285 nn25–6
McGuffey series of readers 62, 248 n61, 263 n54
McGurl, Mark 8, 23–4, 241 n25, 261 n43, 285 n26
McHenry, Elizabeth 300 n23
Macherey, Pierre 33, 34, 37, 69 n72, 254 n97, 255 n101
Machine in the Garden, The (Marx) 64, 265 n72
Macmillan (publisher) 159–60, 162
McTeague (Norris) 26, 127, 143, 149–52, 154–7, 164, 165, 285 n25, 286 n37
Madame Bovary (Flaubert) 83–4
magazines *see* periodicals and magazines
Maggie: A Girl of the Streets (Crane) 140
Main Currents in American Thought (Parrington) 59
Maira, Sunaina 243 n27
Major Writers of America (Miller) 262 n48
Making of American Civilization, The (Beard and Beard) 163
Making of Americans, The (Stein) 127
Mall, Franklin Paine 127
"Man with the Muck Rake, The" (Roosevelt) 140
Mann, Horace and Mary Peabody *viii*, 54, 56, 144–5, 257 n5, 282 n4, 283 n12
Manxman, The (Caine) 16
March, Frank A. 19
marketing: educational services 13, 15
Marrow of Tradition, The (Chesnutt) 212, 301 n34

Marsh, Herbert *vii*, *viii*
Marxism 7, 252 n86, 255 n105, 304 n60
Marxism and Literature (Williams) 282 n7
Marx, John 137, 138, 249 n63
Marx, Leo 57, 64, 68, 265 n72
Massachusetts 32, 144–5, 283 n12
mass culture 33, 34, 44, 72, 254 n99
mass education 202–3
Masterson, Henry 47
Matthews, Brander 57, 65, 66, 67, 247 n55
Matthiessen, F. O. 57, 64, 68, 70, 71–2
Mattson, Kevin 289 n61
"May Day Massacre" 304 n62
meatpacking industry (Chicago) 159, 160–2, 163–4
mediate interest 146, 148
Media U (Cooper and Marx) 137, 138, 249 n63
Melamed, Jodi 230
"Melanctha" (Stein) 127, 130–3, 134–5
Melville, Herman *viii*, 44, 53, 68, 70, 103
"Merely Interesting" (Ngai) 284 n18
meritocracy 173, 183–8, 199, 203, 231, 233
metanarrative and metanarration 83, 269 n22
"Methods of Teaching" (Chesnutt) 299 n19
Michael, Arthur 1
Michaelis, Johann David *vii*, *viii*
Michaels, Walter Benn 198–200, 202, 295 nn68–9, 298 n11
Michigan, University of 113
Mid-Atlantic 238 n8
middle classes *vii*, *xv*, 8, 11, 12, 93, 169, 173, 204, 232–3, 252 n82
  African American writers and literature 206, 207–8, 210, 212, 213, 219
  disgust and 141–2, 286 n37
  education as social control 32, 33, 35, 36, 37, 56, 58, 232, 254 n99, 263 n53
  institutional time 110, 111, 115, 137, 138
Miller, D. A. 228, 229
Miller, Perry 262 n48
Millikan, Max 181
Milton, George Fort 201
Mimesis (Auerbach) 141, 142
Mitchell, Nick 243 n27
Moby-Dick (Melville) *viii*, 53
"Model System of Contemporary Literary Criticism, The" (Poovey) 261 n43
'modern consciousness' 118
modernism and modernists 44, 57, 59, 71, 93, 118, 125, 261 n43
Montana, University of *xi*
Mont Saint Michel and Chartres (Adams) 119–20, 121
Moral Enterprise (Pacheco) 257 n5

Morning Chronicle 48
Morrison, Toni 229–30, 234, 235
Morton, Sarah Wentworth 266 n77
Mosses from an Old Manse (Hawthorne) 66
Mount Holyoke College 256 n3
muckraking 142, 149, 165–6
multiculturalism 230, 233, 296 n83
Munsey's 182
Münsterberg, Hugo 127

N
"Narrate or Describe?" (Lukács) 153
Narrative Discourse: An Essay in Method (Genette) 275 n8
Nasaw, David 253 n94
Nast, Thomas 13–14
National Council of Negro Women 213
National Defense Education Act (1958) 12
National Education Association (NEA) 8, 113–14
nationalism and national literary/cultural identity 57, 58, 62, 67, 93–4
Native Americans 31, 253 n94
naturalism (literary) 142, 152–3, 165, 286 n33, 286 nn37–8
  denaturalization/de-romanticization of literature 100–3
Nature (Emerson) 70
NEA *see* National Education Association
Nef, John Ulric 1
Negro Masonry, Being a Critical Examination of Objections to the Legitimacy of the Masonry Existing among the Negroes in America (Upton) 206
Neighbors (film) 174
Neither Black Nor White Yet Both (Sollors) 297 n7, 300 n29
neoliberalism 102, 209, 230, 231, 255 n105, 274 n68, 274 n70, 296 n83, 303 n59
"New Americanists: Revisionist Interventions into the Canon" (Pease) 266 n73
New Critics 44, 61, 68, 258 n6, 262 n48, 263 n53, 265 n72
New England 57, 58, 67
New England Farmer 4
Newfield, Christopher 6–7, 102, 240 n18
New Historicist critique (romance tradition) 44, 69, 100, 101, 102, 258 n6
'Newland Archer' (fictional character) 21–2, 24, 25, 90, 251 nn75–7
New Left 7
"New Negro" 220, 221, 222
New Schools for Old (Dewey) 79
News and Courier (Charlestown) 189

336   INDEX

newspapers   85–6, 98, 144
New York   62, 259 n12
New York Times   16–17, 18 n59, 157–8, 159, 160, 169, 177, 180–1, 287 n42
New York University   44–5
Ngai, Sianne   164–5, 284 n18
non-literary writing   71
not-reading *see* reading and not-reading
No Place of Grace: Antimodernism and the Transformation of American Culture 1880–1920 (Lears)   118–19
"Normal Motor Automatism" (Stein)   127
Normal School for Colored Teachers (Fayetteville)   95
Norrell, Robert J.   294 n56
Norris, Frank   *xiv*, 26–8, 127, 142, 143, 149–57, 164, 165, 285 nn25–6, 285 n29, 286 nn37–8
Northanger Abbey (Austen)   83
North Carolina, University of   189
North, Joseph   240 n16, 274 n68
North, Michael   93–4, 134–5, 135–6
Norton, Charles Eliot   80, 268 n15
noticing   229–30, 234–5
Novel Art: Elevations of American Fiction after Henry James, The (McGurl)   261 n43
"Novelists of the Future: The Training They Need" (Norris)   152
Novels of Frank Norris, The (Pizer)   285 n29
Novel, The   *ix-x, xi*, 10, 16, 17, 21–3, 109, 247 nn55–6, 247 n59
  revolutionary politics and disgust   157–65
  violence and disgust   149–57

O

Odd Fellows   170
offbeat reading   109, 110, 279 n43
Official History of Freemasonry among Colored People in North America (Grimshaw)   205, 206
Ogden, Robert C.   189
Ohio   12, 256 n3
Ohio School Library   62–3
Oil! (Sinclair)   166
Oklahoma   12
Oklahoma, University of   246 n49
Old School (film)   174
Oldstyle, Jonathan *see* Irving, Washington
On Being Included (Ahmed)   171–2
"'One Place Where Money Makes No Difference, The'" (Findeisen)   33, 290 n12
one-room schoolhouse   144, 172, 221, 238 n6, 245 n42, 271 n48, 282 n4
  relevance of formal education   3, 11, 12, 13, 21, 30, 50

On Native Grounds (Kazin)   141
"On the Teaching of Modern Literature" (Trilling)   265 n72
"Ophelia" (fictional educator)   54–5
"Oratory, Embodiment and US Citizenship in Sutton E. Griggs's 'Imperium in Imperio'" (Karafilis)   301 n41
Order of Forms, The (Kornbluh)   253 n90
Organizing Enlightenment (Wellmon)   244 n33
Origins of the American High School, The (Reese)   248 n61, 264 n55
Origins of American Literature Studies, The (Renker)   43, 256 n3
Orlando Furioso (Ariosto)   48
"Osric Dane" (fictional author)   88–90
Our America (Michaels)   198, 200, 295 n69
Outline Sketch of American Literature, A (Beers)   66–7
outreach programs   12, 14–15, 34, 182
Overshadowed (Griggs)   226, 227
overstyle/understyle   228–9

P

Pacheco, Derek   257 n5
Paine, Tom   163
Palumbo-Liu, David   298 n11
Paraliterary (Emre)   241 n25, 282 n7
Parker, Francis W.   78, 143
Parrington, Vernon Louis   57, 59, 68
Parsons, Elaine Frantz   294 n66
"party pathway"   187, 293 n47
Passeron, Jean-Claude   15, 31, 32, 171, 254 n96
passing   217–18, 300 n29
Pattee, Fred Lewis   57, 66, 67, 68, 97, 262 n48, 265 n69, 267 n4, 271 n53
Paulding, James Kirke   48
Paying for the Party (Armstrong and Hamilton)   293 n47
Peabody, Elizabeth   257 n5
Pease, Donald   266 n73
pedagogical editions   *xiii*, 42, 60–1, 63, 64, 65, 66, 264 n60
pedagogical setting   28–9
pedagogues *see* educators
Penn State University   67, 267 n4
Penn State Yankee (Pattee)   267 n4
Pennsylvania, University of   13, 137
Père Goriot (Balzac)   86
"Perfecting the Political Romance: The Last Novel of Sutton Griggs" (Warren)   301 n41
periodicals and magazines   8, 33, 58, 98, 254 n99
period and periodization   *xi, xiif, xiii, xiv*, 111, 114, 119, 122–3, 124, 125–6
Perry, Bliss   57

Pestalozzi, Johann Heinrich 99, 144
Phelps, Christopher 163
Phelps, William Lyon 16, 17, 18, 23, 247 nn55–56, 247 n59
Phillips, David Graham 140
photojournalists 182
Pickens, William 299 n20
Pillars of the Republic (Kaestle) 237 n6, 238 n4, 238 n8, 259 n12
'Pindar Cockloft' (fictional character) 49
Pinnacle of Feeling: American Literature and Presidential Government (McCann) 279 n45
Piper, Andrew 49
Pitch Perfect (film) 174
Pizer, Donald 285 n29
Playing in the Dark (Morrison) 229–30, 234, 235
plot twists 225–8
Poe, Edgar Allen 65, 67
poetry and poets viii, x, 80, 98, 241 n25, 257 n5, 263 n53, 265 n69, 271 n56
  school and society 48, 66, 67
Pointing the Way (Griggs) 301 n37
Poirier, Richard 57
political and economic struggle 10, 32–3, 243 n27
"Political Economy of Anti-Racism, The" (Michaels) 199, 200
Poovey, Mary 248 n62, 261 n43
Porter, Noah 20
Porter School (Indiana) 79
Portrait of a Lady, The (James) 74, 76, 84
"Portraits and Repetition" (Stein) 133, 134
"Po' Sandy" (Chesnutt) 95
"Possibilities of the Negro" (Du Bois) 299 n20
postbellum period 2, 13–14, 21, 34, 64, 219, 263 n53
  counter-reflexive gestures and reading 94–100
  literary culture x, xi, xiii, xiv, xv, 30–7, 257 n5
  reading and not-reading 85–90, 103
  regionalism and reading 90–4
  temporality and 109, 110, 112
  see also antebellum period
"post-critique" movement 241 n25
Postethnic America (Hollinger) 200
Postmodernism, or, the Cultural Logic of Late Capitalism (Jameson) 100, 101, 273 n62
poststructuralism 69, 99, 100, 101, 272 nn59–60
Power of Sympathy, The (Brown) 54
Practicing New Historicism (Gallagher and Greenblatt) 101
Pragmatic Modernism (Schoenbach) 251 n81, 265 n72
Pratt, Lloyd 275 n7

Prescript of the Order of the Invisible Empire, The (Ku Klux Klan) 196–7
primary education *see* elementary education
Primer of American Literature, A (Howes) 65
primers 18
"Prince Hall Freemasonry" 206
Princeton University 19, 20, 175, 176, 182, 204, 247 n55
printed-ness and print culture 109
  reading and not-reading 76, 77, 85, 94
Prisoner of Zenda, The (Hope) 16
Pritchett, Henry S. 115, 136
private venture schools 3
privatization: education 102, 274 n70
"Problem with Classroom Use of Upton Sinclair's *The Jungle*, The" (Sinclair) 163
Professing Literature: An Institutional History (Graff) 101, 240 n16, 265 n70, 266 n75, 274 n65
"Professionalization and the Rewards of Literature" (Warner) 101, 246 n48
professional-managerial classes (PMC) 27, 102
'professional scholars' 67, 246 n48
Program Era, The (McGurl) 8, 23–4, 285 n26
Progressive education xiv, 57, 59, 241 n25, 279 n45, 287 n45, 289 n62
  reading and not-reading 78, 79, 81, 268 n11
  relevance of formal education 3, 11, 12, 20–1, 35, 36
  secret societies 171, 176, 177–8, 183–8, 189, 197, 198, 199, 293 n49
  student interest 143–4, 148, 151, 152, 163, 166
  see also formal education
proto-Program Era 8, 23–4, 285 n26
Psychology and Pedagogy of Reading, The (Huey) 79
Public School and the Private Vision, The (Greene) 241 n25
public speaking 79
publishers and publishing industry 41, 43, 49, 55, 58, 98, 159–60, 287 n48
Puck (magazine) 13
Pudd'nhead Wilson (Twain) 16
punctuality 110, 280 n60
punishment *see* discipline and punishment
Pure Food and Drug Act (1906) 159, 160, 287 n47, 288 n54
Putnam, G.P. 47
Putnam's (publishers) 182

Q

Q. E. D. (Stein) 107, 109–10, 127, 130, 132, 280 n60
Quincy Method 143
quota systems 187, 188, 293 n49

R

"Race into Culture" (Michaels) 198–200, 295 nn68–9
race and racial difference xiv, xv, 35, 36, 44
  secret societies 171–2, 179, 183–4, 185–6, 188, 206, 289 n3
  white supremacy 188–94, 195, 196–204, 296 n83
Race and Reunion (Blight) 296 n83
Radcliffe College (Annex) 126–7
Radical Innocent (Arthur) 287 n48, 289 nn61–2
Ransom, John Crowe x
"reach" (metric) 249 n63
readers (reading aids) 248 n61
reading and not-reading xiv
  counter-reflexive gestures 83, 84, 85, 86, 87, 88, 90, 91, 92, 94–100, 103, 271 n50
  literary culture 75, 77, 94, 96, 98–9, 101 n64, 102–3, 267 n5, 272 nn59–60, 274 n70
reading lists 33, 264 n55
reading and not-reading xiv, 20–3, 24, 25–6, 28–9, 59, 63, 65, 251 nn75–77
  denaturalization/de-romanticization of literature 100–3
  Dreiser/Wharton and not-reading 85–90
  educational hostility towards 74–82, 97, 99, 102
  educators and 75, 78, 79, 98, 103, 267 n4, 271 n46
  James and not-reading 76, 82–5, 87, 88, 90, 95–6, 100
  literariness 71, 77, 85, 94, 97, 101, 102
  regionalism in postbellum era 90–4, 96
  Romanticism 77, 88, 98, 99, 100, 272 n60, 272 n61
Readings, Bill 249 n63
realism and reality 57, 67, 68, 87, 88, 97, 103, 225
  see also disgust
Reconstruction Trilogy (Dixon Jr.) 35, 188, 189, 191, 192–4, 195f, 197, 201, 294 n66, 295 n68
Red Strings, The 191, 192
Reed, Adolph 298 n9
Reed College (Stanford) 182
Reese, William J. 248 n61, 264 n55
reflexivity 24–5
regionalism 90–4, 96–7
"Relations of American Colleges to Each Other" (Eliot) 116, 117
"remainder theory of humanism" 6, 240 n18
Renker, Elizabeth 43, 57–8, 256 n3
Report of the Committee on Secondary School Studies (National Educational Association) 113–14

Reproduction in Education, Society and Culture (Bourdieu and Passeron) 31, 32, 171, 254 n96
Republic for Which It Stands, The (White) 289 n3, 298 n10
researchers 14, 67, 246 n48
research universities 5, 7, 13, 19, 61, 137
"Review of Our America by Walter Benn Michaels" (Sollors) 200, 295 n75
revolutionary politics 142, 157–65, 166, 263 n53
"Revolution" (London) 157, 160
rewards 146–7
Rhetoric of Romance, The (de Man) 59, 272 n60
Rice, John H. (Reverend) 4
Rice, Joseph Mayer 143
Riegal, Robert E. 163
"Rip Van Winkle" (Irving) 45, 63, 64, 121, 278 n33
Rise of Gridiron University: Higher Education's Uneasy Alliance with Big-Time Football, The (Ingrassia) 244 n37
Rise of the Novel, The (Watt) x
Rise of Silas Lapham, The (Howells) 16
Riverside series (Houghton, Mifflin & Co (publishers)) 59
Robinson, Benedict 283 n8
Robinson Crusoe (Defoe) viii, 78, 267 n10
Romaine, Benjamin (educator) 47, 48
Romanticism ix, 286 n38
  denaturalization/de-romanticization of literature 100–3
  fictional educators 44, 45, 48, 49, 57, 61, 63, 258 n6
  institutionalization of American literature 64, 68, 265 n72
  reading and not-reading 77, 88, 98, 99, 100, 272 n60, 272 n61
'Romola' (Eliot) 79
Rooks, Noliwe 274 n70
Roosevelt, Theodore 140, 160, 163
Rostow, Eugene 181
Rousseau, Jean-Jacques 98, 99, 100, 144, 272 n60, 273 n61
Rowe, John Carlos 119
Rowson, Susanna 54
Royce, Josiah 1, 6
Rudolph, Frederick 175, 176, 291 n15, 291 n22
"Rudolph Rediscovered" (Thelin) 291 n15
rural district schools 3, 12

S

Salmagundi (literary paper) 48, 49, 50
Sampson, Martin Wright 20
Sanderson, James Gardner 174

INDEX 339

Santayana, George 13, 127
Saturday Evening Post (periodical) 33, 182, 189, 190
Savio, Mario 7
Scarlet Letter, The (Hawthorne) 41
Schoenbach, Lisi 251 n81, 265 n72
scholastic culture *viii*
"School as a Conservative Force: Scholastic and Cultural Inequalities, The" (Bourdieu) 296 n81
"School Days" (song) 245 n42
Schooled to Order (Nasaw) 253 n94
School of Hawthorne, The (Brodhead) 262 n45
Schooling Readers (Speicher) 257 n5
Schoolroom Poets (Sorby) 241 n25, 257 n5, 263 n53
School and Society, The (Dewey) *viii*, 78, 146, 147–8, 267 n10
Schools of To-Morrow, The (Dewey and Dewey) 78, 79, 146, 268 n11
Schryer, Stephen 252 n82
science, technology, engineering and mathematics (STEM) 1–2, 6
Scudder, Horace 59
secondary education 2–3, 11, 14, 34, 61, 64, 67, 201, 202, 304 n61
　academic standards 107, 108, 113–14
　reading and not-reading 78, 79, 96, 102 n70, 271 n50
　revolutionary politics 163, 165–6, 263 n53
　see also elementary education; higher education; high schools
secret languages 210–11
secret societies *xv*, 35–6, 115, 169–73, 204, 207, 291 n15, 291 n22
　black identity and 219–29
　campus fiction 172–3, 173–82, 183, 290 n12
　hidden identity 205–9, 210–11, 298 n10
　ideological state apparatuses (ISAs) 187, 197–204
　institutionalization of African American literature 209, 229–35
　meritocracy and 173, 183–8, 199, 203
　Progressive education 171, 176, 177–8, 183–8, 189, 197, 198, 199, 293 n49
　significance of secret societies in African American literature 209–19
　white supremacy 188–94, *195*, 196–204
Sedgwick, Catherine 54, 56
Seltzer, Mark 286 n37
Sensational Designs (Tompkins) 261 n36, 262 n48
sentimentalism 45, 55, 68, 71, 72, 266 n77

educators and 54, 56–60, 61, 63, 260 n33, 261 n36
"Serious Crises: Rethinking the Neoliberal Subject" (McClanahan) 255 n105
Seventh Annual Report of the State Commissioner of Common Schools to the Governor of the State of Ohio 62–3
sexism 44
Shumway, David 258 n6
"signification"/ "Signification" 234–5
Silas Lapham (fictional character) 16
Simmel, Georg 169, 170, 171
Simms, William Gilmore 262 n46
Sinclair, Upton *xiv*, 26, 142, 143, 157–66, 252 n83, 287 n42, 287 n45, 287 nn47–48, 288 n50, 289 nn59–62
Sister Carrie (Dreiser) 23, 83–8, 95, 140
Sketch Book, The (Irving) 45, 46, 49, 50, 63, 64
Sketch Book– Six Selections, The (Irving, ed. Sprague) 60–1
Skulls, The (film) 174
slave system 54–7, 59, 206, 207, 208, 209–10, 212, 213–17, 220, 238 n8, 301 n34
'Slingsby' (fictional schoolmaster) 50
Small, Albion Woodbury 170
Small Wonder (Zimmerman) 245 n42
Smith, Henry Nash 57, 64
Snap the Whip (painting) (Homer) 245 n42
So Black and Blue: Ralph Ellison and the Occasion of Criticism (Warren) 298 n11
Social Darwinism 153–4
Social Darwinism in American Thought (Hofstadter) 153
"Social Equality for the Negro" 189, 190
social experience 109, 110, 147–8, 171, 177, 214
　reading and not-reading 83, 85–90, 103
socialism 157, 158, 159, 163
social reproduction 31, 45, 137, 156, 254 n96, 259 n18
　secret societies 171, 172, 173, 199, 200
"Social Usurpation of Our Colleges, The" (Johnson) 178, 179, 292 n29
"Sociology of Secrecy and of Secret Societies, The" (Simmel) 169, 170
Sollors, Werner 200, 295 n75, 297 n7, 300 n29
Solomons, Leon 127
Son of the Middle Border, A (Garland) 66
Sorby, Angela 241 n25, 257 n5, 263 n53
Souls of Black Folk (Du Bois) 296 n83
Sound and the Fury, The (Faulkner) 138, 281 n68
Southworth, Gertrude Van Duyn and John Van Duyn 201
Southworth, (Mrs) E.D.E.N. 70

Speicher, Allison 257 n5
spellers (reading aids) 18
Spencer, Herbert 152, 153–4, 285 nn28–9
Sport of the Gods, The (Dunbar) 208, 298 n9
Sprague, Homer B. (editor) 60–1
standardization 107, 108, 110, 113–14, 115–18, 136–9
Standish, Burt 174, 220
state common-school system 3
State Nobility, The (Bourdieu) 171, 172
Steffens, Lincoln 176
Steiner, Wendy 134, 136
Stein, Gertrude xiv, 26, 27, 252 n83
  institutional time 107, 109–10, 111, 112, 118, 126–36, 139, 279 n45, 280 n60
STEM *see* science, technology, engineering and mathematics
Stevens, Thaddeus 191, 193–4
Stonequist, Everett 217
Story of Our America, The (Southworth and Southworth) 201
storytelling 79
Stover at Yale (Johnson) 35, 36, 173–4, 176–82, 183, 191, 207, 220, 290 n12, 291 n22
Stowe, Calvin (Harriet's husband) 54, 56
Stowe, Harriet Beecher 54–7, 58, 59, 66, 67, 163, 235, 262 nn45–46, 266 n77
Street and Smith (publishers) 182
student-centered pedagogy 141, 143–8
"student-hour" 137
student interest 141, 142, 145–7, 154, 155, 165, 284 n18, 289 n62
  Progressive education 143–4, 148, 151, 152, 163, 166
students 35, 50, 66, 72, 80, 175, 199, 304 n61
  humiliation of educators 30, 31, 32, 50–3, 64, 221, 224
  protest movements 7, 175, 230, 231
study abroad program 241 n25
Summer (Wharton) 90–1
Sumner, William Graham 154
Sunday Schools 144
Sundquist, Eric 301 n34
synchronicity and asynchronicity: time 111, 118, 126, 130–1, 132, 134
Synnott, Marcia Graham 204, 293 n49

T
"Tables Turned, The" (Wordsworth) 98, 271 n56
Tales of a Traveller with Selections from the Sketch Book (Irving, ed. Krapp) 60, 61, 63–4
Talks on Pedagogics (Parker) 78, 143
Tap Day ceremonies 178, 179–80, 181, 183, 184, 186, 187

Tate, Allen x
Taylor, Frederick 137
teachers *see* educators
Teacher's College (Columbia University) 60
temporality xiv, 28
  Adams and institutional time 111, 112, 118, 119, 120–6, 130, 131, 139, 276 n12, 277 n27, 278 nn34–5
  institutional time 107, 108, 109, 110, 111, 112, 118, 126–36, 275 nn7–8, 276 n10
  politics of standard time 136–9
  Stein and institutional time 107, 109–10, 11, 112, 118, 126–36, 139, 270 n45, 280 n60
  time travel 111, 118–26, 131
Tetlow, John 107, 108, 112, 275 n4
Texas, University of 13
textbooks 61, 62, 201, 263 n54, 295 n79
textuality and nontextuality 93–4
Thelin, John 2, 176, 187, 245 n40, 237 n4, 291 n15, 291 n22
"Theodore Dreiser at Indiana University" (Katz) 270 n45
This Side of Paradise (Fitzgerald) 174, 182, 290 n14
Thoreau, Henry David 44, 53, 70, 99, 241 n25, 265 n69
Three Lives (Stein) 26, 111, 130
Through Other Continents (Dimock) 109, 275 n7, 279 n43
Ticknor and Fields (publishers) 58, 59, 262 n45
Time: An Essay (Elias) 110, 276 n10
time *see* temporality
time travel 111, 118–26, 131
To Advance Knowledge (Geiger) 245 n40
Tocqueville, Alexis de vii–viii
Tompkins, Jane 261 n36, 262 n48
"Too-Close Viewer" 228
"Topsy" (fictional character) 54–7
Torracinta, Simon 232
To Wake the Nations: Race in the Making of American Literature (Sundquist) 301 n34
Trachtenberg, Alan 93, 94
Tract Society 261 n36
Traitor, The (Dixon) 192, 194, 197
transferred interest 148
Transformation of the School, The (Cremin) 268 n17
transparency 35, 36, 211, 223
  black identity 215–16, 217, 222, 224, 225
  campus fiction 178, 179, 180, 185, 292 n29
  white supremacy 191, 194, 196, 197
"Treason of the Senate, The" (Phillips) 140
Treatise Concerning Religious Affections, A (Edwards) 144
Trent, William P. 67

Trilby (Du Maurier) 16
Trillin, Calvin 182
Trilling, Lionel 68, 69, 87, 88, 265 n72
Trinity Hall (Cambridge) 95
Trollope, Anthony 88
Trouble with Diversity, The (Michaels) 199, 298 n11
tuition fees 231, 232, 233
Turner, James 19, 249 n63
Turn of the Screw, The (James) 82–4, 95–6
Tuskegee Institute 188, 189, 191, 207, 213, 294 n56, 297 n5
Tuttle, Joseph F. 275 n2
Twain, Mark 16, 53, 65, 68, 103, 121–2
Twenty Years at Hull-House (Addams) 20–1, 79
Twice-Told Tales (Hawthorne) 70
Twilight of the Middle Class, The (Hoberek) 252 n82
Tyler, Moses Coit 57
Tyler, Royal 266 n77

U
UC Berkeley 7
Ugly Feelings (Ngai) 164–5
Uncle Tom's Cabin (Stowe) 54–7, 58–9, 163, 235
Understanding Fiction (Warren and Brooks) *x*
Undoing the Demos (Brown) 303 n59
UNESCO 8
Unfettered (Griggs) 206, 223, 227
Union League, The 191, 192, 194, 196–7
United States of America: A History (Riegal and Haugh) 163
universities *see* higher education
Universities and the Capitalist State (Barrow) 136
University of Chicago Magazine 170
University Missourian 181–2
University in Ruins, The (Readings) 249 n63
Up from History (Norrell) 294 n56
Upton Sinclair: And the Other American Century (Mattson) 289 n61
Upton, William H. 206
urbanization 141–2, 151
Uses of Literature (Felski) 29, 252 nn86–87

V
"Value of College Education for Women, The" (Stein) 127, 128, 129
Vanderbilt, Kermit 57, 263 n52
Van Doren, Carl 65
Vandover and the Brute (Norris) 127, 151, 285 n25
Vásquez, Mark 241 n25, 257 n5
Veblen, Thorstein 12, 136, 138, 172–3, 175

Veysey, Laurence 6
violence: disgust (literary) 142, 143, 149–57, 164, 165, 285 nn25–26, 285 n29, 286 nn37–38
Virginia, University of 31, 65, 67
Virgin Land (Smith) 64
Viswanathan, Gauri 2, 237 n3
voluntary associations 169–70
vomiting: disgust and 164, 289 n59
"Voyage, The" (Irving) 63

W
Wade, Louise Carroll 163
waiting: temporal alienation 111, 126–36
Walden (Thoreau) 53
Ward, Lester Frank 154
Warner, Michael 101, 246 n48
Warner, Susan 70, 266 n77
Warren, Fred 159
Warren, Kenneth 235, 298 n11, 301 n41
Warren, Robert Penn *x*
Washington, Booker T. 188–9, 190–1, 207, 208, 213, 294 n56, 297 n5, 299 n20
Washington University (St. Louis) 113
Watkins, Mildred Cabell 65
Watt, Ian *x*
Wayland, Francis 14, 31, 113
Webb, Vanderbilt 181
Weber, Max 25–6, 169–70, 171
Webster County (Nebraska) 30
Week on the Concord and Merrimack (Thoreau) 70
Weeks, Mabel Foote 127, 280 n46
Wellmon, Chad 244 n33
Wendell, Barrett 57
West, Cornel 235
West Point 67
Wharton, Edith *xiv*, 21–5, 140–1, 251 nn75–7, 269 n35
  reading and not-reading 85–91, 94–5, 96
"What Is Clark University" (*Worcester Telegram*) 5, 18, 239 nn11–14
What a Library Means to a Woman (Liming) 269 n35
Wheatley, Phillis 266 n77
Whipple, Edwin P. 41
White, Andrew 31, 100
White, Morton *ix*
White, Richard 289 n3, 298 n10
white supremacy 188–94, 195, 196–7
Whitman, Walt 44, 53, 70, 99, 260 n33
Whittier, John Greenleaf *x*, 67, 245 n42
"Who Can Save the University?" (Clover) 243 n27

"Wider Range of Electives in College Admissions Requirements" (Tetlow) 107, 108, 112, 275 n4
Wide, Wide World, The (Warner) 70
Wilder, Craig Steven 253 n94
Wilderson, Frank 304 n60
Williams College 100
Williams, Raymond 101, 273 n64, 282 n7
Williams, Stanley T. 47, 63, 66
William Watkins Academy for Negro Youth 213
Wilson, Woodrow 19, 176, 189
Wings of Death, The (Dane) (fictional novel) 88–90
Wings of the Dove, The (James) 84
Wirt, William 79
Wissenschaft (scholarship) 5, 12, 18, 244 n33
Women, Compulsion, Modernity (Fleissner) 119, 286 n33
Worcester Telegram 5–6, 18, 239 nn11–14
Wordsworth, William 98–9, 100, 271 n56, 272 n57
workingmen's organizations 239 n8
World Publishing Company 59
World War I *see* First World War
writers 8, 44, 59, 110–11, 152–3, 204, 257 n5, 262 n46
    institutionalization of American literature 61, 65, 66, 67, 70, 71, 265 n69
literary production 21, 26–7, 29, 252 n85
literature of disgust 141–2
reading and not-reading 80, 92–3, 94–5, 97, 98
see also African American writers and literature
writing and composition 75, 267 n4

X
"Xingu" (Wharton) 88–90, 96

Y
Yacovone, Donald 201
Yale College (University) *vi*, 16–17, 18, 20, 31, 113, 247 n59, 287 n42
    Progressive Education 183–8, 293 n49
    revolutionary politics 157, 158–9, 162
    school and society 53, 65, 66, 68
    secret societies 169, 173–4, 176–82, 291 n22
    see also Harvard University
"Yale Report, The" *vi*, 245 n45, 247 n56
"Yale's Society Elections" (New York Times) 169
yearbooks 187
Yoncalla (Oregon) *vii*

Z
Zboray, Mary Saracino and Ronald J. 49
Zimmerman, Jonathan 237 n6, 245 n42
Zola, Émile 152–3